ARCHAEOLOGY AN

THE BEST OF

Volume Two

Archaeology in the World of Herod, Jesus and Paul

Archaeology and the Bible
THE BEST OF BAR

VOLUME TWO

Archaeology in the World of Herod, Jesus and Paul

•

EDITED BY
HERSHEL SHANKS
& DAN P. COLE

BIBLICAL ARCHAEOLOGY SOCIETY
WASHINGTON, D.C.

Library of Congress Catalog Card Number: 90-81696
ISBN 0-9613089-6-6 (Volume Two)
ISBN 0-9613089-3-1 (Set)

Printed and bound in the United States of America

Biblical Archaeology Society
3000 Connecticut Avenue, NW
Washington, DC 20008

Table of Contents

SECTION C

The Dead Sea Scrolls—Jewish Texts from the Time of Jesus

SECTION D

By the Sea of Galilee Where Jesus Preached

SECTION E

The Tomb of Jesus 226

SECTION F

The World of St. Paul's Missionary Journeys 271

CONTRIBUTORS

Hershel Shanks, co-editor of this volume, is editor of *Biblical Archaeology Review* and *Bible Review*. He is the author of *The City of David, A Guide to Biblical Jerusalem* and *Judaism in Stone*, on the history and archaeology of ancient synagogues. He edited *Ancient Israel, A Short History from Abraham to the Roman Destruction of the Temple* and *Recent Archaeology in the Land of Israel*, both published by the Biblical Archaeology Society.

Dan P. Cole, co-editor, is professor of religion at Lake Forest College in Illinois. He wrote the descriptive captions accompanying three Biblical Archaeology Society slide sets: Biblical Archaeology, Jerusalem Archaeology and New Testament Archaeology. Cole has excavated at Shechem, Gezer and Tell Halif and is the author of *Shechem I: Middle Bronze II B Pottery*. He serves on the Editorial Advisory Board of *Biblical Archaeology Review*.

Nahman Avigad is emeritus professor at Hebrew University and formerly headed the Israel Archaeological Council. During his illustrious career, he has led digs throughout Israel, including the Judean desert caves, Beit Shearim, Masada and the Jewish Quarter in Jerusalem. Avigad is the author of *Discovering Jerusalem: Recent Archaeological Excavations in the Upper City*.

Dan Bahat specializes in Jerusalem archaeology. He teaches at Bar-Ilan University in Tel Aviv and is the author of *Carta's Historical Atlas of Jerusalem* and co-author of *Jerusalem in Time and Eternity*. Formerly district archaeologist for the Galilee, he has directed excavations at Beth-Shean, Tel Beit Mirsim and Caesarea. Bahat received the Jerusalem Prize for Archaeology and serves on **BAR**'s Editorial Advisory Board.

Gabriel Barkay is senior lecturer in archaeology at Tel Aviv University and also teaches at the American Institute of Holy Land Studies. He has excavated at Susa and elsewhere in Iran and at Lachish, Megiddo, Mamshit, Jezreel and Jerusalem, all in Israel. Barkay is a member of **BAR**'s Editorial Advisory Board.

Meir Ben-Dov, field director of the archaeological expedition around the Temple Mount in Jerusalem since 1968, has served as archaeological adviser for the Nature Reserve Authority and the Ministry of Religious Affairs. Ben-Dov is the author of *In the Shadow of the Temple* and other books.

Magen Broshi has served since 1965 as curator of the Shrine of the Book, the Israel Museum's special museum housing the Dead Sea Scrolls. He directed excavations on Mt. Zion and elsewhere in and around Jerusalem, and at Tel Megadim.

Robert J. Bull, professor of church history at Drew University, New Jersey, directs the university's Institute for Archaeological Research. He has excavated at Shechem, Tell Balatah, Ai, Pella, Tell-er-Ras and Khirbet Shema, and directed the Joint Expedition to Caesarea. He is co-author of *King Herod's Dream: Caesarea on the Sea*.

Robert L. Hohlfelder is professor and chairman of the history department at the University of Colorado. A specialist in numismatics, underwater archaeology and late Roman/early Byzantine history, he has excavated on land and below water in Greece, Italy, Spain and Israel. He is co-director of the Caesarea Ancient Harbour Excavation Project and co-curator of the touring exhibit "Caesarea Beneath the Sea" sponsored by the Smithsonian Institution Traveling Exhibition Service.

Jerome Murphy-O'Connor is a Dominican Father and professor of New Testament and intertestamental literature at the École Biblique et Archéologique Française in Jerusalem. He is the author of *The Holy Land, An Archaeological Guide from Earliest Times to 1700* and *Saint Paul's Corinth*.

Ehud Netzer, architect and archaeologist, is senior lecturer at the Hebrew University's Institute of Archaeology. Netzer has excavated at Masada, Herod's desert palace/fortress at Herodium and Herod's winter palance at Jericho, as well as at Caesarea and Sepphoris. He is a member of **BAR**'s Editorial Advisory Board.

Joseph Patrich is a lecturer at the Institute of Archaeology at Haifa University in Israel. He served as field director of the excavations at Rehovot-in-the-Negev, Hammat Gader and Beth-Shean, and has investigated the caves near the Dead Sea.

Kathleen Ritmeyer and **Leen Ritmeyer** met in 1975 while working on the Temple Mount excavations. Leen has worked as an archaeological architect at numerous digs in Israel, including the major Jerusalem excavations — the Jewish Quarter, the City of David and the Citadel. Kathleen has excavated at sites in Ireland, Scotland and at Tel Acco in Israel. As partners in the firm Archaeological Design, the Ritmeyers produce educational materials on the restoration of ancient sites in Israel.

Hartmut Stegemann, professor of New Testament Science at the University of Göttingen, West Germany, specializes in the study of the Dead Sea Scrolls. He directs the university's Qumran Research Center. Stegemann is preparing a dictionary of the non-Biblical texts found at Qumran.

James F. Strange is professor of religious studies at the University of South Florida. He has directed the university's excavations in Lower Galilee since 1983, working in recent years at Sepphoris. Strange serves on **BAR**'s Editorial Advisory Board. He is co-author of *Archaeology, The Rabbis and Early Christianity*.

Lindley Vann, associate professor of architecture at the University of Maryland, is co-director of the Caesarea Ancient Harbour Excavation Project. Vann has excavated in Turkey, Tunisia, Sri Lanka, Israel and Jordan and is the author of *Unexcavated Buildings of Sardis*.

Shelley Wachsmann is nautical archaeologist for the Israel Antiquities Authority, responsible for discovering, recording and protecting Israel's nautical heritage. He has dived extensively in the Mediterranean Sea, the Sea of Galilee and the Red Sea and has directed a number of nautical surveys and excavations.

Yigael Yadin was Israel's most celebrated archaeologist until his death in 1984. A former Chief of Staff of the Israeli army, Yadin led the excavations at Hazor and Masada. He also discovered the Bar-Kokhba letters and helped obtain four of the Dead Sea Scrolls for the state of Israel. He was the author of *The Message of the Scrolls, Art of Warfare in Biblical Lands, The Temple Scroll, Masada* and *Hazor, the Head of All Those Kingdoms*.

Introduction

This series of volumes is not meant to present simply the "Best of BAR" (as *Biblical Archaeology Review* has come to be called). The objective has been to group together thought-provoking articles on related themes from different periods of Biblical history. As such, the volumes also serve as an excellent introduction to Biblical archaeology at its exciting, often controversial, best. Each volume contains a series of articles selected and organized as a coherent, progressive whole. The first volume focuses on Israel during the period of the Hebrew Bible; the second, on the world of the New Testament. Subsequent volumes will cover other discrete areas.

The series has been designed to serve the interests and needs of both the general reader and the student of Biblical studies and archaeology.

Each volume covers a range of recent scholarly discoveries and interpretations. The reader will also become familiar with the process of archaeological discovery and interpretation, as well as with some of the problems involved in that process.

Archaeology holds a natural fascination for most of us. It allows us to retrieve from the dusty earth some personal reminders of our own past. Uncovering an ancient artifact somehow brings us into contact with our distant ancestors, especially when it connects us with the Bible.

But archaeology involves more than a mere nostalgic diversion—like spending a rainy afternoon rummaging through a box of childhood mementos. Sometimes the excitement comes from retrieving a better understanding of our past. In this way, we better understand ourselves. That **BAR** tries to foster this understanding perhaps explains why it has become such a popular journal over the past fifteen years, with over a quarter million readers, and why an increasing number of teachers have been using its articles in their classrooms.

The attraction of having a series of such articles in a single volume is obvious. No need to fight over a single library copy. No need to worry about back-issue availability. It's OK to mark up your own copy to use for future reference. You may even want to read unassigned articles.

And for the general reader: You can read articles grouped together in a meaningful way.

Occasionally, in this volume—*Archaeology in the World of Herod, Jesus and Paul*—articles from **BAR**'s sister publication, *Bible Review* (**BR**), provide useful supplements to the selections drawn from **BAR.**

The pictures here primarily appear in black and white, while in the original most were in color. Unfortunately, only by using black-and-white reproduction could the price of the volumes be kept within reasonable limits.

Readers will note that the articles within each volume have been arranged as much as possible in accord with the chronological development of Biblical history. Brief introductions to each section call attention to the implications of the articles for Biblical understanding and to the way particular articles illustrate facets of the archaeological process or issues of scholarly interpretation. Supplementary After Words follow the articles and call attention to matters more readily discussed after the articles have been read, occasionally adding follow-up comments by readers, or by the authors, in subsequent issues of **BAR**.

For those interested in pursuing a subject further, additional related articles in **BAR** and **BR** have been listed in For Further Reading at the end of each topical section. In most instances, the back issues containing these articles are still available and may be purchased individually from the Biblical Archaeology Society.

The rest is up to you. We hope you enjoy it.

A Word About Volume II

The articles drawn together in this volume of *Archaeology and the Bible* focus on Judea during the century before the Roman destruction of the Temple in 70 A.D. and on the Mediterranean world that saw the early expansion of Christianity.

Three successive figures dominate the landscape covered here: Herod the Great, Jesus of Nazareth and the apostle Paul. Our articles carry us from the impressive building projects of Herod—the Temple Mount in Jerusalem, at Caesarea on the sea and his mountain-high palace/fortress of Herodium—to the humble home in Galilee where Jesus may have stayed and the spartan tomb in Jerusalem where his body probably was placed, on to the terrain over which Paul spread the new gospel of Christianity westward into the gentile Roman world.

The sites described include three of the most impressive cities of the Roman world: Herod's beautifully adorned Jerusalem, his grandiose port city of Caesarea Maritima and the cosmopolitan Roman center of Ephesus. Architectural structures range from a modest private dwelling to Jerusalem's Temple Mount and include along the way synagogues and tombs and column-lined boulevards. The archaeological problems encountered range from how to investigate harbor installations buried beneath the waves to how to raise a fragile wooden boat from the mud of the Sea of Galilee to a reassessment of a purported tomb of Jesus with the help of comparative typology of tomb architecture acquired from other excavations. The archaeological materials reported on range from scraps of papyrus and corroded coins to massive Herodian wall blocks weighing a hundred tons.

To make this volume easier to use, we have made two changes in the articles. Since all illustrations are now black and white, references to colors in captions have been deleted, except those in "Reconstructing Herod's Temple Mount in Jerusalem" found in Section A. This article appears in color in this collection because we were able to print additional copies of it at the same time we printed the November/December 1989 issue of **BAR**. References to particular pages within the articles—except "Reconstructing Herod's Temple Mount in Jerusalem"—have been changed to correspond to the pagination of this volume. When an article in a specific issue is mentioned it will appear like this if it is included here: May/June 1980, p. 42 [112]. The page number in brackets is the page where the article will be found in this volume.

Acknowledgment

Like all the projects of the Biblical Archaeology Society, *Archaeology and the Bible* was produced by the devoted and careful efforts of numerous members of our staff. Our special thanks for these volumes go to Carol Andrews, Steven Feldman, Lauren Krause, Susan Laden, Suzanne F. Singer and Judith Wohlberg.

Jerusalem—From Herod the Great to the Roman Destruction

Excavations in Jerusalem over the past three decades have uncovered more detailed information about the ancient city's character than had been gleaned over the previous century and a half, when serious scholarly investigation of the city began.

This is dramatically apparent in the area of the Temple Mount, the uniquely sacred space in Israel's religious heritage. Herod the Great magnificently enlarged and embellished the Temple precincts and rebuilt the Temple itself in the most important of the many ambitious building projects instigated during his reign. The first-century A.D. Jewish historian Josephus gave a detailed description of Herod's Temple Mount building program, but excavations carried out by Israeli archaeologists Benjamin Mazar and Meir Ben-Dov since 1968 have now provided dramatic visual confirmation of Josephus's description and have greatly clarified some of the specific elements.

Hershel Shanks' opening article, "Excavating in the Shadow of the Temple Mount," provides an introduction to the subject by describing the recent excavations alongside the Temple Mount, including an account of the way they were marred by religious squabbling, political infighting and the use of archaeological methods that have been heavily criticized. He also summarizes the multilayer history of the Temple Mount from the time of Herod on through the eras when Jerusalem was controlled by others—Romans, Byzantine Christians and Moslem caliphs.

The second selection, "Herod's Mighty Temple Mount" by Meir Ben-Dov, field director of the dig through most of its seasons, integrates the information gained from the excavations with the ancient historical sources, particularly Josephus, to describe in detail the historical setting of Herod's building activity and the building program itself.

In the third selection, "Reconstructing Herod's Temple Mount in Jerusalem," Leen Ritmeyer, latest of a series of architects associated with the excavations, and Kathleen Ritmeyer provide an even fuller description of Herod's enlarged Temple Mount as it can now be understood. They also provide updated interpretations for the features along the Temple Mount retaining wall, some of which had been incorrectly identified.

Unlike the other articles in this volume, the Ritmeyers' article appears in color, because we were able to print it for inclusion in this collection at the same time we printed the November/December 1989 issue of **BAR**. To make the page references within the text intelligible, we have retained the pagination as it appeared in the magazine.

The fourth selection, "Reconstructing the Magnificent Temple Herod Built" by Joseph Patrich, supplements these descriptions with a reconstruction of the Temple itself as Herod lavishly rebuilt and adorned it. Nothing remains of the Temple for study, of course. If any fragments did survive the Roman burning of 70 A.D. and subsequent dismantling of the Jewish Temple, they remain buried and inaccessible to archaeologists under the Moslem shrine erected on the same spot and preserved to this day as a sacred area. Patrich draws upon Josephus's extensive descriptions, however, correlating them with descriptions in the second-century A.D. Jewish Mishnah, especially the tractate *Middot*. He also refers to depictions on Jewish coins of the Second Jewish Revolt period (only 60 years after the Temple's destruction) and to architectural features of other ancient temples, such as the Egyptian temples of Hathor at Dendara and Horus at Edfu.

The net result of these articles is to provide us with a heightened appreciation of the very ambitious—indeed, grandiose—nature of Herod's building program at Jerusalem's Temple Mount.

The final two selections draw our attention to materials uncovered by Nahman Avigad from 1969 to 1983 in excavations to the west of the Temple Mount in Jerusalem's Jewish Quarter, its ancient Upper City. Avigad's investigations revealed that this area, with its elevated position directly across the Tyropoeon Valley from the Temple, had attracted aristocratic occupation during the final century of the Second Temple period. In "Jerusalem Flourishing—A Craft Center for Stone, Pottery and Glass," Avigad illustrates some of the array of fine craft items uncovered by the excavators, reflections of the wealth that some Jerusalemites enjoyed during the time of Herod and his immediate successors. By contrast, "Jerusalem in Flames—The Burnt House Captures a Moment in Time" provides graphic documentation from the burnt house of the violent destruction that ended an era for Jerusalem and for the Jewish state in 70 A.D.

NOTE: In Meir Ben-Dov's "Herod's Mighty Temple Mount," the last sentence should read: "From a distance, the walls of the Temple Mount looked like the sides of a pyramid with its top lopped off. The meticulous attention to detail in such a monumental project is one of the factors that made the Temple Mount one of the most renowned wonders of the Roman world."

Excavating in the Shadow of the Temple Mount

HERSHEL SHANKS

RICHARD NOWITZ

IT SHOULD HAVE BEEN THE JEWEL IN ISRAEL'S ARCHAEOLOGICAL CROWN. IN FACT, ISRAEL'S EXCAVATION OF THE AREA ADJACENT TO JERUSALEM'S TEMPLE MOUNT, ON THE SOUTH AND SOUTHWEST SIDES OF THE SACRED PRECINCT, HAS BEEN THE SUBJECT OF CONTINUING CONTROVERSY AND CRITICISM. EXCAVATION RESULTS HAVE BEEN SPECTACULAR, TRUE, BUT THEY FALL SHORT OF WHAT MIGHT HAVE BEEN—INDEED, WHAT SHOULD HAVE BEEN.

Preceding Pages: *The Temple Mount in Jerusalem. In the last quarter of the first century B.C., Herod the Great built the Second Temple, with porticoes, courts and a vast trapezoidal esplanade. Supporting the entire complex were four immense retaining walls. Here we see the full extent of the western wall that is not still buried or hidden by other structures. Large portions of this wall are Herod's original construction. Today, a section of this Herodian wall—to the left of the ramp—is one of Judaism's holiest places of prayer, a reminder of the Temple destroyed 2,000 years ago. Above this wall, on the great platform where the Temple once stood, rises the golden-domed seventh-century "Mosque of Omar" (center, p. 2).*

The first-century historian Flavius Josephus reported that conquering Romans burned all of Jerusalem and razed its walls to the ground in 70 A.D. But, in fact, archaeologists have discovered that large sections of the Temple Mount's enormous retaining walls still thrust up from bedrock, in some places to heights of 65 feet. (According to Ben-Dov, field director of the Temple Mount excavations, the highest walls of the Temple Mount originally rose 165 feet!)

Almost two decades of archaeological excavations by Professor Benjamin Mazar and Ben-Dov have uncovered numerous architectural features of the Temple Mount and of the structures outside the walls, filling in substantial gaps in the Jewish, Moslem and Christian history of this holy city. Many of these features are pictured on the following pages.

To identify some of the Herodian features seen here, refer to the drawing on pages 8-9.

EVEN BEFORE PICKAX BROKE earth, resistance to the excavation came—this will seem ironic only to the uninitiated—from Israel's twin-headed Chief Rabbinate. But for this resistance, the dig might have begun at the so-called Wailing, or Western, Wall of the Temple Mount, a site Jews have venerated for centuries. The Sephardi* chief rabbi was fearful that the archaeologists might prove that the Wailing Wall was not the western wall of the Temple Mount—and besides, it was holy ground anyway. The Ashkenazi** chief rabbi had other fears: What if the archaeologists found the Ark of the Covenant? "That would be wonderful!" exclaimed Hebrew University's Benjamin Mazar, the director of the projected dig. Not at all, said the rabbi: Since Jews of this generation are not "pure" in terms of religious law, they are forbidden to touch the Ark of the Covenant. Excavation would be unthinkable until the Messiah comes!

Excavation began—at the southern rather than at the western wall of the Temple Mount—by using a deliberate diversionary tactic. The archaeologists occupied some vacant rooms in a building south of the Temple Mount that was being used by the Rabbinical High Court. The Sephardi chief rabbi ordered the archaeologists to vacate the rooms. Meanwhile, the excavation began outside. A full-blown public dispute developed between the archaeologists and the Rabbinate—but over the rooms; no one seemed to notice the dig outside. The archaeologists held their ground, in the rooms, for several days until they had 80 people outside excavating. Finally, they gave in to the rabbis and vacated the rooms. The dig, however, was now a *fait accompli*. It was, however, confined to the southern wall and that part of the western wall south of the Jewish prayer area.

Arabs also objected to the dig. The Moslem authorities feared it would yield "Jewish" discoveries that would be used to show who the "original owners" of the site were.

The relationship between the archaeologists and the Moslem authorities was a curious one. It is true that the local Moslem authorities never actually came around to supporting the excavation. But over the years, their attitude slowly changed from opposition to cooperation, at least beneath the surface. On the other hand, the international Arab community, through the United Nations, continued to press annually for condemnation of Israel because of its archaeological activities near the Temple Mount.

Meir Ben-Dov, field director of the excavation, in an introductory chapter to his fascinating new book on the dig,* explains why the opposition of the local Moslem authorities gradually dissipated: One of the earliest discoveries of the excavation was an Omayyad palace built in the seventh or eighth century A.D. by Moslem rulers of Jerusalem. Ben-Dov invited the Moslem notables to view his finds. They saw the care taken to preserve these Islamic walls, which still stood as a glorious monument to a vigorous and largely unknown period of Jerusalem's history under Moslem rule. This visit dispelled many of the fears the Moslem notables had previously expressed. Thereafter they regularly toured the excavations and even allowed the archaeologists to explore and study otherwise inaccessible, Moslem-controlled areas under the Temple Mount. The archaeologists for their part scrupulously adhered to the Moslem prohibition against excavating under the Temple Mount.

As it turned out, the dig revealed extremely rich finds from the periods of Moslem rule, filling in large gaps in Moslem history. The Israeli archaeologists have not slighted the Islamic periods in any way. The Islamic remains have been preserved on the site, and over 100 pages in Ben-Dov's book are devoted to Moslem history and to the archaeological finds that illuminate that history.

Ben-Dov tells the story of a visit to the excavation by Rafiq Dajani, the deputy director of the Jordanian Department of Antiquities. Dajani remarked to Ben-Dov, "If we could leave politics to the politicians, I would heartily congratulate you on your work, revealing finds of which we knew very little up until now. The finds from the early Moslem period are thrilling, and frankly I'm surprised the Israeli scholars made them public." A foreign correspondent overheard Dajani's remarks and included them in his story. Two weeks later

* "Sephardi" designates the community of Jews that traces its ancestors to Spain, southern Europe and North Africa.

** "Ashkenazi" designates the community of Jews that descends from Jews dispersed in Russia and eastern Europe.

* Meir Ben-Dov, *In the Shadow of the Temple* (New York: Harper & Row, 1985) 381 pp., $24.95.

Tons of earth *were removed by archaeologists to reveal a patchwork of remains from different historical periods. Here, along the Temple Mount's 900-foot-long southern wall, Herodian structures mingle with early Iron Age structures and later Byzantine, Persian, Turkish, Crusader, Mameluke and Ottoman buildings, while traffic on the modern road to Jericho cruises by. Byzantine houses at the far left of this photo can be seen close up on page 16.*

The excavations continue around the southwest corner and along the western wall (see photo, pp. 6-7), covering a total of nine acres.

Dajani was summarily dismissed and later died in the prime of life.

In contrast to the local Moslem authorities, the international Arab community continued to pillory Israel at the United Nations. For years, UNESCO ritually passed resolutions condemning Israel. Charges were made and rumors spread that the excavations were undermining the base of the great Al Aqsa Mosque on top of the Temple Mount, that the excavations were destroying Islamic cultural property, and that the Israeli archaeologists were using unacceptable excavation methods.

As early as 1968, UNESCO passed its first resolution that "urgently called on Israel to desist from any archaeological excavations in the city of Jerusalem." Similar resolutions were adopted regularly.

In 1974, the UNESCO director-general dispatched his personal representative to Jerusalem to report on the archaeological situation. Raymond Lemaire, a Belgian professor of architecture and secretary-general of the International Council of Monuments and Sites, arrived in Jerusalem in September 1974 and, according to his report, "enjoyed the full cooperation of the Israeli authorities." His report concluded that there was no danger to the Al Aqsa Mosque. With respect to alleged methodological inadequacies, the report concluded:

> "Perusal of some of the documents prepared gives one the impression that some of the criticisms that have been levelled at the methods used in the excavations are groundless. The excavations are being carried out by a perfectly well-qualified team of experts of various kinds, who are extremely attentive to all aspects and to all the periods of which remains have been found on the site. The same care is expended on the preservation of remains of the Ommiad [Omayyad] palaces as on those of the Herodian period."

This report had little effect, however. In November 1974 UNESCO condemned Israel in a resolution that withheld UNESCO funds for Israel and effectively expelled Israel by refusing to assign her to any of the five regional groupings through which UNESCO conducted its activities. The condemnation and expulsion of Israel was clearly not on archaeological grounds, but on political grounds.

Although Ben-Dov does not discuss this episode in any detail in his book (he says only that Israel was ousted from UNESCO "ostensibly because of our excavation"), the fact is that the dig could have been—and privately was—subjected to criticism on methodological grounds by professional Israeli and American archaeologists. UNESCO's hectoring and politically motivated ritual condemnation may well have suppressed this legitimate criticism of the dig's methods. Legitimate criticism of a dig—always controversial among archaeologists—may well have been muted in this case because it would immediately have been used for political purposes, to attack Israel. The private methodological criticism of this excavation was hardly criticism that placed the dig beyond the range of acceptable methodology. It was criticism that could be leveled at other digs and other archaeologists as well. The methodological issues involved, however, were and continue to be the subject of discussion within the profession. But they were perhaps not voiced more loudly at the time because in the then-current political climate such criticisms would be used as a stick to beat Israel.

What were—and are—the criticisms? Here are some. The dig was simply too big. It continued for 12 years throughout the year. Most digs are conducted for a month or two in the summer. Theoretically, there is no reason that a dig cannot operate all year round if it has adequate professional staff and controls. This dig, in the opinion of many archaeologists, did not. As a result, it was poorly supervised, and the careful records of each locus, which are kept at the best excavations, are reportedly unavailable here. Within the profession, it is widely recognized that, using the records kept at this dig, it will probably be impossible to write an excavation report of the kind produced by first-rate excavations. Without such a detailed report, other archaeologists cannot check the Temple Mount excavation results for themselves.

On the platform *where the Temple of Solomon and the Temple of Herod once stood, two mosques now dominate a 1,300,000-square-foot plaza, their gold and silver domes reflecting the bright Jerusalem sun. Around the plaza's massive retaining walls, archaeologists have uncovered 25 layers of civilization.*

Above the excavations, at the rear left of the photo, is a segment of the western wall of the Temple Mount exposed before the excavations began. Formerly called the Wailing Wall and today simply the Western Wall, this remnant of Herodian construction is holy to Jews as a reminder of their Temple, destroyed by Titus in 70 A.D. At the corner where the south and west walls of the Temple Mount meet, bottom center, a tower once stood; at its pinnacle a trumpeter would sound the blast announcing the Sabbath.

At the bottom right of this photo we see about half of the vast excavations south of the Temple Mount, up to the silver-domed Al Aqsa mosque, right center. The excavations continue to the east of Al Aqsa, as seen in the photo on page 5.

Moreover, it is impossible to tell what was missed in the haste to excavate this enormous area. Ben-Dov says he "wanted to conclude this dig in our own generation." In fact, it was finished in just 12 years, and much information has been lost.

Another criticism is that the excavation did not leave any areas unexcavated. This denies future generations of archaeologists areas to work on at such time that archaeological methodology might be greatly improved.

In five years of excavation, Ben-Dov says 300,000 cubic meters of dirt was removed—a world record, he claims, that will not soon be broken. Some earth was removed by a bulldozer. Here is Ben-Dov's justification for using a bulldozer, an excavation method most archaeologists regard as anathema, especially in an area like the Temple Mount.

> "Working at an accelerated pace produced an appreciable amount of earth and fill that had to be disposed of. For this purpose we called in a bulldozer—after checking through the detritus by sinking a number of investigatory shafts—and thus saved precious time. A bulldozer is the last thing an archaeologist would normally expect to find at a dig, but the experience I had acquired excavating the Belvoir fortress taught me that if its operator is graced with a sensitive soul, and if an archaeologist is stationed permanently beside its scoop, it can be a very helpful instrument. As time went on a quiet revolution took place, and today you can see bulldozers working at many sites."

Many archaeologists will find it difficult to accept this defense of a bulldozer. Nor would they agree that Ben-Dov's "quiet revolution" has in fact occurred.

Within the archaeological community, the criticisms of this dig are controversial issues. Assessing their validity is often difficult because the pertinent evidence is voluminous and often unavailable. Few archaeologists really want to get involved in someone else's dig. It is not very pleasant to be critical of one's colleagues. Some of the criticisms that have been privately leveled at this dig have also been directed at other digs and other archaeologists. Yet, despite all these reservations, it is not helpful simply to sweep the issues under the rug. Within the profession, this dig has privately been the subject of serious criticism, much more than most.

As if all these problems weren't enough, near the end of the dig a rift developed between Benjamin Mazar, the distinguished dean of the Israeli archaeological community and director of the excavation, and Meir Ben-Dov, the dig's field director. The two men are now operating independently, each having seized what records he could. According to most reports, Ben-Dov was the more successful in sequestering excavation records.

In 1969 and 1971 two preliminary reports were published on the first three seasons of excavation. Additional preliminary reports would appear, one would expect, at regular intervals. None has.

In 1975 a book entitled *Mountain of the Lord** was published by Mazar "assisted by" Gaalyah Cornfeld, with David Noel Freedman as consultant. The subject was the archaeology of Jerusalem. The book includes materials from the Temple Mount, Mazar's dig. Reportedly, Mazar was so dissatisfied with the book—he supposedly had little to do with writing it—that he requested that it not be reviewed in the *Israel Exploration Journal* or the *Revue Biblique*. It was not.

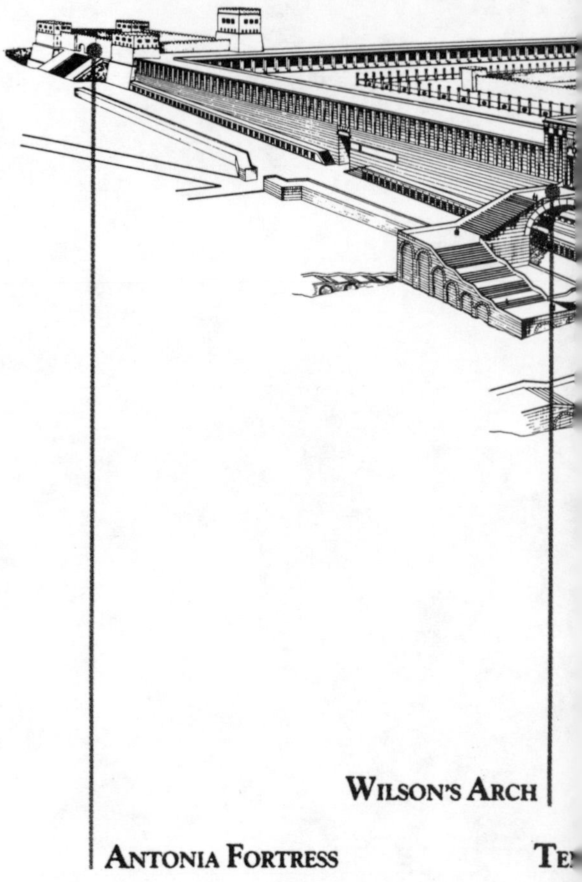

Now we have a new popular book by Ben-Dov—*In the Shadow of the Temple*. The Hebrew edition, a bit more modestly and accurately entitled *In the Shadow of the Temple Mount*, was discussed in a Hebrew Jerusalem newspaper* by Dan Bahat, Israel's district archaeologist for Jerusalem. Bahat characterized Ben-Dov's book with an expletive unprintable in the pages of **BAR**. According to Bahat, "the book is a scandal of the first degree." At a reception for the book's publication, the archaeological community stayed away in droves. Neither Mazar, the dig director, nor Joseph Aviram, the executive secretary of the Israel Exploration Society, attended. When queried by a newspaper as to why his fellow archaeologists stayed away from the reception, Ben-Dov

Y. RACHLIN

WILSON'S ARCH

ANTONIA FORTRESS

TE

* New York: Doubleday.

* *Kol Ha'ir*, October 29, 1982, p. 21.

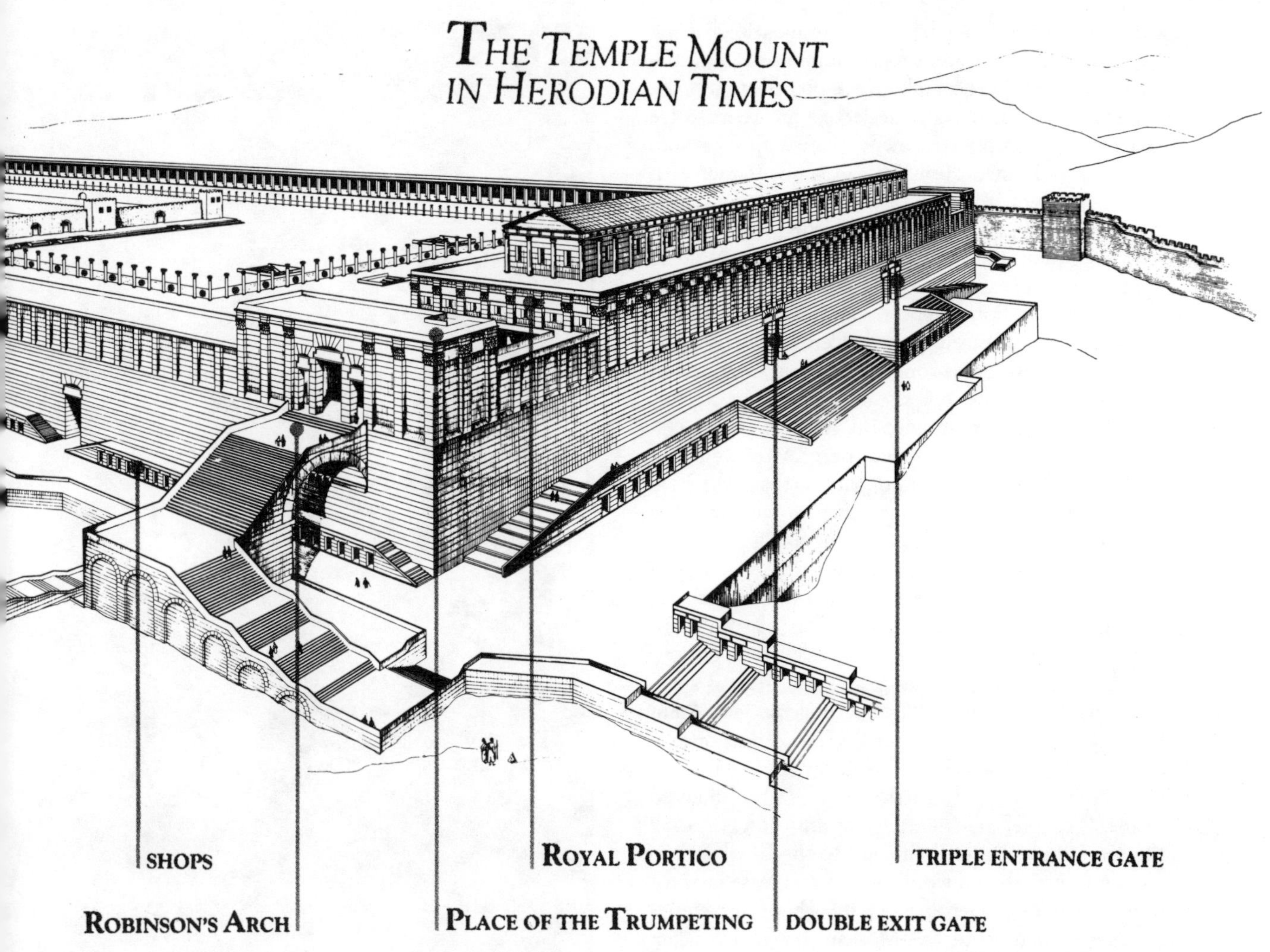

explained that he is "a tiger who hunts alone"—and indeed he is: He has almost no close colleagues in the archaeological community and is generally considered a pariah by the archaeological establishment. He has no university affiliation, and it is safe to predict that the *Israel Exploration Journal* will either ignore his book or damn it.

Despite all the criticism and controversy that has surrounded this dig and despite all the scorn that has been heaped on Ben-Dov's book, it is a wonderful reading experience. It is informative, even riveting, not to be missed by anyone to whom Jerusalem is close at heart. The finds are amazing and Ben-Dov writes extremely well—an attribute not common among archaeologists.

In 380 pages Ben-Dov describes the finds from what he claims are 25 strata and 12 distinct periods, beginning with First Temple period tombs from the kingdom of Judah (c. ninth century B.C.) and ending with pottery and pipes from the period of the Ottoman Turks, who ruled the area from the early 16th century A.D. to the early 20th century. No period is neglected or sloughed over.

The most important finds come from the Herodian period (37 B.C.-4 B.C.), followed by the times of the Byzantine Christians (325-637 A.D.) and of the Moslem Omayyads (seventh to eighth centuries A.D.).

Each chapter begins with a masterfully written historical description that provides a setting for the account of the excavation and the finds related to that period.

One of the most exciting discoveries of the dig was a monumental staircase (on the southern side of the Temple Mount) that led up to the two main pilgrim entrances to the Temple area in the Herodian period. Interestingly enough, excavation here was possible only because of the archaeologists' excellent relationships with the local Moslem leadership and their understanding cooperation. The land in this area belongs to the *waqf*, the Moslem religious trust. Ultimately, the archaeologists obtained consent to excavate both from the tenants to whom the *waqf* had leased the land and from the *waqf* itself. In Ben-Dov's words:

> "Once again we invited a number of Moslem notables to visit the excavations, and once again they were convinced that the finds relating to Islam, together with the rest of the discoveries enabling us to decipher the secrets of ancient Jerusalem, were of major import. They were also convinced that there was no political motive behind our work and that the charges

about our desire to undermine the foundations of the Al Aqsa Mosque were totally unfounded. On the contrary, all the structurally weak points around the mosque, which had been neglected for years, were now receiving proper treatment. Many cups of savory coffee were downed during my subsequent talk with the trustees of the *waqf*, and the conversations rambled from one subject to another, in the best spirit of Oriental hospitality, before we got round to the matter of excavating south of the city wall. Here, again, we spent hours upon hours talking and drinking at a calm, leisurely pace before a contract was drawn up placing areas south of the Old City wall at our disposal for the purpose of excavation, reconstruction, and preservation of the remains.

"Not that the matter ended there. After we began working on the site, certain parties that will here remain unnamed used the agreement as an excuse to vilify a number of Moslem religious dignitaries. One of the *qadis* who signed the lease with us was even forced to relinquish his post, though he honored his signature and obligations anyway. The judge in question came from one of the leading Palestinian nationalist families of the previous generation (he was a relative of the former *mufti* of Jerusalem, Haj Amin el-Husseini), and his traditional rivals seized on the opportunity to blacken his name in the local Arab press. Sometime later I met the ex-*qadi*, who lamented to me, 'You see, my friend, there are those who sell their land to Jews and their souls to the Devil and no one says so much as a word. But when I lease land for the purpose of a scientific project whose discoveries tell us so much about the Moslem past in Jerusalem and of the kings and prophets whom we, too, venerate, see what happens. Still, you should know that I do not regret what I have done—not one whit. I am old, and in standing before God I am confident that what I did is for the best.' "

The magnificent staircase that was uncovered on the *waqf* land connected a public square in front of the Temple Mount with the Hulda Gates—entrance and exit gates to and from the Temple platform.

On these steps tens of thousands of pilgrims climbed to the Temple platform. One of them was doubtless Jesus of Nazareth.

Ben-Dov describes a visit to the site by an Ethiopian patriarch:

"The patriarch of the Ethiopian Church happened to visit the dig soon after we had uncovered these steps.

'Is it possible that Jesus and the Apostles walked up these stairs?' he asked. 'There's no doubt about it,' I told him. 'This is the main staircase that led to the Temple Mount, and it was the only one used by pilgrims bound for the Temple.' Upon hearing my answer, a wave of emotion swept over the patriarch and his retinue, and we paused so that they could offer up prayers on the spot."

The Hulda Gates opened into tunnels that led up to the esplanade on which the Temple was built. To get to

RICHARD NOWITZ

Jesus of Nazareth *undoubtedly walked down these steps, as did thousands of other Jews when they passed through the double-arched exit gate in the southern wall of the Temple Mount after leaving the Temple esplanade. Now sealed and blocked by a medieval building, the two arches are indiscernible, but a Herodian lintel fragment (above) from the 20-foot-high gate preserves for us a hint of the gate's original splendor.*

Always careful to avoid animal or human images—prohibited by the Second Commandment—Herodian stonecarvers chose flowers, fruit and geometric patterns to adorn the Temple Mount.

On the east part of this same southern wall, to the right of the steps, are three arches of another gate, also sealed. (See close-up on p. 12. The Double and Triple Gates are also called the Hulda Gates.) Similar steps 50 feet wide (not restored) led up to this triple gate, the main entryway to the Temple Mount. The steps are not high, only 7 to 10 inches, but their depths alternate—one step is 12 inches deep, the next 35, then 12 again, and so on. Thus the architect created an ascent that was not arduous, but that did require the climber to slow down and approach the holy site in a deliberate, unrushed way. (See artist's reconstruction, pp. 8-9.)

WERNER BRAUN

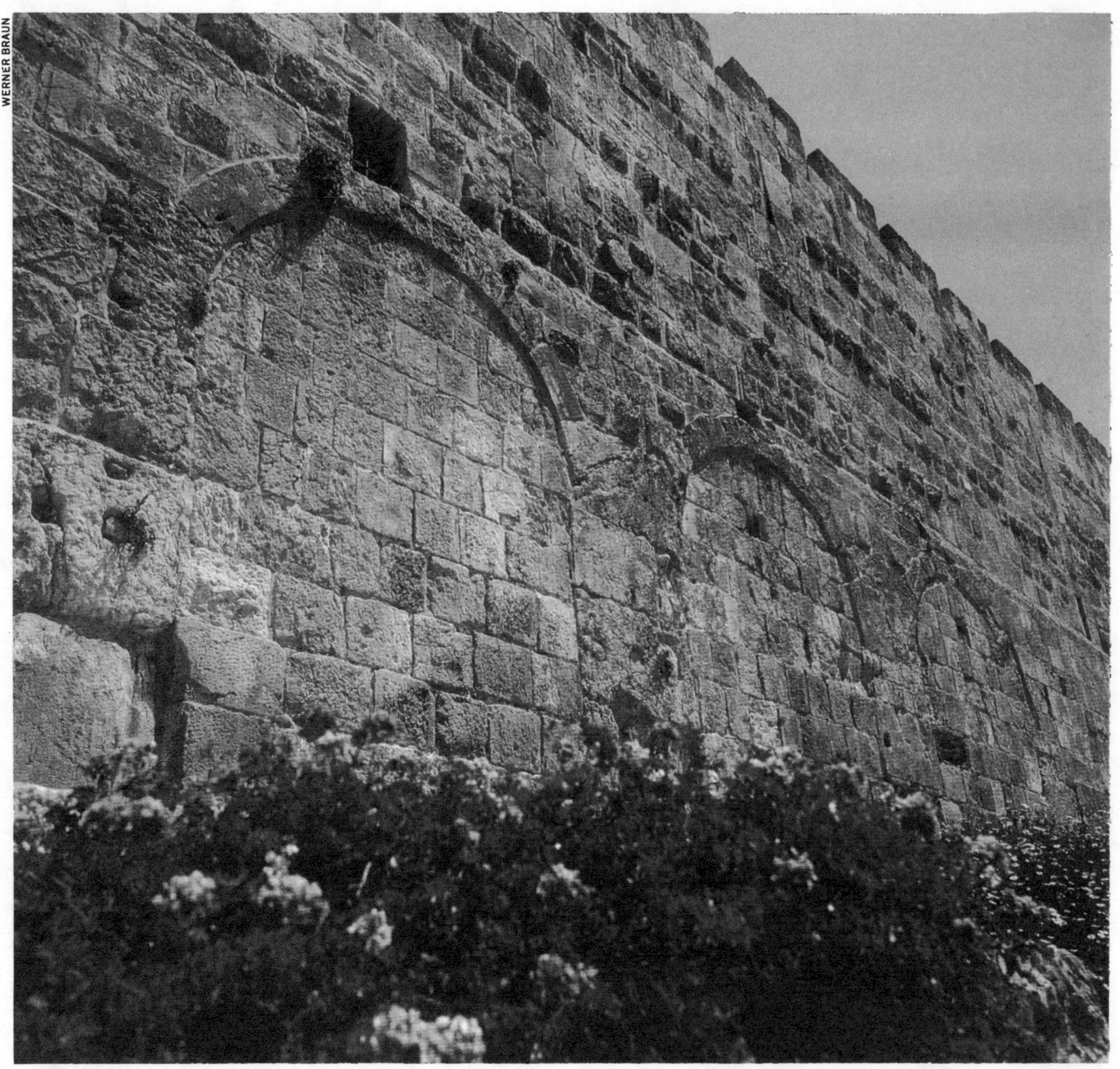

Sealed triple entrance *to the Temple Mount.*

the esplanade, pilgrims would walk through the triple gates, enter a sloping tunnel and walk up. To descend, they would walk through another tunnel that sloped down to the double exit gate. Today, these tunnels are under the Temple Mount, and no excavation can be undertaken there.

The Hulda Gates have long been blocked from the outside. The triple entrance is still easily visible, but only a bit of the lintel of the double gate is still exposed. Most of the gate is covered by a medieval building that rests up against the southern wall of the Temple Mount. Both tunnels can be entered, however, from inside the walls, although few Westerners have done so. For more than a hundred years before the recent study reported in Ben-Dov's book, no Western scholar had studied these tunnels. The Israeli archaeologists requested the *waqf's* permission to undertake a new study, and the request, in Ben-Dov's words, "was readily granted. We were even offered assistance in the form of lighting and ladders."

The original triple-gate tunnel, known in the New Testament as the Beautiful Gate (Acts 3:2), according to Ben-Dov, had been almost completely destroyed and rebuilt. The double-gate tunnel, however, was in significant part preserved in its original Herodian state. The western gatepost was preserved to a height of nearly 20 feet. According to Ben-Dov, the lintel above the gatepost is probably the original Herodian lintel.

The decorated domes inside the double-gate's entrance, as well as the inner walls of the tunnel and the

Flowers and geometric designs *covered the ceilings of the Hulda Gates' tunnels. These tunnels connected the Temple esplanade with openings in the southern wall.*

The flowers, though stylized, represented specific local species. The author and his excavation team discovered some 300 fragments like these carved stone decorations, which probably adorned the Triple Gate (opposite). In the Double Gate vestibule, carvings still decorate the ceiling, but they cannot be seen without permission of the Moslem authorities.

These fragments give us tangible evidence of how the decorations on the entrance to the Temple itself may have appeared. Probably painted in realistic colors, the decorations were by all reports magnificent. Josephus exclaims that the Temple was "the most wonderful edifice ever seen or heard of, both for its size and construction and for the lavish perfection of detail and the glory of its holy places" (Jewish War VI.267).

MEIR BEN-DOV

MEIR BEN-DOV

tunnel's central pillar are all original, dating to the Herodian period. The walls of the tunnel are built of ashlars worked to a fine smooth finish without margins or bosses (unlike the ashlars used in the facing wall of the Temple Mount itself).

The domes in the ceiling of the gates are over 16 feet in diameter. They are among the earliest surviving domes known to us from classical architecture. These domes were embossed with a variety of floral and geometric decorations that left no open spaces. Nor was there even a hint of an animal or human image—in strict conformity with the Second Commandment's prohibition of graven images. The predominant floral motif was the vine with clusters of grapes—a symbol of blessing, happiness and productivity. From literary sources, we know that the entrance to the Herodian Temple itself was decorated with a fruited vine motif fashioned entirely of gold. The same motif in the Hulda Gate gives us a clear idea of how this decoration must have appeared on the Temple itself. The flowers in the domes of the Hulda Gate tunnels were originally painted in appropriate colors. Ben-Dov concludes, "Without actually seeing these domes and their ornamentation, it is impossible fully to appreciate Jewish art of the Second Temple period." Alas, the public cannot enter this area.

In the excavations outside the Hulda Gates, the archaeologists found nearly 300 stone fragments that apparently came from destroyed domes in these tunnels. Although these tunnels are not open to visitors, we can get some idea of what they look like from these fragments and from Ben-Dov's descriptions and drawings.

Just as Ben-Dov was able to maintain excellent relations with local Moslem authorities, despite their initial objections to the dig, so was he successful with the rabbis. When the Ministry of Religious Affairs itself decided to undertake archaeological clearance north of that part of the Temple Mount's Western Wall dedicated to Jewish prayer (the Wailing Wall), the rabbis asked Ben-Dov to be their archaeological supervisor. Ironically enough, his study of that area's most famous and impressive monument—the mighty span known as Wilson's Arch—led him to redate it from King Herod's time to the Moslem period—to support a bridge from the Temple Mount across the valley to the Upper City. Although it was originally built in the Herodian period, Wilson's Arch was apparently destroyed and then rebuilt, most probably by the Moslems.

After the Roman destruction of Jerusalem in 70 A.D., the area around the Temple Mount lay in ruins. The Romans later rebuilt Jerusalem as a Roman camp, renaming it Aelia Capitolina in honor of its founder, the Roman emperor Hadrian, whose full name was Publius Aelius Hadrianus. Roman legionaries camped at the foot of the Temple Mount. A memento of a Celtic calvary unit—a large figurine of a spear-carrying Celtic soldier seated on his horse—was found in the excavation at

MEIR BEN-DOV

Celtic rider. *Bearing a shield and a spear, this bronze figurine is a memento of a Celtic cavalry unit that served in Jerusalem with the Roman garrison in the second century A.D. Only 2.5 inches tall, it was found near the southwest corner of the Temple Mount, in remains from Aelia Capitolina, the Roman city established by the emperor Hadrian on the site of Jewish Jerusalem.*

this level. Another find from this period was a Latin inscription mentioning Titus, who was the conqueror and destroyer of Jerusalem.

In 324 A.D. Jerusalem passed into Christian hands. Jerusalem soon became a pilgrim and tourist center. Ben-Dov tells us that "it was important to the Byzantines that the [Temple Mount] remain in ruins as tangible evidence that Jesus' prophecy of the Temple's detruction had been borne out." The area around the Temple Mount became a residential quarter. Many of the Byzantine houses, especially from the late Byzantine period (early seventh century), have been preserved to the second story and are beautifully reconstructed in an archaeological garden that now adorns the site.

For one brief moment in the Byzantine period, the Jews harbored the illusion that their Temple might be restored. In 361 A.D. the Emperor Julian assumed the helm of the Roman empire. A thorough-going Hellenist, he wanted to restore the glory of classical Rome to the empire. He sought to undo the alliance between the empire and the Church and to re-introduce religious freedom. In pursuit of this policy—and because he wanted Jewish assistance in a military campaign he was planning against the Persians in the east—Julian encouraged the Jews to return to Jerusalem and rebuild their Temple. The Jews immediately made plans, but in 363 Julian was killed and was succeeded by a loyal Chris-

Titus inscription (right). *Latin letters carved into a stone column include the name of Titus, the general who led the catastrophic assault on Jerusalem in 70 A.D. The complete Tenth Roman Legion dedicatory inscription appears in the drawing below.*

According to Josephus, Titus destroyed the Temple on the ninth of the Hebrew month of Av, the same date the Babylonians destroyed Solomon's Temple. The ninth of Av has been and continues to be a day of fasting and prayer for Jews throughout the world. Ben-Dov writes of the inscription's discovery: "The year was 1970, on the eve of the ninth of Av. We were filled with emotion because of the uncanny symbolism of the find. One thousand nine hundred years ago to the day, Titus had briefed his troops on the storming of the Temple Mount. And now, in the renewed State of Israel, standing in Jerusalem, digging alongside the Temple Mount, we had come into tangible contact with Titus and his legions. What more could an archaeologist ask for?"

The inscription states Titus's name and surname Vespasianus and his imperial titles as in Imperator Augustus, etc., and also mentions the Tenth Roman Legion.

IMPCAESAI
VESPASIAN
AVG IMPT
SARVESPAVG
L
AVG PR PR

MEIR BEN-DOV

tian. As Ben-Dov relates, "The wheel of history turned back again."

From the time of Julian's brief reign, the excavators uncovered a Hebrew inscription carved into the wall of the Temple Mount—a variant of Isaiah 66:14 expressing hope for the national resurrection of the Jewish people, as well as the resurrection of the dead. It was apparently carved by those who intended, by permission of the Emperor Julian, to rebuild the Temple on the esplanade above: "And when you see this, your heart shall rejoice, and their bones shall flourish like an herb . . . ."

In the late Byzantine period, the houses were more extensive and palatial. In addition to the remains of walls, vaults and stairways, the excavation found pottery, cooking equipment, ovens and even a bathroom with a seat built to hold a chamber pot. Ben-Dov remarks, "This particular toilet did not flush, but in other houses we found the equivalent of flush toilets with pipes leading directly into the sewage system."

In 614 A.D., the period of Byzantine splendor in Jerusalem ended. The city fell to the Persians. The Persian empire had long been the rival of the Byzantine empire; in the early seventh century, war between these great empires broke out in earnest. As Ben-Dov explains: "In contemporary terms, one could call this confrontation a world war."

Jewish assistance was important to the Persians in their drive on Palestine.

> "The Persians asked for their aid and were rewarded with Jewish support in the form of funds, food, and primarily manpower, as many young Jews flocked to join their forces. In addition, appreciable assistance was profferred by the Jewish community within the Persian Empire itself. The Jews participated in this war not as mercenaries but as a nation with its own stake in the victory, since they regarded the war as a struggle for national liberation . . . . It seemed almost as if the Messiah's tread could be heard in the distance, and the entire nation dedicated itself to the battle. When Jerusalem fell to the Persians in 614, the hammering of the stonemasons who would reconstruct the Temple was already echoing in Jewish ears.
>
> "The Christian community of Palestine suffered greatly at the hands of the Persians (as had the Christians of Syria and the other conquered lands), and of the many Christians who were put to the sword, particularly vulnerable were men of the cloth. For Christianity, the official state religion, had been used to advance the political aims of the empire, and the Persians chose not to distinguish between the political regime in the strictest sense of the term and the reli-

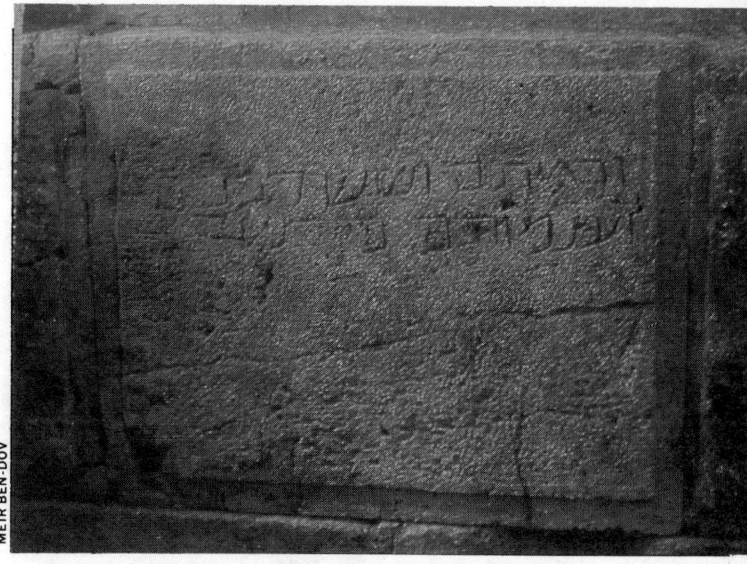

MEIR BEN-DOV

וראיתם ושש לבבכם
ועצמותכם כדשא

Silent testimony *to hopes of rebuilding the Temple. Carved into a wall of the Temple Mount in the fourth century, this Hebrew inscription (above), a variant of Isaiah 66:14, bespoke the mood of optimism that the Temple would soon be rebuilt: "And when you see this, your heart shall rejoice, and their bones shall flourish like an herb . . ."*

In 361, Julian, a Hellenist, was emperor. Working to restore religious freedom to the Roman empire, Julian encouraged the Jews to return to Jerusalem and rebuild the Temple. But Julian was killed in 363, and his successor, Jovian, once again aligned the Empire with Christianity. The prophecy of Isaiah was not realized.

MEIR BEN-DOV

"Blessed be they *who dwell in this house" reads a Greek inscription (right) in an elegant mosaic floor of a Byzantine-period house. Almost every substantial Jerusalem house built in the Byzantine period had a mosaic floor in one or another of its rooms, thanks to the availability of a large work force of mosaic artisans.*

gious functionaries who had incidentally served its ends. The damage to the Christian community was particularly notable in Jerusalem, where two forces joined to wreak havoc: the Persians, who rightly believed the city to be one of the underpinnings of Christianity and of the empire's strength in the East; and the Jews of Palestine, who harbored a deep grudge over the Byzantines' general hostility toward the Jews throughout the empire, no less than for the deeds of Justinian and his successors in Jerusalem—and particularly on the Temple Mount. Hence the chronicles of the day are replete with acts of murder, plunder, and wanton destruction."

Jerusalem was reconquered by the Byzantines in 629.

"The return of the Byzantines was a heavy blow to the Jews of Palestine . . . the stage had been set for a national and religious revival. The Jews could almost see the restored Temple standing before them—and all that it implied. And then, so quickly and abruptly, everything had been reversed. Jewish families that had clung to their faith for generations, despite a policy of bloody persecution and attempts to convert them to Christianity, now abandoned Judaism and converted out of sheer despair."

The war had changed few boundaries:

CLAUDIA HIMMELMAN

Jewish life in Jerusalem ***saw a renaissance beginning in 614, when the Persians defeated the Byzantines. Jewish settlement in the holy city—sharply curtailed by Roman and Byzantine law—picked up quickly. Some families moved into houses which the previous tenants had decorated with symbols of their own religion. On this house, a cross on the lintel was plastered over and Jewish symbols, seven-branched candelabra*** **(menorot)*****, ram's horns*** **(shofarot)*****, and incense shovels*** **(machtot)** ***were added.***

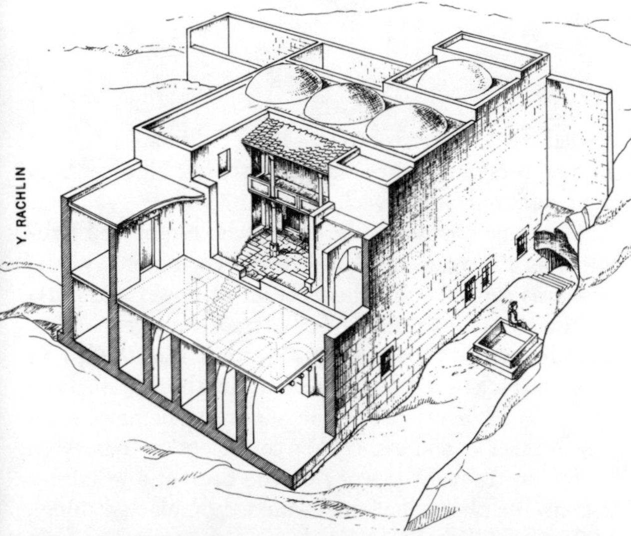

Y. RACHLIN

Byzantine houses ***(early seventh century) alongside a wall from the Omayyad period (660-750 A.D.), left. One elegant home, center, had a peristyle court; its columns have been returned to their original positions. Under the Roman-Byzantine emperor Constantine at the beginning of the fourth century A.D., Jerusalem became a Christian city. The emperor promptly began a campaign to encourage European Christian settlement in Palestine, and home-building boomed.***

Later in the Byzantine period (sixth century A.D.), houses were also built around courtyards (reconstruction drawing, above), but the columns were structural, supporting partial roofs, not decorative as they had been in the early Byzantine period. Usually built on bedrock, these houses often rose several stories. The inhabitants seem to have been oblivious to air pollution: They installed workshops in ground floor rooms (for tanning, dyeing and finishing cloth, refining copper, or other light industries), while they made their living quarters in the upper story.

"Tens of thousands of lost lives and the harrowing damage to the world economy had brought the sides right back to where they had started. With one major difference: The economic turmoil of the age, particularly among the peoples inhabiting the ravaged outlying areas, and the weakness of the exhausted rival armies practically invited the rise of yet a new rival—the Moslem Arabs. So it was that the Moslem Empire rose in the wake of the relentless clashes between two older, declining powers."

The Pyrrhic Byzantine victory was short-lived. In 638 the Arabs entered Jerusalem and received the surrender of the city from the local patriarch. Thus began Moslem rule.

From the few years of Persian rule and from the few years of Byzantine rule after that, the excavators found houses decorated with Jewish symbols, including seven-branched candelabra (*menorot*), palm branches (*lulavim*) and ram's horns (*shofarot*). In the doorpost of one of the buildings, a niche was carved to hold a *mezuzah*, a small case holding a parchment inscribed with two passages from Deuteronomy. (*Mezuzot* can still be found in Jewish homes today, in fulfillment of the Biblical command to place these words on the doorposts [*mezuzot*] of your gates [Deuteronomy 6:9; 11:20].) But this same house

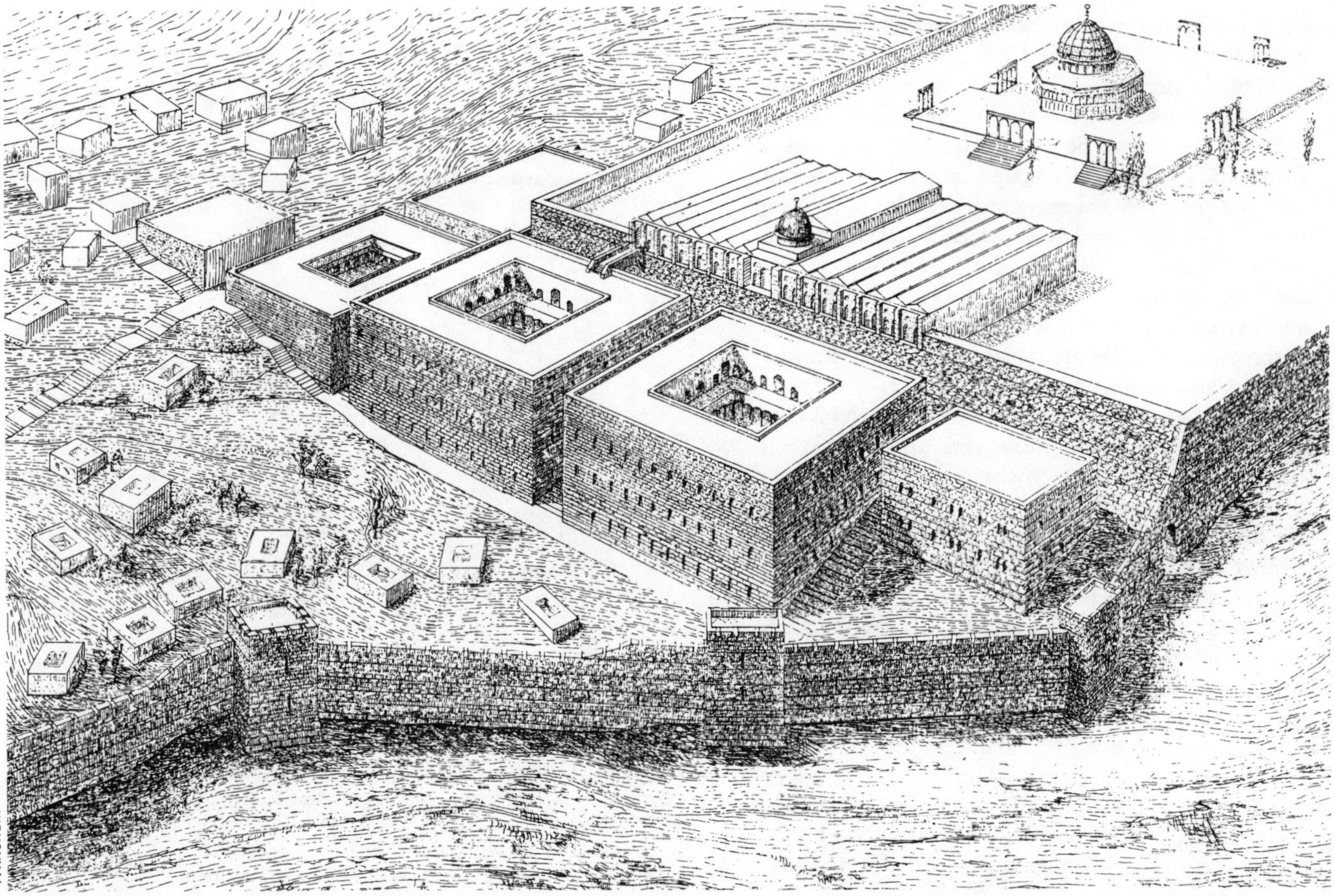

Y. RACHLIN

Y. RACHLIN

bore on its lintel a cross, a reflection of a previous inhabitant's faith.

In the late seventh century and early eighth century, the Omayyad Moslems built the Dome of the Rock and Al Aqsa mosques on the Temple Mount. Ben-Dov calls these structures the "two jewels and among the earliest achievements of Moslem architecture."

The origins of these magnificent buildings are obscure, however, because the Abbassid dynasty that succeeded the Omayyads attempted to obliterate not only all members of the preceding dynasty but all records of their achievements as well.

It was the Omayyads, however, who established Jerusalem as a Moslem religious center. Their primary purpose was geopolitical. Their center of power was Syria and Palestine, not Arabia. To buttress these geopolitical considerations, a religious justification was needed to make Jerusalem a Moslem center. In the Koran, Ben-Dov tells us, every detail but one in Mohammed's life has a specific address. The sole exception relates to Mohammed's night journey on the back of a wondrous animal—half horse, half man—named Burak (Lightning). Mohammed rode Burak to the "outer mosque" where the angel Gabriel raised Mohammed on his horse up to heaven to meet Moses, Elijah and Jesus. The location of the "outer mosque" is not clearly identified in the Koran. Many scholars believe the reference is to the outer mosque in Medina. But in the Omayyad period, the tradition developed that the outer mosque was in Jerusalem. Thus a rationale was provided for constructing Al Aqsa Mosque, which means "the outer." The rock mass beneath the Dome of the Rock is said to bear Burak's hoofprint as he pushed off on his ascent to heaven.

Ben-Dov notes that a similar phenomenon occurred in the development of Jewish tradition. When King David made Jerusalem the capital of his kingdom in about 1000 B.C., it too needed the enhancement of a

Floral designs *(right) painted shades of red on white plaster originally decorated an Omayyad caliph's palace from the seventh or eighth century. An enormous building, 300 feet long and 250 feet wide, the palace had an immense central courtyard (reconstruction drawing, opposite, below) and a roof bridge that gave the caliph direct access to the Al Aqsa mosque (see drawing, opposite, above).*

The palace was part of a large-scale building complex that included an adjacent identical building and a bathhouse. Devastated by an earthquake in 747, this magnificent achievement of Moslem architecture was then buried by newer buildings erected by the Abbassids, the dynasty that succeeded the Omayyads. It remained unknown for 1,200 years, until Israeli archaeologists brought it to light.

MEIR BEN-DOV

religious consecration, especially since the Temple to house the Ark was to be built there. Like the Koran, the Bible assigns a specific location to most events. But there is no location specified for Mt. Moriah, where Abraham offered to sacrifice Isaac. So the tradition arose that the rock mass on the Temple Mount, now inside the Dome of the Rock, was the very spot on Mt. Moriah where Abraham, in obedience to God's command and to show his complete devotion, drew his knife to sacrifice his son Isaac and was stopped by the angel of the Lord (Genesis 22).

At the foot of the Temple Mount, the archaeologists found one of the many surprises of the dig. During the Omayyad period, the Moslems had built a series of magnificent palaces in this area, right over the ruins of the Byzantine houses. These impressive Omayyad structures have been preserved in the archaeological garden that now covers the site. Because the palaces were built by the Omayyads, the Abbassid histories omitted all reference to them, so they were completely unknown until excavated by the Israelis.

Interestingly enough, excavations in this area had been conducted in the 1960s on behalf of the Jordanian Department of Antiquities in order to decide whether a school could be built on the site. These excavations were directed by two of the world's foremost archaeologists, Dame Kathleen Kenyon of the British School of Archaeology and Père Roland de Vaux of the French École Biblique. However, they limited themselves, as their methodology required, to several small squares. They mistakenly identified the walls of an Omayyad palace as Byzantine. King Hussein therefore concluded that the school could be built on the site. The plan was aborted by the Six-Day War in June 1967.

Ben-Dov is critical of Kenyon and de Vaux's methodology:

> "The sad fact is that not only did these scholars fail to define the plan of the structure because of the limited scope of their excavations, even their dating of the remains was wrong . . . I realized that our excavation in the vicinity of the Temple Mount would have to be conducted very differently from the approach taken by Kenyon and de Vaux. The only way to achieve reliable results would be to dig up the whole area."

Ben-Dov explains his own methodology:

> "We began to expose the area by conducting the excavation on two planes. One was horizontal, meaning the investigation of broad, single-stratum areas. The other was vertical by means of sinking a shaft at the periphery of the area and going down through several strata in order to tentatively identify them and plan the continuation of the dig downward. Based on this thinking . . . I called in a bulldozer and put it to work. With the heavy equipment backed by the efforts of hundreds of laborers and volunteers, within a relatively short time we had opened up the western area below the southern wall and realized that it was occupied by a single immense building. All the exposed walls, including the sections discovered by Kenyon and de Vaux, belonged to one and the same structure: an almost perfectly square 2-acre building that was flanked on the north by a broad paved street."

The building itself—an Omayyad palace—had been coated with white plaster and had been painted with lovely frescoes and beautifully embossed stones—"an edifice of unusual splendor." Unfortunately, only fragments of the decorations survived. A bridge led from the palace to the Al Aqsa Mosque on the Temple Mount, so the palace probably belonged to the caliph himself.

Ben-Dov concludes his account of this discovery:

> "For 1,200 years the remains of these Omayyad buildings awaited their redemption. For 1,200 years the Abbassids succeeded in their mission of wiping out all trace of the Omayyad enterprise in Jerusalem, but now the archaeologist's spade had brought them to light. It is one of the ironies of this city's history that this remarkable discovery was made by Israeli archaeologists, while King Hussein—a scion of the Hashemite dynasty, which traces back to the family of the prophet Mohammed—was responsible for further bury-

ing all trace of this glorious palace by building yet another structure over its ruins in the belief that they were the remains of a Christian building."

Ben-Dov proceeds to trace the history of the site in the days of the Abbassids, the Fatamids, the Seljuk Turks, the evidence of Jewish pilgrims, the Crusaders, the Mongols, the Mamelukes. Then, probably in the Ottoman period, a long, enclosed market or bazaar was built south of the Temple Mount, containing small shops. Stone troughs for feeding sheep and goats were found in some of the stalls. So the area remained until the end of the 19th century when the marketplace shifted. Then the area became partly the city dump and partly agricultural land, marked off with small vegetable plots—until the excavation that led ultimately to the archaeological garden that now covers the site.

There is much to criticize in Ben-Dov's book. Most important is that the author's archaeological conclusions often come down to mere assertions: He says they are so; we must accept them on faith. His reconstructions are sometimes unsupported by evidence. Too often we want to know more of his reasoning and more of the evidence. This is especially true regarding many of the controversial matters Ben-Dov discusses. As to these, Ben-Dov usually omits discussion of other views and sometimes even fails to note that there are other views.

For example, the mysterious word *millo*, which is referred to in Samuel, Kings and Chronicles and is usually untranslated, in fact denotes, we are told, the earth fill south of the Temple Mount that Ben-Dov removed (with a bulldozer!). Kathleen Kenyon argued, perhaps more persuasively, that *millo* referred to the stone terraces that supported structures further south on the eastern slope of the City of David. More recently, the stepped-stone structure excavated by Yigal Shiloh has emerged as a candidate for the *millo*.* But none of these other possibilities is mentioned in Ben-Dov's book.

In the second century B.C., the Seleucid king Antiochus IV (Epiphanes) ravaged Jerusalem and desecrated the Temple in his effort to impose Hellenism on the Jews. To control the Jews and their activities on the Temple Mount, Antiochus built a mighty fortress called the Acra. When the Jews regained their freedom at the time of the Maccabean revolt, the Jewish rulers (Hasmoneans) razed the hated Acra to the ground. Its location has long been a matter of intense scholarly dispute. Ben-Dov claims to have excavated remains of the Acra just south of the Temple Mount. But we are given very little of the evidence. Is he correct in his claim? He does mention that there are other theories, and he considers and rejects the suggestion of his friend Yoram Tsafrir (whom he does not name). But the discussion is so incomplete that the reader cannot reach his or her own conclusion.

Perhaps the greatest church of the Byzantine era was the famous Nea, lost to history for 1,400 years. Just inside the Old City walls, Nahman Avigad, one of Israel's most highly regarded archaeologists, found unmistakable remains of the Nea. Ben-Dov claims to have found part of an apse of the Nea extending outside the Old City wall. The two men disagree on the precise location of the church, its plan, and the interpretation of the remains. Ben-Dov makes no mention of Avigad's interpretations.

Ben-Dov will reply to these charges of omission—with considerable validity—that there was simply no room to go into further detail. The book is already 380 pages. In his introduction, he confesses that when he agreed to write the book he had no idea how difficult it would be to include everything in a single volume. As it is, the publisher agreed to extend "the book's length to a third more than originally planned."

Moreover, it is in the nature of popular books not to give the detailed evidence. This is no less true of Yadin's popular books, or more recently, of Nahman Avigad's *Discovering Jerusalem*, in which he summarizes his own excavations in the Jewish Quarter of Jerusalem's Old City.*

In short, the criticisms of Ben-Dov's conclusions will have to be thrashed out in the scholarly journals. But can this occur before the scientific report is published? And when, if ever, will this report come out?

There are other criticisms. Professional archaeologists will point out the many errors in details and even in plans, as well as the inconsistencies and omissions. There is no index or list of illustrations—again probably because of lack of space. There are no footnotes and only rare citations to sources.

Roman legionaries are called legionnaires. Father Bargil Pixner is referred to as Father Bargil Fixner. On one occasion, Aelia Capitolina is referred to as "Aelia Capitolonia." The author fails to mention that it was the excavation architect, Brian Lalor,** who first suggested that Robinson's Arch supported a monumental stairway, rather than a bridge.

But all this is caviling. Ben-Dov's book is a splendid one, despite its deficiencies. There is an enormous amount of material here—beautifully illustrated, often in color—that can be found nowhere else. For this, we must all be grateful. And the story is told very well indeed—with engagingly written historical background and an exciting, even suspenseful way of relating the finds and their interpretation. Ben-Dov asks meaningful questions of his material and vividly brings the past to life, giving the reader an exciting sense of "You are there."

* See "Has Jerusalem's Millo Been Found?" **BAR**, July/August 1982 and "*New York Times* Misrepresents Major Jerusalem Discovery," **BAR**, July/August 1981.

* See "Jerusalem Flourishing—A Craft Center for Stone, Pottery and Glass," by Nahman Avigad and "Jerusalem in Flames—The Burnt House Captures a Moment in Time," **BAR**, November/December 1983 [78-102]. See also Philip J. King's review of *Discovering Jerusalem: Recent Archaeological Excavations in the Upper City* by Nahman Avigad in the same issue.

** The failure to mention Lalor may stem from the fact that Lalor wrote to senior members of Israel's archaeological community charging that Ben-Dov had improperly confiscated part of the dig records, in effect ousting the dig director, Benjamin Mazar.

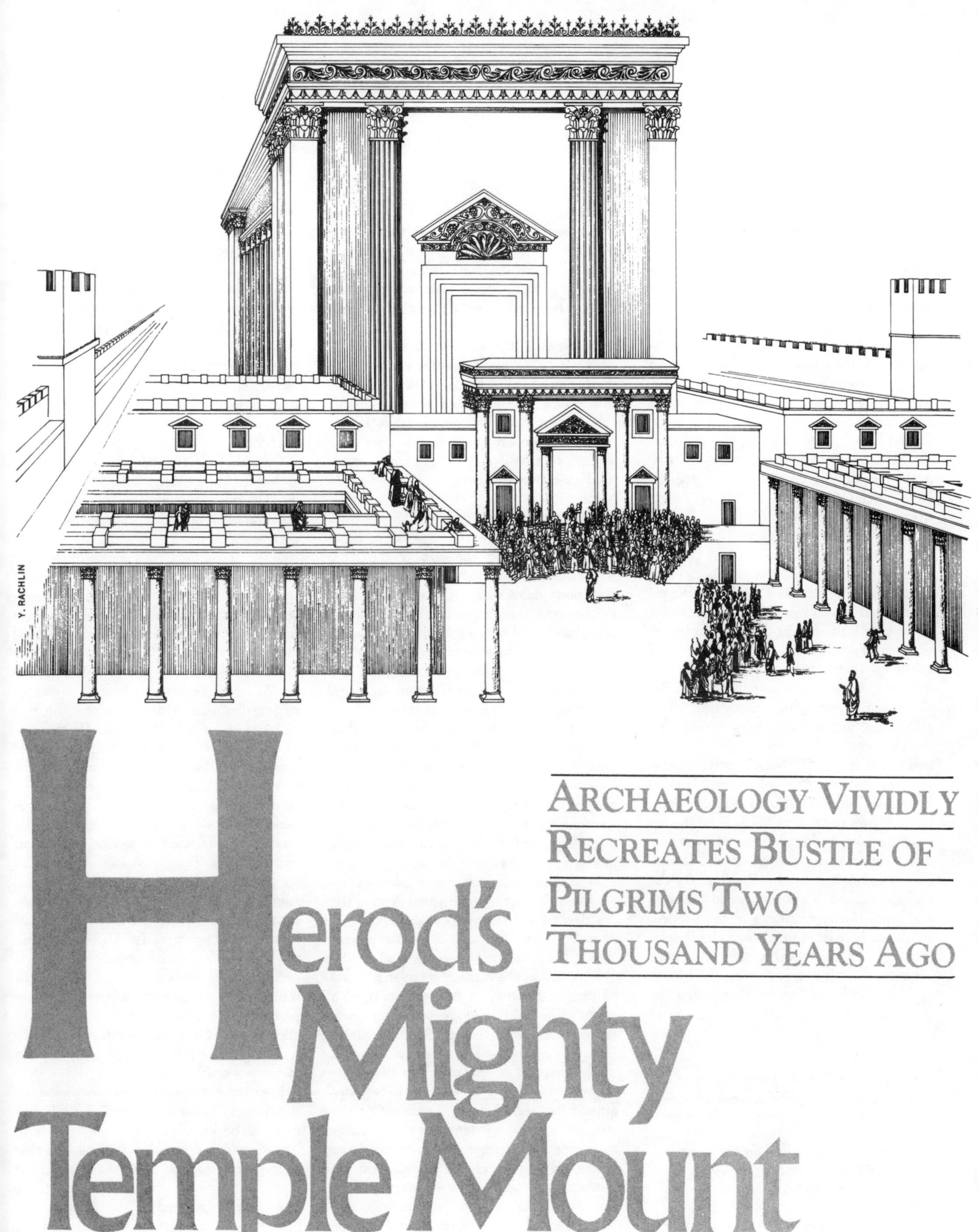

Herod's Mighty Temple Mount

Archaeology Vividly Recreates Bustle of Pilgrims Two Thousand Years Ago

SOLOMON'S TEMPLE was destroyed by the Babylonians in 586 B.C. when they conquered Jerusalem. A half century later, the returning exiles, under the leadership of Ezra and Nehemiah, built the Second Temple, a modest structure that gradually fell into disrepair. This temple was remodeled and rebuilt during the last quarter of the last century before the Common Era by Herod the Great. So complete was this rebuilding that some scholars refer to Herod's temple as the third temple. But in Jewish tradition it is the Second Temple, only rebuilt by Herod. When the Roman army conquered Jerusalem in 70 A.D., the Roman general Titus destroyed Herod's rebuilt Second Temple, thus ending what scholars call the First Jewish Revolt. (Another Jewish revolt against Rome was to follow in 132 A.D.)

Perhaps the best way to appreciate the magnificence of Herod's Temple and the reconstructed and enlarged esplanade on which it was built is to begin at the end, just before the Roman destruction. Titus's siege of Jerusalem was at its height in 70 A.D., the culmination of a four-year war that had begun as a Jewish revolt against increasingly intolerable, and incompetent, Roman rule. The Romans conducted their siege operation slowly but surely. Within the city, frustration ate away at the beleaguered Jews as hunger stalked them and a pall of failure hovered over their strongholds. Even though it was clear that the fall of the city was only days away, a week at most, no one considered surrendering to the Romans. As the end approached, Titus summoned his General Staff, the commanders of the Legions, to discuss how to proceed once the Roman forces had broken into the city. Their consultation was apparently held on the Mount of Olives, with the Temple Mount, in all its glory, laid out at their feet.

Overleaf: *The Second Temple, built by Herod the Great in 20 B.C., where tens of thousands thronged to worship at the major Jewish holidays and pilgrimage festivals. Fragments of Corinthian columns, grape arbors and flowers carved in stone have recently been discovered in extensive archaeological excavations next to the Temple Mount, allowing an artist to suggest this reconstruction.*

An account of this discussion is preserved in the works of Tacitus, one of the greatest of Roman historians: "It is said that Titus, who called the council, declared that the first thing to decide is whether or not to destroy the Temple, one of man's consummate building achievements. A few of [the officers] felt that it would not be right to destroy a holy building renowned as one of the greatest products of human endeavor . . . ."

The fact that hardened army officers at the end of a brutal war were troubled by the question of how to proceed after their conquest is an eloquent tribute to the unparalleled majesty of the Temple and the Temple Mount. It was a custom of the age to punish rebellious nations by destroying their temples, and one would expect this rule to apply all the more so in the case of the Jews, whose defiance and obstinacy stemmed from a religion, philosophy, and national outlook in which the Temple and the Temple Mount played a central role. However, the Temple had earned itself a reputation as one of the greatest cultural attainments of all time, and such distinction had to be taken into account.

Testaments to the glory of Herod's Temple and the Temple Mount he designed as its podium are naturally found in contemporaneous Jewish sources as well. The sages of Israel—who had seen many lavish edifices and were familiar with such cities as Rome, Alexandria, Antioch and Athens—had a saying: "Whoever has not seen Herod's building has never seen a beautiful structure."

Most of all, however, a sense of the Temple Mount's magnificence emerges from the descriptions and impressions of Flavius Josephus, the Jewish historian of the war against Rome. Josephus lived at a time when the Temple was at the acme of its splendor, and he became a witness to its destruction. As a native of Jerusalem and the son of a priestly family, he knew the Temple and the Temple Mount down to the last detail and devoted whole chapters of his works to describing them. These accounts provide us with so astonishing and detailed a picture of the structure's power and grandeur that in many cases they sometimes strike the reader as the product of an overactive imagination. In summing up a series of descriptions praising the Temple, for example, Josephus tells that "The external facade of the Temple had all that it takes to excite wonder in the eye and in the heart." Some scholars were indisposed to accept his descriptions at face value, treating them instead as oriental flights of fancy or, at best, hyperbole. With a measure of condescension, one scholar attempted to defend these ostensible exaggerations by saying that Josephus undoubtedly suffered a lapse of memory as a result of his distance from the Temple and his being distracted by the hustle, bustle, and pleasures of life at the Roman emperor's court where, after the Temple's destruction, he lived while writing his books.

On the basis of finds uncovered in our archaeological investigations, we are able to say that the details given in Josephus's works are not only far from exaggerations, they correspond amazingly to what has been uncovered in the field. As a matter of fact, the degree of precision in the factual information Josephus imparts to us is quite remarkable—though one may well take issue in some cases with his analyses and historical judgments.

Herod is often perceived as a hard-hearted despot who was more interested in immortalizing his name than in serving the best interests of his subjects. It was for this reason, scholars often contend, that he invested most of his kingdom's resources into his monumental building project in Jerusalem, confident that it would bring him eternal fame. Jewish sages of the past reasoned that Herod felt the need to repent for his sins and built the Temple Mount as an act of contrition. In assessing the deeds of political figures, however, we must be wary of personalizing motives to arrive at simple answers. Herod's motive for undertaking this ambitious construction project was far less personal—and more prosaic, if you will. It was an attempt to solve a constellation of problems created by the mass movement of pilgrims to and from the Temple Mount. Put simply, Herod needed to relieve his city of a monstrous traffic jam.

Ever since it was first built by Solomon, the Temple stood at the top of a hill that came to be known as the Temple Mount. The summit was a relatively small area that sloped off steeply on all sides except to the north. As a result of this topography, the masses that streamed to the Temple were forced to crowd into the small area of the summit, most of which was occupied by the

H*erod could not increase the size of the central jewel, the Temple, but he was unrestricted in providing it with a magnificent setting.*

Temple itself. The first builders of the Temple Mount dealt with this problem by constructing retaining walls on the slopes to support an esplanade around the Temple, thus making it possible for more people to take part in the events centering on it. This same solution was adopted by Herod and his engineers in enlarging the Temple Mount to its present dimensions.

In Herod's day, although most Jews still lived in Judea, large and important Jewish communities existed throughout the civilized world—in the Parthian empire between the Tigris and Euphrates rivers, in Syria, Phoenicia, and Anatolia, in the lands bordering on the Mediterranean, such as Egypt and North Africa, in Spain, Italy, Greece, and in the islands in the Mediterranean Sea. Most renowned for its power and eminence was the Jewish community of Rome itself. The Jews of the Diaspora* held important positions in public administration, international trade, and other branches of economic life and surely left their mark on the cultures of their countries of residence.

Considering this unparalleled dichotomy, the Jews of Judea grappled with the question of how to relate to their co-religionists in the Diaspora. Should the Diaspora Jews be considered fellow Jews in every way, or were Jews to be defined only as people who lived in the land of Judea? Clearly, from both the emotional and the political and economic standpoints, the more a sense of national unity could be maintained among the dispersed communities, the better it would be for all concerned. The problem was how to translate this sentiment into action, and one answer was by placing stress on the absolute exclusivity of the center of Jewish ritual in Jerusalem: the Temple. All efforts, together with the longings of the people in dispersion, had to be channeled toward that site.

To this end, the pilgrimage to Jerusalem on the Jewish holidays and festivals was actively promoted and soon became the goal of Jews everywhere. This custom brought crowds of pilgrims from abroad and within the country as well. Some scholars have estimated the number of pilgrims during the Roman period at 80,000 to 100,000 people on each festival. This swarm of visitors turning up on the holidays presented the city fathers with a major logistical headache. Above all it was imperative that this huge congregation be able to visit the Temple Mount at one and the same time. Jerusalem was then one of the largest cities in the world, with a population of 150,000 to 200,000. Add to this number the tens of thousands of pilgrims from outside the city and you have a constituency of over 200,000 people massed together in one spot. An equivalent volume of traffic to a single site is rare even in our day. Herod designed his extension of the Temple Mount to host this formidable crowd on an esplanade so that it could witness the ritual ceremonies performed in the Temple courts.

When Herod decided to rebuild the Temple Mount to accommodate the mass pilgrimage to Jerusalem, he knew that he would have to overcome opposition from various quarters. This resistance was born of suspicions about the King's real intentions. Considering that Herod was in the good-graces of the Roman emperors, it was only natural that such misgivings should arise. Herod therefore decided to address the leaders of the people and apprise them of the details of his plans. His speech is preserved for us by Josephus, who evidently copied it from the court archive. Here, in part, is what Herod told his subjects.

"That the enterprise which I now propose to undertake is the most pious and beautiful of our time I will now make clear. For this was the temple which our fathers built to the Most Great God after their return from Babylon, but it lacks 60 cubits in height, the amount by which the first temple, built by Solomon, exceeded it. And yet no one should condemn our fathers for neglecting their pious duty, for it was not their fault that this temple is smaller. Rather it was Cyrus and Darius, the son of Hystaspes, who prescribed these dimensions for building, and since our fathers were subject to them, and their descendants after them to the Macedonians, they had no opportunity to restore this first archetype of piety to its former size. But since, by the will of God, I am now ruler and there continues to be a long period of peace and an abundance of wealth and great revenues, and—what is of most importance—the Romans, who are, so to speak, the masters of the world are [my] loyal friends, I will try to remedy the oversight caused by the necessity and subjection of that earlier time, and by this act of piety make full return to God for the gift of this kingdom (*Jewish Antiquities*, XV, II. 382-387)."

This speech, following the stock formula of a ruler showing deference to his subjects, must have achieved its aim, because we do not hear of any pockets of resistance to Herod's plan. On the contrary, enormous forces were rallied to execute the task. But local support was not enough. After taking care to defuse potential opposition at home, Herod still had to obtain a "building permit" from Rome.

Extending the area of the Temple Mount required the construction of massive retaining walls to bear the weight of the structures above them. Jewish religious law (*halakhah*) regarding the entrance to the Temple Mount demands that it contain only two gates, and this restriction on access accorded the area the appearance and properties of a fortification. The fact is that during the Jewish revolt that culminated in the destruction of the Temple, a group of Zealots barricaded themselves on the Temple Mount and held out there for quite a while. How was it, then, that the Roman authorities permitted Herod to build a complex that could conceivably become an obstacle to them in governing Jerusalem?

No known source contains Herod's request for permission to rebuild the Temple Mount. Neither does any source suggest that the Romans made any attempt to foil the operation. But a talmudic legend based on the Baba Batra Tractate 4:71 tells that Herod had a healthy fear of the Romans and therefore consulted with a sage by the name of

* The Diaspora is the term used for Jews dispersed outside the Land of Israel. The word is used for both the people and their communities.

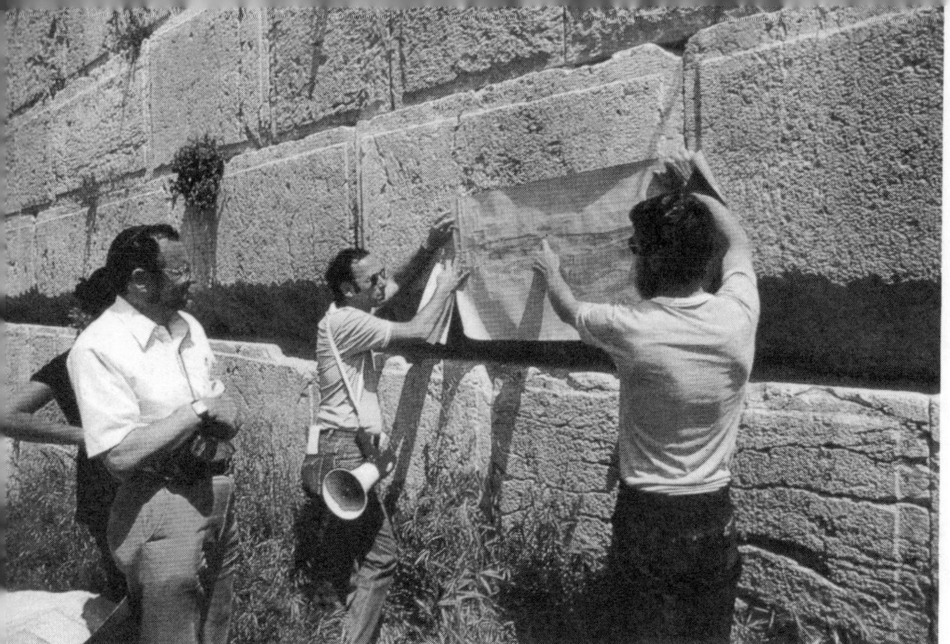

Massive ashlars *quarried near Jerusalem were set in place with a precision that astounds even modern engineers. Masons chiseled margins 3.5 to 7 inches wide and less than an inch deep around each block to guide the workers who would set the blocks in place. So tight and exact was the fit that no adhesive was used between the stones; today tufts of persistent greenery sprout from cavities worn by time into the once-smooth facade.*

Here at the western wall of the Temple Mount, a guide points out features of the ancient Temple complex in a reconstruction drawing.

Bava, who advised him as follows:

"Send an envoy [to Rome to request permission for the project] and let him take a year on the way and stay in Rome and take a year coming back, and in the meantime you can pull down the Temple and rebuild it. [Herod] did so, and received the following message [from Rome]: If you have not yet pulled it down, do not do so, if you have pulled it down, do not rebuild it; and if you have pulled it down and already rebuilt it, you are one of those bad servants who do first and ask permission afterward."

We cannot know whether or not this legend contains a kernel of historical truth but, in fact, the deed preceded the authorization. It is entirely possible that things happened just this way, though we could equally well assume that Herod's keen political instincts guided him in "packaging" and "selling" his idea to the powers that be and that he knew how to worm his way into the hearts of the Roman rulers and extract their permission to build. In any event, there is no evidence that Rome interfered.

Herod's Temple Mount is the largest site of its kind in the ancient world. The southern wall, the shortest of the four retaining walls, is 910 feet long (the northern wall is somewhat longer); the western wall, the longest, is 1,575 feet (the eastern wall is somewhat shorter). The Temple Mount is thus a trapezoid covering the equivalent of 12 soccer fields—bleachers included!

The retaining walls rose 98 feet above the paved avenues at the foot of the mount—to about the height of a ten-story building. The towers at the corners soared at least 115 feet above the street level. In some places the foundations of these retaining walls reached down as far as 65 feet below the street, making the walls there a total of more than 165 feet high. (All these measurements relate to the actual architectural finds.)

The size of the Temple itself was dictated by law and could not be altered so much as an inch. Although Solomon's Temple was an imposing building in the age of the kings of Judah, in Herod's day, 900 years later, its dimensions were closer to those of a standard house. One could try to improve the appearance of the Temple—plate it in gold and precious stones or otherwise adorn it in splendor—and that was indeed done; but it had to remain exactly the size Solomon established when he first built it. Although Herod could not increase the size of the central jewel, he was unrestricted in providing its setting. And this he did in the retaining walls of the Temple Mount. These magnificent retaining walls not only supported the spacious plaza or esplanade built around the Temple, they also magnified the impression made by the Temple itself. Indeed, the very enormity of these retaining walls helped to balance the relatively modest proportions of the Temple itself. This was the great achievement of the Temple Mount's architect: creating the setting of retaining walls with the precious stone—the Temple—crowning it all.

The construction of the new Temple Mount was certainly not the only project Herod undertook in the capital. On the contrary, the king embarked on an orgy of construction that included a new royal palace near today's Jaffa Gate, the adjoining citadel with its three famous towers (Phasael, Hippicus, and Miriamne), the Antonia Fortress, the repair and restoration of the walls, cultural arenas such as a theater and a hippodrome, and a number of markets. What's more, Herod did not restrict his building activities to Jerusalem; his entire kingdom underwent a striking architectural transformation. Caesarea changed from an anonymous fishing village into the largest port in the Mediterranean basin (larger even than Piraeus, the port of Athens), and Sebaste (Samaria) was enhanced by new walls, markets, a theater, and other imposing structures—to mention just two of these remodeling schemes. At the same time, Herod developed the Jordan Valley by establishing a vast agricultural farm there and built palaces and fortifications in Jericho, Cypros, Terrex, Geba, Heshbon, and Masada. He rebuilt and expanded the Hasmonean fortresses of Alexandrium, Hyrcania, and Macherus and carried out many other projects throughout the country. Herod's passion for building was not even restricted to his own kingdom; he donated funds to erect markets and other public structures in a number of cities in both the East and West, far from the borders of Judea. In short, the man just loved to build. But public building on such a grand scale took more than love to accomplish. Untold sums had to be produced to finance it, not to speak of the manpower—tens of thousands of laborers—to execute it.

The obvious question is where did Herod get the capital and manpower for all these building projects. Here again, the prejudice of earlier scholars held their minds in thrall: The capital, they believed, came mostly from the heavy taxes he imposed on the inhabitants of the country, and a good part of the manpower came from slave labor. A more penetrating investigation of the subject produces very different insights into the origin of those resources.

WERNER BRAUN

As Herod explained to his people in the address quoted by Josephus, "there continues to be . . . an abundance of wealth and great revenues," and it was with the aid of these riches that he intended to execute his plans. If Herod's income had derived solely from taxes, it is doubtful that he would have had either the backing of the masses for rebuilding the Temple Mount or the audacity to appear before his subjects and deliver the speech he did. Moreover, if we examine the country's sources of income as an agrarian economy, even if we calculate all the income from agriculture as if it were a tax, there still wouldn't have been nearly enough money to finance Herod's building spree.

Logically, then, Herod must have had other sources of income. Foremost among them was his toll from controlling the international routes of what was known as the spice or luxury trade, which proved to be a lucrative source of profit for all associated with it. The main beneficiaries of this bounty were the Arab tribes and the Nabateans living on the marches of Judea. The Hasmoneans had tried unsuccessfully to cash in on this flourishing branch of commerce, but Herod succeeded where they had failed. The "spice trade" was undoubtedly the real motive behind Herod's wars, the reason for regional friction and for his ties with the Nabateans. It also explains his territorial expansion into the districts of Batanean (Bashan) and Trachonitis to the north and east. This was also the reason for Herod's penetration into Moab (Transjordan) and the fortification of Heshbon. As a matter of fact, the construction of the large harbor at Caesarea should also be seen in the same light, as the small harbors of Jaffa, Gaza, and Ashkelon were swamped by the volume of trade.

The second major source of income for Herod's coffers was the development of special agricultural farms in the Jordan Valley. The entire area north and west of the Dead Sea (Jericho, Phasaelis, Archalais, and Ein Gedi) and east of the Jordan (Beit Haram and other sections) was transformed into a gigantic hothouse for the cultivation of spices, medicinal plants, and dates. Herod mobilized hydraulic engineers to get spring water flowing over many miles to these plantations. The dry, warm climate did its part, and the income from the yield proved to be enormous. Jericho dates, for example, were renowned for their quality throughout the Roman empire; one strain was even named after Nicholas of Damascus, the Greek historian who was Herod's friend and a denizen of Augustus's court. Dates were so valuable to the Judean economy because they served as the principal sweetener in those days, before the lands of the Mediterranean discovered the pleasures of sugar cane. Nor was this elaborate operation kept secret. When Mark Antony wanted to give Cleopatra a special gift and told her to choose any place in the East (within the Roman empire), she asked for Herod's farm in Jericho. Since she lacked the manpower to run it, however, she leased it back to Herod, who calculated that even with the added expense of rent, it would still be a lucrative operation for him. (Incidentally, Augustus subsequently returned the farm to Herod.)

As to where the second major element—labor—came from, we have noted that Palestine was essentially an agrarian country whose Jewish inhabitants made their livelihoods from working the land. Their encounter with the Roman world introduced them to new technologies, such as hydraulic engineering and metal forging, and the Jews were quick to apply these technologies to the sphere of agriculture. Hydraulics, which made it possible to conduct water over great distances in aqueducts, was originally developed in Rome to enhance urban architecture through the construction of public fountains and to heighten the emperor's pleasure by the spectacle of water games. In Judea, however, water was harnessed to serve the needs of agriculture through irrigation.

Iron forging was developed in Rome to augment the power of the Roman army—the main prop of the empire—by equipping it with the best weaponry; the Jews learned the techniques from the Romans but used them to make such agricultural tools as plows, pruning hooks, and spades. These technologies, coupled with the cultural sophistication of the Jews of Judea, greatly boosted the level of agricultural productivity. In practical terms, these improvements meant that the individual farm required fewer working hands to generate an appreciable yield. Augustus's long reign was an age of peace for the Roman empire. Natural population increase occurred as a matter of course, creating an excess of working hands and, consequently, pockets of unemployment.

It was a combination of the abundance of capital in the royal coffers and this surplus of working hands throughout the country

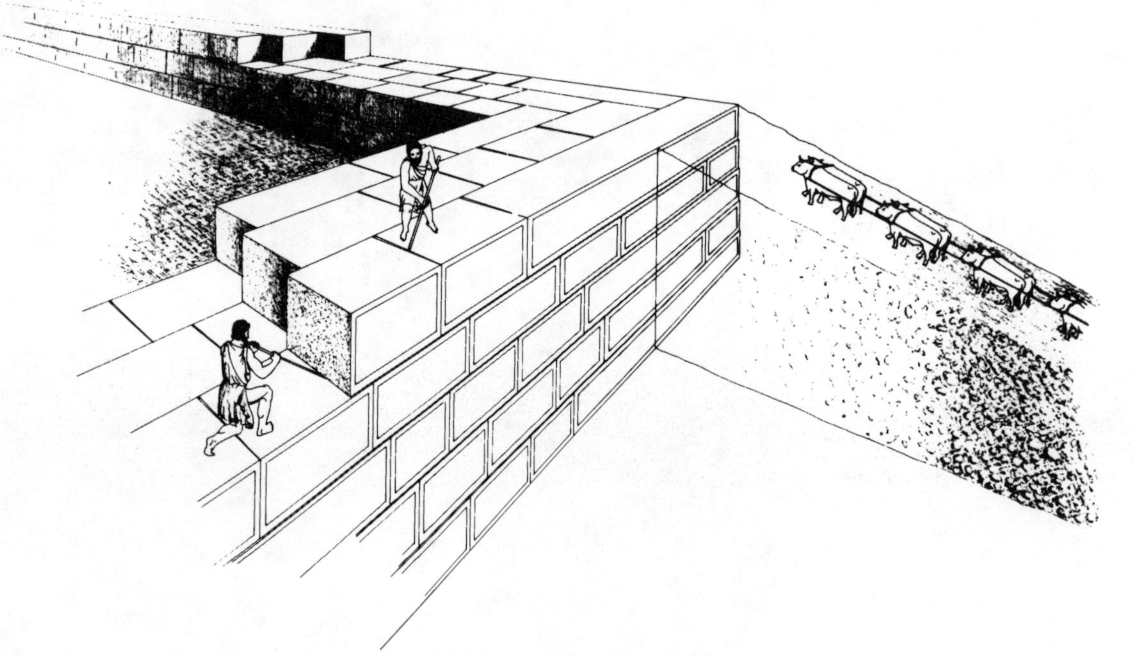

MARTA RITMEYER

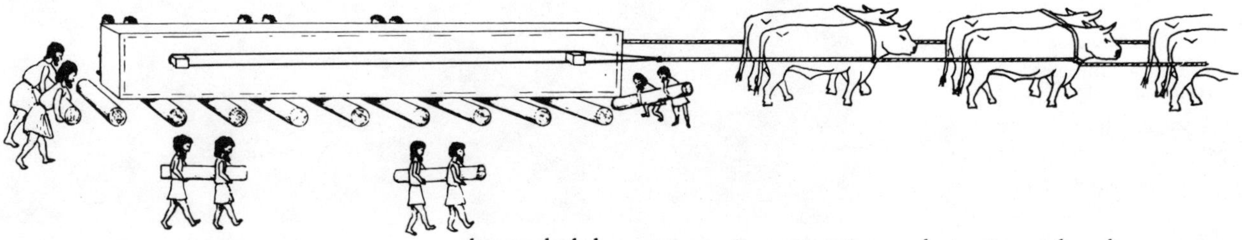

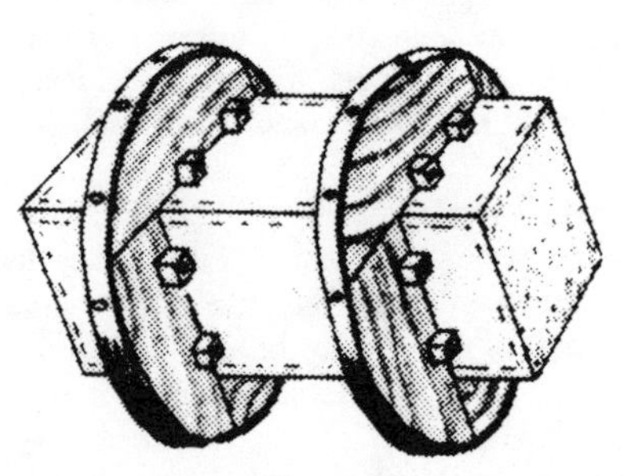

Hauling stones *from the quarry to the construction site usually required oxen, but sometimes wooden wheels were simply fixed to the stones (bottom). Once on-site, oxen would pull the stone up an earthen embankment to the top of the wall.*

Masons dressing one column (p. 25) left the job unfinished—probably because the stone cracked—and never moved the column from the quarry. It has remained where it was abandoned; today, this spot is by the side of a road in Jerusalem's Russian Compound. The column was probably destined for one of the Temple Mount's porticoes (see artist's reconstruction, p. 29).

that sparked the great surge in construction in Herod's day. In fact, throughout history, whenever we come across an extraordinary spasm of building, these same two factors are found lurking in the background. Certainly they were salient economic features of Herod's age.

Herod's masons invested eight years in preparations alone—quarrying, dressing, and transporting stones to the building site—before the king gave the green light for actual construction work to begin. Another three years passed between the initiation of work and the dedication of the Temple, with lavish ceremonies that included the sacrifice of hundreds of offerings. The Temple itself was built by the priests over a period of 18 months.

Throughout those 11 years, Josephus informs us, it rained in Jerusalem only at night, so as not to interfere with the construction work. A talmudic legend that refers to this same phenomenon adds that at dawn "the wind blew and the clouds dispersed, the sun shone so that the people were able to go out to their work, and then they knew they were engaged in sacred work" (Jerusalem Talmud, Berachot 1:8; Babylonian Talmud, Ta'anit 23:71). Before our dig this colorful description might well have appeared to be an exaggeration, but now, at the end of 14 years of excavation, with 13 winters behind us, we can confirm this detail as a realistic one. Throughout this period we lost an average of only five workdays a year because of rain and snow, as most of the precipitation fell at night.

The stone used for building the Temple Mount came from quarries near the building site. Jerusalem stone is found in natural strata about a meter high, and the Temple builders cut the stones full height for most of the courses of the Temple Mount's walls. To free the stone from the bedrock, holes were drilled delineating the size of the blocks desired by the builder. Then the holes were plugged with wooden pegs and filled with water. When the wood absorbed the water, it expanded and cracked the stone, releasing it from the bedrock. Once the block of stone had broken away, it received its initial treatment in the quarry and was then transported to the building site over the dirt roads cut especially for that purpose. The usual transport vehicle was an ox-drawn wagon, though in some cases wagon wheels were attached directly to the block of stone, and it was rolled to the building site where the blocks were set in place on the walls.

In the course of the construction work,

pulleys based on multiple gears were used to hoist and manipulate the building materials. The stones were hauled up to the topmost course over gently sloped earth embankments, then placed on rollers that moved over the thick walls. No adhesive was used. Each massive block was planed down and set flush against the next one with polished precision.

This construction venture demanded great physical effort and enormous energy but, even more, it required impeccable organization and planning, first-class engineers and construction technicians, talented foremen, and motivated workers of a high professional standard. And today, even knowing this, all who lay eyes on these monumental stones find it hard to credit the construction process of Herod's time. Let us look more closely at how these monumental walls were built.

Two thousand years have passed since these retaining walls were built, yet they are still as solid and sturdy as if they had been built rather recently. All the more striking is the fact that they were built by the "dry" method of construction, meaning that no adhesive—concrete, cement, or mortar of any kind—was spread between the stones. Sometimes cracks are visible in the ashlars, but these are simply flaws in the Jerusalem stone. Unfortunately, Jerusalem stone is not particularly strong; it has many natural veins and cracks, and it is susceptible to changes in weather from dampness to dryness and back again. Yet if we examine the spots where these monumental walls meet, we can see that they have not moved at all in 2,000 years, not even so much as a millimeter. In fact, they are so stable that were it not for the dressing around the edges, we would sometimes be unable to distinguish between one stone and the next.

How can we account for this remarkable durability? There are three explanations: the way in which the foundations were laid and built, the weight of the stones, and the way the problem of fill on the inside of the retaining walls was handled.

The secret of the strength of these retaining walls lies first and foremost in their remarkable foundations, which were always built on bedrock. Sometimes the masons dug down only six feet before reaching bedrock, sometimes they had to go down 35 feet or more. But there was absolutely no exception to the rule that the wall's foundations must be built on the natural rock. The face of the bedrock was planed down and prepared to take the stones of the first course, on which the subsequent layers were built.

The sturdiness of the Temple Mount's retaining walls is also a function of the extraordinary weight of their stones. The smallest of these blocks—and the majority of the stones used in the walls—weighed 2 to 5 tons. Many others weighed 10 tons or more. Some stones (particularly at the corners) exceeded even that weight; the southwest corner of the Temple Mount contains ashlars that weigh about 50 tons apiece! These ashlars are 40 feet long, 3 feet high and 8 feet thick.

A number of massive stones in the western wall north of Wilson's Arch are unequaled in size anywhere in the ancient world. One of these blocks is 40 feet long, 10 feet high, about 13 feet thick, and weighs close to 400 tons!

The use of such monumental stones solved the problem of stability and is responsible for the fact that the walls still stand in our own day, 2,000 years after being built.

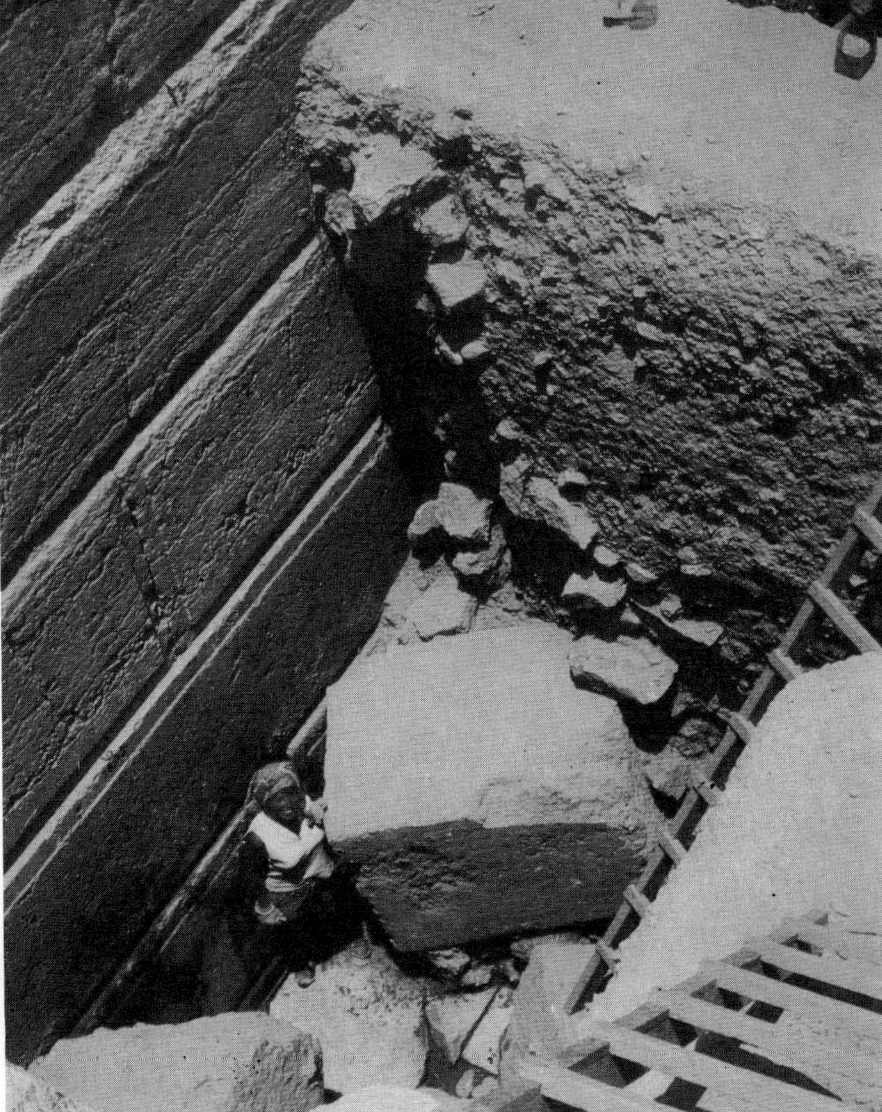

MEIR BEN-DOV

Toppled during the Roman destruction ***of Jerusalem in 70 A.D., fragments of Herodian ashlars lie on the paved street that skirted the Temple Mount's southern wall.***

Yet it is questionable whether stability was the sole reason for building with such mammoth blocks of stone. Sturdiness could have been achieved even if the walls had been built with small stones, but that would have ruled out the possibility of employing the "dry construction" method, making it necessary to use mortar or cement as an adhesive material. That was how buildings were constructed in Rome, for example.

High-grade mortar, however, was made out of a mixture of 50 percent lime and 50 percent river silt or gravel with the addition of soil. The production of lime required a considerable output of energy, and the main source of energy at the time came from burning wood. The amount of cement needed for building with small stones was equal to half the volume of a wall, making the necessary amount of lime equal to a quarter of the volume of a wall! Production of the lime necessitated running ovens for a full day and night, sometimes two full days and nights, as the process entailed burning blocks of limestone at high temperatures. There was no shortage of trees in Rome and the rest of the countries north of the Mediterranean. Indeed, the great struggle there was to turn forest land into agricultural land.

In the lands of the East, however, and particularly in Judea—which was a heavily populated country—the demand for wood proved to be a major problem in the Second Temple period. Wood was prized both as a source of energy and as the main raw material in construction, crafts, and industry. It was used to make tools, plows, sickles, furniture, scaffolding, doors, and ceilings, not to mention its common use as a fuel for running ovens and to produce the coals used for household cooking and heating. Wood therefore played a vital role in daily life.

The trees of Judea during that period were mostly pines, oaks and terebinths. Because of the warm climate and meager rainfall, it took many years to replace trees that had been cut down. Sensitive to this problem, the sages of the Mishnah and Talmud went so far as to forbid the raising of small cattle, particularly goats, which were (and continue to be) the scourge of the forest.

Whenever the country was dominated by foreign rulers, little consideration was given to the quality of life of its inhabitants, and it was then that the forests were exploited to the point of depletion, without any thought for the future. Anyone who wanted to build could simply hack down trees to his heart's content, whether for quality timber or for the wood needed to produce lime. Obviously this led to the exhaustion of energy sources and, as a consequence, to an appreciable decline in the standard of living.

Any responsible regime was obliged to pursue an intelligent policy regarding both the felling of trees and the development of new approaches to saving on wood, including the use of alternative sources of energy, raw materials, and building techniques. The

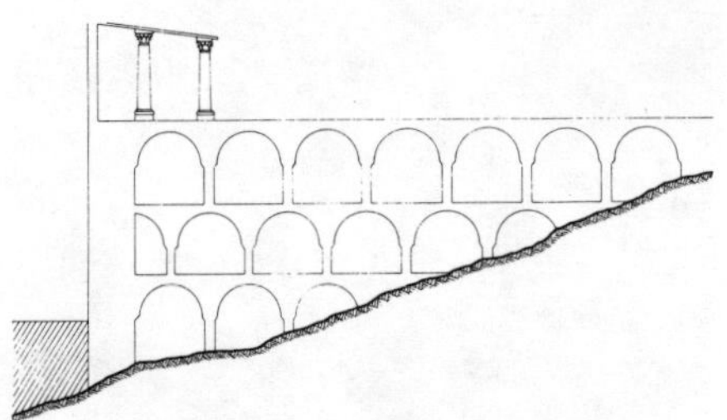

Layers of vaults ***filled the space behind the Temple Mount retaining walls. A paved plaza was laid above the upper story of vaults. Striving to be faithful to Jewish law, Herod insured that the priests officiating in the Temple could not become "impure" by walking over any unmarked graves in the earth below. Jewish law prescribes the construction of vaults, which create voids, over graves as a way of "neutralizing" the power of graves to make those who walk over them ritually impure.***

stone dome, for example—a construction technique imported from Rome—proved to be an excellent means of economizing on wood. Instead of building roofs and ceilings out of timber beams, as was then the custom, the houses were topped off with domes built of local stone. This solution called for expertise in stonecutting and a high level of construction skills, but it led to a saving of countless square meters of timber. Likewise "dry construction" spared the wood needed to produce mortared construction.

Lime was indeed produced in Judea, but it was used to make plaster, especially to waterproof cisterns, but also to cover walls. Wherever it was possible to economize on lime—and therefore on wood—the saving was welcomed.

Building walls without cement or mortar as an adhesive called for an immense investment in dressing the stones, planing them down, and meticulously working them into a shape that would enable them to adhere to the stones laid around them. Moreover, the construction of high, massive walls like those of the Temple Mount required not only hewing the stones and dressing them properly but starting off with huge blocks that had to be transported to the building site. The extra effort was worth it, however: an initial calculation shows that building the Temple Mount's retaining walls by the dry-construction method saved 100 square kilometers of forest that would otherwise have gone into the production of lime.

Building with large stones also made it possible for the project to proceed at an incredibly fast pace. When a 40-foot-long stone was set in place, the structure advanced by 40 feet in a single stroke! We can hazard a conjecture that by using large ashlars instead of conventional-size building blocks the building time was cut by more than half.

To these pragmatic reasons for using huge ashlars, we should add the majestic appearance they accorded the long, high walls of the Temple Mount and the strength and awe they bestowed upon their surroundings. The use of massive stones answered all the needs of the hour and the place.

Using retaining walls to support a plaza implies that they will be fully visible on the outside but covered on the inside by the earth fill that underlies the esplanade. Modern construction demands that the ratio between the height of a support wall and its thickness be 4:1 in order for it to withstand the pressure of the fill. The height of the Temple Mount's retaining walls at its southeast corner is about 65 feet. If Herod's masons had studied modern engineering, they would have built the walls to a thickness of about 16 feet. How thick were these walls? Fortunately, we found a spot in one of the upper courses of the eastern wall where a stone was missing, and it happened to be one of the original stones from the Second Temple period. With the approval of the Moslem authorities, we cleared away the detritus at that spot and penetrated the wall to discover that the wall at that point was built of three rows of stones that firmly adhere to each other. Even though Herod's engineers did not have access to the textbooks we consulted, they had built this wall precisely 16.25 feet thick!

The irony of our discovery was that although Herod's engineers followed the rules of advanced architectural doctrine, they did not have to build the walls that thick at all. For these support walls were not subject to the pressure of earth behind them; the inside of the retaining walls faced onto a void. Instead of filling the area within the support walls with earth and building the esplanade above it, Herod's architects constructed layers of vaults in the open space between the mountain's natural slope and the projected plaza. At the outer end, adjoining the retaining walls, there were three stories of vaults; at the other end, close to the mountain's summit, the gradient dictated a reduction to one story. Above the upper story of vaults, a paved plaza was constructed.

In effect, then, the Temple Mount was

Y. RACHLIN

Royal Portico interior. ***A grand hall in the southern end of the Temple Mount extending across the compound from east to west*** *(see p. 9)**, the Royal Portico contained 162 Corinthian columns, each 27 feet high. "The thickness of each column," Josephus tells us, "was such that it would take three men with outstretched arms touching one another to envelop it."***

constructed of vaults covered, at the desired height, by an open plaza. The vaults provided ample space for storage and other needs.

The architect of the Temple Mount wanted to distinguish visually between the lower part of the walls, which served for support, and their upper part, which comprised the exterior wall of the porticoes on top of the Temple Mount. He did so by building the retaining wall flat and adorning the portico wall with stone projections that resembled pilasters. In the seventh century A.D., the Temple Mount's walls were destroyed down to the point where the pilasters began. So how do we know they were built that way? First of all, at the northern end of the western wall (today within the confines of a building), we found a section of the original wall that contains part of the pilasters *in situ*. Second, in order to fashion the pilasters, masons dressed the stones in a special way. We uncovered examples of this unique dressing among the debris at the foot of the western and southern walls. Some of these stones turned up in the rubble created by Titus's soldiers in 70 A.D.; others were found among the ruins from the late Byzantine era, when Jerusalem was recaptured from the Persians by the Emperor Heraclius in 628 A.D.

Each corner of the Temple Mount was graced with a tower from which guards could monitor what was going on in the Temple's precincts and head off the build-up of crowds. The northwest corner even boasted a military fortress, called the Antonia Fortress, which served Herod's troops (and, in days to come, would serve the soldiers of the Roman Legions). The other three corners of the Temple Mount had standard towers manned by lookouts and guards of the priestly class, who were responsible for the Temple's security and personnel. (We should also note that the state treasury was kept in the Temple, as was customary in temples throughout the ancient world.) In addition, the considerable length of the eastern and western walls required the construction of additional towers somewhere around the middle of these walls.

When our dig reached the level of the paved street that skirted the Temple Mount at the southwest corner, we came upon a stone that could well have been the cornerstone of the tower above. It was dressed on three sides—on two sides and the top—which indicates that it was not only a cornerstone in the literal sense of the term but the topmost stone of that corner.

Ron Gardiner, one of our archaeologists, was examining the stone when suddenly we heard shouts of joy coming from his direction. Ron is a level-headed Welshman who first came to Palestine as a policeman in the mid-1940s, toward the end of the British Mandate, and has since returned from time to time to join archaeological expeditions. It's not every day that you can see him succumb to excitement, and shouts were a sure sign that he had discovered something. And a delectable something it was. "There's a Hebrew inscription engraved on the stone!" he called up to us. The inscription was easily deciphered because its letters were clear and deeply engraved, and we soon realized that it was incomplete. It read: "To the trumpet-call building to pr . . ." At that point the stone was broken, and the rest of it could not be found. "What a pity!" was the universal response. I suppose it's human nature to moan over what we lack rather than to rejoice over what we have.

After we recovered from the excitement, we set our minds to figuring out the missing part of the inscription and establishing the significance of the stone being found at that particular spot. One suggestion was that the inscription originally read: "To the trumpet-call building to pr[oclaim]." But what would have been proclaimed there? None of the sources at our disposal—neither Josephus's description of the Temple Mount nor the mishnaic sources—seemed to touch upon this subject. Then I recalled a passage by Josephus that mentioned the Temple Mount towers in a completely different context:

> "They, moreover, improved this advantage of position by erecting four huge towers in order to increase the elevation from which their missiles were discharged: one at the northeast corner, the second above the *Xystus*, the third at another corner opposite the lower town. The last was erected above the roof of the priests' chambers, at the point where it was the custom for one of the priests to stand and to give notice, by sound of trumpet, in the afternoon of the approach, and on the following evening of the close, of every seventh day, announcing to the people the respective hours for ceasing work and for resuming their labors. (*The Jewish War*, IV. 580-583)."

Josephus assumed that anyone familiar with Jerusalem would be able to identify the towers easily, so he stressed that the outermost tower was the one from which the trumpets proclaimed the start and the end of the Sabbath. The southwestern corner was the most suitable one for this purpose, since it rose above the Lower Market, Jerusalem's main commercial center.

What did the inscription mean? The Hebrew prefix consisting of the letter *lamed* (ל) can mean "to" or "toward," indicating direction as in "to Jerusalem." In the case before us, an inscription beginning with the word "to" could have graced a sign post directing the priest to the place where he was to blow his trumpet. On the other hand, the inscription was engraved at the top of the tower, so that by the time the priest got up there he no longer needed directions. Another possibility is that the letter *lamed* connoted association or possession, as in "belongs to" the trumpet-call building. It took three years to build the Temple Mount's walls and eight before them to prepare the stones and other raw materials for the operation. Perhaps during that time certain stones were keyed with inscriptions or markings indicating to the foremen where they should be placed in accordance with the architect's blueprint. This is a common practice in construction, but the problem with the theory is that such markings were usually abbreviations or initials, never so elaborate a rendition as we have here.

The final possibility is that we had before us a dedication stone. While the Temple Mount was being built, many people made donations to the project. The standard contribution was apparently a building stone—not the actual stone, of course, but a sum equal to the cost of one stone or a portion thereof. An ancient legend tells that one of the sages of the period was so wretchedly poor that he couldn't afford a donation to the holy enterprise. But he was aided by Heaven, took heart, and carried a stone on his back all the way from the Judean Desert. This tale alludes to the custom of "donating stones" to the Temple Mount. The system apparently worked like a contemporary custom of planting trees in Israel, whereby the donor doesn't actually furnish or purchase a specific tree but contributes the cost of having a tree planted for him. If someone has the means and the desire to donate an entire forest, he or she will surely want to have a sign or plaque posted at the entrance acknowledging that generosity or perhaps even have the forest named in his or her honor. Our cornerstone may have represented a similar convention: a person of means had donated a tidy sum for the entire wing of the trumpet-call building, and his generosity was duly immortalized by a dedication stone. If indeed that was the case, the full inscription probably read: "For the Trumpet-Call Building, to Proclaim the Sabbath, Donated by John Doe"—or, rather, the Hebrew equivalent of his time. Similar instances are known to us from dedicatory inscriptions found in ancient synagogues throughout the country. We even have a precedent from the Temple itself: The Nicanor Gates were donated by a man named Nicanor. Beyond offering this conjecture, however, we can only hope that the broken part of this stone will turn up in the future so that the puzzle will be solved. (For another interpretation, see Aaron Demsky, "When the Priests Trumpeted the Onset of the Sabbath," Nov./Dec. 1986.)

The dressing of the stones used in the Temple Mount's walls was of the highest quality, with the ashlars being worked to a smooth surface on five of their sides (all except the vertical face opposite the front surface). The consummate construction of stones placed next to and above one another in perfect alignment coupled with the smooth surface of the stones, created the look of a massive stone wall whose individual components were invisible to the naked eye. Each wall appeared to be an evenly textured, consistently white, plastered surface. At the same time, the architects' intent was to create the sensation that the walls were a composite of stones—and they succeeded in that, too. For anyone who views the Temple Mount from a distance is able to see that its walls are built of distinctively individual blocks. The walls are not a monolithic surface but a patchwork that is manifest because of the stones' special dressing. Scholars call it marginal dressing, and its purpose is to create a frame, or margin, around the block. After the stone's outer face was smoothed down, masons chiseled a frame one or two centimeters deep around its edge. The length of the margin is of course identical to that of the stone; its width varies from 9 to 18 centimeters, a variance that obtains not only between one stone and the next but on the same block and does not seem to be guided by any method or consistency. The area of the stone's surface enclosed by the margins is called the boss and is also completely smooth; yet the fact that it stands out some two centimeters more than the margins is sufficient to make each stone distinguishable from those around it.

This method of dressing stones was obviously meant only for the visible parts of a wall. The margins served as a guide for setting the stones in place with precision and were therefore required on all the stones of a wall. But the bosses of those ashlars destined to be used in the foundations, and consequently covered with earth, did not have to be dressed. Indeed, when we uncovered the foundations of the southern wall, we found that the bosses of the ashlars set below street level were left rough. The architects were undoubtedly interested in saving both time and money on the dressing work, and we can better appreciate their reasoning when we recall that the foundations sometimes extended 65 feet below street level.

We have already noted that despite this method of highlighting the individual stones, the support walls retained something of a flat appearance. But the same cannot be said of the upper section of the walls, or the exterior of the porticoes, which were adorned with pilasters. Further to avoid the possibility of this upper section appearing flat, highly prominent square bosses were worked into the centers of a number of stones. The dimensions of these protrusions were 7.8 x 7.8 inches in length and height, and they extended about 8 to 10 inches outward, like cubes attached to the center of the stones. Each of them cast a deep shadow on the area around it, creating a play of light and shade that de-emphasized the flatness of the wall. The stones bearing these cube-like bosses were scattered throughout the wall at random: sometimes they are found on two adjoining stones, sometimes considerably further away from each other.

One final note concerning the high degree of technical precision exhibited in the construction of the Temple Mount's walls and the detailed engineering calculations invested in them. Every course of the retaining wall is set about an inch further in than the one below it. Calculated over a stretch of 65 feet, this brings the top of the wall to a position some two feet further back than its bottom. This method of laying the courses was not adopted to make the walls stronger or sturdier but solely for aesthetic reasons: From a distance, the walls of the Temple Mount looked like the sides of a umental project is one of the factors that made the Temple Mount one of the most renowned wonders of the Roman world.

TEMPLE MOUNT

Reconstructing Herod's Temple Mount in Jerusalem

KATHLEEN AND LEEN RITMEYER

erod the Great—master builder! Despite his crimes and excesses, no one can doubt his prowess as a builder.

One of his most imposing achievements was in Jerusalem. To feed his passion for grandeur, to immortalize his name and to attempt to win the loyalty of his sometimes restive Jewish subjects, Herod rebuilt the

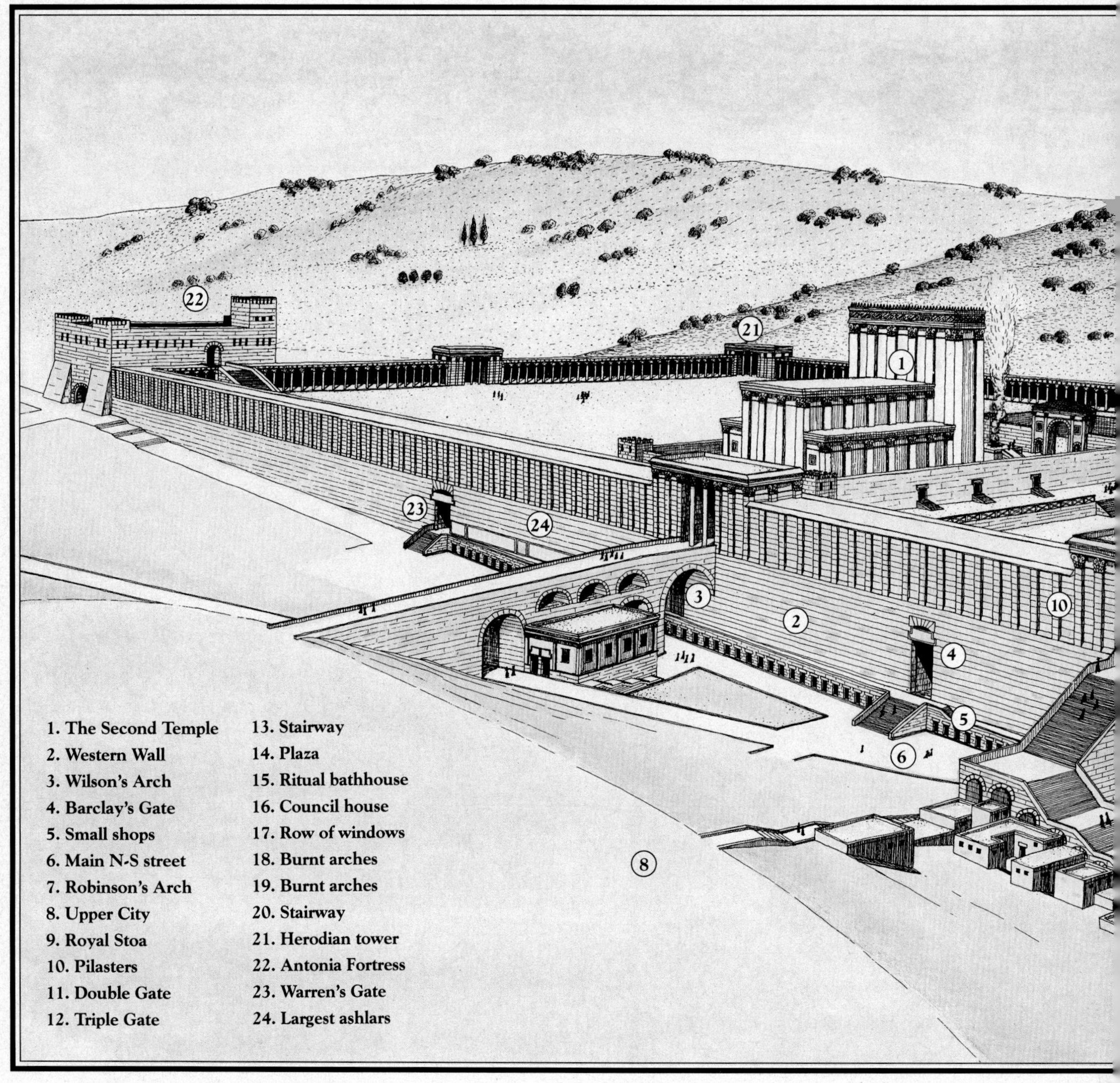

Temple (1 on the reconstruction drawing above) in lavish fashion. But first he extended the existing platform—the Temple Mount—on which it was built, doubling its size.

Herod ruled from 37 to 4 B.C. Scarcely a generation after the completion of this unparalleled building project,* the Romans ploughed the Temple Mount and built a temple to Jupiter on the site. Not a trace of Herod's Temple was left. The mighty retaining walls of the Temple Mount, however, were deliberately left lying in ruins throughout the Roman (70-324 A.D.) and Byzantine (324-640 A.D.) periods—testimony to th destruction of the Jewish state. The Islamic period (640 1099) brought further eradication of Herod's glory Although the Omayyad caliphs (whose dynasty laste from 633 to 750) repaired a large breach in the souther wall of the Temple Mount, the entire area of th Mount and its immediate surroundings was covered b an extensive new religio-political complex, built in par from Herodian ashlars that the Romans had toppled Still later, the Crusaders (1099-1291) erected a city wa in the south that required blocking up the souther gates to the Temple Mount. Under Ottoman rul (1517-1918), Jewish prayer at the western wall was agai permitted, but the Turkish sultans changed the entir character of the Temple Mount by Islamicizing it, s as to make it virtually unrecognizable.

* According to the first-century Jewish historian Josephus, Herod began to build the Temple in the 18th year of this reign (19 B.C.); the Temple itself took only 18 months to build and the cloisters were completed within eight years. However, a reference in the Gospel of John 2:20 ("It has taken 46 years to build this Temple") suggests that the project continued for a much longer time.

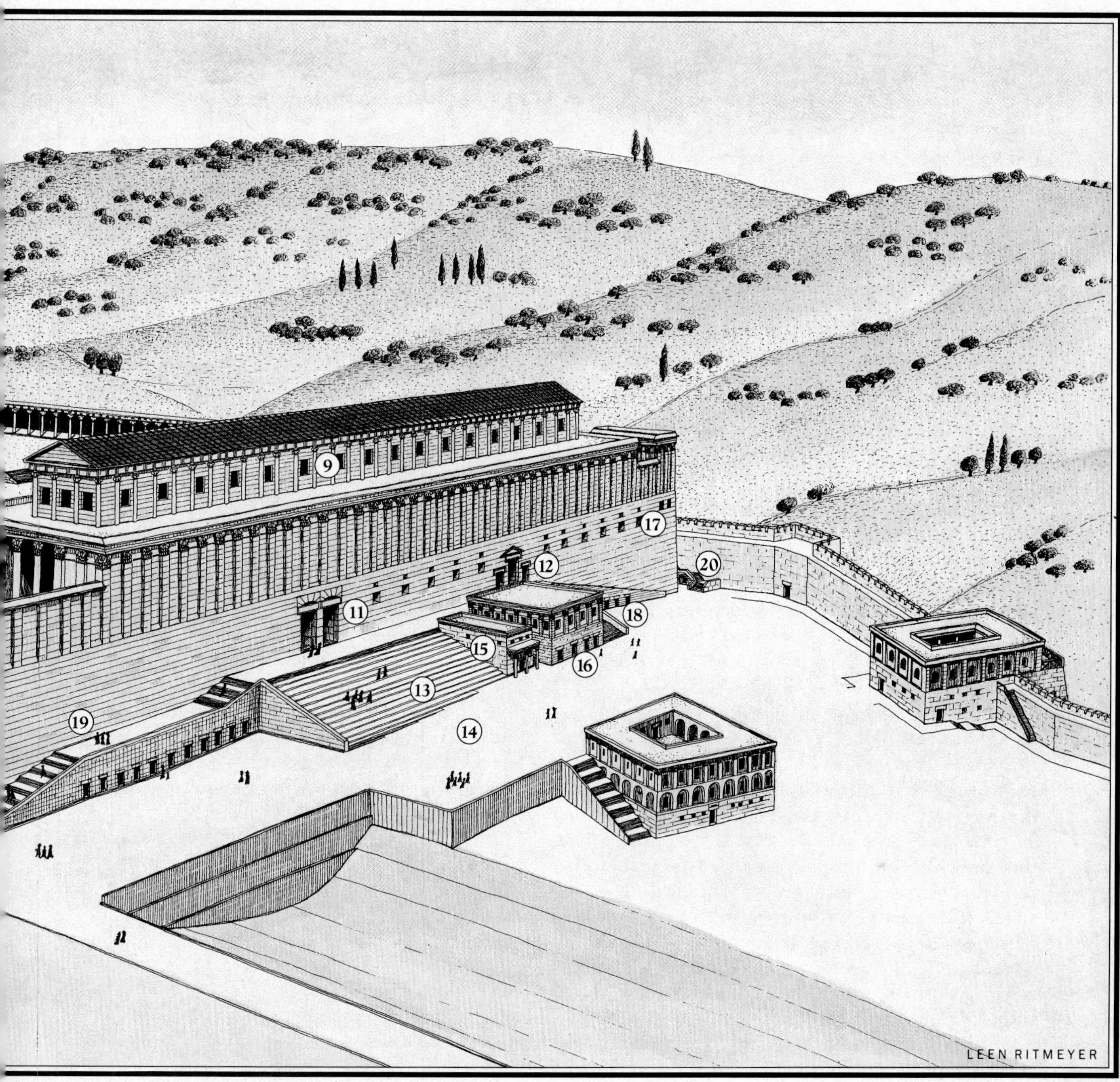

THE TEMPLE MOUNT

hen King Herod (37-4 B.C.) rebuilt the mple (1), he carried out the project on a ındiose scale. Not satisfied with the size of : Temple Mount that Solomon had built, rod doubled its extent by lengthening the stern wall, in the background, at each end d by building a new wall on the other ee sides. To this he added the numental Stoa (9) along the southern ll, right foreground, a series of gates— ne with simple stairways, others adorned th magnificent stairways—and a bridge), at left, linking the Mount with the Upper City (8). The Antonia Fortress (22), at the far left, was built to guard the Temple Mount's vulnerable northern side, the only side lacking a natural valley that could give protection to the Mount.

This glimpse at grandeur is the product of painstaking excavations, insightful interpretations, and the skilled hand of architect-artist Leen Ritmeyer, who translates the evidence into a vision of the past. Using photos, drawings and words, Ritmeyer and his wife Kathleen conduct the reader on a tour around the wall surrounding the Temple Mount. They employ archaeological and literary evidence and relevant other structures to reconstruct the ancient appearance and function of all the major features of the wall and its gateways during the Herodian period. The reconstruction seen here, with the western wall extending to the left and the southern wall extending to the right, can serve as a visual guide to the accompanying article. Features discussed in the text, and photos and plans that illustrate it, are keyed by numbers to their locations in this drawing.

With nothing to go on but literary sources (principally the first-century Jewish historian Josephus) and the bare outline of the retaining wall, it is no wonder that the imaginations of artists over the centuries reigned supreme as they sought to reconstruct the Temple Mount and its immediate environs.

A realistic reconstruction of the area around the Temple Mount became possible only when systematic excavation of the area south and west of it began in 1968, soon after the 1967 Six-Day War. Directed by Professor Benjamin Mazar, on behalf of the Israel Exploration Society and the Hebrew University of Jerusalem, the excavation continued without a break until 1978.

Also of considerable assistance in reconstructing this area are the records of the British explorer Sir Charles Warren, who investigated the Temple Mount environs during the 1860s on behalf of the London-based Palestine Exploration Fund. Warren and his companions dug numerous shafts down to bedrock, as well as horizontal underground tunnels off the shafts to trace long-buried walls and other structures. During the Mazar excavations, we rediscovered some of Warren's tunnels, which amply demonstrated the daring and courage his digging methods required.

As Professor Mazar's dig progressed, each wall and stone was surveyed, each architectural element examined. Gradually a complete plan of the multi-period site—from the eighth century B.C. in the Iron Age to the Turkish period—emerged. To reconstruct what the area was like in the time of Herod the Great, the Herodian elements were separated from the other periods. Then we re-examined the ancient sources and searched for parallels in other monumental Hellenistic buildings in an effort to arrive at an accurate reconstruction. A series of architects assisted the archaeologists, of whom Leen Ritmeyer, one of the authors of this article, was the latest.*

Of the Temple itself, we shall not speak.** The Moslem authorities, under whose jurisdiction the Temple Mount lies, do not permit archaeological investigation of the platform. Suffice it to quote Josephus's observation, "To approaching strangers [the Temple] appeared from a distance like a snow-clad mountain; for all that was not overlaid with gold was of purest white" (L., *The Jewish War* 5.5.6).†

Our reconstruction concentrates on the wall of the Temple Mount, the means of access to the Temple Mount, the gates in the walls and the adjoining streets and buildings. In short, we will make a circuit around the Temple Mount and trace the remains that tell the tale of Herod's greatness.

Let us begin at the western wall (**2**).†† It was this fragment of masonry that became the focus for the longing of dispersed Jews throughout the centuries. Then it was known as the Wailing Wall; now it is called the Western Wall or simply *ha-Kotel*, the Wall. Today it is again a center of worship, and also a site of national celebration. Contrary to common understanding, this wall is not a remnant of the Solomonic Temple Mount.

In order to build his Temple to the Israelite God Yahweh, Solomon needed to construct a level platform on the highest hill of Jerusalem. To accomplish this, Solomon built a retaining wall to support the earthen fill of the platform, the Temple Mount. Herod doubled the area of this platform by building a new wall on three sides—west, south and north—and by extending the fourth wall (the eastern wall) north and south to meet the new southern and northern walls. Today's western wall is a section of the massive retaining wall Herod built to support the Temple Mount.

In enlarging the Temple Mount, Herod not only doubled the original area of the Temple podium, he also wrought a complete change in the topography of the area. The Tyropoeon Valley, which bordered the Temple Mount on the west, was filled in, as was a small valley to the north of the old Temple Mount. In the south, the upper slope of the Kidron Valley was filled in, leaving only the line of the eastern wall unchanged.

Josephus described Herod's retaining wall as "the most prodigious work that was ever heard of by man" (W., *Antiquities of the Jews* 15.11.3).

An idea of the size of Herod's Temple Mount can be conveyed by stating that it would take approximately five football fields to fill its area from north to south and three football fields from west to east. Its exact dimensions are shown in the drawing, opposite; note that it is not exactly rectangular.

At the present time, only seven courses of Herodian

* The original architect on this excavation was Munya Dunayevsky, who had collaborated closely with Professor Mazar on many earlier excavations for over 30 years until his untimely death in 1969. Dunayevsky made a major contribution to the initial stratigraphical analysis of the site, and his drawing of the southwest corner of the Temple Mount shows the preliminary understanding of the superstructure of the western wall.

Following Dunayevsky's death, the Irish architect Brian Lalor introduced the technique of three-dimensional reconstruction drawing to the dig. The basic concept of the reconstruction of the area around the Temple Mount is his. Lalor's catalogue of architectural elements provided an overview of the composite style employed in Herodian architecture. It was he who first suggested that Robinson's Arch supported, not a bridge, but a monumental stairway.

Following in Lalor's footsteps came David Sheehan, another Irish architect, and Leen Ritmeyer, from Holland. David Sheehan worked out some of the problems of the street adjacent to the western wall, adding the shops for which evidence had been found and the flight of steps that led up over them alongside the western wall. Details of Leen Ritmeyer's contribution are contained in this article.

** For a detailed description of Herod's Temple, according to Josephus and Mishnah *Middot* (a rabbinic source), see Joseph Patrich, "Reconstructing the Magnificent Temple Herod Built," *Bible Review*, October 1988. (Drawings in this article by Leen Ritmeyer.)

† The quotations from Josephus's works come from the Loeb Classical Library edition (abbreviated "L.," comprising *The Jewish War*, tr. H. St. J. Thackeray, and *Jewish Antiquities*, tr. Ralph Marcus and Allen Wikgren) or from *The Works of Josephus*, tr. William Whiston (abbreviated "W.").

†† Numbers in parentheses in this article correspond to numbered features in the drawing on pp. 24 and 25.

Wilson's Arch

Discovered by the British engineer-excavator Charles Wilson in the mid-19th century, Wilson's Arch (3) supported a bridge and aqueduct that spanned the Tyropoeon Valley to connect the Temple Mount with the Upper City. Today's arch is apparently a later restoration rather than the original Herodian structure. Originally the arch rose some 74 feet above the bedrock of the Tyropoeon Valley, but partial filling of the valley has reduced the arch's height to 25 feet above the present pavement. The arch is 45 feet wide. Today the reconstructed arch shelters an area where Jews pray and where Torah scrolls—often carried outdoors to be read in the plaza before the western wall—are stored. The first-century A.D. historian Josephus mentions the Hasmonean forerunner of this bridge in connection with the Roman siege of Jerusalem by Pompey in 63 B.C. The Hasmonean forces retreated into the Temple area and "cut the bridge."

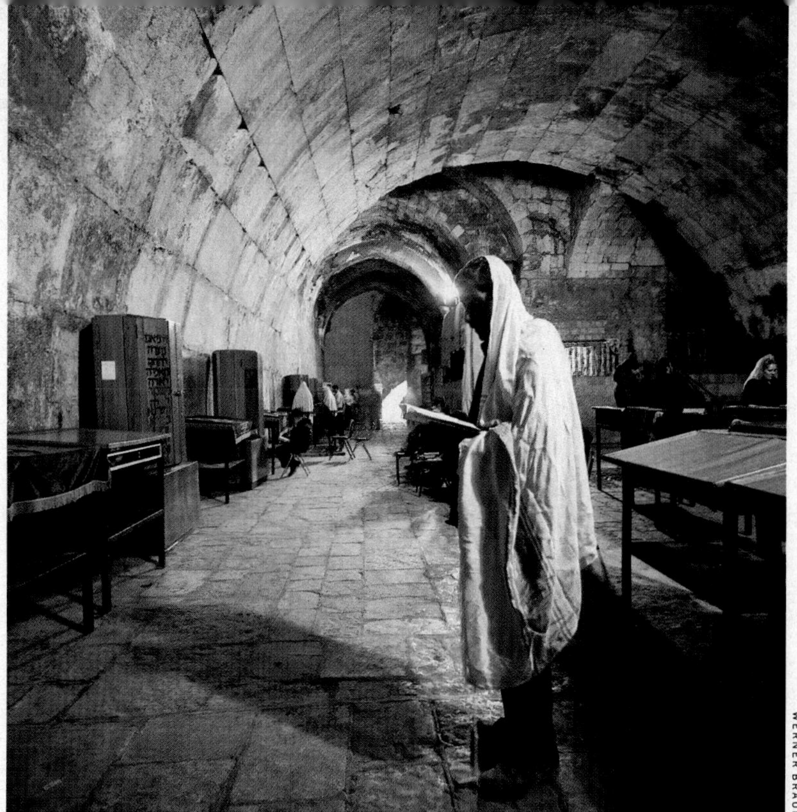

WERNER BRAUN

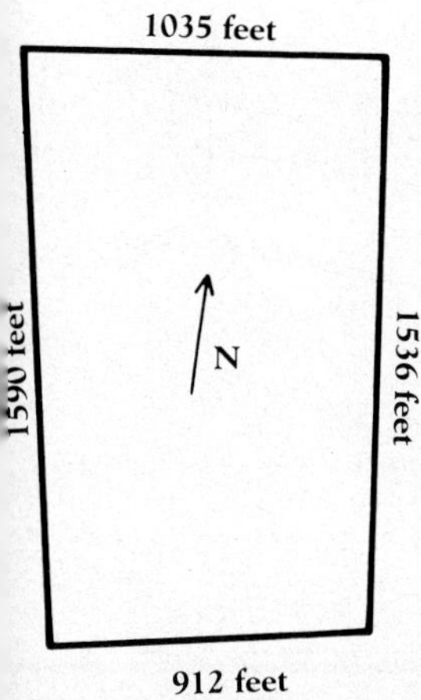

Plan of Temple Mount Wall

ashlars are visible above the prayer plaza in front of the western wall. Below the plaza level are 19 additional courses of Herodian ashlars. This means that bedrock lies a staggering 68 feet below the plaza. (The shafts dug by Warren adjacent to the wall show us how many courses lie below the surface. These shafts can still be seen north of the prayer area. They are well lit; coins thrown by tourists reflect from the bottom.)

It is not difficult to distinguish Herodian ashlars from those of later periods above them. Herodian masonry has a fine finish, a flat, slightly raised center boss and typical flat margins around the edges. The stones were cut with such precision that no mortar was needed to fit them together perfectly. Some of these ashlars are as much as 35 feet long and weigh up to 70 tons.

North of the open prayer area, under overhead construction, is Wilson's Arch (3), named after Charles Wilson, the British engineer who first discovered it in the mid-19th century. As it exists today it is probably not Herodian, but a later restoration, the first of a series of arches built to support a bridge that spanned the Tyropoeon Valley, linking the Temple Mount with the Upper City to the west. In Herodian times, an aqueduct also ran over this causeway, bringing water from "Solomon's Pools" (not really Solomonic) near Bethlehem to the huge cisterns that lay beneath the Temple platform.

Moving south from Wilson's Arch, we come to a gate in the western wall. Known today as Barclay's Gate (4), after its discoverer—J. T. Barclay, a British architect who worked in Jerusalem a short time before Wilson and Warren—it has been almost completely preserved. The only section now visible, however, is the northern half of its massive lintel (almost 27 feet long and 7 feet high) and the top three stones of its northern doorpost. These form part of the western wall at the southern end of the area today reserved for women (by Orthodox Jewish law, men and women worship separately). The remainder of the gate is obscured by the earthen ramp leading up to the Moor's Gate, which is the present-day access to the Temple Mount from this area.

We know the level of the original threshold of Barclay's Gate from Warren's records. Our excavation revealed the level of the Herodian street in front of the gate. There is a difference of about 13 feet between the level of the street and the level of the threshold of Barclay's Gate. This difference rather baffled us until another bit of seemingly trivial information, recorded by the indefatigable Warren, provided the missing piece of the puzzle.

Warren tells us that while digging in the area, he saw the remains of a vaulted chamber protruding from below the threshold of Barclay's Gate. Warren assumed that this must have been part of a lower viaduct that crossed the Tyropoeon Valley, but on a much smaller scale than the bridge supported by Wilson's Arch. Additional clues from our excavation have led us to conclude that this vault supported a staircase that led up to Barclay's Gate from the main Herodian street. At the southern corner of the western wall, we found a flight of six steps, 10 feet wide, leading north. Somewhat farther north (about 46 feet south of

Barclay's Gate

Although most of Barclay's Gate (4) survives, little of it can be seen today. Named for its discoverer, the 19th-century British architect J. T. Barclay, this gate in the western wall of the Temple Mount has mostly disappeared behind later construction and beneath the risen street level. The sketch (below, top right) indicates the original Herodian elements visible in the larger photo, as well as the unseen parts of the gate. Seven courses of Herodian ashlars are visible in the western wall. The first three courses above plaza level formed the upper part of the gate's northern doorpost. Small stones now block half of the upper part of the gate's former doorway. The other half of the blocked doorway is obscured by the earthen ramp and wall leading up to the Moor's Gate, the present access to the Temple Mount. The wall at right in the larger photo, perpendicular to the Temple Mount's western wall, supports the ramp. A sign is visible, upper right, above the arch of the Moor's Gate. Almost half of Barclay's Gate's massive lintel is visible (outlined in the photo), extending from above the doorpost across the top of the blocked doorway. In its entirety, the lintel measures about 27 feet long and 7 feet high.

Excavation in front of Barclay's Gate revealed that the Herodian main street (6) (smaller photo) in front of the gate lies 13 feet lower than the gate's original threshold. It had been a mystery how people reached Barclay's Gate from the main street, so far below. But now we have an answer.

The reconstruction drawing (below, bottom right) shows Barclay's Gate as it would appear if sliced down the middle, an then viewed from the north. A vaulted chamber between the main street and the gate threshold above apparently supported upper street and a stairway from the main street. This upper street ran along the western wall from the southwest corner (where steps leading up to the upper street were found; see photo, p. 35) to Warren's Gate (23). The space beneath the upper street was probably partitioned into small rooms by walls built perpendicularly to the western wall. Two such walls were excavated. These rooms may have been sho (5), serving the bustling traffic of pilgrims and residents.

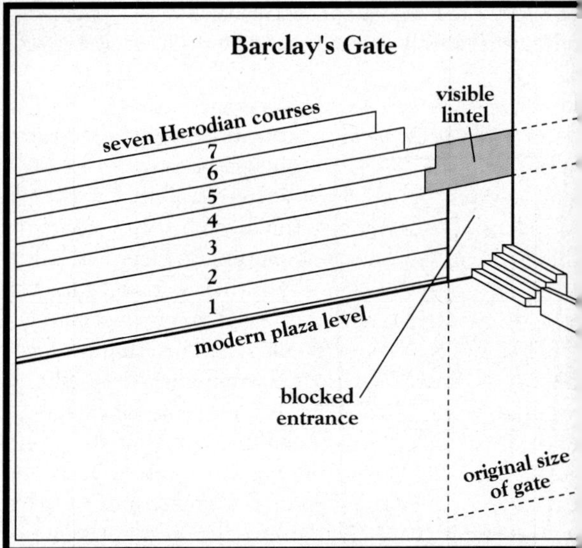

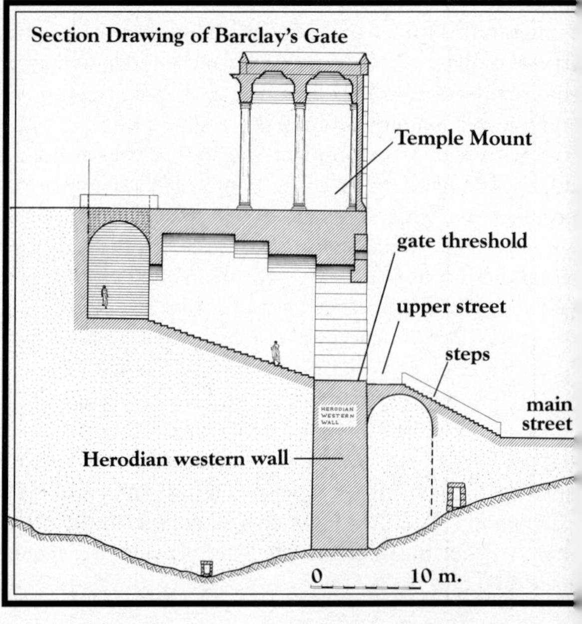

ırclay's Gate), we found two walls built perpendicular) the western wall. A row of many similar walls, ɛrpendicular to the southern wall, had been found ırlier. These we assume to be the remains of ɔmmercial premises frequented by visitors to the emple. If that is true, the two walls perpendicular to ıe western wall probably also formed part of a similar rangement of small cells on this side (5). The flight steps at the southern end of the western wall must ıerefore have led up to a narrow street that ran *over* ıe roofs of these shops. Finally, the vault observed by /arren must have carried a staircase that connected ıe lower street (the main street [6]) with this narrow pper street, giving access to Barclay's Gate. Thus, the 3-foot difference between the level of the main erodian street and the threshold of Barclay's Gate was ow explained.

The fact that the main Herodian street stopped short f the western wall by 10 feet strongly supports this ɛconstruction. The small shops adjacent to the western ıd southern walls formed part of the Upper and Lower larkets of the city, as described by Josephus. The main erodian street ran from Damascus Gate in the north) the Siloam Pool in the south, through the Tyropoeon alley; the shops adjacent to the western wall of the emple Mount fronted on this street.

The next element we will examine is Robinson's rch (7), which protrudes from the western wall south f Barclay's Gate. In fact, Robinson's Arch is barely the ɔring of the arch, in contrast to Wilson's Arch, which complete. Robinson's Arch is named after the merican orientalist Edward Robinson, who in his avels in Palestine in the second third of the 19th ɛntury correctly identified dozens and dozens of iblical sites. It was he who first identified this arch that ɛars his name. From its discovery until the time of our xcavation, it was generally assumed that Robinson's rch was the first of a series of arches that supported ıother causeway spanning the Tyropoeon Valley in the ıme way as the bridge that began at Wilson's Arch. t the beginning of our excavations, a hypothetical ɛconstruction based on this theory was indeed drawn p. However, when we found no other piers in addition) those that had supported Robinson's Arch, and that ad already been discovered by Warren, we turned in erplexity to Josephus. He described the gate to the emple Mount that must have existed above Robinɔn's Arch as follows:

> "The last gate [in the western wall] led to the *other* city where the *road descended down into the valley* by means of a *great number of steps* and thence up again by the ascent" (W., *Antiquities of the Jews* 15.11.5).

According to Josephus, this gate led from the Temple lount, not *over* the Tyropoeon Valley via a bridge to ıe Upper City (8) on the west, but rather to "the alley" below by means of "a great number of steps." ccess to the "other city," the Upper City on the west, was obviously via steps leading up from the valley.

Excavations proved the accuracy of Josephus's description. The archaeologists discovered a series of piers of arches of graduated height, ascending from south to north. The arches were equidistant. At the top is a turn eastward over Robinson's Arch. On this basis a monumental stairway has been reconstructed, leading from the Royal Stoa (9) on the Temple Mount down to the street in the Tyropoeon Valley. From there one could ascend to the Upper City or south to the Lower City.

Beneath Robinson's Arch, weights, coins, stone vessels and other evidence of commercial activity were found in four small cells. Above the lintel of the entrance to each of these shops was a relieving arch, designed to distribute the downward pressure of the superstructure.*

The stairway that ascended over Robinson's Arch provided an impressive entrance to the Royal Stoa, which Herod built on the southern end of the Temple Mount. Josephus describes this royal portico in some detail (*Jewish Antiquities* 15.11.5). It was built in the shape of a basilica with four rows of 40 columns each. Each of the huge columns in this veritable forest of columns was 50 feet high. The thickness of each was such, Josephus tells us, "that it would take three men with outstretched arms touching one another to envelop it" (L., *Jewish Antiquities* 15.11.5). Fragments of columns found in the excavation validate Josephus's description. Most of these fragments, however, had been reused in later Byzantine and Islamic buildings.

It was probably from this Royal Stoa that Jesus

> "drove out all who sold and bought in the Temple, and he overturned the tables of the moneychangers and the seats of those who sold doves. He said to them, 'It is written, "My house shall be called the house of prayer"; but you make it a den of thieves' " (Matthew 21:12-13; also compare Mark 11:15-17; Luke 19:45-46).

Lying on the main north-south street adjacent to the western wall, the excavators found massive amounts of rubble, testifying to the extensive destruction of the complex inflicted by the Roman general Titus in 70 A.D. Among the various architectural remains found in

(text continues on p. 32)

* A relieving, or discharging, arch is an arch built into the wall above the lintel of a doorway. Without it, the pressure of the wall construction would break the lintel stone. The relieving arch diverts the pressure that comes from above through the arch stones to the side parts of the opening, as illustrated in the drawing at right. Arrows show diversion of pressure from above.

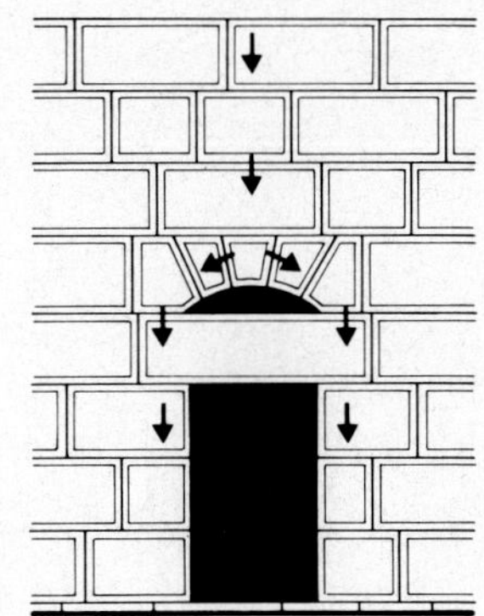

Robinson's Arch

Discovered by Edward Robinson (1794-1863), often hailed as the "father of Biblical geography" (below), Robinson's Arch (7) was assumed to be the first of several supporting a bridge over the Tyropoeon Valley from the Temple Mount to the Upper City, similar to the bridge that began at Wilson's Arch (3). Before excavation, only a trace of an arch's spring (below, right), jutting from the deeply buried western wall, hinted at the original Herodian structure. Excavation uncovered the full extent of the arch's spring, the protruding stones halfway up the wall at left (opposite), but failed to find the piers that would have supported a bridge across the valley. Instead, the archaeologists discovered a series of piers of graduated height in a north-south line south of Robinson's Arch. The piers were supports for the arches of a monumental stairway, which led up from the main street in the valley and then turned right to the entrance to the Royal Stoa. Robinson's Arch, in this reconstruction (right), would have supported the upper portion of the stairway, attached to the Temple Mount wall. Shaded areas in the drawing identify Herodian remains visible today.

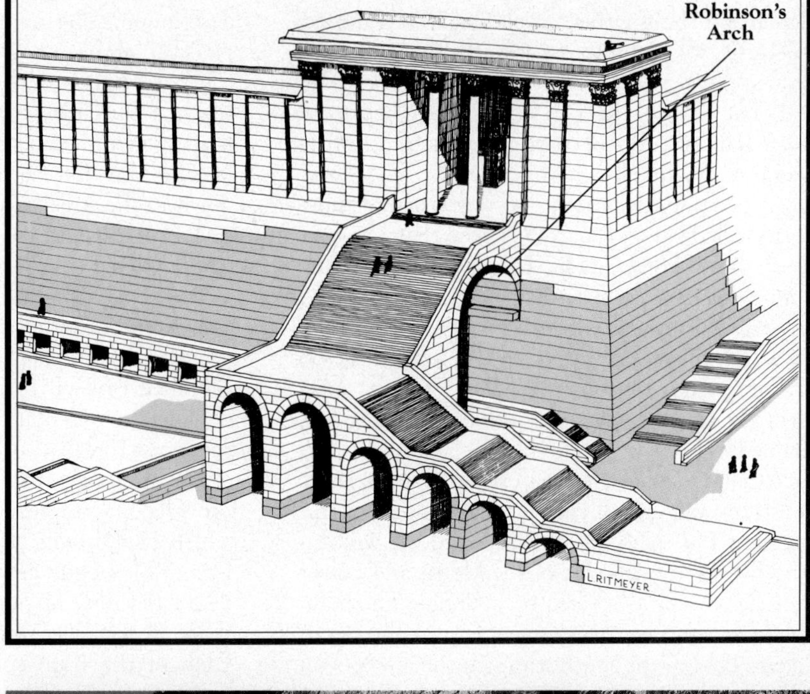

COURTESY UNION THEOLOGICAL SEMINARY, NEW YORK, NY

WERNER BRAUN

(continued from p. 29)

the rubble were steps from the original monumental stairway, archstones, columns, capitals, friezes and pilasters.

These pilasters are of special interest because they confirm the architectural style of the wall of the Temple Mount: flat in the lower part, with pilasters, or engaged pillars (**10**), in the upper part. These rectangular engaged pillars were set into the wall and topped with capitals.

A complete Herodian wall in this same style has survived intact in the structure surrounding the Tomb of the Patriarchs (Machpelah) in Hebron.*

On the Herodian street near the southwest corner of the Temple Mount, the excavators found a large stone block with a Hebrew inscription carved on it. Unfortunately, the end of the inscription is not on this fragment. The piece containing the final letters of the inscription had broken off, leaving the inscription open to various interpretations. The surviving part of the inscription can be vocalized *l'bet hatqia l'hak . . .*, which may be translated "to the place of trumpeting *l'hak- . . . .*"

Various possibilities have been suggested to complete *l'hak—l'ha-kohn* (for the priest); *l'hekal* (toward the temple); or *l'hakriz* (to herald [the Sabbath]).** Whatever the correct ending, it is clear that this inscription was a direction to the place where the priest stood to blow the trumpet to announce the commencement of the Sabbath and feast-days as mentioned in Josephus (*The Jewish War* 4.9.12). Most scholars have assumed that the direction was for the priest himself, to mark the place where he was to stand. Another possibility, however, is suggested by traces of fine white

* See Nancy Miller, "Patriarchal Burial Site Explored for First Time in 700 Years," **BAR**, May/June 1985; and Dan Bahat, "Does the Holy Sepulchre Church Mark the Burial of Jesus?" **BAR**, May/June 1986.

** See Aaron Demsky, "When the Priests Trumpeted the Onset of the Sabbath," **BAR**, November/December 1986.

THE ROYAL STOA

The largest structure on the Temple Mount, this grand hall extended across the southern end of the great platform, from east to west (see drawing, pp. 36-37). Built in the style of a basilica, the stoa was divided into a central nave and side aisles by four rows of 40 columns each (plan, right).

One row consisted of pilasters built into the southern wall. A second row, 40 monoliths topped by Corinthian capitals, created an aisle adjacent to the nave. A third row divided the nave from an aisle on the other side. The fourth, northernmost row formed an open colonnade, not a wall as on the southern side. Through this open row of columns one could proceed into the Temple court.

At the eastern end of the nave, the apse (drawing below) was the setting for meetings of the Sanhedrin—the supreme Jewish legislative, religious and judicial body. In his proud description of the Temple Mount, Josephus called this stoa "more deserving of mention than any under the sun" (Antiquities of the Jews XV:430).

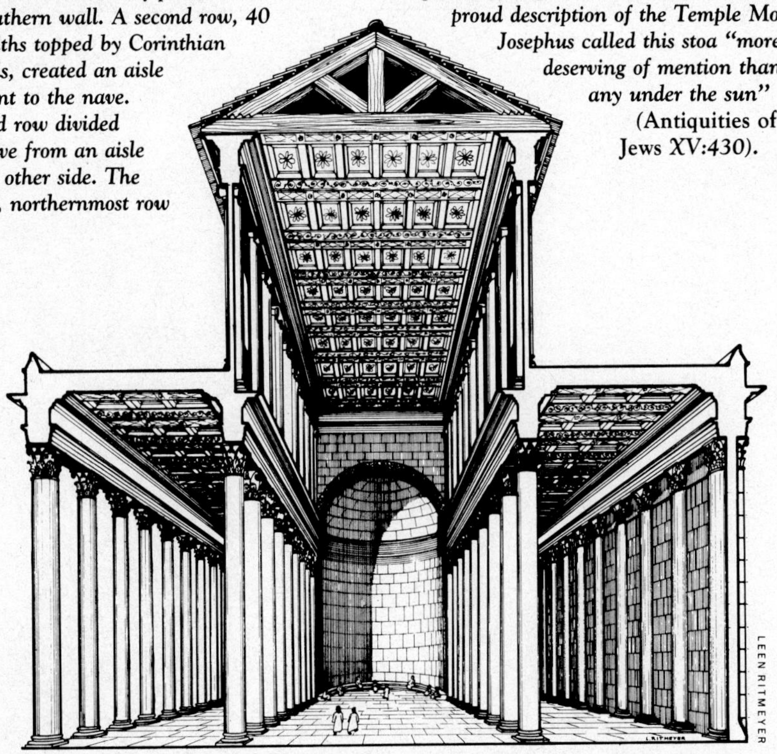

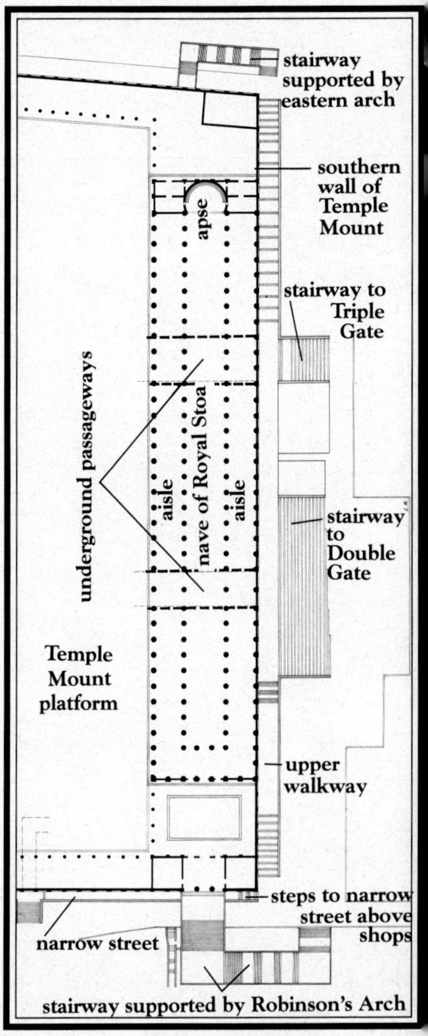

The Korban Vessel

fragment of a stone vessel (two views, low, right), found in the fill near the uthern wall, bears the inscribed word krbn orban), which means "sacrifice." As seen this wax impression (below, left), two udely drawn birds, identified as pigeons or doves, also appear, upside-down and below the word, on the fragment. The vessel may have been used in connection with a sacrifice to celebrate the birth of a child, since these birds were traditional offerings on such an occasion. The sale of these birds was targeted by Jesus when he "drove out all who sold and bought in the Temple, and he overturned the tables of the moneychangers and the seats of those who sold doves" (Matthew 21:12; Mark 11:15).

ERICH LESSING/ISRAEL DEPT. OF ANTIQUITIES AND MUSEUMS

ISRAEL DEPT. OF ANTIQUITIES AND MUSEUMS

Pilasters

ctangular engaged pillars, or pilasters, orated the upper portion of the Temple unt wall (10). An example from another rodian structure, the enclosure wall of the nb of the patriarchs (Machpelah) in bron, appears in the drawing at right. mains of the Temple Mount pilasters were nd in the rubble in front of the pier of binson's Arch (below). In this view we nd in front of the Temple Mount's stern wall, out of sight at lower left. The nelated southern wall of the Old City pears at upper left. The large, broken stone in the foreground is a wall fragment with a piece of a protruding pilaster; it lies in front of the nearly buried entrance to one of the shops beneath the upper street. The shop's beautifully dressed lintel is topped by two semi-circular stones. Just to the left of the semi-circular stone on the left is another pilaster fragment, with fine carved margins. At lower left, three stone steps formerly supported by Robinson's Arch (bearing red identification numbers) lie where they fell, still in neat order.

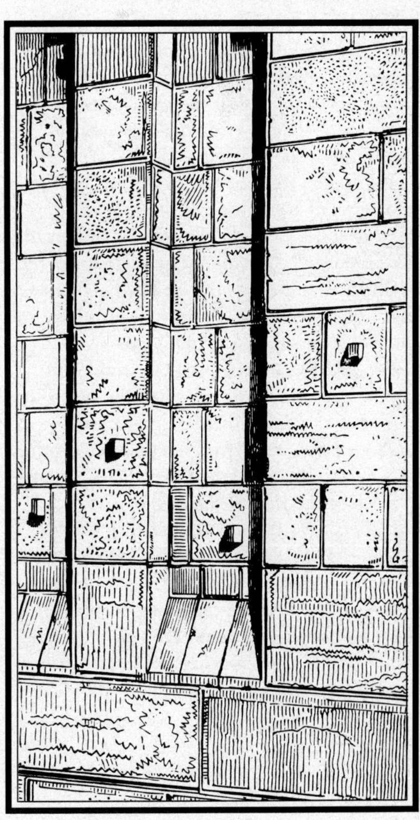

DE VOGUE *LE TEMPLE DE JERUSALEM*

THE PLACE OF THE TRUMPETING

Many courses of fine Herodian masonry still stand at the southwest corner of the Temple Mount (opposite, top). Beneath the unexcavated bank of earth abutting the Temple Mount's western wall, four steps are exposed—the first in a stairway. This stairway once ascended to a narrow street that ran over the rooftops of a row of shops (5) along the Temple Mount's western wall. Another, major street (6) ran in front of the shops.

On the smooth paving stones of the Herodian street in front of the steps, at the right of the photo, a wooden frame erected by the excavators protects a large stone that fell there in 70 A.D. The eight-foot-long ashlar bears a dramatic, but incomplete, Hebrew inscription (right), "to the place of trumpeting to [or "for"] . . ." Although the excavators who discovered the stone in 1969 made an earnest search for the missing fragment, it was never found. Very likely, 19th-century explorer-archaeologist Charles Warren (left) inadvertently broke the stone. Digging his excavation shaft, seen as a broken line in the drawing (opposite, bottom), through fill that buried the southwest corner, Warren pierced the Herodian pavement at this corner and probably cracked the edge of the trumpeting stone, which lay where it had fallen on the pavement, one end protruding into his shaft. In the photo (opposite) the wooden frame just right of center protects the newly discovered inscribed stone.

PALESTINE EXPLORATION FUND

What does the inscription mean? Scholars have offered several suggestions for the missing words: "to the Temple," "to herald the Sabbath," "for the priest." However the inscription ended, it gives us hard evidence that atop the Temple Mount walls, above the southwest corner shops, there was a designated place for a priest to stand and announce with a trumpet blast the beginning or end of the Sabbath (drawing, right). Josephus, the first-century Jewish historian, in The Jewish War, describes this very spot:

"Above the roof of the priests' chambers, . . . it was the custom for one of the priests to stand and to give notice, by sound of trumpet, in the afternoon of the approach, and on the following evening of the close, of every seventh day, announcing to the people the respective hours for ceasing work and for resuming their labors."

LEEN RITMEYER

plaster found on parts of the stone. This indicates that the inscription itself may not have been visible after the stone was in place. The entire inscription may simply have been a mark inscribed in the quarry to indicate to the builders where to place the stone. The fact that the carving is not particularly beautifully executed would support this theory.

One thing is clear, however: the stone could have come only from the top of the southwest corner of the Temple Mount. Found lying on the Herodian street, underneath other stones that had fallen from the tower above, it could not have been transported here from any other place. The tower at the southwest corner of the Temple Mount stood at a height of approximately 50 feet above the level of the Temple court. The Romans would never have moved the stone from another part of the Temple precincts and then hoisted it up to the tower and dropped it on the pavement before destroying the tower. The fact that the inscription is incomplete gave rise to theories that the original location of the trumpeting stone was elsewhere.* Here is one instance where Warren's excavation method—the digging of shafts and tunnels—detracted from, instead of supplemented, our understanding of the remains. Warren almost certainly cut off the remainder of the inscription on this stone while digging his shaft in darkness at the southwest corner of the Temple Mount. Happily, he was unaware of the controversy that would rage when the stone was uncovered some hundred years later.

Let us turn now to the southern wall of the Temple Mount (see drawing, pp. 36-37). Even before our excavations began, the locations of its two main features, the Huldah Gates (called after the prophetess of that name—see 2 Kings 22:14; 2 Chronicles 34:22), were known. The remains of these gates are visible in the wall we see today. They are now referred to as the Double Gate (**11**) and the Triple Gate (**12**). Few people are aware, however, that the Double Gate has been preserved in its entirety inside the Temple Mount. Its original lintel and relieving arch are still intact. On the outside, the western half and most of the eastern half of the Double Gate are concealed by a Crusader structure built against the southern wall of the Temple Mount in order to protect the Double Gate during the Crusader period. At that time, the southern wall of the Temple Mount served as the city wall, and the center of government itself was located on the Temple platform. The security of the Double Gate required the erection of a massive tower outside it to provide a zigzag entrance. Standing perpendicular to the southern wall of the Temple Mount, the wall that obscures most of the Double Gate on the outside was part of this Crusader tower.

Over the remaining part of the Double Gate still

* See Asher S. Kaufman, "Where Was the Trumpeting Inscription Located," letter in **BAR**, May/June 1987.

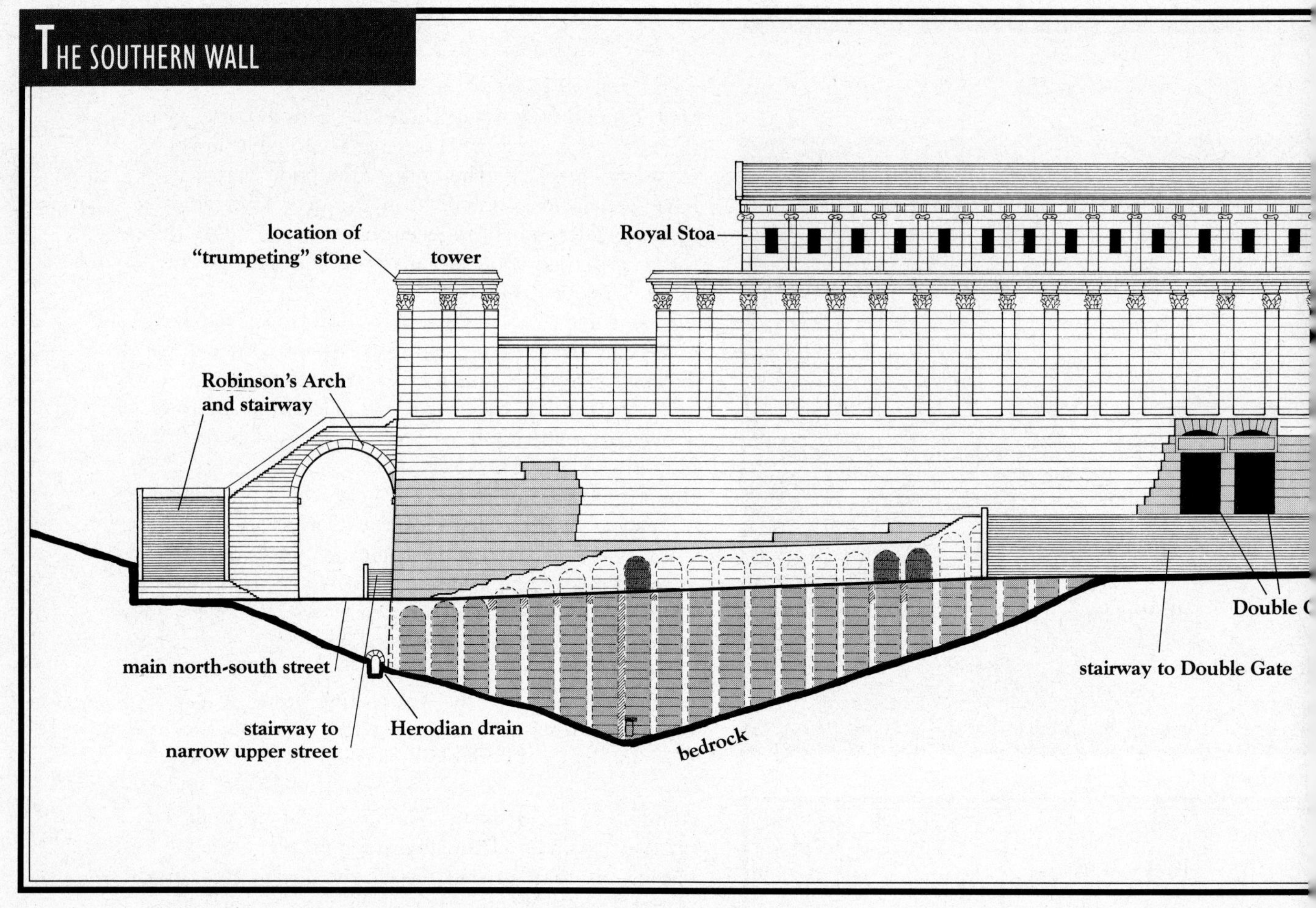

visible on the outside is a decorative applied arch that dates from the Moslem Omayyad period. Originally, however, there was no decoration, or even molding, on the outside.

Inside the Double Gate, which gave access to the Temple court, two pairs of domes still delight the eye with their stone-carved decoration. Using floral and geometric motifs, the unique decoration is a fine example of how Herodian craftsmen adapted Roman decorative styles while still conforming to Jewish law, which forbade the representation of human or animal figures.

Some earlier reconstructions of the outside of this gate included additional decoration, such as a pediment (a triangular, roof-shaped decoration above the lintel of a doorway) or a frieze. However, by counting each of the Herodian courses and drawing up an accurate elevation of the whole southern wall, we were able to determine that the top of the relieving arch above the lintel of the Double Gate was level with the internal court. So there would have been no room for any additional decoration. Today's courtyard level—2,420 feet above sea level—is the same as the Herodian court level. I (Leen) was able to confirm this in 1977 during repairs to the floor of the El Aqsa mosque, which lies above the Double Gate. At that time, just below the floor, I saw a circular keystone—the top of the dome of the Double Gate.

In Herodian times, access to the Double Gate from outside was chiefly by means of a broad stairway (**13**), founded on the natural bedrock of the Temple Mount slope. The stairway's eastern end extends 105 feet east of the centerpost of the Double Gate. In our reconstruction, we have assumed that the stairway was built on the central axis of the Double Gate so that it therefore also extended 105 feet west of the Double Gate's centerpost. Accordingly, the total width of the stairway is shown to be 210 feet—an impressive entranceway indeed! The 30 steps, which were laid alternately as steps and landings, were conducive to a slow, reverent ascent. This monumental stairway also provides a moving pictorial setting for an incident described in the Talmud,* in which we are told, "Rabban Gamaliel and the elders were standing at the top of the stairs at the Temple Mount" (Tosefta, *Sanhedrin* 2:2).

* The Talmud (tahl-MOOD) is a collection of Jewish laws and teachings comprising the Mishnah and the Gemara (a commentary on the Mishnah). There are two Talmuds. The Palestinian (or Jerusalem) Talmud was completed in the mid-fifth century A.D.; the Babylonian Talmud, completed in the mid-sixth century A.D., became authoritative.

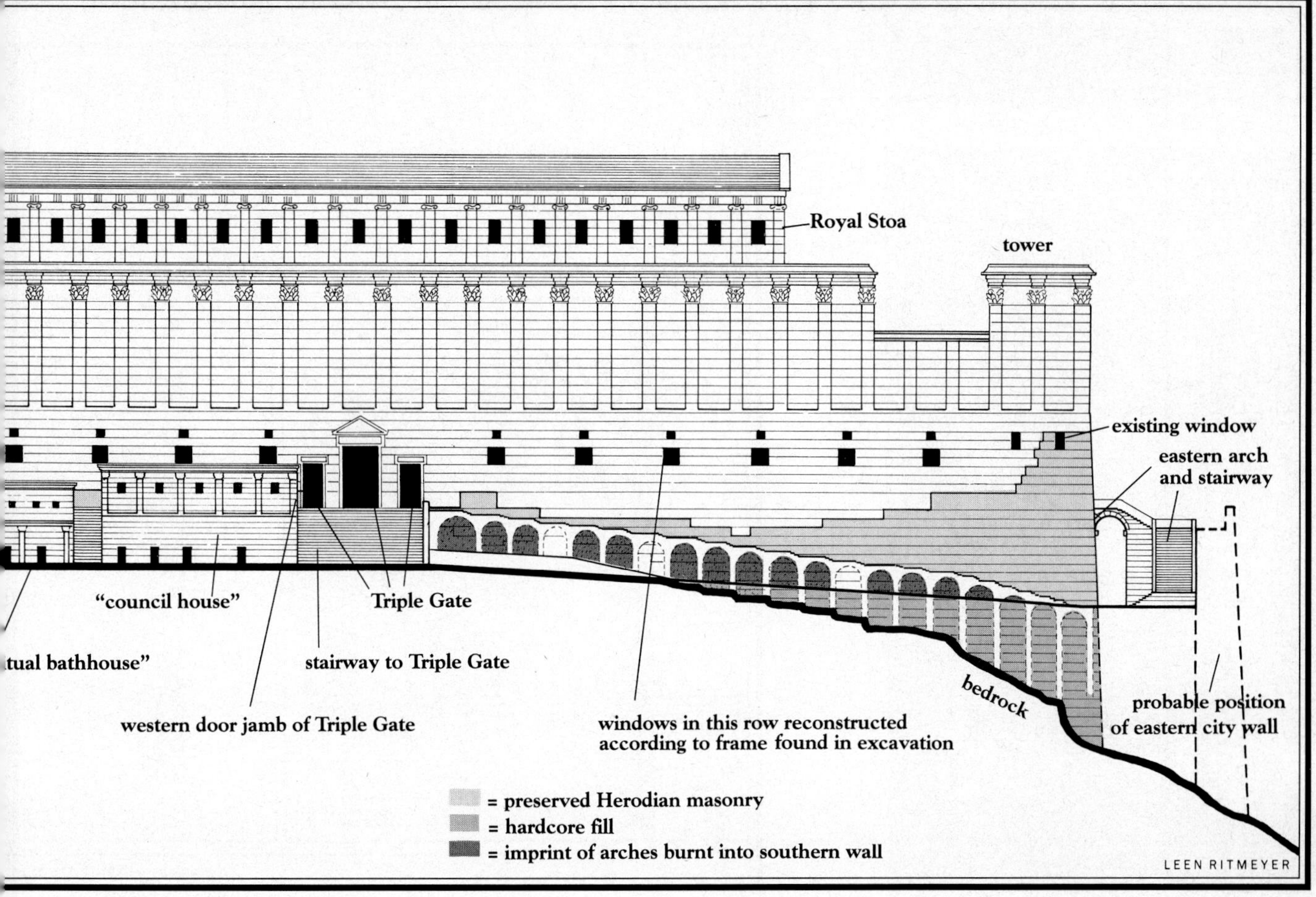

From the viewpoint of design and town-planning, it ; evident that a wide plaza (**14**) must have existed outh (in front) of the steps leading to the Double Gate. 'aving stones in a small area, approximately 16 feet quare, withstood the ravages of time to confirm the xistence of this plaza. The rest of the paving slabs were aken by later builders who needed construction naterial. Approximately 100 feet south of the steps, the rchaeologists found evidence of what was probably the oundation of the plaza. This suggests that the imensions of the plaza were what we should expect hem to have been. Its size was apparently comparable o similar plazas in the ancient world, at such places s Athens, Priene and Assos.

Between the Double Gate and the Triple Gate, our econstruction drawing shows two buildings. The one o the west (**15**) was a bathhouse for ritual purification; nany *mikva'ot* (ritual baths) cut into the bedrock have een found there. The building to the east (**16**) was robably a council house, indicated by the many edrock-cut Herodian chambers (rooms) found near the Triple Gate. This building may have been the first of he three courts of law located in the Temple precincts, s mentioned in the Mishnah:* "One [court] used to it at the gate of the Temple Mount, one used to sit t *the gate of the Temple Court* and one used to sit in the Chamber of Hewn Stone" (Babylonian Talmud, *Sanhedrin* 11:2).

If the Double Gate was for pilgrims to enter and exit, the Triple Gate was used by members of the priestly order to reach the storerooms where the wine, oil, flour and other items needed in connection with the Temple service were kept. From there, of course, they could also reach the Temple platform.

On either side of the Triple Gate, we have reconstructed a row of windows (**17**). Their existence has been supposed on the basis of a finding in the immediate area, a window frame with grooves for metal bars. Some provision for light and air was needed for the underground storeroom. This fact, combined with the window frame, is the basis for the windows we have reconstructed.

Excavations found the area near the southeast corner of the Temple Mount to be devoid of architectural remains, as it had served as a quarry for construction during later periods. Our workers cleared away the accumulated rubble from the wall, thereby exposing the original stones. One day, while surveying the bedrock foundations of Herodian rooms that adjoined the

(text continues on p. 40)

* The Mishnah is the collection of Jewish oral laws compiled and written down by Rabbi Judah the Prince in about 200 A.D.

The Double Gate

RICHARD NOWITZ

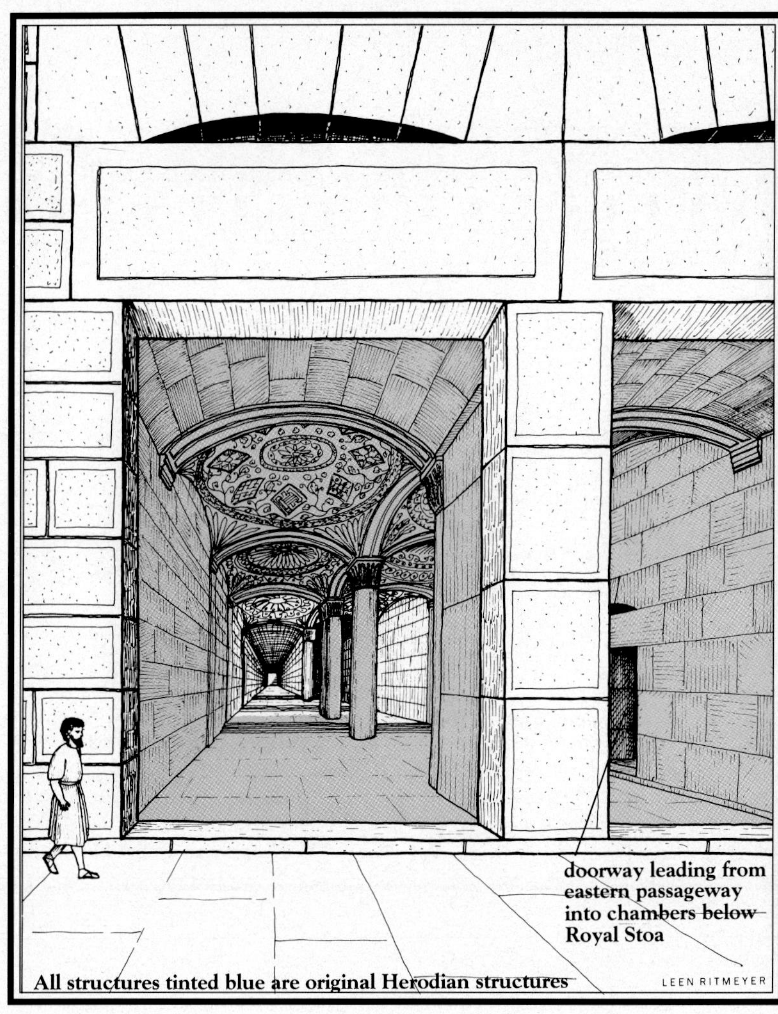

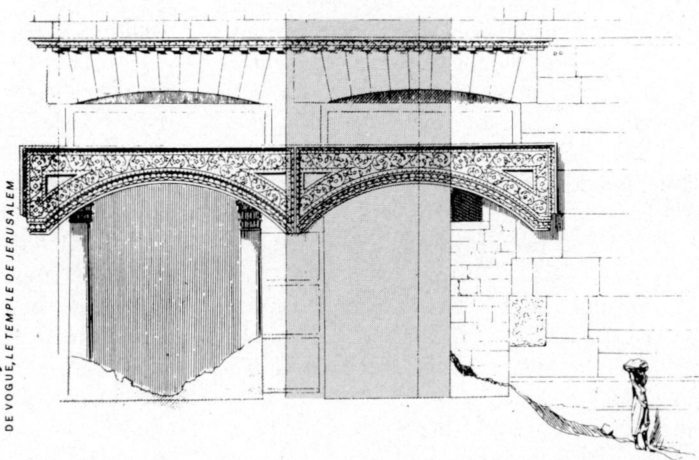

DE VOGÜÉ, LE TEMPLE DE JERUSALEM

The main entrance to the Temple Mount at the time of Herod is marked today by half of an arch (photos, left) built over the Double Gate during the Omayyad period (633-750 A.D.). Used by pilgrims and residents of Jerusalem, including Jesus, to approach and exit the sacred precinct, the Double Gate originally was not decorated at all on the outside. Instead it was surmounted by a plain lintel and above this, a relieving arch (drawings above). The Herodian lintel and relieving arch are visible in the photos (left) directly above the applied Omayyad arch. A fragment of another, smaller Omayyad decoration protrudes from the wall above the relieving arch.

The wall extending perpendicularly from the gate at the left of the photos is part of an entrance tower erected by Crusaders. The Crusaders walled up the eastern opening of the 20-foot-high Double Gate and built their entrance tower in a zigzag shape to protect

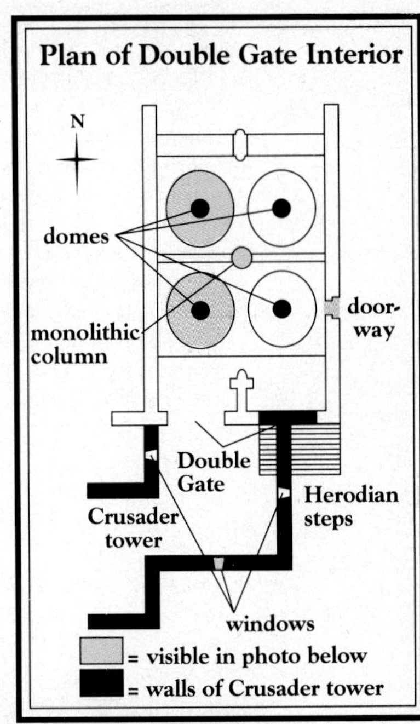

the Double Gate's western opening, which they used (drawing, above right). In the fine reconstruction drawn by Count Melchior de Vogüé in 1864 (opposite, below) we can see how the arches looked before the Crusader tower blocked them. The tower wall is distinguishable by a rectangular gray tint overlay. The architectural features to the right of the tinted area are those visible in the photos (opposite, far left). Everything beneath and to the left of the tint is now hidden by the remains of the Crusader tower.

Thirty steps—partially original and partially restored—led up to the Double Gate. Their heights are roughly equal, between 7 and 10 inches. However, their depths alternate—12 inches, then 35 inches, then 12 inches, and so on. In this way, the Temple Mount architect created an ascent that required each worshipper to approach the Temple slowly and with some deliberation. In the photo (opposite, left top), at the top of the steps, huge Herodian ashlars form the first course of stones in the southern wall east—to the right—of the Double Gate. The smaller stones above date from rebuilding work in the Omayyad period.

Although the exterior of the Double Gate was modest, within it elaborately carved columns and domes adorned a passageway to the Temple Court, giving the visitor a preview of the Temple's splendor. As shown in the drawing (opposite, right top), the first four domes and the supporting side walls and columns stand today in their original form; in this drawing, all features tinted blue are original construction. Here we see the interior of the gate from the outside; we are looking north.

In the photo (right) we see the two intact western domes from the opposite direction—from within the passageway, looking south toward a sunlit window in the wall of the Crusader tower. Flowers and geometric designs cover the dome ceilings. Though stylized, these flowers represent specific local species. In the northwestern dome, a border of acanthus leaves frames a scallop design. In the southwestern dome a grapevine twines among eight decorated squares (drawing, above).

In the lit area on the left of the photo (above), beyond the large horizontal concrete beam, is the eastern passageway of the Double Gate. On the eastern wall of the passageway—at the far left of the photo—a doorway leads into side chambers located below the Royal Stoa. The doorway's extant Herodian lintel and relieving arch are visible behind and left of the modern, concrete frame around a white Herodian column. In the drawing (opposite, right top) this doorway is at the right.

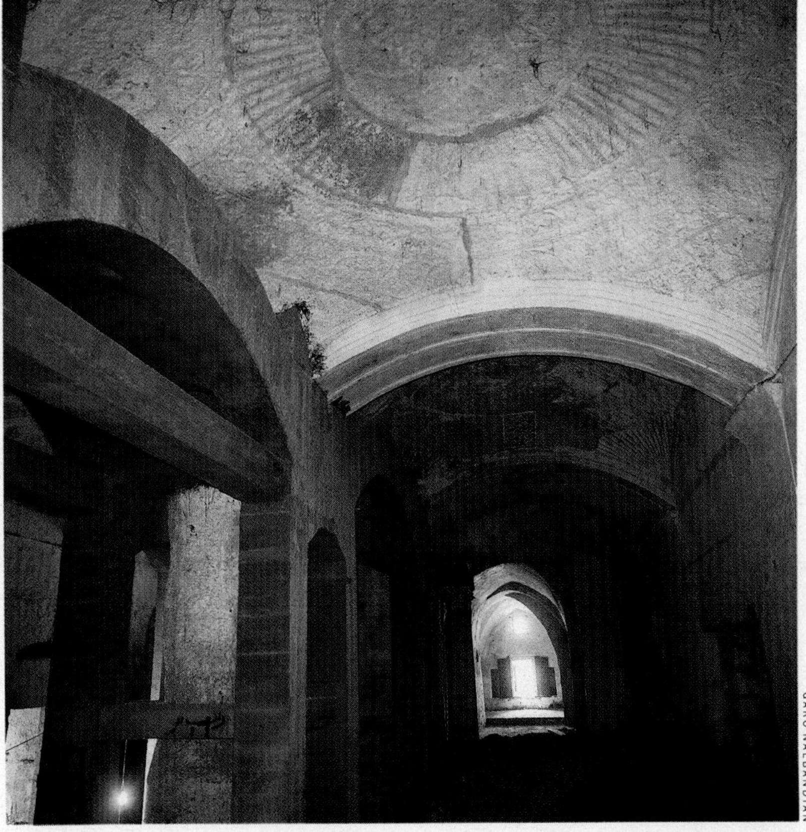
GARO NALBANDIAN

SHOPS ON THE SOUTHERN WALL

Burnt into the Temple Mount wall, the imprint of an arch provides a ghostly reminder of the eighth day of the Hebrew month of Elul, 70 A.D. On that day in August, Roman soldiers overran the Temple and its precincts, putting everything to the torch. This small, arched cell—probably a shop—burned along with many like it on the southern wall. This arch imprint is the first one east of the Triple Gate (see drawing, pp. 36-37).

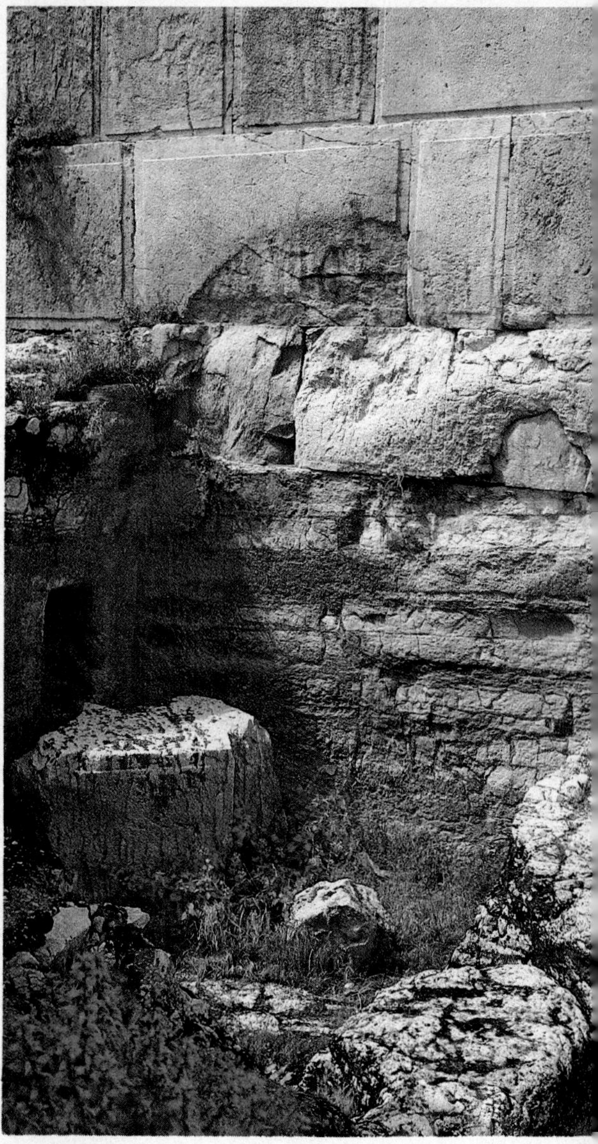

(continued from p. 37)

southern wall on the outside, east of the Triple Gate, we noticed something unusual. The imprint of arches burnt into the stones was clearly discernible on the Herodian wall. These arches descended in height toward the southeast corner of the Temple Mount. They were all that remained of small cells, probably shops (**18**), that lay below the stepped street that skirted the Temple Mount wall.

The tragedy of the Roman destruction comes vividly to life as we imagine the only possible scenario that would have left such an indelible imprint on the southern wall. The limestone ashlars used in the Herodian construction can be reduced to powder when exposed to very high temperatures. The Roman soldiers must have put brushwood inside the chambers and the blaze created when this was set alight would have caused the arches to collapse. The street that was carried by these arches also collapsed. Before the arches collapsed, the fire burnt into the back wall of the chambers, leaving the imprint of the arches as evocative testimony to the dreadful inferno. Josephus writes that, after having burnt the Temple, "The Romans, thinking it useless, now that the Temple was on fire, to spare the surrounding buildings, set them all alight, both the remnants of the porticoes and the gates . . . " (L., *The Jewish War* 6.5.2).

In the western part of the southern wall (**19**), three similar arches were subsequently discovered burnt onto the wall. Two flights of three steps each, with a landing in between, still exist near the southwest corner. The continuation of this pattern of steps and landings along the southern wall from west to east reaches exactly to the top of the first visible burnt arch. From the third visible arch (which is, at its center, 282 feet east of the southwest corner), a sharp flight of steps has to be inserted to reach the level of the top of the stairway leading to the Double Gate.

Now let us proceed to the eastern wall of the Temple Mount, which today has a Moslem cemetery in front of it. Some 130 feet of this ancient wall was exposed by a bulldozer prior to 1967. Despite the lack of scientific excavation on this side of the Temple Mount, many clues to its former appearance are preserved in the jigsaw of stones that make up the wall. Three Herodian windows, one with its lintel still in place, can be discerned in the Herodian tower just north of the southeast corner. This tower loomed high above the Kidron Valley and is sometimes identified as the "pinnacle of the Temple" referred to in Jesus' temptation in the wilderness (Matthew 4:5; Luke 4:9).* Some 100 feet north of the corner (directly opposite Robinson's Arch on the western wall) the beginning of an arch-spring can be seen. The springing arch was set on impost-blocks with large bosses (raised center portions) still visible. This arch apparently supported a stairway (**20**) that descended to the road that ran along the eastern wall. (In this, it paralleled the stairway over

* The devil took Jesus up to the "pinnacle of the Temple" and told him to throw himself down in order to prove he was the Son of God. Jesus replied, "It is written, 'You should not tempt the Lord your God.' "

THE EASTERN WALL

Preserved on this eastern side of the Temple Mount (right) are many Herodian features that mirror those on the opposite, western wall. Three windows, a double gateway and the spring of an arch set on impost blocks are all visible if you use the drawings (below) to guide your eye. The drawing (below right) identifies features in the photo (right). Like Robinson's Arch on the western wall, the arch on the eastern wall supported a stairway that led from the Temple Mount to a road below (see drawing, p. 30).

Two stones to the left of the arch spring, a strong vertical line begins, created by slight projections of the ashlars from the face of the wall. The projections gradually deepen from course to course. The vertical line thereby created on the wall was the visual continuation of the northeastern corner of a tower that once projected above the corner of the Temple Mount wall (drawing, below left). Above the arch, a double doorway provided access to storage vaults that lay below the level of the Temple court.

Between two small trees, an obvious vertical "seam" extends from the base about halfway up the wall, just north of the arch spring. This seam, called the "straight joint," identifies the beginning of the Herodian expansion of the Temple Mount to the south. The seam separates smoothly dressed Herodian ashlars on the left from rough ashlars on the right belonging to the earlier wall.

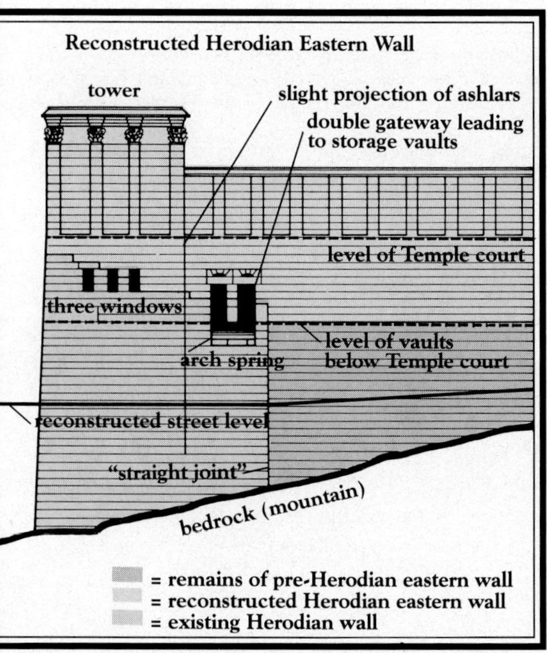

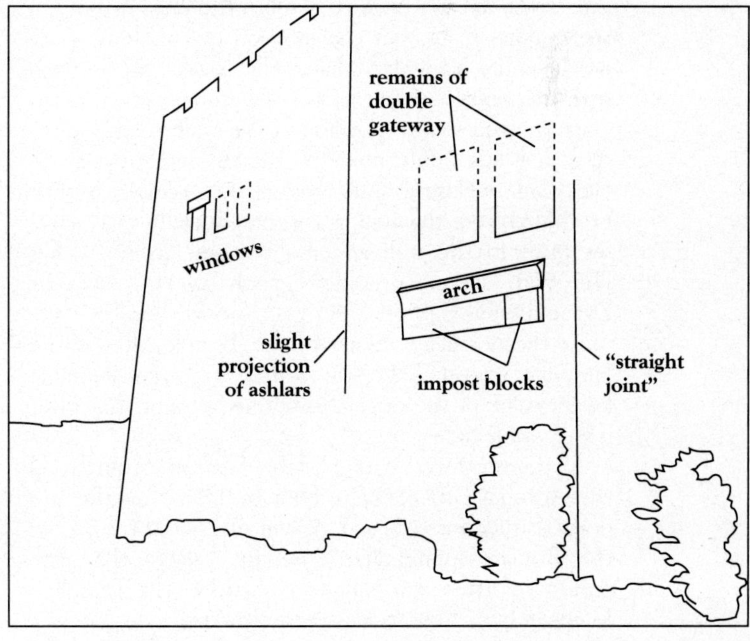

Robinson's Arch on the other side of the Temple Mount.) At the top of the stairway, a double doorway, also partially preserved, led into storage vaults, erroneously called Solomon's Stables. Although above street level, these vaults lay below the level of the Temple court. Perhaps wine, flour and incense for Temple rituals were stored here. The vaults were probably connected with the Triple Gate passageways, which led up to the Temple court and which were used by the priests.

At a point in the eastern wall, 106 feet north of the southeast corner, is a seam in the masonry—the famous "straight joint." Obviously the part of the wall south of this seam was added to the earlier wall. The masonry on the two sides of this seam are quite distinct from one another. The southern extension is clearly Herodian and is remarkably well-preserved. The date of the wall north of the "straight joint" is still the subject of heated controversy.*

The location of the gate to the Temple court in the eastern wall is, as yet, undetermined. The only visible entranceway, the Golden Gate, dates from the Early Islamic period (seventh century). The arch of another gate** lies directly beneath the blocked entranceway of the Golden Gate, but the location of this lower gate precludes its being Herodian. This lower gate is flush with the Golden Gate that is visible today. The Golden Gate protrudes from the line of the wall, so the lower gate does also. But none of the other gates of the Herodian enclosure wall around the Temple Mount protruded from the wall as this one does. In fact, gates set flush in the wall are also the rule in the other Herodian sacred precincts, such as the ones at Damascus and Hebron.

At the northeast corner of the Temple Mount, the Herodian tower (**21**) still stands to a considerable height. One of the original shooting-holes of the tower is still visible today.

At the northwest corner of the Temple Mount stood the Antonia Fortress (**22**), built by Herod on the site of an earlier fortress and named after Mark Antony, the Roman commander. Josephus relates that the Antonia Fortress was built as a "guard to the Temple." Manned by a Roman legion, the fortress had a tower on each of its four corners. The southeast tower w 70 cubits high (approximately 112 feet) "and commanded a view of the whole area of the Templ (L., *The Jewish War* 5.5.8). Josephus tells us that tl Antonia Fortress was erected on a rock 50 cubi (approximately 80 feet) high and was situated on a gre precipice. Archaeologists believe it was located on tl rock scarp where the Omariya School now stand Although not a trace of the fortress itself has bee found, one of the large buttresses of the fortress w revealed in the tunneling conducted along the wester wall by the Ministry of Religious Affairs.

This project has also brought to light the wester wall's remaining Herodian gate (**23**), previous discovered by Warren while tunneling under rigoro conditions. Since its original discovery by him, it h been known as Warren's Gate. Immediately to tl south of this gate, the largest stones (**24**) in the Temp Mount have been found. They are almost 11 1/2 fe high. The largest of four especially impressive stones 47 1/2 feet long. It weighs approximately 400 tons.

We have now made the full circuit round the Temp Mount wall. In our own way, we have followed tl injunction of Psalm 48:

"Walk around Zion, circle it;
count its towers,
take note of its ramparts;
go through its citadels,
that you may recount it to a future age."

(We wish especially to thank Professor Benjamin Mazar of the Hebre University, who has always encouraged us and has allowed us publish material from the Temple Mount excavations in this articl

Photos and drawings, unless otherwise credited, are by Lee Ritmeyer.

* For one view and a review of the arguments, see Ernest-Marie Laperrousaz, "King Solomon's Wall Still Supports the Temple Mount," **BAR**, May/June 1987.

** See James Fleming, "The Undiscovered Gate Beneath Jerusalem's Golden Gate," **BAR**, January/February 1983.

A Pilgrim's Journey

KATHLEEN RITMEYER

Jerusalem is bathed in the clear light of early morning. A pilgrim has come for one of the great festivals, and his journey is almost over. He begins the ascent from the Siloam Pool at the bottom part of the Lower City (see drawing on pp. 44-45). The sun is not yet casting its harsh glare on the stepped street paved with large limestone slabs, which is the path he must take to the Temple Mount. The pilgrim's eyes rest for a moment on the glittering spikes of the Temple in the distance; then he moves on. The houses of the Lower City are spread out before him like the crescent of the moon; higher up, on his left, he can see the magnificent palaces of the nobility in the Upper City. As he proceeds up the valley past the oldest part of the city, established by David and Solomon, he can still see, on his right, some of the splendid old palaces.

All along the street the merchants of the Lower Market are busy setting up their stalls for the day's business. The pilgrim is jostled by the farmers and traders who have come to buy and sell and by their beasts of burden. Baskets of luscious fruit, piles of cheeses, jars of wine and mounds of bread are set out hurriedly on the rough wooden tables. The unloading of bales of richly colored silks from a wagon causes an outbreak of excitement and arguing.

At the end of this stepped street, the pilgrim comes to a busy intersection. Visitors from many lands—Ethiopians, Macedonians, Cretans, Parthians and Romans from every part of the Roman empire—are moving toward the great plaza that fronts the monumental staircase leading up to the Double Gate of the Temple Mount. A different language from each group of people creates a cacophony of sound.

Our pilgrim climbs the first flights of the imposing staircase that leads to a gate in the western wall. The hubbub of the markets becomes fainter. He reaches the central platform of the staircase, which affords him a fine view and an opportunity to rest. The whole of the Lower City and a large portion of the Upper City are spread out before him.

On the west, the Upper City has the appearance of an impenetrable wall, the houses are so densely packed together. The Hasmonean Palace, built before Herod's time, rises high above its surroundings, and people can be seen moving about on its roof. Looking north, he sees the archives building and the Xystos, the open-air plaza where athletic games were held during the Hellenistic period, in front of the old city wall. On the other side of the plaza, opposite the Xystos, stands the elegant Council House, or Bule, whose outer walls match the walls of the Temple Mount for beauty. A procession of priests moves solemnly over the bridge that spans the Tyropoeon Valley, a bridge that gives the priests and nobles direct access from the Upper City to the Temple Mount. The thronged street below veers off to the northwest in the direction of the city gate that leads to Damascus. As far as the eye can see, the Upper Market is crowded with milling traders, buyers and visitors attired in strange costumes.

The pilgrim braces himself for the remaining climb up the staircase that leads to the Temple Mount. Flanked by two massive limestone pillars, so highly polished that they resemble marble, the gate evokes deep awe from the pilgrim. Looking up, he admires the gold-plated Corinthian capitals that crown the pillars. Inside the propylaeum, or gate-building, the shade is refreshing. Groups of people linger, luxuriating in the respite from glare and bustle.

A different scene greets the eye as he enters the Royal Stoa proper on the Temple Mount. A long hall, supported by four rows of thick columns stretches out in front of him. The northern side is open and leads to the Temple court. Long shafts of dust-flecked sunlight are filtered through the windows in the upper part of the stoa and glance off a scene of frenzied commercial activity. At the tables of the moneychangers, the pilgrim exchanges coins bearing the image of Caesar for silver shekels without the forbidden graven image. Women who have recently given birth are crowded at the stalls nearby, haggling over the price of the doves and pigeons they will sacrifice in gratitude for the happy conclusions of their pregnancies. Those who successfully complete a purchase walk away bearing small cages. Oxen and sheep to be sacrificed are also offered for sale; the smell of their droppings permeates the entire area.

At the eastern end of the portico is a partition through which members of the Sanhedrin are emerging after a session. The pilgrim observes on the other side of the partition the beauty of the apse, specially constructed to accommodate the Sanhedrin. A magnificent stone arch covered with a rich variety of geometric and floral patterns forms the backdrop for the Sanhedrin conferences. The tiers of smooth stone steps on which they sit while conferring are now empty.

Leaving behind the noise of the cooing doves and the bleating animals, the pilgrim moves on and passes through the open portico in the direction of the Temple. Soon, merging with the crowds pouring out of the underground stairway leading up from the Double Gate, he becomes part of the great throng who have come to worship at the "House of the Lord."

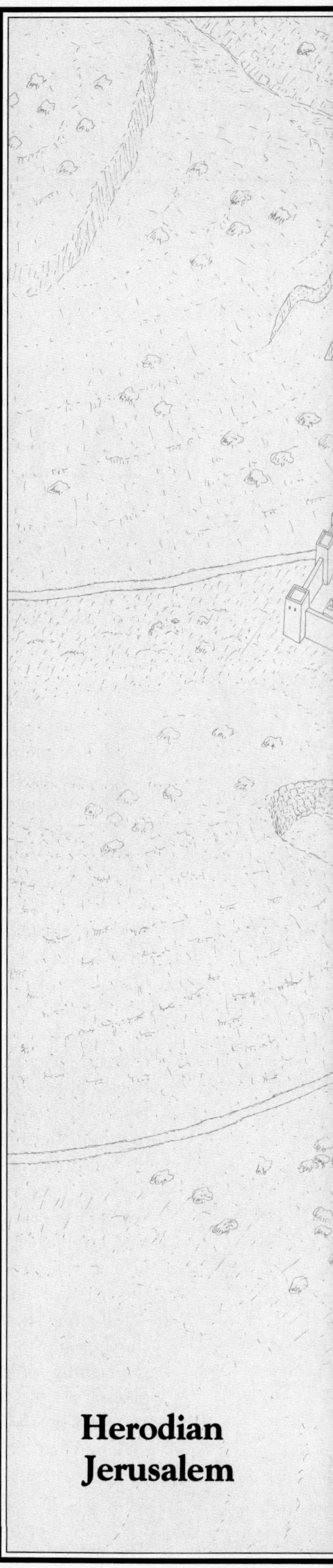

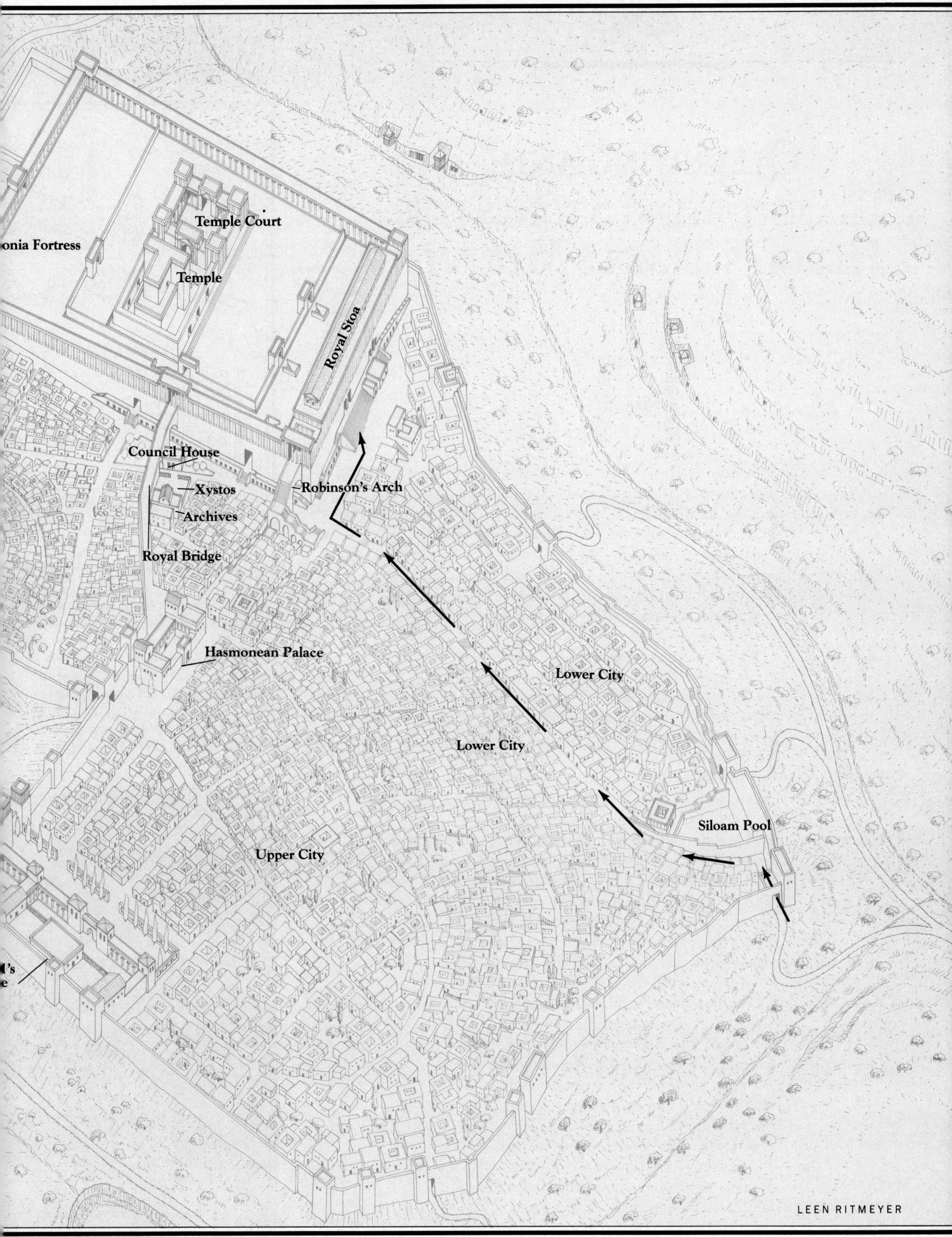
Temple Court
onia Fortress
Temple
Royal Stoa
Council House
Xystos
Robinson's Arch
Archives
Royal Bridge
Hasmonean Palace
Lower City
Lower City
Siloam Pool
Upper City
LEEN RITMEYER

Quarrying and Transporting Stones for Herod's Temple Mount

LEEN RITMEYER

Herod's construction in the Temple Mount area, like the construction of most of Jerusalem's buildings, used local limestone.

The mountains around Jerusalem are composed of Turonian and Cenomanian limestone that has a characteristic horizontal layering. These horizontal layers vary between about 18 inches and 5 feet thick. In exceptional cases, the layers are even thicker.

To quarry this limestone the stonecutter first straightened the face of the stone. This consisted of chiseling the rock in such a way as to produce a flat vertical surface—the side of the incipient stone—and a flat surface on top. Next, with a pickaxe he dug narrow channels 4 to 6 inches wide on all sides except the bottom of the incipient stone. In two of these grooves, at right angles, the quarryman would insert dry wooden beams, hammer them tightly into place and pour water over them. This caused the wood to swell, and the consequent pressure caused the stone to separate from the lower rock layer.

The next stage required squaring-off the stones and preparing them for transportation. The smaller stones were simply placed on wagons, according to Josephus. Some of the corner stones in the Temple Mount. however, weighed 50 tons and sometimes more. Special techniques were developed to transport these stones on large wooden rollers. While shaping the stones, the masons left 12-inch-long projections on opposite sides of each stone. These projec-

STONE QUARRYING

Stone quarrying in Herod's time (above). A stonecutter, right, uses a pickax to cut a channel in a limestone block. Meanwhile another worker, left, pours water over some logs stacked in the channel between two blocks. The water will cause the wood to swell, exerting lateral pressure on the block and splitting the block off of the bedrock to which it is attached at bottom. Because the

Stages of quarrying and moving ashlars (below). In the background, at left, the unworked bedrock exhibits the natural horizontal layering of the limestone in the Jerusalem vicinity. Blocks cut, but not yet removed, appear at upper right. The thickness of the limestone layers determined the height of the blocks that were quarried.

At lower left, a stonecutter dresses some rough blocks, taking care to leave projections on opposite sides of each block. The finished product, an ashlar with a projection and margins on its outer face, lies to his right.

Ropes are looped around the stone projections. Using a crane, lower right, a foreman supervises as the crane hoists one end of the block off the ground and lowers it upon a wooden roller.

At center, an ashlar begins its journey out of the quarry. Hitched to the stone by ropes looped around the projections, a team of oxen pulls the block. Wooden rollers ease the ashlar's movement. As the ashlar inches forward, rollers left behind at the rear are moved to the front.

LEEN RITMEYER

nestone lay in natural horizontal layers, e blocks would cleave along a relatively ·at, horizontal line.

Remains of an ancient quarrying ·eration (below) can be seen at a tomb mplex near the Siloam Pool. Shallow, complete channels cut around incipient ocks appear in the bedrock.

HERSHEL SHANKS

tions were later removed. In the meantime, however, ropes were placed around these projections, and two short, but strong, cranes outfitted with winches lifted the stones on one side and lowered them onto rollers. Oxen could then pull the stones with ropes placed around the projections. According to Josephus, 1,000 oxen were used in this work.

The quarries were probably located near what we know today as the Russian Compound, in the heart of modern Jerusalem. There a 50-foot-long column, still attached to the bedrock, can be seen. In the process of quarrying the column, a natural fissure was observed in the rock, so the workmen simply stopped work and left the damaged column in place. The quarries in this area are 125 feet higher than the Temple Mount, so the journey of over a mile to the Temple Mount was downhill. Using the force of gravity obviously made transportation easier.

Once the stones arrived at the building site, they had to be put in place. At both the southwest and southeast corners of the Temple Mount, stones weighing over 80 tons are still in place at a height of at least 100 feet above the foundations. How did they get there? At our excavation site, some of the more pious local laborers who worked with these stones were so awed by their size that they attributed their placement to angels. It would have been impossible, they said, for mere man to lift them into place. In a sense, they were right; no man could have lifted these stones to such a height, notwithstanding all the sophisticated Roman engineering equipment available at the time.

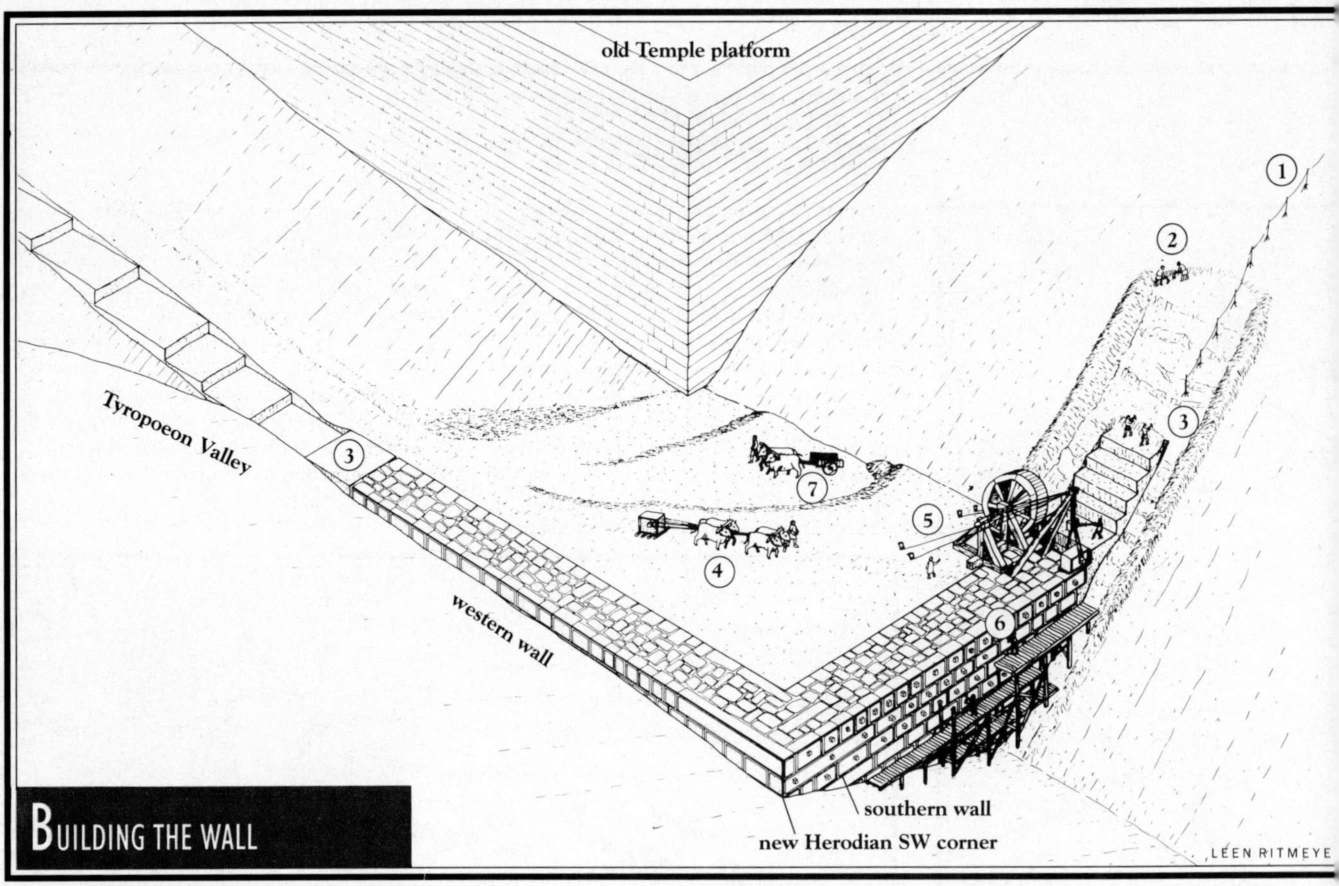

old Temple platform

Tyropoeon Valley

western wall

southern wall

new Herodian SW corner

LEEN RITMEYE

BUILDING THE WALL

Building Herod's Temple Mount wall involved several steps, as illustrated in this drawing (above). First the line of the wall was laid out by markers (1). Then the construction site was cleared down to bedrock (2). Next the bedrock itself had to be cut and leveled before the ashlars could be put into place (3). Oxen hauled the ashlars from the quarry on rollers (4) for a mile or so down to the construction site, which was 125 feet lower than the quarries, north of the Temple Mount. A crane powered by a treadmill lowered the blocks into place (5), and once the courses had been laid, workers chiseled off the projections (6). In a few cases, a projection was not chiseled off for some reason, as this example from the southeast corner shows (below), thus providing archaeologists with excellent evidence of the construction process.

Herod's builders solved the problem of how to hoist huge ashlars onto a rising wall. They worked from inside the wall. At the completion of each course of ashlars, the area within the retaining wall was filled in, up to the top of the latest course, with cartloads of "hard core" (7), which consists of broken stones and rubble such as quarry chips. Thus a new working level for the nex course was created that allowed the stones t be moved into place with minimal lifting by the crane.

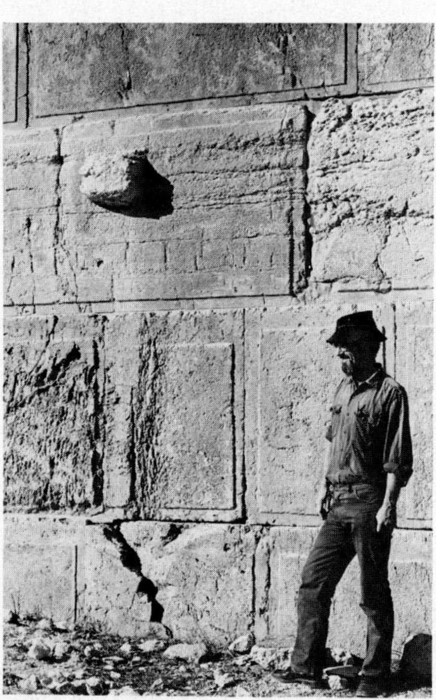

In fact, the stones did not have to be lifted from below. They were actually lowered into place from above. The 16-foot-thick walls of the Temple Mount are basically retaining walls, built to retain the high pressure of the fill that was dumped between the previous platform and the new Temple Mount wall. This was Herod's way of enlarging the previous platform to twice its original size. Herod's engineers solved the construction problem by pouring the internal fill simultaneously with the construction of the walls. Thus, the first course of stones was laid in the valley surrounding the previous Temple Mount. Then the area between the new and old walls was filled up to the level of the top of this course. This created a new work-level on top of which, from the inside, a second cours of stones could be laid. Again fill woul be added on the inside, so that a thir course of stones could be laid. And s on, course after course, until the whol of Herod's extension was raised up t the level of the previous Templ platform.

The buildings on the Temple Moun were built of smaller stones. Stone from these structures were throw down into the street below when th Romans destroyed Jerusalem in 70 A.D Most of them were later scavenged fo other construction. But a few wer found in the excavations. Thes weighed between two and three ton Stones of this size would have posed n problem for the skilled builders o Herod's Temple Mount.

Reconstructing The Triple Gate

KATHLEEN AND LEEN RITMEYER

Reconstructing the Triple Gate required that we answer three principal questions. What was the gate's original width? Was it originally a double gate or a triple gate? For whom was it built?

The discovery of a vault in front of the Triple Gate—about 23 feet south of the facade—gave us critical information for understanding the gateway in its earliest form. A vault is a wide arch that forms the roof or ceiling of a chamber. This vault supported a stairway leading up to the Triple Gate. (A stairway was required in order to ascend from the plaza to the threshold of the Triple Gate; some of the steps from this stairway were actually found in the excavation.) The width of the vault provided us with the width of the stairway leading up to the gate. Although the vault is only about three-quarters preserved, it is easily reconstructed on the basis of symmetry. The west side of the vault aligns perfectly with the west door jamb of the Triple Gate. (This door jamb with its beautiful molding is the only original element of the Triple Gate exterior that has survived. Additional Herodian construction is evident inside the gate. The present-day western wall of the passageway that originally led from the gate up to the Temple court (as in the Double Gate) is constructed on bedrock foundation. One Herodian column-base is still visible within the gateway. This column-base is a double-width pilaster, that is, a column attached to and protruding from a wall.) A narrow wall divides the vault in front of the Triple Gate into two chambers. We know the width of the eastern chamber from the width of the preserved western chamber. The total width of the vault is 50 feet.

The width of the vault, as we said, tells us the width of the stairway and this, in turn, tells us the width of the Triple Gate to which the stairway led. We confirmed our reasoning when we observed that the width we were assigning to this gateway was identical to the width of the gates that stood over Robinson's Arch and Wilson's Arch on the Western Wall of the Temple Mount.

The blocked Triple Gate visible today is of Omayyad (seventh century A.D.) construction, but its width reflects the original dimensions of the Herodian gate. But was this gate originally a triple gate? Or was it a double gate? We assume that even originally it was a triple gate—for two reasons: (1) at 50 feet, it is considerably wider than

Triple Gate

The arches of the Triple Gate (right) have been sealed since the gate was rebuilt in the seventh century A.D. A two-chambered vault excavated below and in front of the Triple Gate shows us exactly the gate's original width. This vault supported a stairway that led up to the Triple Gate.

A narrow wall separated the two chambers of the vault (plan, opposite page). Remains of this narrow wall are visible below and just right of the center of the middle gate of the Triple Gate. The chamber to the left of this dividing wall has survived intact and enables us to calculate, with the assumption of symmetry, the measurements of the right-hand chamber. The total width of the two chambers and dividing wall give us the width of the Herodian stairway and, thus, of the Triple Gate.

The only Herodian element of the Triple Gate still preserved stands at the end of a row of Herodian ashlars that extends from the center left edge of the photo to the base of the left arch of the Triple Gate. The last ashlar in this row, abutting the Triple Gate, displays fine vertical molding and originally was part of the gate's door jamb (see the reconstruction of the Temple Mount southern wall on pp. 36-37).

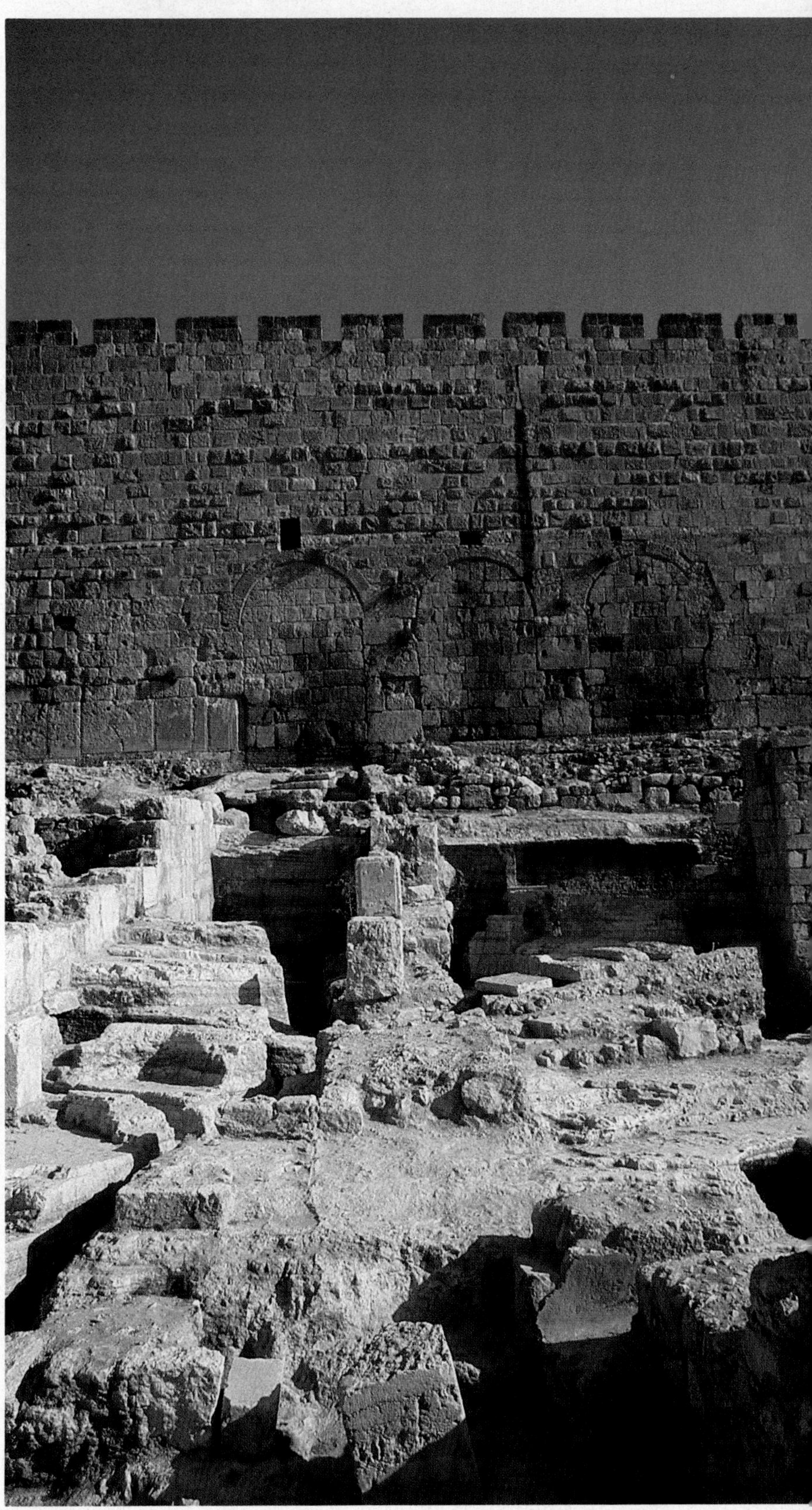

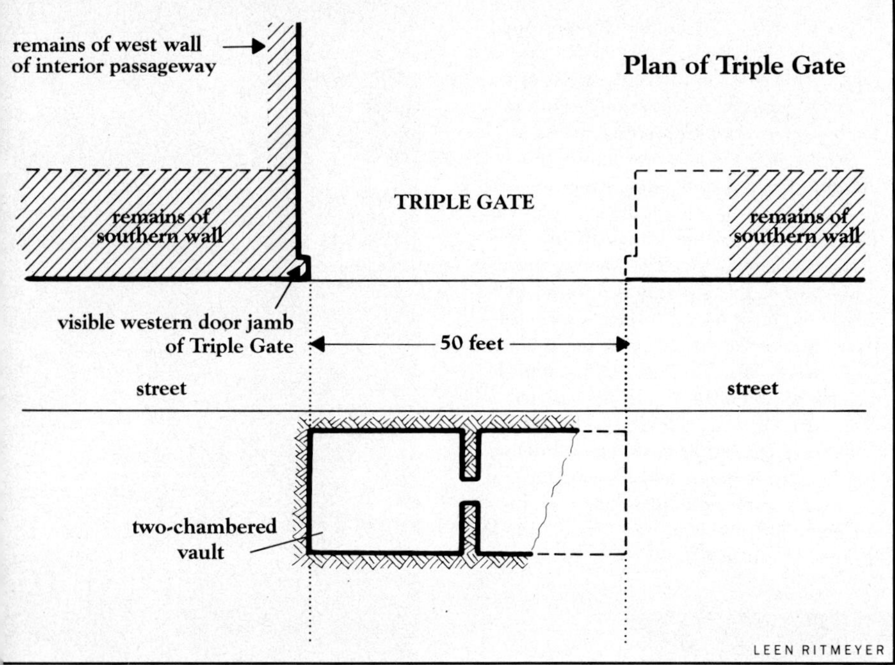

the 39-foot-wide Double Gate (in the southern wall, to the west of the Triple Gate); (2) classical gates were, with only few exceptions, either single or triple—and clearly 50 feet is too wide for a single gate.

The Mishnah tells us that there were "two Hulda gates at the south, serving for entry and exit" (Middot 1:3). Scholars and exegetes have long argued over whether the two Hulda gates referred to in this passage were the Double Gate and the Triple Gate or, on the other hand, the two passages of the Double Gate. Some say pilgrims went in one side of the Double Gate and came out the other. Others would have the pilgrims going in via the Double Gate and coming out via the Triple Gate (or vice versa).

Our view is that the Mishnah refers to the two passages through the Double Gate and that pilgrims entered through one passage and exited from the other. Let us explain why.

First, as we have already noted, the Double Gate has a very broad—210-foot—staircase leading up to it; the staircase leading up to the Triple Gate is much narrower—50 feet. Second, as we have also noted, a double gate is a rare phenomenon in classical architecture. When found—for example, at the Porta Negra in Trier, Germany—it always involves the circulation of two-way traffic: one side for going in and the other for going out. Third, the Double Gate opens into a passageway that led directly up and onto the Temple court. The Triple Gate also had a ramp that gave access to the Temple court, but it seems to have been more directly connected with the underground vaulted storerooms that are today quite erroneously called Solomon's Stables.

What did the Triple Gate originally look like? Unfortunately, so little of the Herodian construction of this gate has been preserved that we have little guidance in reconstructing it.* However, we believe we have located a parallel to the Triple Gate—described below—which may tell us what the gate looked like. Features of this parallel structure also suggest that the Triple Gate had a priestly function. (For this reason, too, we believe that the Double Gate was used by ordinary pilgrims.)

Josephus tells us (*The Jewish War* 5.12.2) about a tomb complex built for the family of the high priest Ananas. It seems, from Josephus's description, that the tomb complex was located near the Siloam Pool, where the Hinnom Valley leads into the Kidron Valley. In the early part of this century, remains of a splendid tomb complex were investigated in this area—near where the Monastery of St. Onuphrius now stands. This investigation was undertaken first by the Irish archaeologist R. A. S. Macalister[1] and then by the German scholar Knut Olaf Dalman.[2] This area is some distance from the Temple Mount, so it escaped the horrible destruction inflicted by the Romans in 70 A.D. Only fragments of architectural elements have been found in the Temple Mount area. By contrast, here at the mouth of the Hinnom Valley, magnificent Herodian remains still stand to their full height. The decoration used in this tomb complex closely resembles what we see on the fragments from the Temple Mount excavations. We believe many elements in these tombs, which—as Professor Benjamin Mazar pointed out to us—are in view of the Triple Gate, duplicate elements of the gates to the Temple.

One particular tomb is especially noteworthy. A triple gate cut out of the bedrock originally provided the entrance to the anteroom of this tomb. The proportions of the triple gate in the facade of this tomb seem to have

* In our earlier reconstructions, we drew only a single building in this area—a bathhouse—between the Double and Triple Gates. But this was only a tentative decision. With the discovery of a drainage channel (a feature usually found under Herodian streets) running south through this area, we concluded that a stepped street must have separated the area between the two gates into a western and an eastern half, with separate buildings on either side. This called for a new interpretation of the function of these buildings between the Double and Triple Gates—buildings that were heavily reconstructed in later times. The building west of the stepped street, now drawn at a considerably reduced size from our original reconstructions, was designated as a *mikveh* (ritual bathhouse) for purification before entering the sanctuary. Locating one of the courts of law east of the stepped street provides a very probable solution to the puzzle of the function of the rest of the building complex.

TOMBS RESEMBLING THE TRIPLE GATE

In clear view of the Triple Gate, an elegant Herodian-style tomb complex (right) may be the burial place of the family of Ananas high priest of the Temple. The tomb may have been carved to resemble the Triple Gate, through which priests entered and departed the Temple precincts. Many architectural elements of this tomb complex survive intact, giving us examples, perhaps even artistic duplicates, of the proportions and decorations of the Triple Gate.

The darkened doorway to a burial chamber pierces the back wall of the tomb's anteroom. Projecting forward above the doorway, remains of the front wall of the anteroom display a seashell decoration. Originally a full semicircle, this seashell was carved above the central entrance of a now-destroyed triple gate to this tomb anteroom (reconstruction drawing, below, right). In the reconstruction of the Temple Mount's Triple Gate (p. 37), author Ritmeyer used the proportions of this tomb's triple gate as a model. However, he varied the styles of the three doorways to reflect examples in the tomb complex and excavated remains.

Instead of a seashell over the central entrance of the Triple Gate, Ritmeyer drew a pediment. One of these pediments appears in the tomb complex, above an Attic mock-doorway (below, left). The opening in the lower part of this doorway is a burial niche. Above the three burial niches, a scalloped dome mimics the domes inside the Double Gate (see p. 39). The side entrances in the Temple Mount Triple Gate are modeled after Attic doorways without pediments (opposite page and reconstruction drawing, below, right bottom), which were found in the tomb complex and also were found as architectural fragments scattered around the Temple Mount walls.

GARO NALBANDIAN

LEEN RITMEYER

GARO NALBANDIAN

HERSHEL SHANKS

been a kind of miniature of the Triple Gate in the southern wall of the Temple Mount. It seems likely that a priestly family built this tomb. Perhaps they wanted to transfer to their last resting place some of the magnificence they were accustomed to seeing as they approached the Temple court from the Triple Gate.

Inside the tomb, the chambers, like others in this complex, have side-molding that closely corresponds to the molding of the western jamb of the Triple Gate.

In our reconstruction of the Temple Mount's Triple Gate, we have used the proportions of the tomb's triple gate and the side-molding found inside many of these tombs to outline the doorways in the Temple Mount's Triple Gate. We have reconstructed the style of the three entrances as Attic doorways, based on the Attic doorways found in these tombs. (We also found fragments of Attic doorways in the Temple Mount excavations.) The molding on the lintel of Attic doorways extends beyond the jambs (see drawing, p. 52, bottom right). Finally, in our reconstruction of the Temple Mount Triple Gate, we have placed a pediment over the center entrance, just as we found it on three Attic mock-doorways inside the tomb.

Putting all the evidence together, we now conclude that the narrower stairway leading to the Triple Gate was used by the priests. The magnificent broad stairway leading to the Double Gate was trod by pilgrims on their way up to, and down from, the Temple Mount. But the facade of the Triple Gate—the priests' gate—was far more elaborate than the undecorated facade of the Double Gate—the gate of the masses.

[1] R. A. S. Macalister, "The Rock-Cut Tombs in Wady er-Rababi, Jerusalem," *Palestine Exploration Fund Quarterly Statement* 1900-1901.

[2] Knut Olaf Dalman, Uber ein Felsengrab im Hinnomtale bei Jerusalem," *Zeitschrift des deutschen Palästina-Vereins* 1939, Bd. 62, pp. 190-208.

Reconstructing the Magnificent Temple Herod Built

JOSEPH PATRICH

WITH DRAWINGS BY LEEN RITMEYER

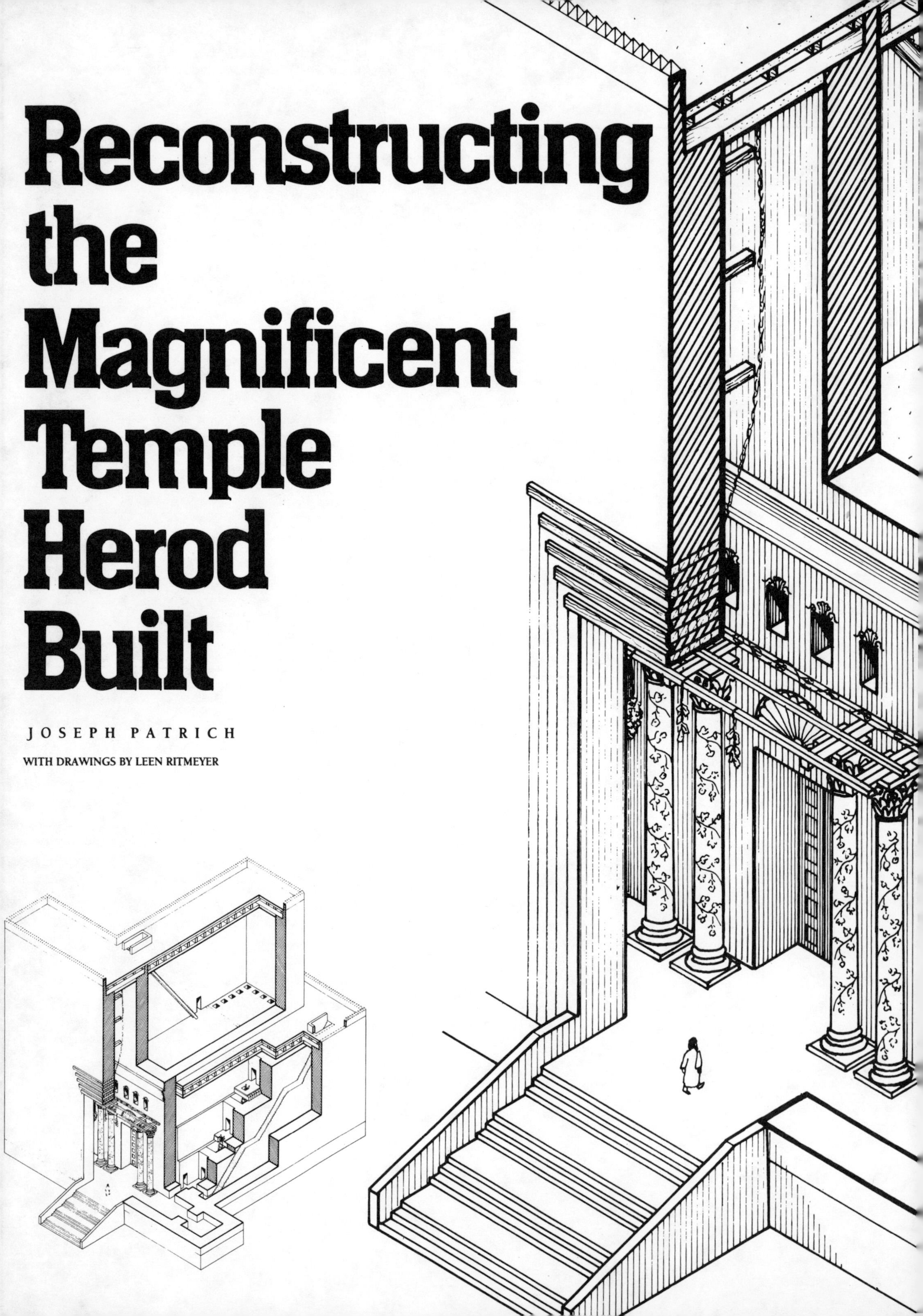

"In the fourth year of his reign over Israel, Solomon began to build the House of the Lord" (1 Kings 6:1). Bible scholars call this the First Temple. King Solomon built this Temple on the Temple Mount in Jerusalem, on a stone threshing floor bought by Solomon's father, David, for 50 shekels of silver from Araunah the Jebusite (2 Samuel 24:18-25).

The First Temple stood on the Temple Mount for more than 350 years, until its destruction by the Babylonian king Nebuchadnezzar, in 586 B.C. Second Kings relates that Nebuchadnezzar "carried off from Jerusalem all the treasures of the House of the Lord and the treasures of the royal palace; he stripped off all the golden decorations of the Temple of the Lord—which King Solomon of Israel had made—as the Lord had warned" (2 Kings 24:13). Nebuzaradan, the Babylonian chief of the guards, "burned the House of the Lord, the king's palace, and all the houses of Jerusalem" (2 Kings 25:9).

The Babylonians "exiled all of Jerusalem [to Babylon]: all the commanders and all the warriors—ten thousand exiles—as well as all the craftsmen and smiths; only the poorest people in the land were left" (2 Kings 24:14).

Then in 539 B.C., in the first year of the reign of King Cyrus of Persia, an edict was issued by the king:

> "All the kingdoms of the earth the Lord God of heaven has given me. And he has commanded me to build Him a house at Jerusalem which is in Judah" (Ezra 1:2).

> "King Cyrus also brought out the articles of the house of the Lord, which Nebuchadnezzar had taken from Jerusalem . . . thirty gold platters, one thousand silver platters, twenty-nine knives, thirty gold basins, four hundred and ten silver basins . . . and one thousand other articles" (Ezra 1:7,9,10).

According to the Bible, there were successive waves of repatriations of Jews under Persian rule. The first was led by Sheshbazzar, the son of King Jehoiachin, who had been taken into captivity in 597 B.C. This first return, marking the beginning of a new era in the history of Israel—the Second Temple period—occurred not long after 539 B.C., when Cyrus issued his decree to start rebuilding the Temple in Jerusalem. Sheshbazzar was entrusted with the Temple vessels (Ezra 1:7, 5:14-15) and is reported to have laid the foundation for the rebuilt Temple (Ezra 5:16). The actual work of rebuilding the Temple, however, remained uncompleted.

A major wave of returning exiles was then led by Zerubbabel, grandson of Jehoiachin, and by the priest Joshua/Jehoshua, apparently during the early years of the administration of the Persian king Darius (522-486 B.C.). In the second year of Darius's reign, Zerubbabel and Joshua established an altar on the Temple Mount in Jerusalem and began their work of Temple construction.

> "The house [Temple] was finished on the third of the month of Adar in the sixth year [516/5 B.C.] of the reign of King Darius. The Israelites, the priests, and the Levites, and all the other exiles celebrated the dedication of the House of God with joy" (Ezra 6:15-16).

Some 60 years later, during the reign of King Artaxerxes (465/4-424/3 B.C.), Ezra and Nehemiah came to Jerusalem, Ezra as a "scribe skilled in the law of Moses" (Ezra 7:6), and Nehemiah as governor of Judea. Of Nehemiah's varied accomplishments during those turbulent times, the one for which he is most remembered is rebuilding the walls of Jerusalem—a major move in the establishment of national security and a political statement that Nehemiah's adversaries understood very well.

In 37 B.C. Herod the Great became king of Judea. In keeping with the grandeur of his building plans throughout his kingdom, he completely rebuilt the 500-year-old Temple. Herod's rebuilding of the Jerusalem Temple both enlarged and glorified it. With thousands of workmen, the work started in the 18th year of his reign (20/19 B.C.) and was completed after 17 months, during the year 18 B.C., so we are told by the first-century A.D. Jewish historian Flavius Josephus. This Temple was destroyed by the Romans in 70 A.D.

Detailed descriptions of Herod's Temple have come down to us in tractate *Middot* of the Mishnah* and in the two principal works of Josephus, *The Jewish Wars* (a detailed description of the First Jewish Revolt against Rome, 66-74 A.D.) and *Antiquities of the Jews* (a history of Israel from the beginning to Josephus's time).

Tractate *Middot* is attributed to Rabbi Eliezer ben Jacob, a *tanna*** who lived at the end of the Second Temple period and who had firsthand knowledge of the Herodian Temple before it was destroyed. His description is generally thought to be realistic, although some scholars claim that it is idealized.

* The Mishnah is the compilation of Jewish oral law redacted, arranged and revised by Rabbi Judah HaNasi about 200 A.D. The Mishnah is divided into six orders; each order is divided into tractates.

** The Aramaic word *tanna* (plural, *tannaim*) generally designates a teacher mentioned in the Mishnah, or a sage who lived in mishnaic times, about 20-200 A.D.

A comparison of the descriptions in *Middot* and in Josephus reveals certain discrepancies, as does a comparison between Josephus's own descriptions in *The Jewish Wars* and *Antiquities of the Jews*. The differences relate, for the most part, to the dimensions of the Temple's apertures and of certain parts of the Temple. Taken as a whole, however, all three sources generally agree with one another. Josephus is conversant not only with the essential elements of the Temple—the Portico (*ulam*; sometimes translated "porch"), the Sanctuary (*heikhal*) and the Holy of Holies (*kodesh ha-kodashim*)—but also with the Upper Chamber, the cells and even the *mesibbah*, or stepped passageway, referred to in tractate *Middot*. Because the differences between *Middot* and Josephus are not fundamental,[1] we can use details supplied in one source to supplement the others. Using these sources we can reconstruct, with great fidelity, Herod's Temple, the Temple that Jesus knew.

Our reconstruction aspires to a degree of detail never before achieved: a precise scale drawing of the Temple as a whole, as well as of each of its components. We attempt to remain faithful to the descriptions found in the sources and to refrain from hypotheses not grounded in these written sources. We present in our drawings not only our innovations, but all the parts of the Temple, as they may be understood from tractate *Middot* and Josephus. In the following description of the elements of the Temple, we frequently have not indicated the source of our information so as to preserve the flow of the discussion. But on page 76 you will find a box with source references from *Middot* and from Josephus's writings related to the individual architectural elements of the Temple.

Before turning to pages 70-71 to see the architectural details of Herod's Temple—room by room—let us try to envision it as a whole.

The splendors of Herod's Temple made a tremendous impression on all who saw it. Rabbinic sages taught: "Whoever has not seen Jerusalem in her splendor has never seen a lovely city. He who has not seen the Temple in its full construction has never seen a glorious building in his life."[2] And again in another tractate of the Talmud: "He who has not seen the Temple of Herod has never seen a beautiful building."[3]

What made the exterior of the Temple so magnificent? The Talmud informs us that, according to one opinion, it was constructed of yellow and white marble, or, according to a second opinion, of blue, yellow and white marble. Mention is also made of Herod's intention to cover the edifice with gold. And in fact, Josephus relates that the entire facade was covered with massive plates of gold; at sunrise, the Temple facade radiated so fierce a flash that persons straining to look at it were compelled to avert their eyes in order not to be blinded. The other walls were also plated with gold, but only in the lower sections. The upper parts of the building were of purest white, so that, from a distance, the building looked like a snow-clad mountain. Presumably, this effect was achieved by the application of whitewash to the upper section of the building, renewed once a year before Passover (*Middot* 3:4). Gold spikes lined the parapet wall on the roof. Such was the external splendor of the Temple.

Dimensions of Architectural Elements of the Temple as Recorded in Middot
(all dimensions are in cubits: 1 cubit = 52.5 cm = 20.7 inches)

East/West Dimensions	
Portico wall	5
Portico	11
Sanctuary wall	6
Sanctuary	40
Dividing space	1
Holy of Holies	20
Sanctuary wall	6
Cell	6
Cell wall	5
TOTAL	100

North/South Dimensions	
Mesibbah wall	5
Mesibbah	3
Cell wall	5
Cell	6
Sanctuary wall	6
Sanctuary	20
Sanctuary wall	6
Cell	6
Cell wall	5
Space for draining water	3
Its wall	5
TOTAL	70

Vertical Dimensions	
Solid basement	6
Sanctuary	40
Sanctuary ceiling:	
Coffers	1
Water drain	2
Roof beams	1
Plaster work	1
Upper Chamber	40
Upper Chamber ceiling:	
Coffers	1
Water drain	2
Roof beams	1
Plaster work	1
Parapet	3
Scarecrow	1
TOTAL	100

Interestingly enough, neither ornately decorated columns nor capitals nor friezes with reliefs are mentioned, either on the facade or on the other sides of the building. Therefore one cannot claim that it is the exterior facade of the Temple that is depicted on the Bar-Kokhba coin on page 72. This coin clearly shows four columns and capitals, two on each side of an entryway. We believe these are the columns standing in the Portico before the Sanctuary entrance. (See the discussion of the columns beginning on p. 69.)

However, another coin (below right) from the time of the Second Jewish Revolt probably represents the exterior facade of the Temple. The Temple's facade was on the eastern side of the building—facing the rising sun. From east to west, on the lowest level, the Temple consisted of the Portico, the Sanctuary and the Holy of Holies. An Upper Chamber extended above the Sanctuary and the Holy of Holies. Surrounding the Sanctuary and the Holy of Holies on the north, west and south were cells—small windowless rooms—arranged in three stories. The cells did not surround the Upper Chamber, so that beyond the Portico, the Temple was wider in the lower part than in the upper level.

On the northern side, beyond the cells but within the exterior wall of the Temple, was the *mesibbah*, or stepped passageway, leading from the front of the building up to the roof at the back of the building. The counterpart of the *mesibbah* on the southern side was a channel for draining away water from the roof (*beit horadat hamayim*).

The Portico was the widest part of the Temple. In *Middot** it is said, "The Sanctuary [here referring to the Temple in its entirety] was narrow behind and wide in front and it was like a lion . . ." (*Middot* 4:7).

Exact dimensions of the Temple components are recorded in *Middot*. The measurements are all given in cubits.** Describing the overall exterior dimensions, *Middot* observes: "And the Sanctuary [including the Portico and the Holy of Holies] was a hundred cubits (172 feet) by a hundred cubits with a height of a hundred cubits" (*Middot* 4:6). The interior dimensions are specified from bottom to top, from north to south and from east to west. The horizontal dimensions are given at

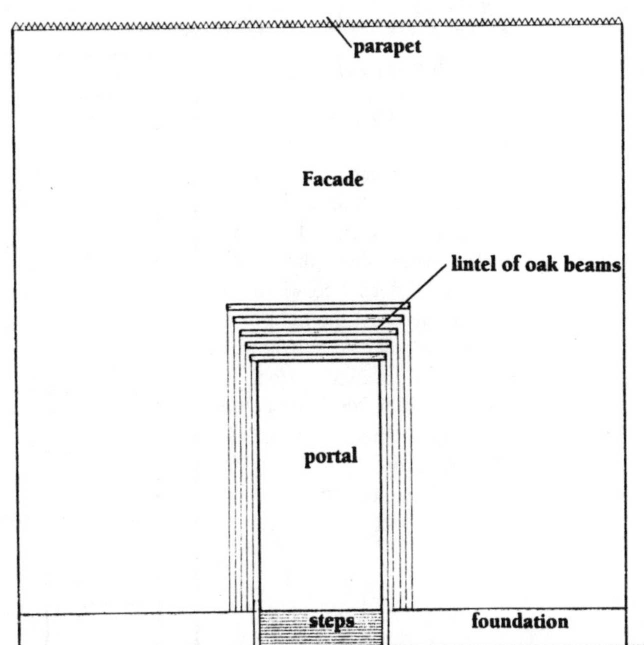

The Outer Facade of the Temple

Covered entirely with gold, the facade of the Temple reflected the glow of the morning sun. The 70-foot-high portal, without doors or curtains, was surmounted by oak beams whose length gradually decreased from top to bottom. The beams penetrated the thickness of the wall. Doorposts were formed by the extension of the beams at a 90-degree angle.

OUR ONLY PICTURE of the entrance to the Portico of Herod's Temple appears on this rare, silver *di-drachma* coin minted during the Second Jewish Revolt against Rome (132-135 A.D.). The stairs at the bottom of the picture and the lintel at the top indicate that this depiction represents the outer entrance rather than the portal to the Sanctuary. Two apparent columns on each side may really be doorposts. In confirmation of textual information, the coin shows that the lintel widened from bottom to top. The object between the doorposts may represent the table of the shewbread, as suggested by Professor Dan Barag. The coin's inscription spells "Shimon" (Simon), the first name of Bar-Kokhba, the leader of the Second Jewish Revolt.

* Mishnah translations follow Herbert Danby, *The Mishnah* (London, 1933).

** One cubit equals 52.5 centimeters (20.67 inches). This cubit is called the long or royal cubit to distinguish it from the short cubit, which was about 45 centimeters. The use of two different cubits is reflected in the Bible. For a discussion of cubits mentioned in the Bible, see Gabriel Barkay, "Measurements in the Bible," *Biblical Archaeology Review*, March/April 1986, p. 37.

The Facade of the Sanctuary

The central focus of the Sanctuary facade was the magnificent Sanctuary portal flanked by freestanding columns and draped with a golden vine. Above the portal were small decorated windows. In the doorway, the right half shows the outer door; behind it, unseen, is yet another door. In the left half of the doorway, the outermost tapestry veil hangs. The "chambers of the slaughter knives" are seen in the lower corners of the section.

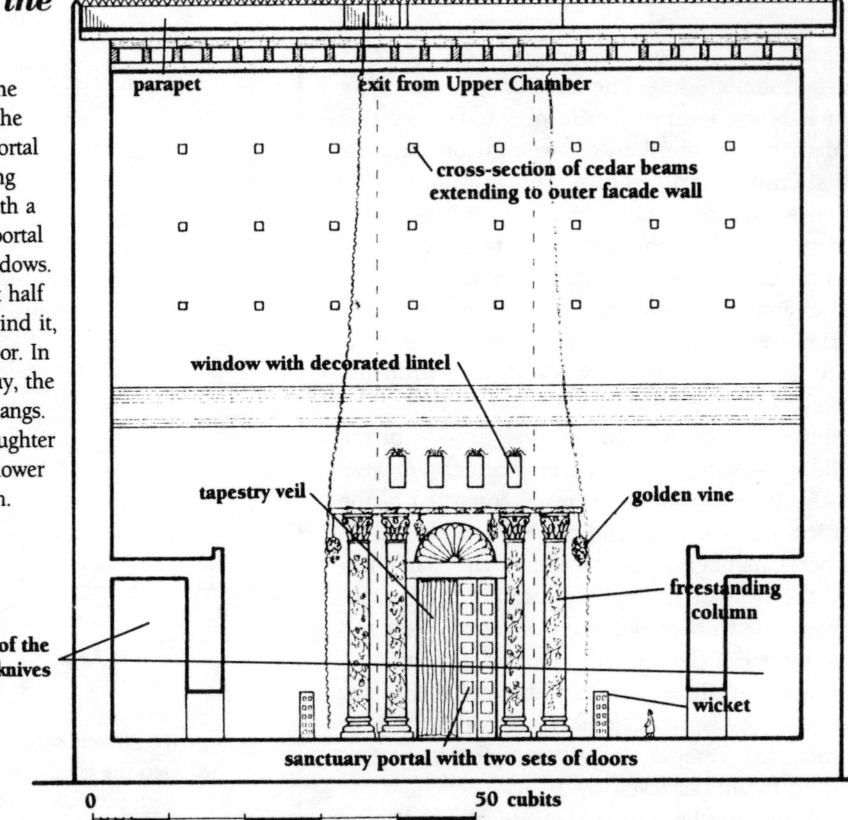

the level of the second story of the cells, as if a horizontal slice was made across the Temple at this level. Using the dimensions, summarized in the chart on page 66, we were able to produce scale drawings of the Temple plan viewed from above, drawings of cross-sections, as if looking at the surface of vertical north-south and east-west slices, and precise renderings of certain features.

We are ready now to consider, in detail, the architectural elements of Herod's Temple. As you read what follows, refer to the drawings on pages 67-71 in order to visualize, as we have, how the Temple appeared to those who lived in Jerusalem and to those who came as pilgrims three times each year to celebrate the festivals of Sukkot (Feast of Tabernacles), Shavuot (Feast of Weeks) and Pesach (Passover, the festival of the Exodus from Egypt). Our descriptions will proceed from east to west, as if we were approaching and then entering the awesome Temple.

The Outer Facade and the Portico (ulam)

Twelve steps led up to the entrance to the Portico. Each step was 0.5 cubit (10 inches) high, so that the floor of the Portico was 6 cubits (10 feet) above the level of the Court of the Priests, an outside courtyard that surrounded the Temple. Six cubits is exactly the height of the substructure—the solid foundation upon which the walls of the Temple stood. The facade of the Portico was a plain, square surface, 100 cubits (172 feet) to a side, interrupted only at its center by an impressively large portal with a lintel above it. Aside from the fact that the facade was covered with gold, there is no information in the sources as to additional ornamentation, with the exception of the lintel above the entrance. The portal was 40 cubits (69 feet) high and 20 cubits (34 feet) wide. Neither doors nor curtains covered the opening. Like the entire outer surface of the facade, the inner walls of the portal were gilded. The lintel of the portal was constructed with five, one-cubit-thick, carved oak beams (*maltera'ot*, from the Greek, meaning primary ceiling beam) placed one above the other. The beams extended through the entire thickness of the facade wall and were separated from each other by courses of stones, each course one cubit high. The lowest beam was 22 cubits (38 feet) in length, the shortest of the five; each subsequent beam extended an additional cubit on each end, so that the topmost was 30 cubits (52 feet) long.

A portal of this kind is depicted on a rather rare, silver *di-drachma* coin (see p. 67) minted by Bar-Kokhba, the leader of the Second Jewish Revolt against Rome (132-135 A.D.).[4] Although the Herodian Temple had already been destroyed for more than 60 years when these coins were minted, the memory of it was still relatively fresh. The depiction on these coins almost certainly represents the entrance to the Portico, with stairs in front and a lintel diagonally cut at its ends. What appear to be two columns may simply be doorposts of the entryway into the Portico. It was above this entrance that Herod set the golden eagle, which was later removed by pious Jews, but only at the end of his reign.[5]

As mentioned above, the facade of the Portico was 100 cubits (172 feet) wide. After passing through the open portal, one entered the Portico itself, a long, narrow anteroom extending from north to south along the entire width of the building; it was 11 cubits (19 feet) across from east to west. The walls of three sides of this anteroom were 5 cubits (9 feet) thick. (The wall of the Sanctuary, opposite the Portico facade, was 6 cubits [10 feet] thick.) The Portico extended to the full height of the Temple, 85 cubits (146 feet) from the floor to the ceiling.

The Portico exceeded the width of the Sanctuary of the Temple by 15 cubits (26 feet) on each side. The excess width, which stuck out like wings, formed two rooms, one at each end of the Portico, called the Chambers of the Slaughter Knives (*beit haḥalifot*). In these rooms were kept the knives for the sacrifices. The width of the Portico, exclusive of the two side chambers, was 60 cubits (103 feet).

The eastern Portico wall—that is, the Temple facade—measured from the top of the solid basement to the top of the roof parapet, was 94 cubits (162 feet) high (85 cubits [146 feet] from floor to ceiling and 9 more cubits [15 feet] of roof construction and parapet), but only 5 cubits (9 feet) thick—or perhaps I should say thin, because 5 cubits is very thin to support a wall of this great height. In order to prevent collapse of such a tall but thin wall, cedar beams were set between the Portico facade wall and the Sanctuary wall. The drawings opposite and on pp.70-71 illustrate one of several possible arrangements for these beams.

The Sanctuary Facade and Portal

On the facade of the Sanctuary itself—unlike the almost unadorned and less sacred Portico facade—Herod expended great effort and expense on magnificent decorations.

In the center of the Sanctuary facade wall was the portal, 20 cubits (34 feet) high and 10 cubits (17 feet) wide. This wall was 6 cubits (10 feet) thick.

Two sets of panel doors controlled access to the Sanctuary—one exterior and one interior (see opposite). Each panel door was 5 cubits (9 feet) wide. The exterior panel doors opened inwards, almost covering the 6-cubit (10-foot) thickness of the wall; the interior panel doors opened into the Sanctuary itself, resting on the inside wall of the Sanctuary (*aḥar hadelatot*). According to another opinion also found in *Middot* 4:1, these doors were all folding doors, with each panel folding in half; when open, all of the door panels folded inside the entry and their combined width (2.5 cubits plus 2.5 cubits), together with that of the wooden doorposts (0.5 cubit each), covered the 6-cubit thickness of the wall.

The Sanctuary facade and the portal doors were all overlaid with gold.

On each side of the portal was a small, low wicket or doorway (see pp. 68, 70-71). The northern wicket led into a cell from which one could enter the Sanctuary.* (The cells will be described in full on page 74.) The southern wicket was sealed, having never been used.

The Columns and the Golden Vine
(see drawings on pp. 68 and 70-71)

Between the low wickets and the large entrance doorway into the Sanctuary, we have reconstructed four columns, two on each side of the main doorway, freestanding in the open area of the Portico. Columns are mentioned in this place only in the Latin version of *Antiquities of the Jews* 15.394-395, describing the golden vine (see below). The number of columns, however, is not specified in this passage of Josephus. At this point, our reconstruction is based on the depiction of the portal on the Bar-Kokhba *tetradrachma* (p. 72) and upon a fresco above the Holy Ark in the early third-century A.D. Dura-Europos synagogue, excavated in the 1930s in Syria. Both the coin and the fresco appear to refer to the Temple, and they clearly have four columns. In placing the columns where we have, we differ from other scholars,[6] who consider these depictions as representations of the exterior facade of the Temple rather than of the Sanctuary facade. However, as was mentioned above, no such decoration is mentioned in our sources, when describing the Temple's facade.

The people of Israel are often compared to a vine, as for example in Jeremiah 2:21: "I planted you with noble vines, all with choicest seed; alas I find you changed into a base, an alien vine." (See also Psalm 80:9-12 and Ezekiel 17:5-8.) A

text continues on page 72

* Alternatively, one could pass through the wicket, then through a passage within the wall, into the space between the two sets of main doors to the Sanctuary.

Plan of the Temple's Lower Story

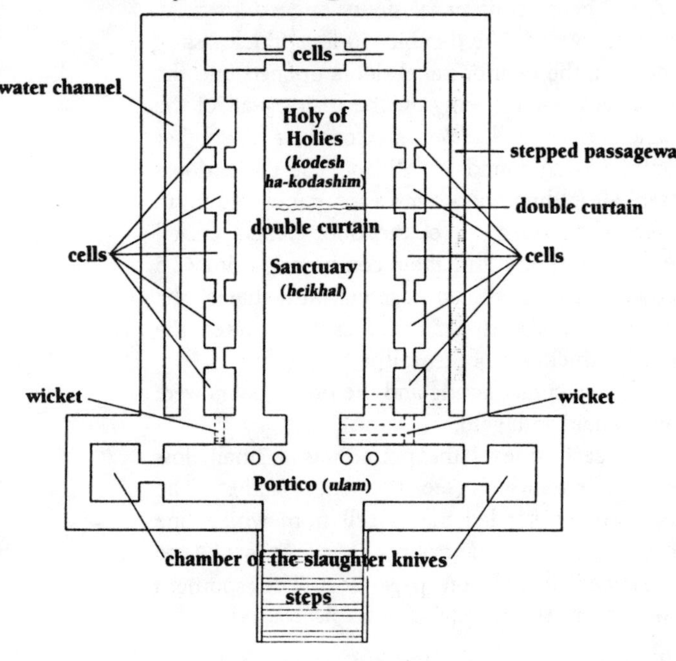

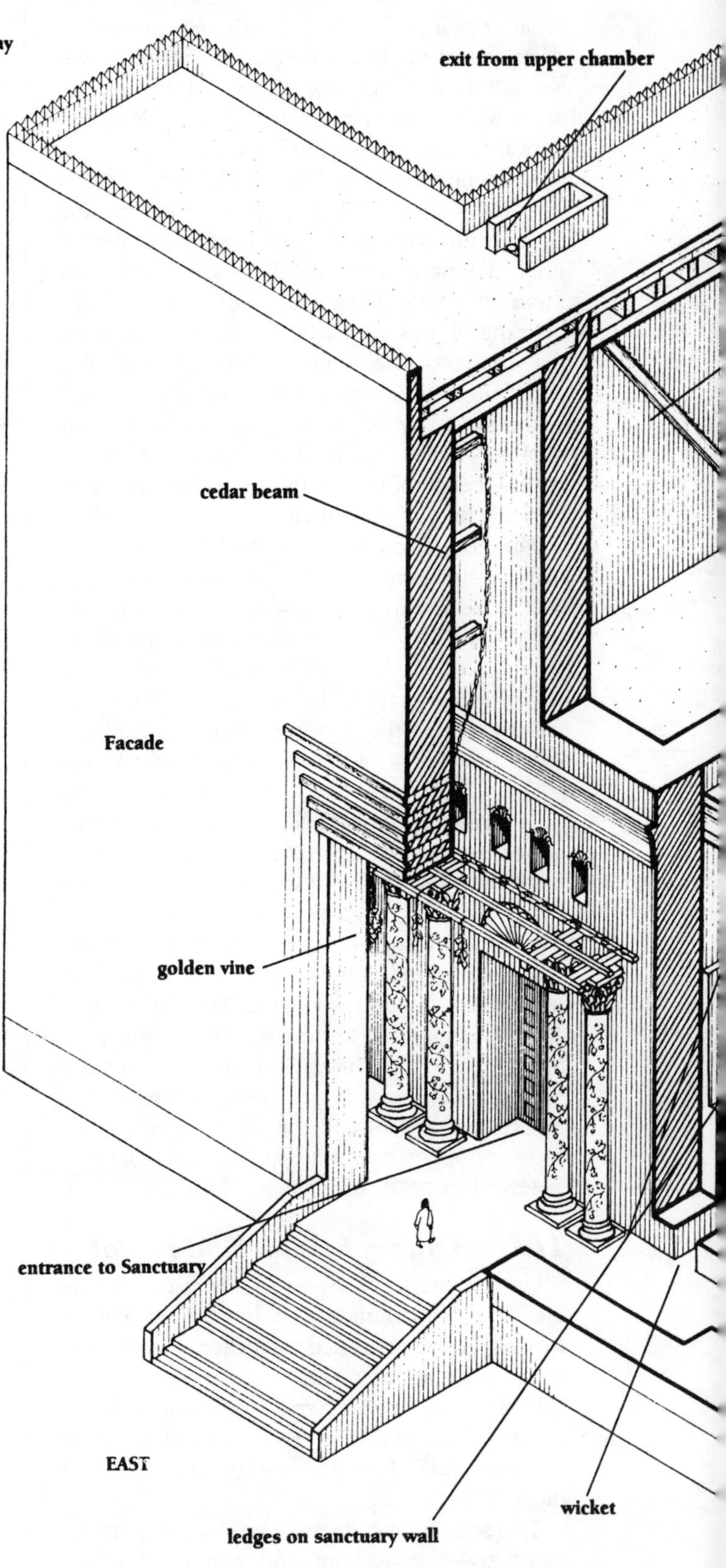

To help you understand the Temple from both the inside and out, three different types of drawings appear on these pages: a cutaway three-dimensional view (center), a plan (above) of the Temple's lower story, and a vertical section (far right) through the center of the Temple.

In the three-dimensional view, artist Leen Ritmeyer has peeled away the outer walls of one half of the structure. In this drawing, climb the steps on the eastern side of the Temple, pass through the outer facade, and enter the Portico. Walk through the Portico, in the direction of the Sanctuary (*heikhal*) entrance, flanked by columns and draped with the golden grapevine.

To the right of the Sanctuary entrance, a small, low doorway, or wicket, leads into the first of a series of cells that enclose the building on three sides. From the cell entered through the wicket, doorways lead, left, to the Sanctuary, forward, to the adjacent cell, and right, to the stepped passageway that gives access to the roof of the cells.

The cutaway exposes the three stories of cells along the northern wall of the Sanctuary. However, we see only a few of the five cells that actually occupied each level. And, of course, we see none of the cells that wrapped around the western and southern sides of the Temple. Ladders allowed vertical communication between the cells.

The Templ

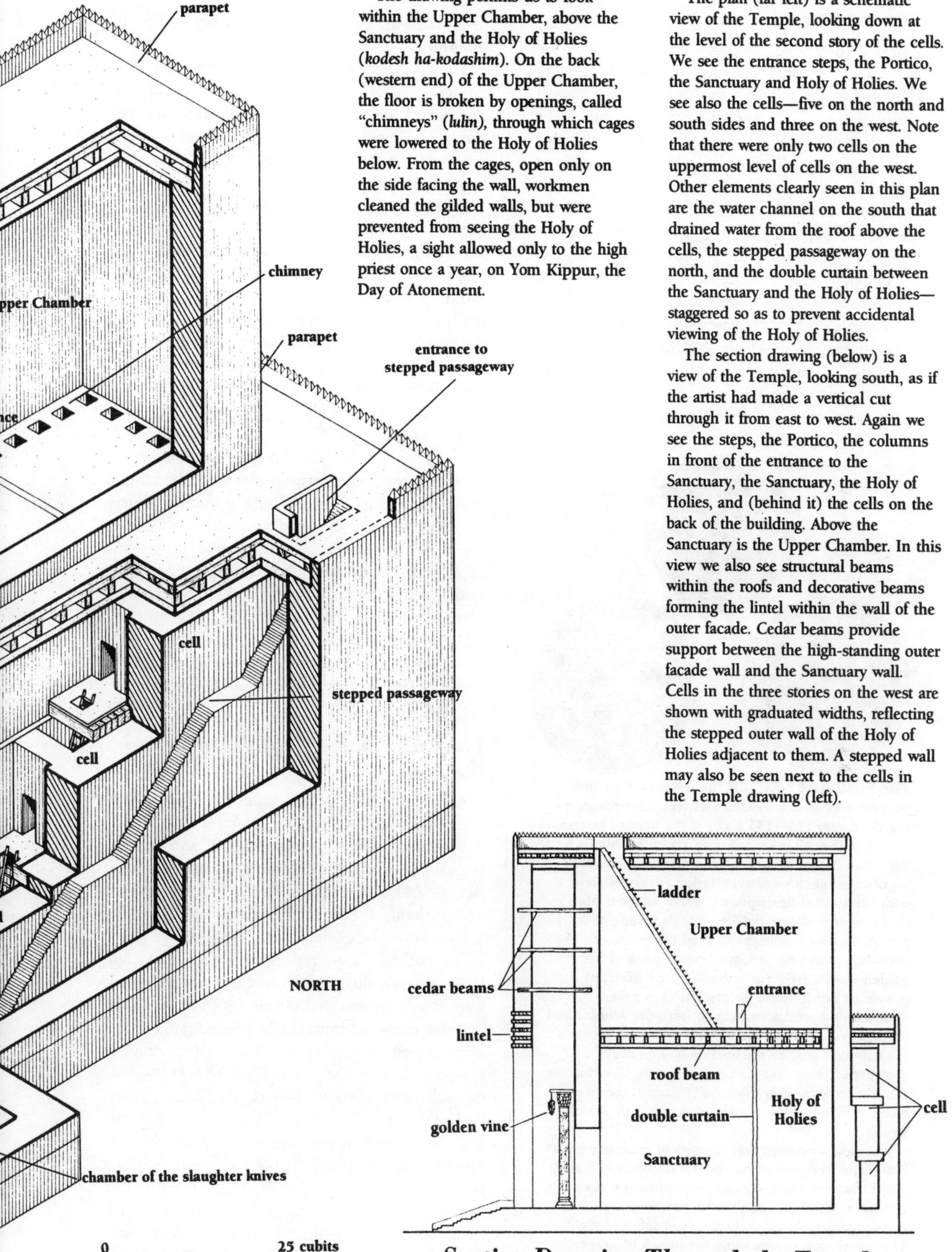

The drawing permits us to look within the Upper Chamber, above the Sanctuary and the Holy of Holies (*kodesh ha-kodashim*). On the back (western end) of the Upper Chamber, the floor is broken by openings, called "chimneys" (*lulin*), through which cages were lowered to the Holy of Holies below. From the cages, open only on the side facing the wall, workmen cleaned the gilded walls, but were prevented from seeing the Holy of Holies, a sight allowed only to the high priest once a year, on Yom Kippur, the Day of Atonement.

The plan (far left) is a schematic view of the Temple, looking down at the level of the second story of the cells. We see the entrance steps, the Portico, the Sanctuary and Holy of Holies. We see also the cells—five on the north and south sides and three on the west. Note that there were only two cells on the uppermost level of cells on the west. Other elements clearly seen in this plan are the water channel on the south that drained water from the roof above the cells, the stepped passageway on the north, and the double curtain between the Sanctuary and the Holy of Holies—staggered so as to prevent accidental viewing of the Holy of Holies.

The section drawing (below) is a view of the Temple, looking south, as if the artist had made a vertical cut through it from east to west. Again we see the steps, the Portico, the columns in front of the entrance to the Sanctuary, the Sanctuary, the Holy of Holies, and (behind it) the cells on the back of the building. Above the Sanctuary is the Upper Chamber. In this view we also see structural beams within the roofs and decorative beams forming the lintel within the wall of the outer facade. Cedar beams provide support between the high-standing outer facade wall and the Sanctuary wall. Cells in the three stories on the west are shown with graduated widths, reflecting the stepped outer wall of the Holy of Holies adjacent to them. A stepped wall may also be seen next to the cells in the Temple drawing (left).

Section Drawing Through the Temple

text continued from page 69

huge golden vine stood above the portal of the Sanctuary. *Middot* 3:8 tells us, "A golden vine stood over the entrance to the Sanctuary, trained over posts . . . . " According to Josephus (*The Jewish Wars*), "[The opening of the Sanctuary] had above it those golden vines, from which depended grape-clusters as tall as a man." *Antiquities of the Jews* provides further details:

> "He [Herod] decorated the doors of the entrance and the sections over the opening with a multicolored ornamentation and also with curtains, in accordance with the size of the Temple and made flowers of gold surrounding columns, atop which stretched a vine, from which golden clusters of grapes were suspended."[7]

Our reconstruction of the golden vine, trained over columns, is based upon this description by Josephus.

The golden vine made a great impression upon foreign visitors to Jerusalem, as well, and is mentioned in the late first-century/early second-century A.D. writings of Florus and Tacitus,[8] when they refer to the 63 B.C. conquest of Jerusalem by Pompey.

Adding to the weight of gold of the vine itself, freewill donations and vow-offerings of gold were also hung on the vine. The statement in *Middot*, that in view of the great weight of the gold, "three hundred priests were appointed" to remove it, may be somewhat exaggerated; however, Josephus, describing the vine itself, claims that the golden grape clusters were the size of a man, so that a specially massive structure was needed in order to bear the weight of the tendrils and the clusters that hung above the 20-cubit-high (34-foot) portal.

Some of the Bar-Kokhba *tetra-drachma* coins show a wavy ornamentation above the horizontal beams straddling four columns, a motif that may be interpreted as the tendrils of a vine. Neither the hanging clusters nor the grape leaves are depicted on these coins; they do appear, however, as the central motif in other Bar-Kokhba coins of lower denominations (see at left). The strip of half-circles that appears in the third-century A.D. fresco of the Dura-Europos synagogue, at the top of the facade, is probably a late transformation of the golden vine.

THE SANCTUARY FACADE, as it appears on the obverse side of a *tetra-drachma* (top), attributed to the third year (134-135 A.D.) of the Second Jewish Revolt. Although other scholars consider this to be a depiction of the Temple's outer facade, the author argues that such an interpretation is inconsistent with the textual descriptions, which support his view that this coin shows the Sanctuary's facade and portal. The four columns flanked the entrance. The wavy line above the columns may represent the golden vine, a frequent symbol, in the Bible, of the people of Israel and a decoration above the Sanctuary's portal according to both the *Middot* and the historian Flavius Josephus. The object between the columns may be the narrow face of the shewbread table. The coin's inscription, like that on the *di-drachma*, says "Shimon" (Simon), the first name of Bar-Kokhba, leader of the Second Jewish Revolt.

Josephus also says that clusters of golden grapes hung from the vine above the portal. Although such grape clusters and leaves do not appear on the *tetra-drachma*, some Bar-Kokhba bronze coins of lower denomination do show them (lower left and right). The inscription surrounding the bunch of grapes (lower left) says, "First Year of the redemption of Israel."

The Curtain, the Golden Lamp and the Tables

A veil of Babylonian tapestry, woven and embroidered in four colors—scarlet (*tola'at shani*), light brown (*shesh*), blue (*tchelet*) and purple (*argaman*)—hung at the entrance of the Sanctuary (see p. 68). The colors were highly symbolic: *tola'at shani*, a scarlet dye extracted from the scarlet worm, symbolized fire; *shesh*, a fine linen in its natural color, represented the earth that produced the fiber; *tchelet*, a blue dye extracted from snails, represented the air; *argaman*, a purple dye also extracted from snails, represented the sea from which it originated. The veil portrayed, Josephus says in *The Jewish Wars* 5.5,4 (212-214), "a panorama of the heavens, the signs of the Zodiac excepted." The veil hung on the outside and was visible even when the doors of the Sanctuary were closed. In the Hellenistic period, before the erection of the Herodian Temple, the veil had hung on a long golden rod concealed in a wooden beam. In 53 B.C., this beam was given by the priest responsible for the veils to Crassus, governor of Syria. The false hope of the priest was that his bribe would prevent further looting of the Temple treasures (*Antiquities of the Jews* 14.105-109).

In front of the veil, at the entrance to the Sanctuary, hung a golden lamp—a gift of Queen Helena of Adiabene (in what is now northern Iraq). Two tables also graced the entrance in front of the veil, one of marble and the other of gold. On the marble table, the priest placed the new shewbread to be introduced into the Temple, and on the gold one, the old bread, which had been brought out of the Sanctuary. (On the *di-drachma* coin, p. 67.) The object between the doorposts of the open entryway may be a table or tables, standing before the Sanctuary entrance on the western side of the Portico.

In our reconstruction we have shown four windows above the portal of the Sanctuary (see pp. 68 and 70). We know from *Middot* 3:8 that golden chains hung from the ceiling of the Portico to be used by the young priests to climb up and inspect, repair and clean window decorations. Above each of the four window lintels, my reconstruction shows a decoration, wreath- or crown-like ornaments attached to the wall. *Middot* 3:8 implies that there were four such crowns, reminiscent of those fashioned from the silver and gold collected from the returnees from the Babylonian Exile, and placed upon the head of Jehozadok the High Priest (Zechariah 6:14).

Those who stood in the Court of the Priests outside the Temple could look through the wide, high opening, into the Portico and see the exquisite golden ornaments hanging on the Sanctuary facade, as well as the tapestry veil and the tables with shewbread. But they could not see into the Sanctuary.

*The Sanctuary (*heikhal*) and the Holy of Holies (*kodesh ha-kodashim*)*

The Sanctuary and the Holy of Holies composed one long room, 60 cubits (103 feet) long, 20 cubits (35 feet) wide and 40 cubits (69 feet) high, separated by curtains. Entered from the Portico, the Sanctuary was 40 cubits long. It was separated from the Holy of Holies by two curtains (*amah traksin*) hung 1 cubit apart (see p. 70). The eastern curtain—on the side of the Sanctuary—was slightly open at the southern end, while the western curtain—on the side of the Holy of Holies—was slightly open at its northern end, an arrangement that prevented unauthorized people from seeing the Holy of Holies. Only the High Priest was permitted to enter the Holy of Holies; to do so he passed through the space between the two curtains.

The very beautifully worked curtains, embroidered with lions and eagles, were displayed to the public before being hung in the Temple. As we find in *Sheqalim* 8:5, another tractate of the Mishnah:

> "The veil was one handbreadth thick and was woven on [a loom having] seventy-two rods, and over each rod were twenty-four threads. Its length was forty cubits and its breadth twenty cubits; it was made by eighty-two young girls and they used to make two in every year; and three hundred priests immersed it [to purify it before hanging]."

The interior of the Sanctuary was completely overlaid in gold save only the area behind the doors. The overlay consisted of gold panels 1 cubit square and as thick as one gold denarius (a Roman coin). The gold panels were taken down at the three pilgrimage festivals and displayed outside, at the ascent to the Temple Mount, after which they were re-hung in the Sanctuary. Within the Sanctuary were the lampstand, the shewbread table (to be distinguished from the marble and gold tables in front of the entrance to the Sanctuary, mentioned previously), and the incense altar, all made of gold. The seven branches of the lampstand recalled the seven planets, while the 12 loaves of bread placed upon the Table of the Shewbread recalled the 12 signs of the Zodiac and the 12 months of the year. The altar held 13 different types of incense, taken from the sea, the desert and the earth.

The Holy of Holies was devoid of all furnishings. No one was permitted to enter or even look inside, save the High Priest and even he could do so only once a year, on the Day of Atonement (Yom Kippur), when he went in and out four separate times.[9] The only thing inside the Holy of Holies was a rock, three fingers high, called *even hashtiya*, upon which the High Priest made incense offerings.

Artisans, on the other hand, who were responsible for the maintenance of the building, entered the Holy of Holies from above, in closed cages lowered from the Upper Chamber through openings (*lulin*) in the floor, cut right through the ceiling of the Holy of Holies (see p. 71). The cages were closed on three sides and open only to the walls so as to prevent the artisans from stealing a glance into the Holy of Holies.

Contributions of gold, made in payment of vows, were set aside for the sole purpose of preparing the beaten gold sheets that covered the walls of the Holy of Holies.

Above the Sanctuary and the Holy of Holies was the Upper Chamber, while surrounding the Sanctuary and the Holy of Holies on three sides—north, west and south—were the cells. Together, the Upper Chamber and the cells enveloped the most sacred parts of the Temple on three sides and from above.

The Cells

The Sanctuary and the Holy of Holies were surrounded on three sides with small chambers, or rooms, that are referred to as cells. In all, there were 38 cells arranged in three stories. They were on each side and extended to the full height of the Sanctuary. The Upper Chamber (over the Sanctuary and Holy of Holies) remained unenveloped by cells.

Here is the description of the cells in *Middot*, which we guarantee you will understand if you read to the end of this article and look closely at the drawings:

> "And there were thirty-eight cells there, fifteen to the north, fifteen to the south, and eight to the west. Those to the north and those to the south were [built] five over five and five over them, and those to the west, three over three and two over them. And to every one were three entrances, one into the cell on the right, and one into the cell on the left, and one into the cell above it. And in the one at the north-eastern corner were five entrances: one into the cell on the right, and one into the cell above it, and one into the *mesibbah* and one into the wicket and one into the Sanctuary" (*Middot* 4:3).

The lowest story of cells stood on the same solid basement as the walls of the Portico and the Sanctuary.

Josephus also refers to cells arranged in three stories around the Sanctuary and the Holy of Holies, but not around the Upper Chamber:

> "Around the sides of the lower part of the Sanctuary were numerous chambers, in three stories, communicating with one another; these were approached by entrances from either side of the gateway. The upper part of the building had no similar chambers, being proportionately narrower . . ." (*The Jewish Wars* 5.5, 5 (220-221).

Josephus mentions here neither the total number of cells nor their exact arrangement around the walls, but in reference to the Solomonic Temple (the First Temple), he refers to 30 cells that encompassed the building, a fact for which there is no Biblical source (*Antiquities of the Jews* 8.85). It is possible that this figure actually relates to the Temple of Josephus's own times, but even then, only to the sum of the cells on the northern and southern sides (15 each, as stated in *Middot*).

We believe the description of the cells in *Middot* is the more accurate and we have adopted it in our reconstruction. On each of the long sides are 15 cells, five on each of the three floors. The cells are interconnected by openings. On the back of the building are similar cells in three stories, but only three on each of the first two floors and two on the third floor.

These cells were probably used for storage of ritual vessels, material required for the ritual itself (such as oil and spices), and for the Temple treasures. These same purposes could also have been served by many of the chambers in the courtyards round about the Temple. An interesting parallel to these cells is found in the "crypts" surrounding the Egyptian temple of Hathor in Dendara, as well as the temple of Horus at Edfu, also in Egypt, both belonging to the Hellenistic period and both completed in the first half of the first century B.C., shortly before the erection of Herod's Temple.

The ceiling supports of the first and second stories of cells were not extended into the Sanctuary wall; instead, they rested upon 1-cubit-wide ledges on the exterior face of the Sanctuary wall (see p. 71). The lower ledge was built out more than the upper one from the surface of the Sanctuary wall. Hence, from bottom to top the walls of the Sanctuary receded in steps. At the level of the lowest story, the Sanctuary wall was 7 cubits (12 feet) wide; at the level of the second story, 6 cubits (10 feet) wide; and at the level of the upper story, 5 cubits (9 feet) wide. Thus the cell rooms in each story had a different width depending on the thickness of the Sanctuary wall against which it was built: the first-story rooms, 5 cubits wide; the second, 6; and the third, 7 cubits.*

* The length of the cells is not mentioned in *Middot*. The present reconstruction assumes a barrier wall 4 cubits (7 feet) wide between the cells, and an overall length, on the north and south, equal to the length of the interior of the building; that is, 61 cubits (105 feet). The total length of the western cells was limited on the north and on the south by the cell walls, giving them a total length of 44 cubits (76 feet). Thus by subtracting the thickness of the divider walls from the proposed total length of the cells on the north and south and on the west and dividing by the total number of cells on each side, we arrive at 9 cubits (16 feet) for the length of the northern and southern cells in the three stories and 12 cubits (21 feet) for the length of the western cells on the first and second stories. It is not clear how the two cells of the western third story were divided; it may be that the division was asymmetrical so that they had different lengths.

The height of the cells is not recorded in *Middot*. It is

(note continues opposite)

The Stepped Passageway (mesibbah), and the Water Drain (beit horadat hamayim)

Between the cells and the outer wall, on the northern side of the building, there was a 3-cubit-wide (5-foot) space called the *mesibbah*. A parallel space on the southern side, also 3 cubits wide, was called "the space for draining away the water" (*beit horadat hamayim*). The *mesibbah* ascended within the width of the wall. Josephus mentions this ascent, but only in conjunction with the Solomonic Temple (*Antiquities of the Jews* 8.70) and not as part of the Herodian Temple. As there is no Biblical support for the *mesibbah* as an element of Solomon's Temple, we assume (as we assumed with Josephus's description of the cells surrounding the Solomonic Temple) that Josephus was extrapolating from the Herodian Temple with which he was personally acquainted. According to our reconstruction (see pp. 70-71),[10] the *mesibbah* was a sloping, stepped passageway 66 cubits (114 feet) long and 45 cubits (78 feet) high, leading from the ground level to the roof above the top story of cells. Each step had a rise of half a cubit (10 inches) and a tread of half a cubit, according to the dimensions recorded in *Middot* 2:3. This allowed for the incorporation of a number of horizontal landings, with a total length of 21 cubits (36 feet). Our depiction assumes the following structure (from bottom to top): a landing 7 cubits (12 feet) long; a flight of stairs 14 cubits (24 feet) long; another landing of 7 cubits; another flight of 14 cubits; a third landing 7 cubits long; and a third flight up to the outer roof, 17 cubits (29 feet) long. This calculation places the three landings at the floor level of the three cell stories.

A *mesibbah*, in the form of a graded ascent within a wall, is found among the largest and most famous Hellenistic and Roman temples: for example, the Egyptian temples of Hathor in Dendara and of Horus in Edfu both have them; the palace-temple at Hatra in Parthia, the temples of Zeus in Baetocece (Hossn Solieman), Syria and Qasr Bint Fara'un in Petra, the Nabatean capital also have them. And it is quite possible that Herod installed such an ascent at the temple of Augustus that he built in Sebaste (Samaria).

The "space for draining away the water," in the southern wall, opposite the *mesibbah*, served to drain off the rain water from the Temple roofs (see p. 70, left). It is reasonable to assume that this was a sloping channel that enabled the water from the cells' roof to run off. Assuming symmetry, we would then suggest that the channel sloped downwards from west to east, like the *mesibbah*, but the opposite slope is also a possibility. Such an ascent, with a moderate slope, could also have been used by workers to move building materials upward during the construction of the roof of the lower stories, as well as of the Upper Chamber which formed the second story of the Sanctuary. The workers might have made use of the *mesibbah* in the same manner. Moreover, the external walls as well as the cell walls, between which these ascending passageways ran, could serve both as scaffolding and as "curtains in the courtyard," concealing in this manner the building work going on within the Sanctuary and the Holy of Holies from the curious eyes of the people (Mishnah *'Eduyot* 8:6).

The Upper Chamber

The Upper Chamber, which formed a second story above the Sanctuary and the Holy of Holies, was 40 cubits (69 feet) high; its walls were 5 cubits (9 feet) thick. A mosaic strip of paving (*r'ashei psifasin*) 1 cubit (21 inches) wide, separated the eastern part of the Upper Chamber extending over the Sanctuary from the western part over the Holy of Holies. Like the double curtain between the Sanctuary and the Holy of Holies, a curtain probably hung here as well. The entrance to the Upper Chamber, reached by walking from the top of the *mesibbah* upon the roof of the cells, was on the south; the entrance itself certainly opened into the area over the Sanctuary rather than the area over the Holy of Holies. Close by the entrance were two cedar posts that served as a ladder by which one could climb to the roof of the Upper Chamber, 45 cubits (78 feet) above the floor level.

In the western part of the Upper Chamber, above the Holy of Holies, there were chimneys (*lulin*) (see p. 71) or holes cut in the floor, through which maintenance artisans were let down in boxes open only towards the walls of the Holy of Holies. In this way the workmen could not see inside the Holy of Holies.

In our reconstruction, these chimneys are 2

possible to deduce from *Middot* 4:5 that the cells encompassed the entire height of the Sanctuary, since the roof surface of the cells is on exactly the same level as that of the floor of the Upper Chamber. Presumably, the entire roof structure of the third-story cells formed a continuation of the roof structure separating the lower level of the building from the Upper Chamber. This roof structure was 5 cubits (9 feet) thick. If we assume that the ceilings of the first and second cell-stories were 2 cubits (3 feet) thick each, then we are left with a space 12 cubits (21 feet) high for each cell. These are the measurements adopted in the present reconstruction. According to our assumption, these ceilings, which rested upon the walls of the Sanctuary, consisted of wooden beams that ran across the cells.

cubits (3 feet) square, 1 cubit away from the wall and 2 cubits from each other. These dimensions would have allowed the artisans to comfortably carry out their work of cleaning and repairing the walls with only minor overlapping of the surface area covered by any two adjacent chimneys.

The location of the chimneys, their dimensions and the spaces between them were dictated by the function they performed. On the other hand, the chimney location determined the layout of the beams supporting the ceilings of both the Sanctuary and the Holy of Holies. The main roofing beams, as well as the second layer of roof beams that crossed them, would have had to be positioned in such a way as to create squares of 3 x 3 cubits (5 x 5 feet), through which the chimney openings could be cut. These considerations led us to the solution proposed in our reconstruction of the roof of the Temple's first story.

The Temple Roofs, the Parapet and the Scarecrow

The Temple had two levels of roofs: the lower level over the cells and the upper level over the Portico and the Upper Chamber (which itself was over the Sanctuary and the Holy of Holies). At the edges of both roofs was a 4-cubit-high (7-foot) parapet, topped by 1-cubit-high gold spikes, intended to prevent ravens and other birds of prey from perching, soiling the walls with their droppings and interrupting the order of sacrifice. *Middot* refers to these spikes as "scarecrows"* (*kalah 'orev*); the sages were divided as to whether they were included in the calculation of the 4-cubit-high parapet or were additional.

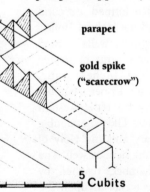

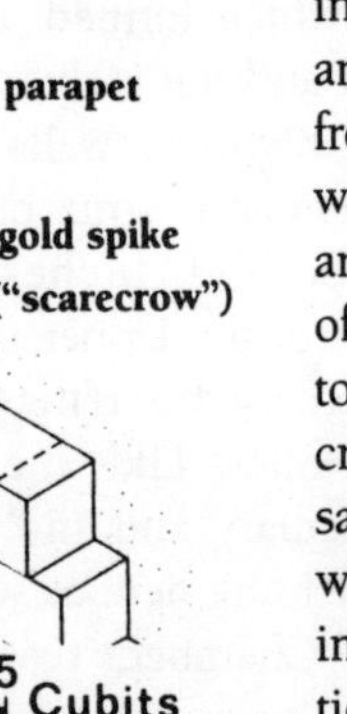

Installations of this sort, to ward off birds of prey, are also found in temples of other nations where sacrifices formed an important part of the cult. In our reconstruction, the upper course of the parapet consists of stone pyramids 1 cubit square at the base and 1 cubit high. The golden spikes stood at the top of each pyramid, a design that we think would have achieved its aim as a bird repellant.

The squared-off denticulated ornamentation commonly found on the top of temples is insufficient, in our opinion, to prevent birds of prey from perching there. We must assume that, in order to effectively keep birds away from the Temple precinct and from the freshly killed sacrifices that would attract them, it was necessary to install special devices not only on the Temple roofs but elsewhere around the altar.

We are not the first to render a reconstruction of the Second Temple in Jerusalem. Many have tried with more or less devotion to fact rather than fancy. But we believe that our reconstruction, intimately bound to a careful reading of those

* The golden spikes are mentioned by Josephus. In contrast, there is a suggestion in the Gemarah (Babylonian Talmud *Shabbat* 90a; *Menahot* 107b) that the "scarecrow" consisted of iron plates.

Literary Sources for Details of Temple Reconstruction

General: *Middot* 3:6-4: 7; *Wars* V, 5, 1-8 (184-247); *Antiquities* XV 380-425.
Splendor: *Sukkah* 51b; *Baba Batra* 4a; *Tosefta Menahot* 13,19; Braitha in *Pesahim* 57a; *Wars* V, 5, 4 & 6 (208-213, 222-227).
Whitewashing: *Middot* 3:4; *Sukkah* 51b; *Baba Batra* 4a.
Dimensions and External Shape: *Middot* 4:6, 7; *Wars* V, 5, 4 & 5 (208-221); *Antiquities* XV 391, 393.
Portico Steps: *Middot* 3:6; *Wars* V, 5, 4 (207).
Facade and Portico Portal: *Middot* 2:3, 3:7. (In *Wars* V, 5, 4 (208) the height of the Portal is 70 cubits and its width, 25 cubits.)
Golden Eagle: *Wars* I, 33, 2-3 (648-653); *Antiquities* XVII 149-155.
Portico Dimensions: *Middot* 4:7. (In *Wars* V, 5, 4 [207, 209] the excess is given as 20 cubits on either side; the Portico measurements are 20 cubits [depth] x 50 cubits [width] x 90 cubits [height].)
Cedar Beams Between the Portico Wall and the Sanctuary Wall: *Middot* 3:8.
Gilding of Portico Walls: *Tosefta Menahot* 13, 19.
Window Crowns on Sanctuary Facade: *Middot* 3:8. (Windows are mentioned in Codex Kaufmann, Cambridge, Parma-De Rossi 138, Paris 328-329, as well as in the Mishnah Commentary of the Rambam [ed. Kappah] and 1 *Maccabees* 1:22 and 4:57.)
Sanctuary Portal: *Middot* 4:1; *Wars* V, 5, 4 (211) (the height of the Portal is 55 cubits and its width, 16 cubits); *Antiquities* XV 394 (Latin version); *Eruvin* 2b.
Golden Vine: *Middot* 3:8; *Wars* V, 5, 4 (210); *Antiquities* XV 394-395 (Latin version); Tacitus, *Historiae* V.5.5; Florus, *Epitoma* I, 40:30.
Wickets: *Tamid* 3:7-8; *Middot* 4:2; *Yoma* 39b.
Door Panels: Gilded (*Wars* V 208); *Tamid* 3:7; *Eruvin* 10:11; *Eruvin* 102a.
Veil: *Wars* V, 5, 4 (212-214); *Antiquities* XV 394 (Latin version); *Letter of Aristeas* 86; 1 *Maccabees* 1:22; *Antiquities* XIV 105-109; *Tamid* 7:1; *Tosefta Sheqalim* 3, 13; *Yoma* 54a; *Ketubot* 106a *Matthew* 27:51.
Gold Lampstand: *Yoma* 3:10 and parallels; *Yoma* 37a and Braitha (*ibid.*) 37b; *Jerusalem Talmud (JT) Yoma* 3, 8, 41a.
Tables: *Sheqalim* 6:4; *Menahot* 99a,b; *Tamid* 31b; *JT Sheqalim* 6, 3.
Sanctuary and Holy of Holies Dimensions: *Middot* 4:6, 7; *Wars* V, 5, 5 (215) (60 cubits in height).
Curtains of Holy of Holies: *Yoma* 5:1; *Sheqalim* 8:4, 5 (for the correct version of Mishna 5, see: J. N. Epstein, *Introduction to the Mishnaic Text* [Heb.], p. 952); *Tosefta Sheqalim* 3, 15; *JT Sheqalim* 51b; *Yoma* 51b-52a; *The Apocalypse of Baruch* 10, 19; *Pesikta Rabbati* 26 (ed. Ish-Shalom 131a); *Protoevangelium Iacobi* 10, 1.
Gold Overlay in Sanctuary: *Middot* 4:1; Braitha in *Pesahim* 57a.
Sanctuary Vessels: *Wars* V, 5, 5 (216-218); *Yoma* 5:3; *Tosefta Yoma* 2, 12; *Menahot* 11, 5-6; *BT ibid.* 98b-99a; *Yoma* 21b; 33b; 51b-52a; *JT Sheqalim* 6, 3.
The Holy of Holies: *Middot* 4:5; *Wars* V, 5, 5 (215-219); *Sheqalim* 4:4; *Tosefta Kelim, Baba Qama* 1, 7; *Tosefta Sheqalim* 3, 6.
Even Hashtiya: *Yoma* 5:1, *Tosefta Yoma* 2, 14.
The Structure of the Ceiling and the Roofs: *Middot* 4:6.
Building Materials: *Wars* V, 5, 4 & 6 (208-213, 222-224; *Sukkah* 51b; *Baba Batra* 4a; *Middot* 3:4.
The Cells: *Middot* 4:3, 4; *Wars* V, 5, 5 (220); *Antiquities* XV 393.
Mesibbah and the Space for Draining Away the Water: *Middot* 4:5, 7.
The Upper Chamber: *Middot* 4: 5, 6; *Wars* V, 5, 4, 5 (209, 211, 221); *Antiquities* XV 393.
The Curtains of the Upper Chamber: *Tosefta Sheqalim* 3, 13-15; *JT Yoma* 42b; *Yoma* 54a.
The Parapet and the Scarecrow: *Middot* 4:6; *Wars* V, 5, 6 (224); *Shabbat* 90a; *Menahot* 107b; *Eruvin* 6a.

sources that contain "eyewitness" accounts, may be as close as it is possible to come to depicting the Temple as we would have seen it, gleaming in Jerusalem's transparent light, 2,000 years ago. BR

(The photos of the *di-drachma* and *tetra-drachma* coins [on pp. 67 and 72] are published here by courtesy of the Israel Department of Antiquitites and Museums. The photos belong to the Israel Museum, and I am indebted to Prof. Ya'akov Meshorer for permission to publish them. The photos of the bronze coins [on p. 72] are published here by courtesy of the Institute of Archaeology, Hebrew University, Jerusalem.)

[1] Many scholars, such as Emil Schürer, Kurt Watzinger, Abraham Schalit, Michael Avi-Yonah and others, find the *Middot* descriptions of the Temple preferrable to that provided by Josephus.

[2] Braitha in Babylonian Talmud *Sukkah* 51b.

[3] Babylonian Talmud *Baba Batra* 4a.

[4] I am indebted to Prof. Dan Barag for bringing this coin to my attention. See also: Barag, "The Table for Shewbread and the Facade of the Temple on the Bar-Kokhba Coins," *Qadmoniot* 20 (1987), pp. 22-25.

[5] Josephus, *The Jewish Wars* 1.33,2-3 (648-653) and *Antiquities of the Jews* 18.149-155.

[6] Kurt Watzinger, Michael Avi-Yonah, Yaakov Meshorer, Leo Mildenberg and Dan Barag, to mention just a few of them.

[7] This translation by Lea Di Segni is from the Latin version, which, in this instance, is better than the corrupt Greek version.

[8] Tacitus, *Historiae* 5.5.5; Florus, *Epitoma* 1.40:30.

[9] *Tosefta Kelim, Baba Qama* 1,7.

[10] For details see Joseph Patrich, "The *Mesibbah* of the Temple According to the Tractate *Middot*," *Israel Exploration Journal* 36 (1986), pp. 215-233, Pl. 27A.

JERUSALEM
A Craft Center for St

By Nahman Avigad

If Jerusalem is famous for one thing, it is for being a religious center. But our interest in the Holy City lies also in its everyday life, of which so little is known. Recent investigations revealed that in ancient times, especially in the late Second Temple period (50 B.C.-70 A.D.),various arts and crafts, such as stonework, painted pottery and glass industry, flourished in Jerusalem.

To understand these crafts is to add a new dimension to our understanding of life in the Holy City. From these crafts we learn about the world of the craftspeople who produced the artifacts, about the art and culture their products reflected, and about the people who used them. A knowledge of these crafts breathes a new reality into the ancient world we are trying to understand.

For 14 years, between 1969 and 1983, I directed archaeological excavations in the Jewish Quarter of the Old City, within the area of Jerusalem where its Upper City was located. The Jewish Quarter of the Old City had been largely destroyed by the Jordanians in 1948. When the Jewish Quarter was reconstructed after the 1967 Six Day War, we took the opportunity to investigate the site, which had never been excavated before. Our archaeological excavations provided some of the most impor-

LOURISHING

ne, Pottery, and Glass

tant evidence yet uncovered concerning Jerusalem as an ancient craft center. Foremost among these crafts was one that utilized the common raw material naturally available locally—stone.

Even before our excavations, Jerusalem stonework was well-known. The well-developed art of stoneworking is evidenced by the Second Temple Period tombs scattered around the city. The architectural carvings and ornamentation in these rock-hewn tombs, as well as on carved stone sarcophagi and ossuaries,* which are found in such large quantities in Jerusalem, are witness to the local skill in this craft, which eventually evolved into a typical Jewish style. Although no sepulchral discoveries were made in our excavations, I have reproduced here one of the finest of the sarcophagi (p. 84) discovered on the campus of the Hebrew University on Mount Scopus, which superbly illustrates the high standard attained by these Jerusalem artisans.

Other excavations in Jerusalem over the last decade have also uncovered artistic stonecarving. For example, the ornamented stones with geometric and floral patterns discovered near the Southern Wall of the Temple Mount fully display the ornamental richness and variety that typified the Royal Portico of the Temple Enclosure at the end of the Second Temple Period. One stone ornamented in a

*An ossuary is a rectangular box with a lid, usually hewn out of limestone, which was used as a depository for secondary burial of a deceased person's bones.

Elegant *terra sigillata* *pottery vessels have been restored. Some of the finest pottery produced in late Hellenistic times, these vessels were probably imported from an eastern Mediterranean country.*

similar style was found in our excavations, and it, too, was apparently from a monumental building somewhere in the so-called Upper City, which was where our excavations were located.

Our excavations in the Upper City have shown that Jerusalem artisans also produced such practical wares as stone tables and household vessels. In other words, Jerusalem had a flourishing and varied stone industry, employing many artisans and craftsmen.

OVERLEAF Triangles and diamonds ***of different-colored stone and marble, polished with care and inlaid with precision around a square of veined white marble, once formed the top of a small decorative table. This tabletop fragment, found in a large, elegant Herodian home in Jerusalem's Upper City, attests not only to the wealth of the Upper City residents but also to the high level of skill the Jewish stonecrafters of Jerusalem had attained by the first century B.C.***

Until we discovered stone tables in our excavations, as far as the archaeologist was concerned, the furniture of the Second Temple Period in Israel had been unknown. Even now this is the only type of furniture actually found. The ordinary tables in the Jerusalemite home were, of course, made of wood; but they long ago disintegrated under moist climatic conditions. We now know that Jerusalemites also had stone tables, decorative in nature and quite expensive, that had specific functions within the house.

Our first stone table was found in the so-called Burnt House, which was burned in the Roman destruction of Jerusalem in 70 A.D. (See "Jerusalem in Flames—The Burnt House Captures a Moment in Time," p. 96.) Later we found more of these tables in many houses in the Upper City. Fragments of such tables had been discovered in other excavations in Jerusalem—some of them long ago—but these fragments had not been recognized as parts of tables. Fragments of the small columns that form the legs of these tables had also been found, but long puzzled excavators.

We found two types of stone tables, one rectangular and high, the other round and low. The rectangular tables have a single central leg and a rectangular top. A projec-

Low, three-legged table *with stone top. Reconstructed wooden legs have been set into the three depressions under this tabletop excavated in the Jewish Quarter. The restoration is based on similar tables depicted in contemporaneous paintings and coins. Sometimes these animal-shaped table legs had bronze "paw" fittings like the one below. From the height of this and other tables found in the Jerusalem Upper City excavations, we can deduce that these were dining tables around which guests would sit, relaxing on couches while eating.*

tion on the underside of the table slab fits into a corresponding depression in the top of the leg, joining the two together. The leg is fashioned in the form of a column, with all the usual elements including base, shaft, and capital. These tables were the same height as modern tables, 28 inches to 32 inches, and the tops measure about 18 inches wide by 34 inches long.

One unusually elegant table had a thin top and a foot in the form of a tall, well-designed column; it is made of a hard, polished stone that was shattered into dozens of fragments and splinters by the fire in the house where it came to light. Our search for its pieces continued over two seasons, during which time we carefully sifted all the earth removed from rooms of the house.

Another table is more typically proportioned, with a thick top and stubby central leg. The fore-edge of the top bears a stylized leaf pattern also found on Jewish ossuaries from Jerusalem; its leg has a capital in Doric style. The top and leg of the table were found in different buildings and

Serving pieces *grouped as they might have been used in the home of a wealthy Jerusalemite in the first century A.D. The tabletop is a replica, and portions of the column leg and large stone vessels under the table have been restored. The bronze vessels on the table were found intact.*

This arrangement of table and vessels is based on a scene carved into a tabletop fragment that was found in an Upper City building called the Burnt House. Above is an artist's drawing of this ornamented fragment, which was stolen from the excavations and then recovered by the Israel Department of Antiquities after it was found at an antiquities dealer's shop.

Eretz Israel. Vol. X. 1970.

did not originally compose a single table. They do, however, go together quite admirably.

The edges of these tables are generally ornamented on three sides with geometric and floral patterns; the fourth side is most often plain. This suggests that the tables originally stood against a wall.

On the edge of one table fragment there is an unusual motif—two crossed cornucopias with a pomegranate between them. Until recently, this motif was known only from Hasmonean (first century B.C.) coins; this is the first instance of this Hasmonean emblem being found on an object other than a coin. An unusual motif on another tabletop, a fish, is particularly noteworthy because it is the only animal figure found in ornamental use (see photo p. 86). This period in Jerusalem is known for its strict adherence to the proscription against human or animal representation.

The smaller round tables are about 20 inches in diameter. Their tops are usually of soft limestone, though some fragments are of either a hard, reddish Jerusalem stone, a blackish bituminous stone, or imported black granite. On the bottom of these smaller tabletops are three depressions, where wooden legs had been affixed. Nothing survives of the legs, but on the basis of Hellenistic and Roman paintings and reliefs, we can suggest that they were in the form of animal legs, sometimes with bronze fittings at the bottom. A round table of this sort appears in a wall painting in a Hellenistic tomb at Marisa, some 22 miles southwest of Jerusalem, as well as on several of Herod's coins.

The group of tables from the Jewish Quarter thus reveals a hitherto unknown aspect of home furnishing in ancient Jerusalem. Hellenistic and Roman paintings and reliefs depicting rectangular tables with a single leg reveal that they were used as serving tables to hold drinking vessels. The round tables with three legs are depicted in use for meals, surrounded by guests reclining on couches.

Stone tables like these were in widespread use throughout the Roman Empire, although they originated in the Hellenistic East. The Roman historian Livy, who lived in Herod's day, mentions "tables with one leg" among the booty brought from Asia Minor in the second century B.C., when they were apparently still considered a novelty in Rome. The Roman scholar Varro (first century B.C.) describes "a stone table for vessels, square and elongated, on a single small column . . . many placed it in the house alongside the central pool. On and near it, when I was a lad, they would put bronze vessels." A graphic representation of such a group is also found on a Roman pottery oil lamp. Even today, the visitor to Pompeii will find such decorative tables in the dining rooms and patios of the luxurious villas there. In Jerusalem, too, these attractive stone tables added beauty and culture to the home. The basic technique of the Jerusalem stonecarvers who made these tables, as well as the style of their ornamental motifs, was deeply rooted in the local tradition of stoneworking and, although their work was patterned after foreign models, it had a decidedly local flavor.

An ornamented fragment of a stone tabletop was recently purchased from an antiquities dealer in Jerusalem by Dr. L. Y. Rahmani on behalf of the Israel Department of Antiquities and Museums. The dealer claimed that i

Richly decorated stone sarcophagus. *Found on the Mt. Scopus campus of the Hebrew University of Jerusalem, this elegant sarcophagus dates to the time of Herod. Both the box and lid are decorated with finely chiseled leaves, flowers and grapevines, attesting to the skill attained by Jerusalem stoneworkers in the first century B.C.*

Courtesy Hebrew University of Jerusalem

Hasmonean coin and fragment *of a stone table. Both are decorated with the same "still life": a pomegranate flanked by horns of plenty. Although this motif was previously known from Hasmonean coins like this one, the Jerusalem table fragment is its first appearance on an object other than a coin.*

The only animal figure *discovered in the excavations, this open-mouthed fish decorates a fragment of a stone table from Jerusalem's Upper City. In first-century B.C. Jerusalem, Jews for the most part observed a strict interpretation of the second commandment, reading it to forbid the making of all graven images.*

Flowers and geometric patterns like those on either side of the fish were common decorative motifs, but the fish is an anomaly.

had been found at Turmus-Aya near Samaria. Dr. Rahmani showed this fragment to me before his Department bought it and asked if I thought that it might have been stolen from our excavations, for we had just found the first such tables in the "Burnt House." The stone offered for sale bore the typical traces of soot, as did ours. I was in an embarrassing position, because we had carried out the excavation of the burnt rooms under strict supervision, employing only staff members and volunteers, and the site was guarded after working hours and at night by a special guard. Since a heavy fragment of a stone table was no mean item to put in your pocket and smuggle away, I told Rahmani that I didn't think it was ours. I began having second thoughts, however. One of the day workmen, in cahoots with the night watchman (who also worked for us during the day) might have been able to remove such a bulky item. It might have been placed to one side during the day and then removed at night, to be sold to a waiting antiquities dealer. Other factors also seemed unexplainable. For instance, at the very time we were uncovering the first such rare objects in the Jewish Quarter, a similar fragment of a Jerusalem table came to light at a site far away in Samaria, where no excavations were currently known to be in progress, and this fragment, too, bore traces of fire. I reluctantly came to the conclusion that the fragment Rahmani bought from the antiquities dealer had indeed been taken from the Burnt House in our Jewish Quarter excavation.

According to Rahmani's published description, various motifs are incised on the edge of the tabletop: on the long side is a ship, while on the shorter side there is a table with a single leg, bearing various vessels and flanked by two large jars with high bases. This latter depiction appears to be a precise graphic counterpart to Varro's description noted above and is also in surprising agreement with the depiction on the Roman oil lamp also mentioned above. In ornamenting this tabletop, the Jerusalem artisan had simply chosen the motif of the table itself, with all the vessels usually associated with it; in other words, a page straight out of the book of the everyday life of his period. On the basis of these depictions, both literary and pictorial, we have been able to restore such a grouping, using finds from our excavations.

In addition to stone tables, we found an abundance of stone vessels. Indeed, the discovery of stone vessels became routine. Whenever we approached a stratum of the Second Temple Period in which a building was burnt by the Romans during the destruction of the city in 70 A.D., stone vessels invariably made their appearance as well. Thus, even in the absence of other specific chronological clues, we were often able to date a structure as Herodian solely on the basis of the presence of even a single stone vessel—or even mere fragments of a stone vessel. Generally, these vessels were accompanied by traces of fire, obviously from the destruction of 70 A.D.

Our discovery of stone vessels came as no surprise, for their existence in Jerusalem had long been known from previous excavations. What did surprise us was the great number and variety of complete vessels. Our discovery of them in almost every house soon led us to realize that stone vessels, previously regarded as isolated luxury items, were in fact widely used. Some of the stone vessels served

Roman reliefs *showing serving and dining tables. In the above relief, from Italy, two servants are kept busy waiting on groups of diners seated on couches around low three-legged tables. Pitchers and drinking vessels for the diners are kept on a higher one-legged table between the two groups. This one-legged table stands away from the wall. The table in the relief at right stands against the wall, a position that explains why tabletops found in the Jerusalem excavations were decorated only on three sides. On either side of the stylized lion leg of the table in the scene at right are large pitchers, probably refill sizes for the smaller pitchers on top of the table. As one servant reaches for a pitcher, another pours a beverage into a drinking vessel he has just taken from the table.*

Scenes like these, showing one- and three-legged tables, how they were used and the arrangement of beverage vessels around them, have enabled Israeli archaeologists to reconstruct similar tables and vessels from fragments salvaged from the fiery debris of Jerusalem's destruction.

the same functions as their pottery counterparts; others were of special shapes for special uses. In general, the stone vessels are a rich and variegated addition to the types of utensils known to have been in use in the Jerusalem household in antiquity.

Stoneware production in Jerusalem during this period reached a pinnacle of both technical skill and design. Stone vessels were of course produced in other lands. For example, some stone vessels found in Delos in Asia Minor are quite similar to ours. The Jerusalem artisans undoubtedly learned much from others, but the peculiar and specific need for stoneware in Jerusalem (for reasons explained below) led Jerusalem artisans to outstanding achievements. The products of Jerusalem were undoubtedly famous and were apparently unrivaled within Palestine. The one large stone jar found at Ain Feshkha and the several smaller stone vessels found at Masada and other sites were surely made in Jerusalem.

The stone vessels are generally made of a soft, readily carved limestone, found in abundance in the vicinity of Jerusalem. Among the smaller vessels found in our excavations, a few are made of other types of stone, such as alabaster or marble.

On the basis of form and finish, it is possible to distin-

guish between stone vessels made on a lathe and those carved by hand. In either case, the craftsmen would use chisels to give the vessels their general form and then usually would drill to extract the material from the interior before finishing.

The lathe-turned vessels have open and cylindrical shapes, as is dictated by that technique of manufacture. Among such vessels are the very impressive large jars in goblet form, standing on a high foot. The rim has a molded profile, as does the high base, and the surface is well smoothed and often ornamented with horizontal bands or vertical ribbing. Where ledge handles are present, the strips between the two handles are rougher, giving them an ornamental effect. It is possible that these jars are to be identified with the stone "jar" (*kallal*) mentioned in the *Mishnah** (*Parah* 3, 3), a large stone or pottery vessel that was used for holding the ashes of the Sin Offering. Long ago, the late J. Brand described the *kallal* of the Mishnah as a goblet-shaped vessel with a broad rim, straight sides, curved bottom, and a high base—a description that fits our vessels perfectly.

The blocks of stone from which these jars were fashioned weighed several times as much as the finished products, which were 26 inches to 32 inches tall. This makes it all the more surprising that the ancient lathes could support such a mass, and we can only wonder how they were powered.

Most of the lathe-turned vessels, however, are much smaller than the jars: plates, bowls, and handleless cups,

*The *Mishnah* is the body of Jewish oral law, specifically, the collection of oral laws compiled by Rabbi Judah the Prince in the second century.

Machine-made stone bowls and cups, *a small sample of the attractive and varied shapes and sizes Jerusalem stonecrafters were producing by the first century A.D.*

The abundance of stone vessels found in the Jewish Quarter houses surprised archaeologists, but they quickly saw the explanation. Stone, unlike porous pottery, cannot be ritually unclean and therefore unusable according to Jewish dietary laws. If a stone vessel was designated for use with meat dishes, for example, and then accidentally came in contact with milk, it could be purified and then reused. But a pottery vessel subject to the same accident had to be destroyed—it could not be made clean and then reused. Thus, stone plates and bowls were in demand. And stonecrafters perfected their art producing an abundant supply of these dishes for the rich residents of the Upper City.

Relish dish? *Several handmade stone vessels with multiple compartments like this were found. Perhaps it was used as a serving dish for olives and relishes, or perhaps it was an individual dinner tray.*

which are also rather attractive, some of the forms clearly imitating imported pottery vessels. These smaller vessels were readily made on a bow-powered lathe, somewhat resembling a primitive drill.

Hand-carving of stone vessels was employed for special forms where a lathe could not be used—as in the case of vessels with a vertical handle (which would interfere with the turning of the lathe) or of vessels that were not round. Of the types with handles inconvenient for turning, we may note two examples. A cup of fine form, resembling a modern coffee cup, has a delicate handle apparently imitating some pottery form of foreign origin. Ordinary cups of the period are in the form of a deep bowl; indeed bowls were generally used for drinking in antiquity. Another sort of stoneware cup was cylindrical with a pierced, vertical handle; its surface was not smoothed but rather pared vertically with a knife or an adze. These cups often have a short spout at the rim, not opposite the handle but at a right angle to it.

These two types of cups were the most common stone vessel found, and we encounter them often outside Jerusalem as well. The fact that they were made in various sizes, from large (6 inches high) to small (2 inches high) has led archaeologists to consider them to be "measuring cups" for liquids and for dry measures; one opinion is that their standard corresponds with that mentioned in the Mishnah, but this requires further investigation.

Handwork is, of course, also necessary on vessels that are not round, as is especially obvious on deep, square bowls—a shape not found in pottery but one apparently considered very convenient for kitchen use. Another noteworthy vessel has multiple compartments, with two, three, or four divisions; one such vessel is reminiscent of a salt and pepper shaker, while another resembles an army "mess tin" or a serving dish for a selection of relishes.

Round or elongated serving trays of stone with ornamental handles have also been found. Such trays are depicted in Roman mosaics loaded with food. In one depiction, a tray of our type bears a large fish.

Another handcarved vessel worthy of note is a stone oil lamp, the only example known to us. Additional stone objects were found whose original function cannot even be guessed.

All in all, we were astonished by the rich and attractive variety of stone vessels. Neither the local abundance of raw material nor the attractiveness of their shapes would alone explain this phenomenon. Moreover, their manufacture is much more costly than that of pottery, and stone vessels are more restricted and less convenient to use because of their weight and the softness of their material. Why, then, did they appear so suddenly and in such quantities in the Jerusalem household?

Stone cup. ***Before the Jewish Quarter excavations, stone vessels like these were thought to be luxury items. But the author found them in almost every Jewish Quarter house—so many, of different shapes and sizes, that he concludes that these stone vessels were as common as coffee cups today.***

Most stone drinking cups of this period were deep handleless bowls made on a lathe. But this cup with its carefully styled handle is handmade, probably the Jerusalem potter's imitation of a style popular somewhere "abroad."

The answer lies in the realm of *halakhah*, the Jewish laws of ritual purity. The *Mishnah* tells us that stone vessels are among those objects that are not susceptible to uncleanness (*Kelim* 10, 1; *Parah* 3,2), but no further details are given. Stone was simply not susceptible to ritual contamination. When a pottery vessel, on the other hand, became ritually unclean through contact with an unclean substance or object, it had to be destroyed. In contrast, a stone vessel would preserve its purity and thus its usability, even if it had come into contact with uncleanness.

One of the clearest literary witnesses to the Jewish ritual of purity relating to stone vessels is preserved in the New Testament, in the episode of the wedding at Cana in Galilee. There Jesus performed the miracle of changing water into wine. The text reads: "Now six stone jars were standing there, for the Jewish rites of purification, each holding two or three gallons" (John 2:6). These were most probably jars of the very type we have been discussing.

With the destruction of Jerusalem in 70 A.D, the flourishing production of stone vessels and stone tables came

Bowls found near the Temple Mount, *painted in red, brown and black floral designs. Although locally made, these bowls have been called "Pseudo-Nabatean" because like Nabatean pottery, they are thin-walled and painted with flower motifs. But their composition and style are in fact unique, and thus far these fragile vessels have been discovered only in Jerusalem. The author now prefers to call them "Jerusalem Painted Pottery."*

to an end, and the tradition of their manufacture was never revived.

The most common article in any household in antiquity was, of course, its pottery. The corpus of Palestine pottery during the Herodian period is not especially rich, but in the light of the recent excavations in Jerusalem, it turns out to have been more variegated than previously thought. The most common vessels were those most used in the house: cooking pots and storage jars. Most of these vessels were not found in the kitchens and storerooms which, at least in our excavations, were mostly looted and destroyed; rather, they came to light in the cisterns and pools of the houses, which had been turned into refuse dumps.

The cooking pots are almost invariably blackened with soot—evidence of their daily use. We would expect, in keeping with the large number of cooking pots in which food was prepared, that there would be a correspondingly large number of bowls or plates for serving. But the pottery of this period includes few locally made bowls or plates, types that are generally found in large quantities in other periods. In this particular period, only small, thin bowls are found here, suitable only for small portions. This raises an interesting gastronomical question, for which we have no ready answer. We do know from other souces that the wealthy people of the period generally enjoyed, if anything, excessive culinary delights.

Most of the storage jars used for water, wine and oil have elongated bodies. We also found some with a more globular, sack-shaped form.

Another basic vessel-type, in this as in all periods, is the jug in its various forms, including juglets and small bottles for small quantities of oil or perfume. Equally common were the thin-walled asymmetrical flasks.

In addition to these common vessels, we also found several types of unusual pottery. Foremost are the painted bowls sometimes known as "Pseudo-Nabatean" ware. Curiously, this type of bowl was entirely unknown during the first hundred years of excavations in Jerusalem, and only since 1968, with the commencement of excavations near the Temple Mount, have these painted bowls made their appearance. They have since become a regular feature in our excavations in the Upper City as well, among the finds of the first century A.D. These bowls are very fragile, and they are seldom found intact; but even so we have been able to mend and restore an impressive group.

These thin-walled bowls, which measure about 5 inches to 6 inches in diameter, are of very fine quality and are painted on the inside in stylized floral patterns in red and, sometimes, in brown or black. Two styles of painting are evident. One employs symmetrical compositions taking up the entire area of the bowl; the motifs are usually arranged radially, but sometimes they are in concentric circles, as on one example found in the house we called the Mansion. In the second, more carefree style, the painter often used a few quick strokes of the brush, much in the manner of abstract artists today.

When these painted bowls were first found, they were called "Pseudo-Nabatean," for they superficially resemble the Nabatean bowls, famous for their thinness and painted motifs. But the bowls from Jerusalem are different in the form of their motifs, in their composition and even in the quality of the ware itself. They seem to be a sort of Jewish alternative to the fine Nabatean bowls, which simply did not reach the Jerusalem market in significant quantities. Since these locally produced bowls have been found thus far only in Jerusalem, it would be appropriate to recognize them as a class by themselves and to call them "Painted Jerusalem Bowls."

No one would have previously thought that Jerusalem was famous for its glass, but now we know it held an important place in the technological history of ancient glass. This came to light through one of our most unusual discoveries—the refuse from a glass factory (see pp. 92-94). This waste material included a rich variety of glass fragments—some of them distorted by heat—unfinished products, hunks of raw glass, and lumps of slag. Where the glass factory itself was located, we do not know, except that it must have been somewhere in the vicinity.

The reader may ask what value scrap glass could have for us. Scientific research is not a treasure hunt for finished products in perfect condition, and the archaeologist treasures material that can provide an insight into methods of manufacture and their development as well as he cherishes finished products. It would of course be nice to find a complete workshop, with all its various installations, tools and products in various stages of manufacture, but no such glass factory has ever been found, and the next best thing are the waste materials that derive from one. Even such refuse is infrequently found, and its rare discovery in our excavations can thus be considered a blessing in disguise.

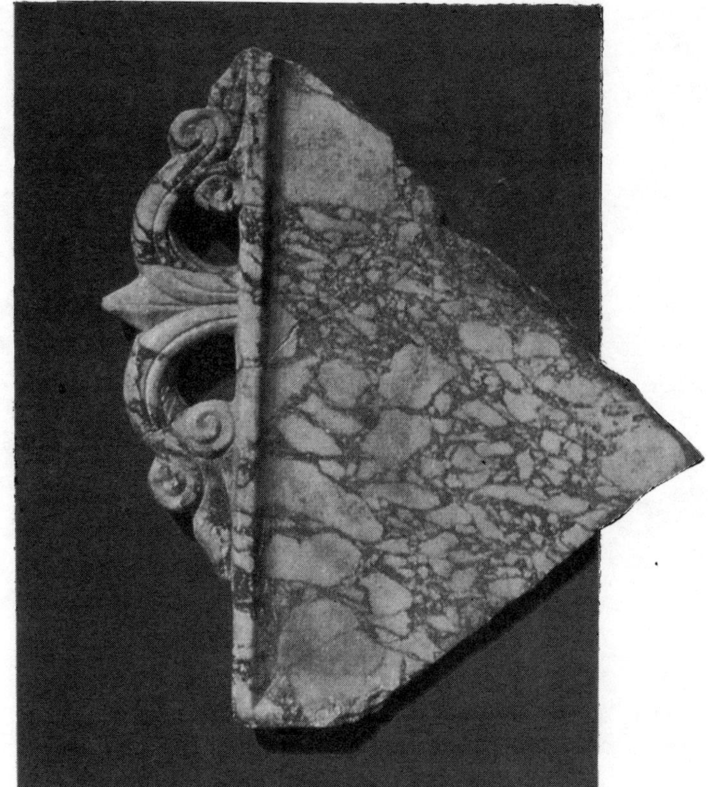

Stone trays. ***Scenes on some Roman mosaics show serving trays like the deep stone one (bottom) and the marble fragment (top) filled with food for banquets. The delicate rims and ornamental handles display the skill of the master Jerusalem stonecrafters.***

Among the vessel fragments, we could distinguish two major types of glass products, each based on a different

Text continues on p. 95

Refuse From a First-Century Glass Factory

Glass molding and glass blowing existed side by side in a Jerusalem glass factory during the Herodian period. Here we see the refuse from this factory—evidence of an industry in transition. The Upper City excavations present archaeologists and ancient glass experts with a unique opportunity to study a pivotal phase in the history of glass manufacture.

Clockwise from left: broken bowls; chunks of unprocessed glass; a heap of stems and pipes; a striped blowing pipe and fragments of a flask blown from it (reassembled in an artist's reconstruction); mouth and neck fragments of flasks; and pipes broken just as egg-shaped globs of glass were being blown. Before these pipes were discovered, scholars thought that glass vessels were blown from glass globs at the ends of metal pipes, but these finds show that in the earliest stage of glass blowing, the globs of hot soft glass were stuck onto pipes that were themselves made of glass.

Below are fragments of glass bowls that were molded, not blown. Simple concentric circles are incised along the inside of their rims. Alongside the fragments an artist has shown what complete bowls would look like, as projected from the shape and design of each fragment. The top bowl is rounded and the bottom bowl has a ribbed body and is carinated—sharply angled just under the shoulder.

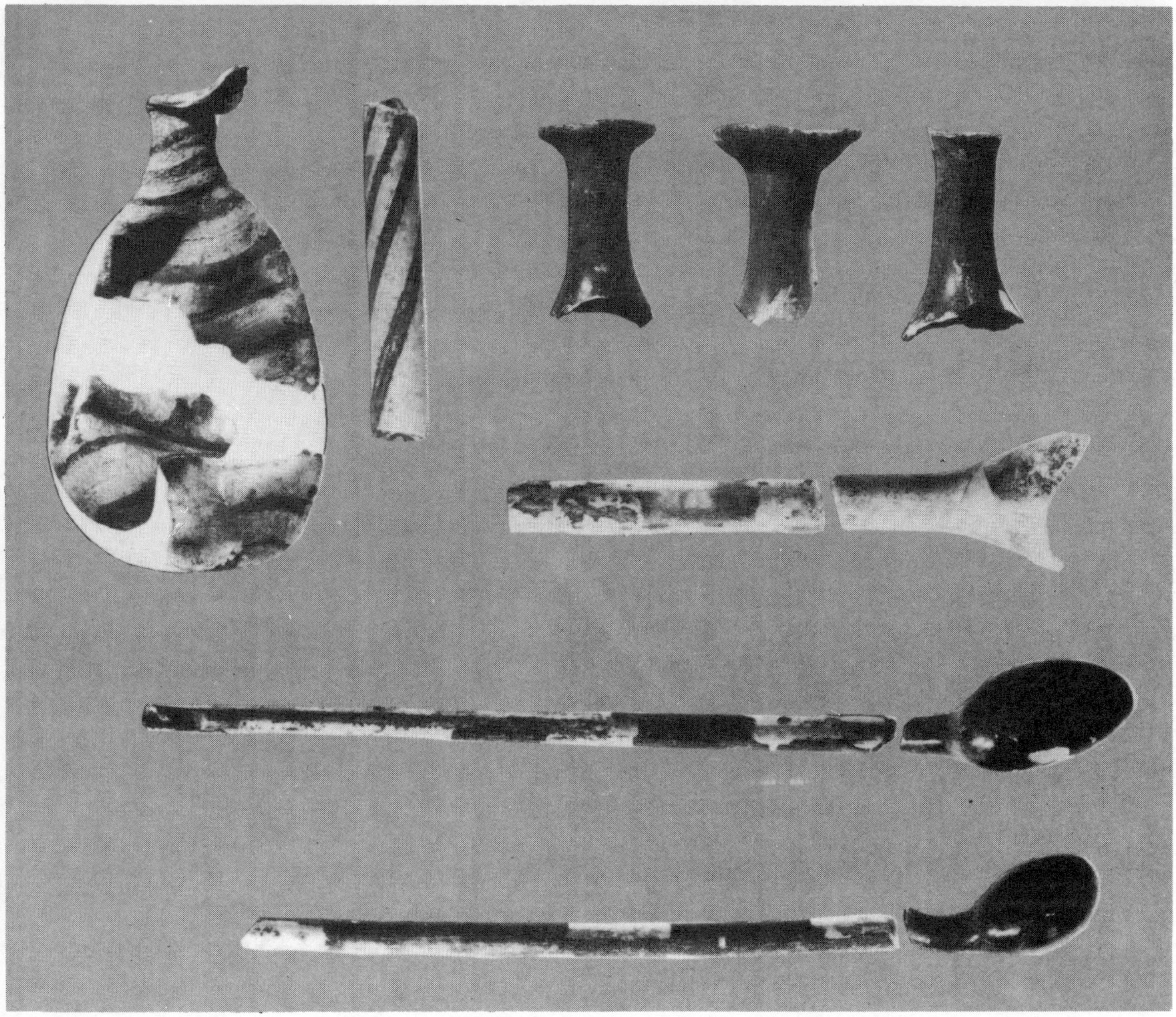

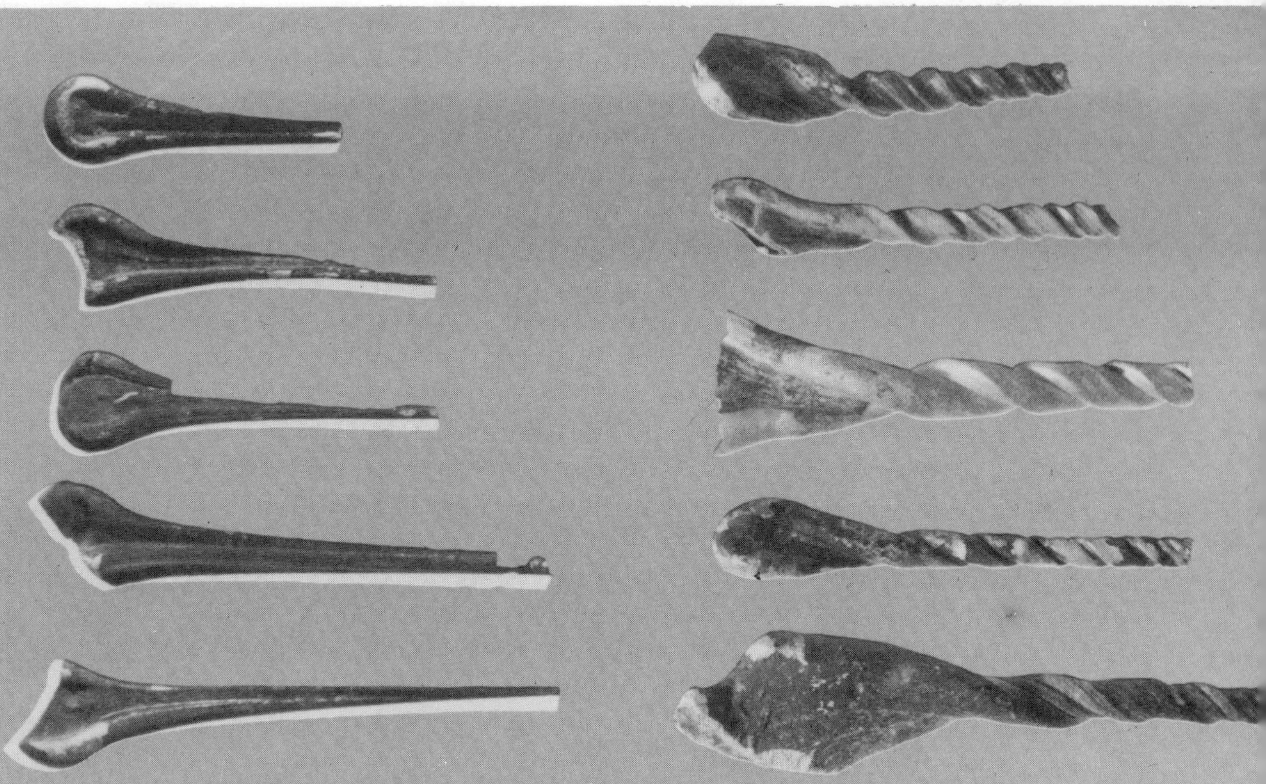

Making Kohl Sticks

Phases of "kohl stick" manufacture. These fragments have been grouped to illustrate the steps of manufacturing the thin twisted glass rods that are called kohl sticks because they were used to apply the black eye paint kohl. Above left are glass sticks strengthened by heat; above right are sticks that, while still hot, were partially twisted with pincers. Below we see fragments of the finished product.

Kohl sticks are rarely found in excavations but can be seen in some museums. In the Jerusalem glass factory, archaeologists discovered an abundance of them as well as the smooth rods that are the raw material for their manufacture.

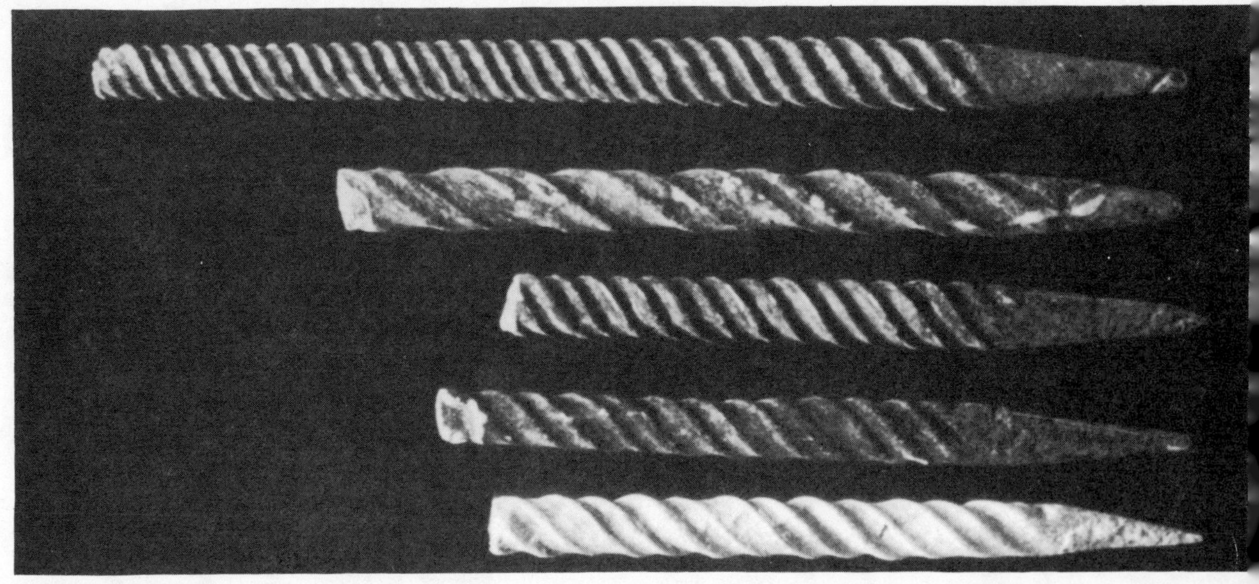

method of manufacture. For one type, the artisan formed vessels in molds; for the other type, the artisan shaped the hot glass into the desired form by blowing through a tube.

Chronologically, the molding process is the earlier of the two. We found hundreds of fragments of thick glass bowls, hemispherical or conical in shape, all of the molded type. The glass itself is greenish, but the surface is now generally covered with a layer of thick, black patina. These bowls, attractive in their simplicity, were very common in the Late Hellenistic period (second to first century B.C.), and similar examples have been found in many places in Palestine. Alongside these fragments were a small number of fragments from another type of bowl, also molded, but of thinner material, either rounded or carinated (sharp-angled), with rims that are modeled and bodies that are ribbed—a very common mode of decoration in the Hellenistic period.

The fragments of the second type of glass product are of closed vessels, such as small bottles of the "perfume bottle" type. This is the simplest shape to obtain using the glass blowing technique. It was probably the first shape ever produced by this process.

Our mixed find of molded and blown glass is especially interesting, for we see here a single factory using two different techniques side-by-side. Despite the numerous excavations in Israel and abroad of sites rich in glass finds, never before has such clear-cut evidence for the initial stage of glass blowing come to light. This process revolutionized the production of glass vessels and facilitated their "mass production," relatively speaking. The invention of glass blowing can be compared to that of the potter's wheel in ceramic production. In our glass finds we can see at least a partial explanation for the actual beginning of glass blowing.

Scholars have long believed that, from the initial invention of glass blowing, vessels have been blown from a gob of hot, plastic glass stuck on the end of a metal tube or pipe, as is still the practice today. But our finds from Jerusalem now indicate that the earliest glass blowing was done with glass tubes. These glass tubes are perhaps the very first stages of experimentation at glass blowing, followed later by the use of the blow-pipe. Our pile of glass refuse included many thin glass tubes, some of them with the beginning of a swelling at one end, though the continuation was broken off. There were also bulbs of glass the size of birds' eggs, which had clearly been blown from glass tubes. In other words, both the pipes and the bulbs of glass composed a single element, the initial phase of blowing a glass vessel. For one reason or another, the blowing ceased on these pieces, and the vessels were never completed. It is not quite clear yet how blowing with a glass pipe was accomplished in the heat of an open hearth. The matter requires further specialized study.

Dr. Gladys Weinberg and Professor Dan Barag, well-known experts on ancient glass, examined the glass refuse soon after its discovery, and they tell me that no evidence of this sort has been found at any other site in the world, and that this find of the earliest phase of glass blowing is of revolutionary significance for technological research. In their opinion, Jerusalem is the first site at which the meeting of the two techniques, glass molding and glass blowing, has been encountered. This discovery, then, represents a transitional phase in which the production of glass continued in the older molding technique alongside the newly introduced technique of glass blowing. This occurred around the middle of the first century B.C.

Another glass product reflecting the process of manufacture was thin, twisted rods, most of them found broken but originally about six inches long with one end rounded and the other pointed. Generally known as "kohl sticks," and probably used for cosmetics, they are rarely found in excavations but can be seen in some museums. Here we suddenly uncovered an abundance of them. We also found the smooth rods that were the raw material employed in their manufacture. We can follow the process of their manufacture into twisted sticks from smooth rods, through the phase of twisting, to their actual finishing. The marks of the pincers used to hold the hot, plastic rods are still clearly visible. Other glass objects discovered among the refuse included spinning whorls, conical gaming pieces, discs, and inlay plaques.

It is odd that we should find such significant remains in Jerusalem, for scholars have generally assumed that the centers of glass production were located close to sites rich in silica sand, the principal raw material of glass. However, the production of glass vessels, like that of pottery or metal wares, was not restricted to a single area. Chunks of raw glass could readily be transported from place to place, and glass artisans in various locales, however remote, could use them in whatever manner they desired.

Much research still needs to be done on this material. From it, glass experts will no doubt be able to clear up many of the longstanding questions relating to the earliest history of blown glass. One of these questions concerns the part played by the Jews in the production of glass in antiquity, for it is commonly thought that their role was a major one. Though this has not been proved conclusively, our finds from Jerusalem may well be a valuable contribution to that discussion.

Unless otherwise noted, all photos and drawings in this and the following article are courtesy of Nahman Avigad.

This article has been adapted from Chapter Three, section 10, of *Discovering Jerusalem: Recent Archaeological Excavations in the Upper City* by Nahman Avigad (Thomas Nelson Publishers: Nashville, 1983). Printed by permission of Thomas Nelson Publishers.

The Burnt House Captures a Moment in Time

By Nahman Avigad

WE CAME UPON IT SUDDENLY, in the very first year of our excavations. At that time we had not yet excavated a single house that had witnessed the catastrophe of 70 A.D., when the Romans destroyed Jerusalem. We were still emotionally unprepared for the impressions and associations raised by the prospect before us. In subsequent years, after several other burnt houses had been discovered, our emotions became somewhat blunted to the sight of such stark violence. But not only was this Burnt House the first such discovery, its preservation of traces of destruction and fire and the quantity of objects found in it were never exceeded. In January 1970, after heaps of rubble and refuse had been cleared away, we removed a rather thick layer of fill and refuse containing nothing ancient. Then stone walls suddenly began sprouting out of the earth. We saw immediately that these were the walls of rooms. As a first step in stratigraphic excavation, we dug a trench the breadth of one of the rooms, in order to determine the sequence of the layers. At a depth of about a meter, we encountered a floor of beaten earth. Already, the sides of the trench were providing a clear and impressive cross section, which we were able to read like an open book.

The upper layer contained fallen building stones that had changed color as the result of a fire. The layer beneath was a mixture of earth, ashes, soot and charred wood; at the bottom of the cross section, overlying the floor, were pottery fragments and parts of scorched stone vessels. The plastered walls were also black with soot. The picture was clear to any trained eye. There was only one phase of occupation, and its composition was unambiguous: the building had been destroyed by fire, and the walls and ceiling had collapsed along with the burning beams, sealing over the various objects in the rooms. When did this occur? The pottery indicated that it was sometime in the first century A.D.

Was the destruction of this building, so close to the Temple Mount, connected with the Roman destruction of Jerusalem in 70 A.D.? We seemed to have before us a unique picture of a house sacked by the Roman legions. The household effects were buried and left just as they had been, undisturbed by later activities.

In the excavation diary I wrote: "On the same day (13 January 1970) I was somewhat excited." But after the

Caught in the fire *when the Romans attacked, a young woman who was in the kitchen of the Burnt House sank to the floor and was reaching for a step near the doorway when she died. The fire had spread so fast, perhaps fed by oil used in this kitchen, that she could not escape and was buried by falling debris.*

initial excitement came moments of doubt. My initial impression might merely have been wishful thinking, and the facts might not lend themselves to such far-reaching conclusions. My chief assistant at the time, Ami Mazar, was away, and Roni Reich, the area supervisor, was as carried away as I was. I therefore invited several of my fellow Jerusalem archaeologists to visit the site, each one separately, to see their reactions to the cross section. All of them arrived at the same conclusion as ours.

Systematic excavation of the entire area only served to increase our tension as well as our expectations. The salient question was whether the same phenomenon would be found in the other rooms as well. As we cleared each room, an identical picture emerged. First we would come across stone debris from the collapsed walls, which filled the rooms. The dressed blocks were of the soft, local *nari* limestone, which had been baked to various colors by the great heat of the fire. Some had become lime-white, while others were gray, red, and yellow, and mostly very crumbly. Among the debris filling the rooms were a mixture of ash and soot and large quantities of charred wood.

Soot reigned over all, clinging to everything. It covered the plastered walls. Even the faces of our workmen turned black. There was no doubt that the fire had rampaged here, apparently fed by some highly flammable material contained in the rooms. It may well have been some oil, which would account for the abundance of soot. The traces were so vivid that one could almost feel the heat and smell the fire.

When we reached the floor level, objects began appearing, scattered about or in heaps: pottery, stone vessels, broken glass, iron nails, and the like. The known types of pottery gave us a general dating in the first century A.D. for the destruction of the building. But the many coins strewn over the floor—partly from the Roman Procurators of Judea and mostly from the First Jewish Revolt against

LOCATION OF JERUSALEM'S UPPER CITY DURING THE TIME OF THE SECOND TEMPLE

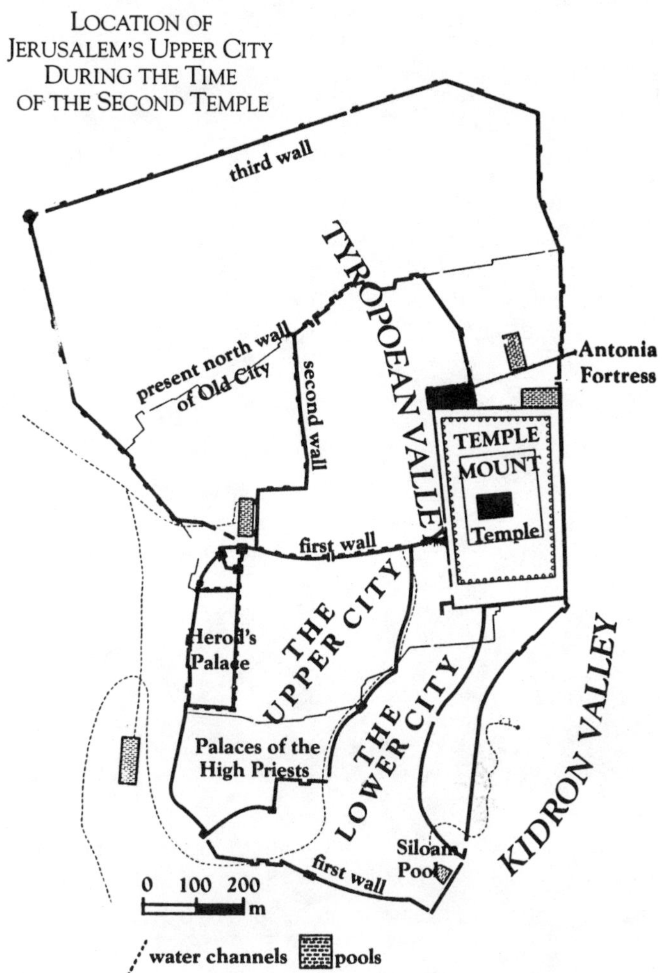

Rome—permitted a more precise dating. The coins of the revolt bear the legends "Year Two/The Freedom of Zion," "Year Three/The Freedom of Zion," and "Year Four/Of the Redemption of Zion." The latest, from the fourth year of the revolt, date to 69 A.D.

It was now quite clear that this building was burnt by the Romans in 70 A.D., during the destruction of Jerusalem. For the first time in the history of excavations in the city, vivid and clear archaeological evidence of the burning of the city had come to light. We refrained from publicizing this fact immediately, in order to keep from being disturbed by visitors. But word of the discovery soon spread and people began thronging to the site to see the finds on the spot.

The already considerable excitement upon seeing the scorched objects being recovered from the ashes increased with the discovery of a spear leaning against the corner of a room. Beyond the image of the destruction, each of us pictured in his mind the scene so vividly described by the first-century Jewish historian Josephus: the Roman soldiers spreading out over the Upper City, looting and setting the houses alight as they slaughtered all in their path. The owner of this house, or one of its inhabitants, had

Looking toward the Temple Mount, ***excavators pause in their work of uncovering a building in Jerusalem's Upper City.***

During Second Temple times, a priest would stand at the pinnacle of the southwest corner of the Temple Mount, the wall angle in front of the silver dome, and blow the shofar, or ram's horn, to herald the Sabbath and important festivals. But on August 28, 70 A.D., the Jews of the Upper City who looked toward the Temple Mount saw not the trumpeter but their Temple in flames. Perhaps the sight gave them courage because, according to Josephus, they held out against the Roman assault for nearly a month after the destruction of the Temple. Finally, on September 20, the Romans overran the city, slaughtering the inhabitants and putting the entire city to the torch.

managed to place his spear so it would be readily accessible, but he never got to use it.

Something amazing occurred in the hearts of all who witnessed the progress of excavations here. The burning of the Temple and the destruction of Jerusalem—fateful events in the history of the Jewish People—suddenly took on a new and horrible significance. Persons who had previously regarded this catastrophe as stirring but abstract and remote, having occurred two millennia ago, were so visibly moved by the sight that they occasionally would beg permission to take a fistful of soil or a bit of charred wood "in memory of the destruction." Others volunteered to take part in uncovering the remains, regarding such labor as sacred. The latent sentiment released—by people normally quite composed and immune to showing their emotions—was unbelievable.

The series of rooms uncovered was from the basement level of a large house whose continuation lies under a new dwelling on the north, so it could not be excavated. On the west, the building is abutted by an earth fill and building remains from the Israelite period. This is a good example of how a house from the days of the Second Temple was built over a site from the First Temple period.

The plan of the Burnt House(p. 102), as far as it could be recovered, included a small courtyard paved with stones (1), three medium-sized rooms (2, 3, 4), a small room (5) that was the only one not burnt and that contained no finds, a small kitchen (6), and a small, stepped ritual bath (7). The walls of the rooms were generally preserved to the height of about one meter; they were coated with a thin white lime plaster, while the floors were of beaten earth. The ovens sunk into the floors of these rooms are evidence that these were not dwelling quarters but probably a workshop. Although a variety of small objects were scattered in disarray throughout the rooms, the outstanding feature in each room was a heap of broken objects, including stone vessels, stone tables, and pottery. Before the building collapsed, the violent hand of man had cast unwanted belongings into heaps on the floor—seeing this, we recalled Josephus's description of the Roman soldiers looting the houses after the city had been conquered.

One fine day in January 1970, while we were still excavating the Burnt House, our registrar of finds, Sara Hofri,

At the ready, ***this spear was propped against a wall in the Burnt House where its owner could quickly grab it to defend himself against the invading Romans. But the Romans burned this house so quickly that the spear was never touched; instead it was buried in place by the fiery debris of collapsed walls and ceiling, preserving for 2,000 years this image of resistance and tragedy.***

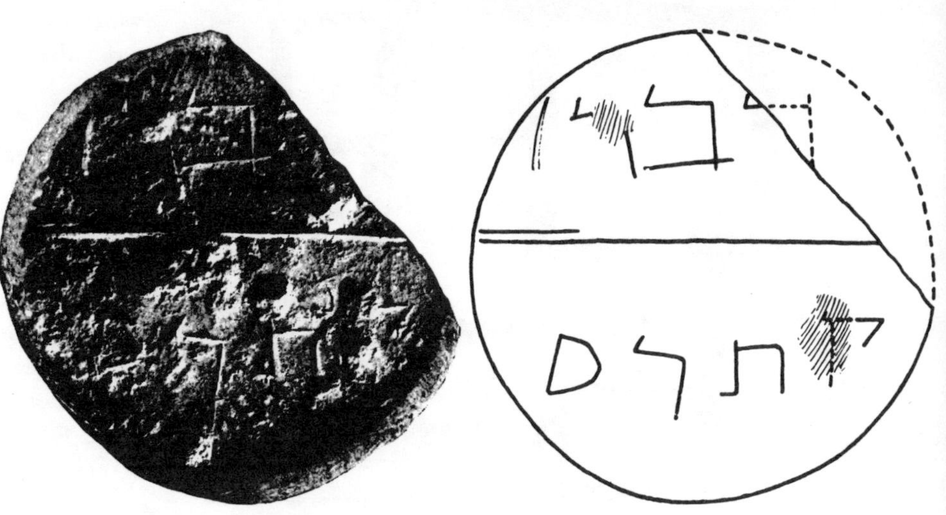

"Of Bar Kathros," *proclaims the Hebrew inscription on this stone weight (left) found in the Burnt House. An artist's drawing of the weight (right) shows the partially broken letter* dalet *(the first letter, reading right to left) which means "of." Now archaeologists can give a name and even a family history to the owners of this workshop. The Bar Kathros family was infamous—as High Priests, they served as overlords of their fellow Jews during Roman rule and abused their power through nepotism and libel.*

came running over from our expedition office with a stone weight in her hands, shouting: "Inscription"—a word that electrifies any archaeologist working on a dig. This weight, one of the many found in the Burnt House, had been washed and was then found to bear letters incised in thin lines. The inscription was not in the Greek script so often found on such weights but rather in Hebrew (to be more precise, in the "square" Aramaic script). Except for the first letter in the upper line, of which only the tip remains, and the first letter in the lower line, which was partly blurred, the inscription was intact and could clearly be read: "(of) Bar Kathros," or "(of) the son of Kathros."

Brief inscriptions of this sort, which lend a personal touch to the silent finds, are invaluable to the excavator. They bring bone-dry discoveries to life by adding the historical dimension of the material itself. This inscription opened up the possibility of identifying the owner of the house and ascertaining the sort of people who lived there. Did the name Bar Kathros fit into the picture of the period, the locale and the events being revealed before us through the archaeological discoveries? The "House of Kathros" is known as one of the families of High Priests who, in practical terms, ruled the Jews of Palestine in the days of the Roman procurators. They had taken over important offices in the Temple and abused their position there through nepotism and oppression. A folksong preserved in Talmudic literature relates the corruption of these priests:

Woe is me because of the House of Boethus,
 woe is me because of their slaves.
Woe is me because of the House of Hanan,
 woe is me because of their incantation.
Woe is me because of the *House of Kathros*,
 woe is me because of their pens.
Woe is me because of the House of Ishmael, son of
 Phiabi,
 woe is me because of their fists.
For they are the High Priests, and their sons are
 treasurers, and their sons-in-law are trustees,
 and their servants beat the people with staves."
 (Babylonian Talmud, Pesahim 57, 1=Tosefta,
 Minhot 13, 21)

This refrain gives vent to the groanings of a people under the oligarchic rule of a priesthood that used any means to further its own interests. Apparently, each of the priestly families mentioned here practiced its own form of oppression: the one through a sharp tongue, the next through a sharp pen, and most of them through simple brute force. The members of the "House of Kathros," who are accused of misusing the written word, were infamous for their libelous slander.

It can be assumed that our Bar Kathros was a scion of this same Kathros family. He lived in the same period, and his name—not a common one—was unknown outside that family. (The word *bar*, literally "son of," without a personal name before it, indicates that the name here is a family name rather than that of an actual father.) The house in which his inscription was found is situated opposite the Temple Mount, in a neighborhood that was populated by the nobility of Jerusalem.

We have defined a small room (6) at the northern edge of the Burnt House as a kitchen. This room, too, was entirely burnt out during the fire. Near its northern wall was a crude hearth of small fieldstones, built in two parts. The left-hand section contained a round pottery oven.

A unique find came to light near the doorway on the east, where more of the wall was destroyed than at any other spot. Leaning against the preserved fragment of the wall were the skeletal remains of the lower arm and hand of a human being, with the fingers still attached. The hand was spread out, grasping at a step. Dr. B. Ahrensburg, who examined these remains, determined that they

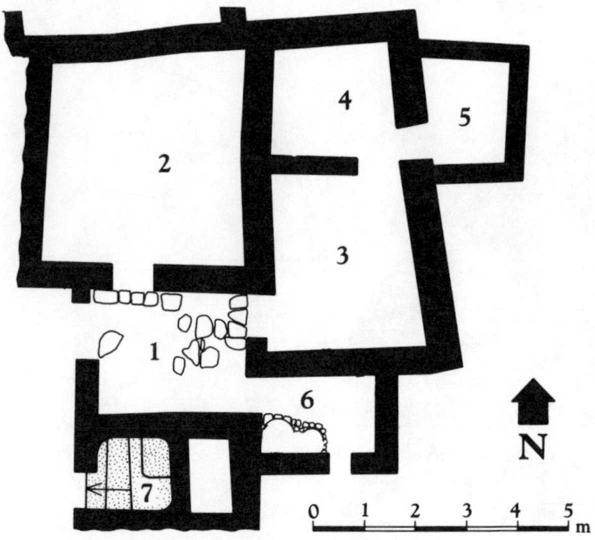

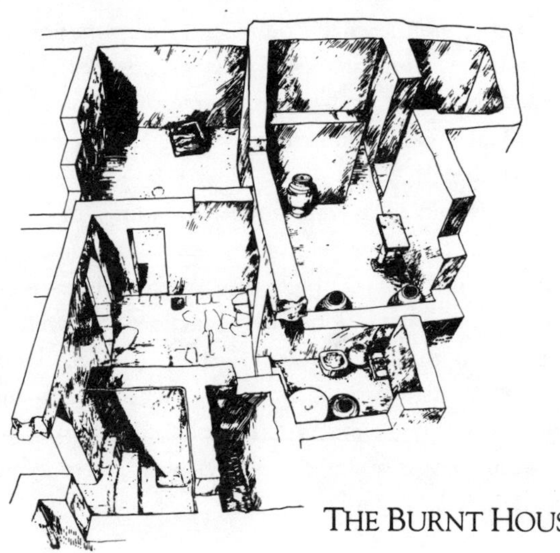

THE BURNT HOUSE

were of a woman in her early twenties. The associations conjured up by this spectacle were rather frightful. We could visualize a young woman working in the kitchen when the Roman soldiers burst into the house and put it to the torch. She tried to flee but collapsed near the doorway, only to perish in the flames. This arm seems to be the first and only human remains discovered so far that can definitely be associated with the great human tragedy that accompanied the destruction of Jerusalem in 70 A.D. This tangible evidence, surprising in its freshness and shocking in its realism, gave us the feeling that it had all happened only yesterday.

We are well aware of the events of this tragedy: The Romans captured the Temple and burnt it on the ninth of Ab (28 August, 70 A.D.), taking the Lower City at the same time. But the Upper City on the Western Hill, above the scarp facing the Temple Mount, held out stubbornly. On the eighth of Elul, a month after the Temple had been burnt, the Romans attacked the Upper City with full fury, taking it, setting the houses afire and slaughtering the inhabitants. Josephus describes the fighting in detail:

> Caesar, finding it impracticable to reduce the upper city without earthworks, owing to the precipitous nature of the site, on the twentieth of the month Lous [Ab] apportioned the task among his forces. The conveyance of timber was, however, arduous, all the environs of the city to a distance of a hundred furlongs having, as I said, been stripped bare. . . . The earthworks having now been completed after eighteen days' labor, on the seventh of the month Gorpiaeus [Elul], the Romans brought up the engines. Of the rebels, some already despairing of the city retired from the ramparts to the citadel, others slunk down into the tunnels. Pouring into the alleys, sword in hand, they [the Romans] massacred indiscriminately all whom they met, *and burnt the houses with all who had taken refuge within*. Often in the course of their raids, on entering the houses for loot, they would find whole families dead and the rooms filled with the victims of the famine. . . . Running everyone through who fell in their way, they choked the alleys with corpses and deluged the whole city with blood, insomuch that many of the fires were extinguished by the gory stream. Towards evening they ceased slaughtering, but when night fell the fire gained the mastery, *and the dawn of the eighth day of the month Gorpiaeus [Elul] broke upon Jerusalem in flames*—a city which had suffered such calamities. . . . The Romans now set fire to the outlying quarters of the town and razed the walls to the ground. Thus was Jerusalem taken in the second year of the reign of Vespasian, on the eighth of the month Gorpiaeus [20 September, 70 A.D.].

(*The Jewish War* VI, 8-10)

The story of the Burnt House, which so dramatically and vividly illustrates a most tragic and fateful chapter in the history of Jerusalem, thus comes to an end. But although the house met its end, the story itself is actually not yet complete, for in our own days, two thousand years later, when the descendants of the slaughtered returned to the site, they uncovered the physical traces of the destruction and rebuilt their homes over the ruins. Now they too, like Bar Kathros, can look out through their windows and see the Temple Mount, where the "previous tenant" had apparently worshipped. History has repeated itself. We hope that no other folksong beginning with the refrain "woe is me" will ever be heard here again.

This article has been adapted from Chapter Three, section 5, of *Discovering Jerusalem: Recent Archaeological Excavations in the Upper City* by Nahman Avigad (Thomas Nelson Publishers: Nashville, 1983). Printed by permission of Thomas Nelson Publishers.

In the first article of this section, Hershel Shanks discusses the severe criticisms raised against the Temple Mount excavations directed by Benjamin Mazar and Meir Ben-Dov. Some of the initial criticisms were religiously motivated; they emerged in the politically charged atmosphere following Israel's occupation of Jerusalem's Old City in the Six-Day War of 1967, when many people's sentiments were strongly pro-Israeli or pro-Arab.

It remains one of the hazards of practicing archaeology in the Near East that religious or political factors—sometimes both—can lead to misunderstanding and even disruption of the archaeological process.

This does not diminish, however, the seriousness of the charges raised concerning faulty archaeological methods employed in the Temple Mount excavations. The complaints by other excavators, as listed in the article, were that the digging was done too fast (not allowing for adequate controls or recording), that it uncovered too much (not preserving any undisturbed deposits for future investigation which could employ more sophisticated methods) and that it used equipment too gross for careful work (bulldozers!).

Dan Cole and others of the Gezer excavation staff, while on an official visit, observed digging by teams of novice volunteers using big picks without a supervisor in sight. Pottery was being saved in boxes labeled not by some discrete locus but by the day and general area.

These criticisms do not simply reflect archaeologists' preferences for using this or that methodology. They point out flagrant disregard for basic archaeological standards as developed and used for a decade prior.

There is a serious ethical issue involved here, and it applies as much to the "scholar" directors of "authorized" excavations as to the weekend pothunter or the professional tomb robber. Ancient remains in the soil are part of our common heritage—and potentially the heritage of our children's children. We cannot investigate that heritage without at least partially dismantling the context in which it lies buried. Archaeology is a destructive process. It is also nonreversible, once we remove something we cannot put it back. As Darrell Lance used to warn new volunteers at the Gezer excavations in the mid-1960s, "If you blow it here, you've blown it for all eternity!"

By the late 1960s, work being done in Israel and Jordan by numerous British, American and Israeli scholars reflected the developing awareness of two archaeological imperatives: (1) Materials should be separated as carefully as possible according to the soil layer or installation in which they are found. That will generally necessitate small teams using small hand-tools under close supervision. (2) Meticulous recording should make it possible to reconstruct on paper each architectural element in its exact relationship to other materials and the exact context from which each object comes. That will normally necessitate a supervisor in regular attendance in each area making close separations of digging loci and taking frequent three-dimensional measurements to be entered on a daily top-plan and in an ongoing notebook. A third imperative had already been articulated by some scholars: (3) Digging should not extend beyond what is necessary to answer the legitimate questions of the current project. Some of the archaeologically significant area should be left for the future, when digging controls and analytical techniques are further refined.

Turning to other matters, Meir Ben-Dov's speculations on the sources of Herod's wealth drew the following comment from another Israeli archaeologist, Magen Broshi, in **BAR**, July/August 1987:

> Meir Ben-Dov suggests two reasons for Herod's ample supply of manpower: hydraulic engineering and metal forging. Application of these technologies, according to Ben-Dov, saved labor and thus freed farm hands to be employed in Herod's gigantic enterprises.
>
> It is easy to show that hydraulic technology, i.e., irrigation, achieves just the opposite effect: it requires *more* labor, not less. Irrigation adds new areas to the cultivated land, new tracts that were never tilled or which had lain fallow; therefore, more farm hands are needed. Moreover, multiple cropping (the use of the same field for two or more crops successively in the same year), introduced by irrigation, demands much more labor than dry farming. In the 1920s an Arab fellah in the Jezreel Valley invested only 147 working days a year in his dry farm (75 by his wife, 31 by his children). [G. Stanhill, "The Fellah's Farm: an Autarkic Agro-system," *Agro-Ecosystem* 4 (1978), p. 438.] Multiple cropping, in contradistinction, is labor-intensive and occupies the farmer all year round.
>
> But even if Ben-Dov were right about the technology, it should be observed that irrigation never played a significant role in the agriculture of ancient Palestine. It is true that Herod and his successors developed the irrigation of the oasis of Jericho, but in almost all other parts of the country (except the Beth Shean area) irrigation was almost of negligible significance. In the hills west of Jerusalem only 0.6% of the total area of the terraces were irrigated in antiquity. In the Hebron Mountains today only 0.28% of farmed land is irrigated. In antiquity, the figures must have been similar. [Z.Y.D. Ron, "Development and Management of Irrigation System in Mountain Regions of the Holy Land," *Transactions of the Inst. of British Geographers*, N.S. 10 (1985), pp. 149-151.]
>
> Ben-Dov's iron-forging theory is also ill-founded. Iron tools were used in the country for over a thousand years before Herod, and from the very beginning we find implements of good—and often very good—quality. [Cf. J.D. Muhly, "How

Iron Technology Changed the Ancient World—And Gave the Philistines a Military Edge," **BAR**, November/December 1982, and Vol. I, p. 228.] The truth is that we have no information on labor-saving iron technology in the Roman period.

> A partial answer to the ample availability of Herod's manpower can be found in the fact that dry farming occupies the farmer only part-time—sometimes less than half a year. As a great deal of Herod's building was done by non-professionals (e.g., hauling the stones), this must have been done by peasants who sought employment in their free time.

Meir Ben-Dov replied in the same issue:

> To answer Mr. Magen Broshi seriously I would need to write another book! But even so, just to refer to the main points he raised, this would be my argument:
>
> 1. Agricultural Economics: To compare farming in the Herodian period with the Arab fellahin of the 19th century is irrelevant, to say the least. The standard of living of the Jewish farmer in the Herodian period was much higher than that of the fellahin. Suffice it to say that the Jewish farmer of those days was obligated to educate his children and pay for it himself. In order to support this standard of living, a farmer had to be resourceful. If a comparison is to be made, a better one would be to the modern Israeli agriculturalist. In other words: When using one's brains, the land will respond!
>
> 2. Water Supply: Engineering during the Herodian period reached its peak. The Arab farmer, especially of the 19th century, never achieved this level. In Palestine as well as in Babylon, the written sources (such as the Mishnah and the Talmud) support this thesis.
>
> 3. Iron Technology: Highly developed iron technology is reflected in the products of the Herodian period—tunneling, quarrying, stone-dressing, rock-cut tombs, the Temple Mount itself and thousands of pillars in places like Jerusalem and Caesarea. All this demonstrates highly skilled iron technology. The Roman army, as reflected in its weaponry and chariots, demonstrates the same skill and the same high technology.

This exchange demonstrates that even scholars can sometimes resort to weak arguments when drawn into debate; let the reader beware!

As Ben-Dov points out, Broshi has argued about irrigation here by analogy to agricultural practices of a vastly different era without establishing why the early 20th-century (not 19th as Ben-Dov carelessly states) and Herodian periods in Palestine should be treated as at all comparable. Simply saying that "the figures must have been similar" does not automatically turn the figures into evidence.

It is not necessarily "irrelevant, to say the least" (as Ben-Dov charges) to refer to modern studies of traditional cultural practices in trying to assess conditions of an earlier era. The potential insight from such information is better than relying on mere speculation. Broshi has here called attention to studies of recent-era farming practices that might, in fact, be worth considering. Unfortunately, he applies them to the Herodian period simplistically and dogmatically. Ben-Dov has responded in equally dogmatic fashion, dismissing Broshi's observations out-of-hand and countering with his own oversimplified "evidence" that the Herodian-era farmer had a higher standard of living. If, in fact, "the Jewish farmer of those days was obligated to educate his children and pay for it himself" (we are not given a source), it remains to be determined, (a) how rigorously such a regulation was observed or enforced, (b) how much education was deemed adequate, (c) how great or modest was the expense involved and, finally, (d) whether this regulation should be seen as evidence of farmers' level of prosperity or as a further form of oppressive taxation holding them in poverty. Ben-Dov, like Broshi, asserts rather than marshalling clearly relevant evidence.

Other logical lapses can be observed in both letters, but the most critical flaw in both scholars' arguments is their failure to consider the conditions of autocratic rule. For Herodian Palestine, the most important factors in the economic equation are likely to have been Herod's insatiable ambition and his ability to impose taxes and conscript labor. Indeed, if we are going to engage in speculation, it is as easy to suggest that it was neither "abundance of capital" nor surplus of workers with "free time" that resulted in Herod's building projects, but rather that it was Herod's driving ambition for his building projects, which led to heavy taxation and conscription of laborers which, in turn, might well have forced on farmers the *need* to squeeze more income from their soil through such methods as extensive irrigation.

For Further Reading

Concerning the Temple Mount

Benjamin Mazar, "Excavations Near Temple Mount Reveal Splendors of Herodian Jerusalem," **BAR**, July/August 1980

Murray Stein, "How Herod Moved Gigantic Blocks to Construct Temple Mount," **BAR**, May/June 1981

Michael A. Zimmerman, "Tunnel Exposes New Areas of Temple Mount," **BAR**, May/June 1981

James Fleming, "The Undiscovered Gate Beneath Jerusalem's Golden Gate," **BAR**, January/February 1983

Aaron Demsky, "When the Priests Trumpeted the Onset of the Sabbath," **BAR**, November/December 1986

Concerning Jerusalem in the Roman Period

Nachman Avigad, "How the Wealthy Lived in Herodian Jerusalem," **BAR**, December 1976

Magen Broshi, "Estimating the Population of Ancient Jerusalem," **BAR**, June 1978

Rivka Gonen, "Keeping Jerusalem's Past Alive," **BAR**, July/August 1981

Ehud Netzer, "Herod's Family Tomb in Jerusalem," **BAR**, May/June 1983

Menahem Magen, "Recovering Roman Jerusalem—The Entryway Beneath Damascus Gate," **BAR**, May/June 1988

Caesarea and Herodium— Reflections of Herod's Other Mighty Works

Recent investigations of Herod's extensive building projects outside of Jerusalem give us further graphic evidence of his extraordinary ability, his ambition and his energy.

Robert Bull's article, "Caesarea Maritima—The Search for Herod's City," encapsulates the results of the first decade (1971-1981) of the continuing excavations at what has proved to be a major port city built by Herod where previously there had not even been a modest harbor.

Without some reflection, the reader might not appreciate several very important elements in the work by Bull and his associates at Caesarea that make this report as comprehensive and clear as it is. Herod's city proved to be a huge one, spreading out over 164 acres; its Byzantine successor grew to extend five miles along the waterfront and two and a half miles inland. Digging at such a huge site and investigating it by modern painstaking standards, there had to be first of all a well-defined research design. Digging could not proceed randomly or simply extend from trench to trench in the expectation of uncovering a whole city. A deliberate listing in advance of what questions were most important was necessary, and intelligent decisions had to be made about where answers to those questions might most likely be found. Then, excavating teams had to be efficiently deployed, selectively uncovering only enough elements of a building complex or wall or street system to interpret it relevantly and to determine its extent; after that, moving on to the next project. The research design then had to be reconsidered and refined each year on the basis of the most recent season's discoveries. Only in this manner was it possible to glean so much information about so extensive a site after only a decade of summer field seasons.

Robert Hohlfelder's report on "Caesarea Beneath the Sea" and the following year's report by Lindley Vann, "Herod's Harbor Construction Recovered Underwater," carry a double impact. They provide dramatic evidence for the ambitious nature of Herod's harbor installations at Caesarea, and they give some idea of the tremendous contribution that underwater investigators have begun to make in the archaeological enterprise. Vann's reconstruction of the process used by Herod's marine engineers to pour massive concrete blocks on the sea floor as much as 1,500 feet from shore makes exciting reading, both as a reflection of ancient technical prowess and as a reflection of modern underwater detective work.

The last selection, Ehud Netzer's report of "Searching for Herod's Tomb," takes us into the desolate Judean wilderness southeast of Jerusalem to view a completely different kind of Herodian building complex: a fortress-palace erected for his personal use and—if we can trust Josephus—as his final resting place. While Netzer's primary focus in the article is on his unsuccessful search for Herod's tomb, he also provides us with a good view of the opulence of one of Herod's private royal retreats. As Netzer notes, in its size alone Herodium's 45-acre expanse was exceeded in ancient Mediterranean private complexes only by the later Hadrian's Villa (at Tivoli, near Rome) and by Nero's palace at Rome.

C·A·E·S·A·R·E·A

THE SEARCH FO

M·A·R·I·T·I·M·A
HEROD'S CITY

BY ROBERT J. BULL

Herod, the ancient world's master builder, constructed a magnificent port city on the Mediterranean coast of Palestine. He called it Caesarea in honor of his Roman patron Augustus Caesar. Maritima distinguished it from the many other cities that bore this much honored name, notably Caesarea Philippi, another city in Herod's kingdom, located inland at the source of the Jordan River.

Overleaf: *Still standing on the beach north of Caesarea, the graceful arches carrying the water channels of the high-level aqueduct are reminders of the grandeur of this ancient city. Built in two sections parallel along their lengths, the aqueduct is seen here from the west. Inscriptions found on this western channel (see p. 114) tell us that this channel was built by the soldiers of the Roman legions commanded by Hadrian in the second century A.D. Photo by Charles O'Gorman/Scanner*

According to the first century historian Josephus, who left us a detailed description, the port of Caesarea Maritima was as large as Piraeus, the port of Athens. If so, Caesarea was one of the two or three largest ports on the Mediterranean, indeed in the world.

The port of Caesarea was all the more remarkable because it was located on a 40-mile length of the Mediterranean shore that had no natural harbor, bay or inlet. The Mediterranean coast in the area of Caesarea is an uninterrupted line of sand and cliffs. Here, for the first time in history, Herod constructed a port on the open sea without benefit of any natural features whatever.

Herod chose the site precisely because the coast was so inhospitable to navigation. Commercial vessels of the period, for the most part, had to sail before the wind in the manner of square-rigged ships. To use nautical language, they could not sail very close to the wind or tack with ease. Moreover, ancient pilots used headlands and structures along the coastline to take their bearings. The stars, widely used at this time by desert travelers to determine direction, were only of secondary use to coastal shipping. Commercial vessels stayed close to shore not only to gain their bearings but also to take advantage of the breezes generated by the land. The prevailing winds in the eastern Mediterranean are out of the southwest, and it is from that direction that most storms come. This prevailing wind, combined with a strong north-flowing current, could make any trip along the eastern Mediterranean coast difficult.

The dangers of sailing along this coast were well-known, of course, since this was the route of the long-established Phoenician-Egyptian run. In a storm, a vessel sailing this coast would find itself wind-driven toward shore, its course affected by the strong in-shore current, and in danger of shipwreck on the sands. The ship's master could either drop anchor and attempt to ride out the storm, or put into a nearby harbor at the first sign of heavy weather—if there was a harbor nearby.

Between Dor (Dora) 8 miles north of Caesarea, and Jaffa (Joppa), 32 miles south, lay a 40-mile stretch of inhospitable Mediterranean coastline without any natural haven for ships. Josephus describes how vessels on their way to Egypt "had to ride at anchor in the open, when menaced by the southwest wind; for even a moderate breeze from this quarter dashes the water to such a height against the cliffs that their reflux spread a wild commotion far out to sea."[1] Caesarea, built from scratch, provided such a haven.

The site Herod chose for his harbor had been a small village, probably built in the fourth century B.C., but by Herod's time, it was dilapidated and in ruins. According to the limited literary sources that have survived, the little Hellenistic village was called Strato's (Straton's) Tower, after what may have been a prominent structure used by navigators. The Greek geographer Strabo reported a small ship's landing at Strato's Tower, but little else is known about it.

Herod, on the other hand, built on a grand scale. That is how he did everything. And at Caesarea, "as nowhere else," Josephus tells us, "[Herod] displayed the innate grandeur of his character."[2]

The centerpiece of Caesarea was of course its harbor. Out from the shore for a distance of one-third of a mile, Herod built a great stone breakwater more than 200 feet wide. This breakwater, located on the southern side of the harbor, curved to the north at the seaward end and formed the major protection of the harbor against the storms out of the southwest. A smaller, less massive stone mole extended out 800 feet from the shore on the northern side of the harbor to a point only about 60 feet away from the return curve of the southern breakwater. This opening is thought to mark the location of the northern entrance into the harbor mentioned by Josephus. Both mole and breakwater have long since been destroyed by earthquake action, but their outline underwater against the white sand of the Mediterranean Sea bottom can be seen from an airplane overhead. Clearly visible is the opening that marks the northern harbor entrance. (See picture on p. 127.)*

In 1960, the Link Mission for Underwater Exploration excavated the remains of this ancient Herodian harbor and found that the area encircled by the two breakwaters was about 3½ acres. Josephus, with his customary eye for detail, tells us that the blocks of stone used to construct the breakwater were 50 feet long, 18 feet wide and 10 feet high; they had to be let down in water 120 feet deep. Lofty towers adorned the wall creating the mole.

> "Numerous inlets in the wall provided landing places for mariners putting into the harbor, and the whole circular terrace fronting these channels provided a broad promenade for disembarking passengers . . . at the harbor mouth stood colossal statues, three on either side, standing on columns."[3]

The city itself matched the harbor. It was built largely of

*An article by Robert L. Hohlfelder about the underwater archaeological excavations of Herod's harbor at Caesarea starts on page 124.

imported white marble, pursuant to a "magnificent plan" devised by Herod. The city took between 10 and 12 years to build[4] and was inaugurated in 13/12 B.C. The city included a palace, civil halls, an amphitheater, a hippodrome for athletic events, a system of aqueducts, warehouse vaults, sea-flushed sewers and a high defense wall surrounding the city. On a height facing the harbor Josephus described a temple dedicated to Rome and Augustus (Caesar Augustus). The temple was "remarkable for its beauty and grand proportions; it contained a colossal statue of the emperor, not inferior to the Olympian Zeus which served as its model."

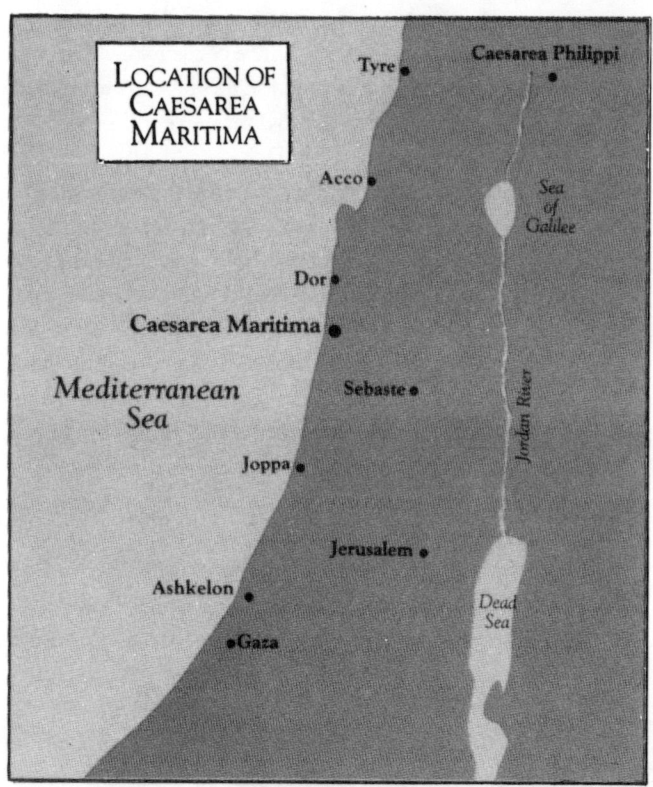

Students of near eastern archaeology are accustomed to finding ancient cities buried in tells, those flat top mounds with steep sides containing one city upon another in stratified layers. Most of these tells vary in size between 10 acres and 50 acres.

Caesarea is different. The visitor will find no easily observable tell. And the city itself is vast. The Herodian city contained about 164 acres. After Herod's death, the city expanded far beyond the Herodian city wall. During the time of the *pax Romana*, a defense wall was no longer considered necessary to protect the city against invaders. Roman legions on the borders of the empire provided protection enough. As a result, the city spread out laterally along the coast and inland beyond the Herodian wall.

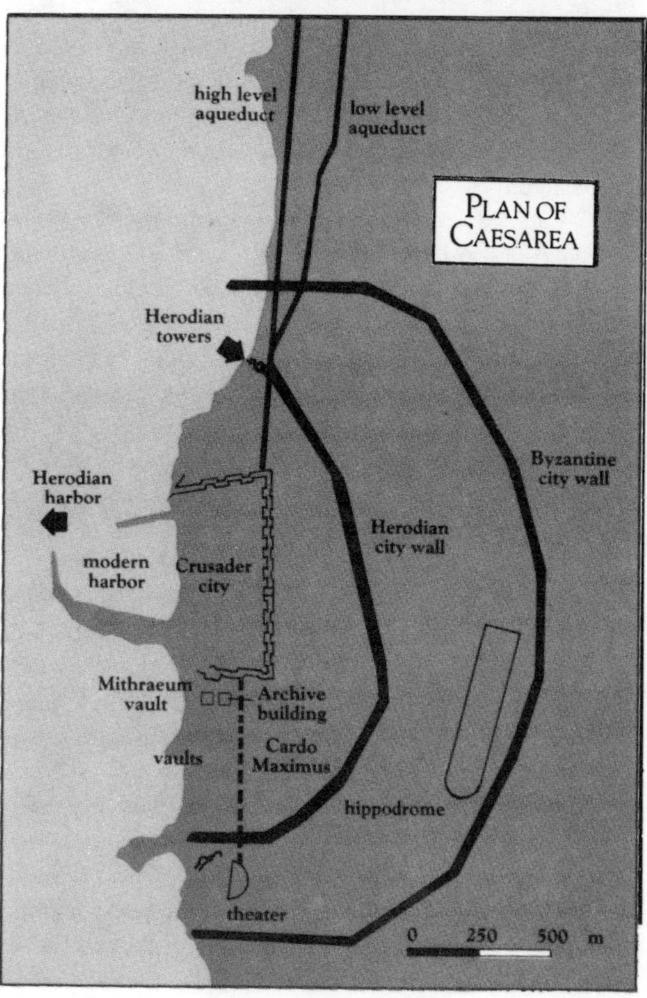

In the Byzantine period (seventh century) a defense wall was again built around the inner city. This was the defense wall of the city in 639/40 A.D. when Caesarea was conquered by the Moslems, but by that time Caesarea had already expanded about five miles along the coast and as much as two and one half miles inland.

The absence of a tell in the traditional sense does not mean, however, that there are no stratified remains at Caesarea. On the contrary, our excavations have uncovered nine different major strata in the city. Previous excavators have also uncovered a number of strata.

Herod died in 4 B.C. Shortly afterward, in 6 A.D., the Romans annexed Judea and chose Caesarea as the seat of the provincial Roman administration. Roman Procurators charged with the administration of taxation and with overseeing civil affairs of the province resided in, and governed from, Caesarea. The Roman Procurators established local courts in Caesarea and recruited detachments of auxiliary legionnaires from the local population. These troops were garrisoned and supplied at Caesarea. The mint of Caesarea under Roman license struck bronze coins to pay the troops. The coins were also widely used as exchange in the rapidly developing economy.

Except for a brief period (41-44 A.D.) when Herod Agrippa became a client king, like his grandfather Herod, and governed Judea from Jerusalem, the seat of government remained at Caesarea. It was from Caesarea that the province of Judea, later the province of Syria-Palestina, was governed without interruption for the next six centuries, that is, during the Roman and Byzantine Periods—until the Moslem conquest in 639/40 A.D.

Caesarea figures prominently in several events in The New Testament. In the book of Acts it is said that Philip, one of seven evangelists sent out of Jerusalem to preach in all the towns, completed his tour, and settled in Caesarea. His presence marks the first continuous leadership of the Christian community in Caesarea. His arrival may have occurred at the time when Pontius Pilate was still Procurator. In Acts 10, Cornelius, a converted centurion in the Italian Cohort stationed at Caesarea, sent to Joppa for Peter. Peter responded to his call and then preached in Caesarea to a gathered community of relatives and friends in the house of Cornelius. This incident is the first recorded preaching of the gospel to the gentiles. Paul visited the Christian community at Caesarea after a sea voyage from Ephesus at the end of his second missionary journey (Acts 18:22). Later, Paul was arrested in Jerusalem and was sent to Caesarea for safekeeping. He was imprisoned for two years in Herod's palace in the area reserved for the Procurator Felix. His case was heard by King Herod Agrippa. Paul, as a Roman citizen, appealed to Caesar in Rome and was sent there by ship from the Caesarea harbor (Acts 23-27). Little else is known of the development of the Christian church in Caesarea after that time until the early third century.

Caesarea was, however, the scene of some bloody preliminaries to the Roman destruction of Jerusalem in 70 A.D. At that time, Caesarea was a polyglot city of Jews, Christians, Samaritans, and gentiles, Greeks and Syrians, each group living in separate city districts. A disagreement between the Jews and Greeks over access to a synagogue in a gentile district of Caesarea led to open conflict and the subsequent desecration of the synagogue. Besides their frequent conflict with Roman subjects resident in Caesarea, Jews were often subject to Roman persecution.

The Jews found themselves increasingly at odds with their Roman rulers. Soon after the conflict over the desecration of the synagogue, word leaked out that soldiers of the Caesarea garrison, attempting to put down a Jewish insurrection in Jerusalem, had plundered the Temple treasury. The Jews of Caesarea attacked Roman troops garrisoned in the city. The troops responded, killing 20,000 Caesarea Jews. This atrocity catalyzed the First Jewish Revolt (66-70 A.D.), which ended in the Roman destruction of the Jerusalem Temple and the burning of the city. Vespasian, who directed the suppression of the revolt until he became emperor, made his headquarters and supply base at Caesarea. Titus, operating with supplies from Caesarea, completed the job left unfinished by Vespasian and after five months captured Jerusalem. Titus returned to Caesarea with Jewish captives. During the festivals and games held at Caesarea to celebrate his victory, 2,500 Jews lost their lives in gladitorial sports in the Caesarea amphitheater.

Vespasian, in gratitude for the support Caesarea had given him in suppressing the Jewish revolt, granted the city the status of a Roman colony.

Sixty years later, a second Jewish revolt against Roman rule broke out. Again the Roman legions were supplied from Caesarea. This time, however, Jerusalem was leveled. On its remains, the limits of a new city were marked out by a plowed furrow and the name of the city was changed to Aelia Capitolina. The Tenth Roman Legion was then stationed on the site. With the complete destruction of Jerusalem, Caesarea's place as chief city and capital of Palestine was secure. The governor of the Province of Judea was raised to senatorial rank and Caesarea became the capital of the Roman Province of Syria-Palestina.

Caesarea continued to grow in size, wealth and prestige during the second, third and fourth centuries. Prices were low, food was plentiful, gardens abounded, and public incense burners sent the aroma of spice floating on the evening air.

The Biblical theologian Origen (185-254) taught daily for 23 years at Caesarea. Here he established a major library and wrote extensively. His biographer said that in his lifetime Origen wrote 6,000 works. One of these was the *Hexapla*, a six-column comparative text of the Old Testament in fifty volumes. This early effort to arrive at a critical Biblical text widely influenced the early church, but unfortunately, apart from a few quotations, it is now lost. The church historian Eusebius (263-339), a friend and advisor of the emperor Constantine, also wrote extensively, utilizing the 30,000 volume library at Caesarea begun by Origen. When the Emperor Constantine ordered 50 Bibles to be copied for the new churches of the empire they were copied in the *scriptorum* at Caesarea. In the last years of his life Eusebius was bishop of the city in which he was born.

At about the same time that Origen first taught at Caesarea, Rabbi Hoshaya (d. 250) founded a school for the study of Judaism which produced a succession of outstanding rabbis including the famous Rabbi Abbahu.

After the fourth century, the literary record of Caesarea is almost nonexistent. In 614 A.D. the city was overrun by the Persians, and in 639/640 A.D. Caesarea was captured by the Moslem forces that conquered the whole of the middle east and north Africa. Cut off from the west and the long-established religious, commercial and intellectual contacts, Caesarea began a slow decline, becoming a village living in the remains of an ornate city.

Then the village became a quarry. The marble of its

walls, the statues of its streets were burned for lime. The village residents were farmers who needed lime for crops rather than palaces and ornate decoration. The marble and the Aswan granite of Caesarea were mined to build cities elsewhere. In order to transport these huge stone and marble blocks, a ramp and shallow-draft wharf were built in the harbor—made from the magnificent Corinthian columns. They were laid three-deep by the hundreds in the silted harbor so that the heavy stones could be moved to the sea and shipped to Acco.

In 1251 A.D. the Crusaders built a fortified city at the harbor. The wall of that city remains a major Caesarea monument to this day.

In 1884 Moslem refugees from Bosnia established a colony on the remains of the Crusader city. Their mosque can still be seen inside the Crusader walls.

Before we began our excavations in 1971 a number of ancient structures were visible in addition to the fortress walls of the Crusader city and the mosque of the Bosnian refugees inside. Perhaps the most famous is the Caesarea aqueduct. It has been romantically portrayed on a hundred tourist brochures. Actually there are several aqueducts that supplied water to the city in various periods of its existence.

The most famous aqueduct, however, is the so-called high-level aqueduct which, as it approaches the city, is supported on a 6½-mile line of arches. This aqueduct, upon close examination, will be seen to consist of two aqueducts joined together side by side, both originating at a spring near the foot of the Carmel range northeast of the city. Since the spring water was not of sufficient volume to supply the two water channels, a search for additional water was made in the limestone foothills east of Mt. Carmel. About 10 miles due east of Caesarea, a farmer showed us a shaft 8 feet by 5 feet by about 33 feet deep, hewn at a steep angle into the side of the limestone hill. Down the shaft ran a series of steps and at the bottom of the shaft was a rock-hewn tunnel approximately 3½ feet by 4 feet which ran eastward from the bottom of the shaft. Pick marks on the sides of the tunnel ran in two directions, indicating that the tunnel was cut by teams working in both directions. On the walls are niches for oil lamps that lit the tunnel as work progressed. This tunnel, cut some 6 miles through the limestone of the hills east of Caesarea, taps a water collection point 10 miles east of the city and conducts that water along a circuitous but constantly declining channel until it joins the high level aqueduct on the side of Mt. Carmel. The aqueduct then carries the water another 6½ miles into the city. In short, Caesarea was supplied with an aqueduct nearly 13 miles long, half of which was a rock-hewn tunnel (for purposes of purity and security) and the other half of which was carried on a series of arches to the city.

Joint Expedition to Caesarea

Converging on the horizon *at the city of Caesarea, the high-level aqueduct and the low-level aqueduct appear as scars in the Mediterranean sand north of the ancient port. The high-level aqueduct is the prominent straight line to the right; it was probably first built by Herod when he founded Caesarea and then later enlarged by Hadrian in the second century to double its capacity. The water that flowed in the 6 1/2-mile-long high-level aqueduct came from springs deep in the flank of Mt. Carmel, over 12 miles from the city. The spring water was first carried for 6 miles through a rock-hewn tunnel* *(see p. 112)* *within the mountain; it then flowed into the high-level aqueduct to continue its journey to Caesarea.*

To the left of the high-level aqueduct is the fainter line of the much shorter low-level aqueduct. This fifth-century A.D. addition to Caesarea's water supply system brought less pure water to the city from a river 4 1/2 miles north of Caesarea. The water-carrying capacity of the high- and low-level aqueducts together indicates that in the fifth century, when both aqueducts were used, the demand for water of an enlarged Caesarea was five times the city's need in the second century.

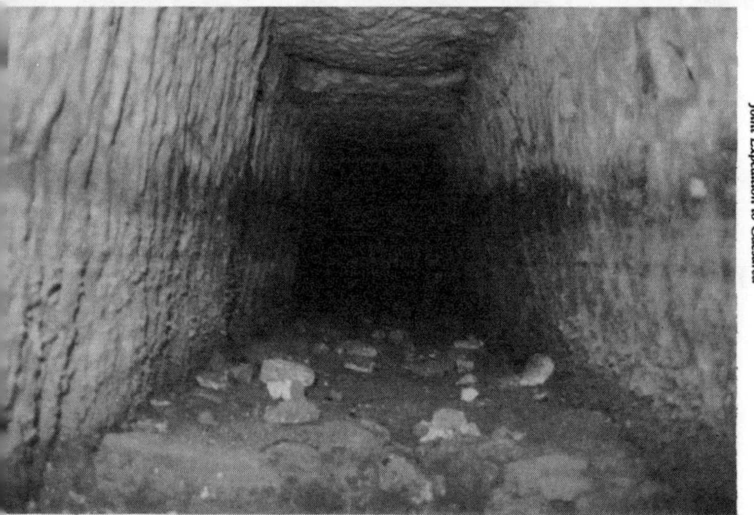

Joint Expedition to Caesarea

Herodian masons, ***working from opposite ends, cut this 6-mile-long tunnel through the bedrock of Mt. Carmel. At its eastern end it gathers the water of underground springs. At its western end it joins the eastern channel of the high-level aqueduct that carries the water south an additional 6 1/2 miles along the shore to its destination at Caesarea. Along the left-hand wall of the tunnel, above the dark line, a series of niches in the rock are visible. These held oil lamps to illuminate the tunnel as masons chiseled away the limestone.***

A second aqueduct, the low-level aqueduct, has its source in a river 4½ miles north of the city. This aqueduct, dated by pottery taken from beneath its concrete foundation, was in use in the fifth century. The volume of water carried in each of the aqueducts has been calculated and indicates that in the fifth century the water demand of the growing city was about five times as much as it had been in the second century.

Experts agree that the high-level aqueduct is the older. Was the high-level aqueduct built by Herod? The difficulty in providing a definitive answer is illustrative of the difficulty encountered time and again in deciding what parts of the ancient remains at Caesarea were actually built by Herod and what parts were built later. The London-based Palestine Exploration Fund examined the high-level aqueduct in 1873 and attributed it to Herod himself, largely on the ground that Herod must have built an aqueduct to supply the city with water. Since then, several formal Latin inscriptions have been found on the western face of the western aqueduct that have led some scholars to date the structure to Hadrian's reign (117 A.D.-138 A.D.). These inscriptions contain references to Roman legions that served in Caesarea at that time and according to one inscription "the Emperor Caesar Trianus Hadrianus Augustus made it." The Latin word is *fecit,* which means make or build, and seems to refer to original construction rather than to a repair.

The fact that the high-level aqueduct consists of two distinctly different but adjacent aqueducts helps to solve the dating problem. Investigations by an Italian team in 1961 and by Abraham Negev of the Israeli Department of Antiquities in 1964 showed that the two channels of the high-level aqueduct were built independently. The eastern aqueduct was finished on both sides. Later the western one, the one toward the sea, was added, and was, according to the inscriptions, built by Hadrian. The eastern aqueduct was built earlier. It was probably built by Herod. In 1975, our excavation team made several attempts to date the eastern aqueduct by carefully digging beside it in an effort to find the trench in which the builders of the aqueduct would have laid the foundations of the arches. Unfortunately, we were unable to define the outline of the trenches or to recover any datable material.

However, our excavation team was able to locate the foundation and the foundation trench of another structure, the great defense wall built by Herod as part of his city plan. Beneath the wall and within the trench located 650 meters (one-third mile) north of the harbor, we uncovered pottery dating to the Herodian period.

Caesarea's imposing theater, almost half a mile south of the harbor, is very likely Herodian. Josephus refers to a theater built by Herod. Today this theater still commands a magnificent view of the sea. How much of the existing structure is original and how much is reconstruction is difficult to tell.

The theater was completely uncovered by an Italian excavation team at Caesarea between 1959 and 1963. Clearly, it underwent extensive repairs and alterations during the 400 or 500 years when it was in use. The stage was renovated, vaulted entrances were added, and ornamental capitals, lintels and cornices were built into existing architectural elements. It has now been restored and reconstructed, so that it can be, and is, used for concerts by the Israeli Philharmonic and other world-renowned orchestras, ensembles and soloists. In the Herodian period, Greek and Roman classics were probably performed here. The theater

Carved into the bedrock *of Mt. Carmel, this stepped shaft led to springs deep within the western flank of the mountain. From the base of the shaft a rock-cut tunnel carried the spring water to the high-level aqueduct which transported the water to the city of Caesarea.*

Joint Expedition to Caesarea

is approximately 300 feet in diameter and accommodates about 4,000 people.

Finds from the theater excavation included a magnificent, many-breasted statue of Diana of Ephesus. But the most sensational find uncovered by the Italians in the course of their theater excavation was an inscription. In the theater steps a stone was found containing a Latin inscription naming "Pontius Pilate, Prefect of Judea." The inscription was originally a dedicatory plaque for a Tiberieum Pilate built. A Tiberieum was a structure—probably a temple or shrine—honoring the Emperor Tiberius. After the Tiberieum fell into disuse, the dedicatory plaque was used to repair one of the steps of the theater. This inscription is the only known lithic inscription referring to Pontius Pilate. It reads as follows: "Pontius Pilate, the Prefect of Judea, has dedicated to the people of Caesarea a temple in honor of Tiberius."

This broken portion *of the high-level aqueduct and the section drawing of it (below) show clearly that the aqueduct was built in two parts, side by side. We are looking at a vertical slice perpendicular to the length of the aqueduct. The outer lip of the right-hand (eastern) channel is broken away completely (see arrow in drawing in which it has been restored). Just below the point where this outer channel wall should be is a pointed protrusion that was part of a decorative cornice running along the length of the eastern channel. A matching cornice pointing to the left can be seen in the drawing below and circled in the photograph in the shadow of the vertical crack separating the eastern and western channels. This cornice, now hidden by the adjacent channel on the left (west) shows that both sides of the earlier eastern channel were finished and exposed to view until the later (western) channel was added in the second century.*

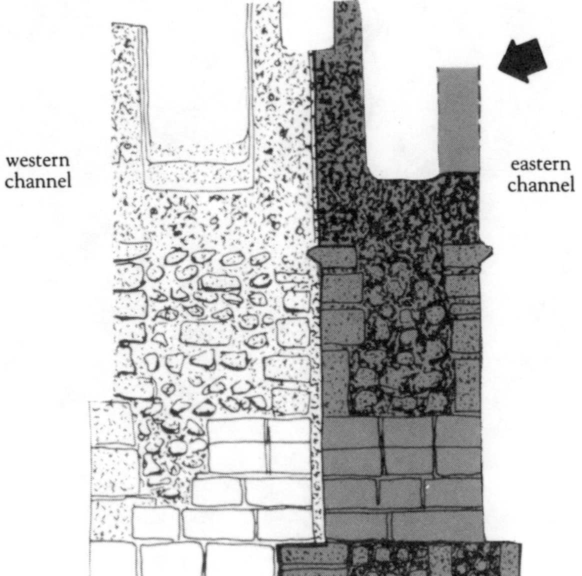

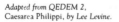

Adapted from QEDEM 2,
Caesarea Philippi, *by Lee Levine.*

Joint Expedition to Caesarea

Joint Expedition to Caesarea

Inscribed in Latin, *this stone identifying the builders of a section of the high-level aqueduct was found on the western channel of this aqueduct. It reads, "A detachment of Legion Ten Fretensis [dedicates its work] to Emperor Trajan Hadrian Augustus." Additional inscriptions naming the sixth and second Roman legions were found in other sections of the western aqueduct. It is likely that Roman soldiers serving Hadrian in about 130 A.D. were assigned to public works projects, such as building this additional 6½-mile-long western channel next to the existing eastern channel—a useful distraction for restless legionnaires.*

The hippodrome, used primarily for chariot racing, lies east of the harbor. It has been dated to the second century on the basis of the coins found in the earliest of five sand tracks in the area of the hippodrome. From the beginning, however, Caesarea was a center of sporting events in the Mediterranean world. Much of this activity—gymnastic exercises, boxing and wrestling matches—may have occurred in another structure, the amphitheater. The outline of this oval amphitheater, still unexcavated, can be seen from the air in the northeast section of the city. The huge hippodrome was approximately 1,500 feet long and over 250 feet wide and could seat as many as 38,000 people. Among the remains of the hippodrome are several Aswan granite *metae* or turning posts for the chariot races. An obelisk stood in the center of the field. Three large pieces of this obelisk now lie broken in the hippodrome. The obelisk, like the *metae,* was made of Aswan granite imported from 600 miles up the Nile River in Egypt. The obelisk may have stood as high as 72 feet.

Both a synagogue and the remains of several churches have been uncovered, evidence of the polyglot nature of the Caesarea population. The synagogue is located north of the wall enclosing the Crusader city and overlooks the sea. Like many structures at Caesarea, it was built and rebuilt several times. It was first built in the fourth century A.D.,

Joint Expedition to Caesarea

Joint Expedition to Caesarea

One of the most sensational *discoveries at Caesarea was this inscribed stone mentioning Pontius Pilate. Found in a step of the theater, it was originally part of a nearby temple honoring the emperor Tiberius. The stone was moved to the theater to repair a step after the temple fell into disuse. The Latin reads: "Pontius Pilate, the Prefect of Judea, has dedicated to the people of Caesarea a temple in honor of Tiberius."*

and was used until about the middle of that century. In the middle of the fifth century a new synagogue was built on the ruins. In the ruins of these buildings, excavators found mosaics, inscriptions, columns, and a hoard of 3,700 bronze coins from the mid-fourth century. A menorah, the seven-branched candelabrum, was found carved on a marble plaque as well as on the capitals of the columns. Several mold-made oil lamps bearing menorahs were also uncovered. A mosaic inscription contained a reference to the archisynagogus, an official like today's synagogue president. This inscription also mentions a *triclinium*, or Roman-style dining room that once was probably part of the synagogue.

Below the fourth-century synagogue was a square building that had originally been constructed as a residence. Herodian lamps, spindle-shaped bottles and so-called pseudo-Nabatean pottery suggested to excavators from the Israeli Department of Antiquities that the structure was of the Herodian period. Some of the walls of this building had been incorporated into the fourth-century synagogue. The excavators accordingly concluded that the Herodian residence had at an early stage been converted into a synagogue and served thereafter as a house-synagogue. This house-synagogue may have been the famous "Synagogue of the Revolt," as it is referred to in the Talmud, the center of the conflict described above that sparked the First Jewish Revolt against Rome (66 A.D.-70 A.D.)

Apart from the cathedral remains in the Crusader city and the so-called roofless church found northeast of the Byzantine defense walls, no church structure has been archaeologically defined at Caesarea. Our own expedition has uncovered fragments of two chancel screens from churches and a 2½-foot-long by 6-foot-high fresco of an assembly of 13 saints in a vault. But we have not found a structure we can demonstrate to be a church building.

The most prominent monument at the site, however, is the massive Crusader enceinte which enclosed Crusader Caesarea. Originally it enclosed the city on four sides, but on the seashore it has been almost completely washed away by erosion. While the Crusader ruins contain structures that date from early in the Crusades, the prominent visible remains today—the moat, escarpment, citadel and walls containing some sixteen towers—date from 1251 when King Louis IX of France spent a full year restoring the fortifications at Caesarea, the King himself assisting in the actual building.

Our excavations at Caesarea began in 1971 and are still continuing.[5] They are slow and painstaking, involve hundreds of volunteers and staff each year, and have barely scratched the surface, so to speak. This must therefore be considered a very preliminary report. Like previous investigators, we found remains from many periods.

Dramatic evidence for the varied religious character of Caesarea in the third century A.D. was uncovered on one occasion when we confidently expected to be excavating authentic Herodian construction. We were excavating south of the Crusader enceinte in a building near the sea, trying to understand the wall structure of a third-century

The tiers of stone seats *in the Herodian theater face the sea that laps against the beach directly to the west (lower left corner). By the sixth century, performances in the theater had ceased and the eastern side of the structure was incorporated into a fortress. A substantial portion of this fortress, identifiable by two round towers projecting from it, still extends toward the sea on the north side of the theater. Another incomplete tower may be seen projecting to the east (upper right). In the early '60's an Italian excavation cleared and restored the theater. Today audiences fill the ancient benches to hear performances by the Israel Philharmonic.*

building, when we hit a floor level consisting of a thick layer of hydraulic concrete, a waterproof cement. On top of the hydraulic concrete were four-inch-high limestone blocks set at regular intervals that served as supports for thick ceramic roof tiles. Traces of marble indicated that the tiles had once been covered with white marble sheets so that an elaborate marble floor 60 feet long and 15 feet wide covered the area. A series of columns too short to be roof-bearing columns was found on the remains of the floor. The columns bore inscriptions honoring hitherto unknown procurators of the third century A.D. On some were signs that they were once topped by sculpture. They seem to have been ranged along the sides of this structure. The evidence of the elaborate marble floor, columns, sculpture and inscriptions led us to name this structure the "Honorific Portico."

Under the marble floor in the Honorific Portico was an elaborate but puzzling drain. There is an aphorism among Near Eastern archaeologists which counsels, "The answer lies below." We decided to follow this advice in the hope of better understanding the drain and the Honorific Portico. Within a few hours we exposed a large barrel vault made of sandstone blocks. The vault was originally 96 feet long, 16½ feet wide, and 15 feet high, and oriented east and west. The huge vaulted room was two thirds filled with sand. Although the roof of the vault took only a few hours to uncover, we spent the next two years excavating the material deposited inside the vault.

It turned out to have been built, as we expected, as a warehouse for the Herodian harbor. The lowest courses of the vault rested on bedrock. We found embedded in the lowest floor level, which also rested on bedrock, huge quantities of amphorae fragments. Sometimes enough of a single one of these large storage jars was found so that it could be reconstructed. The amphorae dated to the first century and were typical of those used in trading vessels from Gaul,

A shaft of light *pierces the ceiling in the Mithraeum at Caesarea. Originally built by Herod in the first century B.C., this 96-foot-long vault was part of a huge seaside storage complex composed of, perhaps, 100 such vaults. This one was converted in the third century A.D. to a place where Romans could worship the god Mithra, an ancient deity of life and truth. Benches were built along the walls, a small square stone altar was placed in the area between the benches at the innermost end of the vault, and the walls were plastered and covered with frescoes. Now badly deteriorated, the frescoes depicted events in the life of Mithra. Once a year, at the time of the summer solstice, a shaft of sunlight passing through this hole in the vault roof would fall directly upon the altar. A beautiful marble medallion (see p. 118) bearing scenes from Mithra's life was found on the floor near the altar and helped to assure the excavators that they had indeed discovered a Mithraeum.*

Joint Expedition to Caesarea

Joint Expedition to Caesarea

This marble medallion, *found behind the altar in the Mithraeum at Caesarea, was a key to the identification of this vault as a third-century sanctuary for the worship of Mithra, an ancient deity of light and truth popular among Roman soldiers. Mithra (center left), slays the sacred bull (center right) on the upper panel of this marble medallion. Three other scenes from the life of Mithra appear across the lower panel: from left, Sol, the sun god, kneeling before Mithra; the banquet of Sol and Mithra; and Mithra riding a bull toward a reclining figure. The medallion is 7.5 cm in diameter and 1 cm thick.*

Italy, Spain and elsewhere in the western Mediterranean.

Some of the amphora handles had stamps impressed in them indicating that they had once contained *garum*, a kind of fish sauce. We also found coins in the beaten earth floor—dating from the time of Nero (54-68 A.D.) and probably minted at Caesarea. Clearly, we had uncovered a warehouse that had had heavy use in the first century A.D. and because it is part of a large complex of similar warehouses it can safely be called part of Herod's massive harbor installation.

Contiguous to this vault on the south side was another similar vault and beside these there were other vaults. These vaults were so filled with debris that exploration was hindered for lack of crawl space, as well as lack of oxygen and light. However, we did manage to measure 10 of the estimated 20 vaults in this block of vaults. We now believe that there are as many as five such blocks of vaults along the harbor front.

Seven of the western vaults in this block opened onto a paved road 18 feet wide that ran along the shore. Six other vaults opened onto roads that ran inland and later, as we shall see, helped us to understand the street system of Herodian Caesarea. Another seven vaults faced eastward and opened onto a road that was probably the main street of Caesarea, known in Caesarea as in other Roman towns, as the Cardo Maximus. Obviously these vaults constituted a huge warehouse complex and shipping installation dating from Herodian Caesarea.

This huge warehouse complex and the amphorae filled with goods bound for Italy and Spain are evidence that Caesarea was indeed a harbor rivaling Piraeus, an eastern terminus for traffic between the Mediterranean, Damascus, Arabia and beyond. The income from this trade, coupled with that derived from sea traffic calling at Caesarea on its way between Egypt and the northern Mediterranean coastal cities must have been enormous. Here we have an explanation for the source of the vast revenues Herod needed to finance his extensive building programs. Even though Herod taxed his subjects severely, the tax return from four million subjects living on what was primarily an agrarian economy could hardly account for the huge sums Herod used and gave away during his reign. Herod's lavish building activity was not confined to his own kingdom, where he built at least three cities, including Caesarea, a network of fortresses and palaces that ringed the kingdom of Judaea, as well as the Temple that stood resplendent in the center of it all at Jerusalem. His largesse extended to cities and colonies both east and west of Caesarea. He gave to Damascus a theater and a gymnasium; to Ashkelon, baths; to Tyre, a colonnade and fountains; to Beirut, temples and market places; to Laodica, an aqueduct; to Antioch, a colonnaded street; to Rhodes, a Pythian temple; and gifts to Cos, Samos, Pergamum and other cities, some as far away as Athens.

But let us return to the first storage vault we uncovered, the one under the Honorific Portico, that we completely excavated over a two-year period. The reader may be wondering how this vault evidenced the polyglot character of third-century Caesarea, as I earlier indicated. The fact is that the vaulted building had been built as a warehouse in the Herodian period, but it had been turned into a Mithraeum in the third century A.D. The walls of this vault had been plastered and were at one time completely covered with elaborate frescoes from the life of Mithra. The ceiling was painted blue. Beside the altar at the end of the vault were three scenes from the life of Mithra. Unfortunately, the frescoes were in a very poor state of preservation. When the old warehouse vault was converted into a Mithraeum, stone benches were added along the side walls and an altar was built at one end of the vault. Both the benches and altar were covered with plaster.

Behind the altar we found a very well-preserved white marble medallion; its upper segment shows Mithra slaying the sacred bull. This beautiful medallion was one indication that the warehouse had been converted into a Mithraeum and was a big factor in its identification.

The vault had been converted into a Mithraeum at the same time the Honorific Portico had been built above it—this helped to explain both that building and the elaborate drain that had so puzzled us. The drain was intended to protect the frescoes in the Mithraeum from water from above that would otherwise leach through the voussoir of the vault.

Now, in light of the Mithraeum, we better understood the building above it. As the Mithraeum was excavated we noted an opening near the eastern end of the vault's ceiling. This opening was offset from the vault's center line and admitted a shaft of sunlight into the vault. As we were digging we observed that the shaft of light admitted to the vault by this opening transcribed an arc during the course of each day. And each day the arc of light moved closer to the altar at the end of the vault. Just after noon on June 21, the summer solstice, the shaft of light had progressed to the altar, illuminating it with a blaze of light. The opening in the ceiling had been purposely and precisely placed and was known to the builders and users of the Honorific Portico above.

Since the inscriptions in the Honorific Portico all honor military personnel we believe that the Mithraeum was a military Mithraeum for the use of the Roman legionnaires. More than 800 Mithraea are known; the vast majority, however, have been found in Europe and North Africa, in places where the Roman legions were stationed. Only about 30 Mithraea have been found in Asia. The Mithraeum at Caesarea is the only one ever found in Israel.

Even though many Mithraea have been discovered, little is known about the Mithraic cult, liturgy or beliefs. It is apparent, however, that Mithra was a savior god who brought a new order of life to his followers. Mithra was an ancient deity of light and truth mentioned in Persian and Indian literature. In the first century after the turn of the era, the worship of Mithra became popular among the Roman military troops. Graded membership in the cult was obtained through rigorous initiation rites. Membership was secret and was confined to males. Adherents professed and practiced a high moral code. By the third century, Mithraism was so popular that it was a rival to Christianity, but by the fourth century, it began to wane.

In this article we can only briefly touch upon the extensive Late Roman and Byzantine structures uncovered at Caesarea, such as the Honorific Portico and the Mithraeum. These, and a wide variety of other structures, went out of use sometime before the fifth century. A patterned mosaic, almost two acres in area, was laid over their remains to form a courtyard almost a city block wide. It was contemporary with the last phases of the Archive Building. At the eastern end of this courtyard, above the vaults and overlooking the sea, a series of grand Byzantine buildings was constructed. Their purpose is still unknown to us, but something of their quality can be seen in the marvelous mosaics found on their floors. One floor originally was decorated with four portraits, the first figural mosaics found at Caesarea. Each of these magnificant portraits represented a season of the year, and two, winter and spring, have been preserved (see p. 120).

Joint Expedition to Caesarea

A stone altar *to Mithra, seen in the foreground, was set in place in the third century A.D. Stone benches were constructed along the walls of the Herodian storage vault. On the bench along the narrow end of the vault, a short post (top center) probably once held the beautiful Mithraic medallion found on the floor nearby. A round depression, the exact diameter of the medallion, was found in the post's upper surface, evidence that the medallion was once attached there.*

From the beginning, we knew that one thing we wanted to discover was the street plan of Herodian Caesarea. If Caesarea was built like other Roman cities of its day, it was laid out in squares with parallel streets running both east-west and north-south. The major north-south axis was called the Cardo Maximus or simply Cardo. The Cardo and the other parallel north-south streets would have regularly intersected the east-west cross streets, each of which was called a *decumanus*.

In the hope of getting at least some clues to the Herodian street plan, very early in our excavation we decided to dig under several unusual sand dunes. South of the 13th century Crusader city near the sea's edge are four large sand dunes and a broad stretch of level sand east of the dunes. Each of the four elongated dunes is about 250 feet long; each lies on a north-south line; and each is approximately equidistant from the one adjacent. The dunes rise 60 feet above the sea and 25 feet above the fields immediately to the east. From old photographs and from even earlier draw-

Joint Expedition to Caesarea

An exquisite mosaic *of a woman's face, one of the finest floor mosaics ever discovered in Israel, decorated a Byzantine building at Caesarea. Constructed above the Herodian storage vaults in about the sixth century, this building overlooked the sea. Originally there were four such panels in the corners of the floor—each representing one of the seasons. Here we see Spring; Winter was also preserved but Fall and Summer had been destroyed. Nine different colors of tesserae, or cut pieces of marble and glass, were used to create the subtle modulation of the face.*

ings, we learned that these dunes have been in this location and in approximately the same configuration for centuries.

Dunes normally move at a predictable rate. Stable dunes like these must contain some kind of anchor inside that holds them in place. The size and stability of the Caesarea dunes suggested that they were being held in place by the remains of major port or port-related installations.

In 1960 Abraham Negev of Hebrew University had conducted soundings in this area that indicated that a complex of buildings lay buried here, some buildings within the dunes. According to Professor Negev, the buildings were in use during the Byzantine period (fourth to seventh centuries). In one building Professor Negev found a mosaic containing an inscription from the New Testament—Romans 13:3: "If you would not fear the authority, then do good."

We decided we would try to excavate this entire building. This excavation gave us our first clue to the location of the Cardo. The Cardo was from the Byzantine period—but because Caesarea's growth had been uninterrupted we hypothesized that the Byzantine city still followed the street plan of Herod. Under the Byzantine street we hope to find the Roman street and under that the Herodian street.

But first the building. Initially we called it simply Structure I. Later we named it the Archive Building because mosaic inscriptions indicated that the municipal archives of Caesarea during the Byzantine period were housed here. The building was probably part of a municipal center or perhaps even part of the governor's complex.

The building was 60 feet long and 48 feet wide. It contained eight rooms. Three of the rooms were on each side of a large central hall oriented east/west. The entrance to the central hall was in the east. At the end of the central hall was the eighth room. Almost every room in the building contained a mosaic inscription.

The building had been destroyed in the Islamic conquest of Caesarea in 639/640 A.D. A thin ash layer in an earlier stratum indicated that the buildng had probably also been burned when the Persians conquered the city in 614 A.D. The general plan of the building had been established in the third or fourth century. In the intervening period there were a number of rebuilds and modifications, although the basic outline remained the same.

One mosaic floor was laid upon the previous one, and we were able to identify three different mosaic floors. The uppermost was laid sometime in the late fifth or early sixth century A.D. Beneath this floor was another mosaic floor. Under the second floor we found pottery indicating that the second mosaic floor was constructed at the beginning of the Byzantine period in the fourth or fifth century. A third mosaic floor has been dated on very minimal evidence to the third or fourth century.

I already mentioned one inscription—from Romans 13:3—found in the northeast corner of the building. In the central hall of the building a heavy calcium deposit partly obscured another inscription. When we scraped off the calcium deposit with the help of some hydrochloric acid, we found a mosaic medallion 28 inches in diameter containing a five-line inscription which, like all the others, was in Greek. It read, "Christ, help Marinus the President and

Joint Expedition to Caesarea

"If you would not fear *the authority, then do good and you will receive praise." This admonition from Romans 13:3, written in Greek on a mosaic floor in the Archive Building, greeted visitors in the late fifth or early sixth century A.D. It is one of several mosaic inscriptions found in this public building which opened onto the Cardo Maximus—the colonnaded north-south thoroughfare of Caesarea.*

Ampelios and Musonius."

In one of the southern rooms we discovered a multicolored mosaic medallion containing an inscription which was a longer version of the Romans 13:3 inscription already found: "If you would not fear the authority then do good and you will receive praise." A small encircled cross surmounts the inscription.

In yet another room, at the doorway, was an inscription reading: "Peace be upon your entrance and your exit." This inscription is in a *tabula ansata* (a rectangle containing an inscription, with a triangle on each side pointing to the inscription).

The largest inscription was found in a room at the western end of the central hall. It reads, in four lines, "Christ, Help Ampelios, the keeper of the archives and Musonius, the financial secretary [or accountant], and the other archivists of the same depository." On the basis of this inscription, we called the structure "The Archive Building." The inscriptions in a central location admonishing recognition of the governing authority also suggest this was a municipal or governmental edifice. A fragmentary inscription on a sandstone bench found in one of the rooms contains only two words "break" and "laws," further support for the theory that the building served a government function. Lead seals of a type attached to books and codices during the Byzantine period have also been found in the area. Today's Caesarea residents tell us that during a road clearing operation beside the Crusader City many more of these seals were found. Five such seals said to come from this road clearing are now in the museum of Kibbutz Sdot Yam, just south of Caesarea. For all of these reasons we feel justified in naming the structure the Archive Building and in identifying it with a municipal function.

All of the inscriptions I have described are from the uppermost mosaic floor. We have investigated the two lower mosaic floors only in limited areas where the upper floor was already broken or did not contain either a design or an inscription.

Even from this limited investigation, it appears that these lower mosaic floors also contain inscriptions. However, their contents will not be discernable until we remove the later mosaics that still cover the earlier floors.

The main entrance to the Archive Building was to the east. The back of the building was toward the Mediterranean. Outside the main entrance to the building a previous investigator had uncovered part of a patterned mosaic 18 feet wide. While we were examining the eastern edge of this mosaic we uncovered a three-foot-wide stylobate, that is, a continuous base for a row of columns. On top of the stylobate were found *in situ* white marble column bases, spaced about ten feet apart. At first it was thought that the column bases and the mosaic were part of a portico in front of the Archive Building. This initial conclusion was supported by the subsequent discovery that beneath the 18-foot-wide mosaic were two additional mosaic surfaces, and that the dates of the three mosaic surfaces corresponded to the dates of the three mosaic floors found inside the Archive Building. Subsequent excavation, however, proved that we were wrong in concluding that this was a portico of the Archive Building.

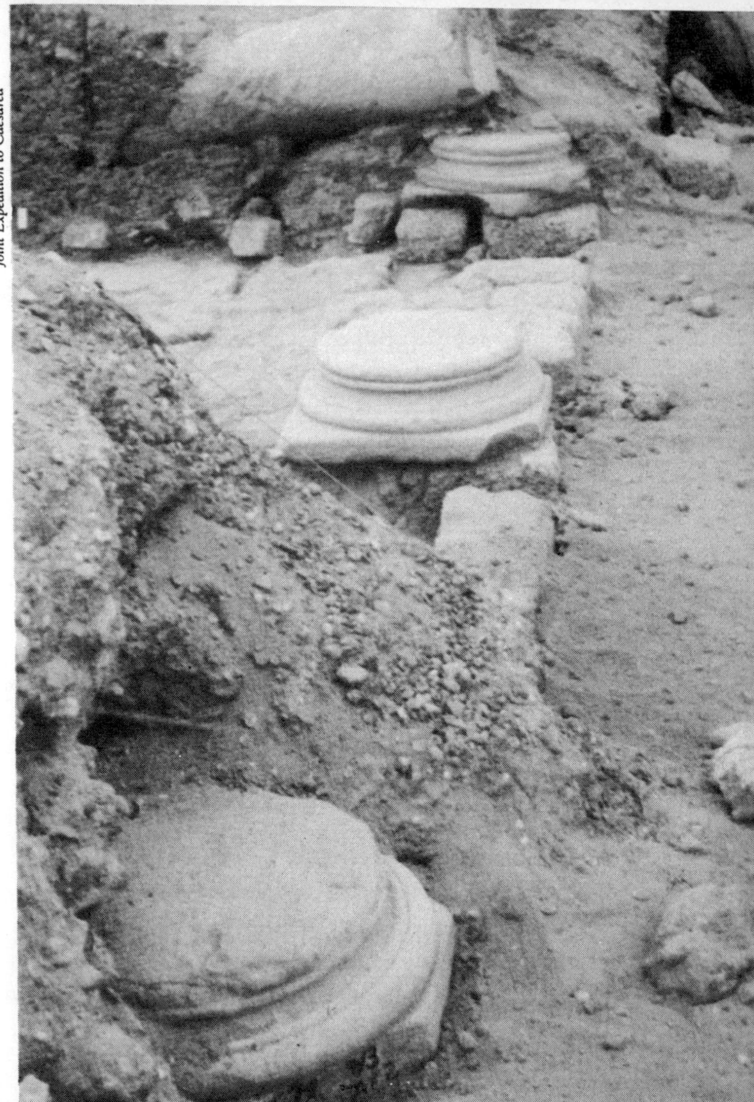

Joint Expedition to Caesarea

The three column bases *are remains of the splendid colonnade that once lined the Cardo Maximus of Caesarea. As many as 700 columns in two rows may have lined the mile-long main north-south street. The two rows of columns, one on either side, separated the 18-foot-wide, paved central roadway from mosaic-covered sidewalks of equal width adjacent to the roadway. Alongside the column base in the upper part of the picture is a fallen column shaft that once held a Corinthian capital. Roof tiles uncovered in the excavation indicate that originally the sidewalks on either side of the central roadway were covered.*

Beyond (east of) the stylobate, we found a street, also 18 feet wide, paved with heavy limestone pavers laid in a herringbone pattern. On the other side of this street but at a location south of the Archive Building we found another stylobate of similar size, shape and construction as the first. East of the second stylobate we found evidence for another mosaic pavement, although we do not yet know its exact width.

What we had thought was a portico of the Archive Building was in fact part of a major north-south city street. This thoroughfare consisted of an open vehicular street built of limestone pavers, on either side of which was a line of marble columns. Beside each row of columns was a patterned mosaic sidewalk 18 feet wide, the same width as the open street. Both the street and the two mosaic sidewalks appeared to extend south for one third of a mile precisely to the exit of the Herodian theater. Our excavations uncovered not only the column bases still on the stylobates, but also some of the fallen column shafts beside the bases and fragments of Corinthian capitals. We also found some of the roof tiles that served as part of the covering for the sidewalks on either side of the open street. Here, obviously was, the grand concourse of Caesarea—the Cardo Maximus.

But in all three phases this street dated to the Byzantine period or the late Roman period at the earliest.

When we projected the northern continuation of the Cardo on our plan, we discovered that it ended in what was probably the Roman forum in the center of the city, now under the Crusader fortress. More important, the Cardo, on its way to the Herodian theater exit, follows the line formed by the eastern end of the blocks of Herodian vaults mentioned above. Thus, the Roman and Byzantine Cardo fits the city street plan determined by the regular block pattern of Herod's warehouses. This seems to indicate that the Herodian street followed the same line as the one we have been excavating. But until now we have found no trace of a street we can call the Herodian Cardo or even of an early Roman Cardo underneath the layers of the Byzantine Cardo. We have not given up the search, however. Thus far, we have examined this thoroughfare at three different points along its projected course and found the Cardo there under 12 feet of overburden, frequently repaired, partly destroyed, often robbed out—but there.

In the center of the paved street we found drain openings, actually manholes, some of which went down ten feet. At the bottom was an arched layer of brick covering the elaborate sewer system of ancient Caesarea. So far we have explored only one vault of this sewer system, which was ten feet wide and just as high. Unfortunately almost all of the sewers have been blocked by debris and by the remains of later sewers built inside the older ones.

The original sewers were probably Herodian, lending further support to the suggestion that the street above marks the line of the original Herodian street. City planning in Roman times called for sewers to be placed under streets rather than under buildings. Josephus tells us that half the time spent constructing Herodian Caesarea was devoted to putting sewers under the city and that these were flushed by the sea. He relates that "some [of the sewers] led at equal distances from one another to the harbor and the sea, while one diagonal passage connected all of them, so that rainwater and refuse of the inhabitants were easily carried off." (*Jewish Antiquities* XV:340). Thus far in the excavations at Caesarea we have cleared one huge sewer, 10½ feet high. This sewer tunnel opens toward the sea. It is uncertain as yet how these sewers were flushed by the sea because the tides along the Mediterranean shore are not high enough to provide that action. One possible explanation is that the "diagonal passage" referred to by Josephus, may have flushed out all the parallel sewers under the streets by means of sea water diverted into it. Eight hundred meters south of the center of Caesarea we have located a mole or breakwater positioned in the sea counter to the current. Perhaps this mole diverted seawater into a sewer opening—still undiscovered—at the seaward end of the diagonal passage. If so—this water would have continuously flowed into and cleaned the sewers beneath the streets of the city. In future seasons, we hope to explore the Caesarea sewer system more extensively.

We also discovered several of the cross streets that run perpendicular to Caesarea's Cardo Maximus. Each cross street is called a *decumanus* (plural: *decumani*). To describe this discovery and to understand our eventual projection of the Herodian street plan we must go back to the Herodian vaults or warehouses. While all the vaults could not be examined, we were able to determine that they were built on bedrock in blocks of 20. This 20 vault unit, we speculated, was the size of the original city block of structures. Four, and perhaps five, of these blocks line the shore from the crusader fortress to Herod's theater. We dug probes where we projected spaces between the blocks of vaults. In each case we found a cross street or decumanus from the late Roman period. Since these streets were built on top of an earlier Herodian street, we have been able in this case to lay out Herod's city plan in this area of Caesarea. And so, gradually, with the aid of the trowel and sometimes even of the teaspoon, a picture of Herod's city has begun to emerge.

[1]Josephus, *The Jewish War* I, 408-415 (5)
[2]Josephus, *The Jewish War* I, 408-415 (5)
[3]Josephus, *The Jewish War* I, 408-415 (7)
[4]Josephus, *Jewish Antiquities* XVI, 136 (V.1) states 10 years; *Jewish Antiquities* XV, 343 states 12 years.
[5]The Joint Expedition to Caesarea was authorized by the American Schools of Oriental Research and licensed by the Israel Department of Antiquities.

PONTIUS PILATE INSCRIPTION

To the Editor:
The May/June **BAR** (p. 33 [115]) carried an interesting photo of a stone found at Caesarea Maritima, bearing a damaged Latin inscription which was translated: "PONTIUS PILATE, THE PREFECT OF JUDEA, HAS DEDICATED TO THE PEOPLE OF CAESAREA A TEMPLE IN HONOR OF TIBERIUS": the underlined words, or parts of words, are translations of the Latin words shown in the picture, but everything else is not represented on the stone by even one Latin letter.

It would be interesting if you could inform us if most of the translation is just an educated guess, or if perhaps the entire inscription is known from another source.

Msgr. Archibald V. McLees
St. Pascal Baylon Rectory
St. Albans, New York

Robert Bull replies:
Msgr. McLees's surmise that part of the translation given in **BAR** *is an educated guess is correct. That guess is based on what looks to some of us like the remains of the letter "S" found just before* TIBERIEUM *in the first line of the inscription from Caesarea.*

I record the inscription as follows:

1. *[——] S Tiberieum*
2. *[. Po]ntius Pilatus*
3. *[praef]ectus Iuda[ea]e*
4. *[didit dedicavit]*

Translated it reads "_____ Pontius Pilatus, prefect of Judea, offered and dedicated the Tiberieum to . . ." If there is a broken "S" in the first line of the inscription, it could, among other possibilities, be the second "S" in [Caesarien]s(ibus). This was the reading of Antonio Frova (Scavi di Caesarea Maritima, *Milano, 1965, p. 217f). If [Caesarien]s(ibus) is the correct reading along with the other additions given above, then it would be possible to translate the inscription as it was in* **BAR** *"Pontius Pilate, the Prefect of Judea, has dedicated to the people of Caesarea a temple in honor of Tiberius."*

CAESAREA TUNNEL VISION

To the Editor:
An avid **BAR** reader, I much enjoyed Robert J. Bull's "Caesarea Maritima, the Search for Herod's City" in the May/June 1982 issue. Alas, I can not understand how two teams of "Herodian masons, working from opposite ends [to] cut a 6-mile-long tunnel through the bedrock" (pp. 29 & 30 [111 & 112]), found each other under Mt. Carmel.

I would be very thankful to know what instruments and knowledge, besides Divine Guidance, steered the masons for about 3 miles in stone obscurity to meet their target with an accuracy of about 4 feet. Also, did I comprehend correctly that the poor masons had to bend themselves down all the length of the four-foot-high tunnel and that each three-mile-long, 3½ x 4 foot, dead-end tunnel supplied enough air to keep them alive and active?

Sergey Samoilov
Morristown, New Jersey

Robert Bull replies:
Only a small part of the six-mile-long Herodian tunnel could be examined. Four shafts similar to the one shown on page 30 [112] of **BAR** *were found. At the bottom of each shaft, the tunnel branched east and west. We were able to crawl into the tunnel about 164 feet; we found oxygen supply greatly diminished and our way blocked by rubble. We assumed that the rubble had entered the tunnel from a yet-unexcavated shaft. Our conclusion was that the six-mile tunnel was cut by crews working toward one another at two cutting faces begun at the bottom of pairs of shafts approximately 230 feet apart. Since the shafts were 230 feet apart, the cutting faces were never more than 115 feet from a shaft. Presumably this distance assured an adequate air supply for the masons and for their oil-burning lamps. The complete excavation of the shafts and the tunnel has yet to be accomplished; we would of course welcome help.*

The instruments used by the ancient masons at Caesarea to "guide" them in the survey and planning of each of the 230-foot sections of the tunnel, as well as the whole aqueduct, were probably similar to those used to build the aqueduct and tunnels that supplied water to Rome and to many other Roman cities of that period. The water table (chorobate) *used for leveling and the measuring stick* (groma) *used for determining right angles, among other instruments, allowed Roman engineers to plan and build with accuracy over even greater distances than those evidenced at Caesarea.*

I believe the masons had to remain bent over in the 4-foot-high tunnel. Whether they were citizens, slaves, soldiers or criminals, I do not know.

MORE ON THE CAESAREA AQUEDUCT TUNNEL

To the Editor:
Your November/December 1982 issue contains a letter inquiring about the knowledge and instruments used to construct the tunnel for the aqueduct at Caesarea Maritima.

A device that enables a tunnel to be dug from both ends is described in the "Dioptra" by Heron of Alexandra (60 A.D.). A picture of this device and how it is used is found on pages 102-104 of *Science Awakening* by Bartel L. Van Der Waerden (Oxford University Press, 1961). While it is not known that such a device was used, the knowledge certainly existed.

Incidently this is not the first tunnel dug from both ends. About 530 B.C. Eupalinus of Megara constructed a tunnel approximately one kilometer long as part of an aqueduct on the island of Samos. This is also described in Van Der Waerden's book.

Roger C. McCann
Starkville, Mississippi

C·A·E·S·A·R·E·A
BENEATH THE SEA

By ROBERT L. HOHLFELDER

OF ALL THE GREAT SEAPORTS of antiquity, Caesarea Maritima is the only one readily accessible to underwater archaeologists.[1]* Many ancient ports, like Piraeus, the port of Athens, cannot be carefully examined because they are still in use. Other harbors of antiquity have silted in over the centuries and today serve a variety of purposes that preclude archaeological investigation. Such has been the fate of Ostia, the ancient port of Rome, where modern Rome's airport now sits.

But Caesarea Maritima lies partially submerged along a section of Mediterranean coast that has seen no significant development or use for the past seven centuries. For at least the next few years archaeologists can pursue their quest for the submerged port of Caesarea.

Scholars have long known that a unique record of human activity exists in the depths of the Mediterranean Sea. But until the development of SCUBA (Self-Contained Underwater Breathing Apparatus) during World War II, scientists could not effectively explore this repository of history and artifacts. SCUBA allowed divers, for the first time, to move about unencumbered by heavy helmets and by air lines attached to a ship on the surface.

From time to time before the development of SCUBA, fishermen and commercial or military hard-helmet divers made significant discoveries of art works and shipwrecks. These discoveries only confirmed the obvious, that the Mediterranean Sea is a museum of the history of human life on this planet. Still today chance finds are made, but such random salvage is not what is meant by underwater archaeology.

The year 1960 marked the beginning of modern underwater archaeology. That year at Cape Gelidonya, Turkey, Professor George Bass of Texas A & M University, utilizing SCUBA, undertook the first systematic exploration and excavation of what turned out to be a Phoenician shipwreck from about 1,200 B.C., the oldest ship excavated underwater to date.[2] In the same year, off the coast of Israel, Edwin Link, working in conjunction with Professors Charles Fritsch and I. Ben-Dor, began the underwater excavation of Caesarea Maritima, the Roman and Byzantine capital of Palestine, with a team of professional SCUBA divers operating from the research vessel, Sea Diver.[3] Link's expedition confirmed the site of Caesarea Maritima's main harbor, previously thought to have been south of its actual location, and recovered evidence to suggest that it had been badly damaged by earthquakes early in its existence. More important, each project established that the techniques of stratigraphic land archaeology—the careful recording of all finds in relationship to each other and to the context in which they were discovered—could be employed in the sea.

Columns tossed ***against the shore are silent reminders of a time long past. Other columns lie like matchsticks in the harbor or were incorporated into breakwaters by the Crusaders. All stood originally in the colonnades of Caesarea's elegant north-south street, the Cardo Maximus.***

*Endnotes for this article will be found on page 135.

Garo Nalbandian

With these two excavations, a new branch of classical archaeology was defined. Underwater archaeology with its two divisions—shipwreck archaeology and the archaeology of submerged coastal sites—emerged as an exciting new frontier in the study of human history.

The search for ancient ships is the most publicized aspect of underwater archaeology. Some results have been spectacular, such as the discovery, excavation, lifting and restoration of a fourth-century B.C. shipwreck off Kyrenia, Cyprus, by Michael Katzev.[4] Since the zone of concern of a shipwreck is usually fairly compact and related to a single historic period, the archaeological problems associated with such sites are, as a rule, limited. Diving considerations, on the other hand, tend to be paramount. Because sport divers regularly loot the more accessible shipwreck sites in the Mediterranean, shipwreck archaeology is often conducted in deeper water. Here physiological limitations add a dimension of danger to the already romantic aura that surrounds the search for lost ships on the bottom of the sea. There can be little wonder why this type of underwater archaeology has captured popular fancy.

The underwater archaeological investigations of ancient coastal sites, such as submerged harbor installations, projects a much less romantic image. Yet coastal investigation holds greater promise than shipwreck archaeology for enhancing our understanding of the role of the sea in antiquity. Since Link's work at Caesarea Maritima in 1960, numerous other similar sites throughout the Mediterranean have been systematically excavated. These projects, such as the explorations at Kenchreai and Halieis in Greece or at Populonia and Cosa in Italy, have all added substantially to our awareness of maritime activities in the ancient past. Most artifacts recovered are mundane, not adding greatly to our knowledge, but some finds have been extraordinary, such as the discovery of 120 glass panels in a submerged temple of the goddess Isis at Kenchreai.[5] During the past two decades the techniques of excavation and exploration, as well as the tools employed, have improved significantly. For example, an inexpensive probe has been developed to detect ancient structures beneath the present ocean floor. The work of these twenty years has firmly established the legitimacy and importance of coastal site archaeology, even

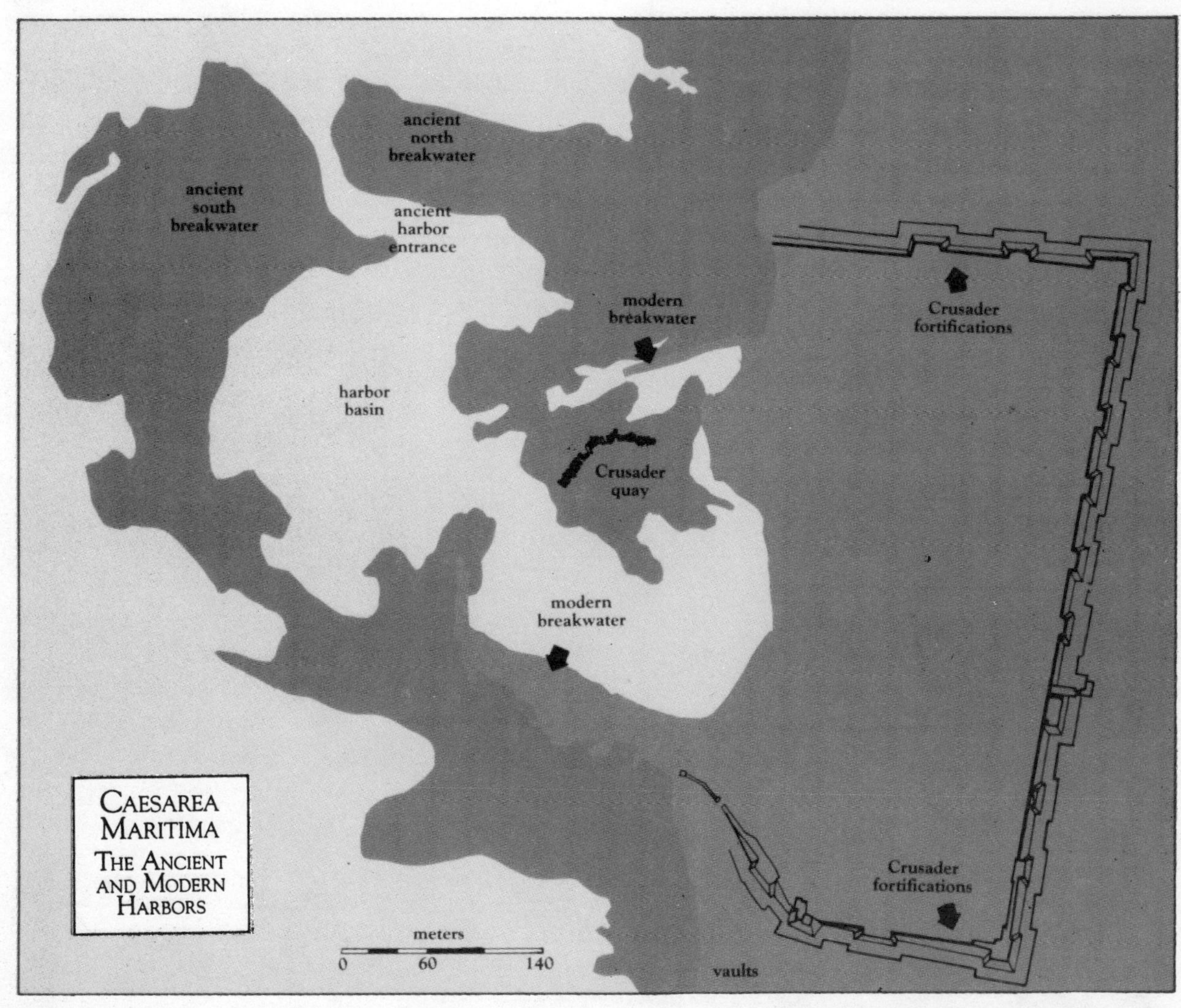

CAESAREA MARITIMA
THE ANCIENT AND MODERN HARBORS

The submerged remains *of the massive breakwaters from Herod's harbor appear as a dark gray circular area in this infrared aerial photograph. A white boat in the upper left corner marks the entrance to the 2,000-year-old harbor constructed by Palestine's master builder. Above the boat is the northern breakwater. Below the boat is the 100-foot-long, curved southern breakwater which Josephus accurately described as 200 feet wide. Josephus wrote that Herod built this wall to "break the surge" of water created by the fierce prevailing southwest winds.*

The structures on the right side of the picture are portions of the modern breakwater which extend from the shore. The modern harbor and its breakwater are small, almost tiny, compared to the harbor Herod built.

if public awareness of it is still limited.

In 1979 the Caesarea Ancient Harbour Excavation Project (CAHEP) was formed by the Center of Maritime Studies of the University of Haifa to complete the work started at Caesarea in 1960 by Edwin Link. Professors Elisha Linder and Avner Raban of Haifa University were instrumental in the creation of CAHEP, an international scholarly consortium. Professor Raban and the author currently serve as co-directors of this project.[6] In 1979, 1980 and 1981, surveys and excavations were undertaken at various locations within the submerged structures of the ancient port. At least two more major seasons of field work are scheduled for 1983 and 1985, with limited operations planned for 1982 and 1984.

The starting point for CAHEP's explorations was the description by Josephus of the design and construction of the enormous harbor built by Herod the Great at the end of the first century B.C. Josephus' account of the building of Sebastos, as he named the harbor of Caesarea Maritima, has long been thought to be lavishly extravagant. Who could believe that once, on this barren strip of coast, there was a harbor at whose mouth "stood colossal statues, three on either side, resting on columns; the columns on the left of vessels entering port were supported by a massive tower, those on the right by two upright blocks of stone clamped together, whose height exceeded that of the tower on the opposite side."* Could the skeptical reader accept that 2,000 years ago Herod's engineers performed seemingly im-

**Jewish War,* I, 413.

Harry Wadsworth

Two divers *of the Caesarea Ancient Harbour Excavation Project (CAHEP) plot a site plan underwater, just as their counterparts do on dry land. Over the last two decades, development of SCUBA breathing systems and simple underwater tools has made maritime exploration an important component of coastal site archaeology.*

Robert L. Hohlfelder

A large stone anchor, *c. 1,200 B.C., was salvaged from the bay south of Caesarea's harbor. It may be the oldest artifact found in any Caesarea excavation and indicates that ships plied this route in the earliest days of the Iron Age, more than a thousand years before Herod built his grandiose city.*

possible engineering feats to make a huge protected anchorage safe from fierce prevailing winds?

As CAHEP's explorations have proceeded, it has become increasingly clear that Josephus' description of the design and size of Caesarea Maritima's harbor is substantially accurate. Sebastos was indeed one of the engineering marvels of the ancient world. Several architectural features mentioned by Josephus have been discovered, such as the remains of both the promenade on the inner face of the harbor and the towers that marked the entrance. His dimensions for the main components of Herod's harbor approximate the actual measurements of extant structures. For example, he states that the width of the southern breakwater was 200 feet. Its actual size is 195 to 243 feet at the various points surveyed. He speaks of huge blocks of stone 50 by 9 by 10 feet that were lowered into the sea to build the main mole. In fact, blocks have been discovered even larger than those described. It also appears that Josephus omitted some distinct elements of Caesarea Maritima's port facilities. Underwater investigation has revealed that the harbor Josephus described is but one component of a larger system of moorings and anchorages in use at the time of its construction.

We have also discovered on land a section of a seawall from an inner harbor to the east of the one described by Josephus but connected to it. Carved from sand dunes, this inner harbor provided a small but safer basin for the ships that were hauled into it by tugboats or stevedores. (The inner-outer harbor concept employed at Caesarea Maritima would be used again by Roman engineers in the next century when work began on Ostia, the harbor constructed for Imperial Rome itself.) To the south of the inner-outer harbor was a secondary anchorage almost equal in size to the main port. Several stone anchors discovered to date suggest that this bay, formed by a small headland and a natural reef that were augmented over the centuries by man-made structures, was used by ancient mariners as far back as 1,200 B.C. To the north of Sebastos about a third of a mile, another small harbor has been discovered that antedates by several centuries Caesarea Maritima's foundation and may be associated with the Phoenicians and a much earlier chapter of the history of Palestine. The forthcoming 1982 season will concentrate on land and underwater excavations in this location to learn more about this harbor and its role in Caesarea Maritima's history. If all these facilities

Divers discovered *this huge stone block at the terminus of Caesarea's northern breakwater. It is believed to be from one of the towers Josephus described at either side of Herod's harbor entrance. The block is 13 feet (4 meters) long, 4.5 feet (1.35 meters) high and weighs several tons.*

Two semi-circular lead projections on the top of the block fit into two matching depressions in another stone discovered in the harbor. The projections and depressions were part of a building method for securing the massive stones together, probably one on top of another.

Harry Wadsworth

Harry Wadsworth

On land, this archaeologist *would need a shovel, a basket and a strong back to clear away rubble. In the sea, he just needs an air lift, the basic excavation tool of underwater archaeology. The large hose sucks up silt and sand for drying and sifting on shore.*

served the city during its early years, as is now suspected, then Caesarea Maritima did indeed have one of the greatest harbors in the Mediterranean in antiquity and perhaps the largest in terms of working space. An archaeological record of the life, vicissitudes and use of this complex has only begun to emerge in the past three years of excavation by the CAHEP underwater team.

In addition to finding structural features of Caesarea's harbor not mentioned by Josephus, we were also surprised by the engineering skills and design employed in the harbor's construction. Herod's engineers showed a mastery of technology rivaling that of our own age. There are remains of a sluice system designed to enable sand-free water from the open sea to enter the enclosed harbors at several locations to facilitate circulation within the enclosed basins and thus inhibit silting. In addition, excavations have uncovered the remains of a subsidiary breakwater system. Employed for the first time at Caesarea Maritima, this subsidiary system was intended to reduce damage to the main enclosing arm of the harbor at its most vulnerable point. Also, the maritime engineers made extensive use of a new high quality concrete that hardened underwater and was practically impervious to the destructive action of the sea. Blocks of this hydraulic concrete weighing more than 50 tons and surpassing in size those mentioned by Josephus have been discovered. At the time of its construction, this harbor was the largest maritime facility to feature this building material. Although it was constructed in antiquity, we may be well-justified in calling Caesarea Maritima the first modern harbor.

News From the Field

★Caesarea

Herod's Harbor Construction Recovered Underwater

By Lindley Vann

Two thousand years ago, divers whose only air supply was their lungs pushed and pulled at a 50-foot-long rectangular wooden frame suspended in the water from cranes. First one, then another of the divers swam to the surface to breathe, then dove again. Bit by bit, the wooden frame descended, finally hovering inches above the ocean floor. The divers edged away. All at once, the ropes holding the frame were cut and it sank deep into the silt and sand on the ocean bottom. The divers swam ashore. Large wood and leather tubes like elephants' trunks were lowered into the water inside the frame. Roman hydraulic concrete, three times denser than water, poured through the tubes, gradually displacing the water in the frame. When the pouring was done, the concrete hardened underwater to form a huge foundation block for a harbor breakwater.*

In the summer of 1982, scuba divers from the Caesarea Ancient Harbor Excavation Project (CAHEP)[1] uncovered two intersecting beams that had been the bottommost pieces of the wooden frame, or form, into which this concrete was poured. The sand and silt covering these beams had protected them both from rot and from the destructive appetite of shipworms, thus preserving the timbers where they had been positioned 2,000 years ago.

Caesarea Maritima and its harbor (called Sebastos) were the vision and product of one man, Herod the Great.[2] He was a prodigious builder, keenly aware of the political advantage of embellishing the cities within his kingdom and those in neighboring lands. A list of his works recorded by the first-century A.D. Jewish historian Josephus[3] included temples, theaters, amphitheaters, gymnasia, baths, porticoes, aqueducts, fountains and colonnaded streets. The variety of these projects indicated not only the generosity (or ego) of the man but also reflected the religious, cultural and political needs of his varied constituencies. The Temple in Jerusalem was rebuilt for the Jews; theaters, gymnasia, porticoes, and colonnaded streets satisfied those who wanted cities to have a Hellenistic appearance; and temples dedicated to Roma and Augustus, baths, amphitheaters and aqueducts reflected the strong influence on Herod of Roman technology and institutions.

The harbor at Caesarea was an engineering marvel. On a stretch of eastern Mediterranean coastline known for its dangers to mariners and lacking sheltered anchorage, Herod built a harbor as large as Piraeus, the port of Athens. Two breakwaters, one on the north and one on the south, with a 60-foot entrance between them, enclosed a protected anchorage. The breakwaters extended as much as 1,500 feet from the shore. Within the main harbor was a sheltered inner harbor.

This past summer, CAHEP divers uncovered two massive concrete blocks, as well as parts of the wooden forms into which they had been poured. One block (see p. 134) was located at the northwest corner of the north breakwater. It measured 39 x 49 feet with a maximum preserved height of 5 feet and an irregular upper surface. The remains of the wooden form into which the concrete had been poured were located on the north and west sides of the concrete block and at its northwest corner (see drawings on pp. 132 and 133). These timbers, 11 inches wide, which ran along the lower edge of the block, intersected in a simple lap joint at the corner of the block. Cut into the upper surface of the beams were slots to receive a series of uprights with cross-sections averaging 6 inches by 9 inches. Fragments of these uprights were found in the beams.

When the forms were constructed, horizontal planking was nailed to two sides of the vertical posts, creating an inner and an outer wall. Then the hollow space between the inner and outer walls was filled with a blue-green mortar mixture containing large particles of tufa, pumice,** and lime, the same mixture as that of the block itself. Remains of the double wall filled with mortar were found along the west side of the block. The upper portion of the formwork was reinforced with additional vertical posts and horizontal tie beams. The tie beams and upper vertical posts decayed, but left their impressions, which appeared as square holes, in the concrete block, as seen in the drawing on page 133. The original height of the block was not preserved, but we assume that another layer of horizontal tie beams was present at the top of the form, as shown in the reconstruction drawing on page 133.

Herod's harbor was completed in 10 B.C. Two important events occurred just before this time; one definitely influenced the final form of Herod's great harbor at Caesarea. This was the invention of hydraulic concrete by Roman engineers. The significant property of hydraulic concrete was that it hardened underwater. The special ingredient for Roman concrete† was a volcanic sand known as pozzolana, a bonding agent similar to our portland cement.

The second event was the publication of a treatise in 25 B.C. called *On Architecture* by a Roman architect and engineer named Vitruvius. Although we cannot assume that Herod read Vitruvius, this book became the "state of the art" of its time. Vitruvius describes structures ranging from harbor installations to private dwellings. Vitruvius writes of pozzolana:

> "There is also a kind of powder which from natural causes produces astonishing results. It is found in the neighborhood of Baiae and in the country belonging to

*This is an imaginative, but plausible, reconstruction of a technique for pouring hydraulic concrete underwater.

**The tufa and pumice, or volcanic rocks, used in the construction of Caesarea's harbor may well have come from the Bay of Naples.

†The term "Roman concrete" is also used to refer to *opus reticulatum* walls (see "Herod's Family Tomb," **BAR**, May/June 1983), walls built with uniformly cut small stones laid in a diagonal or other pattern. The concrete that was the core of *opus reticulatum* walls had the same composition as the concrete used in the breakwaters at Caesarea.

When used with respect to *opus reticulatum*, "Roman concrete" refers to the entire wall including stones *and* binding concrete; but as it is used to describe the material poured into forms at Caesarea, Roman concrete refers to the concrete blocks.

the towns about Mt. Vesuvius. This substance, when mixed with lime and rubble, not only lends strength to buildings of other kinds, but even when piers of it are constructed in the sea, they set hard under water."

On Architecture II.6.1

The process of pouring concrete underwater was probably much the same as it is today. The semi-liquid mass of concrete was poured into a tube (most likely made of wood with flexible leather joints); the other end of the pouring tube was held close to the ocean bottom. As pouring continued, the mouth of the tube was kept below the surface of the concrete already in place, so that the newly poured concrete remained in a proper mixture and gradually displaced the sea water within the form. (If the concrete had simply been dumped into the water, the heavier materials would have fallen and the lighter sand and cement would have remained in suspension.) The texture of the first-poured concrete on the bottom of the block was uneven until enough concrete was poured to cover the mouth of the pouring tube; then the concrete acquired a uniform consistency. A block about 50 feet by 40 feet by 5 feet required more than 10,000 cubic feet of concrete. Multiple tubes, each manned by a separate crew, were no doubt necessary for each pouring.

The second concrete block discovered this past summer projected from the sand 20 feet north of the first block, clearly separated from the breakwater. This block was built of the same materials and in the same manner as the first block and both blocks had approximately the same orientation, with their west faces aligned. Fragments of wooden formwork were found on the west side of the second block near its south corner. This block was not part of the breakwater but was probably the foundation of a tower standing northeast of the harbor entrance. (Previously, in 1981, the bases of two other towers southwest of the entrance had been identified by divers.) The positions of these tower foundations match those described by Josephus in the Caesarea harbor:

> "The entrance to the port faced northwards, because in these latitudes the north wind is the most favorable of all. At the harbor-mouth stood colossal

Text continued on page 134

The harbor at Caesarea. *This infrared photograph taken in 1960 reveals the remains of Herod's massive breakwaters (dark gray) now underwater. The white ship in the upper left is the research vessel* Sea Cloud *of the Link Expedition, the first underwater expedition at Caesarea. Immediately above the ship is the entrance to the ancient harbor and the end of the northern breakwater. At the northwest corner of this breakwater, CAHEP divers found remains of 2,000-year-old wooden beams (shown in the photo, p. 134), that formed part of a frame into which concrete was poured for the breakwater's foundations; unseen in this photograph is the tower block discovered underwater beyond the northern breakwater.*

Below the Sea Cloud *is the ancient harbor's curving southern breakwater. The irregular shape of this breakwater is the result of centuries of damage inflicted on the structure by the prevailing southwest currents. By contrast, the inner face of the northern breakwater was well protected and has retained its original form.*

Parts of the small modern breakwater extend from the shore on the right of the picture.

How Herod Built a Harbor

2.

L. Herbots

Herod's harbor at Caesarea *was the first artificial harbor in the ancient world. It is shown here (1), partially reconstructed (but not drawn to exact scale) as it probably appeared in 10 B.C. when Herod completed it. The reconstruction is based on descriptions of harbor construction by Vitruvius (On Architecture), and on the descriptions of Caesarea's harbor by Josephus in The Jewish War and Jewish Antiquities and on archaeological remains discovered in recent years.*

The harbor was formed by two breakwaters, built on concrete foundations, extending up to 1,500 feet into the Mediterranean Sea. The larger southern breakwater enclosed an inner basin. The northern breakwater was 150 feet wide; the southern breakwater was approximately 200 feet wide. Between the two breakwaters was the 60-foot-wide entrance to the harbor. Outside the entrance to the harbor, in the foreground, stood three large concrete piers resting on the sea bottom. The two on the right were said by Josephus to have been joined together as part of a platform for monumental sculpture. The single tower on the left also supported monumental sculpture (2). Ships entering the harbor would have passed between the two groups of sculpture. Based on evidence from other harbors and from the writings of Josephus, it is possible, although far from certain, that a tower stood on the end of one or both of the breakwaters flanking the entrance to the harbor. It is likely that one of these towers served as a lighthouse. In times of siege a chain may have stretched between the ends of the breakwaters to prevent the passage of ships. In the summer of 1982, divers discovered a concrete foundation block at the northwest corner of the terminus of the northern breakwater and a second block—not connected to this breakwater —20 feet north of the first one (see arrows). The second block formed the foundation of the outer tower seen on the left.

The aim of Herod's engineers was to build an artificial anchorage where there was no natural harbor to shelter ships. They did this by laying immense concrete blocks on the sea bottom, starting at the shore and building seaward from the blocks already in place.

First a wooden form was constructed and placed on the sea bottom. The bottommost corner of one of these wooden forms was found with the concrete block that had been poured into it (3). The sides of the form consisted of a double wall of planks. Between the inner and outer parts of this double wall was concrete packing, poured into the double wall and allowed to set in order to strengthen the form before it was lowered into the sea. The drawing (4) is a detail of the wooden remains in situ; the drawing (5) illustrates the simple lap joint that connected the two beams. Horizontal and vertical wooden tie beams added stability to the form.

The tie beams and the rest of the wooden form are gone—destroyed by shipworms and decay—but the images of the wooden vertical and horizontal tie beams remain in the concrete block. An exact drawing (6) of the top surface of the two blocks discovered last summer—shows the block at the end of the northern breakwater (right) and the block forming part of the base of the tower outside the harbor entrance at the end of the northern breakwater (left). The block from the breakwater measures 49 feet by 39 feet by 5 feet; the block from the tower foundation was only partially excavated. Shown in white are the holes that once contained the vertical wooden members of the form's inner structure. Seen in gray are the five cavities left in the block by some of the horizontal wooden tie beams that joined the vertical pieces. From this information we are able to reconstruct the probable appearance of a form (7). Here the artist has drawn one complete form in the water, waiting to receive concrete. It seems likely that the concrete would have been poured through large tubes located on the upper level of the breakwater where a person stands and perhaps also from barges anchored nearby. This upper level was constructed of stones and smaller concrete blocks placed on top of a previously poured concrete form identical to the one shown to its right.

By using each concrete block as a base from which a new form could be put in place, the breakwaters were gradually extended to their final length.

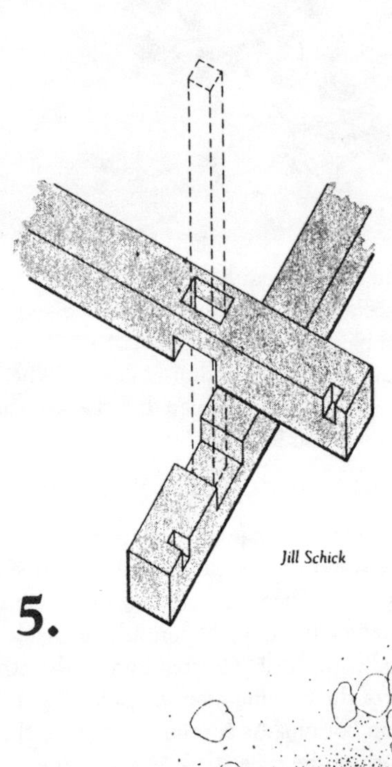

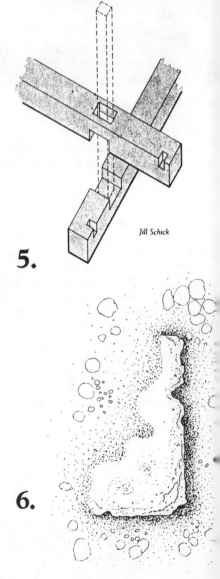

Jill Schick

5.

6.

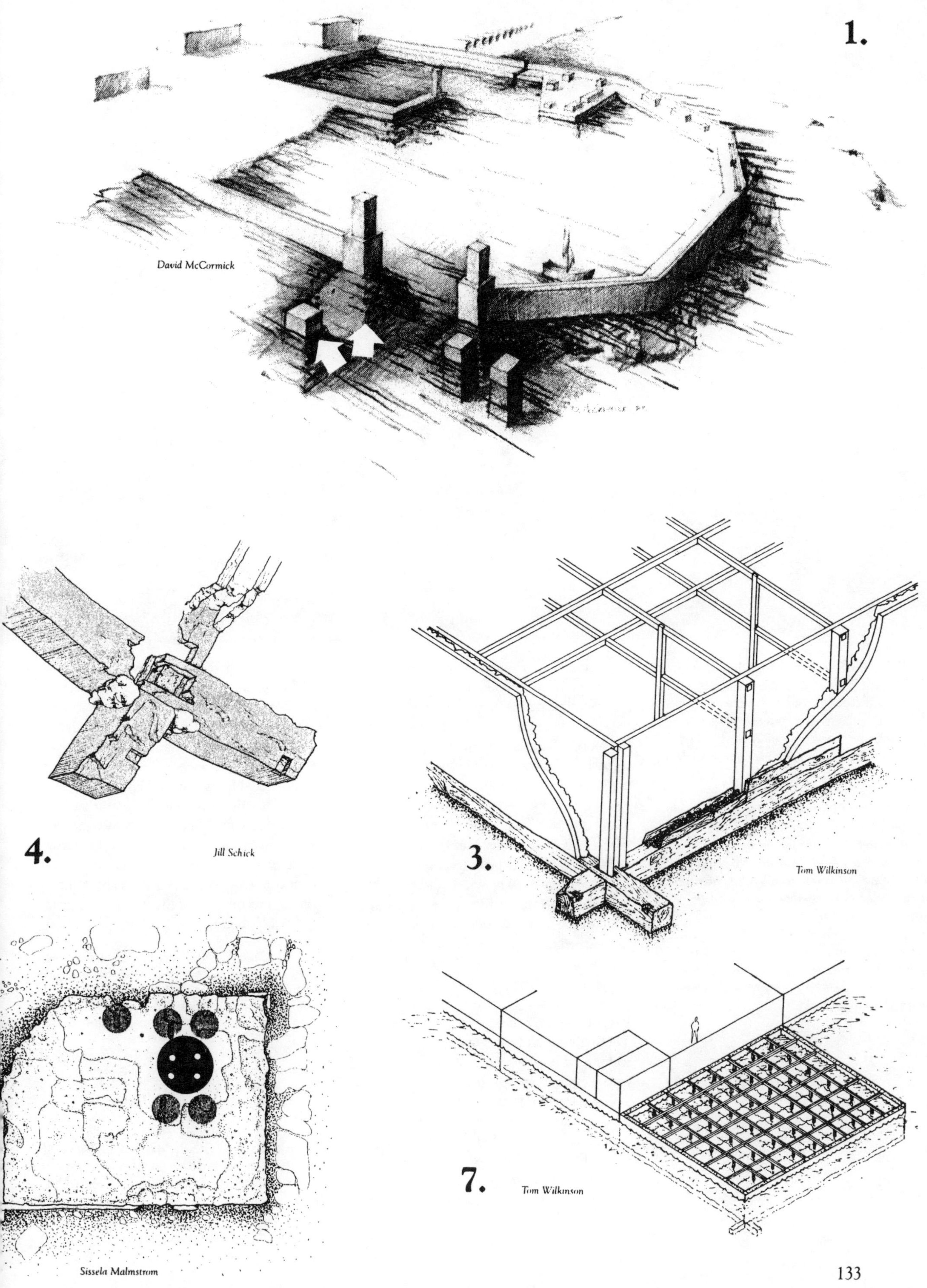
1.
David McCormick
4.
Jill Schick
3.
Tom Wilkinson
7.
Tom Wilkinson
Sissela Malmstrom

Two-thousand-year-old wooden beams *lie on the sea floor in Caesarea's harbor. These beams were part of a wooden frame into which concrete was poured in order to make immense concrete foundation blocks for the breakwater. Behind the measuring stick is the north face of the concrete block located at the northwest corner of the northern breakwater. The block measures 39 feet wide by 49 feet long by 5 feet high and was originally higher. Running along the lower edge of the block and continuing beyond the block to the right is one wooden beam; perpendicular to it, coming out toward the viewer to the right of the measuring stick, is another beam. Both are 11 inches wide and cross in a lap joint. Details of the wooden remains and the block and a reconstruction drawing of the complete form may be seen on pages 132 and 133.*

statues, three on either side, resting on columns; the columns on the left of the vessels entering port were supported by a massive tower, those on the right by two upright blocks of stone clamped together, whose height exceeded that of the tower on the opposite side."

Jewish War I, 413.

No statues have been found near the Caesarea harbor towers, but contemporaneous depictions of sculpture at harbor mouths are known. A marble relief was found in 1863 or 1864 near the Torlonia villa on the northeast side of the port at Ostia (the port serving Rome). This relief depicts a colossal statue on the third story of the four-story lighthouse built by the Emperor Claudius. It also shows two other large statues on pedestals at the harbor. These statues on towers bear witness to the widespread popularity of this type of architecture in ancient harbors.

Towers with statues are also depicted on a small commemorative medal about the size of a dime, which was found by the Link Expedition during the first underwater excavations at Caesarea in 1960. This medallion contains a representation of the entrance to a port. Two letters, KA, found on the medallion might be an abbreviation for Caesarea. Perhaps we are looking at the Caesarea harbor, but it is also possible that the scene depicts a similar harbor at Alexandria.

Concrete blocks and wood fragments are not as exciting visually as the marble statues, mosaic floors and huge vaults found on land at Caesarea. But mundane as these concrete blocks and wood frames are, our discovery of them confirms important details about the plan and technology of the world's first great artificial harbor.

[1]The Caesarea Ancient Harbor Excavation Project is sponsored by the Center for Maritime Studies at the University of Haifa and led by Professor Avner Raban. Other co-directors and representatives of their supporting institutions are Robert L. Hohlfelder of the University of Colorado, John P. Oleson of the University of Victoria, and Lindley Vann of the University of Maryland.

[2]For more information on the archaeological excavation of Caesarea and its harbor, see Robert Bull, "Caesarea Maritima—The Search for Herod's City" [106] and Robert Hohlfelder, "Caesarea Beneath the Sea," **BAR**, May/June 1982 [124].

[3]For more information on Josephus, see the review of *Josephus—The Jewish War*, **BAR**, May/June 1983, p. 18.

Endnotes from "Caesarea Beneath the Sea"

(see p. 124)

[1]An expanded version of this article was presented as a public lecture at the annual meetings of the American Association for the Advancement of Science, Washington, D.C., January 5, 1982.

[2]George F. Bass, *Cape Gelidonya: A Bronze Age Shipwreck, Transactions of the American Philosophical Society,* Vol. 57, Pt. 8, Philadelphia, 1967.

[3]C. Fritsch and I. Ben-Dor, "The Link Expedition to Israel," *Biblical Archeologist* 24 (1961), pp. 50-56.

[4]Although Professor Katzev has written extensively about the Kyrenia ship, the most enjoyable introduction to this project for readers of **BAR** would be a viewing of his excellent documentary, "With Captain Sailors Three—The Ancient Ship of Kyrenia," co-produced by the Cyprus Broadcasting Corporation and the National Geographic Society (1978). This film is the best ever made on shipwreck archaeology in the Mediterranean.

[5]Robert L. Scranton, "Glass Pictures from the Sea," *Archaeology* 20 (1967), pp. 163-173 and Leila Ibrahim, Robert Scranton and Robert Brill, *Kenchreai, Eastern Port of Corinth, Vol. II: The Panels of Opus Sectile in Glass,* Leiden, 1976.

[6]CAHEP's field work has been funded by the National Endowment for the Humanities, the Rothschild Foundation, the University of Colorado Foundation, the University of Haifa, and numerous private donors. This article was completed during the tenure of a faculty fellowship awarded by the Council on Research and Creative Work, the University of Colorado. I wish to thank these agencies, institutions and individuals for their generous support. Other senior staff members include Professor John P. Oleson, University of Victoria, B.C., senior underwater archaeologist; Professor R. Lindley Vann, architect; and Mr. Harry Wadsworth, underwater photographer. For a preliminary report on CAHEP's activities, see Robert L. Hohlfelder and Avner Raban, "The Ancient Harbors of Caesarea Maritima," *Archaeology* 34 (1981), pp. 56-60.

SEARCHING FOR HEROD'S TOMB

Somewhere in the desert palace-fortress at Herodium, Palestine's master builder was buried.

By Ehud Netzer

*Dedicated to the memory of David Rosenfeld.**

I had no idea of searching for Herod's tomb when I began my archaeological work at Herodium. But I confess it has now become something of a minor obesssion with me. Whether I will eventually achieve my goal is still an open question, but the search itself is instructive and enjoyable. Although I cannot, in all honesty, conceal my desire to find the tomb of the Holy Land's greatest builder, I shall nevertheless consider myself richly rewarded even if I continue to fail.

We know that Herod was buried at Herodium because Josephus tells us so.[1] On a matter such as this, there is no reason to doubt the accuracy of this well-known, first-century Jewish historian, who was born in Palestine about 40 years after Herod's death in 4 B.C.

Herodium, *a man-made mountain in the Judean wilderness. In 23 B.C., Herod the Great built a magnificent palace-fortress here on top of a natural hill. Seven stories of living rooms, storage areas, cisterns, a bathhouse, and a courtyard filled with bushes and flowering plants were laboriously constructed; then the whole complex was surrounded and partly buried by a sloping fill of earth and gravel. This massive fill reached a height of 60 feet, providing the palace with a virtually impenetrable defense and creating the unique and dramatic cone shape we still see today.*

Herodium is a magnificent palace complex in the barren Judean hills eight miles south of Jerusalem and three and a half miles east of Bethlehem. Herod's decision to build a palace at this spot was not an accident. In 40 B.C., Herod had fought a crucial battle here against Mattathias Antigonus, the last Hasmonean (Maccabean) king. Antigonus had rebelled against his Roman overlords in collaboration with Rome's traditional enemy, the Parthians from Iran. Herod, the consummate politician, refused to join Antigonus's revolt. Instead, Herod fled south from Jerusalem with his close family and bodyguards, heading for the safety of

*On July 3, 1983, David Rosenfeld, a young Israeli guard at the Herodium excavations was brutally murdered by Bedouin who belonged to Fatah—the largest of the terrorist groups comprising the PLO. The murderers chose Friday to perpetrate their vicious crime because our regular Arab guards were observing the Moslem sabbath and David was alone. David was stabbed nearly 100 times. In their ecstasy, the murderers also managed to stab themselves and as a result they were apprehended.

Two days after David was killed, Arab and Jew, American and Israeli cleaned up the caked blood and said the Kaddish, the traditional Jewish prayer for the dead. Then, together, we continued our work on the excavation.

David left a wife, Dorit, and two small children, Daniel, 2½, and Alexander, 1½.

This article is dedicated to David. May his memory be a blessing.

his fortress at Masada. Antigonus and his troops pursued and at the site of what would someday be Herodium, Herod turned and fought, winning a decisive battle that allowed him to continue his escape. Passing with difficulty through Arabia and Egypt, Herod finally reached Rome, where Mark Anthony nominated him king of Judea. With Mark Anthony's nomination, Herod was quickly elected by the Roman Senate, but it took three years of constant war with Antigonus before Herod was able to assume his new position.[2]

Only hours before the crucial battle with Antigonus at the future site of Herodium, Herod lived through another terrifying experience. Josephus tells us that as Herod and his family were fleeing Jerusalem, the chariot carrying Herod's mother overturned, seriously injuring her. Herod was so shocked and anguished that he nearly committed suicide. Indeed, he had drawn his sword and was about to stab himself when his friends restrained him. Herod then ministered to his injured mother, who eventually recovered. (See Josephus's text in the box on page 144.)

This traumatic personal experience and the crucial battle with Antigonus that followed no doubt left a deep impression on Herod. Twenty years passed before he returned to the battlefield, this time as an established and active king, as well as an experienced builder. His feelings toward the place were so strong that he decided not only to commemorate his victory there but also to name the site after himself—the only site to which he gave his name.* More than that, he decided to be buried there.

Although Herodium consists of both a mountain palace-fortress and a lower complex of buildings, when people think of Herodium, they immediately focus on the spectacular, cone-shaped, artificial mountain. Through the ages many scholars have believed and even now believe that Herod's tomb lies somewhere undiscovered within this unique mountain palace-fortress.

Herod built this mountain palace-fortress on top of a natural hill. The main feature of the structure is a cylinder-like wall. The cylinder, approximately 200 feet in diameter, consists of two concentric circular walls with a corridor 39 feet wide between the two walls. When this cylinder was constructed, it rose about 90 feet above bedrock. Between the two concentric walls there were seven stories—two substructural cellars with barrel-vaulted ceilings and five stories of corridors that also served as storage areas. Today the two or three uppermost stories are no longer extant.

When the cylinder wall was completed, a massive fill of

*Josephus mentions another site named Herodium "on the Arabian frontier" (*The Jewish War* I, 419). The parallel passage in Josephus's *Jewish Antiquities* (XV, 323-325) does not mention it, so its existence is doubtful, although possible.

The 45-acre site of Greater Herodium is dominated by the cone-shaped mountain palace-fortress, excavated in the 1960s by Father Virgilio Corbo. At the base of the mountain, on the north slope (at the bottom of the picture above), Ehud Netzer has uncovered additional extensive remains of Herod's elaborate desert retreat. The pre-excavation photograph above served as Netzer's map and guide, helping him decide where to dig in Lower Herodium, below the mountain palace-fortress. Shapes and contours not apparent at ground level became, from this distant view, strong suggestions of buried architectural features. In this photograph, Netzer saw the outline of the Course (an artificial terrace), the Monumental Building at the Course's western end, and the palace area to its south. Excavations revealed many architectural elements of Lower Herodium. These are identified on the plan (top right). The author noted four architectural axes at Herodium that bisect important structures to create what appears to be planned symmetry. These axes are shown as heavy dotted lines. The Monumental Building's position on a direct line between the eastern tower—the largest tower of the mountain palace-fortress—and the pavilion in the center of the pool suggests an as yet undiscovered significance to the Monumental Building: Could the Monumental Building be related to the place of Herod's burial?

THE PLAN OF GREATER HERODIUM

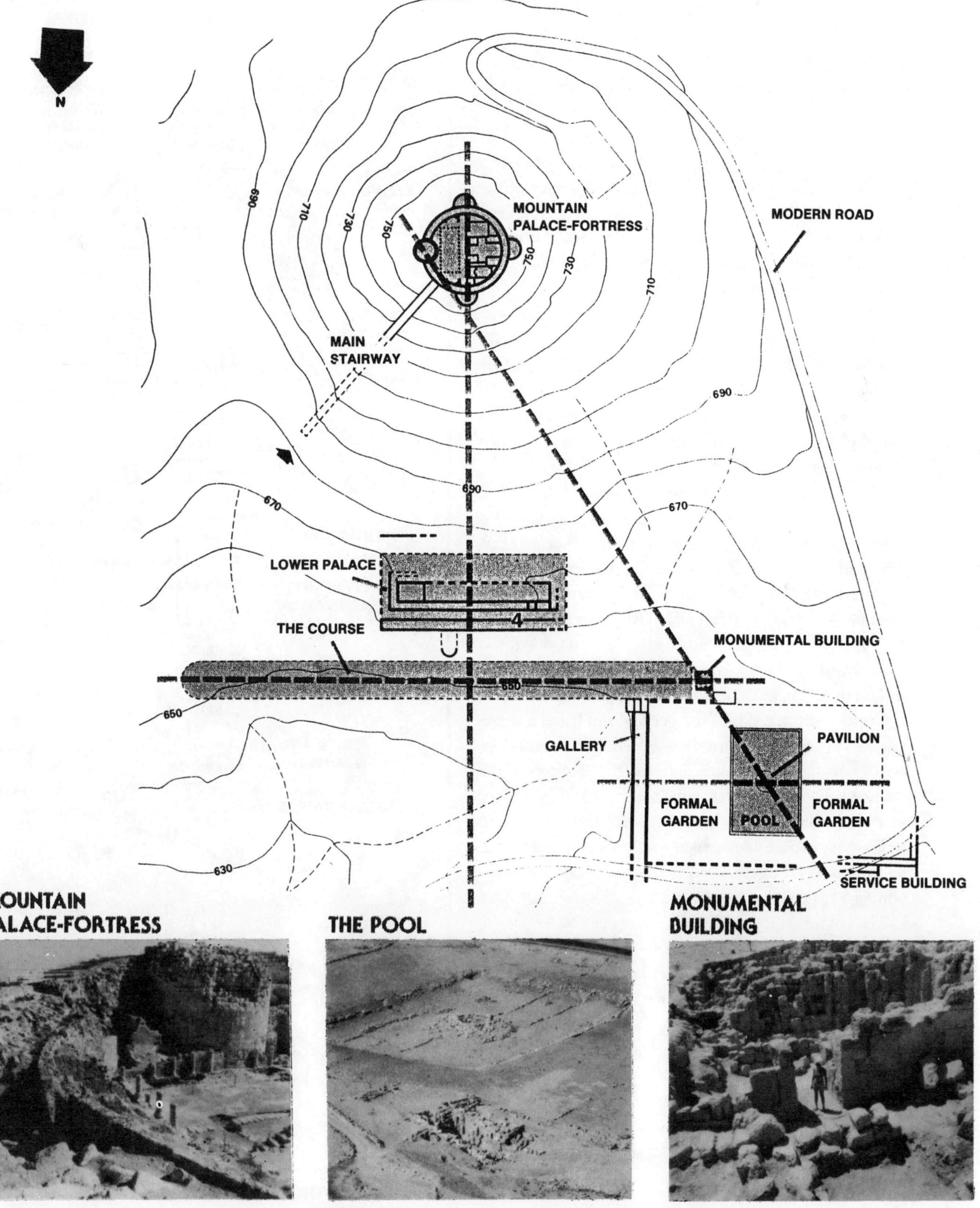

MOUNTAIN PALACE-FORTRESS

THE POOL

MONUMENTAL BUILDING

earth and gravel was added on the outside. The fill reached to about the fifth floor (counting the lowest of the two subcellars as the first floor), or to approximately two-thirds of the height of the cylinder. Thus, only about one-third of the cylinder wall was exposed after the fill was heaped up outside. Inside, Herod built a spacious, private palace on a level platform he created on top of the natural hill. The outside fill reached three stories above this platform!

This fill imparts to the huge structure a cone-like shape, with the palace inside far below the top of the wall, giving the mountain the appearance of a volcano with building remains inside its crater.

The fill-created conic shape transformed the structure into a distinctive monument. The steep slope formed by the fill, together with the upper free-standing part of the cylinder walls and the towers built into them, made it extraordinarily difficult to penetrate the fortress. No doubt the fill was not added later, but was planned from the beginning as an integral part of the structure.

Within the cylinder walls, Herod built a private, intimate, exotic and protected palace, divided into two equal parts. In the eastern half was an oblong courtyard surrounded by a peristyle. At either end was a semicircular niche, or *exedra*, for a statue. Originally, the courtyard was full of planted bushes and colorful flowers, with pathways between them.

The western half of the palace contained the living quarters. Sleeping rooms and living rooms surrounded a cross-shaped room that probably included a square, open courtyard in the center. South of the sleeping and living rooms was the triclinium—the official reception and dining room (45 feet long by 30 feet wide). At a later stage (during the First Jewish Revolt against the Romans), this room was transformed into a synagogue by the addition of benches around the walls and four columns to support a new roof.

On the northern side of the sleeping and living quarters was a complete Roman bathhouse. Here Herod, accompanied by his intimate friends, enjoyed the comforts of the bath. A fairly large, barrel-vaulted room served as the hot room (caldarium). From there one passes through a round warm room (tepidarium), which is still covered by a beautiful stone cupola, to the small cold room (frigidarium) containing a stepped water basin.

The palace on top of the hill was about 180 feet above the base of the cone. It could be entered in only one way: by a steep stairway nearly 500 feet long that went directly up the mountain, first outside for about 300 feet, then through a tunnel in the mountain for the remaining 200 feet. Josephus counted 200 steps, but I assume there were many more. I doubt if the stairs were made of white marble, as he described them. They were probably of hewn stone.

Four prominent towers on the outside of the cylinder

Text continued on page 144

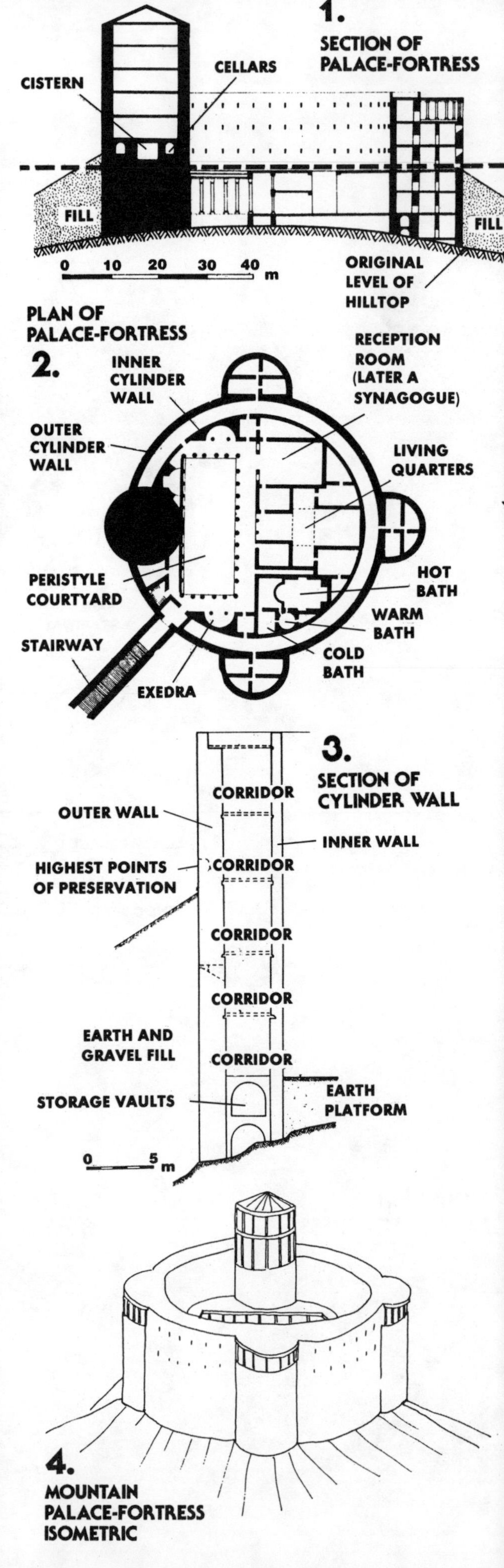

MOUNTAIN PALACE-FORTRESS

UPPER HERODIUM

From as far away as Jerusalem, eight miles to the north, Herodium is easily recognized by its distinctive silhouette. Here we see elements of the mountain palace-fortress, which nestles out of sight within the mountain's cone.

The section drawing (1) is a vertical slice through the palace-fortress along an east-west plane, facing south. The stippled slopes on the outside of the towers represent the earth and gravel fill poured around the palace-fortress above the level of the natural hill. The elements of the round eastern tower are clear: the solid lower portion, the cistern and two small cellars, and the five levels of rooms. In contrast, the western tower contains rooms down to its base; on the very top floor, we see a colonnaded balcony.

The single dotted line on the section shows its relationship to the circular plan (2). This plan shows a bird's-eye view of what one would see if a horizontal slice were made at the level of the dotted line, with the upper floors removed. Note that the plan is made at a level where the eastern tower is still solid and where we can see the tops of the columns in the peristyle courtyard and the walls of the reception room, living quarters and bath. Each of the three semicircular towers is divided into four rooms; none had windows since this level was surrounded by fill.

All four towers were connected at each level by corridors that ran within the double-walled enclosing cylinder of the mountain palace-fortress. These corridors are seen in the section (3) as horizontal double-dotted lines between the vertical inner and outer cylinder walls.

Before the fill was laid against the outer walls of the cylinder, the mountain palace-fortress would have appeared as it does in drawing (4).

Hurled from the top of the cylinder walls, rolling stones (below left) became lethal weapons. These stones may have been used by Jewish defenders occupying the mountain palace-fortress in 66-70 A.D. against the Romans attacking from below.

A niche or *exedra* (below right) was built at either end of the long peristyle courtyard in the mountaintop palace. Here we see the southern *exedra*. A statue originally stood in this semicircular niche and in an identical niche at the opposite (northern) end of the courtyard.

Zev Radovan

MOUNTAIN PALACE-FORTRESS

UPPER HERODIUM

Inner and outer cylindrical walls (left) curve around the mountaintop palace-fortress. The huge solid base of the eastern tower (left and below) was constructed first. Then the cylinder walls were built; the cylinder consists of two concentric walls, with diameters of 207 feet and 166 feet, respectively. The area between the cylinder walls was divided into seven stories of storage areas and corridors connecting the towers (see section drawings, p. 140).

The eastern tower of the mountain palace-fortress, 55 feet in diameter and solid to its extant height (except for two small rooms and a barrel-vaulted cistern visible in the photo below, near the top of the tower), is the largest of Herodium's four guard towers. Unlike the other three, which are semicircular towers, the eastern tower is circular and extends through both the inner and outer cylinder walls surrounding the palace; the tower protrudes into the peristyle courtyard. Several stories of rooms atop this tower, now missing, once provided a royal retreat from the windowless palace within the mountain; here there was always a breeze and a spectacular view of the Dead Sea and the Judean wilderness.

Many scholars expected Herod's tomb to be found within this tower, but the author counters that because Jewish law forbids burial inside a dwelling, the eastern tower could not contain Herod's tomb.

Zev Radovan

wall overlook the palace and command a wide view of the surrounding countryside. They precisely mark the points of the compass. Three of these towers are substantially the same. They are semicircular and are built against and bonded to the outer cylinder wall. Originally, each contained about 20 rooms distributed over five or six stories (60 rooms altogether in the three semicircular towers). Only in the upper stories did these rooms have windows; no windows were present in the lower floors of the towers, because these floors were covered with fill piled outside the walls. The illuminated rooms above the fill were probably used for palace staff or guards, perhaps even for guests of the king. The unlit rooms in the lower stories served either for storage or as dormitories for servants or soldiers.

The eastern tower is unique. It is round, not semicircular. It extends through both the inner and outer cylinder walls and into the oblong courtyard. An examination of its construction reveals that it was the first structure built at Herodium—even the cylinder walls were built later. The walls of the cylinder are not bonded to this tower. Its diameter, 55 feet, makes it larger than the other three towers. Moreover, to its extant height it is solid, except for a water cistern and two small cellars. Originally the cellars, which served now-missing upper stories, were entered from their roof.

Several levels of apartments must have topped the eastern tower at Herodium—making up a secondary dwelling unit, just as Josephus suggests existed on top of the towers Herod built in Jerusalem. At Herodium this secondary dwelling unit must have been especially important because

HEROD FLEES FROM THE PARTHIANS AND DEFEATS ANTIGONUS AT THE PLACE HE WOULD LATER CALL HERODIUM

While the Parthians deliberated what they should do—for they did not like the idea of openly attacking so powerful a man—and postponed the matter to the next day, Herod, who was in great perturbation and gave more weight to what he had heard about his brother and the Parthians' plot than to the other side, decided when evening came to take this opportunity to flee and not to delay as if there were some uncertainty of danger from the enemy. Accordingly he set out with those soldiers whom he had there, and mounted the women on beasts of burden, including his mother and sister and the daughter of Alexander, the son of Aristobulus, whom he was to marry, and her mother, who was a daughter of Hyrcanus; he also took his youngest brother and all the servants and the rest of the crowd that was with them, and unknown to the enemy followed the road to Idumaea. And no enemy would have been found so hard of heart that on witnessing what was taking place at that time he would not have pitied their fate as the wretched women led their infants and with tears and wailing left behind their native country and their friends in chains; nor did they expect anything better for themselves.

Nevertheless, Herod let his spirit rise above the blow caused by this misfortune, and being himself of good courage in the face of misfortune, went to the others along the road and urged each of them also to have courage and not give himself wholly over to grief, for this, he said, would hinder them in their flight, in which alone their safety lay. And so at Herod's exhortation they tried to bear their troubles. But once when a wagon overturned and his mother was in danger of death, he was near to taking his own life because of his anguish on her account and his fear that as a result of the delay caused by the overturn the enemy might overtake them in pursuit. Indeed he had drawn his sword and was about to stab himself when those about him restrained him and prevailed upon him by their number and also by telling him that it was not right for him to abandon them and leave them in the power of their foes, for it was not the act of a noble man to free himself from danger and disregard that of his friends. And so, being forced to desist from his rash act against himself by shame at their words and by the number of those who stayed his hand from carrying out his plan, he revived his mother and procured for her such care as was possible in the short time at his disposal, and continued on his way, making the journey to the fortress of Masada at great speed. Many were the battles he fought with the Parthians who harassed him in pursuit, and he was victorious in all of them.

But during his flight he was not safe from the Jews either, for they too attacked his party when they were sixty stades [about seven miles] from the city and engaged them in hand to hand combat along the road; but these too he routed and crushed as if he were in no such helpless and difficult position but were excellently prepared for war and had a great advantage; and later when he became king, he built a wonderful palace on the spot where he defeated the Jews, and founded a city round it, which he called Herodia [Herodium].

Josephus, *Jewish Antiquities* XIV, 352-360.

the palace dwellers inside the mountain suffered from two major disadvantages: the lack of wind (especially on a hot day) and the lack of visual contact with the outside world. The apartments on top of the eastern tower made up for these disadvantages. Here Herod could repair and enjoy a gentle breeze even on the hottest day and gaze at the beauty of the landscape. The view of the Judean desert, the Dead Sea and the distant mountains of Moab is truly breathtaking.

Many scholars believe that Herod's tomb lies at the base of this tower or somewhere within it. I am sure, however, that the tomb is not here.

Text continued on page 149

Zev Radovan

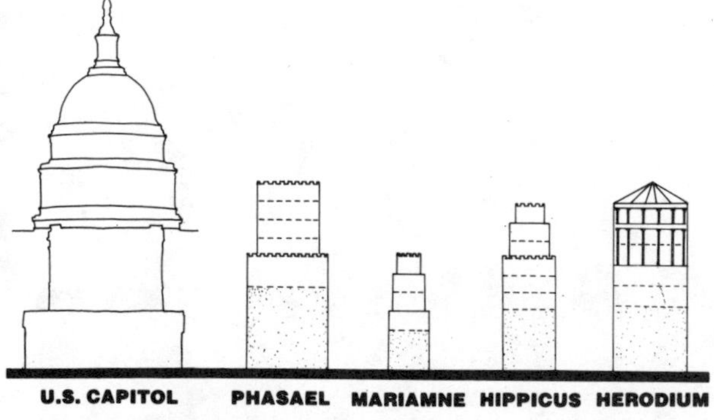

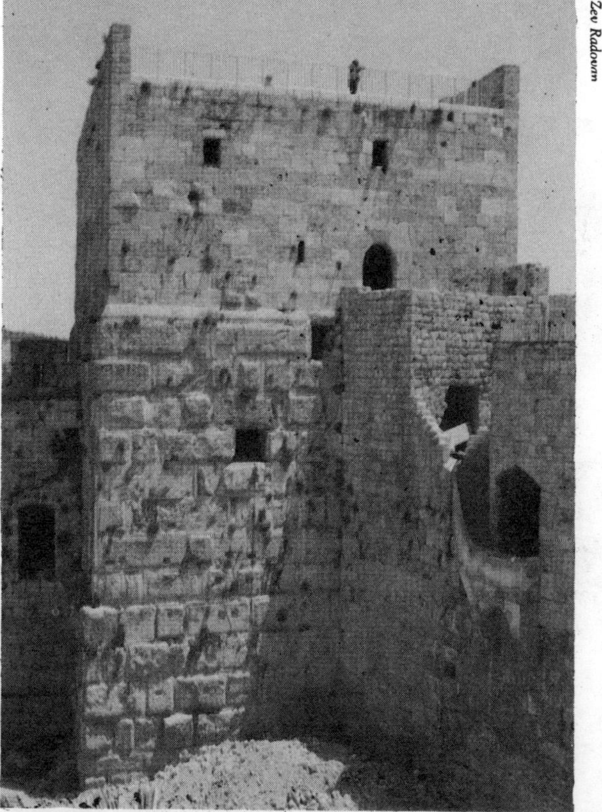

Zev Radovan

Zev Radovan

Herod's towers. *Herod built many towers in Israel, both to guard his palaces and to stand as monuments to friends and relatives. In the photo, right top, we see Hippicus (left), Phasael (center) and Mariamne, three huge towers that protected Herod's palace in Jerusalem. This scale model reconstruction by Professor Michael Avi-Yonah is in the garden of the Holyland Hotel in Jerusalem. Although no traces of Hippicus and Mariamne have yet been found, much of Phasael's solid base (right, middle) still stands within the complex called the Citadel just south of the Jaffa Gate. According to Josephus, Hippicus was "solid throughout" and Mariamne was "solid to a height of ... 20 cubits."*

The four towers at the corners of the Antonia fortress (right, bottom), built by Herod to guard the Temple Mount at its vulnerable northwest corner, were similar in plan to his many other military observation towers, including the towers at Herodium. This reconstruction is also part of the elaborate model of Herodian Jerusalem at the Holyland Hotel. Like these Jerusalem towers, the high eastern tower of the Herodium palace also has a solid base. Herod built the solid-base Jerusalem towers as monuments and observation posts. Since the solid-base round tower at Herodium served a similar function, it is unlikely that this tower was built, as some suggest, to hide Herod's tomb.

Josephus's descriptions of all these towers, together with comparative remains, suggest the possible reconstructions in the drawing (above). Drawn as a scale is the 287-foot-high U.S. Capitol in Washington, D.C., which gives some idea of the original heights of Herod's towers.

THE POOL AND PAVILION

LOWER HERODIUM

Werner Braun

The volcano-shaped artificial mountain rises 2,460 feet (750m) above sea level. This mountain palace-fortress and the related lower palace and residential structures near the mountain's base cover approximately 45 acres. Herod the Great completed this huge building project in one construction stage in 23 B.C.

At the foot of the artificial mountain, Herod built another complex of buildings. The outstanding extant feature of this vast lower complex was the pool, now dry, which covers most of the foreground of this photograph. The walls of large, rough-cut stones are over 9 feet deep, 210 feet long and 135 feet wide. In the center of the pool are remains of an island with a circular pavilion about 40 feet in diameter. A plan of the pavilion (below) shows in dotted lines the base of 16 excavated piers in the pavilion whose exact function is unknown; the black circles show proposed positions for the inner and outer columns of the pavilion.

An aqueduct brought water to the pool even in the scorching heat of summer, from springs three and a half miles away. Here, in the middle of a desert was a true pleasure palace, in size and lavishness unique in Israel, and the third-largest palace in the entire Roman world.

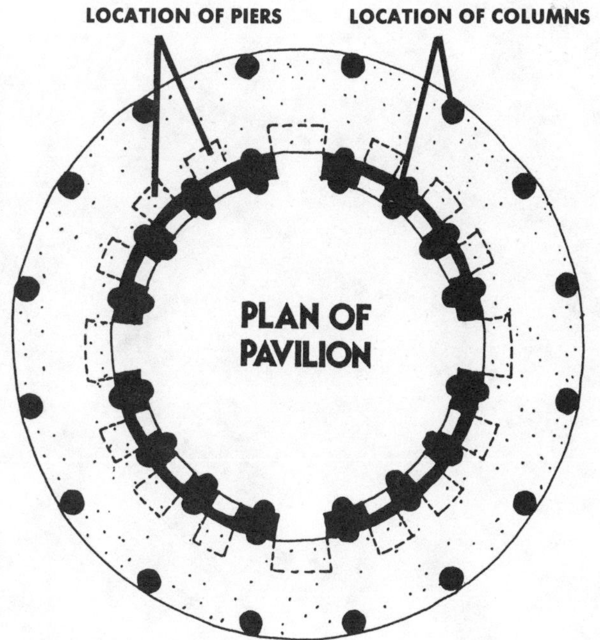

THE POOL
LOWER HERODIUM

The immense rectangular pool in the background of the photograph below was the architectural focus of Lower Herodium. Here the royal family and their guests sailed small boats to the island in the center of the pool, where Herod gave parties in a round, colonnaded pavilion. An early explorer of Herodium, Felicien De Saulcy, excavated the remains of this pavilion, looking for Herod's tomb, but found no evidence of a burial.

In the foreground of the photo is the Monumental Building, roughly 45 feet square and partially cut into bedrock. The purpose of this structure—massively built and isolated from the rest of Lower Herodium— has eluded excavators, and attempts to locate Herod's tomb here have not yet met with success. But Netzer believes the building is somehow related to the as-yet undiscovered tomb of Herod.

In the section drawing (below), facing south, we see the pool on the right bounded by two black walls; in the center of the pool is the colonnaded pavilion. The three elements shown in black are those actually found; other details are reconstructed. On either side of the pool are formal gardens. On the far left is a sheltered gallery that ran along almost the entire eastern side of the pool complex. Perhaps it was here that people could find shade and lounge in the late afternoon breezes.

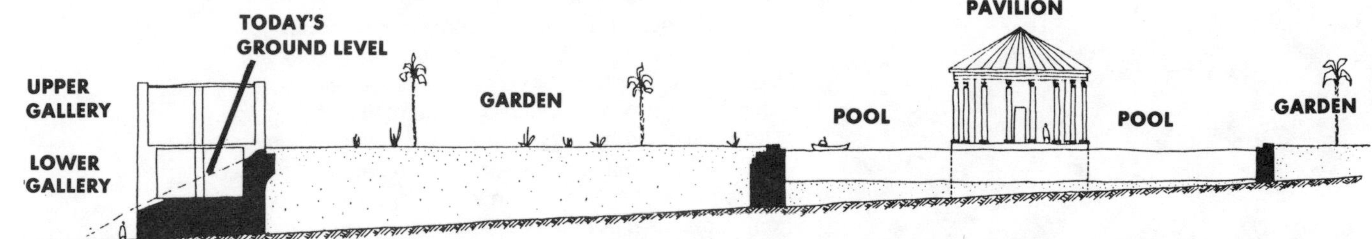

Zev Radovan

The ancient Jews did not bury their dead inside buildings, especially buildings that had been used as dwellings. They did not even use places attached to dwellings for burials. Tombs and cemeteries had to be isolated.

No evidence of a tomb has so far been found anywhere inside the hilltop palace. Although Herod *could* have been buried inside the base of the eastern tower, Jewish religious laws, as I indicated above, preclude this; the solid base of the eastern tower was not built to hide a tomb but as a result of architectural and structural considerations.

Herod built a number of monumental towers with solid bases, several of which are described by Josephus in great detail. In Jerusalem, Herod built three famous towers at the northern end of his palace, one named for his brother Phasael, one for his friend Hippicus and a third for Mariamne, his wife.[3] Hippicus, Josephus says, was "solid throughout" and rose to a height of 80 cubits.* Phasael had a "solid base" and was 90 cubits high. Mariamne was "solid to a height of only 20 cubits." The solid foundations were probably necessary because of the towers' great heights, particularly because of the danger of earthquakes. Josephus tells us that sometimes, as with Hippicus, a water cistern was built on top of the solid foundation. (At Herodium, a water cistern survives on top of the eastern tower.)

The base of the Phasael tower has survived as part of Jerusalem's Citadel; it is adjacent to the Jaffa Gate in the Old City. It has, as Josephus says, a solid base. Herod also built four towers at the four corners of the Antonia fortress in Jerusalem. One Antonia tower was exceptionally high—the one overlooking and commanding the Temple Mount.[4] Another exceptional tower, named Drusion for Caesar's stepson, was built at Caesarea.[5]

Thus, it was common for Herod to build impressively high towers, all probably with solid bases, and to name them in honor of his friends and relatives. These towers served as military observation posts, but more important, as striking monuments. A similar impulse in other historical periods has led to the construction of church towers and minarets. In the Middle Ages, city palaces in Italy had towers. Among the most famous still standing are those of Bologna and San Gimignano.

If Herod's towers were indeed built primarily as monuments and military structures, then the dramatic structure with its towers on the mountaintop was built not as a mausoleum, but as an integral part of the mountain palace, a fortress and a monument both to Herod's great name and to his military victory at this site. It was not his burial place.

If Herod was not buried on the mountaintop, then where at Herodium was he buried? Possibly, Herod's tomb is

*A cubit was approximately equivalent to 18 inches.

THE APPEARANCE OF THE FORTRESS AND THE CITY OF HERODIUM

Herod constructed another fortress in the region where he had defeated the Jews after his expulsion from the realm, when Antigonus was in power. This fortress, which is some sixty stades [about seven miles] distant from Jerusalem, is naturally strong and very suitable for such a structure, for reasonably near by is a hill, raised to a (greater) height by the hand of man and rounded off in the shape of a breast. At intervals it has round towers, and it has a steep ascent formed of two hundred steps of hewn stone. Within it are costly royal apartments made for security and for ornament at the same time. At the base of the hill there are pleasure grounds built in such a way as to be worth seeing, among other things because of the way in which water, which is lacking in that place, is brought from a distance and at great expense. The surrounding plain was built up as a city second to none, with the hill serving as an acropolis for the other dwellings.

Josephus, *Jewish Antiquities* XV, 323-325.

The French explorer ***Richard Pococke visited Herodium in 1738 and drew the first plan of the artificial mountain in modern times.***

inside the hill, far below the level of the palace-fortress. However, the inside of the hill is not totally *terra incognita*. Over the years, we have studied a complex system of tunnels cut into the hill during the second Jewish Revolt against the Romans (132 A.D.-135 A.D.). Herodium had already been occupied by the Zealots during the First Jewish Revolt against the Romans (66 A.D.-70 A.D.). After that, Herodium was neglected, but during the second Jewish Revolt the mountain was again used as a fortress. This time the Jewish warriors decided to improve the defensive possibilities by digging a system of tunnels along the northeastern slope of the mountain, on both sides of the stairway. Three large Herodian water cisterns that had been carved into this side of the mountain were integrated into the tunnel system as junction points. The cisterns were also used to store the debris from the construction of the tunnels. The tunnels were connected at one end with the building on top of the hill; at the other end, they were connected with the outside by a few hidden outlets situated on the steep slopes. This gave the fortress's defenders a hidden underground tunnel system, unknown to the Romans. From here, the Jewish defenders could surprise the Romans or hide from them if they reached the mountaintop. During our investigation of these tunnels—more than 750 feet of them—we found no sign of a tomb. My belief is that Herod's tomb is somewhere near the base of the mountain.

Although I have studied the mountain palace-fortress, measured it and performed some small sondages there, and have even studied the tunnels inside the mountain, the great bulk of my Herodium excavations have been undertaken at what is called Lower Herodium, the complex of buildings at the foot of the mountain. As my studies have shown, these buildings were an integral part of the larger complex that archaeologists call Greater Herodium.

Earlier archaeological excavations focused on the mountaintop. In a way, it was through those earlier excavations that I was first drawn to Herodium.

Father Virgilio Corbo directed the first archaeological excavation at Herodium from 1963 to 1967—a Franciscan mission excavating on behalf of the Studium Biblicum Franciscanum. As an Israeli, I could not visit Herodium during those years. The only spot from which I could view Herodium was the observatory at Ramat Rahel, just south of Jerusalem, atop an Iron Age palace-fortress excavated by the late Yohanan Aharoni. Even from that distance, Herodium was breathtaking.

In 1963, Father Corbo visited Masada, where I was working as an architect in the excavation and reconstruction of that magnificent site. None of the members of the Masada expedition could speak Italian. Neither could I, but since I had picked up a few words of Italian on visits to Italy, I volunteered to escort Father Corbo around Masada. As we walked together, Father Corbo told me of his excavations at Herodium. I listened with excitement.

About four years later, a few days after the Six Day War, I visited Herodium for the first time. It was an unforgettable experience. Now I have been to Herodium hundreds of times, but even after all these years and after four seasons of excavations, I am still awestruck each time by the grandeur of this man-made mountain-monument.

In 1972, I was ready to begin working on my Ph.D. thesis at the Hebrew University of Jerusalem under the direction of Yigael Yadin. It was he who suggested that I take the Herodian remains at Jericho and Herodium as my topic.[6] Though I could have undertaken the project just by sitting in the library studying and analyzing the reports of earlier excavations, I decided in addition to go to the field and to study the site with a pickax and spade, that is, by excavation.

What attracted me most were the widespread remains at Lower Herodium. An aerial photograph of the entire site (see p. 138) was of enormous help while I was deciding where to dig; it revealed just how extensive the remains of Lower Herodium were. Indeed, this aerial photograph was to become my guide and my compass.

HEROD'S FUNERAL AND BURIAL AT HERODIUM

The king's funeral next occupied attention. Archelaus, omitting nothing that could contribute to its magnificence, brought forth all the royal ornaments to accompany the procession in honour of the deceased. The bier was of solid gold, studded with precious stones, and had a covering of purple, embroidered with various colors; on this lay the body enveloped in a purple robe, a diadem encircling the head and surmounted by a crown of gold, the sceptre beside his right hand. Around the bier were Herod's sons and a large group of his relations; these were followed by the guards, the Thracian contingent, Germans and Gauls, all equipped as for war. The remainder of the troops marched in front, armed and in orderly array, led by their commanders and subordinate officers; behind these came five hundred of Herod's servants and freedmen, carrying spices. The body was thus conveyed for a distance of two hundred furlongs to Herodium, where, in accordance with the directions of the deceased, it was interred. So ended Herod's reign.

Josephus, *The Jewish War* I, 670-673.

THE COURSE AND LOWER PALACE

LOWER HERODIUM

The vast artificial terrace (below) called the Course stretches out for almost 1100 feet. Part of the original retaining wall of the Course is still visible on the north (lower) side. In this view looking west, remains of the lower palace appear top left. Excavators have not yet determined the purpose of this enormous flat expanse of earth; but, if the Monumental Building at the western end of the Course housed or was related to Herod's tomb, perhaps the Course was built as a processional terrace for Herod's elaborate military funeral.

At right is a section drawing of the lower palace. The black areas show the few surviving structures uncovered in excavations. Drawn above these structures is a suggested reconstruction of this huge palace, which was more than twice as large as the palace-fortress on the mountaintop.

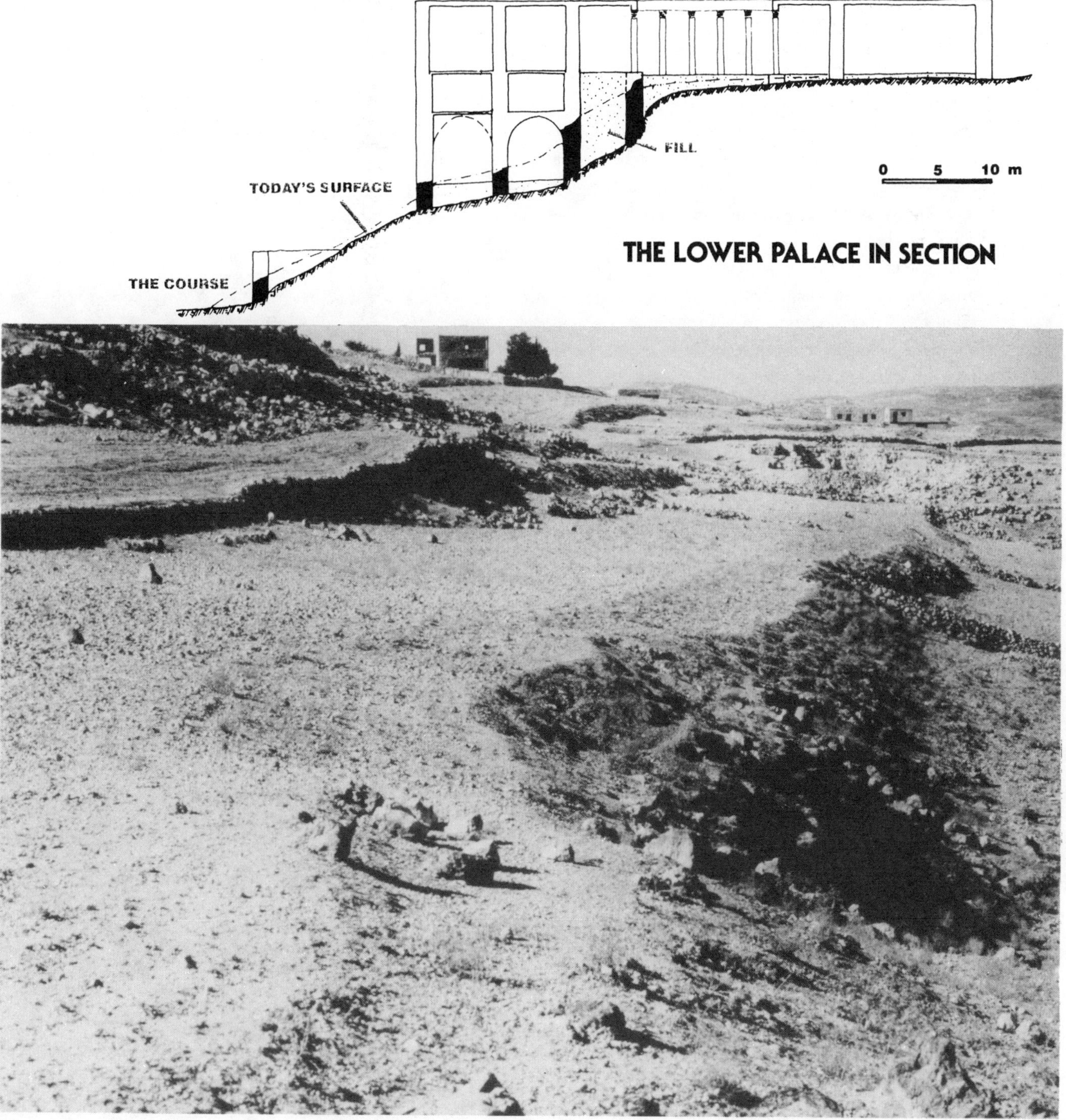

THE LOWER PALACE IN SECTION

The most prominent feature of Lower Herodium is a great pool, now of course dry. Even in its present condition, it is impressive. It is over nine feet deep and measures 135 feet wide by 210 feet long. In one corner of the pool, stairs nearly eight feet wide are preserved.

The walls of the pool, which are five feet thick, are constructed of large, rough, partly drafted stones. A gray hydraulic mortar mixture consisting of lime and ashes was applied to the walls to prevent seepage. The pool itself was partly cut into the bedrock and partly built on top of a fill. Originally the pool was fed by an aqueduct from springs three and a half miles away at Urtas.

Although we found no evidence of colonnades, footpaths or gardens, they must have been part of this large and important pool complex. East of the pool was a large, artificially leveled area whose upper layer was thick, pure, brown-black earth that was probably brought here for the gardens surrounding the pool. At Jericho we found some vivid remains of the garden surrounding the pool. We did not find similar remains at Herodium, probably because the ground here is cultivated yearly and farmers long ago destroyed any evidence of the gardens and colonnades surrounding the pool.

In the center of the pool—on what was a little island—are the remains of a large circular building about 40 feet in diameter. We exposed only part of the remains, but enough to enable us to get a clear picture of the original building—probably a colonnaded pavilion.

One early explorer in Palestine, the Frenchman, Felicien De Saulcy, conjectured that Herod was buried in this island pavilion, but De Saulcy conducted a small dig and found no evidence to support his hypothesis. Our own excavations and analysis of the surrounding area refute any suggestion that this was Herod's tomb.

The pool served as a water reservoir, a swimming pool, a lake for small sailing boats and, most important, as an architectural focus for Lower Herodium. Here were the pleasure grounds of Lower Herodium that vied with the artificial mountain palace-fortress itself in beauty and grandeur. In an area where water was scarce, here was water aplenty.

The island pavilion served as a small exotic reception hall that could be reached only by boat. We have discovered no evidence of a bridge to the island. The elegant pavilion set off the beauty of the pool and its surrounding gardens. From ancient drawings, we know that at each of several other sites a round pavilion or tower was located at the center of a rectangular pool. A similar pavilion was probably part of the middle terrace of the northern palace at Masada.

Between the pool and the mountain, just at the foot of the mountain, are the remains of a huge building. At the

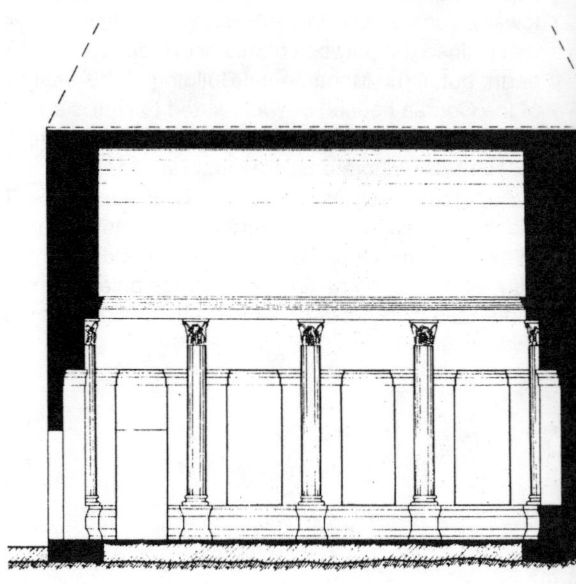

MONUMENTAL BUILDING

LOWER HERODIUM

Ehud Netzer hopes that excavations near the Monumental Building (B28 plan below, right) will reveal the location of Herod's tomb. The north half of this symmetrical building was excavated first in the hope of uncovering the entrance to Herod's burial cave behind the building. No such entrance was found. Then the south half of the building was excavated to determine whether an entrance to a burial cave was under the mountain on the south side of the building. Again, no cave was found.

At left is a reconstruction of the possible appearance of the Monumental Building as seen from the north. The reconstruction is based on the Temple of Diana at Nimes, to which the Monumental Building bears a striking similarity. The almost three-meter thickness of the north and south walls was probably necessary to support a dome and, perhaps, a second story or a monumental roof.

Below, an excavation volunteer stands in an entrance in the ten-foot-thick north wall. Inside, pilasters forming niches project from the south wall. Although some plaster still clings to the stones, nothing remains today of the frescoes that covered these walls in Herod's time.

Zev Radovan

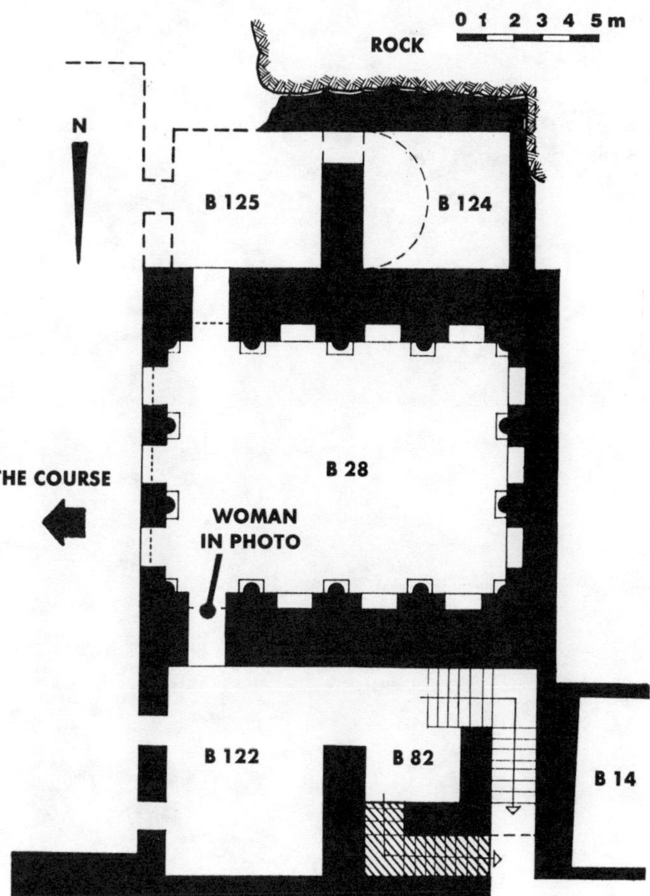

MONUMENTAL BUILDING
LOWER HERODIUM

Rooms adjacent to the Monumental Building yielded unexpected architectural remains. In this view (below)looking east, we see room B124 in the foreground and room B125 at the rear of the photo. Because the southern wall of these rooms abuts the hill of Herodium, Netzer speculated that they might contain an entrance to Herod's burial cave. At the end of the 1980 summer season, both rooms were cleared—but no entrance was revealed. However, while clearing room B124, a great number of magnificent carved ashlars, unlike any other stones at Herodium, were found in front of room B125.

Zev Radovan

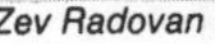

Zev Radovan

Zev Radovan

The large ashlar (below, top) decorated with a triglyph-metope motif and the one (below, bottom) with a carved rosette may have been part of a Doric frieze. Below left is another beautifully carved ashlar decorated with grape leaves. Suddenly, hopes were high—perhaps these unique ashlars were part of Herod's tomb. The next season's work began at the spot where the ashlars had been found. But the evidence the excavators found was disappointing: The ashlars were not part of a tomb, but had been reused in the fifth or sixth century to form part of a church. Below, far left, is a wall of this Byzantine church, built entirely of Herodian ashlars. But the author still hopes to uncover a tomb cave at Herodium, one that originally used these elegant ashlars in a monument to the master builder, Herod the Great.

Zev Radovan

Zev Radovan

end of the last century, Claude R. Conder and H. H. Kitchener of the London-based Palestine Exploration Fund carefully surveyed this 400-foot-long building. We too studied the remains which, unfortunately, are poorly preserved. We concluded from its size and location that this building must have been the central palace at Herodium. It is more than twice as large in area as the entire mountain palace-fortress. Built on an elevated platform (a few of the large, vaulted, substructural halls remain), this lower palace was clearly the most prominent building in Lower Herodium. Herod's retinue stayed in this lower palace, as no doubt did Herod himself when he did not want to go up to the mountain palace-fortress.

From the early stages of our work at the site, we were especially interested in and curious about an artificial terrace in front of the lower palace. We call this artificial terrace simply "the Course." It is instructive to look at the Course in the aerial photograph. To the observant eye it is different from the largely natural agricultural terraces that continue above it on the left. The Course is large. It is almost 1,100 feet long and 80 feet wide, nearly three times longer than the huge palace above it. The eastern end of the Course is clearly defined; beyond it the hillside is covered with natural rocks. On the lower (north) side of the Course parts of the original retaining wall may be seen. At the western end of the Course is perhaps the most significant building we have yet found at Herodium. We call it the Monumental Building.

At first I assumed that the Course was a hippodrome for horse races and chariot races. With this in mind, we paid special attention to the building that we at first thought was a U-shaped structure at the Course's western end. We assumed at this stage that this building was a small theater-like building from which Herod and his friends watched the races. But what we thought was a U-shaped building turned out to be a square building. It was not a theater, but a Monumental Building containing an elaborate hall. Moreover, colleagues more familiar with hippodromes convinced me I was wrong to identify the Course as a hippodrome because the Course was too narrow to be a hippodrome. (A few years later I located and exposed the hippodrome Herod built at Jericho, which was three times as wide as the Course at Herodium.) However, I have no doubt that the Course was connected harmoniously with the Monumental Building.

The Monumental Building measures roughly 45 feet by 45 feet. Its northern and southern walls are over 10 feet thick. Inside, is a single hall with a series of niches between pilasters extending from the walls. In a few places, plaster fragments are preserved, indicating that the inside walls were covered with frescoes. The building was built on bedrock and was even partially cut into bedrock.

After our excavation season ended, we analyzed all our finds, and suddenly the idea occurred to me that this Monumental Building may have been Herod's mausoleum. From then on, the idea shaped our thinking and planning.

In the following season, we excavated the northern half of this structure. Since it is symmetrical, we thought that excavating the northern half would make excavation of the southern half unnecessary. We also thought that excavating the northern half might lead us to Herod's burial cave, which we speculated might be behind the building. Unfortunately, the cave was not there.

In several ensuing seasons, we were unable to explain the function of the Monumental Building—or of the artificial terrace onto which the Monumental Building opens. The Monumental Building is too massively built to be a reception hall or a pavilion or even a library. Its side walls are ten feet thick. The unusual thickness of these walls indicates they supported a barrel-vaulted ceiling, an upper story or perhaps a monumental roof. Not only the size of the Monumental Building but also its dimensions and relatively isolated location puzzled us. There is nothing like it at other Herodian palaces. The possibility that it might be connected with Herod's tomb continued to intrigue us. Connecting the Monumental Building with Herod's burial also suggested a function for the Course. Perhaps the terrace had been built as a parade ground for Herod's elaborate military funeral, described in detail by Josephus.[7]

We next speculated that the entrance to Herod's burial cave might be hidden in the southern wall of the Monumental Building, which abutted the natural slope of the hill. So in 1978, we returned to the site and exposed the remaining half of the Monumental Building. Our excavations revealed that the ruined eastern facade, opposite the

HEROD—THE MAN AND HIS DEEDS

By Nahman Avigad

Herod was the son of Antipater the Idumean. Herod dethroned Mattathias Antigonus, the last of the Hasmoneans. With the support of the Romans, he assumed the throne in 37 B.C. and reigned until his death in 4 B.C. His modern appellation "the Great" is well deserved, for he was great in his deeds—both good and evil. Herod was a cautious politician who, throughout his life, was able to garner unstinting Roman support by appeasing the rulers of Rome. This enabled him to rule without serious competition and to extend his hegemony over more of the Holy Land than any of his predecessors, and even to lands far beyond. He was uncompromisingly cruel in suppressing the Hasmoneans, and relentless in the persecution of his opponents among his subjects and his own kinsfolk. Jewish enmity toward him stemmed from opposition to his foreign origin, and from his being a usurper who exterminated the Hasmoneans, the legal dynasty in Judea.

As a king, Herod aspired to glorify both his kingdom and his name. He was among the most extreme admirers of Hellenistic-Roman culture, and his desire to gain a standing for Jerusalem equal to that of the foremost Hellenistic cities led him to imbue his capital with a decidedly Hellenistic flavor. This found expression in the dominant architectural style of the buildings and their monumental proportions, as well as in the life style, which called for theaters, gymnasiums, hippodromes and "the games"—a cosmopolitan atmosphere and a luxurious court. This was neither entirely new nor unique in Jerusalem, where Hellenistic influence had already taken a hold under the Hasmoneans among the Jews of the city.

Herod's penchant for the grandiose led to one of the most important facets of his rule—especially for us today. He was undoubtedly the greatest builder Palestine has ever known. His craving for construction projects had no bounds. Josephus dwells at length on his many building activities in this country and abroad. Indeed, his impressive monuments, including fortresses, palaces, and even whole cities, have been revealed at various sites scattered about the country. He fulfilled his wish to impress his Roman imperial patrons by building new cities according to the best of Roman standards: his port city of Caesarea, and the town of Samaria, which he renamed "Sebaste" (Greek for "Augustus"), with a Temple of Augustus at its crown. These served well to express Herod's extreme admiration for Roman urbanization, architecture, and art. In the fortresses and palaces which he built at Masada, Herodium, and Jericho, Herod gave full architectural expression to his daring eccentricity, in which he sought to combine security, luxurious living, and tranquility with desert solitude. His winter and summer palaces established norms which deeply permeated the material aspect of the lives of the upper crust in Judea. It is noteworthy that in all these projects he strove to avoid any ornamental motifs which might give offense to the tenets of traditional Judaism—in deference to the customs of his people.

From the English translation of Discovering Jerusalem—Recent Archaeological Excavation in the Old City *by Nahman Avigad, to be published in the fall of 1983 by Thomas Nelson, Inc., Publishers.*

course, once contained three entrances. But for all our efforts and hopes, we found no tomb.

Over the years, we excavated a number of other areas at Lower Herodium and established that Lower Herodium was an integral part of the mountain palace-fortress, built contemporaneously with it. The whole complex of Greater Herodium covered an extensive area of approximately 45 acres, requiring a huge architectural and engineering effort. Indeed, of all the known Roman palaces, only two are larger than Herodium—the Villa Adriana near Tivoli and Nero's Golden House at Rome. Both are considerably later than Herodium. Herodium was no doubt Herod's main summer palace, secondary only to his large central palace at Jerusalem. Herodium was a harmonious integration of a countryside palace, rich in gardens and orchards, with a monument, a fortress, the burial place of Herod and a district capital.

The riddle of the Monumental Building continued to bother me, however, and in 1980 we returned to Lower Herodium for our fourth season. Our main target was the Monumental Building and its adjacent rooms. We still wanted to locate Herod's burial cave—if it was there. And we wanted to leave no possibility open that we had missed the spot, if the cave was not there.

We examined the area north of the Monumental Building and exposed a staircase that connected the Monumental Building to the pool complex, which was about 12 feet higher than the Monumental Building. On the southern side of the Monumental Building we found an adjacent room, part of the Monumental Building, that appeared to be promising. It was full of fallen ashlar stones, and clearing it was slow and difficult. Most of the room had been cut into natural bedrock, a perfect location for a burial tomb. But we were disappointed again. I was close to abandoning hope.

Since we had only a few days remaining before the end of the season, we decided to concentrate our effort in one corner of the Monumental Building in an effort to understand the architectural relationship between the Monumental Building and the southern end of the Course.

Here we were surprised to find a large number of ashlar stones quite different from anything we had seen in all previous seasons. These distinctively Herodian stones were of exceptional quality, with well-carved margins and elevated bosses. Such elegant ashlars had appeared nowhere else at Herodium, not even on the mountaintop. They were lying in the debris as if they had fallen from an adjacent building. We were thrilled! We were on the verge of discovering another monument—perhaps the burial monument—when the season ended.

We returned to the area two months later, in October 1980, only to find that the beautiful ashlars were reused; in about the fifth century A.D., they formed the wall of a Byzantine church. This was the third Byzantine church we had exposed in Lower Herodium. (During the fifth and sixth centuries, Lower Herodium was occupied by a Byzantine settlement.)

We had not expected to find a large church on the slope of the mountain. Indeed, we were expecting to find a Herodian monument. But the church had in fact been built there with reused, beautifully carved Herodian stones. The stones had fallen from the church, and not from the Herodian monument in which they must originally have been used.

These beautiful ashlar stones are tantalizing, for they are unique at Herodium. Although most of the other buildings at the site, including the mountain palace-fortress and the Monumental Building, were built of carefully carved ashlars, they were originally faced with lime plaster. Not only from our work at Herodium but also from our work at Jericho and even at Masada, we knew of Herod's fondness for smooth white plaster as a high quality interior and exterior finish for buildings. The ashlar stones that were found reused in the newly discovered church, however, originally had *not* been covered with coats of plaster. And they were made of a much harder stone, with smoothly cut margins and projecting bosses. They must have been used in a building with a monumental facing surpassing anything found so far at Herodium.

Moreover, some of these stones show evidence of being part of a Doric frieze. Such friezes have been found in Jerusalem tombs of the period, including Absalom's tomb in the Kidron Valley and the so-called "Tomb of the Kings" near St. George's School. I believe that these stones at Herodium were part of a monument related to Herod's burial.

Whether we are close to solving the secret of Herod's tomb, I cannot say. If a burial cave exists, even if we find it, it was probably looted in antiquity. But it would not surprise us to find a cave that used these beautifully carved stones, stones befitting the burial of the greatest builder in the history of the ancient land of Israel.

[1]Josephus, *The Jewish War* I, 670-673; *Jewish Antiquities* XVII, 196-199.

[2]*Jewish Antiquities* XIV, 381-389, 487-488.

[3]*The Jewish War* V, 161-175.

[4]*The Jewish War* V, 242.

[5]*The Jewish War* I, 412.

[6]On my excavations at Jericho, see Suzanne Singer, "The Winter Palaces of Jericho," **BAR**, June 1977, and my article, "**BAR** Readers Restore and Preserve Herodian Jericho," **BAR**, November/December 1978.

[7]*The Jewish War* I, 670-673, *Jewish Antiquities* 196-200.

All drawings, unless otherwise indicated, are by the author.

Many people besides Sergey Samoilov ("Caesarea Tunnel Vision") initially expressed amazement at Robert Bull's discovery of a six-mile-long water tunnel cut through the Mt. Carmel bedrock to feed Caesarea's great aqueduct. When Bull reported from the evidence of pick marks that the tunnel had been cut by "teams working in both directions," others assumed as Samoilov did that each team must have had to negotiate a three-mile-straight length of tunnel in order to meet. Roger McCann ("More on the Caesarea Aqueduct Tunnel") tried to be helpful by noting that a kilometer-long water tunnel had been hewn on the Greek island of Samos in the sixth century B.C. by teams cutting from both ends. He might also have mentioned the eighth-century B.C. Hezekiah's tunnel beneath the City of David at Jerusalem. Although only a third of a mile long (1,750 feet), it is an impressive predecessor from an engineering standpoint since its two cutting teams both followed curving paths.

Professor Bull pointed out in his reply that the cutting of the Caesarea tunnel did not require sophisticated calculations. The Caesarea watercourse apparently was cut by sinking stepped shafts into the mountain at 230-foot intervals and then having teams cut toward each other. Aiming the teams correctly would have been a relatively straightforward process.

What is impressive about the Caesarea tunnel is the vast commitment of manpower involved. If the approximately 230-foot distance between the four shafts which Bull reported proves typical of the entire tunnel length, then the six miles of tunnel must have required over 135 shafts.

The achievement is even more impressive when we consider the other major works at Caesarea—the six and a half-mile-long aqueduct, the one and a third-mile-long defensive wall, the huge harbor breakwaters and moles, the massive complex of warehouse vaults, the colonnaded street and sewer system. Moreover, Caesarea's building programs were initiated at the same time Herod was embellishing Jerusalem and building at Jericho, Masada and Herodium. Even if most of the manpower was slaves or prisoners, they reflect a vast amount of royal wealth and power wielded by a king of consuming ambition.

Both the excavators at Caesarea and Ehud Netzer at Herodium referred to detailed descriptions by the Jewish historian, Josephus. However, digging with Josephus in hand has had mixed results. Excavators were guided by Josephus to investigate and successfully interpret such major features as Herod's harbor installations at Caesarea and his palatial apartments at Herodium. On the other hand, Josephus's assertion about Herod's burial at Herodium lacked any specific topographical reference to aid Netzer in locating Herod's tomb.

Finally, Mary O. Minshall of Redwood City, California, pointed out in a letter in **BAR**, September/October 1982, that

> Professor Bull refers to the men in the Roman army as "legionnaires." However, the term used by classicists and archaeologists for a soldier in a Roman legion is *legionary*, not *legionnaire*. Legionnaire is the correct word for members of other legions, e.g., the French Foreign Legion, the American Legion, and recipients of the Legion of Honor medal. . . .
>
> The sentence, "The Roman procurators established local courts in Caesarea and recruited detachments of *auxiliary legionnaires* from the local population," contains a more serious error. At the time described in the article, the Roman army contained two classes of soldiers: legionaries recruited from among Roman citizens . . . and auxiliary troops drawn from non-citizens. While the better paid legionaries comprised the heavy infantry of the Roman army, the auxiliary troops were the cavalry, light infantry, scouts, etc. When these men completed their terms of service of 25 years, they received Roman citizenship and thus they or their sons became eligible for service in the legions. Hence there was no such Roman soldier as an "auxiliary legionnaire." He was either a legionary or an auxiliary, but not both.

The technical points do not affect the essential accuracy of Bull's report. They illustrate, however, how difficult it is for the present-day archaeologist to command all the data in all the disciplines relevant to the materials being uncovered. They also demonstrate that the lay person reading an archaeological report often may have expertise or knowledge that can supplement or correct a scholar's statement or interpretation.

For Further Reading

Concerning Tunnels

Dan Cole, "How Water Tunnels Worked," **BAR**, March/April 1980 *(see Vol. I, Section E)*

Concerning Herod's Palace at Jericho

Suzanne Singer, "The Winter Palaces of Jericho," **BAR**, June 1977

Ehud Netzer, "**BAR** Readers Restore and Preserve Herodian Jericho," **BAR**, November/December 1978

Concerning Other Investigations at Herodium

Ehud Netzer, "Jewish Rebels Dig Strategic Tunnel System," **BAR**, July/August 1988

The Dead Sea Scrolls — Jewish Texts from the Time of Jesus

Certainly the most dramatic archaeological discovery from the Biblical world within the past century has been the recovery of the Dead Sea Scrolls. The articles in this section focus on a scroll which is both the latest to come into scholarly hands (1967) and the longest (27 feet); it also happens to be a scroll unique in its character.

Both Yigael Yadin and Hartmut Stegemann agree that the so-called Temple Scroll is a heretofore unknown contender for a book of the Torah, the basic law given directly to Moses by the God of Israel at Mt. Sinai. They radically disagree, however, concerning both the date of the original book and just whose Torah it was.

Prior to the accidental discovery of the first of the Dead Sea Scrolls by a Bedouin shepherd in 1947, it was assumed that neither parchment nor papyrus could have survived from antiquity anywhere but in the extremely arid sands of Egypt. Many scholars, therefore, initially refused to believe that the scrolls that began to come to scholarly attention after 1947 could have been written as early as was suggested by paleography (the study of the shape and character of their script) or by the then-new carbon-14 process of dating. (For a brief description of how the carbon-14 process works, see p. 220.)

By now, however, it appears clear from the evidence that the over 800 scrolls, in whole or fragmentary condition, that eventually came to light were written over a period ranging from the second century B.C. into the first century A.D.

The scrolls almost certainly were placed in their cave repositories during the final decades of the Second Temple period and the initial decades of the Christian era. Thus, they can provide invaluable new documentary information concerning Palestinian Judaism in the first century A.D. and the religious environment out of which rabbinic Judaism and Christianity grew.

Many of the Dead Sea Scrolls are copies of Hebrew canonical scriptures. They provide insight into the development of the text of the Hebrew Bible at a very early stage; the scroll examples are a thousand years earlier than the earliest manuscripts in the original language previously available for most of the Hebrew Biblical writings.

Other texts found among the scrolls are Jewish sectarian works: commentaries on Biblical writings, collections of hymns, regulations for a devout religious community and descriptions of the end of the age written out of an apocalyptic religious faith. And then there is the Temple Scroll . . .

The Dead Sea Scrolls have been considered by most scholars to have come from the library of a Jewish sect housed at Qumran, probably the Essenes described by Josephus, although the identification of the scrolls with the Qumran community and the Essene character of the documents have recently been questioned. One new theory is that the scrolls comprised a Jerusalem library taken to Qumran because of the anticipated fall of Jerusalem to the Romans.

In any event, as the articles that follow demonstrate, scholars also hold somewhat differing, although overlapping, interpretations of the character of the Temple Scroll.

The initial pages of Yigael Yadin's article, incidentally, provide a good description of the kind of complicated and prolonged negotiations required to secure several of the most important Dead Sea Scrolls, and the delicate process involved in unrolling and reading them.

DAVID HARRIS

The Temple Scroll

The Longest and Most Recently Discovered Dead Sea Scroll

How it affects our understanding of the New Testament and early Christianity

Yigael Yadin

ON AUGUST 1, 1960, I received a letter from a man who identified himself as a Virginia clergyman. The letter stated that the writer was in a position to negotiate the sale of "important, authentic discoveries of Dead Sea Scrolls." Obviously, he contacted me because of my intimate involvement in Israel's acquisition of the original Dead Sea Scrolls six years earlier.

Preceding page: ***At the edge of the Dead Sea in the desolate landscape surrounding Qumran, the Essenes dreamed of the Temple that would one day be built in Jerusalem. They wrote their precise vision of this Temple onto a scroll containing the laws by which they lived and would live. When the Romans threatened them in the first century A.D., the Essenes hid the scroll in a remote desert cave. Probably discovered by Bedouin, the scroll came into the hands of archaeologist Yigael Yadin in June 1967.***

In this view of Qumran, we look east to the mountains of Moab across the Dead Sea. Atop the barren plateau parallel to the western shore of the sea, excavated remains (far left) mark the ritual baths and communal rooms of the Essenes.

In a subsequent letter, Mr. Z, as I shall refer to him, indicated the price for an entire scroll would be around one million dollars, since the Jordanian dealer who possessed the material (and here he named a well-known dealer involved in previous transactions for the purchase of Dead Sea Scrolls, whom I shall call "the dealer") "knows their true value." I informed Mr. Z of my willingness to negotiate only if the price was reasonable in comparison to the price paid to the Metropolitan Samuel for the original Dead Sea Scrolls.

An exchange of correspondence ensued, and on October 7, I purchased from Mr. Z—or through him—a fragment of the Psalms Scroll from cave 11 at Qumran. The pieces adjacent to this fragment were in the Rockefeller Museum, and how Mr. Z obtained this fragment—before the other fragments were obtained by the museum, or after—we shall never know. In any event, it was clear he had access to authentic materials from the Dead Sea Scroll caves.

Then on May 29, 1961, Mr. Z wrote that he had for sale not a fragment but an entire scroll. Moreover, the price was realistic: $100,000. On June 1, 1961, I replied that I would try to raise the $100,000 and would be in touch with him soon.

Shortly thereafter, I left for London, where I spent some time on sabbatical. There, by letter of August 9, 1961, Mr. Z informed me that he had clarified all details of the sale with the dealer and that the scroll in question was a large one: "nine inches wide, about 15 to 18 feet long." Since, as Mr. Z said in his letter, a purchaser would no doubt be concerned with the authenticity of the scroll, he was enclosing a fragment which had broken off from the scroll.

I examined the envelope and found a fragment of a scroll wrapped in tin foil from a package of cigarettes. The back of the fragment was reinforced with a piece of a British postage stamp.

I immediately saw that the fragment was authentic!

It did not surprise me that Mr. Z would send me the fragment like this. He had previously sent me the Psalms Scroll fragment in a Manila envelope wrapped in a napkin, trusting me to send him the money.

In his letter Mr. Z asked me to make an evaluation of the new fragment and send it back to him by return mail—which is exactly what I did. I advised Mr. Z that the fragment seemed to belong to a genuine scroll of the Dead Sea type and was written by a good scribe.

On August 29, 1961, Mr. Z wrote back that the asking price for the scroll was now $750,000.

Angered by this increase in price, I replied that his letter "baffled and infuriated me since it indicates you never took seriously what I told you regarding the price . . . If things remain as you state in your letter, I am afraid you can rule me out as a customer."

Soon thereafter I left England for the United States where wearisome and often detailed negotiations continued with Mr. Z.

Finally, a deal was struck. The agreed price was $130,000. An intricate six-page agreement to be signed by the dealer was drafted by a lawyer. The agreement provided that prior to payment we would examine the scroll itself for authenticity and for its correspondence to the fragment. We also agreed on a $10,000 down payment, which I gave to Mr. Z, and he in turn once again gave me the fragment I had returned to him so that I could eventually compare it to the entire scroll. I also gave Mr. Z $1,500 to finance a trip to Bethlehem, then under Jordanian control, which he said was necessary to conclude the agreement with the dealer.

The agreement prepared by the lawyer was never signed by the dealer. On December 1, 1961, I received a letter from Mr. Z saying that difficulties had arisen: The price was now $200,000. Since I had the fragment, he decided to hold the $10,000 "in order to work in good faith on both sides since you have the all-important piece."

Further correspondence ensued in January and February 1962, Mr. Z asking for further advances and I trying to get back the $10,000.

The last letter received from Mr. Z was on May 17, 1962. He again made "promises" and again pleaded for more money. That was the last we ever heard from him.*

*I am still keeping his confidence, however, by not revealing his name. I want all these people—whether they are robbers or not (and it is a cloak-and-dagger business)—to know that as far as I am concerned, if they tell me not to reveal their identities, I won't. Otherwise, we have no chance of getting more scrolls. And I believe there still might be another scroll or some fragments here or there. For the same reason, I don't call the dealer by name, even though many know who he is.

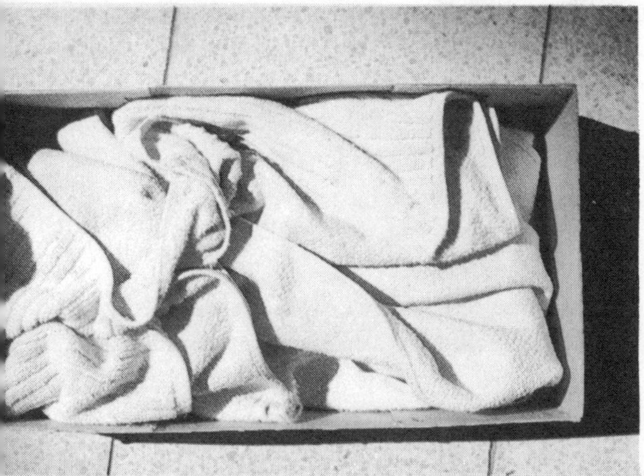

Finding The Scroll

In June 1967, *hours after the Israel Defense Forces had captured Bethlehem and united East and West Jerusalem, Professor Yigael Yadin tracked down a Dead Sea Scroll that was in the hands of an East Jerusalem antiquities dealer. Yadin, who was serving as general advisor to Prime Minister Eshkol, arranged for an Israeli officer to find the antiquities dealer in his East Jerusalem shop. The dealer then took the officer to his home in Bethlehem, where the dealer pulled from their hiding places a flimsy shoe box (left) and a cigar box (p. 164).*

Inside the shoe box, wrapped in cellophane and an old towel, lay a 1,900-year-old scroll (below).

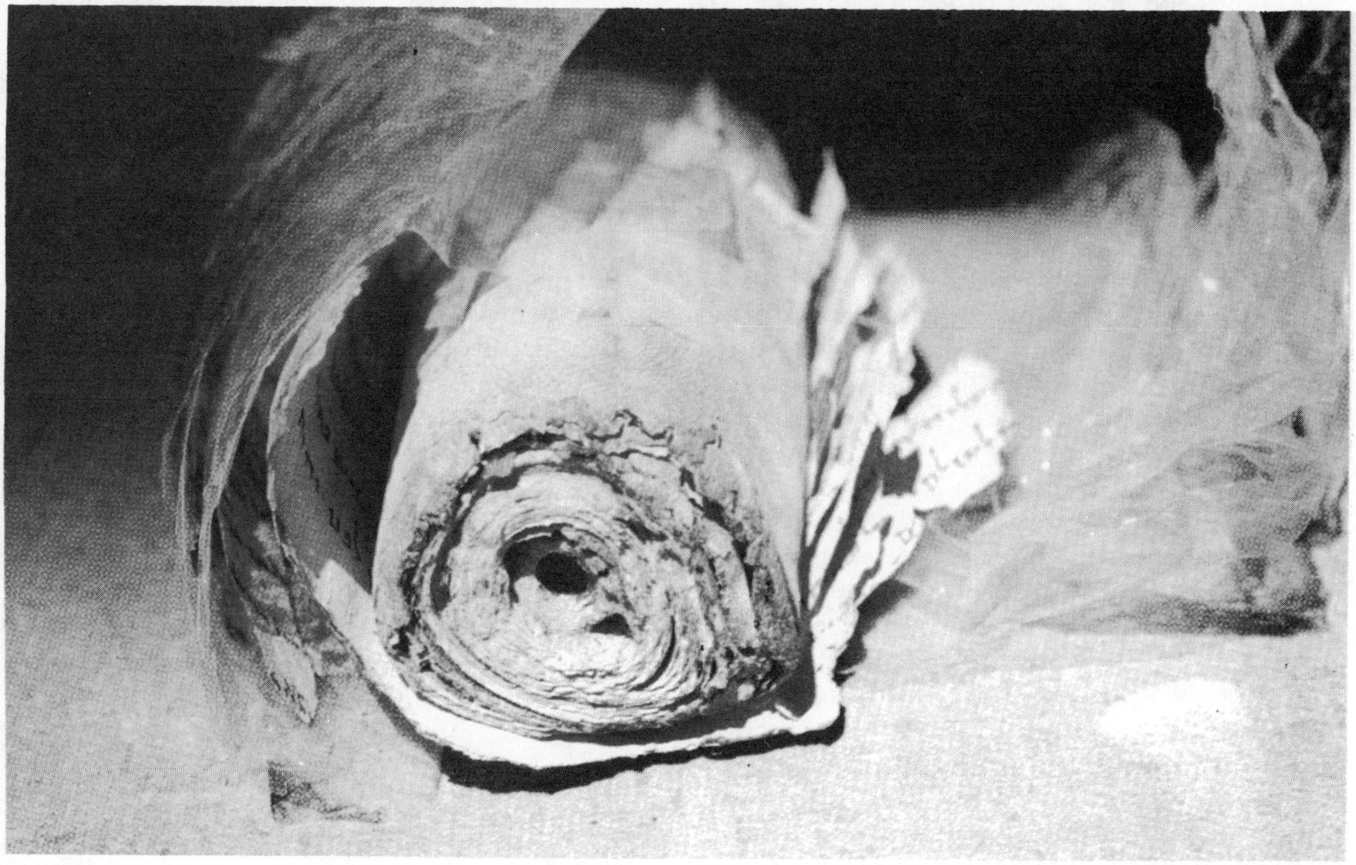

The cigar box ***filled with crumbled and damaged scroll fragments. Although deplorable storage conditions had caused the documents considerable damage, Yadin knew that the scroll he held in his hands on June 8, 1967, would prove to be one of the most important of all inscriptional finds.***

I consoled myself with the thought that at least I had the fragment. I tried to put the matter out of my mind but obviously could not. In 1963 I began my excavations at Masada, Herod's desert fortress and the place where the Zealots made their last stand against the Romans. This excavation was a consuming interest, but I nevertheless continued to peruse the scientific archaeological publications concerning the scrolls, wondering whether I would find some reference to a new Dead Sea Scroll. Nothing appeared, however.

If Masada was not enough to put the matter out of my mind, the Six-Day War in June 1967 was. I was then serving as military advisor to the Prime Minister. On June 7, the Israel Defense Forces captured the Old City of Jerusalem and Bethlehem. Suddenly, I recalled the scroll. The dealer involved had a shop in East Jerusalem and lived in Bethlehem. Both he and his scroll might be within Israeli jurisdiction! I immediately reported this to Prime Minister Levi Eshkol, who put at my disposal a lieutenant-colonel from military intelligence.

After I briefed the lieutenant-colonel about the supposed scroll and the fragment in my possession, he went to the dealer's shop and informed him of the scroll fragment we had obtained from Mr. Z. After brief negotiations, the dealer agreed to take the officer to his home in Bethlehem. There, the dealer removed from beneath some floor tiles a shoe box containing the scroll. He also produced a cigar box containing fragments that had become detached from the scroll. Later, it was discovered that the dealer had hidden additional fragments behind family pictures, both in his own home and in his brother's home.

The military government confiscated the scroll and fragments in accordance with Jordanian law governing antiquities. Although the dealer had illegally concealed the scroll's existence from the Jordanian authorities and had kept it under dreadful conditions that caused extensive damage, especially to the upper part of the scroll, it was nevertheless decided to pay him for the scroll—for the simple reason that we want to encourage such people to come forward if they have additional scroll materials.

The amount finally agreed upon with the dealer, after negotiations lasting almost a year, was $105,000.

Unfortunately, I was given the job of raising the money. This task proved not to be so onerous, however, because of the generosity of Mr. Leonard Wolfson of Great Britain, who contributed $75,000 for this purpose. The balance was paid by the Israeli Government.

Thus ended the saga of the scroll's acquisition. The saga of its unrolling began.

I first held the scroll in my hands on the evening of Wednesday, June 8, 1967, the day Israeli forces united East and West Jerusalem. On June 11, the war was over, and we started the task of unrolling the scroll shortly thereafter. The work was done under the direction of Joseph "Dodo" Shenhav of the Israel Museum, who is already familiar to **BAR** readers as the author of an article on the preservation of the Israel Museum's Dead Sea Scrolls.*

The first part of the scroll we unrolled was a separate wad we call Wad Y, which had been wrapped in cellophane inside the shoebox. The fragments in this wad turned out to be the beginning of the extant part of the scroll. Letters and even words had peeled off some of the columns of script and attached themselves, in mirror image, on the backs of preceding columns (the scroll was rolled with the end on the innermost core). The first extant column of Wad Y had the imprint from a preceding but now lost column; unfortunately, the mirror image was so faint I could not decipher the letters. I could conclude only that there must have been at least one earlier column, so I called the first extant column column II. Wad Y contained columns II through V.

Next we tried to unroll what we call Wad X, which contained columns VI through XIII. Wad X had been rolled so tightly that at times the entire text was preserved in mirror image on the back of the previous column. Sometimes the text was preserved *only* in this manner.

*"Preserving the Dead Sea Scrolls For the Next 2,000 Years" **BAR**, July/August 1981. Shenhav also wrote "Loaves and Fishes Mosaic Near Sea of Galilee Restored" in the May/June 1984 **BAR**.

Other wads were slowly and carefully separated and pieces gradually fitted together and into the main text, based on the contours of the edges. In the end, we were left with a wad consisting of a black macerated mass containing the remnants of two or three columns, but we could neither separate it nor decipher the letters. We photographed the amorphous mass from every angle, with different lightings, with regular, orthochromatic and infrared film—all with negligible results.

Fortunately, the scroll proper was for the most part easier to unroll than the wads. In general, we used the process developed by H. J. Plenderlieth to open the original Dead Sea Scrolls—softening the outer roll by a process of humidification at 75 to 80 percent. When this process did not work, we used another developed by Plenderlieth—applying nearly 100 percent humidity for several minutes, immediately followed by a few minutes of refrigeration. In some cases, we could not use this process, however, because the adjacent writing was in such fragile condition it would have been damaged by the process. In

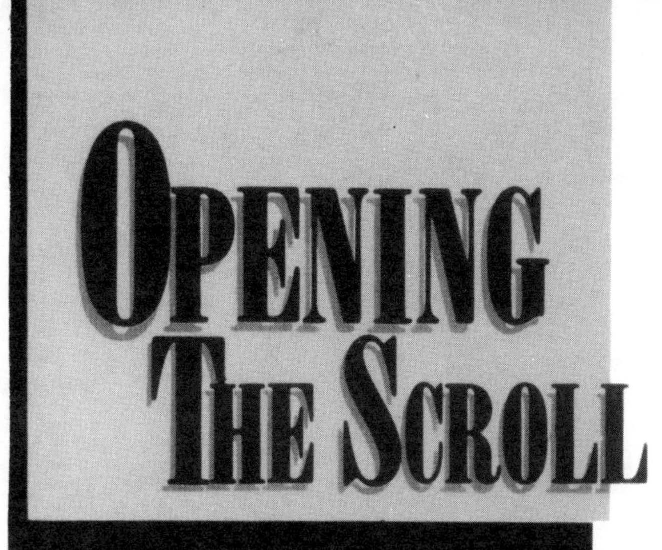

Damaged fragments *of the Temple Scroll are pieced together with surgical delicacy by Joseph "Dodo" Shenhav and Ruth Yekutieli of the Israel Museum. These fragments were part of a "wad," a few pieces that had been separated recently from the main scroll.*

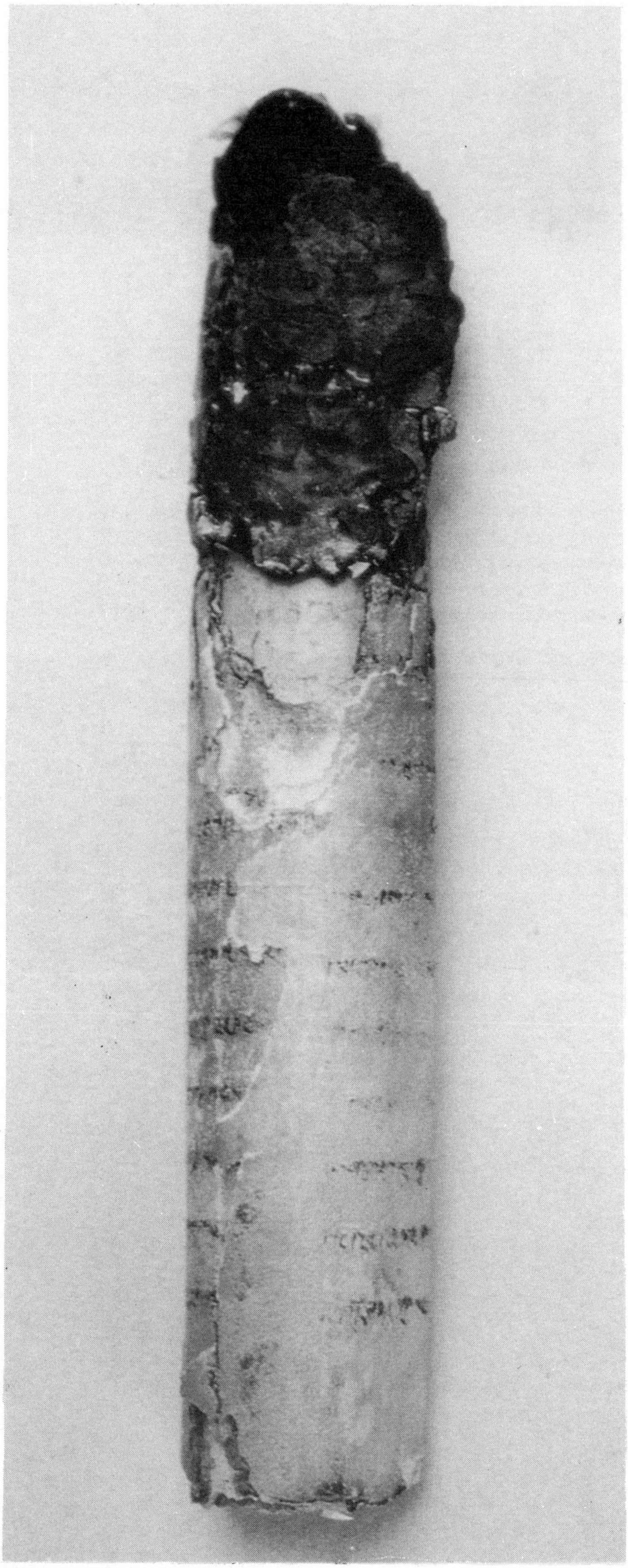

Like the other Dead Sea Scrolls, *the Temple Scroll (above) ended with a page that was blank except for a few lines at the top. Although the top of the Temple Scroll's last page is not preserved, we can assume that four or five lines originally appeared here.*

The last four extant lines of the Temple Scroll text, in column 66 (in the left column of the right page), follow Leviticus 20:17,19 and 28:12-13, and Deuteronomy 27:27. The text reads:

"A man shall not take his sister, his father's daughter or his mother's daughter, for this is an abomination. A man shall not take his father's sister or his mother's sister, for it is wickedness. A man shall not take his brother's daughter or his sister's daughter, for it is an abomination. A [man] shall not . . ."

Part of the last, blank page of the scroll (opposite) was eaten by insects sometime in the not too distant past. The scroll was rolled from the end—it's easy to see the few vertical folds the winding made in the smooth animal skin.

The Temple Scroll (left), *after its outer part was unrolled. (A view of the scroll from the bottom appears on p. 163.)*

In order to unroll the scroll, restorers subjected it to different levels of humidity; sometimes, when humidity didn't work, the restorers cut the columns lengthwise and then glued them back together after photographing their texts.

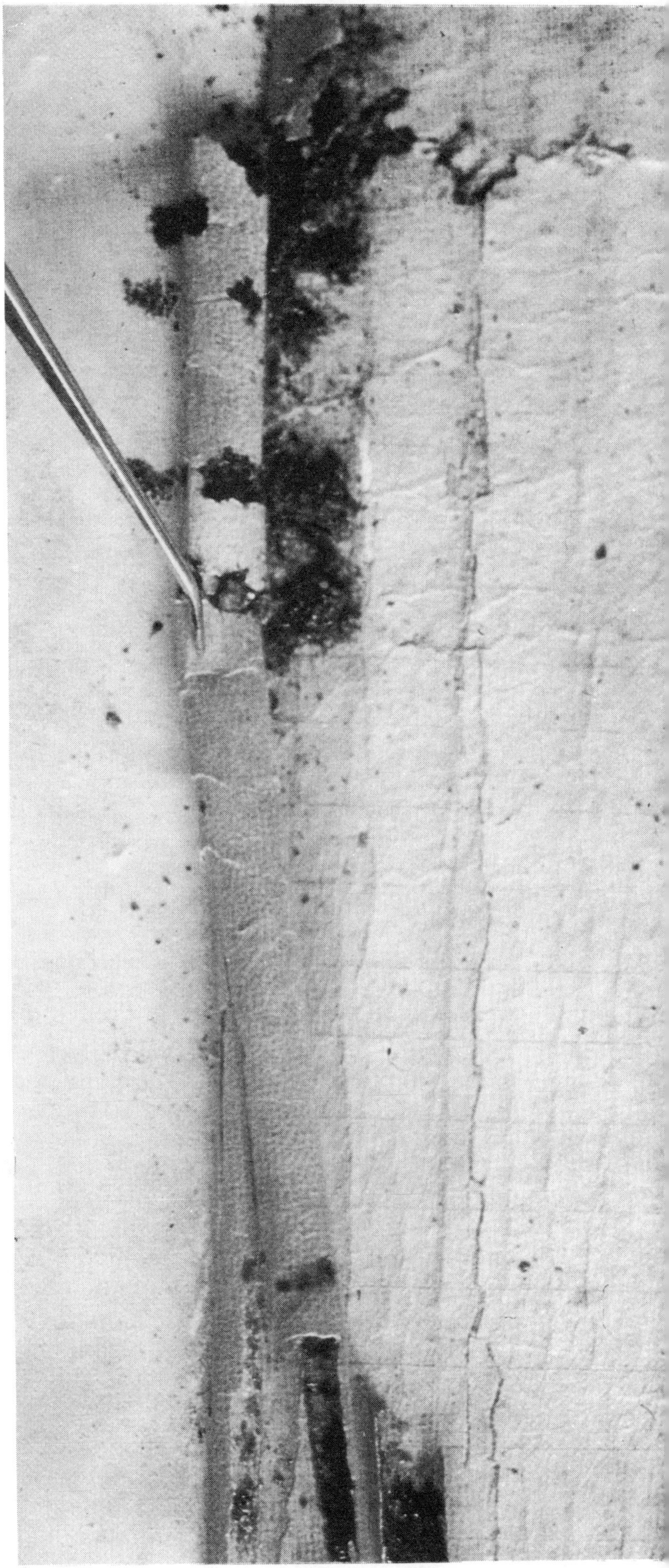

such cases, we had no choice except to leave the pieces stuck together and try to salvage their contents with photographs from back and front against the light. Occasionally, we were compelled to cut the columns lengthwise, a kind of plastic surgery, and then to rejoin them after their separation.

The animal skin on which the scroll is written is extremely thin, indeed the thinnest I have ever encountered. Nowhere is it more than one-tenth of a millimeter thick. Nevertheless, and despite the use of a sharp instrument, the scribe was able to rule in guidelines (so-called "drylines") without making cuts in the skin. Two different hands, called Scribe A and Scribe B, have been detected in the script.

As I have already indicated, the beginning of the scroll is missing, but we know that we have the end because there is a blank sheet at the end of the scroll, as is customary at the end of all Dead Sea Scrolls.

The scroll contains 66 columns of text and is 27 feet long. This makes it the longest of all the Dead Sea Scrolls. Previously, the great Isaiah Scroll—22 feet long—containing the entire text of the book of Isaiah—was the longest of the scrolls, which gives some idea of the length of the Temple Scroll.

On the basis of the script, the scroll can be dated to the Late Herodian period, say mid-first century A.D. or a little earlier. But that is the date of this copy, not necessar-

Infrared film ***does little to illuminate the most badly damaged of the scroll fragments. Fortunately, most of the main scroll was well enough preserved to enable decipherment of the document that the author believes is the torah, or book of law, of the Essenes.***

ily the date of the composition it contains.

I believe the date of the composition of the scroll, however, was much earlier—approximately 150-125 B.C. I have several reasons for this conclusion. One is that we found two unpublished fragments from Qumran Cave 4 in the Rockefeller Museum which came from other, earlier copies of this same composition. The earlier of these fragments was written in a Hasmonean script that can be dated to about the last quarter of the second century B.C. (about 125-100 B.C.), so our scroll could have been composed no later than this. Moreover, I believe I can detect historical allusions in the text that would confirm a dating of 150-125 B.C. This subject is treated at some length in my three-volume edition of the scroll.*

A more interesting question is, what *was* this composition? It is my belief that this scroll contains nothing less than the basic *torah* or law of the Essenes who lived at Qumran on the northwestern shore of the Dead Sea. For them it was a holy book, a part of the canon of what we call the Bible, the Torah of the Lord. Moreover, I believe the scroll was composed by the founder of the sect, the venerated Teacher of Righteousness.

I have several reasons for believing this document was the Essene torah, equal in importance to the traditional Torah, which they naturally also venerated as a holy book. Let me list some of the reasons for believing this scroll was the Essene torah.

**The Temple Scroll*, edited by Yigael Yadin (The Israel Exploration Society, The Institute of Archaeology of the Hebrew University of Jerusalem, The Shrine of the Book: Jerusalem, 1977), 3 volumes.

The scroll contains long passages from the Pentateuch,* sometimes whole chapters, but the scroll is frequently written in the first person, with God himself speaking, instead of Moses referring to God in the third person, as is often the case in the parallel Pentateuchal passages. This change is accomplished by replacing the tetragrammaton** LORD in the Pentateuch by "I" or "me" in the Temple Scroll. Even the supplementary laws in the Temple Scroll, which are not in the Pentateuch, are often written in the first person.

Thus, the text of Numbers 30:3 appears in the Temple Scroll as follows: "When a woman vows a vow *to me* . . . ." Obviously, the author wished to present the Law as if handed down by God himself, rather than through the mouth of Moses.†

On the other hand, the tetragrammaton is also used in a number of instances in the Temple Scroll. These passages, however, also contain an important clue regarding the canonical or holy status of the Temple Scroll. To understand this clue, a little background is necessary.

Hebrew was originally written in a script scholars refer to as Old Hebrew, or Palaeo-Hebrew. When the Jews returned from exile in Babylon, they brought with them a square "Aramaic" script that gradually replaced the previously used script. However, the earlier Old Hebrew script continued to be used in certain archaizing contexts. For example, during the First and Second Jewish Revolts against Rome in 66-73 A.D. and 132-135 A.D., the Jews minted coins using the older Hebrew script on them. In the Dead Sea Scrolls, the tetragrammaton is sometimes written in the Palaeo-Hebrew script, although in general the scrolls themselves are written in the square script. There is a pattern in the Dead Sea Scrolls: the tetragrammaton is written in Palaeo-Hebrew in the midst of a text otherwise written in the square "Aramaic" text that was in common use at the time. In the Dead Sea Scrolls, the archaized, Palaeo-Hebrew tetragrammaton generally occurs in noncanonical, that is, non-Biblical, texts. In the books of the Bible preserved at Qumran, the tetragrammaton is written, by contrast, in the square "Aramaic" script, just like the rest of the text.

In the Temple Scroll, when the tetragrammaton is

*The first five books of the Bible, called in Hebrew translation the Torah of Moses.

**The tetragrammaton is the ineffable and unpronounced name of God, consisting of the four consonants YHWH, often transcribed in English literature as Yahweh.

†Although Moses is never mentioned by name in the existing columns of the scroll, it is clear that God is speaking to Moses, as we know, for example, by a reference to "Aaron your brother" (column 44, line 5).

used, it is written in the square "Aramaic" script, as in the Biblical books found at Qumran. This is another reason to believe that the Temple Scroll was considered by the Essene community as Biblical or canonical.

The subject matter and the fact that such a long scroll—nearly 30 feet—was copied several times at Qumran, as we know from the Rockefeller Museum fragments, also indicates that it was probably considered a holy book.

The Temple Scroll probably even contains excerpts from certain lost books referred to in the Bible, according to the Essene tradition, which are otherwise unknown. This again requires some background to understand.

While still in the wilderness, the Israelites were implicitly commanded to build a temple for the Lord once they were established in the Promised Land. For example, in Deuteronomy 12:10-11, we read:

> "But when you go over the Jordan, and live in the land which the Lord your God gives you to inherit, and when he gives you rest from all your enemies round about, so that you live in safety, then to the place which the Lord your God will choose, to make his name dwell there, thither you shall bring all that I command you: your burnt offerings and your sacrifices, your tithes and the offering that you present, and all your votive offerings which you vow to the Lord."

The building of the Jerusalem Temple was one of the most important tasks enjoined upon the Israelites in the wilderness. But the Bible contains no laws for the plan of the Temple. This is a startling omission. Despite detailed laws and descriptions of the Tabernacle and its utensils, the Torah gives no divine law concerning the plan of the Temple!

Later Biblical writers naturally noticed this unusual omission. The Chronicler explains:

> "Then David gave Solomon his son the plan of the vestibule of the temple, and of its houses, its treasuries, its upper rooms, and its inner chambers, and of the room for the mercy seat; and the plan of all that he had in mind for the courts of the house of the Lord [and the details of all the sacred furniture] . . . . All this he made clear *by the writing from the hand of the Lord* concerning it, all the work to be done according to the plan."
>
> 1 Chronicles 28:11-19

All this was made clear *in writing* from the Lord? Where was this written in the Torah?

According to the rabbis, a scroll existed in which this Torah was written. They even called it the Temple Scroll (*megillat beth ha-mikdash*). It was given to David, said the rabbis, through Moses, Joshua and the prophets:

> "The Temple Scroll which the Holy One Blessed Be He committed to Moses . . . , Moses . . . transmitted to Joshua . . . and Joshua to the Elders and the Elders to the Prophets and the Prophets to David and David to Solomon."
>
> *Midrash Samuel*, Buber ed., xv:3(92)

The scroll we obtained in 1967 contains elaborate plans for the building of the Temple. Indeed, nearly half of the scroll is taken up with the plans for the Temple, sacrifices and the laws of the city of the Temple. That is why I decided to call it the Temple Scroll. I do not claim that this scroll contains the text of the scroll supposedly handed down to David (and definitely not the one the rabbis had in mind). But I do believe that the author of this part of the scroll was writing with knowledge of the existence of a Temple Scroll referred to obliquely in the book of Chronicles. Either believing that he was divinely inspired or basing his descriptions on an older tradition, he considered himself to be preserving this missing part of the Torah, referred to in the Biblical book of Chronicles. It is interesting to note that the Temple Scroll concentrates on precisely those elements detailed in the passage from Chronicles in which God's missing laws for the plan of his Temple are described—the vestibule, the treasuries, the upper rooms, the inner chambers. In the Temple Scroll, God himself speaks in minute detail concerning his Temple to be built by the children of Israel (see pp. 170-171). He is the Master Architect, supplying the plans missing from the Torah. At the end of days, in the New Creation, God himself will build the Temple.

Another major portion of the Temple Scroll—nearly four columns—is devoted to what I call the Statutes of the King. This portion of the scroll could also be called the Torah of the King or the Laws of the King or even the Constitution of the King. This portion of the scroll contains laws relating to the marriage of the king, rules for mobilization during war, limited rights of the king to booty in war, provision for an advisory council (consisting of 12 priests, 12 Levites and 12 lay Israelites), provision for subordinate administrative positions of authority, and other such matters. This too may be related to an otherwise unknown book referred to in the Bible.

While still in the wilderness, the Israelites were commanded to appoint a king after they occupied the Promised Land (Deuteronomy 17:14-15). Yet here too there is a startling omission in the Torah. There is almost a complete absence of laws governing the king. There are a few verses in Deuteronomy 17:15-20 and in 1 Samuel 8:11ff. regarding the rights and duties of the king, but that is all. In 1 Samuel 10:25, however, we learn that "Samuel explained to the people the rights and duties of the king and he [Samuel] *wrote it down in a book* which he laid before the Lord."

THE PLAN OF THE ESSENE TEMPLE

"...I will c

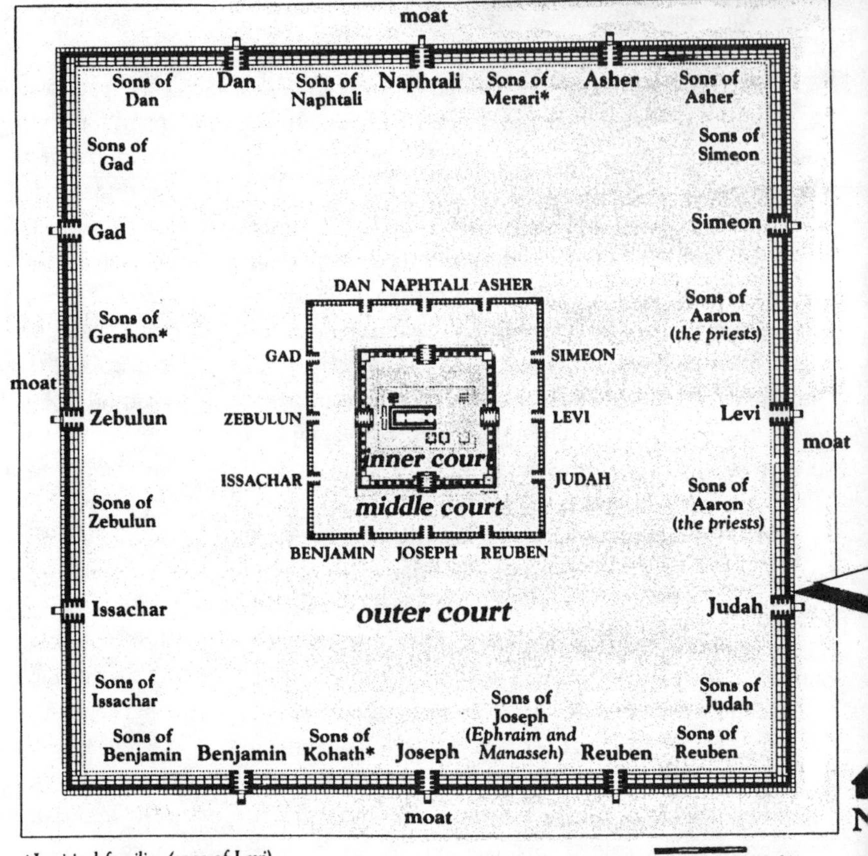

*Levitical families (sons of Levi)

Following elaborate instructions in the Temple Scroll, Yigael Yadin prepared these plans of the Temple that the Essenes hoped would be built in Jerusalem. "To build the Temple in Jerusalem," notes Yadin, "was one of the most important tasks enjoined upon the Israelites in the wilderness." But strangely enough, there are no laws in the Bible detailing how the Temple is to be built, although the Tabernacle and its furnishings are clearly described.

The Essenes in their own "Torah," the Temple Scroll, assigned nearly half of the text to plans for the Temple and to the laws associated with Temple rites.

Yadin is convinced that the Temple concept of the scroll's author "is based on the design of the camp of Israel, set around the Tabernacle in the wilderness, according to tribes and Levitical families." "It was this view," observes Yadin, "and the Biblical mention of the Temple courts of both the First and Second Temples* that formed the basis of the descriptions of the Temple and its courts in the scroll."

The cardinal prescription of the scroll is that there shall be three square courts around the Temple: inner, middle and outer. (The plan of the Temple and its three courts is on the left; an enlargement of the inner court plan is on the right.) To ensure the purity of the Temple and its courts, the scroll ordains two additional precautions: an inner wall (dotted line) to be erected around the Temple within the inner court, and, around the outer court, a fosse (moat) is to be made.

The inner court will have four gates, oriented to the four points of the compass. The middle and outer courts each will have 12 gates named after Jacob's 12 sons and assigned in the same order around each court. The outer court will be divided into 16 chamber areas, 11 allotted to 11 tribes (excluding Levi, from whom the Levites are descended); three to the three sons of Levi—Gershon, Kohath and Merari (the Levitical families); and two to the sons of Aaron (the priests).

Precise dimensions for the inner court gates are given: the entrances are to be 14 cubits wide (a cubit is about 1½ feet) and 28 cubits high from threshold to lintel, with another 14 cubits from lintel to ceiling. Other dimensions given in the scroll are similarly exact.

Lining the inner court stoa, described in column 37 of the scroll, are "s[i]tting pl[a]ces for the priests, and tables in front of the sitting places." The scroll author explicitly refers to these tables to emphasize the separation between priests and laity, "so that [there shall be] no mixing of the sacrifices of the peace offerings of the children of Israel with the sacrifices of the priests."

The scroll tells us there are to be "cooking places," kitchens, on either side of each gate. "In the four angles of the court," the scroll continues, there are to be places for stoves "in which they [the priests] shall boil their sacrifices [and] the sin offerings."

The structures to be found within the

*See 2 Chronicles 33:5; 1 Kings 6:36, 7:12; 2 Kings 20:4; Ezekiel 40-44.

"What happened to this book?" Jews must have asked themselves. In my view, the author of the Temple Scroll believed he was writing down, in the sections of the Temple Scroll I have labeled Statutes of the King, the contents of this missing book, according to his tradition.

In this connection it is interesting that two of the principal points made in 1 Samuel 8:11-12 are that the king "will appoint for himself commanders of thousands and commanders of fifties" and that the king is entitled to a "tenth of your grain and of your vineyards [and] ... of your flocks." These two subjects are among the most important dealt with in the Temple Scroll's Statutes of the King.

In Deuteronomy 17:18 we are told, "And when he [the king] sits on the throne of his kingdom, he shall write for himself in a book a copy of this law (*mishneh ha-torah ha-*

·crate my temple by my glory . . .

on the day of blessing . . . I will create my temple and establish it for myself for all times . . ." **(Column XXIX)**

"You shall make a dry moat around the temple, . . . which will separate the holy temple from the city so that they may not come suddenly into my temple and desecrate it. They shall consecrate my temple and fear my people, for I dwell among them." **(Column XLVI)**

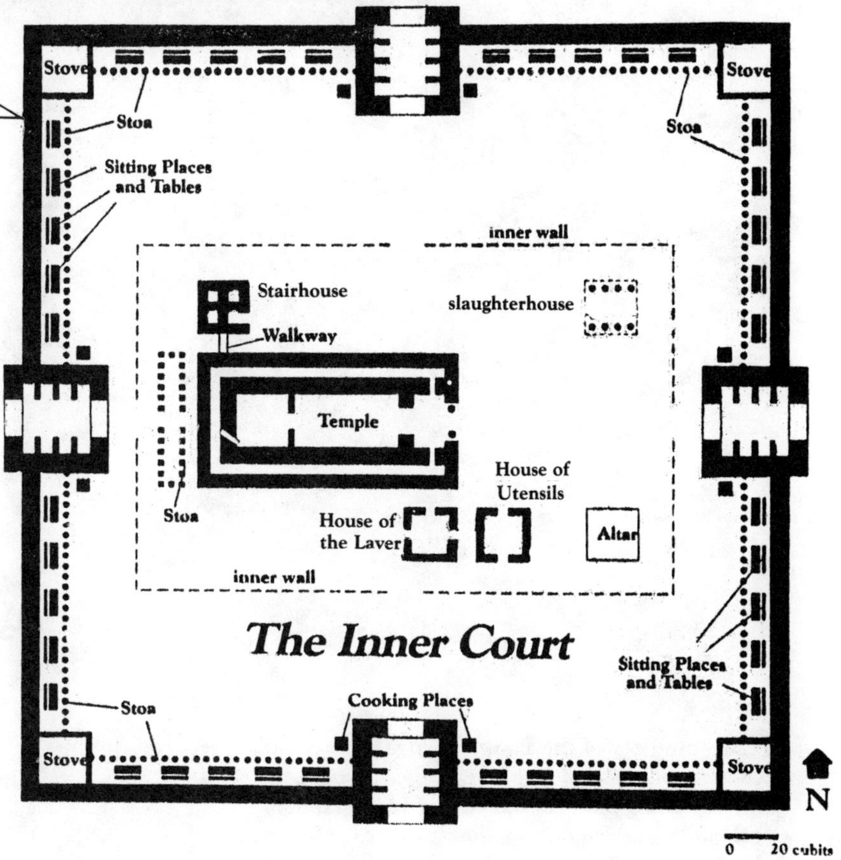

Stove
Stoa
Sitting Places and Tables
inner wall
Stairhouse
slaughterhouse
Walkway
Temple
House of Utensils
Stoa
House of the Laver
Altar
inner wall
The Inner Court
Sitting Places and Tables
Cooking Places
N
0 20 cubits

inner wall of the inner court are described in the scroll in minute detail. They include the Temple's furnishings, such as the cherubim, the golden veil and the lampstand (menorah).

The staircase, next to the Temple, is to be square-shaped, 20 cubits on a side, and located 7 cubits from the northwest side of the *heikhal*, or Temple building. This would be an extraordinary structure—40 cubits high, ascending to the roof of the Temple, and completely plated with gold! (See Morton Smith, "The Case of the Gilded Staircase," **BAR**, Sept./Oct. 1984.)

In the house of the laver, the priests would wash themselves and then put on their holy garments, which were to be kept in gold-plated niches in this structure. The house was to be "square on all its sides one and twenty cubits, at a distance of fifty cubits from the altar."

The commands for the house of utensils list the following altar utensils: basin, flagons, firepans and silver bowls. Even the function of the bowls is defined: "with which one brings up the entrails and the legs on the altar."

The 12 columns with ceiling constituted the Temple's slaughterhouse. Here the sacrificial animal's head would be shackled by a ring embedded in a wooden column. Because the Hebrew phrase denoting roofing is used for this structure, we can assume that it would have either low outer walls or none at all.

To the west of the *heikhal*, there is to be made "a stoa of standing columns for the sin offering and the guilt offering." The columns of the stoa are to be "separated from one another: for the sin offering of the priests and for the male goats and for the sin offerings of the people and for their guilt offerings." To make the separation between priests and laity absolutely clear, the scroll author adds, "for their places shall be separated from one another so that the priests may not err with the sin offering of the people."

The altar itself is mentioned several times, but this portion of the scroll is so badly damaged that commands for the altar's construction are fragmentary at best. We can understand, however, that the great altar of burnt offering was to be built of stone, with a ledge, corner and horns, and that one of its dimensions was to be 20 cubits.

zoth), from that which is in charge of the Levitical priests . . . ." This verse is generally considered by scholars to refer to the whole of Deuteronomy, that is, the second copy of the Law or Torah. The rabbis, or at least some of them, understood this passage to refer to a copy of the previous verses; there were also other speculations. But the author of the Temple Scroll used this verse from Deuteronomy to introduce the Statutes of the King. When he quotes this passage, however, he omits the word "copy," so instead of its being a "*copy* of this law," it reads in the Temple Scroll as if it were the Law itself: "When he [the king] sits on the throne of his kingdom, they [the priests] shall write for him *this* law in a book from that which is in the charge of the priests." Then, as if to emphasize the point, the Temple Scroll adds: "And this is the Law." The Statutes of the King follow.

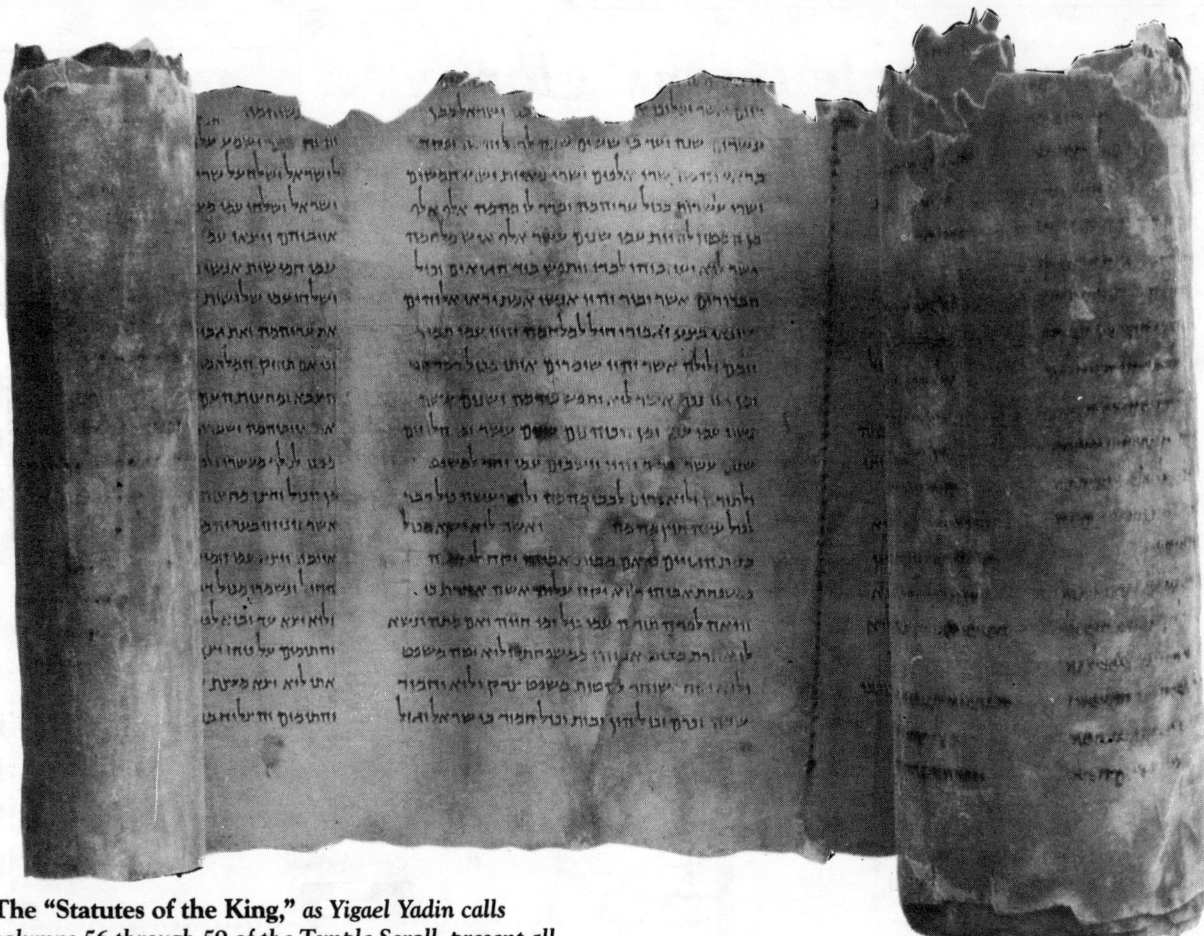

The "Statutes of the King," ***as Yigael Yadin calls columns 56 through 59 of the Temple Scroll, present all the rights and duties of the king of Israel. Here in column 56, which follows closely the text of Deuteronomy 17:14-16, we see some of these rights laid down. "He must not multiply horses for himself, or cause the people to return to Egypt, for war . . . since I have said to you, you shall never return that way again."***

The almost identical verse in Deuteronomy reads, "Since the Lord has said to you." The author of the Temple Scroll changed "the Lord" to "I," so that God, not Moses, gives the people the law.

Other "Statutes of the King" described in the Temple Scroll are the king's duties to organize an army and appoint officers, laws concerning conscription and taking booty during war, the king's marriage, the judicial council and the king's obligation to heed it, and more.

Yadin contends that these "statutes" are based on a book, now lost, that is mentioned in 1 Samuel 10:25: "Samuel explained to the people the rights and duties of the king and he [Samuel] wrote it down in a book which he laid before the Lord."

For all these reasons, it seems clear to me that the Temple Scroll was, for the Essenes, a holy canonical book on a par, for them, with the other books of the Bible.

In a short article, it would be impossible to describe in detail the entire contents of the Temple Scroll. The best I can do here is to provide a summary.

The Temple Scroll is above all a book of the Law, laws for the community both for the present and for the time when the true heirs of the Zadokite priesthood would again reign in Jerusalem. I have referred to the long passages relating to the Temple, its plan, its furniture and utensils, its sacrifices and other cultic laws. I have also referred to the Statutes of the King. Other long sections describe various festivals or holy days, many of which are "additional" holidays not mentioned in the Bible, such as the New Barley festival, the New Wine festival, the New Oil festival (all first-fruits festivals), and the Wood-Offering festival. Other more familiar festivals whose observance is described in the Temple Scroll include the Feast of Booths and the Day of Atonement. Sometimes the observances are the same as those described in other sources; sometimes they are different. Other laws relate to such things as idolatry, vows and oaths, pure and impure animals, ritual impurities, laws of testimony, and so forth.

I have already mentioned some of the characteristics of the scroll: the frequent use of the first person when God speaks, the tetragrammaton (when it appears) in the square "Aramaic" script as in other Biblical Dead Sea Scrolls, and the Herodian and the Hasmonean letter forms which help to date the scroll. Let me allude to a few other characteristics of the scroll.

The author of the scroll is clearly an expert on the text of the Pentateuch. He often merges passages from different parts of the Bible that deal with the same subject into a single smooth-flowing text. Unlike the Bible, the scroll is arranged according to principal themes—the Temple, the festivals, the Statutes of the King, etc., and it brings together disparate Pentateuchal passages bearing on these themes.

More important, the author often harmonizes and unifies duplicate, different, and sometimes even conflicting Biblical laws. In case of simple duplication, the scroll will combine the two texts by contractions and deletions. This approach is in contrast with that of the rabbis who taught, "Whenever a scriptural passage is repeated, it is because of some new point contained in it" (Babylonian Talmud *Sota* 3a).

When several Biblical passages deal with the same subject but their texts contain different, nonconflicting laws, the scroll will combine them into a single integrated text.

For example, in Deuteronomy 12:23-24, the people are commanded to refrain from eating blood; it must be thrown on the ground like water. In Leviticus 17:13, the blood is to be covered with earth. In the Temple Scroll, the two commands are combined: "Blood you shall not eat; you shall pour it on the ground like water; and cover it with earth."

When there are conflicts in Biblical passages, the scroll will often harmonize them, sometimes by splitting the difference.

Perhaps the overriding characteristic of the laws in the Temple Scroll is their strictness. I shall discuss here one of the most important applications of this principle of strictness. The principle of strictness, however, permeates the entire scroll.

The Pentateuch describes the rules of ritual cleanliness applicable to the Israelite camp in the wilderness (e.g. Deuteronomy 23:10-14). How are these laws of ritual cleanliness to be applied after the wilderness tabernacle has been replaced by the Jerusalem Temple and the wilderness camp by the city of Jerusalem? In the approach taken by normative Judaism, the rabbis ruled that the Holy City of Jerusalem was to be divided into *three* different camps: The Temple proper (the Divine camp), the area surrounding the Temple (the Levitical camp), and the rest of the city (the Israelite camp). According to rabbinical interpretation, the harshest bans are applicable only to the Temple proper, the less harsh are applicable to the area surrounding the Temple, and the remainder are applicable to the entire city. To achieve this tripartite division, the rabbis gave different interpretations to different occurrences of the word "camp" in the Biblical text. But these interpretations were not suggested by the text itself. The rabbis applied them in order to ameliorate the harshness that would result if all the restrictions applicable to the wilderness camp were applied uniformly to the entire city of Jerusalem—indeed to other cities as well. The rabbis who resorted to this tripartite division of restrictions by interpreting "camp" in three different ways were—if you wish—the "Reform Jews" of their day in comparison to the Essenes.

The Essenes, as we learn from the Temple Scroll, would have none of this. For them, the City of the Temple (Jerusalem) was equated with the camp where the tabernacle was kept in the wilderness.* All the laws and bans applicable to the wilderness camp were applicable to the *entire city of Jerusalem*. (In some cases, the camp is equated with *any* city, and the bans are applicable to *all* cities.)

We would consider some of the results quite bizarre. For example, in Deuteronomy 23:12-14, we are told there is to be a place outside the camp in the wilderness for defecation. The Essenes applied this injunction literally to the entire city of Jerusalem. The Temple Scroll forbids the building of toilets in the city:

> "You shall make a place for the hand (a toilet) outside the city to which they shall go out . . . 3,000 cubits [outside the city] in order that it will not be visible from the city."

A similar rule is found in another of the Dead Sea Scrolls known as the War Scroll. Because 3,000 cubits is beyond the limit of permitted walking on the Sabbath, Essenes who lived in Jerusalem could not walk to the latrines on the seventh day—and they therefore refrained from relieving themselves on the Sabbath.

Interestingly enough, Josephus, the first-century Jewish historian who in his youth lived among the Essenes in Qumran, confirms that they observed these rules—defecating only outside their settlement and refraining from defecation on the Sabbath. Josephus also describes a city gate in Jerusalem, mentioned nowhere else, that he calls the Essene Gate. This may well be the colloquial name for the gate the Essenes used to go out (or rather, to run out . . .) of the city to relieve themselves. Since the Temple Scroll prescribes the building of public toilets "northwest of the city," this reference provides an important clue as to the location of the Essene Gate. Josephus mentions that near the Essene Gate was a place called *Betsoa*, which is obviously *Beth-Soah* in Hebrew, i.e., a lavatory.

The Essenes applied other bans to the entire city of Jerusalem, according to their interpretation of the Biblical rules of purity related to the camp. Thus all sexual rela-

*This is apparently spelled out in a still unpublished letter from Qumran that, according to the editors, was sent by the Teacher of Righteousness himself. The letter is to be published by John Strugnell and Elisha Qimron. See "Jerusalem Rolls Out Red Carpet for Biblical Archaeology Congress," **BAR**, July/August 1984.

tions were banned in the city of Jerusalem. (This may perhaps explain the fact that the Essenes were celibate. Moreover, this may be the origin of celibacy as a doctrine.) People afflicted with impurity were forbidden from entering Jerusalem and were confined instead to specially built structures east of the city.

The Dead Sea Scrolls are without doubt one of the most important discoveries, if not *the* most important discovery, for Biblical studies ever made in the Holy Land. Their discovery created shock waves among scholars. To change the metaphor, it was as if a powerful telescope with a zoom lens suddenly brought the world of Judaism at the end of the Second Temple period into immediate focus across a barrier of 2,000 years. This period was both a tragic turning point in Jewish history—the Romans destroyed the Temple in 70 A.D.—and the cradle in which Christianity was born and began to grow. The Temple Scroll, like the previously discovered Dead Sea Scrolls, will no doubt be scrutinized by generations of scholars in order to illuminate this critical period in the history of Judaism as well as Christianity.

Since we cannot consider here even a fraction of the problems and insights contained in the Temple Scroll (many of which are discussed in my scientific edition of the scroll), what I would like to do is give a few examples of the way scholars might be using the Temple Scroll to broaden and enrich our understanding of the New Testament and early Christianity.* The importance of the Temple Scroll to Jewish and Biblical studies is more apparent and therefore will not be discussed here.

I have just discussed how strictly the scroll interprets Biblical laws. I mentioned the bans on entering the Holy City of Jerusalem, which the Temple Scroll equates with the Tabernacle camp in the wilderness. One of the locations in which the banned were to be isolated may give us a clearer picture of the nature of the place where Jesus stayed, at the house of Simon the Leper, before he entered Jerusalem (Mark 14:3; Matthew 26:6).

The Temple Scroll, of course, bans all lepers from Jerusalem, just as lepers were banned from the Israelite camp in the wilderness. As noted above, we are told (in Column 46):

> "And you shall make three places *east of the city* . . . into which shall come the lepers and the people who have a discharge and the men who have had a (nocturnal) emission."

From this and a similar passage, we learn that lepers must have been confined in a separate place *east* of the city. We know from the Midrash* that at this time it was thought leprosy was carried by the wind. The prevailing wind in Jerusalem is westerly—from west to east. Therefore, the rabbis prohibited walking east of a leper. According to the Temple Scroll, lepers were placed in a colony east of the city to avoid the westerly wind's carrying the disease into the city. In my view, Bethany (east of Jerusalem on the eastern slope of the Mount of Olives) was a village of lepers. Thus, it was not that Jesus just happened to stay in the house of a leper (Simon) before he entered Jerusalem; he deliberately chose a *village* of lepers. This deliberate choice would have compounded the offense—entering Jerusalem after contact with lepers—in the eyes not only of the Essenes but of the Pharisees as well.

From the doctrinal viewpoint, the influence of the Essenes on early Christianity, as has been noted by various scholars, is more complicated. We must distinguish between the various layers, or strata, to use an archaeological term, of early Christianity. The theology, the doctrines and the practices of Jesus, John the Baptist and Paul, for example, are not the same. The Dead Sea Scrolls shed new light on these differences.

The similarity between the sectarian doctrines reflected in the Dead Sea Scrolls and in early Christianity were, of course, noted immediately after their discovery. Indeed, one of the chief surprises of the Dead Sea Scrolls for some Christians was that some of what were previously thought to be innovative Christian doctrines and practices were in fact known to the Essenes one hundred or two hundred years before Jesus' time.

But these facts must be related to different sources of Christian doctrine. Jesus himself was, in my opinion, quite anti-Essene, as he was anti-Pharisee. Jesus reacted against the strict insistence on ritual purity practiced not only by the Pharisees but even more so by the Essenes.

Indeed, there may well be an anti-Essene reference in the Sermon on the Mount, as was already noted by the Austrian scholar Kurt Schubert. Jesus there says to the multitude, "You have heard it said . . . hate thine enemy. But I say to you, love your enemies" (Matthew 5:43-44). This passage is somewhat of an enigma. Who is it that has said, "Hate your enemy"? We are not told. There is no such doctrine in any Jewish writing. But, as Schubert has shown, in one of the basic texts of the Qumran community called the *Manual of Discipline*, new members of the sect swear an oath of allegiance to love the Sons of Light (that is, the members of the Essene community) and *to hate for all eternity the Sons of Darkness*. The reference in the Sermon on the Mount to those who advise hating your enemies may well be to the Essenes and would thus

*The literature on the Essene-Christian relationship is vast; some of the very best discussions are contained in K. Stendhal (ed.), *The Scrolls and the New Testament* (New York, 1957).

*An early collection of Jewish elaborations on scripture.

reflect Jesus' own anti-Essene stance.

Another enigmatic passage from the New Testament, Mark 8:14-21, may be clarified by the Temple Scroll itself and as we shall see, in a manner that reflects Jesus' anti-Essene position. In the pericope from Mark, Jesus is in a boat on the Sea of Galilee, with only a single loaf of bread. He cautions his disciples, "Beware of the leaven of the Pharisees and the leaven of the Herodians." The disciples are concerned at the lack of bread. Jesus berates them:

> "Having eyes do you not see, and having ears do you not hear? And do you not remember?"

Jesus recalls for them the miracle of the multiplication of the bread:

> "'When I broke the five loaves for the 5,000, how many baskets full of broken pieces did you take up?'
> They said to him, 'Twelve.'
> 'And the seven for the 4,000, how many baskets full of broken pieces did you take up?'
> And they said to him, 'Seven.'
> And he said to them, 'Do you not yet understand?'"

Modern readers have no less difficulty understanding. The passage is full of obscurities. But the Temple Scroll may help us penetrate some of the cruxes: Who were the Herodians and what is the significance of the 12 baskets full of pieces and the seven baskets full of pieces? And why were the disciples supposed to infer that these baskets full of pieces were an allusion to the bread of the Pharisees and the bread of the Herodians?

I previously referred to the many "new" or additional festivals referred to in the Temple Scroll. These were observed by the Essenes but not by normative Jews. One of these additional festivals I did not mention was the annual seven-day celebration known as the Days of the Ordination (or consecration) of the Priests. This celebration is patterned on the seven-day consecration ceremony Moses performed on Aaron and his sons when they became priests of the Lord in the wilderness, as described in Leviticus 8. For normative Judaism, this ordination of the priests was a one-time act. No new consecration or ordination ceremony of this kind was performed on Aaron's descendants. For the Essenes ruled by the Temple Scroll, however, this was a yearly ceremony. It was to be performed annually, forever. So the Temple Scroll tells us. The role of Moses was to be taken by the High Priest. When the High Priest himself was to be consecrated, the role of Moses was to be performed by the priestly Elders. The details of the ordination ceremony are spelled out in great detail in the Temple Scroll. They are quite complicated, but here we need focus only on one aspect. Leviticus (8:2) speaks of one basket of bread used for the offering on each of the seven days of the ceremony. In the Temple Scroll, however, there are seven baskets of bread, one for each day. Indeed, it appears from the Temple Scroll that the Essenes had a special ceremony connected with the seven baskets of bread, although they could not then offer the full sacrifice at the Jerusalem Temple because it was not built according to their plan; it was not pure according to their laws, and the priests were not legitimate according to their view.

Now let us return to the passage in Mark. Jesus tells his disciples to beware of the bread of the Pharisees and the Herodians. He then refers to the miracle of the 12 baskets of bread and the seven baskets of bread. The 12 baskets, I think, alludes to the Pharisees who controlled the Jerusa-

Column 49 ***of the Temple Scroll continues commands begun in column 48 for cleansing after contact with a leper. Then the column details commands for purifying the house of a dead person. The house is to be swept clear of any "defiling smirch of oil and wine and moisture of water." Its floor, walls, doors, doorposts, thresholds and lintels are to be scraped and washed with water. Typically, these rules are stringent; they also require the occupants of the house to bathe and launder on the first day, the third day and the seventh day after the death.***

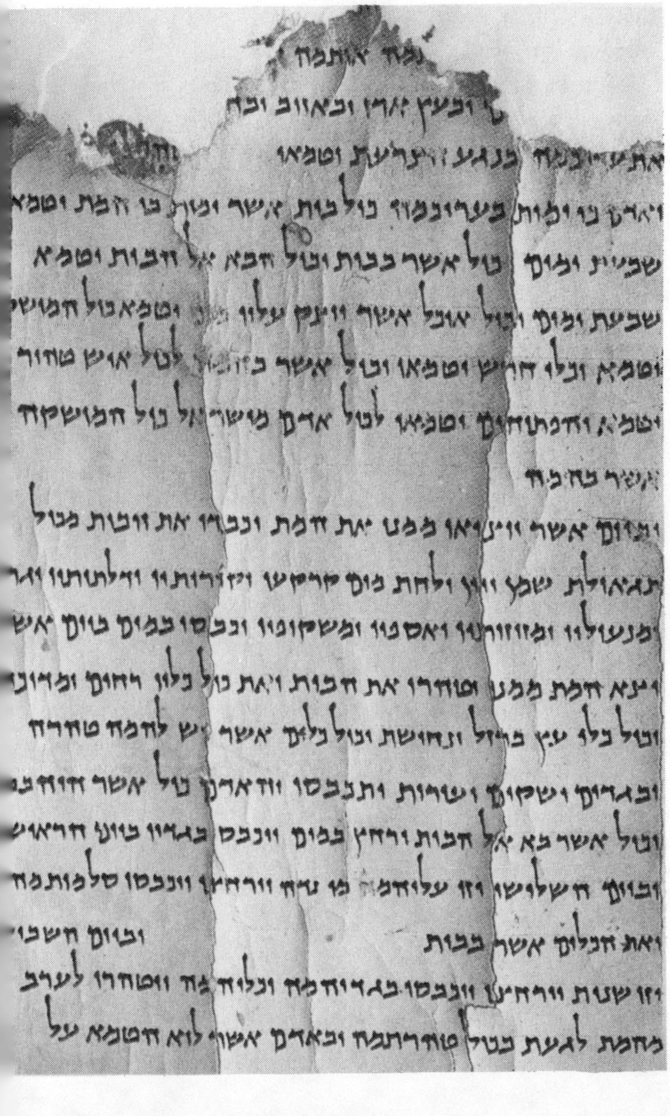

lem Temple. Each week the priests ate the 12 loaves of the presence (Leviticus 24:5-9). In effect Jesus is saying, Do not concern yourself with the 12 loaves in the Pharasaic temple; I created 12 baskets of bread for you.

But what of the seven loaves of the Herodians? What does this allude to? In my view, this refers to the seven loaves the Essenes used in the annual seven-day ceremony of the ordination of the priests. Jesus is telling the disciples not to concern themselves with the Essenes either. Jesus miraculously creates the seven baskets of bread of the Essenes, as well as the 12 baskets of bread of the Pharisees.

But, you may say, the passage from Mark refers to the seven baskets of the Herodians, not the seven baskets of the Essenes. I believe when Jesus refers to the Herodians, he really means the Essenes. I suspect that the Essenes had the nickname "Herodians." Josephus* tells us that Herod was in effect the protector of the Essenes and showed special kindness to them. The suggestion that the Herodians mentioned in Mark, and elsewhere, refer to the Essenes has been made before, but now, from the Temple Scroll, we have considerable evidence for the similarity between Essene beliefs and Herodian beliefs, which strengthens the identification of the Herodians with the Essenes.

Perhaps we can now reply more intelligently to the question Jesus asks: "Do you not yet understand?" Jesus rejects the strict interpretations of the Essenes, as well as the Pharisees. Thus, here again we see Jesus taking an anti-Essene stand.

John the Baptist's relationship to the Essenes is quite different from Jesus'. John may even have been a member of the Essene community. He was active in the area around Qumran; he, like the Essene community at Qumran, was celibate; and he was from a priestly family. Moreover, the type of baptism he was preaching, which gave John his name, was also practiced by the Essenes. We know that the Essenes practiced baptism not only from their literature but also from the baptismal installations found at Qumran.

These baptismal installations are quite different from the ritual baths (*mikvaot*) of the period found, for example, at Masada, in the Jericho area, and in Jerusalem. The normative Judaism ritual baths had to contain "living" water; that is, water either from the rain or from a flowing stream or river. Since this was not available year round, especially in the desert, ritually pure water was saved and preserved in a reserve pool adjacent to the ritual bath. A channel led from the reserve pool to the bath pool so that a small amount of the living water would be added to each bath to purify it, so to say. The Jewish ritual baths are characterized by these twin pools. At Qumran, however, there is only a single pool (with steps) in which people could be baptized.

Baptism as we know it in early Christianity may have been adopted under Essene influence through John the Baptist.

But the most often noted similarities between Christianity and Essene doctrine came not from John the Baptist, and certainly not from Jesus. The principal similarities are to be found in the Pauline Epistles and in the Johannine literature. How do we explain these similarities—such things as the dualism found both in the New Testament and in the writings of the Dead Sea sect, the contrast between the Sons of Darkness and the Sons of Light (a term often used in the Pauline literature), the spirit and the flesh, good and evil. The communal meal is also something we find in early Christianity and in the Dead Sea sect. It is my belief that these similarities came through Paul.

Paul was himself a Pharisee before his conversion on the road to Damascus, but he surely knew well the doctrines of all the sects he was persecuting, including the Essenes. Paul became the apostle to the Gentiles. He was attempting insofar as possible to avoid the burden of the Mosaic law for those whom he converted and who found the Mosaic law an obstacle to their new allegiance. Paul's problem was how to be a Jew without the restrictions of the Mosaic law. I think he found a ready-made theology in many respects in the doctrines of the Essenes. For the

*Jewish Wars XV:372-379.

Essenes, like early Christians (but for different reasons), rejected the Jerusalem Temple and its cult: In my view, the striking similarities between early Christianity and the doctrines of the Essenes entered Christianity after Jesus' time via Paul in the period before the Romans destroyed the Jerusalem Temple in 70 A.D. (and Qumran for that matter).

Yet there is a paradox here: How can it be that a sect (the Essenes) that adhered so tenaciously to the strictest and most legalistic interpretation of all the minutiae of the Law of Moses as prescribed in the Torah, could influence—of all sects—that one (Christianity) which in due course essentially rejected this Law, especially those parts of the Law concerned with Temple observance and ritual purity?

The complete answer is no doubt more complicated than the following hesitant outline suggests, but it is in this area that I believe the answer to our paradox is to be found. As I have said, the early Christians came into contact with the Essenes and were influenced by them at a time late in Essene history (first century A.D.). They met Essenes who maintained their own calendar and repudiated the Jerusalem Temple as well as its laws, for reasons mentioned. Thus bereft of a legitimate temple, the Essenes developed a theology and religious practice that enabled them to live without this cultic institution, especially at their own monastic centers such as Qumran in the wilderness. The following paraphrase of Proverbs 15:8 from an Essene document could have appealed to circles of Pauline or Johannine Christianity: "The sacrifice of the wicked is an abomination, but the prayer of the just is an agreeable offering" (Damascus Document 11:20-21).

The Essenes' rejection of the Jerusalem Temple and its cult, like that of the early Christians, permitted the Essenes to influence the early Christians. Without a temple, the Essenes developed a way of life that was a kind of substitute for the Temple and worship in it. It was this way of life and the theology it reflected that appealed to and influenced the early Christians.

But for the Essenes, the rejection of the Temple was *temporary*. For them, the Jerusalem priests were illegitimate and the Temple polluted because their own rigid legal interpretations of the Law were not applied; even its plan was a wrong one. For the Essenes, the temporary, substitute way of life was applicable only until "the exiles of the Sons of Light return from the Wilderness of the Nations to encamp in the Wilderness of Jerusalem" (War Scroll 3).

What was a temporary substitute for the Essenes, Christianity adopted as a permanent theology, part of their fixed and final canon. In short, what was for the Essenes an *ad hoc* adaptation to their rejection of the Jerusalem priesthood and Temple, applicable only until the end of days when the Temple would be rebuilt by God according to their own beliefs, became for Christianity a permanent solution. Thus, the historical paradox by which the early Christians could be so heavily influenced by a legalistic sect, despite the fact that Christianity itself rejected this legalism.

Let me conclude simply with a few puzzles in the history of Christianity for which the Temple Scroll might provide the hint of a solution.

Of course, even before the acquisition of the Temple Scroll, we knew about the solar calendar used by the Essenes, which contrasted with the lunar calendar practiced by normative Judaism. The Essenes' solar calendar was divided into four sections consisting of three 30-day months, plus one additional day. Thus, the Essene year contained 364 days, divided into twelve 30-day months, plus four intercalated days inserted at the end of each three-month group. (In the course of years, this calendar would need additional intercalated days—or leap years—to maintain the same seasons, but we have no information, for the time being, on how the Essenes did this.) Using this calendar, however, results in holidays always falling on the same day of the week.

I have already mentioned the many "new"—or previously unknown—holidays described in the Temple Scroll, including three new (and one well-established) "first fruits" festivals. The Essenes reckoned the date on which each of these festivals began by counting 50 days after a particular Sabbath (counting the day of the preceding festival as the first day of the new counting), with the result that these festivals always began on a Sunday. Sunday thus begins to appear as a most important day.

In the Statutes of the King, the Temple Scroll considers restrictions on the king's marriages. Rabbinic Judaism interpreted Deuteronomy 17:17 to restrict the king to 18 wives. This was based in part on the fact that King David had 18 wives.

In contrast, the Temple Scroll provides:

> "[The King] shall not take another wife, for she [his first wife] alone shall be with him all the days of her life. But should she die, he may take unto himself another wife."

Here we have a clear-cut ruling against bigamy and divorce, the earliest such ruling in any extant Jewish writing. This may well have been a forerunner of Christian doctrine on these subjects.

As my readers will have noted, I have raised more questions than I have answered. But the scholarly riches of the Temple Scroll have just begun to be mined.

Unless otherwise noted, all photographs in this article are courtesy of Yigael Yadin.

Is the Temple Scroll a Sixth Book of the Torah —Lost for 2,500 Years?

HARTMUT STEGEMANN

The Temple Scroll is the longest and, in my view, clearly the most important of the preserved Dead Sea Scrolls. It was composed, I believe, as an addition or, still better, a supplement to the Pentateuch, as a sixth book of the Torah, on the same level of authority as Genesis, Exodus, Leviticus, Numbers and Deuteronomy.

The 27-foot-long Temple Scroll has been brilliantly published with minute commentary in a handsome three-volume set by the late Professor Yigael Yadin of Hebrew University.[1] His edition of the Temple Scroll is the finest publication of any Dead Sea Scroll that has yet appeared, a masterpiece that will be the basis for all further work on this scroll.*

Yadin almost assumed, however, without seriously discussing the matter, that the Temple Scroll was a sectarian composition belonging to the Jewish group that inhabited the settlement at Qumran near the cave where the scroll was found by Bedouin tribesmen. This group, by extensive scholarly consensus, formed part of the Essenes.

In assuming that the Temple Scroll was an Essene document, Yadin has been followed by nearly all scholars who have considered the Temple Scroll—until very recently.

In my view, the Temple Scroll is not an Essene document. It was composed by other Jews, Jews in the mainstream of Palestinian Judaism in their own time. But it was simply one of the "books," if I may use that term for a scroll, in the Essene library at Qumran, hidden like the others in the caves near their settlement. Its composition had no specific connection whatever with the Essene community at Qumran.

Before explaining the basis for this conclusion, let me set forth several fundamental respects in which I agree with Yadin:

First, the Temple Scroll is, as Yadin emphasized, a *Sefer Torah*, a book of the authoritative religious law, in the strict sense of that term. It is not simply a collection of material pertaining to a particular area of religious life.

Second, like the canonical books of the Torah (Genesis, Exodus, Leviticus, Numbers and Deuteronomy), this Torah, as Yadin also emphasized, was believed to have been given by God himself on Mt. Sinai.[2]

Third, the text of the Temple Scroll is, in Yadin's words, an *"additional" Torah to the Pentateuch*, although on the same level as the Torah. It is not a Torah superior to the Pentateuch,[3] nor a substitute for the Pentateuch. The convincing evidence for this is the fact that the Temple Scroll does not cover such subjects as the creation of the world (Genesis), the Decalogue (Exodus 20:1-17; Deuteronomy 5:6-21), the Aharonite Blessing (Numbers 6:22-27) or the Shema' (the basic monotheistic affirmation: "Hear, O Israel, the Lord our God is one"—Deuteronomy 6:4-9), which were basic to all of the various Jewish religious orientations of the

* Yigael Yadin was a good friend of mine and always supported me in my research. I only wish he had lived to criticize the views I express here that diverge from his own.

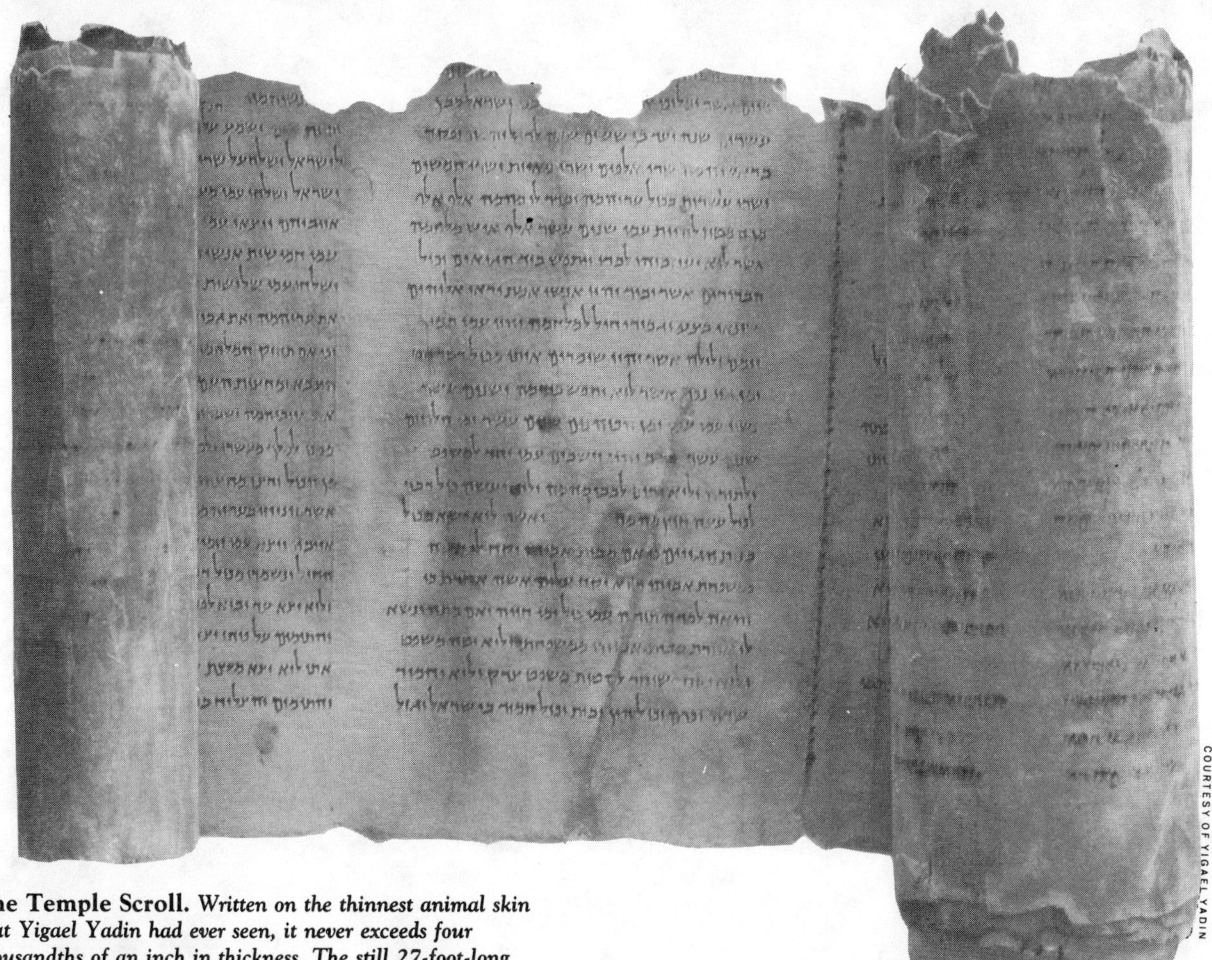

The Temple Scroll. *Written on the thinnest animal skin that Yigael Yadin had ever seen, it never exceeds four thousandths of an inch in thickness. The still 27-foot-long scroll contained at least 66 columns of text. Here we see column 56, the first of four columns that Yadin called the "Statutes of the King," because they enumerate the rights and duties of the king of Israel. Echoing Deuteronomy 17:14-16, the text reads in part, "He [the king] must not multiply horses for himself, or cause the people to return to Egypt, for war . . . since I have said to you, you shall never return that way again." In Deuteronomy, the nearly identical verse reads, "Since the Lord has said to you . . . ." The change from "the Lord" to "I" in the Temple Scroll was apparently made so that God speaks directly to the people, rather than through Moses.*

Found in Cave 11 at Qumran, the Temple Scroll has been understood to be the Torah (law) of the Essene community, the Jewish community that lived in the area of the caves. This was Yadin's conclusion. But Hartmut Stegemann, author of the accompanying article, disagrees. Only two copies of the Temple Scroll, one a mere fragment, have been discovered among some 800 manuscripts taken from the 11 Qumran caves, while other documents are represented by many copies (Deuteronomy, for example, has 25 copies). This and other clues lead Stegemann to argue that the Temple Scroll was not a specifically Essene composition, but was originally intended as a supplementary, sixth book of the Torah, equivalent to the five books of the Pentateuch, and not sectarian in any way.

Second Temple period (515 B.C.-70 A.D.). The Temple Scroll's author only *added* further materials to the given Pentateuch; he did not render the given Pentateuch itself unnecessary or in some way of inferior quality.

Where I differ with Yadin is in his conclusion that the Temple Scroll was a central Torah *of the Essene community*. Yadin believed that the Temple Scroll may even have been written by the Essene community's revered founder, the Teacher of Righteousness himself.

If the Temple Scroll was indeed the central Torah of the Essene community at Qumran, we could expect it to have been widely used by this community in all its affairs. But that was not the case.

Only two copies of the Temple Scroll have been found among the approximately 800 manuscripts recovered from the 11 Qumran caves. One of these copies is Yadin's Temple Scroll itself, which comes from Cave 11—lying about two kilometers north of the central building at Qumran—and which was written about the turn of the era. The second copy is a mere fragmentary scroll, also from Cave 11, but written about 50 B.C. Not a single copy of the Temple Scroll was found in the main library recovered from Cave 4, which held fragments of about 580 different manuscripts.[4]

The Temple Scroll is a very impressive document by its sheer bulk, and it may seem natural to attribute great significance to it in understanding the Essenes among whom it was found. But we must remember that it was only by sheer chance that the main body of this large scroll survived, while most of the other Qumran scrolls are much more fragmentary. It may become less impressive *within the Essene community* when we consider the fact that only two copies of it were found at Qumran, as compared, for example, with 25 different copies of Deuteronomy, 18 of Isaiah and 27 of the Psalter. Of the non-Biblical manuscripts composed by the Essenes or highly esteemed by them, we have at

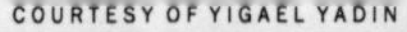

COURTESY OF YIGAEL YADIN

Exercising surgical delicacy, ***Joseph Shenhav and Ruth Yekutiel of the Israel Museum assemble a jigsaw puzzle of damaged fragments from the Temple Scroll. These fragments were part of a "wad," a decayed portion of the scroll that had become separated from the main scroll during its storage in a shoebox in the period before its recovery by Yigael Yadin.***

least eleven copies of the Community Rule, nine of the Songs of the Sabbath Sacrifice, eight of the Thanksgiving Hymns and seven of the War of the Sons of Light Against the Sons of Darkness.

In light of these numbers, we would hardly expect to find only two copies of the Temple Scroll if it was the central law of the Qumran community. Moreover, there is *not a single quotation* from the Temple Scroll in all of the specifically Essene documents, such as the Community Rule, the Damascus Documents or the Thanksgiving Hymns. The Pentateuch is often cited in these writings, from Genesis to Deuteronomy, but not one quotation is from the Temple Scroll. This clearly demonstrates that, regardless of what the members of the Qumran community could learn from copying and reading the Temple Scroll, this text was no legal authority for them, neither a canonical nor an extracanonical one.

When the Essene scrolls quote from the Pentateuch, they often cite the text as coming from the "Book of the Torah" (*Sefer ha-Torah*) or the "Torah of Moses" (*Torath Moshe*). We may conclude that when the community used these terms they were referring to the Pentateuch as it is known to us, and never to the Temple Scroll.

Another important factor that demonstrates that the Temple Scroll was not part of the authorized law of the Essene community at Qumran is that the religious law (*halakhah*) reflected in the Temple Scroll often differs from the Qumran community's known *halakhah*.

At Qumran, every new interpretation of religious law based on an inquiry into the Torah had to be acknowledged by a central body called "The Council of the Community." Thereafter, all members of the community were obliged to follow the new law. In this way, the uniformity of religious law within the group was guaranteed, and no differences in understanding of the Torah could result.

It is true that some religious laws (*halakhot*) reflected in the Temple Scroll agree with specific religious laws of the Qumran community. But these examples simply demonstrate that some of the *halakhot* of the Qumran community come from the same tradition as represented also in the Temple Scroll. There is no direct dependence, however, and the Temple Scroll's text is never quoted. An example of such a correspondence is the concept that the specific holiness of the Temple includes the whole "Holy City" (*'ir ha-qodesh*), that is, the whole city of Jerusalem, an interpretation demanded by the Temple Scroll as well as by the "Laws" of the Damascus Documents[5] (see Magen Broshi, "The Gigantic Dimensions of the Visionary Temple in the Temple Scroll," **BAR**, Nov./Dec. 1987).

But there are also basic *halakhic* differences between the Temple Scroll and the strictly Essene documents found at Qumran. For example, according to the Temple Scroll, the king is permitted to marry only one wife during her lifetime, but he is allowed a second wife after the death of his first wife. But the "Admonitions" of the Damascus Documents in all probability prohibit a second marriage to all Jews "in their own lifetime."

Another example of *halakhic* differences between the Temple Scroll and Qumran law concerns the death penalty. The Temple Scroll demands the death penalty for a particular crime, even if there are only *two witnesses*; Essene law (the "Laws" of the Damascus Documents), however, requires *three witnesses* in all cases. Here we have a direct contradiction, as Lawrence Schiffman has noted.[6] It is difficult to imagine a Jewish community or group whose members differ internally on main points of *halakhah*; the *halakhah* is something like God himself. Yet we would have such differences within the Qumran community if we were to conclude that the Temple Scroll was a central Qumranic document. The differences I have cited are, at the very least, difficult to explain if one adheres to the theory that the Temple Scroll played a normative role for the Qumran community.

As other scholars have noted, from a literary and philological perspective, there is a broad range of differences between the Temple Scroll and the specifically Essene texts. For example, the Temple Scroll refers to the high priest by his traditional title *ha-kohen ha-gadol* (the great priest); this title never occurs, however, in other texts from the Qumran caves. There his title is *kohen ha-rosh* (the high priest) or, perhaps, *ha-kohen ha-mashiah* (the annointed priest).[7]

Another example: In the Temple Scroll, Israel is often called *ha-'am* (the people), and sometimes *'am ha-qahal* (the people of the assembly). These expressions never occur in specifically Essene texts, which prefer *'edah* (congregation) or *yahad* (community). The term *'edah* rarely occurs in the Temple Scroll; and the term *yahad* never occurs there.

It would be easy to produce a long list of such examples, the upshot of which would be to show that the language and the style of the Temple Scroll are *much* more traditional—that is, nearer to the Biblical books—than the equivalents in the specifically Qumranic texts.

The laws prescribing the construction of *the Temple and its courts* consume almost half of the Temple Scroll. But the specifically Essene scrolls reflect no interest whatever in this subject. The specifically Essene texts indeed contain considerable polemic against some conditions at the Jerusalem Temple. But this entire polemic is aimed against the illegitimate priesthood and the sacrifices they offered there, against people who participate in their cult and against some specific cultic customs. Never are the temple building or its courts criticized as being at variance with God's commandments. Nor is there any hint in any of the specifically Essene texts of any desire to change the Jerusalem Temple building or its broader architectural features.

In summation: There is not one mention of the Temple Scroll's text in any of the other specifically Essene writings from Qumran. There is not one quotation from the Temple Scroll in the many Qumran scrolls that otherwise, time and time again, cite all the books of the Pentateuch as their unique law. Further, there are clear differences between the Temple Scroll and the specifically Essene texts in matters of religious law, style, terminology and other linguistic and literary traits. There is also a quite different approach to the Temple buildings in the Temple Scroll, on the one hand, and in the specifically Essene texts on the other. And last but not least, only two copies of the Temple Scroll's text were found in the Qumran caves, both only in Cave 11.

The result is unequivocal in my opinion: Whatever the Temple Scroll was, it was *not* the specific law of the Qumran community, but only some kind of traditional text copied by them once or twice for reasons unknown to us.

But since, as we noted at the outset and as Yadin also observed, the Temple Scroll was composed as a book of the Torah like the other books of the Pentateuch and was regarded as having been given by God himself on Mt. Sinai, we must conclude that the Temple Scroll was an essential part of the Torah for another group of Jews.

But who, where and when?

The argument that I have already given—that the Temple Scroll was not regarded as part of the Torah by the Essenes at Qumran—has been presented to my colleagues at several scholarly meetings and has met with widespread agreement and approval. The argument I am about to make—as to who, where and when, and under what circumstances—has not met with such widespread agreement. It is in fact a matter of great controversy. What the outcome of this scholarly discussion will be, no one can say for sure—but the discussion will be heated and interesting. Nevertheless, it seems permissible to present my views, controversial though they are, to **BAR** readers and to observe that, so far, no one has come up with a better suggestion.

I believe that the Temple Scroll is an early expansion of the Torah—a kind of sixth book to be added to the Pentateuch as it has come down to us. Expanded Torah scrolls are nothing new, although it is certainly unusual to find a whole book representing such an expansion. But even before the discoveries at Qumran, we had both the Samaritan Pentateuch,* with its smaller expansions within the text of the traditional five books of the Pentateuch, and the Greek Septuagint,** with its similar expansions.[8] Now we also have expansions of a similar kind in the fragments of Torah scrolls from the Qumran caves.[9]

In my opinion, most of these early expansions to Torah scrolls represent the initiative of priests at the Jerusalem Temple from the period during which the Judaean exiles returned from Babylonia and rebuilt the Temple (the Second Temple), from the latter third of the sixth century B.C. onwards. The crucial point is that these expansions developed at the Second Temple *before* the canonization of the Pentateuch, that is, before an official textual version of the Torah was authorized and finally established there.

According to the Bible, Ezra the scribe established the canon of the Pentateuch in Jerusalem when he returned from the Babylonian exile, some 50 or 75 years after the Second Temple was built by earlier returnees. The Biblical text gives us enough information to fix the precise date for Ezra's return and canonization of the Pentateuch—458 B.C. As we read in the Book of Ezra, "During the reign of Artaxerxes [465-424 B.C.] . . . Ezra [whose ancestry is here traced back to Aaron the high priest] came up from Babylon, a scribe expert in the Teaching of Moses" (Ezra 7:1-6). In the next verse, we learn that Ezra arrived with other returnees during the seventh year of Artaxerxes' reign (458 B.C.). According to the letter of authority that Artaxerxes gave to Ezra, "The Law of your God . . . is in your care" (Ezra 7:14). The letter continues:

> "Ezra, [you are to] appoint magistrates and judges . . . who know the Law of your God . . . to judge and to teach those who do not know. Let anyone who does not obey the Law of your God . . . be punished" (Ezra 7:25-26).

That is precisely what Ezra did, establishing the Pentateuch as the central authority in Jerusalem.

From form-critical studies of the Pentateuch, we know that when the Pentateuch first took shape, the editors (or redactors, as they are called) used older sources. In the final edition of the Pentateuch, these older sources were combined, augmented and updated, according to the needs and perspectives of a later day. I believe this process occurred in Mesopotamia during the Babylonian Exile. In my opinion, Ezra himself brought this version from Mesopotamia to Jerusalem; he intended it for the future as the only authoritative Torah, proclaiming it *the* Book of the Torah (*Sefer ha-Torah*), and established it in Jerusalem through the authority of the Persian government. Whether compiled in Jerusalem or Babylonia, however, the consequence of Ezra's actions was necessarily that all other Torah scrolls used at the Temple of Jerusalem up to Ezra's time were no longer in force. Every new scroll with books of the Pentateuch had to conform now to the version Ezra proclaimed as authoritative.

Ezra displays the law *in this wall painting from the third-century A.D. synagogue at Dura-Europos, Syria. Although some scholars identify this scene as Moses reading the law after he had received it on Mt. Sinai, the painting seems to better illustrate Nehemiah 8:5, "Ezra opened the scroll in the sight of all the people," for the writing on the scroll faces outward as if being shown to the people. On the floor beside Ezra's right foot rests a cloth-covered box that may be a portable ark, or scroll case, in which the scrolls of the law that Ezra brought from Babylon could be kept. When Ezra in essence canonized the Pentateuch at Jerusalem in 458 B.C., he effectively outlawed other, already-existing additions and expansions of the Torah. Subsequently, Stegemann proposes, portions of other Torah scrolls were collected—together with five additional literary sources—into a new book that we now call the Temple Scroll.*

But what of the many expanded and different versions of Torah scrolls that had developed up to that time, Torah scrolls that contained additions such as

* The Samaritan Pentateuch is the Torah in the form canonized by the Samaritans.

** The Septuagint is the Greek version of the Hebrew Bible, as translated by Jews in Alexandria from the third century B.C. onwards.

survived in the Samaritan Pentateuch and the Septuagint? After all, such traditional expansions had been formulated at the Temple by Jerusalem priests based on the authority of God himself. Could they be invalidated by a human decision—that is, by the authority of the pagan king Artaxerxes I, who stood behind the deeds of Ezra the scribe?

The way out of this dilemma is reflected in the text of the Temple Scroll. Many of the traditional expansions of the hitherto existing Torah scrolls were taken over into this new book, which we now refer to as the Temple Scroll.

At this point, I must explain that the Temple Scroll is itself, like Genesis, for example, a composite document. In a brilliant article by Andrew M. Wilson and Lawrence Wills, with an assist from their mentor, Professor John Strugnell of Harvard,* the authors clearly demonstrate that there are at least five different sources in the Temple Scroll. In different parts of the Temple Scroll, for example, God is referred to in the first person and in the third person, the people are addressed in the singular and in the plural, etc. These five distinct sources were not only combined in the Temple Scroll, but were superficially revised by a final editor, or redactor, who added some further material here and there and created the framework of the final text—the same process that is reflected, for example, in Genesis. In my judgment, Wilson and Wills are basically correct about the different strands of texts combined in the Temple Scroll. On only a few minor points would I favor a solution other than the one they have proposed.

When we examine the setting or *Sitz im Leben* of these five sources of the Temple Scroll, we must conclude that they are all shaped by specific *priestly* interests. Even the final redaction reflects these priestly interests. And there is nothing other than the practice of the priestly cult at the Temple in Jerusalem that is reflected in this setting.

For this reason, it seems clear that the composition of these five sources occurred sometime during the first century of the Second Temple period, and their redaction occurred in reaction to, and not too long after, Ezra's canonization of the Pentateuch in 458 B.C. Once Ezra had established what was essentially a shorter, canonical Pentateuch, in effect outlawing all these former additions and expansions, such additions and expansions were collected and edited to form what we know as the Temple Scroll.

The authority of these old additions and expansions of the Pentateuch was now assumed by the new book as a whole: God himself spoke directly to his people, through this book, as in the Pentateuch, even if all its parts did not conform perfectly to the overall style of direct address. In this way, through the compilation of the Temple Scroll, a sixth book of the Torah was created—the only true Hexateuch that has ever existed historically!

This sixth book of the Torah not only gathered together many of the traditional Torah additions and expansions, but, by the adoption of the five sources, it also brought into the supplemented Torah other materials in which God had spoken to the Fathers in an authoritative way regarding matters of the Temple, its cult, the purity of the participants and the many revised *halakhic* laws.

Yadin himself noted the tendency of the Temple Scroll to combine and harmonize divergent commandments found in the Pentateuch and in the books of the prophets. This in effect illustrates the process of collection and combination out of which the Temple Scroll was created. (A similar method, I might add, can be traced through almost all ages of Jewish tradition and is found not only in the Mishnah and in the Talmuds, but even as late as the *Shulhan 'Arukh*, a 16th-century collection of laws that remains authoritative to this day for observant Jews.)

My basic thesis depends, I realize, on establishing the date of the sources in the Temple Scroll to the early Second Temple period (from the latter third of the sixth century to the fifth century B.C.), and its redaction to the second half of the fifth century B.C. The most important element in establishing this dating has already been discussed—the priestly *Sitz im Leben* of the sources and the historical context of Ezra's canonization of the Pentateuch. No other set of later historical circumstances fits these aspects of the text of the Temple Scroll and its final editing. Moreover, quite apart from all the other arguments, it is difficult to imagine that a supplementary sixth book of the Torah could have been compiled and acknowledged by at least some Jewish priests much later than the fifth—or the fourth—century B.C.

Nevertheless, this is a somewhat radical redating of the Temple Scroll and will not be easily accepted by a scholarly community already accustomed to arguing about dates for the Temple Scroll ranging between about 200 B.C. and 50 B.C. Possible later historical allusions, philology, grammar, etc., will be adduced by my scholarly colleagues to support a particular dating later than my proposed dating. But I have examined all of the arguments adduced thus far, most of them quite technical, and I can say with some degree of confidence that none presents any particular problem for the dating I have proposed.

True, the extant copies of the Temple Scroll that survived at Qumran are much later, from about 50 B.C. onwards, but this says nothing about the sources' date of composition or about the date of their combination and final redaction.

Let me give an example of the kinds of issues involved in this dating debate. One of the sources of the Temple Scroll consists of a reworking of the laws in Deuteronomy 12-26, arranged in a new way, with many additions and alterations as compared with the Biblical text. This source runs from column 51, line 11 of the Temple Scroll to the lost end of the scroll, but is interrupted in columns 57 to 59 by the so-called Statutes of the King. Deuteronomy 21:22-23 requires

* "Literary Sources of the Temple Scroll," *Harvard Theological Review*, vol. 75 (1982), pp. 275-288.

GARO NALBANDIAN

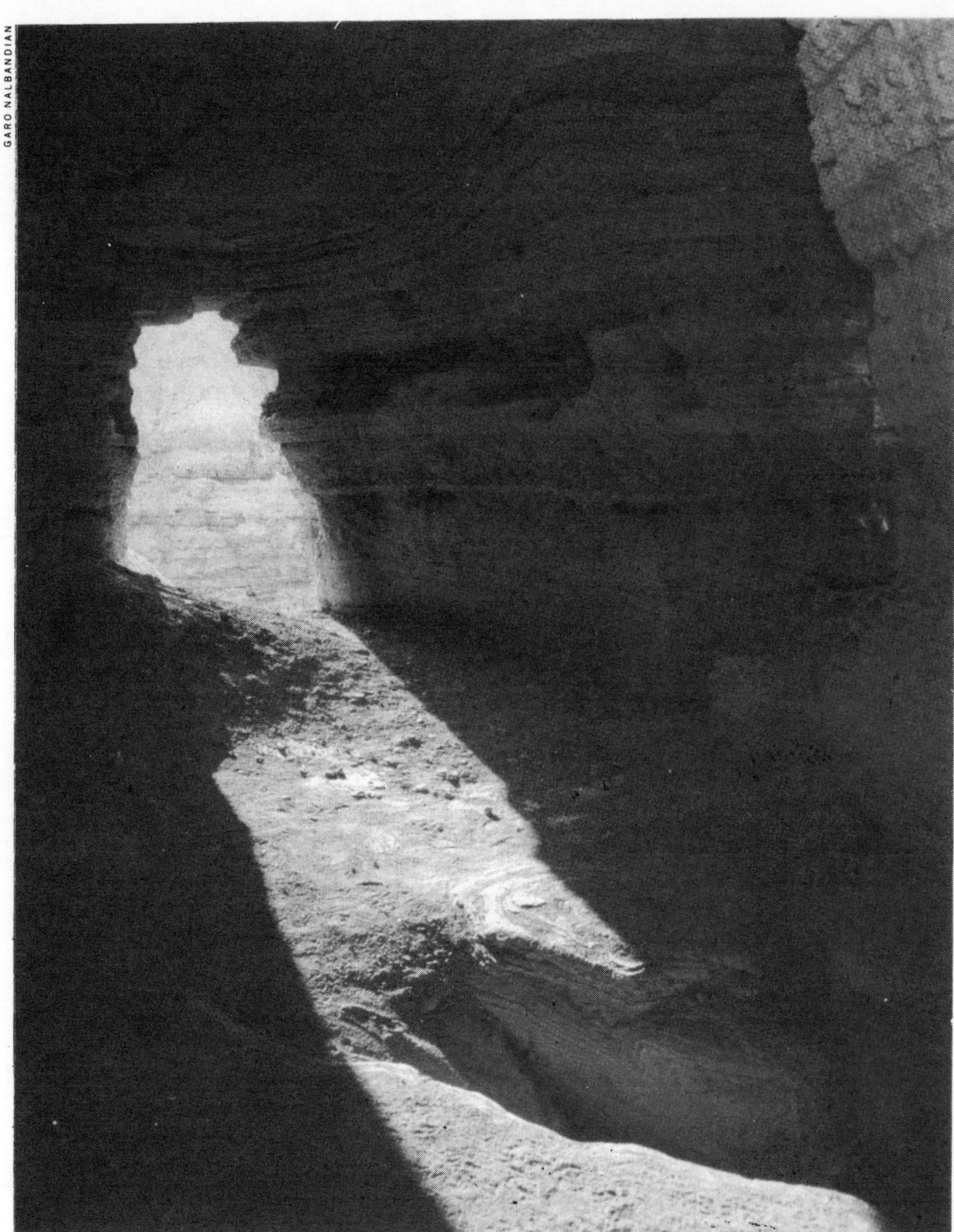

Within caves at Qumran, *such as this one, near the northwest shore of the Dead Sea, the Essenes secreted their manuscripts now known as the Dead Sea Scrolls. On a barren plateau near the caves, they built their community.*

The Temple Scroll, however, was not found with the principal Essene library in Cave 4. Moreover, none of the specifically Essene documents ever quotes from the Temple Scroll, and some of the Scroll's contents differ from the known religious laws of the Essene community, important indications that the Temple Scroll was not a book of legal authority for the Essenes.

Archaeologists dug the small trench in the foreground while searching for scroll fragments.

that a man who has been executed and then publicly exposed by *talah 'al ha-'es*—literally, hanging on a pole—be buried the same day. Otherwise the land will be defiled. In the Temple Scroll, the crimes for which *talah 'al ha-'es* is required is expanded to include, for example, an Israelite who "passes on information about my people and betrays my people to a foreign people." Here the death of the evil-doer will be caused by this "hanging on a pole"—not by killing him before and then "hanging on a pole," as in Deuteronomy. Some scholars have argued that this passage in the Temple Scroll refers specifically to the time of Alexander Jannaeus (first century B.C.), who crucified 800 Jews alive, most of them Pharisees. This is reported by Flavius Josephus and is alluded to in the *Pesher Nahum* from Qumran. But there is no reason whatever to connect the discussion of *talah 'al ha-'es* in the Temple Scroll to this historical incident in the first century B.C. Hanging of people alive by *talah 'al ha-'es* was familiar to the people of Israel, at least as a gentile punishment, from as early as 701 B.C., when Sennacherib, the king of Assyria, conquered the Israelite town of Lachish. The reliefs portraying this conquest show three nude Israelites from Lachish being impaled on stakes. This kind of *talah 'al ha-'es* would thus have been usual from as early as the eighth century B.C.

All other indications of a later date for the Temple Scroll can be shown to be inconclusive in this same way, although perhaps less dramatically.

Accordingly, we may conclude that the Temple Scroll was composed from previously existing sources as a sixth book of the Torah. This occurred soon after Ezra's canonization of the "shorter" Pentateuch, the Pentateuch as we know it. If Ezra canonized this "shorter"

Pentateuch in 458 B.C., the text of the Temple Scroll would have been redacted some time after this, in the second half of the fifth century B.C.

In the early Second Temple period (beginning in the latter third of the sixth century B.C.), there must have been priestly families, or perhaps priestly "schools," in Jerusalem, that composed the expansions and additions that provided the Temple Scroll with its sources. Ezra's "reform"—his canonization of the Pentateuch—stopped this process of further creating expansions and additions. He established the "original" version of the Pentateuch, known to him, I believe, from Mesopotamia, as the only authorized one in Jerusalem as well.

The Temple Scroll incorporated many of the Palestinian "additions" from expanded Torah scrolls and used them to create a new *Sefer Torah*, a new Book of the Law. The editor of this text represents the end of this kind of creativity in Scripture as far as the Torah is concerned. He used these additions and supplementary sources to compose a sixth book of the Torah. The authority behind this new book, however, was still on the same level as the authority of the Pentateuch itself and of its priestly traditions, that is, God himself. The editor did not have to resort to any other source of authority for his new book. He did not intend to replace the traditional Pentateuch; rather, he intended to *complete* it.

Somehow, at least two copies of this sixth book of the Torah found their way to the ancient libraries of Qumran. With what authority the Essenes of Qumran regarded it, we do not know. But we have no reason to believe that for them it was a central document of law. But for many mainstream Jews in Jerusalem, it probably was such a document during the mid-Second Temple period (from the end of the fifth century through the fourth, or even third, century B.C.).[10]

The text of the Temple Scroll will now shed new light on that still rather shrouded period of Jewish life in Jerusalem following the return of the first exiles from Babylonia.

[1] See in addition, Yigael Yadin, "The Temple Scroll—The Longest and Most Recently Discovered Dead Sea Scroll," **BAR**, September/October 1984 [p. 160].

[2] The question of Mosaic authority in the Temple Scroll is still much debated. Indeed, the name of Moses does not appear in the extant text of the Temple Scroll. Compare this with Deuteronomy 12-26. For this reason, Baruch Levine ("The Temple Scroll: Aspects of its Historical Provenance and Literary Character," *Bulletin of the American Schools of Oriental Research* 232 [1978], pp. 5-23, especially pp. 17-21) denies any Mosaic authority for the Temple Scroll. His conclusion was challenged by Yadin ("Is the Temple Scroll a Sectarian Document?" in Gene M. Tucker and Douglas A. Knight [ed.], *Humanizing America's Iconic Book: SBL Centennial Addresses 1980* [Chico, CA: Scholar's Press, 1982], pp. 153-169), who relies on Temple Scroll 44:5 and 51:5-7, where Moses is indeed indirectly addressed. But Levine correctly demonstrates the tendency of the Temple Scroll to replace the traditional authority of Moses with God himself. Probably, this is to be interpreted as polemical—against any human authority in Jewish legal matters.

[3] In this Ben Zion Wacholder is wrong. See his book *The Dawn of Qumran* (Cincinnati, OH: Hebrew Union College Press, 1983), where he claims that the Temple Scroll "may have been intended to supersede not only the canonical Pentateuch but the other books of the Hebrew Scriptures as well" (p. 30).

[4] Yigael Yadin believed that fragments of a document from Cave 4 (Rockefeller Museum No. 43.366, published in Yadin, *The Temple Scroll* [Jerusalem: Israel Exploration Society, 1983], supplementary plates 38 and 40) belonged to a copy of the Temple Scroll. As Professor John Strugnell has correctly pointed out, these fragments are from "a Pentateuch with frequent non-biblical additions" [4Q364 and 365] (quoted in Wacholder, *The Dawn of Qumran*, p. 206), not from the Temple Scroll. In this same reference, Strugnell refers to other unpublished Cave 4 fragments that might quote from, or actually be the text of, the Temple Scroll. The true nature of this text can be discussed, however, only after its publication by Emile Puech. He has kindly shown me the fragments of this scroll, which are unfortunately in very poor condition. They probably come from a late second-century B.C. copy of an expanded text of Deuteronomy, evidently differing from the text of the Temple Scroll. At this time, it is at least very uncertain that even a single Cave 4 manuscript of the Temple Scroll's text exists.

[5] The so-called "Damascus Documents" include two different books, the "Admonitions" represented by columns 1-8 and 19-20, and the "Laws" represented by columns 15-16 and 9-14. Both books were composed separately by the Essenes, and fragments of both of them were also found in the Qumran caves.

[6] See Lawrence H. Schiffman, *Sectarian Law in the Dead Sea Scrolls: Courts, Testimony and the Penal Code* (Chico, CA: Scholar's Press, 1983), p. 77.

[7] Yadin recognized this problem and tried to resolve it with the suggestion that in other scrolls from Qumran we are always dealing with high priests who are mentioned in contexts relating to the End of Days, with specific titles for them. But this is, at least, disputable: In those scrolls, the high priest at the End of Days is called *ha-kohen ha'aharon* or sometimes *meshiah 'Aharon*, while *kohen ha-rosh* seems to be the more usual title used by the Qumran community, but strange to the Temple Scroll.

[8] The Cambridge edition of the Septuagint by Allen E. Brooke and Norman McLean, *The Old Testament in Greek According to the Text of Codex Vaticanus* (Cambridge, UK: Cambridge Univ. Press, 1906-1911), Vol. I, Part I-III.

[9] Yadin mistakenly thought these were references to other copies of the Temple Scroll. They were not that, but were simply fragments of scrolls of the same genre, or expansions within the Pentateuchal books themselves. Unfortunately, some of these are still unpublished, so they can not be treated very thoroughly, even by scholars. In regard to the failure to publish the Dead Sea Scrolls, see the following **BAR** articles by Hershel Shanks: "No Theological Reasons for Failing to Publish Dead Dea Scrolls: Syrian Authorities Commended," January/February 1985; "Failure to Publish Dead Sea Scrolls Is Leitmotif of New York University Scroll Conference," September/October 1985; and "Israel Authorities Now Responsible for Delay in Publication of Dead Sea Scrolls," September/October 1985.

[10] Dating the composition of the Temple Scroll to the second half of the fifth century B.C. results in some provocative suggestions for further research:

First: The Pentateuch as we know it from our Bible must have been finally redacted at least a century before the composition of the Temple Scroll; at least a century would be needed to develop all the additions and alterations of the text used in the Temple Scroll.

Second: Some scholars already noticed that specific aspects of the Temple Scroll are closely related to the Biblical Books of Chronicles—for example, the status of the Levites. The stage of development of the Hebrew language is similar in both Chronicles and in the Temple Scroll. These relationships and similarities are much easier to explain if both Chronicles and the Temple Scroll are contemporaneous compositions, but they would be puzzling if the Temple Scroll was composed about three centuries later as supposed by Yadin and those who agree with him.

Third: Over the centuries, even Palestinian Jews no longer continued to regard the Temple Scroll as a canonical book, as the sixth book of the Torah, as it was in the mind of its author. Nevertheless, the preserved text of Yadin's Temple Scroll demonstrates the way in which some priestly families at the Jerusalem Temple interpreted, augmented and used the canonical Pentateuch during the first century of the Second Temple period. This insight will enable us to understand much better the way priestly teaching developed at the Jerusalem Temple before Ezra returned there.

The differing assessments of the Temple Scroll by Yigael Yadin and Hartmut Stegemann call attention to three further uncertainties, which attach to any one of the Dead Sea Scrolls—uncertainties that often have been slighted or overlooked in discussions of the scrolls: (1) Is a particular scroll a copy of an original manuscript of much earlier date and locale? (2) Did the particular scroll in fact come from Qumran? (3) If it did, is it necessarily an Essene document?

In regard to the Temple Scroll, readers may be interested in evaluating for themselves the relative strength of the arguments Yadin put forward for suggesting that the original document was written between 150 and 125 B.C. by an Essene leader and the arguments advanced by Stegemann for dating the original to the fifth—or at latest fourth—century B.C. and asserting that it was *not* an Essene document.

For Further Reading

Concerning the Discovery, Preservation and Study of the Dead Sea Scrolls

Harry Thomas Frank, "How the Dead Sea Scrolls Were Found," **BAR**, December 1975

Frank Moore Cross, "The Dead Sea Scrolls and the People Who Wrote Them," **BAR**, March 1977

Jack Finegan, "Crosses in the Dead Sea Scrolls," **BAR**, November/December 1979

Joseph Shenhav, "Saving the Dead Sea Scrolls for the Next 2,000 Years," **BAR**, July/August 1981

Raphael Levy, "First 'Dead Sea Scroll' Found in Egypt Fifty Years Before Qumran Discoveries," **BAR**, September/October 1982

Hartmut Stegemann, "How to Connect Dead Sea Scroll Fragments," **BR**, February 1988

Concerning the Temple Scroll

Morton Smith, "The Case of the Gilded Staircase," **BAR**, September/October 1984

Jacob Milgrom, "Challenge to Sun-Worship Interpretation of Temple Scroll's Gilded Staircase," **BAR**, January/February 1985

Hershel Shanks, "Intrigue and the Scroll—Behind the Scenes of Israel's Acquisition of the Temple Scroll," **BAR**, November/December 1987

Magen Broshi, "The Gigantic Dimensions of the Visionary Temple in the Temple Scroll," **BAR**, November/December 1987

Concerning the Content of Other Dead Sea Scrolls

"New Testament Illuminated by Dead Sea Scrolls," **BAR**, September/October 1982

Magen Broshi, "Beware the Wiles of the Wanton Women," **BAR**, July/August 1983

Frank Moore Cross, "The Text Behind the Text of the Hebrew Bible," **BR**, Summer 1985

Frank Moore Cross, "Original Biblical Text Reconstructed from Newly Found Fragments," **BR**, Fall 1985

Concerning Publication of the Dead Sea Scrolls

"Leading Scholar Calls For Prompt Publication," **BAR**, March 1978

"No Theological Reasons for Failing to Publish Dead Sea Scrolls: Syrian Authorities Commended," Queries & Comments, **BAR**, January/February 1985

Hershel Shanks, "Failure to Publish Dead Sea Scrolls Is Leitmotif of New York University Scroll Conference," **BAR**, September/October 1985

Hershel Shanks, "Israeli Authorities Now Responsible for Delay in Publication of Dead Sea Scrolls," **BAR**, September/October 1985

"Debate on Enoch Stifled for 30 Years While One Scholar Studied Dead Sea Scroll Fragments," **BR**, Summer 1987, p. 34

Hershel Shanks, "*At Least* Publish the Dead Sea Scrolls Timetable!" **BAR**, May/June 1989

Hershel Shanks, "Dead Sea Scrolls Scandal—Israel's Department of Antiquities Joins Conspiracy to Keep Scrolls Secret," **BAR**, July/August 1989

Hershel Shanks, "What Should Be Done About the Unpublished Dead Sea Scrolls?" **BAR**, September/October 1989

Hershel Shanks, "New Hope for the Unpublished Dead Sea Scrolls, " **BAR**, November/December 1989

Hershel Shanks, "Dead Sea Scroll Variation on 'Show and Tell'—It's called 'Tell, But No Show,' " **BAR**, March/April 1990

Hershel Shanks, "Leading Dead Sea Scroll Scholar Denounces Delay," **BAR**, March/April 1990

"Why Won't the Scroll Editors Release the Texts? Frank Cross Provides the Answers," **BAR**, March/April 1990

"Dead Sea Scroll Concordance Now Available for Use by Scholars," **BAR**, March/April 1990

"An Unpublished Dead Sea Scroll Text Parallels Luke's Infancy Narrative," **BAR**, March/April 1990

By the Sea of Galilee Where Jesus Preached

For centuries pious Christian pilgrims to the Holy Land have sought out the places where Jesus walked, where he preached, where he healed or performed miracles, where he ate with his disciples, where he prayed and was arrested, where he died, where he rose. . . . So it has been a disappointment to many—indeed, a painful loss—that the effect of modern scholarly investigation so often has been to discredit or throw into question the authenticity of sites that time-honored tradition has associated with sacred events in the Gospel accounts. (See, for example, the following section, which deals with conflicting claims concerning the tomb of Jesus.)

Not all archaeological research has led to negative results regarding Christian holy sites, however. In fact, recent excavations at one of the places associated with Jesus' ministry, Capernaum on the Sea of Galilee, have uncovered not one but two spots that may be the actual locales of significant activities of Jesus recorded in the Gospels. The first two selections describe the evidence that has led investigators to believe they have located Peter's house in Capernaum, where Jesus stayed and effected healings (Mark 1:29-31, 2:1-12), and the synagogue where Jesus preached and also healed (Mark 1:21-28).

On the other hand, the discovery of the Galilee boat in early 1986, reported in "The Galilee Boat—2,000-Year-Old Hull Recovered Intact," shows how easily—even in this day—pious enthusiasm can lead many people to hasty and unsubstantiated conclusions. Shelley Wachsmann describes how in only three days' time a boat buried in the mud of the Sea of Galilee was converted in uncontrolled popular imagination from "ancient" to "a wreck from Jesus' time" to *the* "boat of Jesus." The episode illustrates how easily and spontaneously some of the identifications of sacred objects and sites in earlier centuries may have grown from "it could be" to "it probably is" to "it must be."

Aside from the popular interest generated by the Galilee boat because of its associations—real or imagined—with sacred history, the story of the boat's excavation is particularly fascinating as an illustration of some of the special problems encountered in underwater archaeology and some of the new techniques being developed to deal with those problems.

Wachsmann describes graphically the exceptional challenges the excavation posed and the ingenious processes used to move the fragile frame of the Galilee vessel intact, and then to stabilize it in a new environment where it can be preserved and, eventually, displayed.

Has the House Where Jesus Stayed in Capernaum Been Found?

ITALIAN ARCHAEOLOGISTS BELIEVE THEY HAVE UNCOVERED ST. PETER'S HOME

By James F. Strange and Hershel Shanks

Italian archaeologists claim to have discovered the house were Jesus stayed in Capernaum. Proof positive is still lacking and may never be found, but all signs point to the likelihood that the house of St. Peter where Jesus stayed, near Capernaum's famous synagogue, is an authentic relic.

Nestled on the northwest shore of the Sea of Galilee, the ruins of Capernaum slumbered peacefully for hundreds of years; indeed, some of its remains went undisturbed for thousands of years. Modern investigation of this site began in the mid-19th century, but even now the earth is still

The Capernaum synagogue, *residential area and octagonal church, clustered on the northwest shore of the Sea of Galilee. Beyond the trees is the brick convent of the Franciscan Fathers.*

The synagogue was built on a platform, mounted by steps at its southeast and southwest corners; the southeast steps are visible in this photo. The steps lead to a courtyard, or room, with an intact flagstone floor. This auxiliary room probably served as the synagogue's school room. The interior of the main prayer room was divided by two parallel rows of columns forming a nave and two aisles.

Recent excavations uncovered more ancient buildings beneath this synagogue. Since we know that, historically, the site of a town's synagogue rarely changes, one of these earlier buildings was very likely the Capernaum synagogue in which Jesus preached.

South of the synagogue is a residential area, the remains of private homes. Beyond that (84 feet south of the synagogue) is the octagonal church built over St. Peter's house.

yielding new secrets. What the future holds, no one knows.

An American explorer and orientalist, Edward Robinson, first surveyed the site in 1838. Robinson correctly identified some exposed architectural remains as an ancient synagogue, but he did not connect the site with ancient Capernaum.

In 1866, Captain Charles Wilson conducted limited excavations on behalf of the London-based Palestine Exploration Fund. Wilson correctly identified the site as Capernaum and concluded that the synagogue was the one referred to in Luke 7:5, which was built by a Roman centurion who had admired the Jews of Kfar Nahum (Capernaum*).

As a result of the British interest in the site, local Bedouin began their own search for treasure. They smashed and overturned ancient architectural members looking for small finds to sell on the local antiquities markets. The Bedouin were soon followed by local Arab contractors who appropriated overturned and broken stones for use in new construction projects.

At last in 1894, the Franciscan Fathers acquired the site in order to protect its precious remains. To ensure that the exposed remains would not be carried away, the Franciscans reburied some of them and built a high stone wall around the property.

Naturally, special Christian interest in the site stemmed from Capernaum's importance in Jesus's life and ministry. According to the Gospel of Matthew, Jesus left Nazareth and "settled" in Capernaum (to render the verb literally) (Matthew 4:13). In and around Capernaum Jesus recruited several of his disciples including Peter, who was to become his spiritual fisherman (Mark 1:16-20). Jesus performed a number of miracles in Capernaum—for example, curing the man with the withered hand (Mark 3:1-5). Jesus frequently preached and taught at the Capernaum synagogue (Mark 1:21). In the Capernaum synagogue, Jesus first uttered those mystical words:

> "Whoever eats my flesh and drinks my blood possesses eternal life, and I will raise him up on the last day. . . . As the living Father sent me . . . he who eats shall live because of me. This is the bread which came down from heaven." (John 6:54-58)

The word of Jesus went forth first from Capernaum. Capernaum was not only the center of Jesus's Galilean ministry, but it was also the place of his longest residence.

Where did Jesus live in Capernaum? While we are not told specifically, the fair inference seems to be that he lived

Garo Nalbandian

A Corinthian column capital *from the Capernaum synagogue. A seven-branched candelabrum (menorah) decorates this elaborately carved capital. To the right of the menorah's base is a ram's horn (shofar) and, to the left, an incense shovel; both are ritual objects once used in the Temple in Jerusalem. This capital may have stood atop one of the columns separating the nave from an aisle inside the synagogue.*

at Peter's house. We are told that Jesus "entered Peter's house, [and] saw his mother-in-law lying sick with a fever . . ." (Matthew 8:14). That evening he was still at Peter's house (Matthew 8:16). Apparently Jesus lived there. In Mark we read that "when he [Jesus] returned to Capernaum after a few days, someone reported that he was at home" (Mark 2:1). The home referred to, it seems, is Peter's house. This same passage from Mark speaks of four men digging through the roof of the house to lower a paralytic on a pallet so that Jesus could heal him:

> "And when he returned to Capernaum after a few days, someone reported that he was at home. And many were gathered, so many that they did not have any room, even about the door. And he was speaking the word to them. And they came bringing to him a paralytic, carried by four men. And since they could not get

*Capernaum is the Latinization of the Hebrew Kfar Nahum which means the village of Nahum.

to him because of the crowd, they took apart the roof where he was. And when they had dug out a hole, they lowered the pallet on which the paralytic lay.

"And when Jesus saw their faith, he said, 'My son, your sins are forgiven,' " (Mark 2:1-5). A late Renaissance painting of this Bible scene, "Arise, Take Up Thy Bed and Walk," by Flemish artist Jan van Hemessen appears in **BAR** (Nov./Dec. 1982, p. 24).

Until 1968, the primary focus of excavations at Capernaum was the synagogue. This is understandable. It is indeed a magnificent building of shimmering white limestone that stands out in stark contrast to the rough black basalt of the surrounding houses. The synagogue was constructed on a platform to conform with the rabbinic injunction to build the synagogue on the highest point in the town.* The synagogue is entered by a flight of steps on either side of the platform. The entrance facade contains three doors facing Jerusalem.

Inside the synagogue, two rows of stone benches, probably for elders who governed the synagogue, line the two long walls. The other congregants sat eastern fashion on mats on the floor.

Two rows of columns divide the main prayer room into a central nave and two side aisles. Parallel to the back wall, a third row of columns creates a third aisle in the rear of the main room. Adjoining the main room was a side room that was no doubt used for a variety of community functions—as a school, a court, a hostel for visitors, a dining hall, a meeting place. In antiquity, the synagogue served all these functions.

When this synagogue was first excavated by the Franciscan Friar Gaudentius Orfali in the 1920s, Friar Orfali identified it as the synagogue in which Jesus had preached and performed miracles. Today, however, all competent scholars reject this dating of the Capernaum synagogue. In 1968, the Franciscans renewed their excavations in the synagogue under the direction of two Franciscan fathers, Virgilio Corbo and Stanislao Loffreda. This pair of Italian scholars concluded that the synagogue dated to the fourth or fifth century A.D. Their dating was based primarily on a hoard of 10,000 coins they found under the synagogue floor. This new conclusion set off a lively debate, still unresolved, among scholars who had previously contended that the building should be dated to the late second or third century A.D.

Whatever the date of the surviving Capernaum synagogue, it is likely that the Capernaum synagogue in which Jesus preached stood on this same spot—although this cannot be proved. As we know from other communities, synagogue sites rarely change within a town. A new synagogue is simply reconstructed on the site of the old one. Recently, traces of earlier buildings have been found below the extant Capernaum synagogue. Judging from the size of these earlier buildings and the paving on their floors, they were probably private homes. One of these earlier remains may

*Tosephta. Megillah IV 23.

Garo Nalbandian

The interior of the Capernaum synagogue. *Although this impressive row of white limestone columns looks like a facade, it is actually the narrow north end of the synagogue nave, 27 feet across. On either side of the nave, parallel to its length, is an aisle formed by rows of columns. The intact column in the left foreground and the broken one in the right foreground are two of the columns that separated the nave from the west aisle. The broken column in the rear of the photo is on the east aisle. The columns rest on pedestals, each carved from one stone. Originally, a second story of columns above the aisle ceilings formed an open gallery or balcony overlooking the nave. In the aerial photograph on pages 188-189 one may clearly see the nave with its two flanking side aisles perpendicular to the row of standing columns.*

well be of a home converted into a synagogue in which Jesus preached.

The excavations undertaken by the Franciscans beginning in 1968 went far beyond the synagogue, however. The Franciscans also worked to uncover the town of which the synagogue was a part. It was in this connection that they discovered what was probably St. Peter's house where Jesus stayed when he lived in Capernaum.

Indeed, it was while investigating the context of the synagogue that they became especially interested in the remains of an unusual octagonal-shaped building 84 feet south of the synagogue, opposite the synagogue facade facing Jerusalem. This octagonal building had long been known and, along with the synagogue, it was frequently mentioned in medieval travelers' accounts.

Friar Orfali had done some work on the octagonal building in the 1920s. His plan showed the building as consisting of three concentric octagons. He found only four sides of the largest octagon, which was about 75 feet across; he assumed the other sides had been replaced by later construction. The second octagon was about 57 feet across; and the smallest 26 feet. The smallest octagon had rested

Black basalt walls *remain from houses at Capernaum in which Peter's contemporaries may have lived. The rough black basalt contrasts strikingly with the synagogue's finished white limestone.*

The synagogue was built on a platform—which runs to the end of the photo at right—in order to conform to the rabbinic injunction (Tosephta. Megillah IV 23) to erect the synagogue at the town's highest point.

The construction of the basalt houses is identical to that of the house of St. Peter found beneath the octagonal church. Small stones were pounded between the large ones to strengthen the walls, but no mortar was used. The floors were also made of these rough basalt stones, often obtained from nearby wadis.

on eight square pillars crowned by arches to hold the roof. The building had been paved with mosaics, traces of which remained. Inside the smallest octagon was an octagonal mosaic band of lotus flowers in the form of a chalice; in the center of this mosaic was a beautiful peacock, an early Christian symbol of immortality. Unfortunately, the head and feet of the peacock had been destroyed.

Opinion regarding the octagonal building varied. Local guides invariably pointed it out to gullible tourists as the house of St. Peter, although its identification even as a private residence was not accepted by most scholars. Some suggested the concentric octagons were the public fountains of ancient Capernaum. The best scholarly view, however, was that it was an ancient church. Friar Orfali identified the building as a Byzantine baptistry, citing similar octagonal structures in Europe, such as San Giovanni in Fonte of Ravenna.

When Corbo and Loffreda renewed excavations in 1968, they discovered an apse together with a baptistry on the east side of the middle octagon—which was why the third or outer octagon did not close. The building was oriented by the apse to the east, the orientation of most ancient churches. The discovery of the eastward-oriented apse and the baptistry removed any doubt that the structure was in fact an ancient church. The Franciscans dated it to the middle of the fifth century A.D. In its first phase, the church consisted of but two concentric octagons. The outer partial octagon was added later to form a portico on five of the eight sides—on the north, west, and south. The other three sides were occupied with the apse and two sacristies* on either side of the apse. The precise date of these additions has not been determined.

But why was the church built in the shape of an octagon? The answer is that octagonal churches were built to commemorate special events in Christian history which supposedly occurred at the site. For example, the Church of the Nativity in Bethlehem was built in an octagonal form

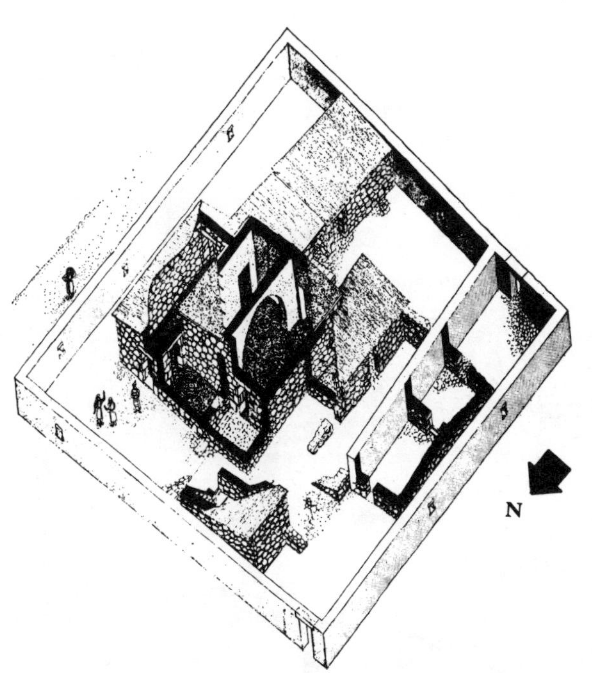

Museum of the Studium Biblicum Franciscanum

House-church from the fourth century. *In this artist's reconstruction, we can see that the main room of St. Peter's first-century house has been renovated. Entrances have been added and an arch built over the center of the room supports a two-story high masonry roof. The original black basalt walls remain but they have been plastered; the room is now the central hall of a church. On the east side of this now venerated room is an atrium, or entryway, 10 feet wide and 27 feet long. Surrounding the house-church compound is a wall about 88 feet square.*

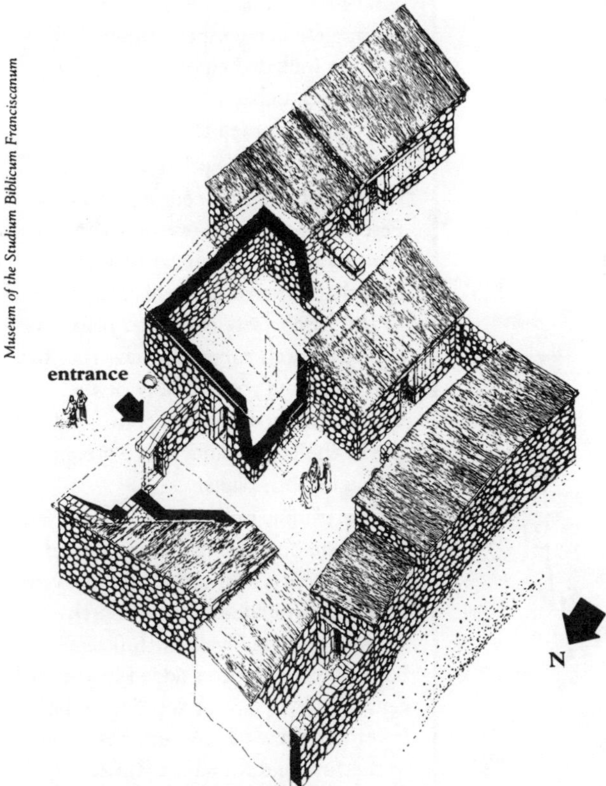

Museum of the Studium Biblicum Franciscanum

An artist's reconstruction *of the first century house that may have belonged to St. Peter. Like most houses of the early Roman period, it was a cluster of rooms structured around two courtyards. The center courtyard served as the family kitchen. Animals may have been kept in the other courtyard. The largest room of the house, delineated in black, later became the central hall of a house-church. At that time, a two-story arch was built inside the room to support an impressively high roof.*

*A sacristy is a room or building connected with a religious house, in which the sacred vessels, vestments, etc., are kept.

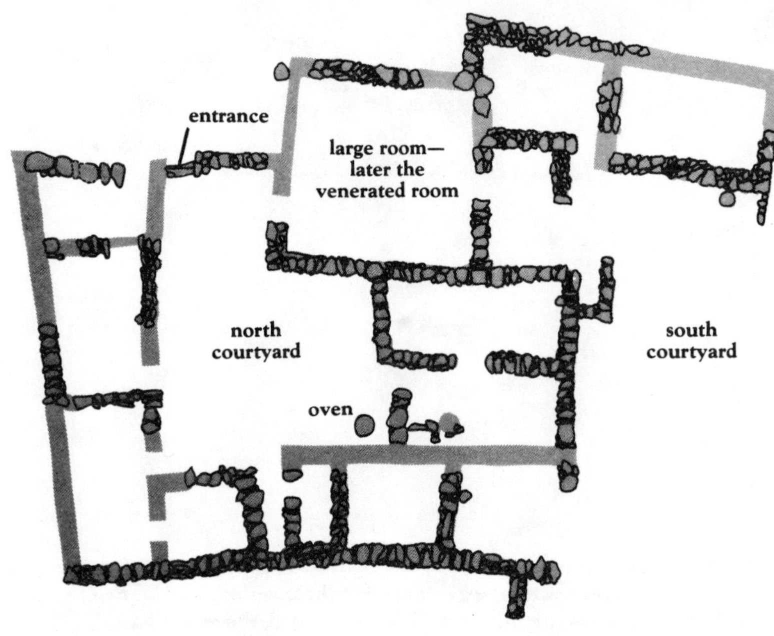

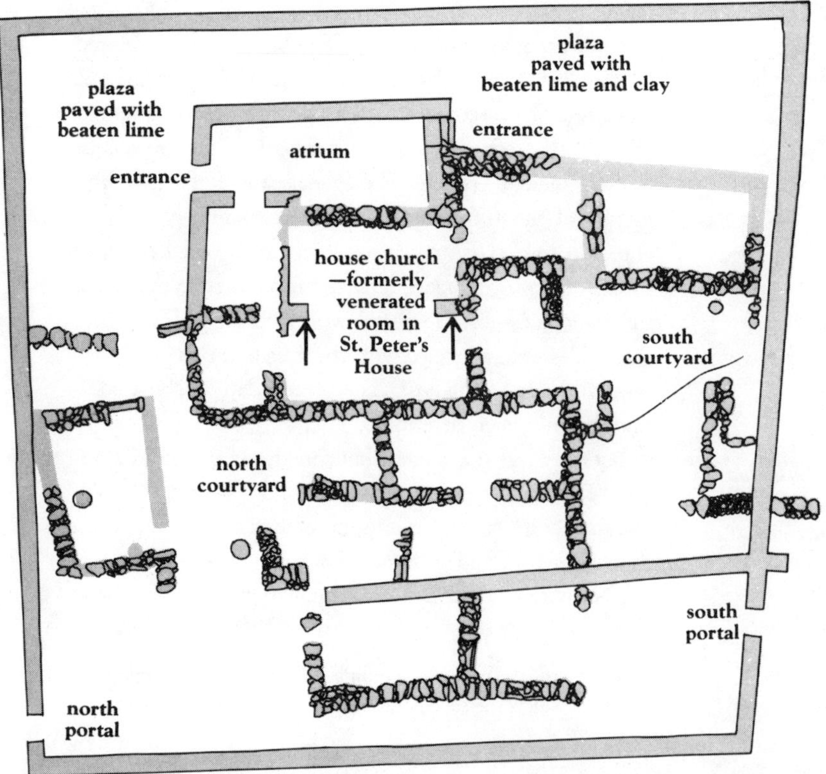

How to Read the Plans

These plans show the archaeological remains of structures from the first to the fifth centuries found at the site of St. Peter's House at Capernaum.

In the first century the simple house of Peter occupied the site. Later in the first century the central room of Peter's house became the venerated room of a house-church. In the fourth century, an arch-supported roof was constructed over the room and a wall was built around the entire complex. In the fifth century, the foundations of the venerated room lay beneath the center of a church composed of two complete concentric octagons and a third incomplete octagon; the innermost octagon included eight square pillars supporting arches which, in turn, supported a domed roof.

In the plan at top left we see the remains of the first-century house of Peter. The plan at lower left shows the remains of the fourth-century house-church. The arrows in this plan point to the basalt piers on which rested a two-story arch supporting the roof over the venerated room. Many of the walls used in the first century continued in use in the fourth and, therefore, are visible in both plans.

The plan at right shows three layers of superimposed remains: gray boulders for first-century structures, black walls for structures added in the fourth century and gray walls within black borders for structures added in the fifth century. The plans at top left and at lower left show all the remains in use in the first and fourth centuries, respectively. The fifth-century church (plan at right), in addition to the black-bordered gray structures, utilized the fourth-century enclosure wall of the complex and the fourth-century long horizontal wall just above the south portal. The plan at right shows certain walls as gray boulders which, although built in the first century, were also used in the fourth century (as can be seen in the plan at lower left).

by the Emperor Constantine in the fourth century A.D., supposedly directly over the cave where Jesus was born. The octagon in the Bethlehem church was intended to mark this spot. Presumably the octagonal church at Capernaum was intended to mark some other site of special importance in Christian history.

It is reasonable to assume, therefore, that this octagonal church at Capernaum was a memorial church. Some scholars believed that the octagonal church was built to memorialize Jesus's temporary residence in Capernaum and may well have been connected with ancient memories or traditions regarding the location of St. Peter's house, also called "the house of Simon and Andrew" in Mark 1:29.

When the Franciscan archaeologists, in their renewed excavations, dug beneath the mosaic floor of the church they found some hard evidence to support this speculation.

Directly beneath the octagonal church they found the remains of another building which was almost certainly a church, judging from the graffiti on the walls left by Christian pilgrims. For example, a graffito scratched on one wall reads, "Lord Jesus Christ help thy servant . . ." A proper name followed in the original but is no longer readable. Another graffito reads, "Christ have mercy." Elsewhere on the walls crosses are depicted. The graffiti are predominantly in Greek, but some are also in Syriac and Hebrew. The presence of Hebrew graffiti suggests that the community may have been composed of Jewish-Christians at this time.

The central hall of this lower church is 27 feet long and 25 feet wide. The roof was supported by a large two-story-high arch over the center of the room. Two masonry piers made of worked basalt blocks, found against the north and

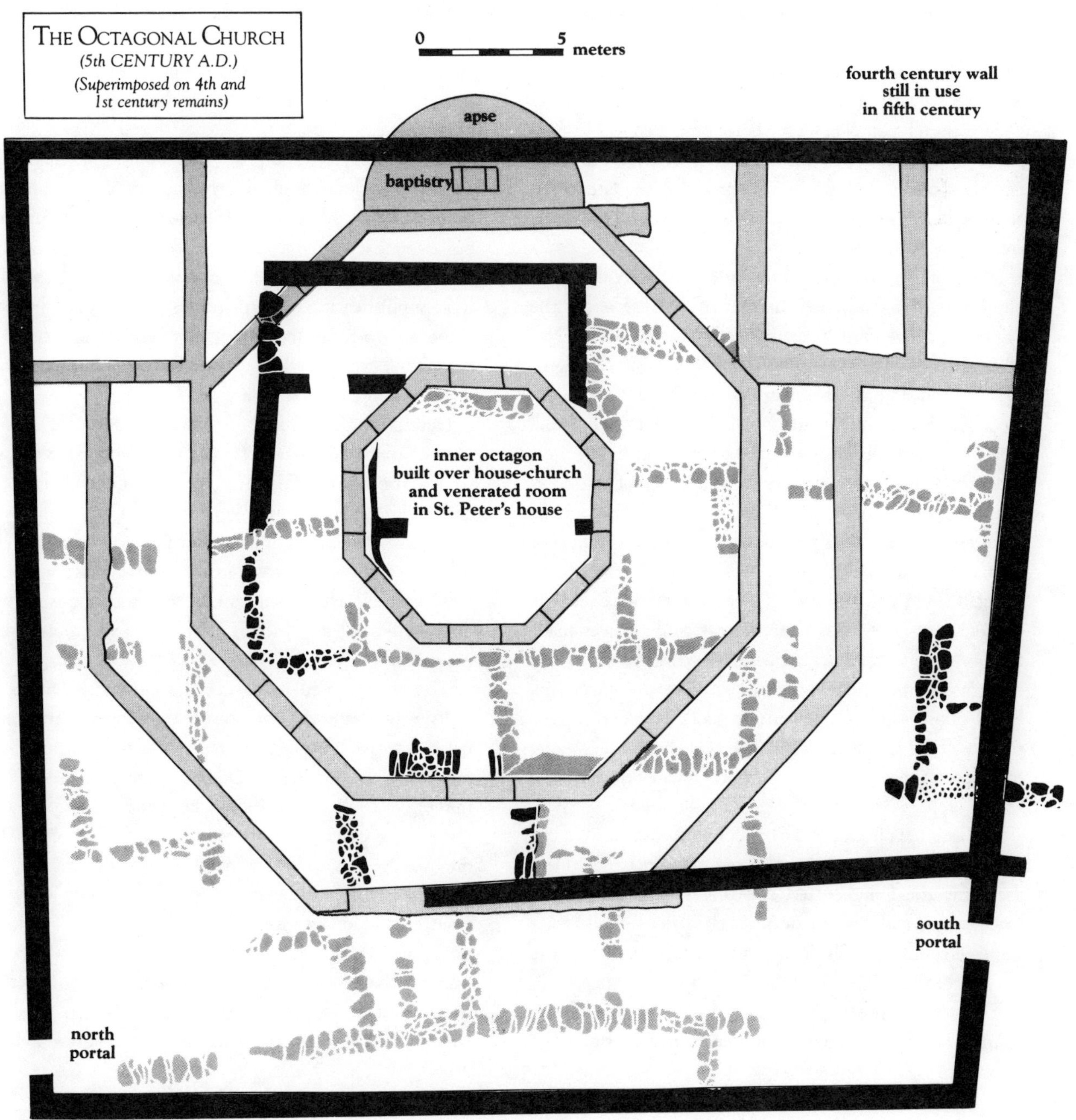

THE PLANS ON THESE PAGES ARE ADAPTED FROM CAFARNAO I: GLI EDIFICI DELLA CITTA (FRANCISCAN PRINTING PRESS: 1975).

south walls of the room, supported the arch. In addition to the bases of the piers, the excavators found two voussoirs, or wedge-shaped stones, from the arch that once supported the roof. The voussoirs were still covered with plaster and paint.

Two doors on the south and one on the north allowed easy access to the central hall. Smaller rooms (9 feet x 12 feet) adjoined the hall on the north. A long narrow room (10 feet x 27 feet) on the east is called the atrium by the excavators. Outside the atrium, which probably served as an entryway into the central hall, is a thoroughfare paved with hard-packed beaten earth and lime, providing a good solid surface for heavy foot traffic.

The central hall was plastered all over and then painted in reds, yellows, greens, blues, browns, white and black, with pomegranates, flowers, figs and geometric designs. Other objects almost surely appeared, but the fragmentary nature of the plaster makes interpretation difficult. The entire church complex was surrounded by a wall about 88 feet long on each of its four sides.

This church complex we have just described was its final phase only, just before the octagonal church was built directly above it. This was how it existed in the late fourth century. However, the origins of this fourth century church are of a far earlier time.

According to the excavators, the central hall of this church was originally built as part of a house about the beginning of the Early Roman period, around 63 B.C. Not all the house has been excavated, but almost 100 feet north to south and almost 75 feet east and west have been uncovered. This house was originally built of large, rounded wadi stones of the rough black basalt that abounds in the area. Only the stones of the thresholds and jambs of the doors had been worked or dressed. Smaller stones were pounded between the larger ones to make the wall more secure, but no mortar was used in the original house. Walls so constructed could not have held a second story, nor could the original roof have been masonry; no doubt it was made from beams and branches of trees covered with a mixture of earth and straw. (This is consistent with the tale of the paralytic let down through a hole in the roof). The archway was probably built inside the central room of the house in order to support a high roof when the house was later converted to a church.

The original pavement of the room also consisted of unworked black basalt stones with large spaces between. Here the excavators found pottery sherds and coins that helped date the original construction. (Such a floor of ill-fitting stones enables us easily to understand the parable of the lost drachma in Luke 15:8.)

The original house was organized around two interior courtyards, as was customary in the Roman period. The outside entrance on the east side opens directly into the north courtyard. This courtyard was probably the main work area for the family that lived here. A round oven, where the family's food was no doubt prepared, was found in the southwest corner of this courtyard.

This courtyard was surrounded by small rooms on the north and west. On the south was the largest room of the house. It was this room that later had the arch built into it so that its roof could be raised after the room became the central hall of the house-church. As originally built, the room had two entrances, one on the south and a second on the north. The room originally measured about 21 feet by 20 feet, a large room by ancient standards.

The southern door of this room led into the house's second courtyard. This courtyard may have been used for animals or for work areas associated with whatever house industry was engaged in by the owners. Curiously enough, several fishhooks were found beneath one of the upper pavements from the later house-church, although this does not prove that the inhabitants of the original house were fishermen.

For all intents and purposes, this house as originally built is indistinguishable from all other houses of ancient Capernaum. Its indoor living area is somewhat larger than usual, but overall it is about the same size as other houses. Its building materials are the usual ones. It was built with no more sophistication than the others in the region. In short, there is nothing to distinguish this house from its neighbors, except perhaps the events that transpired there and what happened to it later.

During the second half of the first century A.D., someone did mark this house off from its neighbors. Perhaps as early as the middle of the first century A.D. the floor, walls, and ceiling of the single large room of the house were plastered. This was unusual in ancient Capernaum. Thus far, this is the only excavated house in the city with plastered walls. In the centuries that followed, the walls were re-plastered at least twice. The floor too was replastered a number of times.

The pottery used in the room also changed when the walls were plastered. The pottery that dates to the period before the walls were plastered is much like the pottery found in other houses designed for domestic use—a large number of cooking pots, bowls, pitchers, juglets, and a few storage jars. Once the room was plastered, however, we find only storage jars and the remains of some oil lamps.

The activities associated with the building obviously changed. No longer was the preparing and serving of food a major activity. Judging from the absence of bowls, people were no longer eating on the premises. The only activity that persisted was the storage of something in the large, two-handled storage jars of the period. Unfortunately, we

Garo Nalbandian, courtesy, Museum of the Studium Biblicum Franciscanum

Reconstruction of a first-century *Capernaum* **house.** ***This bird's-eye view shows a model of a house whose size, number of rooms, and building materials are all typical of houses built in Capernaum about 60 B.C. The simple stone walls of the one-story residence could not support a masonry roof. Instead, a crisscross of tree branches was used, augmented for some rooms with a mixture of earth and straw.***

cannot be sure what was stored. Within the thin layers of lime with which the floor was plastered and re-plastered, the excavators found many pieces of broken lamps.

At this time in early Roman history the only rooms that were plastered in such poor houses were important ones in which groups of people regularly gathered. Plaster provides a reflective surface and aids illumination. Both the plastering and the absence of pottery characteristic of family use combine to suggest that the room, previously part of a private home, was now devoted to some kind of public use. In view of the graffiti that mention Jesus as "Lord" and "Christ" (in Greek), it is reasonable to conclude, though cautiously, that this may be the earliest evidence for Christian gatherings that has ever come to light.

We have already referred to the fact that during the approximately 300 years that the building served as a so-called house-church, over a hundred graffiti were scratched on the plastered walls. These include, by our count, 111 Greek inscriptions, 9 Aramaic, 6 or perhaps as many as 9 Syriac in the Estrangelo alphabet,* 2 Latin, and at least 1 Hebrew inscription. Various forms of crosses, a boat, and perhaps a monogram, composed of the letters from the name Jesus, also appeared.

According to the Franciscan excavators, the name of St. Peter appears at least twice in these inscriptions. Many scholars are highly skeptical of these readings—and with good reason. Unfortunately, the scholarly publication of these very difficult inscriptions does not allow completely independent verification of the excavators' conclusions because of the poor quality of the photographs. But even accepting the Franciscan expedition's drawings of what they see on these plaster fragments, there are still problems.**

Let us look more closely at these inscriptions allegedly referring to St. Peter. One, according to the excavators, is a Latin and Greek inscription that refers to "Peter, the helper of Rome." This of course would be astounding, if this is what it actually said. If we look at the photograph (p. 198 top) of the inscription, it is difficult to see anything more than a "mare's nest" of jumbled lines.

However, the epigrapher of the expedition, Emmanuele Testa, provides us with a drawing (p. 198 center) of the scratchings on the plaster fragment, which appears to be a faithful reproduction of what we called the "mare's nest."

From this, the epigrapher extracted in another line drawing (p.198 bottom) what the excavators see—letters in an inscription.

The excavators see XV scratched over the underlying inscription. We see instead two large XX's apparently scratched over the inscription in an effort to deface it, but this is a small point.

*The Estrangelo alphabet is one of the most common of the Syriac alphabets. It probably first came into use in the first or second century A.D. and was most common in the third and fourth centuries A.D. Although its frequency then declined, it is still in use today.

**See *Cafarnao, Vol. IV (I graffiti della casa di S. Pietro)* by Emmanuele Testa (Jerusalem: Franciscan Printing Press, 1972); and James F. Strange "The Capernaum and Herodium Publications, Part 2," *Bulletin of the American Schools of Oriental Research,* No. 233 (1979), pp. 68-69.

Courtesy Photographic Archive, Archaeological Expedition at Capernaum/Emmanuele Testa

A "St. Peter" graffito? *The name "Peter" may appear in this "mare's nest" of lines (top) scratched on a wall of the Capernaum house-church.*

The drawing (center) is an exact reproduction of the inscription. It was made by Emmanuele Testa, epigrapher for the Franciscan expedition that excavated the building in the late 1960s. To the Franciscan excavators, the lines form the words "Peter, the helper of Rome," but many scholars dispute this reading.

At bottom is another drawing made by Testa, this one an interpretation of the drawing of the "mare's nest" of lines. The excavators read:

RO M AE BO . . .
PETR US

ROMAE *is Latin for Rome;* PETRUS, *Latin for Peter; and* BO(HΘDC) *Greek for helper.*

Some scholars see two large X's scratched over the inscription in an apparent effort to deface it. The strokes the excavators claim form "T" and "U" in the so-called "Peter" are, in fact, part of the two XX's incised over the inscription. Also, the graffito shows horizontal marks above the groups of letters in the first line, indicating that these letter groups are Greek abbreviations. Thus, the meaning of the entire inscription is still a mystery.

The excavators read the underlying inscription:

RO M AE BO . . .
PETR US

The first four letters of the name Peter (PETR), we are told, are in the form of a monogram—a cluster of letters. "Rome" is in Latin, as is "Petrus." BO is taken as a Greek word BO[HΘDC] or some other Greek word from that root, meaning helper.

To the senior author of this article, the strokes which compose two of the letters of the name Peter, T (cocked to the right) and U (appearing as V in the drawing) are rather clearly part of the two XX's incised over the underlying inscription. So we are really left with pure ambiguity.

The word ROMAE is possible, but the MA does not look like anything at all to our eyes. Other readings are possible, especially because horizontal lines appear above the three groups of letters in the first line, which suggests that each of the three groups is a Greek abbreviation.

The excavators see a second reference to St. Peter in another graffito on a plaster fragment, this time in Latin but in Greek letters:

Π	E	T	P
(Pi)	(Epsilon)	(Tau)	(Rho)
V		C	
(Upsilon)		(Lunate Sigma)	

The excavators' photograph and drawing of the fragment are printed together at right.

The first letter (Pi) seems clear on the left. The last letter (C) is broken off at the end of the fragment. According to the excavators, the third, fourth, and fifth letters (Tau, Rho and Upsilon) are combined in a monogram to form a cross, with another cross to the right. To the senior author of this article, however, critical elements in the putative monogram are part of two XX's defacing the underlying inscription, XX's similar to those in the other "Peter" inscription. Moreover, what the excavators see as a sigma appears rather clearly to be an omicron.

Even if these were references to the name Peter, they could well be references to pilgrims named Peter who wrote on these walls, rather than invocations of the name of St. Peter. For these reasons, we are skeptical of this alleged inscriptional support for identifying the original house as St. Peter's.

With what, then, are we left?

Was this originally St. Peter's house where Jesus stayed in Capernaum?

Reviewing the evidence, we can say with certainty that the site is ancient Capernaum. The house in question was located 84 feet south of the synagogue. Although the extant synagogue dates somewhere between the late second century and early fifth century, it is likely that an earlier synagogue stood on this same site.

The house in question was originally built in the late Hellenistic or early Roman period (about 60 B.C.). It was constructed of abundantly available, rough, black basalt boulders. It had a number of small rooms, two courtyards and one large room. When it was built, it was indistinguishable from all the other houses in the ancient seaside town.

Sometime about the middle of the first century A.D. the function of the building changed. It was no longer used as a house. Domestic pottery disappeared. The center room, including the floor, was plastered and replastered. The walls were covered with pictures. Only this center room was treated in this way. Christian inscriptions, including the name of Jesus and crosses, were scratched on the walls; some may possibly refer to Peter. Remnants of oil lamps and storage jars have been recovered. Fishing hooks have been found in between layers on the floor.

In a later century, two pilasters were erected on the north and south walls of this room; the lower parts of the pilasters have been found in the excavations. These pilasters supported a stone arch which in turn supported a new roof, no longer a light roof of branches, mud and straw, but a high masonry roof. On the eastern side of what had now become a house-church, an atrium was constructed in the fourth century about 27 feet long and10 feet wide.Finally, a wall was built around the sacred compound.

This house-church survived into the mid-fifth century. Then precisely over the now plastered central room, an octagonal church was built, covering the same area and with the same dimensions. This was the kind of structure used to commemorate a special place in Christian history.

In addition, we know that as early as the fourth century, Christian pilgrims on visits to the site saw what they believed to be St. Peter's house. Sometime between 381 A.D. and 395 A.D. a Spanish nun named Egeria (Etheria) visited the site and reported in her diary that she had seen the house of St. Peter which had been turned into a church: "In Capernaum a house-church (*domus ecclesia*) was made out of the home of the prince of the apostles, whose walls still stand today as they were." A similar report appears in the diary of the anonymous sixth-century A.D. Italian traveler known as the Pilgrim of Piacenza. However, by this time the octagonal church had been constructed, so he refers to a church that had been built on the site: "We came to Capernaum to the house of St. Peter, which is now a basilica." Thus, even from this very early period, the site was associated with St. Peter's house.

Is this then the house of St. Peter? It cannot be confirmed—certainly not by inscriptions referring to St. Peter. But a considerable body of circumstantial evidence does point to its identification as St. Peter's house. Though we moderns search for proof, that hardly mattered to those ancient pilgrims who scratched their prayers on the walls of the house-church in the belief that this was, indeed, St. Peter's house. So, for that matter, what "proof" does a modern pilgrim need?

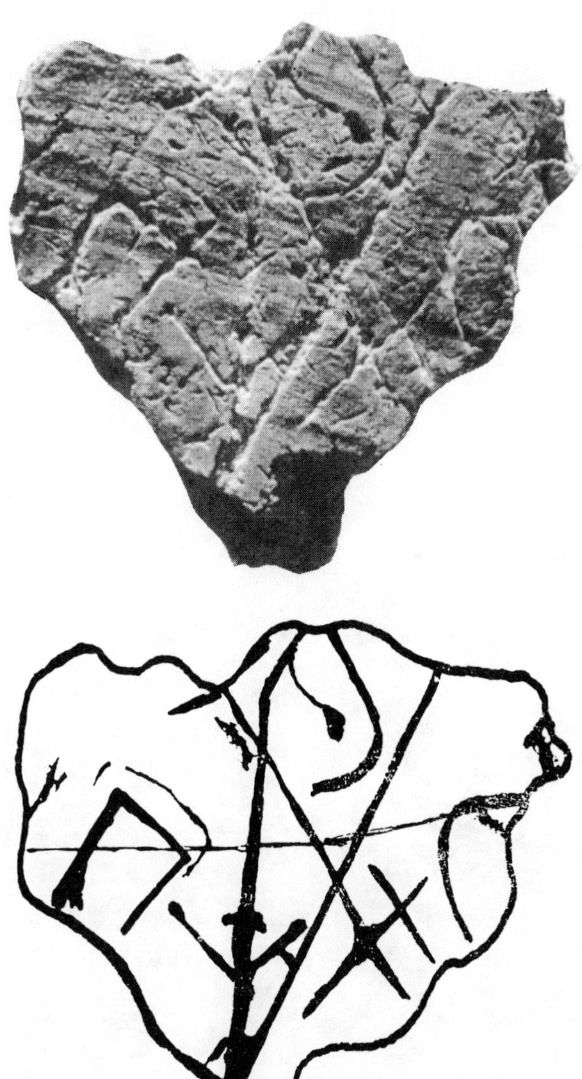

Courtesy Photographic Archive, Archaeological Expedition at Capernaum/Emmanuele Testa

Greek Letters for "Peter." *This inscription is one of a hundred scratched on the walls of the Capernaum building that served as a church from about the mid-first century through the fourth century A.D.*

A drawing (below) shows the various marks on the plaster. The first letter on the left is clearly pi. *The excavators also see the following letters:* epsilon *(E),* tau *(T),* rho *(R),* upsilon *(V) and* lunate sigma *(C). However, another interpretation is that the key strokes of these letters are really part of two XX's incised over the inscription, similar to the XX's in the other "Peter" graffito.*

Even if one accepts the reading of "Peter," perhaps the inscription refers not to St. Peter, but to a pilgrim named Peter who visited the site sometime during these 300 years.

Synagogue Where Jesus Preached Found at Capernaum

By James F. Strange and Hershel Shanks

THE FIRST-CENTURY CAPERNAUM SYNAGOGUE in which Jesus preached has probably been found. Because more than one synagogue may have existed in Capernaum at this time, we cannot be sure that this new find was Jesus' synagogue. But this recently discovered first-century building is certainly a likely candidate.*

At the moment, the synagogue is not a very impressive-looking structure, but it is there nevertheless. And for millions of Christians, that is the important thing. For Jews, too, this find adds important new evidence of how their people worshipped 2,000 years ago. Only a handful of such synagogues are known.**

At present, this ancient Capernaum synagogue has been only partly excavated. It may never be fully excavated and exposed because that would require dismantling the beautiful white limestone synagogue built several centuries later on top of the earlier synagogue.

Franciscan archaeologists initially exposed part of the first-century A.D. synagogue in the mid-1960s, but at that time the evidence was not clear enough for them to make the claim of its first-century date. More excavation was needed—this was undertaken in 1981. Now we have the evidence that was lacking.

The synagogue at Capernaum has been known since

*The Gospels always speak of "the" Capernaum synagogue. Perhaps this was because there was one synagogue in Capernaum or the Gospel writers knew of only one synagogue. But it is also possible they said "the" because all their attention was focused on this synagogue.

**Other first-century synagogues are known from Masada, Herodium, Gamla (probably), Magdala and perhaps Chorazim. In addition, an inscription from such a synagogue has been found in Jerusalem (see Hershel Shanks, *Judaism in Stone*, The Biblical Archaeology Society and Harper and Row: New York and Washington, 1979, pp. 17-19).

Garo Nalbandian

Rough black basalt residences *of first-century A.D. Capernaum stand in stark contrast to the smooth white limestone of the fourth-century synagogue in the background. Under this synagogue, excavators have found another synagogue made of the same black basalt as the residences in the foreground. The lower synagogue was built on nearly the same plan as the upper limestone synagogue visible here. The walls of the lower synagogue were nearly four feet thick—much thicker than those of these residences—and the walls were made of worked stones, rather than the unworked stones builders used in the residences. The upper synagogue has three entrances on the south, Jerusalem-facing facade. Through these entrances can be seen three rows of columns forming aisles on either side of the prayer hall and the back wall.* *A closer view of this interior may be seen on p. 202.*

1838 when the American orientalist Edward Robinson first explored and identified a number of beautiful architectural fragments in the ruins of Tell Hum, as the site was known locally, as the remains of an ancient synagogue.

Over the years, sporadic excavations exposed parts of the synagogue, but this prompted large-scale looting of the stones by local Arab building contractors. In 1894, the Franciscan Order purchased the site to prevent further depredations and even reburied part of the structure to protect it.

Naturally, much of the interest in Capernaum has stemmed from its importance in Christian history and its frequent mention in the Gospels. Shortly after John the Baptist baptized Jesus in the Jordan River, Jesus settled in Capernaum and made it the center of his ministry until he left for Jerusalem. The Gospel of Matthew (4:13) refers to Capernaum as Jesus' residence.

The Gospels also tell us that Jesus preached and ministered in Capernaum and performed at least one miracle in the synagogue there (see Mark 1:21-25). Understandably, special archaeological attention has been focused on the building that was already identified as a synagogue.

From 1921 to 1926, the Franciscans, under the direction of Fr. Gaudentius Orfali, excavated the synagogue. Orfali dated the synagogue to the early first century A.D. It was, he said, the synagogue in which Jesus had preached. This dating, however, has been universally rejected as far too early.

Although Orfali's dating was wrong, the synagogue he exposed and reconstructed was a jewel. Nestled on the shore of the Sea of Galilee and built of shimmering white limestone on a platform above a town built of rough black basalt boulders, the Capernaum synagogue is the most impressive synagogue unearthed in all of ancient Galilee. Flights of steps on either side of the platform give access to an imposing entrance facade with three doors facing Jerusalem.

Inside the synagogue, along the two long walls, are stone benches, probably to seat the elders who governed the synagogue. The other worshipers sat on mats on the floor, eastern fashion.

Two rows of columns in the main prayer room separate a central nave from two side aisles. In the rear of the main room, a third row of columns creates a third aisle parallel

The interior of the Capernaum synagogue, *a large, glistening white limestone structure. Although the synagogue was built in the late Roman style popular in the second and third centuries A.D., Italian archaeologists who excavated the site in 1981 say that the synagogue dates to the Byzantine period—the late fourth or early fifth century A.D.*

In this photo, taken before 1981, we see the rear or north end of the synagogue—the solid structure at left, 27 feet across. Two rows of columns, perpendicular to the north wall, divide the interior into a central nave and two side aisles—one on the west (foreground) and the other on the east (background). On the left, the row of columns creates a third aisle at the back of the synagogue. In 1981, excavators dug an east-west trench across the nave (see p. 207), revealing a black basalt floor. Both ends of this floor ran up to basalt walls that were directly under the stylobates for the limestone columns that create the two side aisles. (Stylobates are low walls supporting columns.) Pottery found in and under this basalt floor clearly dates the basalt structure to the first century A.D. or earlier. Since the site of a synagogue rarely changed in antiquity, this basalt building, which closely follows the plan of the later limestone synagogue, must also be a synagogue, and very likely the one in which Jesus preached.

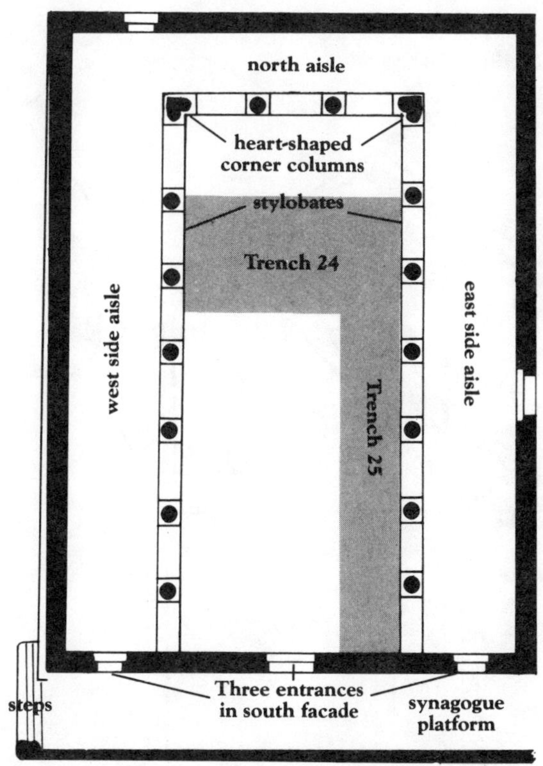

Adapted from Studia Hierosolymitana III *(Virgilio Corbo)*

PRAYER ROOM
OF FOURTH- OR FIFTH-CENTURY
LIMESTONE SYNAGOGUE
AT CAPERNAUM

to the back wall. A side room next to the main room served as a school, a court, a hostel for visitors, a dining hall, a meeting place. In antiquity, the synagogue usually included such an auxiliary "community center" room.

In 1968, the Franciscans renewed their excavations in the synagogue under the direction of two Franciscan fathers, Virgilio Corbo and Stanislao Loffreda.

These excavations touched off one of the most spirited debates in archaeological history—concerning the date of this beautiful ancient synagogue. On one point, all were agreed, however. This synagogue could not be the first-century synagogue in which Jesus preached. Israeli scholars contended that the building dated to the late second or third century A.D. The Italian excavators, however, contended that the building dated to the late fourth or early fifth century A.D.

The debate is fascinating because it involves archaeological, historical and architectural evidence—and each side seems to have a convincing case!

The Italians rely primarily on a hoard of more than 10,000 bronze coins they found under the pavement of the present synagogue building. As we have already noted, the present synagogue building was constructed on a platform created by the use of fill in order to give the structure a more monumental appearance. According to the Italians, a thick layer of mortar was laid on top of this fill, and the synagogue pavement was laid on top of the mortar. The Italian excavators found their coins in the fill and in the mortar which, they claim, sealed the fill below it. Some of the coins were actually embedded in the mortar. These coins have been dated to the fourth and fifth centuries and, according to the Italians, require them to date the synagogue building to the same period.

The Israelis, on the other hand, emphasize the artistic and stylistic parallels to the Capernaum building that clearly point to the end of the second or third century for its construction. That is when 20 or so stylistically similar synagogues were built in the Galilee and on the nearby Golan Heights. Moreover, this late Roman style is entirely different from the Byzantine synagogues with mosaic floors built in the late fourth and fifth centuries, sometimes within miles of the Capernaum synagogue. One such synagogue from the Byzantine period is at Hammath-Tiberias, only ten miles from Capernaum. As one Israeli scholar remarked, were these buildings in fact contemporaneous, "We would probably find this to be the only case of such astounding architectural diversity within so small an area."

Even more important to the Israelis' argument is the fact that barely 30 feet from the Capernaum synagogue, the Italian excavators found a relatively modest fourth-century church built over St. Peter's House (see "Has the

PLAN AND RECONSTRUCTION OF FIRST-CENTURY A.D. SYNAGOGUE AT CAPERNAUM

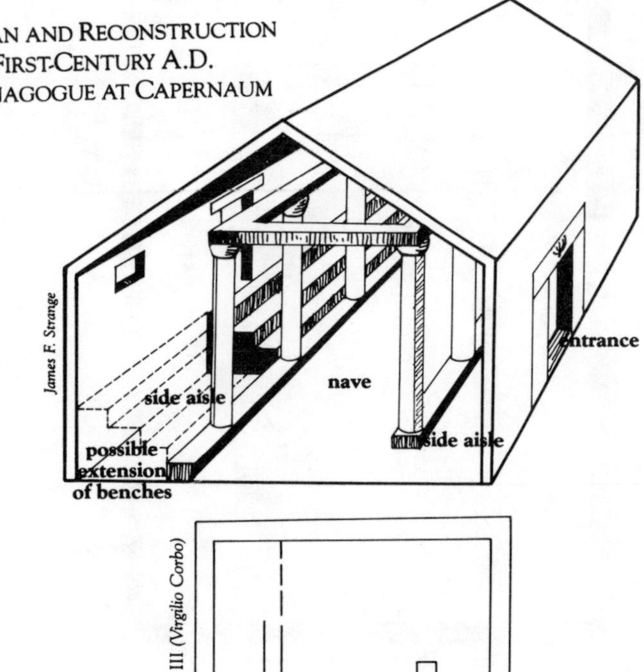

James F. Strange

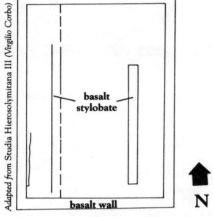

Adapted from Studia Hierosolymitana III (Virgilio Corbo)

House Where Jesus Stayed in Capernaum Been Found?" **BAR**, Nov./Dec. 1982 [188]). It is surely unlikely, argue the Israelis, that so magnificent and richly decorated a synagogue as Capernaum's would be allowed to be built so close to a church whose religion was now the state religion. As one Israeli scholar has commented, "Such a state of affairs might be conceivable in our ecumenical age, but it seems impossible to imagine that it would have been allowed by the Byzantine authorities of the fourth century." No doubt there were synagogues built in the fourth century (probably by bribing local officials, because Byzantine law at the time forbade the erection of new synagogues), but all their splendor was reserved for the interior, not flaunted on the exterior, as was the case at Capernaum. To build a fourth-century synagogue so beautifully adorned on the outside—including the use of explicit Jewish symbols like the menorah, shofar, incense shovel, date palms (which symbolize Judea), lulav (the palm branch used during the Jewish festival of Tabernacles), and a representation of the paneled doors of the ark—would only emphasize the violation of the emperor's law forbidding the construction of synagogues.

For all these reasons, most Israeli scholars adhere to the second- to third-century dating for the Galilean basilica-plan synagogues, including Capernaum.

But what of the coins "hermetically sealed," as the Italian excavators put it, under the synagogue pavement? How did these coins dating from the fourth and fifth centuries get under the floor of a second- or third-century building? Perhaps, say the Israelis, the pavement was relaid in the fourth century, at which time a fill could have been spread inside the building and a layer of mortar placed over it.

The outcome of this debate is still uncertain. If the Italians prove correct, it may require scholars to rewrite the history of the Jews in Palestine during the fourth and fifth centuries A.D. As we know the period today, it was one of persecution and decay, a time when Jews emigrated from the Holy Land instead of coming to it. A fourth- or fifth-century dating of the Capernaum synagogue would indicate that this was a period of prosperity and vigor, a time when Jewish life flourished.

In the midst of this debate a minor point in the Franciscan excavations went almost unnoticed—almost, but not quite.

In the course of their excavation, the Franciscans uncovered what seemed to be part of a wall under the limestone wall of the synagogue. This lower wall was built of worked black basalt blocks, without mortar. This same black basalt was used to construct the residential buildings that surrounded the synagogue, including the building the excavators identified as the first-century house of St. Peter.

In his preliminary report on the synagogue excavation, published in 1975, Corbo described this lower wall as a "foundation" of the south wall of the white limestone synagogue. In Italian, this lower basalt wall is called *muro di basalto,* Wall of Basalt. Corbo therefore labeled it "MB" in his notes—so this is what we shall sometimes call it and the similar walls related to it.

The excavators turned up this wall, or walls very much like it, in no fewer than six of their trenches. It stood to a height of about three feet. They found it beneath all four corners of the limestone synagogue in addition to the section they found beneath the south wall.

Then Corbo exposed this basalt wall for a length of 24 meters (78 feet) along the west wall of the synagogue—the entire length of the west wall of the synagogue.

There was something puzzling, however, about this black basalt wall that served as the foundation wall of the white limestone synagogue. At the southwest corner of the synagogue where the basalt wall appeared most clearly, it was out of alignment with the wall of the synagogue that rested on top of it. The MB or basalt wall extended almost a foot *west* of the southwest corner of the limestone synagogue wall. Why was this supposed foundation wall so clearly out of orientation with the wall it supposedly supported?

Corbo, ever the cautious scholar, refused to speculate. But in fact both Corbo and Loffreda suspected at a quite early stage that the MB or basalt wall may have been the wall of an earlier *building*, which was *later* used as a foundation wall for the limestone synagogue. The earlier building may itself have been a synagogue, perhaps from the first century A.D. More evidence was needed, however.

Even without additional evidence, a prominent Israeli scholar, Michael Avi-Yonah of Hebrew University in Jerusalem, suggested as early as 1967 that the MB (*muro di basalto*) might be the wall of an earlier synagogue.

Additional evidence was uncovered in excavations conducted by Corbo and Loffreda in 1981. The results have now been published in Italian.*

In the nave of the limestone synagogue, in the large central area between the two long rows of columns, two long excavation trenches were sunk in 1981 for the purpose of tracing the basalt wall beneath the limestone synagogue. Corbo's first trench (trench 24) ran east-west across the nave (see pp. 203 and 207). Originally, this area had been paved with limestone pavers used in the limestone synagogue. Beneath the pavers was a layer of mortar that still bore the imprint of the limestone pavers. Then the excavators slowly chipped away at *a foot* of mortar.

Below the mortar was a thin layer of limestone chips. These were the cuttings or debris left by the workers who cut the blocks for the limestone synagogue's walls.

Beneath this thin layer was a fill more than three feet deep consisting of hammer-dressed basalt boulders mixed with dirt. This was the fill set in place by the builders of the limestone synagogue to create the platform on which the limestone synagogue was erected.

Nearly four feet below the surface, under the fill, the excavators hit a patch of rude cobbled pavement of black basalt. This patch was only ten feet long. On the patch of cobbled pavement were potsherds from the first to the fourth centuries A.D. The first-century pottery fixes the earliest date when the patch of cobbled pavement under the potsherds could have been laid.

At a point more than four feet below the nave of the limestone synagogue, the excavators found a pavement of basalt cobbles that extended throughout the entire length of the trench. Obviously, here was the floor of an earlier building. The pottery found in and under this cobbled floor dates to the first century A.D. or earlier. Loffreda published this pottery in extensive groups, and it clearly establishes a first-century A.D. date for the cobbled basalt floor.

At the end of the trench, the cobbled pavement ran up to black basalt walls that, Corbo immediately recognized, were identical to the black basalt walls he had found earlier.

The new basalt walls also appeared beneath the limestone synagogue's stylobates. A stylobate is a special support wall for a row of columns necessitated by the additional load the columns bear. In the limestone synagogue there are rows of columns on three sides of the nave,

*Stanislao Loffreda, "Ceramica Ellenistico-Romana nel Sottosuolo della Sinagoga di Cafarnao," and Virgilio C. Corbo, "Resti della Sinagoga del Primo Secolo a Cafarnao," in *Studia Hierosolymitana* III (1982), pp. 273-357.

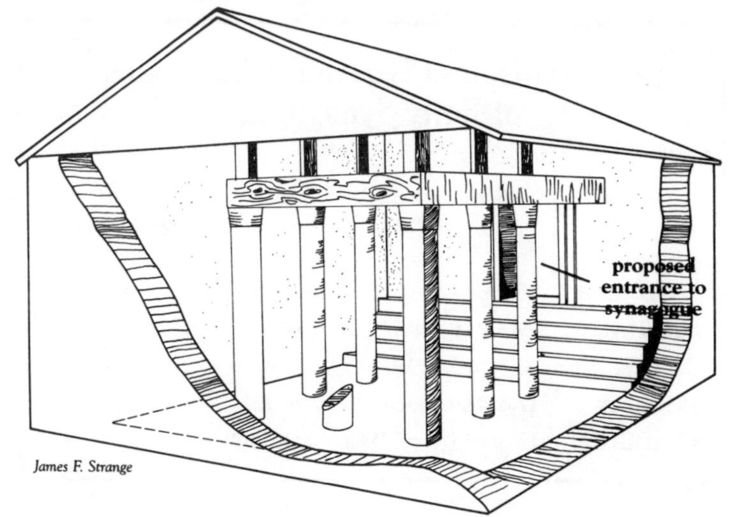

James F. Strange

PLAN AND RECONSTRUCTION OF MAGDALA SYNAGOGUE

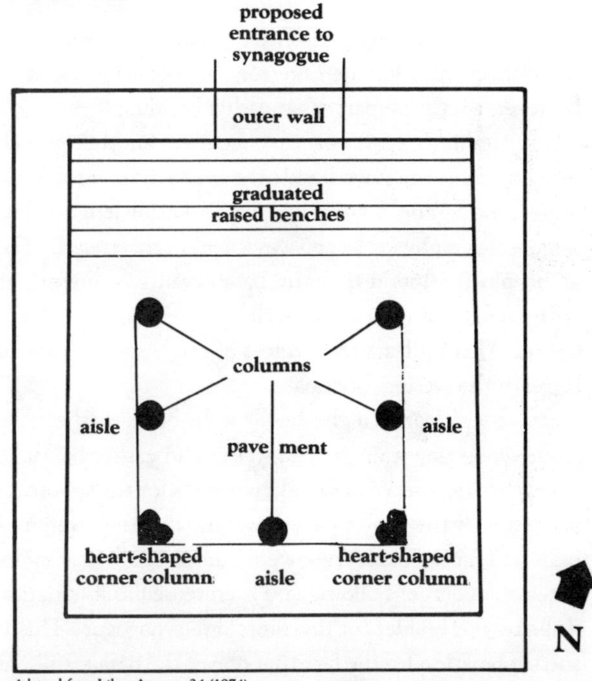

Adapted from Liber Annuus 24 (1974)

Comparison of External Dimensions of Early Synagogues

Synagogue	Width m/*ft.*	Length m/*ft.*	Area sq. m/*sq. ft.*	% of Capernaum area
CAPERNAUM 1st/Century	18.5/*60.7*	24.2/*79.4*	448/*4838*	100
MAGDALA	7.3/*23.9*	8.1/*26.5*	59/*637*	13
GAMLA	15.4/*50.5*	19.4/*63.6*	299/*3229*	67
MASADA	12.8/*42.0*	16.3/*53.5*	209/*2257*	47
HERODIUM	12.3/*40.3*	16.7/*54.8*	205/*2214*	46

creating two side aisles and a back aisle. Each row of columns has its own stylobate. The newly discovered basalt walls that the cobbled floor abutted were under the stylobates for the columns that created the side aisles in the limestone synagogue. These basalt walls served as foundation walls for the limestone stylobates. Originally, however, they were part of an earlier building.

The Italian excavators then opened another trench (trench 25) in the nave beside the eastern, limestone stylobate, extending for the stylobate's entire length. The same stratigraphy (or layers) was found in this trench. The archaeologists found that the basalt wall ran almost the entire length of the eastern stylobate, serving as its foundation. This wall matched traces of the basalt wall found beneath the western stylobate.

It is now clear that the basalt walls beneath the limestone synagogue walls are the walls of an earlier building. True, they now serve as foundation walls for the stylobates and walls of the limestone synagogue. But they were not built as foundations. They were built as walls and stylobates of an earlier building and then reused as foundation walls by the builders of the limestone synagogue. This is the explanation for the fact that one of the basalt walls, as we pointed out earlier, is not in proper alignment with the limestone wall above it.

The consistent structure of the basalt walls (hammer-dressed boulders of uniform size, without mortar) in all the various places they have been found confirms that they all belonged to an earlier building.

There is another reason for this conclusion. As noted, beside the prayer room of the limestone synagogue is a colonnaded room that was probably used as a kind of community center. The entrance to this room is through the east wall of the synagogue's main prayer room. Beneath this side room the excavators did *not* find any of the basalt walls they found under the prayer room. If the basalt walls had been built as foundation walls for the limestone synagogue, we would expect to find them under this side room of the limestone synagogue as well. The absence of basalt walls suggests that the walls under the prayer room, which were later used as foundation walls for the limestone synagogue, belonged originally to a structure that did not extend under the room beside the prayer room.

Another reason to conclude that the basalt walls were the walls of an earlier building stems from the treatment of odd gaps in the basalt walls. For example, there is a nearly five-foot gap in the basalt wall beneath the southern end of the eastern stylobate. The builders of the limestone synagogue needed a foundation here as well as under the rest of the stylobate, so they erected a column of mortar and stone on top of the remains of a floor at the bottom of the gap. In this way they provided support for the southern end of the eastern stylobate.

We can also conclude that this earlier building was not a private house but was, rather, a public building. This is clear from the fact that the basalt walls are nearly four feet thick. Only public buildings have such thick walls. Indeed, the walls of the limestone synagogue are only about 2.5 feet thick.

Moreover, with the additional material from the latest excavations, the plan of the earlier building has emerged with considerable clarity. It appears to follow quite closely the plan of the prayer hall of the limestone synagogue. The walls of the earlier building appear everywhere under the walls of the later building. Basalt walls were also found under the stylobates of the later building. In trench 25, which parallels the eastern stylobate, the excavators were able to follow the basalt wall under the eastern stylobate for a very considerable length. They found that this basalt wall did not extend all the way to the north or south wall of the limestone synagogue. In other words, the basalt wall under the stylobate stopped about where the stylobate of the limestone synagogue stops. This indicates that the basalt wall was, so to speak, freestanding in the earlier building, and may have been used to support an earlier stylobate, rather than enclosing a side room.

As shown in the drawing, based on parallels from other first-century synagogues, the excavators even assume that benches lined the side aisles of the basalt building.

No entrance to the earlier building has been located. However, there is a clear break in the basalt wall on the west side of the building between and beneath the second and third pilasters of the limestone synagogue wall; a door may once have been located here. Such an entrance is also suggested by the plan of a recently excavated synagogue at Magdala which is a parallel to the building we are examining, although much smaller. (The excavators call it a mini-synagogue.[1]) The Magdala plan also tends to confirm the accuracy of our reconstruction of the plan of the earlier building at Capernaum.

The date of this earlier building with basalt walls and a cobbled floor also seems clear. The pottery under the cobbled pavement dates from the third century B.C. to the latter half of the second century B.C. One of the coins found under the cobbled pavement was a coin of Ptolemy VIII Eugertes, who reigned from 146 B.C. to 117 B.C., although the coin may well have continued in circulation for some period after his death. On and in the cobbled pavement, the excavators found pottery sherds dating from the first century A.D. to the fourth century A.D.[2] The floor was doubtless founded in the first century at the latest, and the basalt walls are clearly associated with this floor.

But is the earlier building a synagogue? The answer is yes, for several reasons.

Synagogues, and holy places in general, commonly remain in the same location. A new synagogue is customarily built over the remains of an old one. We know this from numerous excavations. Synagogue locations simply did not move around within an ancient town.

A famous pilgrim named Egeria traveled through Palestine from 381 to 384 A.D. and visited Capernaum at that time (see *Egeria's Travels to the Holy Land*, **BAR**, March/April 1983). Peter the Deacon, writing in 1137 A.D., quotes from a copy of Egeria's *Travels* no longer extant, except as quoted by Peter: "In Capernaum the house of the prince of the apostles [Peter] has been made into a church, with its original walls still standing. It is where the Lord healed the paralytic. There is also the synagogue where the Lord cured a man possessed by the devil [Mark 1:23]. The way in is up many stairs, and it is made of dressed stone" (V1.2). The Franciscan excavator Corbo believes Egeria was referring to the later, white limestone synagogue. Nevertheless, she attests to an ancient tradition even then that this was the site of the synagogue in which Jesus cured the demoniac.

The similarity of the plan of the earlier building to other ancient synagogues of the period also suggests that this earlier building was a synagogue. The plan of the earlier building is similar to the plan of synagogues found at Masada, Herodium, Gamla and Magdala, although, as the accompanying table shows, the earlier building at Capernaum was the largest of them—an indication of its importance.

Architectural fragments that were probably used in the earlier building at Capernaum were found in the fill of the platform created for the limestone synagogue. These fragments are surely consistent with the identification of the building as a synagogue, even if they do not prove it. In the fill below the mortar of the later synagogue, the excavators found impressive column drums—one in beautiful gray granite—and fragments of two kinds of elegant cornice molding. All these fragments probably came from the earlier building and were reused as part of the fill creating the platform for the later building.

Trench 24: ***(1) eastern stylobate (4th-5th century synagogue); (2) pavement (4th-5th century synagogue); (3) basalt wall (MB) (1st century synagogue); (4) basalt pavement (1st century synagogue).***

The conclusion that this was a first-century A.D. synagogue seems inescapable.

Corbo has concluded that this earlier building was the first-century synagogue in which Jesus preached. Luke 7:1-5 recalls certain Jewish elders from Capernaum who tell Jesus of a Roman centurion who " . . . loves our nation, and built us our synagogue." In his recent Italian publication, Father Corbo concludes: "This edifice, after thirteen years of patient labor of excavation and of recording, has been found appropriately under the area of the synagogue of the fourth/fifth centuries. We think therefore with all legitimacy that the edifice of basalt walls excavated under the synagogue is properly the synagogue constructed in the first decades of the first century by that Roman centurion of whom Jesus said, 'Truly I say to you, neither in Israel have I found such faith' (Luke 7:9)."

[1]Virgilio Corbo, "La Citta romana di Magdala," *Studia Hierosolymitana* I, pp. 365-368.

[2]Vigorous discussion in archaeological journals occurred when the Franciscan fathers Corbo and Loffreda first published their proposal for a fourth-century date for the white limestone synagogue at Capernaum (see Virgilio Corbo, Stanislao Loffreda, Augusto Spijkerman, *La Sinagoga di Cafarnao dopo gli scavi del 1969*, Franciscan Printing Press: Jerusalem, 1970. The announcement that fourth-century sherds were found on a first-century floor under four feet of fill and mortar is sure to generate even more debate.

The Galile

Boat

2,000-Year-Old Hull Recovered Intact

COURTESY OF ISRAEL DEPT. OF ANTIQUITIES AND MUSEUMS/PHOTO: DANNY FRIEDMAN

SHELLEY WACHSMANN

A severe drought gripped Israel in 1985 and 1986. The winter rains barely came. Water was pumped from the Sea of Galilee to irrigate parched fields throughout the country. Predictably, the Kinneret (the Hebrew name of the freshwater inland lake also known as the Sea of Galilee) shrank. Wide expanses of lakebed, normally covered with water, were exposed.

Moshe and Yuval Lufan live with their families on Kibbutz Ginnosar on the northwest shore of the lake. Avid amateur archaeologists, Moshe and Yuval frequently explored the newly exposed lakebed for ancient remains.

In January 1986 they were examining an area south of the kibbutz, where a tractor stuck in the mud had churned up some ancient bronze coins. Nearby they found a few ancient iron nails, and shortly afterwards they saw the oval outline of a boat, entirely buried in the mud.

Of course it could have been a 19th- or 20th-century boat as easily as an ancient one. The brothers asked their father, a fisherman of 20 years, whether he had ever heard of a modern boat sinking anywhere near this site. "No" was his reply. Besides, he pointed out, the boat was buried so deeply in the mud that it must have been there for a very long time.

"Ask Mendel," was the father's advice.

Mendel Nun is unique. A member of Kibbutz Ein

The Galilee boat, *resurrected after being buried in lake mud for some 2,000 years, makes its 550-yard voyage to the Yigal Allon Museum at Kibbutz Ginnosar. Subsequently, a crane lifted the boat ashore. The conservator, Orna Cohen, had decided that the sea provided the best means for transporting the 26-foot-long boat from the excavation site to the museum. The boat was wrapped in buoyant polyurethane for protection.*

Based upon the boat's construction techniques, associated artifacts and radiocarbon dates, the boat has been dated to between the first century B.C. and the late first century A.D. It is probably the type of boat that was used by Jesus and his disciples in their many travels upon the Sea of Galilee and by the Jews in the nautical battle of Migdal.

Gev, on the east side of the lake, Mendel has made the Kinneret—in all its aspects from archaeology to zoology—his specialty. He is widely known as Israel's number one "Kinneretologist."

Mendel visited the site, but could offer no opinion as to whether the buried boat was ancient or modern. However, he notified Yossi Stefanski, the local inspector for the Department of Antiquities, of the discovery, and Stefanski in turn notified me as the Department's Inspector of Underwater Antiquities.

On Tuesday, February 4, 1986, I returned from a coastal survey on the Mediterranean to find a note on my desk—something about a boat, possibly ancient, in the Kinneret. The next day I drove to Ein Gev with my colleague Kurt Raveh to pick up Mendel; from there we went to meet the Lufan brothers at Ginnosar.

Over coffee and cake, Yuval and Moshe told us about their discovery. Everyone wanted to know whether the boat was ancient.

I explained that ancient boats found in the Mediterranean were built in an unusual way. The planks of the hull were edge-joined with "mortise-and-tenon" joints that were held in place with wooden pegs. This form of construction has been found as early as the 14th-13th centuries B.C. (it was used in the famous Ulu Burun [Kas] wreck, now being excavated off the coast of Turkey) and continued to be used through the Roman period. All we had to do was scrape away the mud from the top of the uppermost strake (as the continuous lines of planks extending from bow to stern are called) to see whether we could find the dark rectangular remains of the "mortise-and-tenon" joints with round dot-like heads of wooden pegs. This would be the telltale sign that the boat was ancient—assuming, of course, that Kinneret boats developed in a parallel fashion to Mediterranean craft.

Where's the boat? *Buried in the mud beneath Yuval Lufan's feet, the Galilee boat revealed its presence by a faint oval outline. Lufan and his brother Moshe, both residents of Kibbutz Ginnosar, discovered the boat while combing the Sea of Galilee's newly exposed lakebed for remains of ancient craft. Consecutive winters of below average rainfall had caused a dramatic drop in the sea's water level. The mudbed in which the boat was discovered is normally well under water, beyond the reach of amateur archaeologists. Even as the excavation proceeded, the lake returned and threatened to engulf the site. Only the rapid construction of a temporary dike enabled the archaeologists to finish their work.*

The five of us bundled into our jeep and drove to the site. Kurt and I quickly excavated a small section at midship. As we carefully removed the mud, "mortise-and-tenon" joints appeared. They were locked with wooden pegs, the round heads easily visible.

The boat was ancient! This was the first time an ancient boat had been discovered in the Kinneret.

In our excitement, we hardly noticed that it had begun to rain. Suddenly, a torrent of water descended on us. We ran for the jeep. It rained for perhaps a minute and then stopped as suddenly as it had begun. We got out of the jeep and saw a beautiful double rainbow cascading into the Kinneret—straight out of Central Casting, a portent of things to come.

We stood on the shore speculating about the date of the wreck and how it had sunk. Our initial thought was that the boat might have been used by Jews in the First Jewish Revolt against Rome (67-70 A.D.) and sunk by the Romans in the famous Battle of Migdal.

As we stood on the shore watching the rainbows fade, Mendel recounted the story as it was told by the first-century Jewish historian Josephus.

At the outbreak of the revolt in 67 A.D., the Jews prepared a war fleet at Migdal (the home of Mary Magdalene, about a mile south of the site where the boat was discovered). This fleet consisted of fishing boats provisioned for battle. Tiberias, a large town at the southern end of the lake, soon surrendered to Vespasian. The Romans then built a large fortified camp between Tiberias and Migdal.

The Jews from Migdal, under Jeshua Ben Shafat, carried out a daring raid on the camp that caught the Romans by surprise. When the Romans managed to organize themselves, the Jews effected an orderly retreat, and taking to their boats, rowed out into the lake. When they reached bowshot range, they anchored "phalanx-like" opposite the Romans and engaged them in an archery battle.

The Romans then attacked Migdal, massacring the Jews in the city. Many of the Jews sought to escape by boat. Those who managed to do so took refuge on the lake, keeping as far out of range of the Romans as they could.

The next day, Vespasian ordered craft to be built to pursue the Jews in their boats. These were quickly prepared. Roman archers and infantry armed with swords and javelins were stationed on the Roman vessels, and battle was soon joined with the refugees on the lake.

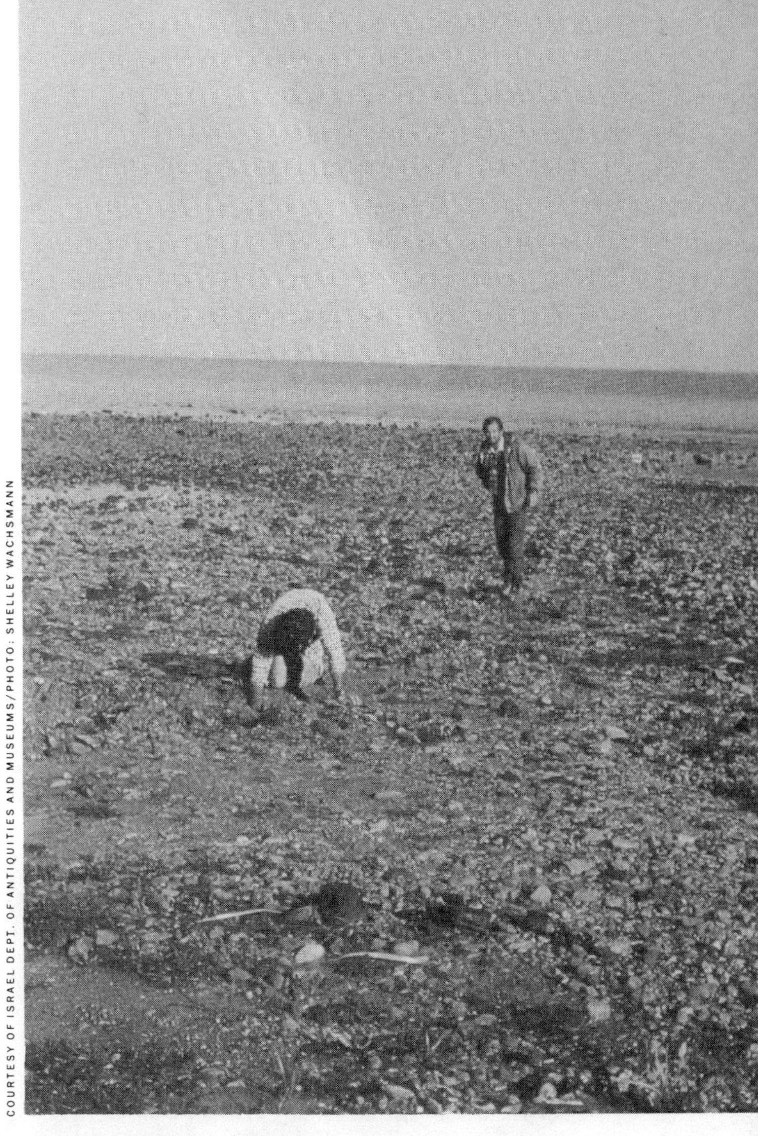

COURTESY OF ISRAEL DEPT. OF ANTIQUITIES AND MUSEUMS/PHOTO: SHELLEY WACHSMANN

A rainbow arcs ***across the Galilee sky. Like a favorable portent, the rainbow appeared shortly after the archaeologists verified that the buried boat was ancient.***

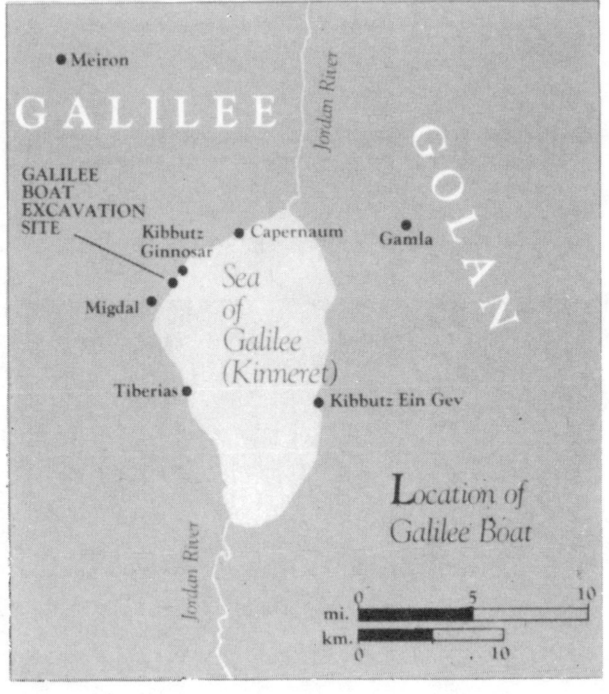

In the ensuing battle the Jews "were sent to the bottom, boats and all." Some tried to escape by breaking through the line of Roman vessels, but to no avail. The Romans reached them with their lances or jumped into their boats and killed them with their swords. Those who fell into the water were dispatched with arrows, while any who tried to climb on to the Roman vessels were beheaded or had their arms cut off by the Romans.

The remaining Jewish boats were driven to land, and the shore became a killing field. Describing the aftermath of the battle, Josephus wrote:

"During the days that followed, a horrible stench hung over the region, and it presented an equally horrifying spectacle. The beaches were strewn with *wrecks* and swollen bodies, which, hot and clammy with decay, made the air so foul that the catastrophe that plunged the Jews in mourning revolted even those who had brought it about. Such was the outcome of this naval engagement. The dead, including those

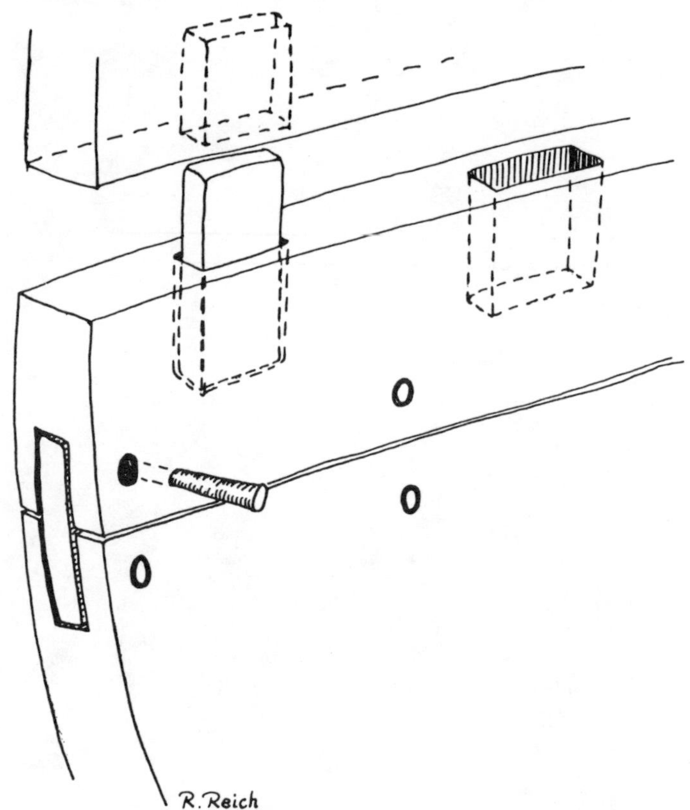

When telltale signs *of mortise-and-tenon joints appeared, the excavators knew they had found an ancient boat. Two round-headed wooden nails, right and left of center (below), peek out of a small section of the uppermost plank. In antiquity, Mediterranean shipbuilders devised the mortise-and-tenon method of joining the hull planks to one another (see drawing, above). Instead of overlapping adjacent planks and fastening them together, shipbuilders placed the planks in an edge-to-edge position and joined them by means of wooden links (tenons) inserted in slots (mortises) carved in the two planks. The tenons were then firmly secured within the mortises by pegs through the plank and its tenon. When the craft was placed in water, the wood swelled, forming a watertight fit. This joining technique has been discovered in vessels dated as early as the 14th-13th centuries B.C.; it went out of use in the Byzantine period.*

who earlier fell in the defense of the town (Migdal), numbered 6,700."

I remember thinking that the battle of Migdal was the nautical equivalent of Masada. Was the buried boat we were looking at a wreck that had washed up on that vermillion beach?

During the next two days we carried out a probe excavation around the boat. We opened a few small sections along its length to determine its state of preservation and to try to date it more accurately. During this excavation, we found two pottery vessels: a cooking pot (or casserole) outside the boat and an oil lamp inside it. Both dated to the early Roman Period (mid-first century B.C. to mid-second century A.D.). The link between this pottery and the wreck was illusive because the pottery was not part of the boat's cargo. Still, these finds did indicate a period of human activity in the immediate vicinity of the boat.

To protect the boat at the conclusion of the probe, we reburied it. Moshe and Yuval brought a tractor from the kibbutz and pushed pieces of jetsam, old pipes and heavy tree trunks around the site so that no one would drive over it accidentally. As an added precaution, they dug two "decoy" excavations farther down the beach to mislead looters and the just plain curious.

The discovery was to be kept secret until the rising waters of the Kinneret safely covered the boat. At that time it would be possible to reveal its discovery and, hopefully, organize a proper excavation.

That was Friday, February 7th. On Sunday, we were startled to read newspaper reports of a wreck from Jesus' time that had been discovered in the Sea of Galilee. Somehow the news had leaked. By Monday the press was writing in front page stories about the discovery of the "boat of Jesus."

The media hype was soon overwhelming. The Ministry of Tourism actively promoted the "Jesus connection" in the hope of drawing pilgrims to Israel. In Tiberias, Ultra-Orthodox Jews, fearful that excava-

Cooking pot, *left, and oil lamp. These beautifully preserved pottery vessels date respectively from the mid-first century B.C. to the mid-second century A.D. and from the first to the second centuries A.D. The oil lamp was found inside the boat, and the cooking pot was unearthed just outside the boat.*

COURTESY OF ISRAEL DEPT. OF ANTIQUITIES AND MUSEUMS/PHOTO: DANNY FRIEDMAN

The boat emerges *from the muck, on the first night of digging. The drought had broken, and forecasts were calling for more rain. Racing the rising lake waters, the team of experts and local volunteers was forced to work day and night. By digging at night, however, they risked damaging or losing smaller artifacts not visible in the warm yellow glow of gas lanterns, their only light source. To avoid any oversights, they removed mud by hand and placed it in plastic boxes precisely labeled according to location. Then, by daylight, they could examine the earth for artifacts.*

tion of the boat would promote Christian missionary work, demonstrated against it.

Soon rumors were circulating that the wreck was full of gold coins. Stories had been making the rounds for years of a ship that sank in the Kinneret during World War I, while carrying payment for the Turkish army. Now our wreck was becoming entwined with these stories, and people began searching for the non-existent treasure.

In Israel it is extraordinarily difficult to keep new archaeological finds hidden. Our boat proved to be no exception. Tuesday night, Moshe and Yuval were watching the site, through field glasses, from Ginnosar. They saw some people with flashlights in the area of the boat. Yuval immediately called me, and I drove to Ginnosar, arriving about midnight. The people had left without finding the boat. The three of us sat in a grove of trees watching the site until 3 a.m. The coast remained deserted. We knew that if we did not excavate the boat soon, there might be no boat to excavate. It was only a matter of time until someone would find and destroy the boat in search of non-existent treasure.

Archaeology throughout the world is dotted with cases of important discoveries destroyed because looters reached them before the archaeologists. We decided we had to excavate the boat immediately despite the fact that the archaeological and organizational logistics were mind-boggling.

A proper excavation takes time to prepare. Funds must be raised, team members recruited and a myriad of details worked out. Months, and sometimes years, go by before a planned excavation goes into the field. We would go into the field *in three days.*

The next day, February 12, I spent preparing a detailed excavation proposal for the Director of the Department of Antiquities, Avraham (Avi) Gitan. I made one condition concerning the excavation. We could assemble a local team for the archaeological excavation and conservation, but we were lacking someone who could make sense of the boat's construction once it was excavated. For this we would have to bring in someone from outside the country. We contacted Professor J. Richard (Dick) Steffy of the Institute of Nautical Archaeology, Texas A & M University, the world's leading expert on ancient ship construction.

Would he be able to come over on such short notice? If so, how were we going to pay for his trip? We called Dick from Ginnosar. He had already heard about the boat from the newspaper accounts and agreed to spend a week with us from February 20 to 25. Getting a ticket for Dick through governmental channels would be difficult on such short notice. However, the new American ambassador to Israel, Thomas Pickering, was a keen amateur archaeologist, and we wondered out loud whether the embassy might have a cultural grant program that could help in such situations. We contacted the American Embassy, and within 14 hours we had an OK on Dick's flight.

Dating the Pottery from the Galilee Boat Excavation

Seventeen identifiable pieces of ancient pottery—including a complete lamp and cooking pot, as well as fragments of cooking pots, storage jars, a jug and juglets—were recovered from the Galilee boat and from the surrounding area during the excavation. The pottery was not significantly water-worn, so we assume that the pieces were deposited near the places where they were found.

The pottery types recovered are all known from other Galilean excavation sites. Several of the more common types were made at Kefar Hananya, a Galilean pottery manufacturing center of the Roman period, located about 8 1/2 miles northwest of the boat site.[1]

None of the pottery is necessarily related to the hull itself; hence it cannot be used to date the boat. To date the boat, only intrinsic evidence may be used: evidence such as the carbon-14 dates obtained for the wood (see box on p. 220), and the method of vessel construction. However, the pottery recovered during the excavation is significant for estimating when there was activity in the vicinity of the boat.

The pottery pieces found near the Galilee boat were the same types as pottery recovered in excavations at Capernaum and Migdal (also known as Magdala), two ancient settlements on the coast of the Sea of Galilee; at Meiron, in the Upper Galilee; and at Gamla, in the western Golan.

The pottery at Capernaum, Migdal and Meiron was dated by its association with datable coins and artifacts and by its location in a dated stratum of remains. By these means, six pottery assemblages from these sites, which were similar to the boat pottery, could be assigned to the period from late first century B.C. to about mid-first century A.D., with one Capernaum assemblage continuing a few decades later. A seventh, similar pottery collection, also from Capernaum, could be dated by three coins in its context to the middle decades of the first century A.D. until about the year 70. One of those coins was from 54 A.D. and two others were from 67-68 A.D.—the former minted at Sepphoris in the 14th year of Nero's reign, and the others from the second year of the Jewish Revolt against Rome. The pottery found at Gamla was all in use before the city was taken by the Romans in 67 A.D., never to be resettled.

By comparing the pottery found near the Galilee boat with these well-dated assemblages from nearby sites, we may conclude that the boat pottery is typical of the period from the late first century B.C. to the decades following the mid-first century A.D., or until about the year 70 A.D. Moreover, later, common Galilean pottery types, first occurring in late first- and early second-century A.D. contexts, are notably absent. The ceramic evidence thus suggests a marked decline or cessation of activity in the vicinity of the boat in the late first century A.D., a conclusion consistent with the Roman victory in 67 A.D. that destroyed the boats of Migdal and left many of its people dead.

Dr. David Adan-Bayewitz, Bar-Ilan University, Ramat Gan, Israel

[1] David Adan-Bayewitz and Isadore Perlman, "Local Pottery Provenience Studies: A Role for Clay Analysis," *Archaeometry* 27 (1985), pp. 203-217; Adan-Bayewitz, *Common Kitchen Ware in Roman Galilee: A Study of Local Trade* (Ramat Gan, Israel: Bar-Ilan Univ. Press, in press).

The excavation was on. Its purpose was to excavate the boat, study it *in situ* and move it to the Yigal Allan Museum at Kibbutz Ginnosar for conservation—if possible, in one piece. We were to start on Sunday, February 16.

Before we could begin excavating, however, a new problem arose—literally arose. The lake was threatening to cover the boat again.

Moshe and I walked out to the site on Saturday night. When I had first seen the boat, less than two weeks before, the waterline was about 100 feet east of the site. Now it had advanced to within about 30 feet of the boat—and the forecast was for more rain. If the rain continued, the site would soon be inundated.

On the way back to Ginnosar, Moshe tried to cheer me up by saying that perhaps water was being pumped out of the lake for irrigation purposes. The Kinneret serves as the main reservoir of Israel's fresh water. There are three huge pumps that take water from it to the National Water Carrier.

This gave me an idea that was definitely on the "Far Side." Perhaps it might be possible to lower the level of the lake by pumping water out of it. I knew that Avi Eitan was meeting with the Minister of Education the next day concerning the boat. I phoned him and asked him to pass on a plea to the Minister of Education to ask the Minister of Agriculture to pump water out of the Kinneret into subsidiary reservoirs that would keep the water level steady until we could finish excavating the boat. In a country where *raising* the level of the Kinneret is a national passion, I doubted that this would be politically feasible, but it was worth a try.

On the day the excavation was to start, we were delayed by an armed band from a nearby settlement that laid claim to the boat. This matter was settled by the police and by a diplomatic effort on the part of the Director of the Department of Antiquities, who quietly explained that all antiquities belong to the state. We had lost half a day.

As we began excavating in the late afternoon, curiosity seekers crowded around, waiting for us to find the "treasure." For the next four hours, we excavated *next to* the boat. It became dark, and the crowd dispersed.

Then we began digging in earnest. With the lake rising steadily, we decided to work around the clock. Gas fishing-lamps lit up the area with an eerie, warm yellow glow. Work went slowly as we removed the mud from inside the boat, being careful to leave a 6-inch layer of mud covering the wood.

Bird's-eye view *of the boat on the second day of excavation. Between the two excavators, at midship line on the far side of the boat, a narrow section of mud was cut out, down to the wooden hull.*

The excavation team slowly formed. Orna Cohen was to be our conservationist; Danny Friedman joined as our photographer. Edna Amos, an archaeologist who had worked previously with Kurt and me in the Mediterranean, heard about the project during that first afternoon of excavation and dropped by to say hello. I immediately drafted her as our recorder. Edna worked through that night till 6 o'clock the next morning and returned the next day to become our permanent recorder.

During the evening we received a visit from members of the Kinneret Authority, the governmental body responsible for the lake. They had received a strange message from the Minister of Agriculture—to lower the level of the lake. They assumed that the message had been scrambled—no one in his right mind would want to *lower* the level of the lake.

I laughed and explained our predicament. They came up with a way to save the site, however, without lowering the level of the lake: Build a massive dike around the site to protect it from the encroaching lake. They promised to return the next morning with workers and supplies.

During the night we cut a narrow section down to the wooden hull at midship. Lying on our stomachs in the cold, wet mud, we excavated it by hand to avoid any possibility of damage to the boat from instruments. The wood slowly appeared; it was beautifully intact.

It was obvious, however, that in excavating clumps of mud in the dark we might miss artifacts. For that reason, all the mud excavated inside and next to the boat was placed in plastic boxes, which were given basket numbers and their positions recorded. The boxes were dumped in numbered piles that were later examined for artifacts. Moshe found an ancient pyramidal arrowhead in this way. More about this later.

Shortly after 6 a.m. Monday morning, the wind suddenly shifted to an easterly. It began pushing the water toward the boat. But it was not long thereafter that the Kinneret Authority team arrived, like the proverbial cavalry, and began building a dike of earthworks and sandbags around the site to protect it from the rising water. The site was saved from the encroaching water. Although the lake continued to rise, there was no longer a problem of water.

It is impossible to describe the effect the excavation had on everyone involved. Kibbutz Ginnosar "adopted" the excavation, supplying volunteers and logistics. The kibbutzniks would finish their own day's work and then join us for another eight or ten hours at night. Volunteers arrived from all over the country. The excitement was infectious. By the second afternoon,

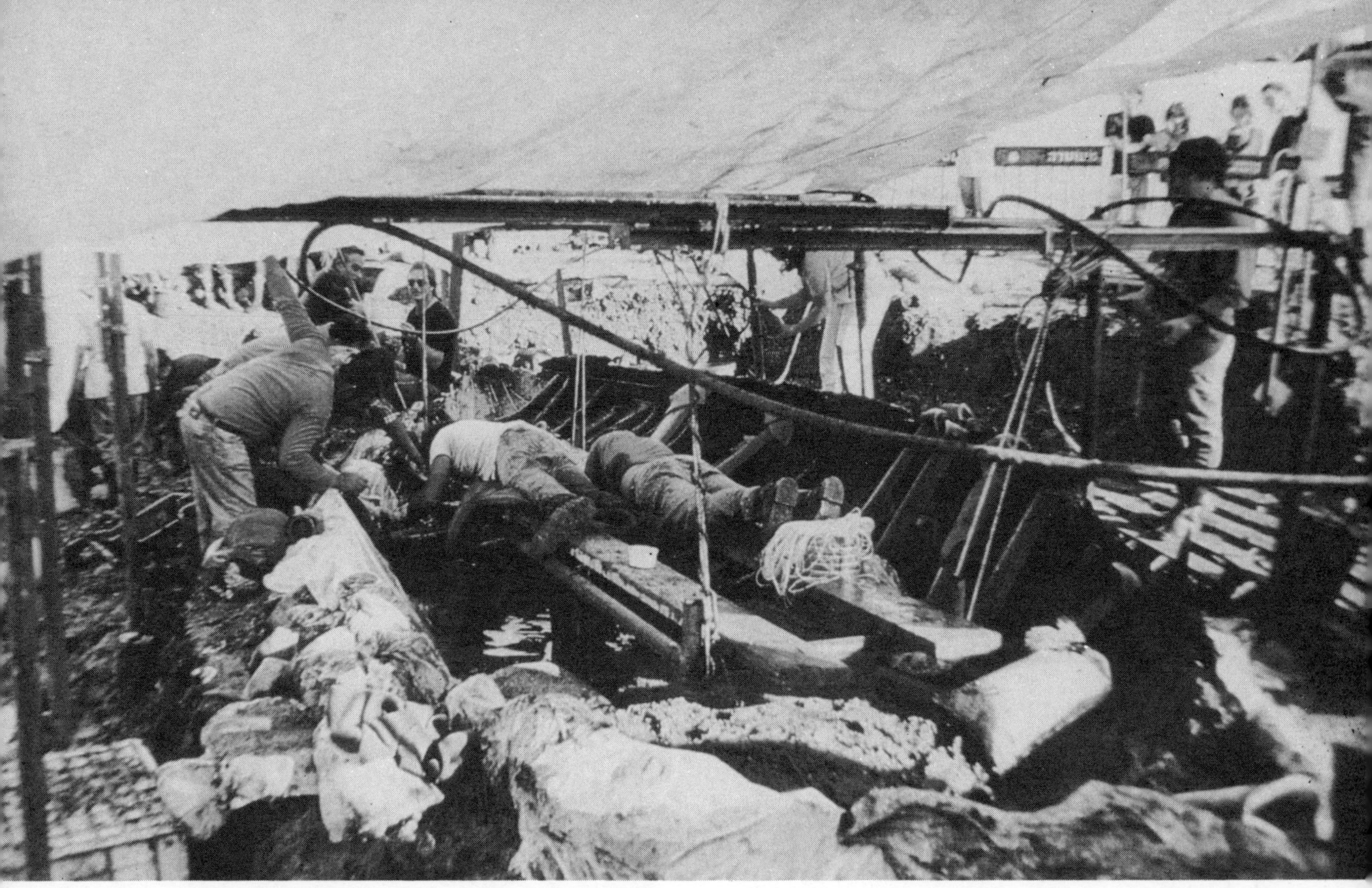

Suspended above the boat *from two bridges of metal poles, wooden planks provided a useful, if uncomfortable, platform from which workers could excavate without touching the fragile, waterlogged timbers. The bridges also supported a white tarpaulin that shielded the boat from direct sunlight, which might otherwise cause the wood to dehydrate and disintegrate.*

members of Moshav Migdal had also joined us. Previous arguments about where the boat would be exhibited were laid aside as we all pulled together in a concerted effort to save the boat. Because of this new-found harmony, we nicknamed it "the Love Boat."

On the second day of the excavation, as we were widening the excavation pit with a backhoe (lent by a moshavnik from Migdal), Zvika Melech, another moshavnik, showed me some pieces of waterlogged wood. We could not stop using the backhoe because enlarging the pit was our top priority, but now each shovel load had to be dumped in front of us and examined. We removed the loose pieces of waterlogged wood. The shovel load was then dumped on the side of the pit where Moshe, using a metal detector, removed iron nails. Suddenly sticking his hand into the pool of water, Zvika yelled, "This wood is connected to something!" Zvika had found what Dick Steffy later identified as fragments of *two* additional boats. The boat fragments were sandbagged, and we began excavating there by hand. Zvika, of course, was put in charge of the area.

On the second evening of excavation, the upper part of the partially excavated stern on the starboard quarter of the boat buckled. We had dug too far on either side without supporting it sufficiently. Someday, when the boat is reconstructed, those timbers will be refitted to the boat. But that evening was one of the worst I can remember. We all felt that despite our best efforts the boat was falling apart.

In order to avoid touching the fragile wood while excavating, Moshe built a series of metal bridges, on which the excavators could lie, over the boat. As the excavation progressed, the bridges were raised, and a platform suspended on ropes was lowered from it. Excavators lay prone on this platform for hours as they dug out the remaining mud by hand.

Each part of the boat was tagged and numbered. White plastic tubing was used to outline the strakes to enhance photographic recording. By the time Dick Steffy arrived on the fifth day of excavation, much of the hull had been exposed. Dick's presence at the excavation site gave us all a feeling of security. His vast knowledge and good common sense were invaluable.

At the conclusion of a *normal* excavation, the excavator gives a few boxes of artifacts to the conservationist. But in our case, the boat itself was one big conservation problem. At the beginning of the excavation I had called in Orna Cohen, an archaeologist turned conservator, who had just returned from a year of studies in England to take charge of this problem.

By the eighth day of excavation, the archaeological aspects of the excavation had been completed. Now the question was how to move the boat. It was Orna's ball game.

The craft's wooden timbers were thoroughly waterlogged. This meant that the cellular material inside the wood cells had been replaced with water to the degree that the wood, according to Orna's study, was now 80 percent water and had the consistency of wet cardboard. Any evaporation of water from such wood is extremely dangerous, causing the cell walls to collapse. This process is irreversible; the wood shrinks and fragments, and it cannot be restored to its former structure. Because of such dangers during the excavation, we sprayed the boat with water day and night, and even covered it with wet sponges and polyethylene sheets, in addition to shading it from direct sunlight.

Moving an entire boat of such soft material was a nearly impossible mission—and yet we had to move it approximately 1,600 feet to the Yigal Allon Museum at Kibbutz Ginnosar.

Orna consulted experts on the transport of large

ZVI MAOZ

Lush planted fields *meet the shore of the Sea of Galilee. At upper left, at the water's edge, stands the Yigal Allon Museum where the Galilee boat is now housed. When this photo was taken, the boat still lay on shore under a tarpaulin, the white speck circled at center, 550 yards to the right of the museum.*

Throughout the complex excavation and transportation of the boat, the two nearby agricultural communities, Kibbutz Ginnosar and Moshav Migdal, enthusiastically volunteered both workers and equipment.

Dotted with numbered tags, *all the wooden sections were meticulously labeled to record their correct locations. Running lengthwise across the boat, white plastic strings outline the planking structure. A dangling sprinkler, brought from Kibbutz Ginnosar, sprayed the boat continually to prevent it from drying out. The wood's micro-structure was supported mainly by water. Any evaporation would lead to the wood's collapse.*

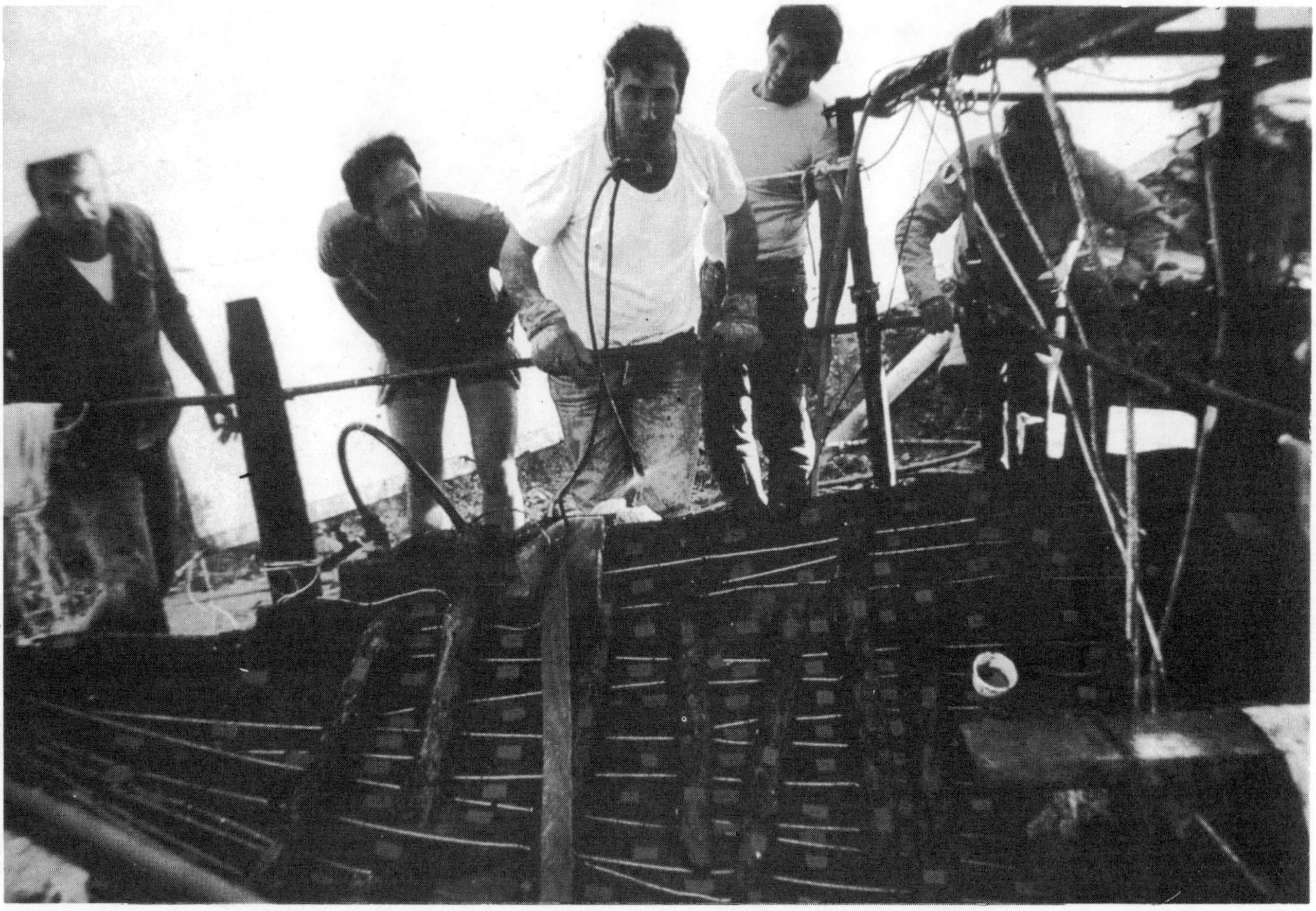

COURTESY OF ISRAEL DEPT. OF ANTIQUITIES AND MUSEUMS/PHOTO: DANNY FRIEDMAN

COURTESY OF ISRAEL DEPT. OF ANTIQUITIES AND MUSEUMS/PHOTO: DANNY FRIEDMAN

Protected by a polyurethane cocoon, *the Galilee Boat floats again, for the first time in 2,000 years. The 550-yard voyage to the Yigal Allon Museum required extensive preparation. Conservator Orna Cohen of Hebrew University planned and supervised the construction of fiberglass and polyester resin frames, fitted inside and outside the boat's hull. The boat was then wrapped in thin plastic sheeting and sprayed with polyurethane liquid, which hardened into a protective shell. Completely encased, the boat was ready to float.*

After a steam shovel, right, cut a channel through the dam that had been built to protect the excavation site from rising water, the Galilee boat sets out on its last voyage.

objects. It seemed that it was impossible to move a 26-foot-long boat of such fragile wood without seriously damaging it.

But Orna devised a method that had never been tried before. She decided to strengthen the boat inside and out with a fiberglass-and-polyester resin frame molded to the shape of the hull. The entire boat would then be encased in a polyurethane foam "straight jacket" to hold it together. We were going to attempt to move the boat intact.

First, frames of fiberglass/polyester (strengthened with old pieces of PVC irrigation hose) were laid down inside the boat. Then the entire hull was covered with fine plastic sheeting, and polyurethane foam was sprayed into the hull. This material sprays on as a dark orange liquid and quickly bubbles up and solidifies, looking every bit like a living entity engulfing the boat.

Next we excavated narrow tunnels under the boat. External fiberglass frames were then molded to the outside of the hull and the tunnels were filled with

polyurethane. These polyurethane strips hardened into external supports for the boat. This allowed the remaining clay and mud beneath the boat to be excavated. Fiberglass trusses were again added and the remaining areas were filled with polyurethane. By the end of the process, the entire boat—without having been moved or shifted—had been wrapped in a protective cocoon that looked somewhat like an overgrown, melted marshmallow.

Now that it was packaged, how would we move it? We considered carrying it overland by truck or helicoptering it out, but the related movement and vibrations were likely to destroy the boat. In the end, Orna opted for the obvious solution.

Once the boat was "packaged," we pumped water back into the excavation pit. Buoyed by the polyurethane, the boat floated at lake level. With a steam shovel, a channel through our precious dike was opened to the lake. The boat was floated through this channel out into the lake. For the first time in two millennia, the boat "sailed" again to the cheers of an onlooking crowd.

The entire excavation had taken eleven exhausting days and nights.

The next day, the boat was lifted onto the shore by a huge crane. Within ten days thereafter, a reinforced concrete pool with white tiles was constructed to serve as the boat's conservation tank. The boat was then raised once again by crane and placed inside the empty conservation pool.

Now began the long and laborious task of removing the polyurethane casing—tantamount to re-excavating the boat. We had not thought of putting trip-wires inside the polyurethane casing; we paid dearly for this mistake. In the tight confines of the conservation pool, the re-excavation was doubly difficult.

We could not fill the conservation pool with water and submerge the boat until all the polyurethane had been removed; otherwise, some parts of the boat would strain to float and the stress would cause breakage. But the boat was now drying out at an alarming rate, no matter how much we sprayed it with water. As time passed, it seemed we were losing the battle. Hairline cracks began to appear. I felt like a doctor about to lose his patient at the end of an extensive operation.

In what was surely the 11th hour, we finally finished the re-excavation of the boat and submerged it in water—and we ourselves nearly dropped from exhaustion.

The boat will now be treated for a period of five to seven years. A synthetic wax called PEG (polyethylene glycol) will be added to the water in slowly increasing concentrations. Simultaneously, the temperature of the water will be gradually raised. In this way, the PEG will penetrate the cellular cavities of the deteriorated wood and replace the water in the cells. At the conclusion of this years-long process, we will be able to exhibit the boat outside the conservation pool and study it in a dry environment. In the meantime, entrepreneurs from Kibbutz Ein Gev and from Tiberias are ferrying tourists across the lake to see "the boat from Jesus' time."

It does seem that the boat fits this time range and is of the type that would have been used by Jesus and his disciples.

I have already mentioned the pottery that gave us a general idea of the date of the boat. Dr. David Adan-Bayewitz of Bar-Ilan University, who studied this pottery, considerably narrowed the time range.

By comparing the datable pot sherds found in the excavation to nearby stratified assemblages, he concluded that the pottery found with the boat is typical of the latter part of the first century B.C. to the decades following the mid-first century A.D., or until about the year 70 A.D. As noted previously, this pottery does not date the boat directly; however, it does indicate a period of human activity in the immediate area of the boat. This period appears to end at the time of the First Jewish Revolt against Rome and may be related to the decimation of the population of Migdal at that time.

How Old Is the Galilee Boat?

The Galilee boat has been dated by a method called radiocarbon dating. This method could be used because the boat was made of wood, a carbon-containing material.

To understand radiocarbon dating, it's important to understand some basic facts about the world of nature. Carbon in the atmosphere exists in three forms—called isotopes—that differ in the weight of their atoms but not in their chemical behavior, so organisms use them as if they were exactly the same. The most abundant form is carbon 12, but for every 10^{12} atoms of carbon 12 there is one atom of the heaviest form, radioactive carbon 14. Carbon 14 is constantly being produced in the atmosphere.

To say that carbon 14 is radioactive means that it decays to the stable, non-radioactive nitrogen at a constant rate. This decay accounts for the fact that the number of carbon-14 atoms in the atmosphere and in living organisms, which continuously exchange carbon with the atmosphere as part of the biological processes of life, does not increase without limit but remains approximately constant.

As long as an organism is alive, the carbon within it is composed of the same proportion of carbon 12 and carbon 14 as the carbon in the atmosphere. But when an organism dies, such as a tree cut for use of its wood, the exchange process stops and decay of carbon 14 proceeds without any replenishment of the supply from the atmosphere.

For any particular radioactive isotope, it is possible to measure its half-life, or the time it would take for one-half of the original radioactive atoms in a sample to decay to a stable form. For carbon 14 the half-life is 5,568 years. This half-life makes it useful for archaeology because the changes are large enough for meaningful measurement in the time periods archaeologists care about.

In the case of the Galilee boat, we assume that the wood used to make it was cut within a short time of the boat's construction. Therefore, the radiocarbon age of the wood represents the true age of the boat.

Samples of the Galilee boat's wood, each weighing several grams, were removed and sent to a laboratory. Using gas proportional counters, which count the radioactive decay events that occur within the carbon 14, the amount of radioactive carbon 14 in the sample relative to the amount of stable carbon 12 was measured. Knowing how long it takes for half the atoms of carbon 14 to decay—namely 5,568 years—it was possible to calculate, based on the current proportion of isotopes present, how old the boat was when it was made (that is, when the living trees used for it were cut). Ten samples from different parts of the boat were counted. The result was that the boat began its life as a fishing vessel on the Sea of Galilee in 40 B.C., plus or minus 80 years, or between 120 B.C. and 40 A.D.

Dr. Israel Carmi, Weizmann Institute of Science, Rehovot, Israel

It therefore seems likely that the boat arrived at the site prior to the battle of Migdal.

Wood from the boat itself was dated by the carbon-14 method.* Dr Israel Carmi of the Department of Isotope Research of the Weizmann Institute carried out analysis on ten samples of wood from the boat and arrived at an average date of 40 B.C., plus or minus 80 years; that is, from 120 B.C. to 40 A.D.**

Dick Steffy independently came to about the same conclusion based on his knowledge of ancient boats. In his hand-written report to the Director of the Department of Antiquities, Dick wrote: "If this were a hull found in the Mediterranean I would date it between the first century B.C. and the second century A.D." He noted, however, that building traditions may have continued in the Kinneret after they had gone out of use in the Mediterranean.

Admittedly, each of the dating methods is insufficient in itself; however, taken together, these different dating techniques suggest a date between the first century B.C. and the late first century A.D.

Dr. Ella Werker of the Department of Botany at Hebrew University examined the wood from which the boat was made. This examination revealed that while most of the boat was constructed of cedar planking and oak frames, there are five other woods represented by single examples. These are: sidar, Aleppo pine, hawthorn, willow and redbud.

The boat is 26 1/2 feet long, 7 1/2 feet wide and 4 1/2 feet high. It has a rounded stern and a fine bow. Both the fore and aft sections were probably decked in, although the boat was not preserved to this height.

Dick Steffy's study of the boat suggests that it had been built by a master craftsman who probably learned his craft in the Mediterranean or had been apprenticed to someone who had. But he had to use timber that was far inferior to what was used on Mediterranean vessels. Perhaps better materials were beyond the financial reach of the owner. Many of the timbers in our boat, including the forward portion of the keel, were apparently in secondary use, having been removed from older boats.

* For an explanation of the carbon-14 method of dating, see the box above.

**However, the carbon-14 test tells us when the wood was cut. Some of the wood on this boat may have been reused from hulls of earlier boats.

The boat must have had a long life, for it had been repeatedly repaired. It ended its life on the scrap heap. Its usable timbers—including the stempost and sternpost—were removed; the remaining hull, old and now useless, was then pushed out into the lake where it quickly sank into the silt.

Did the boat have a mast? Steffy's careful detective work demonstrated that it did. A mast cannot be placed directly on a hull. It normally sits on a construction of wood called a mast step. This may be a simple block of wood or a complicated construction. Steffy found four nail holes where the mast block had been connected to the keel. The impression of the mast block was still visible on the top side of the keel. The mast block, like so many other reusable parts of the boat, had been removed in antiquity.

The boat could thus be both sailed and rowed. It was probably used primarily for fishing, but could also serve for transportation of goods and passengers. During times of armed conflict, it could serve as a transport.

The recovery of an ancient arrowhead in the excavation may indicate that a battle took place in this area. Arrowheads of the same pyramidal design have been recovered outside and next to the walls of Gamla on the Golan heights, another site where, despite an initial Jewish military success, the Romans successfully routed Jewish defenders, after a battle that ended in bloody disaster.* Danny Friedman, our photographer, who also works at Gamla, studied the pyramidal arrowhead found at our site. This type of arrowhead is apparently of foreign origin and was probably a specialty of a foreign auxiliary archer unit attached to the Roman legions. (Only 14 of approximately 1600 arrowheads found at Gamla are of this type.)

* See "Gamla: The Masada of the North," and Flavius Josephus, "The Fall of Gamla," both in the January/February 1979 **BAR.**

Protruding from the mud, *the stern end of the boat's keel terminates in a notch, called a hook scarf, left. Missing is the sternpost, which originally attached to this wooden locking connection. The sternpost was carefully removed in antiquity for reuse in another boat, just as spare parts today are scavenged from old cars.*

COURTESY OF ISRAEL DEPT. OF ANTIQUITIES AND MUSEUMS/PHOTO: DANNY FRIEDMAN

The fact that fragments of two other boats and other wooden debris were found during the excavation suggests to Dick that the area was used for building and repairing boats. This conclusion is also supported by the circumstance that before our boat was sunk, parts that might be used in other boats were removed—much like an old car today might be kept near a garage to serve as a source for used parts.

Was our boat typical of the kind referred to so often in connection with Jesus and his disciples in the Gospels and in Josephus' description of the battle of Migdal?

During the excavation, Dick had suggested that there were probably four rowers on a boat like ours.

At first this seemed to be contradicted by a mosaic picture of a boat found at Migdal. The mosaic shows a boat that apparently had three oars on each side. But when I examined the Migdal mosaic boat more closely I discovered that the two forward oars were represented as a single line of red tesserae (mosaic stones) that stood out against the black and white hull; but the sternmost

COURTESY OF ISRAEL DEPT. OF ANTIQUITIES AND MUSEUMS/PHOTO: DANNY FRIEDMAN

Oars poised, *a boat in a first-century A.D. mosaic remains forever at sea. Decorating a house in the Galilee seaside town of Migdal, only a mile from the discovery site of the Galilee boat, the mosaic boat appears to be propelled by six oars, three on each side. However, the sternmost oar widens at its base and therefore should be interpreted as a steering oar, or quarter rudder. Thus, this mosaic boat may resemble the Galilee boat, which probably had four rowers (two on each side) and a helmsman who steered with the quarter rudder.*

COURTESY OF ISRAEL DEPT. OF ANTIQUITIES AND MUSEUMS/PHOTO: DANNY FRIEDMAN

Ribs of wood *lie bare in the boat's specially built concrete conservation pool. Once inside the pool, the boat had to be stripped of its casing—an excavation in itself. Having outsmarted the Sea of Galilee's encroaching waters, the team now had to work furiously to remove the protective shell before the wood dried out. The boat could be re-immersed only after every shred of polyurethane had been taken off, because the buoyancy of the polyurethane would cause the parts of the boat underwater to rise. This would dangerously strain the boat's fragile frame.*

oar widened at the bottom—it was a steering oar. The boat in the mosaic must have had four rowers, as Dick had predicted for our boat, and a helmsman—a crew of five.

Then I reexamined some passages in Josephus in which he describes how, when he was commander of the Jewish rebel forces in Galilee, he put four sailors in each of the boats; elsewhere he talks of a helmsman—thus each boat again had a crew of five.

How many people could our boat hold? In one passage in Josephus he refers to himself, some friends, and seven combatants in a boat, which, with a crew of five, would total at least 15. In another passage, he tells of ten men of Tiberias who were transported in a single "fishing boat." With a crew of five, this too would total 15 men.

Based on skeletons he has examined, Joe Zias, a physical anthropologist at the Department of Antiquities, estimates that, in the Roman-Byzantine period, Galilean males were about 5 feet, 5 inches tall and averaged about 140 pounds. Fifteen such men would weigh just over a ton and could fit into our boat.

A boat like this could easily accommodate Jesus and his disciples, who regularly used boats on the Sea of Galilee (See Matthew 8:18,23-27, 9:1, 14:13-14,22-32, 15:39, 16:5; Mark 4:35-41, 5:18,21, 6:32-34,45-51, 8:9-10,13-14; Luke 6:1, 8:22-25,37,40; John 6:16-21.) The gospel passages do not indicate precisely, however, how many disciples were in the boat with Jesus during the recorded boat trips on the Sea of Galilee.

While the Gospels do not help in defining passenger capacities, there are two references to crew sizes.

Jesus called James and John, the sons of Zebedee, while they were in their boat tending their nets "and they left their father Zebedee in the boat with the hired servants, and followed him" (Mark 1:20). Thus, the boat of the Zebedee family was crewed by at least five men (Zebedee, James, John and two or more hired servants).

In mid-April 1987, over a year after the conclusion of the excavation, I wrote to Dick, suggesting this working hypothesis: The Kinneret Boat represents a class used on the lake during the Second Temple period. This is apparently the same class described by Josephus and in the Gospels and represented in the Migdal Mosaic.

Dick replied:

"Your working hypothesis sounds okay, but may I

make a further suggestion? Shell construction limited design possibilities, so there probably were not as many different boat designs on the Kinneret in antiquity as there are today. I suspect there were small boats—rowboats for one or two fisherman—and big boats such as ours. They may have varied somewhat in appearance and size, but basically they must have been limited to a couple of different hull forms in any given period. Without propellers to push them along, it seems unlikely that boats much larger than ours would have been practical on such a small body of water."

Is there any historical evidence for the smaller boat types that Dick postulated? Perhaps. Small boats may be inferred from another story Josephus tells about his adventures in Tiberias.

Pursued by an angry crowd, Josephus and two of his bodyguards "advanced to the rear" by commandeering a boat moored nearby and making a dash for it. Considering the speedy exit, it seems likely that they had taken a smaller type of boat.

Mendel Nun explained to me that boats of similar size to our boat were still in use on the Kinneret at the beginning of the 20th century—prior to the introduction of the motor. Known as *Arabiye,* they were used with a seine net. This type of net, used for catching shoals of fish near shore requires a boat 20 to 25 feet long. The net is spread out with its ropes as the boat advances. The net varies in size from about 500 to 1500 feet long, and requires a large stern platform to handle. Known as a *sagene* in Greek, this type of net is referred to by Jesus in the parable in which he compares heaven to a net:

> "Again, the kingdom of heaven is like a net which was thrown into the sea and gathered fish of every kind; when it was full, men drew it ashore and sat down and sorted the good into vessels but threw away the bad. So it will be at the close of the age. The angels will come out and separate the evil from the righteous" (Matthew 13:47-50).

Because a boat that uses this kind of net requires a large stern platform, this might enable us to picture more accurately the episode in which Jesus stilled the waters of the Sea of Galilee. A storm arose while Jesus with some of his disciples was crossing from one side of the lake to the other. In Mark's version of the story, Jesus was "in the stern, asleep on the pillow" (Mark 4:37). The large stern deck may explain why Jesus chose the stern in which to sleep. The stern deck was the station of the helmsman. While it would have been exposed to the elements, the area under the stern platform would have been the most protected area of the boat. Jesus probably slept beneath the stern platform. There he would have had the greatest protection from the elements and been out of the way of the other people on board:

> "And a great storm of wind arose, and the waves beat into the boat, so that the boat was already filling. But he was *in the stern,* asleep on *the pillow;* and they woke him and said to him, 'Master, do you not care if we perish?' And he awoke and rebuked the wind, and said to the sea, 'Peace! Be still!' And the wind ceased, and there was a great calm" (Mark 4:37-39).

More than a century ago, it was noted that the definite article used in relation to the pillow indicates that this was part of the boat's equipment. This may have been a sandbag used for ballast. Such ballast sacks were used on sailboats in the Mediterranean that used the seine net. There were two types of these: one, weighing 110-130 pounds, called in Arabic *kîs ṣābûra,* which means "balance (or ballast) sack"; or two sandbags of about 55 pounds each, used together. The latter was called a "balance (or ballast) pillow" (Arabic: *meḥadet ṣābûra*).

These sandbags were used to trim the boat when under sail; when not in use, they were stored beneath the stern deck where they could be used as pillows by crews resting there.

In conclusion, the Kinneret Boat is *of the class* referred to both in the Gospels in relation to Jesus' ministry in the Sea of Galilee region, and by Josephus in his description of nautical warfare on the lake during the First Jewish Revolt against Rome.

At present we have no proof that our boat played any part in these momentous events. But it does allow us better to understand them and seafaring on the Kinneret nearly 2,000 years ago.

The two articles concerning the Capernaum excavations provide good examples of the problems in separating closely overlaid stratigraphic sequences of building phases as well as problems of dating and interpretation of buildings' functions.

In "Has the House Where Jesus Stayed in Capernaum Been Found?" the authors discuss half a dozen different kinds of evidence which, taken together, have been important in the identification of the purported house of Peter. Note that no one of the different pieces of evidence by itself would be decisive. It is their cumulative weight that provides the strength of the argument. (1) The upper building with its east-facing apse probably was a church; the octagonal shape was used elsewhere to mark sites where sacred events had occurred. (2) This suggestion is reinforced by the discovery of another house below it that appears to have been converted into a church where special attention had been given to the room directly beneath the later octagonal church. (3) Further reinforcement comes from the discovery of over 100 graffiti, including inscriptions of an explicitly Christian nature, supplemented by the occurrence of crosses and, perhaps, even a monogram formed from the letters of Jesus' name. (4) The fact that the inscriptions feature entreaties for divine aid in five different languages including Latin, which was in common use only in the western Mediterranean, further strengthens the likelihood that this had been a Christian pilgrim shrine. (5) The pottery evidence indicates that the initial building had been used for normal household activity until the latter first century A.D., and then had experienced a shift in function away from such domestic activities as food preparation and cooking. (6) The proximity of the building to the Capernaum synagogue further increases the prospect that this was the house-shrine and later church identified by the fourth-century A.D. nun Egeria as Peter's house and that the octagonal building above it is the church that the sixth-century A.D. Pilgrim of Piacenza was told marked the house of Peter.

Note that the identification of the building as the house-church marking Peter's home does not depend on the occurrence of Peter's name in two of the graffiti. The reading of the graffiti by the Franciscan excavators is questioned by the article's authors, in fact, and their caution is appropriate. Indeed, we may have here another classic example of what has been called the Rorschach-blot syndrome in archaeology—the tendency to see in the physical evidence what one is already looking for. If the Franciscan fathers had not already been inclined to identify the building they were excavating as Peter's home, would they be as likely to have seen Peter's name in the graffiti?

Even without these graffiti references to Peter, however, as the authors note in their concluding paragraph, "a considerable body of circumstantial evidence does point to [the house's] identification as St. Peter's house."

Their following statement carries two implications that Dan Cole believes deserve to be spelled out more fully. Strange and Shanks write, "Though we moderns search for proof, that hardly mattered to those ancient pilgrims who scratched their prayers on the walls of the house-church in the belief that this was, indeed, St. Peter's house." Note, on the one hand, that the question in the article's title is left as a question. While the evidence makes it responsible to conclude that this is the house early Christians believed to be St. Peter's home, that does not establish that this actually *was* Peter's home. If the earliest pilgrims did not, in fact, know the exact location of the house where Jesus had stayed and where miracles of healing had been performed, it is quite possible that enthusiastic faith might have focused reverence on a house that seemed appropriately located directly in front of the Capernaum synagogue. It is then possible to envision a process similar to that which occurred for some just recently in regard to the Galilee boat where "it might be" all too easily became "it must be."

On the other hand, the evidence from the Capernaum house-church strongly suggests that the process of Christian pilgrimage began *very early* there (and presumably elsewhere), well before the official encouragement of it by Constantine in the fourth century A.D. Indeed, it would appear that Christian pilgrim activity began at the Capernaum house before the end of the first century A.D. If that can be established, it greatly increases the likelihood that those who established the initial pilgrim shrines were, in fact, able to draw upon living memory rather than mere pious imagination when locating the sites that had become sacred to them.

In "Synagogue Where Jesus Preached Found at Capernaum," the serious student of archaeology will find two matters of special value. First of all, the article provides a good summary of the several kinds of evidence that led to the isolation of an earlier basalt building under the great limestone synagogue and to its identification as an earlier synagogue. Enough information is given, along with supplementary photographs, plans and drawings, to enable the reader to follow that description and to reach an independent assessment of the merits of the excavators' conclusions.

Also of special interest is the discussion of the differing views concerning the date of the upper limestone synagogue. Was it late second to early third century A.D. (as Israeli scholars have tended to claim) or late fourth to early fifth century A.D. (as the Franciscan excavators have claimed)? Note that the arguments for the earlier date give primary importance to *stylistic* criteria (comparison of the synagogue's shape to that of 20 other synagogues now known in the region and datable to the second to third centuries A.D. as opposed to the typical shape of synagogues from the following early Byzantine period). The proponents of the later date, on the other hand, give greater weight to *stratigraphic* evidence (in particular the late coins apparently sealed beneath the synagogue's initial floor).

There was an interesting follow-up to this discussion in Queries & Comments in the May/June 1984 issue of **BAR.** Benjamin Urrutia of Provo, Utah, wrote:

> James F. Strange and Hershel Shanks mention the two different datings for the later Capernaum synagogue (a higher chronology, second-third centuries; a lower chronology, fourth-fifth centuries) and state that "each side seems to have a convincing case"; ergo, no conclusion is drawn in the article. However, it should be pointed out that the lower chronology is based on a single element: the hoard of 10,000 bronze coins from the fourth and fifth centuries. For this, a counterargument has been presented: the possibility that "the pavement was relaid in the fourth century," or more likely the fifth—perhaps with the purpose, precisely, of concealing the coins at a time of persecution and oppression. These same political conditions form part of the complex of arguments for the higher chronology, which also includes architectural patterns (a very strong and convincing point) and the social-economic conditions of the country at the time. For none of these have any counterarguments been presented. One must conclude that the case for a higher chronology [i.e., second-third centuries] is by far the stronger."

James Strange provided this reply in the same issue:

> We bent over backward to be fair to the two positions on the date of the white limestone synagogue at Capernaum, but it seems clear to me that stratigraphy favors the late date. The coins in question are in soil that runs under the floors and beneath the stylobates. The coins are also to be found all the way to the floor of the earlier building. The simplest explanation is that the white limestone building is fourth or early fifth century. We already know that Jewish communities were thriving in Galilee during these centuries, in spite of what the history books say, because of the archaeological evidence from Khirbet Shema and Gush Halav, excavated by Eric Meyers, Carol Meyers and myself, and also from excavation data from Nazareth, Tiberias, Hammath Tiberias, Chorazim, Yaphia, Beth She'arim, Beth Yerah and Beth She'an, all excavated by others.

Turning to the Galilee Boat, readers can appreciate how clearly Shelley Wachsmann itemizes the evidence to date and identify the craft uncovered in 1986 and how carefully he notes the limitations of the evidence. He describes—and the article illustrates—the mortise-and-tenon method of construction used in the boat, which would be consistent with a first-century A.D. date, but he is careful to note that this technique was already in use centuries earlier and continued in use through the Roman period. He discusses the pottery of first-century A.D. type found on top of and near the wreck, but is careful to note that it is not certain the pottery was in the boat when it sank or has anything directly to do with it. (Professor David Adan-Bayewitz, who conducted the technical analysis of the pottery, has provided a helpful summary of his findings in the box on page 214. He also is careful to point out that the pottery is not necessarily related to the boat. Moreover, he only narrows the range of the pottery's age to between the late first century B.C. and 70 A.D.) Dr. Israel Carmi, who carried out carbon-14 analyses of the boat's wood, is careful to note that those tests can only narrow the probable construction date of the boat to somewhere between 120 B.C. and 40 A.D. (His statement in the box on page 220, incidentally, includes a very clear, brief explanation of how the carbon-14 dating process works.)

Although the initial furor that surrounded the discovery of the Galilee wreck focused on its possible connection with Jesus, Wachsmann makes it evident that, for his part, he became more excited by its possible association with the battle of Migdal in 67 A.D., so vividly described by Josephus. Here again, however, note that the author cautiously avoids trying to push the evidence to a definite assertion. He also provides enough information from Josephus's description and from the physical evidence which he finds suggestive so that the reader is able to form an independent assessment.

From the scholar's perspective, the unquestionable value of the Galilee boat is that it provides an intact example of the type of fishing vessel used on the Sea of Galilee at the time of Jesus and his fishermen-disciples, as well as at the time of the dramatic naval engagements of the First Jewish Revolt. As Wachsmann notes in his concluding remarks, the analysis of the boat will enhance our knowledge of seafaring technology during this culminating era of Biblical history. A final reflection: Wachsmann describes the incredible haste with which he and his associates had to uncover and remove the fragile ancient craft, devising their strategy as they dug, all because of the tremendous pressure of public curiosity and the resulting threat from religious relic seekers and (ironically) treasure hunters seeking a rumored hoard of gold coins. How tragic it would have been archaeologically if the Galilee wreck had been lost because of the need to work with such speed.

For Further Reading

Concerning Other Discoveries at Capernaum

Herold Weiss, "Gold Hoard Found at Capernaum," **BAR,** July/August 1983

The Tomb of Jesus

The most potent shrine for Christian pilgrims over the centuries has been the tomb of Jesus, where he was placed after his crucifixion on a nearby hill called Golgotha and from which, according to the New Testament, he rose from the dead on Easter morning. This section focuses on the two sites that differing Christian groups presently revere as the tomb of Jesus and examines some of the archaeological evidence for and against the competing claims made for them.

A capsule review of the historical background might be helpful before plunging into the articles. When the emperor Constantine's mother, Queen Helena, went to the Holy Land on her first imperial pilgrimage in 326 A.D., she paid for and supervised the erection of a magnificent shrine to surround the site identified to her by the local Christian community as the tomb of Jesus. The resulting Church of the Holy Sepulchre became the ultimate goal of Christian pilgrims through the following centuries, the inspiration for successive waves of Crusaders, a place of miracles—where every Easter midnight fresh fire from heaven was claimed to issue for the faithful from within the empty tomb. Until the 19th century, no serious question was raised concerning the authenticity of the site.

The beginnings of modern doubts about the traditional site were given impetus by the American Protestant Biblical scholar Edward Robinson, who made his first visit to Jerusalem in 1838. Robinson brought with him the special curiosity of the historical geographer and the modern scholar's readiness to question earlier assumptions and make fresh assessments. In the subsequent publication of his researches and reflections from this journey (*Biblical Researches in Palestine and in the Adjacent Regions: A Journal of Travels in the Year 1838* [London, 2nd ed. 1860]), he was quick to note that the Church of the Holy Sepulchre stood well within the walls of old Jerusalem, and he judged that the city walls had already expanded to incorporate the area of the church by the time of Jesus' crucifixion. This would eliminate the possibility of the church being the site of either Golgotha Hill or the tomb of Jesus, since both crucifixion and burial invariably took place outside the city walls and the Gospel accounts indicate that the events occurred "near" but outside the city (John 19:17,20; Matthew 27:32). He further argued that it was unlikely that Christians of the fourth century could have drawn upon an accurate memory passed down over the intervening three centuries.

It should be noted that Edward Robinson also brought to Jerusalem a 19th-century Protestant's aversion to the Roman Catholic and Eastern Christian communities, with their more elaborate liturgies, incense and trappings of worship. And it was several of these more ancient Christian communions which he found jostling for position at the Church of the Holy Sepulchre: Roman Catholics, Greek Orthodox, Russian Orthodox, Syriac Christians, Armenians and Egyptian Copts.

Robinson's personal feelings are revealed in his description of his visit to the church on Easter Sunday, 1838, his first day in Jerusalem:

> The annual mockery of the Greek holy fire had taken place just before we entered the city. The Latins too had enacted their mummery, representing the scenes of the crucifixion. In consequence of our late arrival, we thus missed all the incidents of the holy week. This however we counted as no loss, but rather a gain; for the object of our visit was the city itself, in relation to its ancient renown and religious associations; not as seen in its present state of decay and superstitious or fraudful degradation.

He observed the Roman Catholic clergy leading their Easter Sunday service at the church and recalled his impressions as follows:

> I was not less struck with the vulgar and unmeaning visages that peered out from these costly vestments. The wearers looked more like ordinary ruffians, than like ministers of the cross of Christ. Indeed there is reason to believe, that the Latin monks in Palestine are actually for the most part ignorant and often illiterate men, chiefly from Spain, the refuse of her monks and clergy, who come or are sent hither as into a sort of exile, where they serve to excite the sympathies and the misplaced charities of the Romanists of Europe. There was hardly a face among all those before us, that could be called intelligent. . . . The whole scene indeed was to a Protestant painful and revolting . . . and I never visited the place again.

Whether or not Robinson's religious attitudes colored his academic judgment, his skepticism regarding the authenticity of the site marked by the Church of the Holy Sepulchre had a strong influence on many later 19th-century scholars and Protestant clergy who were active in Palestine. There was an increasing tendency among them to look beyond the existing walls of Jerusalem for Golgotha and the locale of the tomb in which Jesus' body was placed.

Attention was drawn more particularly to a hill directly northeast of Damascus Gate by General "Chinese" Gordon when he visited Jerusalem in 1883 and, applying to the city an esoteric kind of spiritual topography well described by Gabriel Barkay in "The Garden Tomb—Was Jesus

Buried Here?" confidently proclaimed that Golgotha, the Hill of the Skull, had to be located there.

Against the background of these pronouncements, a Protestant group in Jerusalem concluded that a tomb discovered earlier on the hill's south scarp was the actual tomb of Jesus. They purchased this Garden Tomb in 1894 and have maintained it in a pleasant garden setting to this day (the only Protestant shrine in Jerusalem). It has become the most moving and meaningful stop on many 20th-century pilgrims' itineraries. Scholars, meanwhile, have carried on periodic debates concerning the strength or weakness of the claims for the competing shrines.

The past few decades, however, have seen several important developments in our archaeological knowledge that throw new light on the arguments for and against both tombs. Barkay, in reinterpreting the Garden Tomb as an eighth- to seventh-century B.C. tomb modified in the Byzantine era, is able to draw upon newly acquired understanding of how other tombs in the area were constructed in successive periods. As recently as 1974, Barkay himself had participated in a reexamination of a cemetery immediately adjacent to the Garden Tomb.

Dan Bahat's "Does the Holy Sepulchre Church Mark the Burial of Jesus?" was occasioned by the publication (in Italian) by archaeologist Virgilio Corbo of a report of excavations begun there in 1960. Bahat also refers to excavations carried out concurrently outside the church at strategic points in the northwest quarter of the Old City to help date the sequence of ancient city walls there. In examining the historic claims for the Church of the Holy Sepulchre, therefore, both Corbo and Bahat were able to draw on information made available because of archaeological data gathered only since 1960.

The investigations seem to establish that at the time of Jesus the area where the church was later built was still outside the city walls and, moreover, that it had been a cemetery—with tombs of the style of Jesus' time found in the immediate vicinity. These discoveries do not establish that the Church of the Holy Sepulchre *must* mark the authentic tomb of Jesus, of course, but they establish that it *is possible* for the church to be in the right place.

Bahat's article also describes the investigations during the 1960s of the church itself, and provides an excellent summary, with plans, of the several stages of building and rebuilding of this most venerated of Christian shrines as they have only recently come to be understood. However one assesses its claims to mark sacred events of the first Holy Week, the Church of the Holy Sepulchre has been the focus of Christian reverence for 16 centuries of successive Holy Weeks since Constantine. We can be grateful, therefore, for the increased knowledge archaeology has given us of the church's building history.

Finally, in "Evidence of Earliest Christian Pilgrimage to the Holy Land Comes to Light in Holy Sepulchre Church," Magen Broshi provides a poignant witness to Christian pilgrimage from the very first decade after Queen Helena's establishment of the Church of the Holy Sepulchre. The ship inscription, sealed under a floor laid no later than 335 A.D., serves as a thematic anticipation of the hardships overcome and faith rewarded on the part of generations of pilgrims who were to follow the ones who left this votive plaque.

The Garden Tomb

Was Jesus Buried Here?

Gabriel Barkay

FIRST-TIME VISITORS to Jerusalem are often surprised to learn that two very different sites vie for recognition as the burial place of Jesus. One is, as its name implies, the Holy Sepulchre Church; it is located in a crowded area of the Christian Quarter inside the walled Old City. The other, known as the Garden Tomb, is a burial cave located outside the Old City walls, in a peaceful garden just north of the Damascus Gate.

The case for the Holy Sepulchre Church as the burial place of Jesus has already been made for **BAR** readers.*

* A new analysis of the Church of the Holy Sepulchre and its claim to be the site of Jesus' burial will appear in the next issue of **BAR**. In the meantime, see the convincing review of Father Charles Coüasnon's book on the Holy Sepulchre Church, *The Church of the Holy Sepulchre in Jerusalem* (London: Oxford University Press, 1974), by J.-P. B. Ross, "The Evolution of a Church—Jerusalem's Holy Sepulchre," **BAR**, September 1976.

Preceding page. *Pilgrims and tourists visit the Garden Tomb, a burial chamber in Jerusalem often proposed as the burial place of Jesus. The tomb's serene setting amid geraniums and oleander provides a place for meditation and prayer, as well as respite from the bustle of modern Jerusalem just a few feet beyond the walls.*

To the tour guide's left, a shadow-darkened doorway marks the entrance to the cave carved into the hill. The dressed stones next to the doorway, topped by a small window, were not built when the chamber was hewn, but sometime after.

On the hill, above, left, a stone wall separates the grounds of the Garden Tomb from the adjacent Moslem cemetery. On the northwest slope of this hill is the Dominican monastery of St. Étienne.

Recent archaeological investigations have revealed that both the Garden Tomb and two cave tombs at St. Étienne were carved into the same rocky escarpment. These tombs were all part of the northern cemetery of Jerusalem during the First Temple period, in the eighth and seventh centuries B.C. The Garden Tomb cave was later reused, but this was in the Byzantine period and in the Middle Ages, not in the time of Jesus.

But what of the Garden Tomb? What is its claim to authenticity?

The year 1983 marked a centennial for the Garden Tomb; in 1883 the newly discovered cave was identified by the military hero of his day, General Charles George Gordon, as the tomb of Jesus. That identification caused, and still provokes, waves of controversy among pilgrims who wish to visit authentic sites of the Gospels. Even today the Garden Tomb is one of Jerusalem's best known sites; it is visited by well over a hundred thousand tourists and pilgrims a year, visitors who imbibe its serene and sacral atmosphere. Indeed, the tranquility of the Garden Tomb provides a striking contrast to the city noise and tumult just outside.

With the development of archaeological research in the Holy Land, it seems appropriate to look anew into this famous cave and the question of its authenticity, especially in light of the increasing accumulation of data on the architectural characteristics of burial caves in Jerusalem and in other areas of Judah during various ancient periods.

The burial cave known as the Garden Tomb was found in 1867 by a peasant who wanted to cultivate the land there. While trying to cut a cistern into the rock, he accidentally came upon the cave. Conrad Schick, the Jerusalem correspondent for several learned societies in Europe, visited the cave soon afterward, and it is from his reports that we first learn of the discovery. One of the few Europeans then living in Jerusalem, Schick assumed the task of keeping up-to-date scientific journals of news from the Holy City. His first report about the cave was published in 1874.[1] It is an innocent enough description of yet another Jerusalem burial cave, similar in style to others about which he periodically reported to his learned societies. According to Schick's account, the cave was filled to half its height with a mixture of earth and human bones. At the entrance to the cave, he saw an iron bar and hinge. He also observed a human skeleton in the balk, or wall, of a trench that had been dug to find the mouth of the cave. After Schick's first visit, the owner of the cave cleared it of its contents in order to use it.

In 1892, Schick published a second report,[2] which was much more detailed because it was written after the suggestion that the cave might be the tomb of Jesus. Obviously, the tomb then assumed far more importance

ARCHIVE OF THE PALESTINE EXPLORATION FUND

Conrad Schick *(1822-1901) came to Jerusalem in 1846 from Germany as a missionary and became a correspondent for the Palestine Exploration Fund and scholarly European journals. In 1867, when a farmer trying to hew a cistern into a rocky hill discovered the cave that would become known as the Garden Tomb, Schick visited the site and wrote up a brief report. Some years later, the suggestion was made that the cave had been the burial place of Jesus. Schick revisited the cave, excavated in front of it and issued a new, detailed report.*

THE LIBRARY OF CONGRESS

MATSON COLLECTION/LIBRARY OF CONGRESS

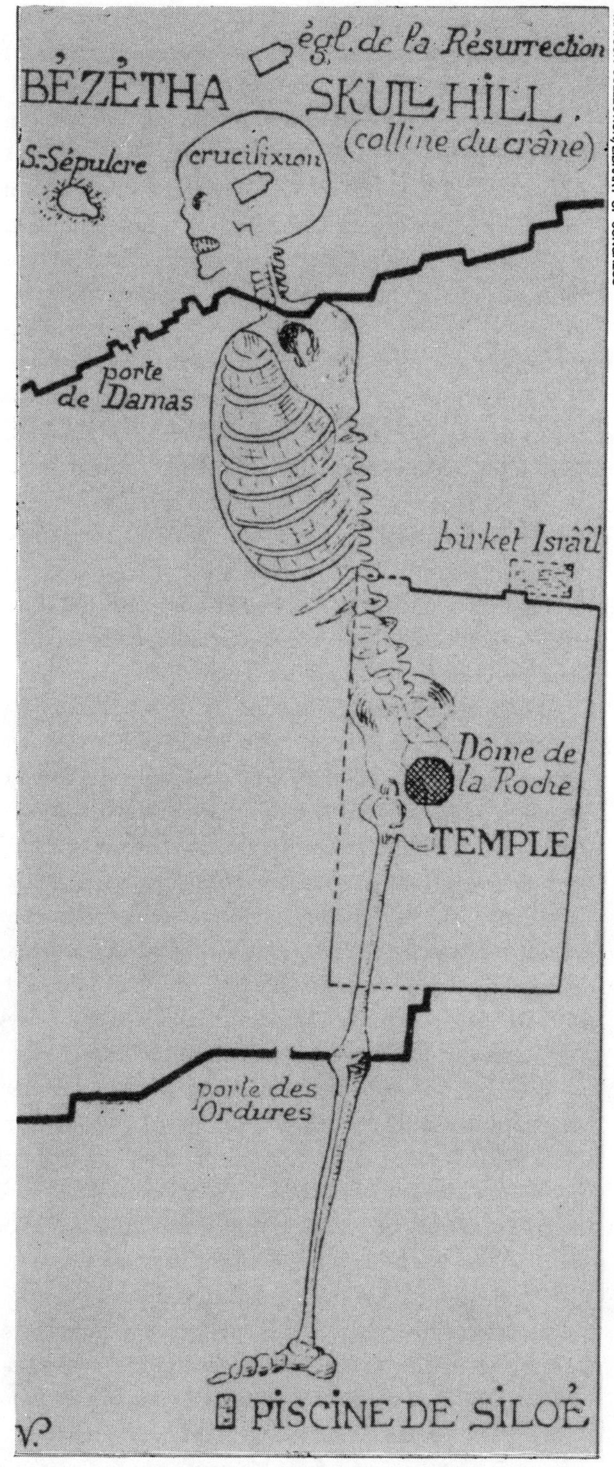

General Gordon. *A renowned British military hero, Charles George Gordon fought in the Crimean War, in China and in Egypt. When he arrived in Jerusalem in 1883, one of his first actions was to combine his religious fervor with a general's skill and confidence in interpreting terrain. After making sketches for a short report, he announced that the hill in which the Garden Tomb cave was hewn was Golgotha ("skull" in Aramaic), the site of Jesus' crucifixion.*

Gordon visualized an imaginary skeleton superimposed on the city of Jerusalem (right): he fixed the skeleton's pelvis at the Dome of the Rock, its legs on the City of David and its feet at the Siloam Pool. With this alignment, the hill containing the Garden Tomb had to be the skull. Gordon even saw a resemblance to a skull in the rocky hill with its dark cave "eyes.

In the same report, Gordon assigned a location for the Garden of Eden. He picked a true tropical paradise of giant trees and lush vegetation—the Seychelles island of Praslin in the Indian Ocean, a thousand miles from the East African coast.

than the hundreds of other caves already known in and around Jerusalem. Schick reported that he had conducted a small dig in front of the cave and had found some vaulted chambers that leaned against the rocky escarpment of the hill in which the cave had been hewn. He also reported the clearing of a large cistern of the Crusader period within the perimeter of the garden, southwest of the cave.

Another description of the Garden Tomb is found in the Jerusalem volume of the *Survey of Western Palestine* conducted in 1884 by Charles Warren and Claude Regnier Conder for the London-based Palestine Exploration Fund. Warren and Conder mention that excavations were conducted in the garden in 1875, unearthing mostly Crusader remains.

In 1883, General Charles George Gordon arrived in

Jerusalem, an event that proved to be critically important in the history of the Garden Tomb. Gordon, the son of a general, was the best-known and best-loved British soldier of his era. He served with distinction in the Crimean War and later went to China in the expedition of 1860, taking part in the capture of Peking. As commander of the "Ever-Victorious Army," he successfully suppressed the Taiping Rebellion. For his service in China, he was decorated by the emperor, and quickly became known as "Chinese" Gordon. In 1873, with the consent of his government, Gordon entered the service of the Khedive, the Turkish viceroy in Egypt. While in this post, he mapped part of the White Nile and Lake Albert. In 1877, he was appointed governor-general of the Sudan, where he waged a vigorous campaign against slave traders. On one occasion, he relieved Egyptian garrisons threatened by a revolutionary force by walking into the rebel camp, accompanied only by an interpreter, to discuss the situation—a bold move that proved successful when a contingent of rebels joined Gordon's forces.

When he arrived in Jerusalem in 1883, Gordon was already a luminary crowned with a halo of heroism. He stayed in Palestine less than a year. In January 1884, he was dispatched to Khartoum to report on the best way of evacuating the British from the Sudan after the revolt of the Mahdi. Although he was eventually ordered to evacuate Khartoum, Gordon took it upon himself to attempt to defeat the Mahdi. Gordon's personal heroism was unexcelled, but finally the Mahdi besieged Khartoum with Gordon trapped inside. Gordon was killed two days before a relief expedition arrived from England.

Even by 1883, when he arrived in Jerusalem, Gordon had a worldwide reputation as a military figure surrounded by an aura of mystery. He was the grand representative of the Victorian era, the personification of heroism, of duty, of loyalty to the British Empire and of faith in God. At the same time, he was an ambitious individualist, an adventurous crusader, and a captivating story-teller. Moreover, his deep religious consciousness went beyond the rational—indeed, reaching into spiritual hallucination. Motivated by a religious compulsion, Gordon came to Jerusalem to meditate on questions of faith that had perplexed him from his youth.

Immediately upon his arrival in Jerusalem, Gordon identified the hill in which the Garden Tomb cave is located as the hill of Golgotha, mentioned in the Gospels as the site of the Crucifixion (Matthew 27:33, Mark 15:22, John 19:17).

This hill is located just north of the northern wall of the Old City. It was and is the site of a Moslem cemetery named Es-Sâhirah (meaning "the place of the awakened"). The hill is separated from the escarpment on

"Hill of Golgotha" *(below). Identified in 1883 by General Charles George Gordon as the site of the crucifixion, this rocky hill stands just north of Jerusalem's Old City. Tombstones of a Moslem cemetery cluster on the hilltop, while a modern bus station crowds its base. Hewn into this hill—farther to the north—are two burial cave complexes: the Garden Tomb, where, some believe, Jesus was laid to rest, and the tombs on the grounds of St. Étienne's monastery.*

In another view of "Golgotha" (right), taken at the end of the 19th century by the famed Jerusalem photographer G. Eric Matson, only a few tombstones dot the hilltop. At the far left, the flying buttresses of St. Étienne's church mark the location of this monastery complex. On the grounds of St. Etienne's, a flight of steps leads underground to one of the burial caves. In the Iron Age (eighth or seventh century B.C.) when these burial caves and the cave of the Garden Tomb were hewn out of the hill, they were all part of the same cemetery.

MATSON COLLECTION/THE LIBRARY OF CONGRESS

HERSHEL SHANKS

GARO NALBANDIAN

Cave "eyes" ***of General Gordon's "Skull hill" are seen here closeup in the sheer Jerusalem hill that conceals a vast underground cemetery.***

which the Old City wall is built by a rock-hewn depression that forms a kind of dry moat. The hill itself, today called El-Edhemîyeh (named after Ibrahim el-Edhem—the founder of a Moslem spiritual sect in the eighth century), has rock-hewn sides creating a vertical escarpment of its own. The Garden Tomb cave is hewn into the vertical escarpment on the western slope of the hill, just 820 feet (250 m) north of Damascus Gate. Today the cave is located in a large, walled garden owned by the Garden Tomb Association.

Just north of the Garden Tomb is the Monastery of St. Étienne (St. Stephen) of the French Dominican Fathers. On the grounds of the monastery is the École Biblique et Archéologique Française—the French School of Bible and Archaeology. On the southern side of the hill into which the Garden Tomb was hewn is located the central bus station of East Jerusalem—across from the Old City wall.

The Garden Tomb is approached by a narrow street now named after Conrad Schick. Schick Street exits onto Nablus Road, which is the main road leading north from Damascus Gate.

Even before Gordon identified this hill as Golgotha, other scholars had mentioned this possibility.* In 1881, Conder suggested that another burial cave cut into a rocky outcrop just west of the Garden Tomb was the tomb of Jesus.** Conder's suggestion was based on the identification of the hill called El-Edhemîyeh as Golgotha.

Although Gordon visited the cave of the Garden Tomb and, no doubt, regarded it as Jesus' tomb, oddly enough, he doesn't mention it in his writings; he concerns himself mainly with the identification of the hill as Golgotha.

This identification was based on some fantastic conclusions concerning the topography of Jerusalem. Gordon visualized the city in the shape of a human skeleton. In his imagination, the skull of the skeleton was in the north (Golgotha means "the skull" in Aramaic); the pelvis of the skeleton was at the Dome of the Rock on the Temple Mount; the legs extended southward on the ridge identified with the City of David; and the feet were at the Pool of Siloam. (See drawing on p. 231.) Since, in Gordon's imagination, the hill north of Damascus Gate formed the skull of the skeleton, Gordon identified the hill as Golgotha.

These speculative identifications were published posthumously in 1885, after Gordon's courageous last stand at Khartoum. His identifications gained fame and publicity, not for any scientific validity, but because of Gordon's compelling personality and his heroically tragic death.

A long and extremely bitter dispute concerning the authenticity of the site followed Gordon's identification of the hill as Golgotha and the consequent identification of the cave in its western escarpment as Jesus' tomb. The authenticity of the tomb was supported mainly by Protestants. It was attacked mainly by Catholics, who held to the traditional identification of Jesus' tomb within the Church of the Holy Sepulchre. The dispute was conducted in scores of articles in a number of journals. Most of these articles have a theological and apologetic, rather than a scientific bent. None concerning the cave, nor any useful analysis of the archaeology of the site.

Capitalizing on the fame of Chinese Gordon, the site was soon named "Gordon's Tomb" or "Gordon's Cal-

* Apparently the first to do so was Otto Thenius, a German scholar, who had already made the suggestion in 1842.

** Today, the grounds of the Franciscan White Sisters Convent on Nablus Road cover Conder's cave.

PEFQS

Iron Age finds *(above) from the Garden Tomb. Excavated in 1904 by Karl Beckholt, warden of the Garden Tomb, this pottery was photographed and published 20 years later by James Edward Hanauer, a Jerusalem scholar who died in the 1930s.*

Hanauer called the objects the handiwork of medieval pilgrims who were filling idle hours in the Holy City. But two of these finds, the animal, middle, and the bed or couch, right bottom, closely resemble objects recently excavated in Jerusalem and Judah, objects that are securely dated to Iron Age II, eighth to seventh centuries B.C. The triangular shaped object that appears to be resting on the couch is probably medieval, and the spindle bottle, left, dates to the Hellenistic period, late first century B.C.

This photograph is all that remains of the 1904 finds. They were "so it was said . . . taken away by a 'Turkish' German officer during the First World War," Hanauer reported.

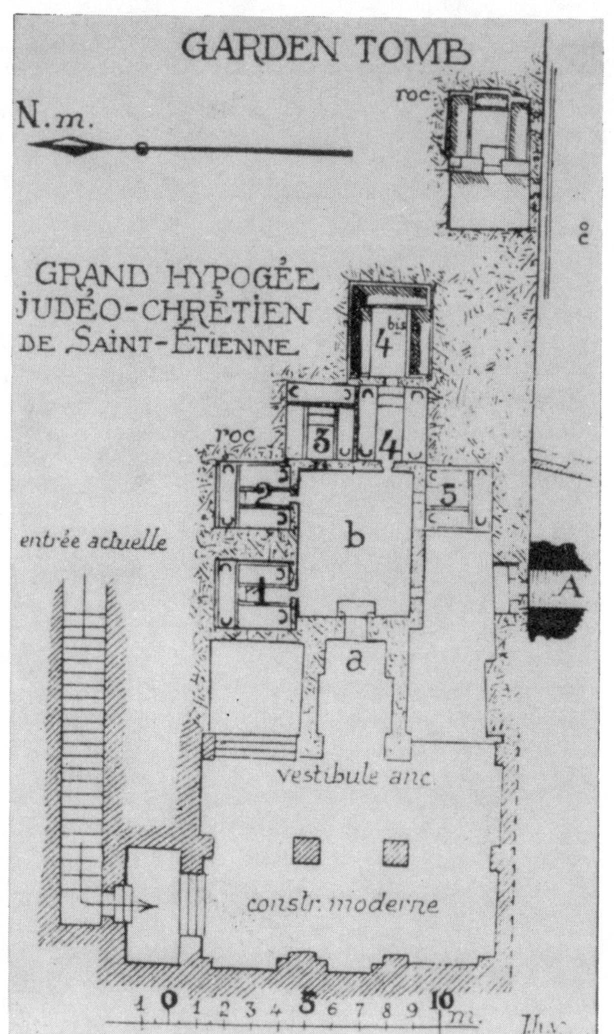

The relationship *between the two-chambered Garden Tomb and the large Cave Complex 1 at St. Étienne's monastery, separated by only two meters, is evident in this plan published by Louis-Hugues Vincent in 1925.*

vary." (Calvary is the Latin form of Golgotha.) Later the name evolved into the "Garden Tomb," perhaps because of the similarity of the words "Gordon" and "garden," but more probably because of the mention of a garden in the New Testament in connection with Jesus' burial. In John 19:41-42, we learn that "at the place where he had been crucified there was a garden, and in the garden a new tomb, not yet used for burial. There, because the tomb was near at hand and it was the eve of the Jewish Sabbath, they laid Jesus."

In 1894, the cave and the surrounding garden were purchased by the Garden Tomb Association for £2,000 sterling raised by an influential group of Englishmen that included the Archbishop of Canterbury. This association still owns and maintains the site. After the purchase, the new owners probably cleared the entire facade of the cave and removed the debris and ruins that had accumulated in front of it, although no reference to the clearing operations is made in contemporary records. The new owners also created a beautiful walled garden of moving serenity.

In 1904, Karl Beckholt, who was serving as Danish consul in Jerusalem and as warden of the Garden Tomb, conducted a small excavation in the yard of the Garden Tomb. He found some objects, which were published 20 years later by a Jerusalem scholar and Anglican clergyman named James Edward Hanauer.*[3] This 1924 publication

* One of the finds was a conical object of white stone covered with small holes resembling windows. Some scholars identified the stone as having some connection with the worship of Venus. This "Stone of Venus" and some of the other objects Hanauer published were, according to Hanauer, probably manufactured by the excavator Beckholt himself, who carved them as souvenirs for tourists. The remaining objects published by Hanauer were unearthed by Beckholt in a pit he had dug somewhere on the premises of the Garden Tomb.

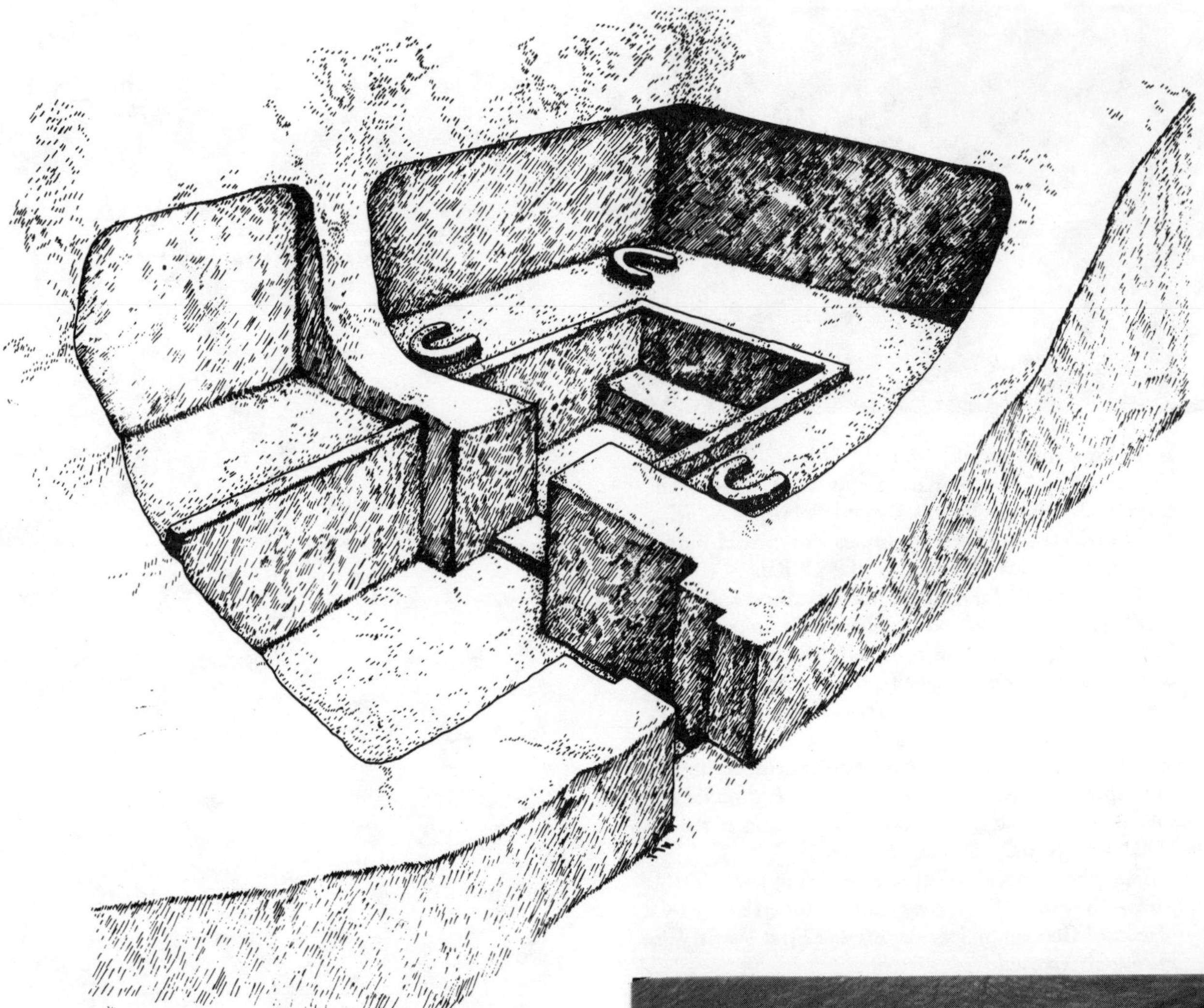

EREZ COHEN

Two-chambered Garden Tomb. *Stepping down from the entrance threshold to the northern room of the tomb, the visitor can see the adjoining southern room through a protective iron screen (right). In the Second Temple period, two-chambered burial caves were usually hewn according to a different plan: the second chamber was cut behind the first, not next to it, as is the case with the Garden Tomb. During the First Temple period, many two-chambered tombs had the rooms one beside the other.*

Originally, these chambers had burial benches with rims and horseshoe-shaped headrests (artist's reconstruction, above). In the inner chamber, steps lead up to the burial benches, where three bodies could be laid to rest. In the Byzantine period, however, these burial benches were carved out to form troughs, or sarcophagi (above, right). The two side benches were completely carved out, leaving a sarcophagus only 57 inches long between them on the far wall—sometimes explained as a burial place for a child.

The chambers have flat ceilings, unlike Byzantine period tomb chambers, which all have vaulted ceilings. Although the Garden Tomb shows clear signs of reuse during the Byzantine period, its flat ceiling is one convincing piece of evidence that it was originally hewn in a much earlier period, the Iron Age.

RICHARD NOWITZ

RICHARD NOWITZ

renewed the bitter dispute about the location of the authentic tomb of Jesus. The opposing positions were summarized in a sharply worded article written from the Catholic point of view by Louis-Hugues Vincent, one of the Dominican scholars at the École Biblique. Father Vincent, a leading scholar on the archaeology and history of Jerusalem, defended the position that the Garden Tomb was of the Byzantine period. He entitled his article "The Garden Tomb—History of a Myth."[4]

In 1955, the Garden Tomb Association sponsored a small excavation in the garden area. Unfortunately, nothing is known about this dig; it was never published.

The dispute over the authenticity of the Garden Tomb was again summarized in 1975 in a book entitled *The Search for the Authentic Tomb of Jesus* by W. S. McBirnie,[5] who advocates the Garden Tomb's authenticity. McBirnie's book, however, is not based on any archaeological information, nor is the author knowledgeable about the history of the area in ancient times.

Thus, almost all published articles dealing with the Garden Tomb from its discovery through 1975 have been polemical, written to prove certain theological presuppositions. Except for the first article by Conrad Schick, who reported the actual discovery of the cave, there has been no objective, factual and archaeological discussion of the Garden Tomb.

To understand why this is so, we need to look at the historical situation in the late 19th century. The growing western interest in the ancient Near East, the Holy Land and Jerusalem brought hordes of visitors and pilgrims who took a new and often critical approach to the traditional holy sites. More and more Protestants came to Jerusalem, and they began to question the authenticity of the holy sepulcher. Located as it is in the midst of a densely built-up area of the Old City, the Church of the Holy Sepulchre did not seem to the Protestants to be a suitable place, outside the city, as Jewish law required, where Jewish dead would have been buried in the early Roman period. The traditional site of the sepulcher within the church was in those days dark, dismal and frequently filthy. It was crowded with priests, monks and pilgrims, mainly from Eastern countries, who often bickered with each other over rights to light candles and to hold ceremonies in various parts of the church. The Protestant newcomers did not feel at home here and could not imagine that this site could be the authentic burial place of Jesus. In this frame of mind, they welcomed any suggestion locating Jesus' tomb in a place that would better fit the tastes of Protestant Westerners, especially because the Protestants were wholly without any proprietary share in the Church of the Holy Sepulchre, which was divided among the Greek Orthodox, Roman Catholic, Armenian and Coptic Churches.

The earliest recorded tradition about Jesus' burial in the Holy Sepulchre is about three centuries after the Crucifixion. The New Testament itself gives no clue whatever as to the location of Golgotha and the tomb of Jesus. The name Golgotha has not been preserved in any form in any written source in antiquity, either Jewish or non-Jewish. It is not attested in geographical names in or around Jerusalem. This was enough to lead many wishful Protestants to reject the authenticity of the Church of the Holy Sepulchre.

On the other hand, there was never any sound scientific basis for locating the tomb of Jesus in the area of the Garden Tomb. The identification of the Garden Tomb as the tomb of Jesus thus reflects the psychology and atmosphere of late 19th-century Jerusalem, rather than any new evidence—scientific, textual or archaeological.

In 1974, I decided to investigate the matter afresh. I did so in a series of visits beginning in the latter part of the year.

I have concluded that the cave of the Garden Tomb was originally hewn in the Iron Age II, sometime in the eighth or seventh century B.C. It was reused for burial purposes in the Byzantine period (fifth to seventh centuries A.D.), so it could not have been the tomb of Jesus. All lines of reasoning support this conclusion.

Although there are numerous burial caves in the area north of Damascus Gate, most of them were excavated about a 100 years ago, when archaeology was in its infancy. Modern scholars, however, have now been able to date these burial caves to the Iron Age. (See "Jerusalem Tombs From the Days of the First Temple" by the author and Amos Kloner.) In addition, a number of newly discovered burial caves have been excavated in various areas of Judah. These, too, are very well dated to the Iron Age, based on well-dated inscriptions and pottery and other artifacts found in the burial caves. All these dated caves now give us a clear picture of the architectural features and layout of Iron Age burial caves.

We now know that the area north of Damascus Gate was an extensive cemetery during the Iron Age. And the Garden Tomb cave is right in the middle of it, between the St. Étienne tombs on the north and two Iron Age tombs on the south, recently published by Amihai Mazar.[6] A chronological, as well as a geographical, link among all these tombs is certainly suggested.

Let us look more closely at some of this evidence.

In 1974-1975, Amos Kloner and I conducted an archaeological investigation and survey of two large and magnificent complexes of burial chambers in the courtyard of the Monastery of St. Étienne, just north of the Garden Tomb. Kloner, then District Archaeologist of Jerusalem, is an expert second to none on early Roman tombs in Jerusalem.

The conclusion of our work on the St. Étienne burial caves was that, contrary to earlier views dating the caves to the Roman period, these tombs date to the Iron Age—the time of the kings of Judah (eighth and seventh centuries B.C.). The Garden Tomb was probably part of the same cemetery as the St. Étienne tomb complexes. It lies only a few feet from Cave Complex Number 1 at St. Étienne and is hewn into the very same cliff.

In 1976, Amihai Mazar, whom **BAR** readers already know well,* published two burial caves near the Damascus Gate in the area just south of the cave of the Garden Tomb. These two burial caves had been discovered in 1937 during the British Mandate, but had never been published. Mazar found the unpublished data of the 1937 excavation in old Department of Antiquities records and

* See "A New Generation of Israeli Archaeologists Comes of Age," **BAR,** May/June 1984, and "Bronze Bull Found in Israelite 'High Place' From the Days of the Judges," September/October, 1983 [see Vol. I, p. 108].

A Detailed Description of the Garden Tomb Burial Cave

The burial cave at the Garden Tomb, on the western escarpment of the hill, was hewn out of limestone from the Turonian geological period.* At the Garden Tomb cave, the escarpment is about 18 feet high.

The Garden Tomb cave consists of two rooms (see pp. 236-237), an entrance chamber and an inner chamber. The two rooms are beside one another. After going into the entrance chamber (on the north), the visitor sees the inner chamber on the right (south).

The rectangular opening into the entrance chamber is about 4½ feet high and about 2½ feet wide. Originally the opening was probably smaller than it is today. The threshold of the opening is about 1½ feet above the ground outside the cave, so that the visitor must step up to go inside.

The entrance chamber itself is roughly rectangular, nearly ten feet long, nearly seven feet wide, and six feet high.

In the east wall of the entrance chamber, opposite the doorway, a horizontal line about three feet above the floor appears in the wall (see p. 236). The dressing of the rock face above this line is different from the dressing below it. Originally, below the line a rock-hewn burial bench probably extended from the wall. This burial bench was later removed, most likely in the Byzantine period.

At some later date grooves were cut vertically into the north and south walls, apparently to hold vertical slabs of stone that extended across the east side of the entrance chamber about 2½ feet from the east wall. The vertical stone slab or slabs held in these grooves created a sarcophagus-like burial trough along the east wall where the original rock-cut burial bench had been removed.

An entryway in the southern wall of the entrance chamber leads to the inner chamber. This entryway measures over 6½ feet high and is only 2 feet wide. Most of the wall separating the two chambers is missing. Part of the remaining wall west of the entrance to the inner chamber has been somewhat decreased in thickness.

More important, a large section of the western wall of the inner chamber is missing. It has been replaced by a wall of stone building blocks in which a window allows light from the garden area to penetrate the inner chamber (see photograph, p. 237). Without this built wall, the inner chamber would be open to the outside.

The floor of the inner chamber is about 8½ inches lower than the entrance chamber, so there is a step down from the entrance chamber.

With a ceiling that measures 7 feet at its highest point, the inner chamber is nearly 8 feet long and 11 feet wide.

Along each of the walls of the inner chamber, except the entry wall, are trough-shaped burial places, resembling sarcophagi, carved from the rock. The outer wall of the troughs is, for the most part, missing. The top edge of the troughs is nearly 3 feet above the floor of the inner chamber. Long grooves, flat on the bottom, were cut into the side walls to support horizontal stone slabs that once covered the burial troughs. This might indicate that these grooves for the slabs that covered the burial troughs were not of the tomb's original phase. If the slabs had been part of the original design, they would probably have been supported by ledges rather than grooves. On each of the side walls, specially carved vertical grooves were cut. Apparently, slabs once fit into these vertical grooves to form the burial space.

The trough-shaped, sarcophagus-like burial place opposite the entrance to the inner chamber is shorter than the burial places on the two side walls. Its length is 4¾ feet, compared to nearly 7½ feet for each of the two side sarcophagi. It has been suggested that this short burial place was intended for a child.

The correct explanation is as follows: Originally, in the Iron Age, three rock-cut burial benches, not troughs, lined the three walls of the inner chamber. In the Byzantine period, when the troughs were cut into the burial benches, one side bench was cut first, then the other. Thus both ends of the burial bench opposite the entrance to the inner chamber were cut off, leaving about 4½ feet of this burial bench into which to cut a burial trough.

On the eastern and southern walls of the inner chamber are Christian symbols—Greek crosses painted in dark red on the rock walls. Above the horizontal crossbar of the crosses are the Greek letters IΣ and XΣ (*iota sigma* and *chi sigma*) marked in the same red paint. *Iota* is the initial of the Greek word for Jesus; *sigma* is the last letter of the Greek word for Jesus. The *chi* stands for the initial letter for the Greek word for Christ, and the *sigma* marks again its last letter. Under the horizontal crossbar of the crosses are the letters A and Ω (*alpha* and *omega*)—the first and last letters of the Greek alphabet, recalling the passage from Revelation 21:6, "I am the Alpha and the Omega, the beginning and the end" (see also Revelation 1:8). These painted symbols clearly belong to the Byzantine (fifth or sixth century A.D.). It is significant that no earlier Christian symbols have been found, nor any evidence of Christian use of the cave before this period.—G.B.

* The escarpment runs generally north-south, winding northwest as it continues northward into the courtyard of the Monastery of St. Étienne. At the end of this northwest bend, in the courtyard of St. Étienne, lies the entrance to Burial Cave Complex Number 1—the most elaborate burial cave known from the period of the kings of Judah.

based his own conclusions on these records. Mazar reported that these burial caves were originally hewn in the Iron Age. His evidence included photographs of pottery taken *in situ* in 1937, pottery he could now identify as having typical late Iron Ag- shapes.

Moreover, not a single tomb from Second Temple times has been found in this area. Just as we now know much more about Iron Age tombs, we also know more about tombs from the Second Temple period. (Jesus lived in the late Second Temple period; the Second Temple was destroyed by the Romans in 70 A.D.) A great number of burial caves from the Second Temple period have been discovered in other areas of Jerusalem, but not one in the area surrounding the Garden Tomb. By the Second Temple period, Jerusalemites had located their cemeteries further north. The southernmost burial cave of the Second Temple period is the luxurious "Tombs of the Kings," about 1,970 feet (600 m) north of the Garden Tomb.*

An examination of various characteristics of the typical First Temple burial caves also leads to the conclusion that the Garden Tomb cave is an Iron Age tomb.

For example, let us look at the basic arrangement of the rooms or chambers. The Garden Tomb cave consists of two adjoining chambers, one beside the other. The entrance from the outside to this two-room burial cave is through the northern room. After entering this northern chamber, one sees, on the right (south), the entrance to the second room or inner chamber. Thus, both the entrance chamber and the inner chamber have one wall formed by the outer face of the escarpment. This is not a natural arrangement for a two-chamber burial tomb. We would expect the inner chamber to be cut *behind* the entrance chamber, further under the rock, rather than at the side of the entrance chamber where there would be a danger, in the course of hewing it out, of accidentally piercing and breaking through the outer wall of the escarpment. To avoid this risk, burial caves of the Second Temple period usually have the two rooms aligned one behind the other. In contrast, a number of First Temple burial caves are cut on the plan of the Garden Tomb cave—with one room beside the other. This is the case, for example, with the famous burial cave of the "Royal Steward" in the Siloam Village, east of the Temple Mount. Two inscriptions were found on the facade of this cave, which leave no doubt as to the date of this tomb. Professor Nahman Avigad identified it as the Royal Steward's tomb. The longer inscription reads as follows: "This is [the sepulcher of . . .] yahu who is over the house. There is no silver and no gold here but [his bones] and the bones of his slave-wife with him. Cursed be the man who will open this." The other inscription refers to the plan of the cave—with one room at the side of the other— *ḤDR BKTP HṢR[YḤ] (ḥeder beketeph hatzariaḥ)*, "a room at the side of the monument." This inscription was intended to prevent someone from hewing out another burial chamber beside the one visible in the outer facade, and thereby accidentally breaking into the inner chamber because he didn't know about the inner chamber hewn beside the entrance chamber.

RICHARD NOWITZ

A crudely drawn cross *marks a wall in the Garden Tomb's southern chamber. During the Byzantine period, fifth or sixth centuries A.D., the Garden Tomb was cleared of its bones and funerary offerings and was then used anew as a burial place. This Byzantine-period cross and other Christian symbols on the tomb walls (see box, p. 239) provide archaeologists with evidence to date the period of the tomb's reuse.*

Another First Temple tomb with this same plan was excavated on the slope of Mt. Zion.* In this tomb, an abundance of pottery vessels and an inscribed seal were found *in situ*, thus enabling us to date the tomb with certainty to the seventh century B.C.

Still a third burial cave with this plan was found quite near the Garden Tomb, on the premises of the convent of the White Sisters on Nablus Road. The architectural features in this tomb, such as right-angled cornices where

* The area surrounding the Garden Tomb is within the line of the Third Wall from the Second Temple period though it was built by Herod Agrippa about one decade after the crucifixion and therefore, located as it was inside the city wall, it would not have been a permissible burial area.

* D. Davis and Amos Kloner, "A Burial Cave of the Late Israelite Period on the Slopes of Mt. Zion," *Qadmoniot* XI, 41 (1978), pp. 16-19 (in Hebrew). It is known as the tomb of Ḥamîohel based on the inscription found on a small seal discovered in the cave.

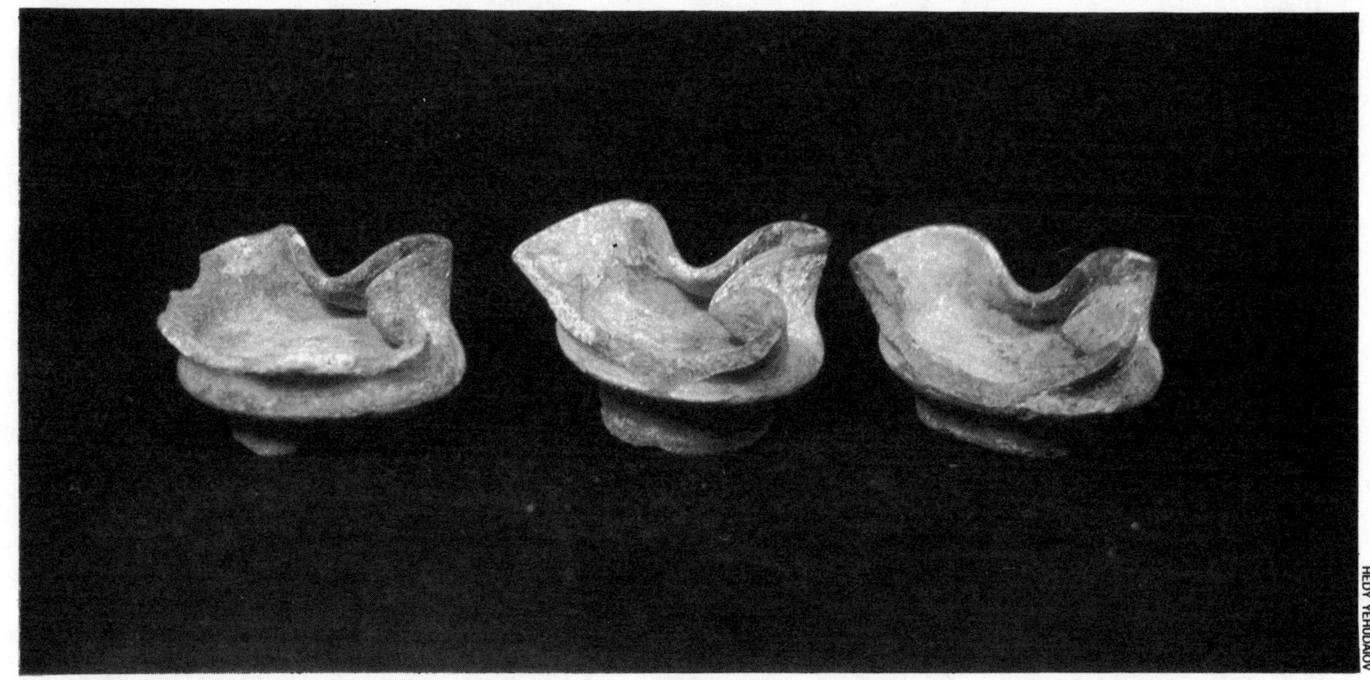

Oil lamps. ***Although their rims are partially broken, these lamps clearly display design features—pinched spouts and high pedestal bases—characteristic of Late Iron Age (seventh century B.C.) lamps in Judah. Discovered by the author in a storage closet near the cave of the Garden Tomb, the lamps may have been originally placed in the tomb during the Iron Age as funerary offerings, and removed in the Byzantine period when the tomb was cleared for reuse. Perhaps they were found in late 19th-century excavations conducted in front of the cave and then were placed in this closet.***

the walls join with the ceiling and raised burial benches, enable us to date it to the Iron Age. (This cave has not yet been published.)

A number of other burial caves from the First Temple period with this same plan have also been found outside Jerusalem—Cave Number 9 in the Iron Age II cemetery at Beth Shemesh and in a recently excavated Iron Age II burial cave at Ṣobah, west of Jerusalem.[7]

Thus, based on the plan of the rooms, the "Garden Tomb" cave appears to be a First Temple period, rather than a Second Temple period, burial cave.

A comparison of the Garden Tomb cave with the numerous Second Temple period burial caves in Jerusalem also emphasizes the very prominent differences. The outstanding characteristics of these Second Temple burial caves are burial niches (called *kokhim;* singular, *kokh*) cut vertically into the cave wall. *Kokhim* are very different structures from the burial benches extending lengthwise along the walls of the chamber, which characterize First Temple burial caves. In Second Temple burial caves we also typically find *arcosolia.* An *arcosolium* is an arch hewn into the wall of the cave forming the ceiling of a resting place or a shelf for stone coffins and ossuaries.* Finally the low burial benches in the niches of Second Temple tombs are carved around sunken floors. The Garden Tomb cave contains none of these elements of Second Temple burial caves. Another telltale sign of Second Temple tombs is evidence of the use of a so-called comb chisel, which had a toothed edge. This kind of chisel left marks that look like small parallel lines, called combing, on the rock surfaces. The Garden Tomb cave, however, contains no sign of comb chiseling. Thus, dating this cave to the Hasmonean or Herodian period (first century B.C.-first century A.D.) seems completely out of the question.

A careful examination of the carving inside the Garden Tomb cave enables us to determine the original appearance of the typical First Temple burial benches in the inner chamber of the Garden Tomb cave, although the tomb was drastically altered in the Byzantine period. Originally, the inner chamber was carved so that a rock-cut burial bench extended from each wall except the entrance wall. On entering, one would see three burial benches in the shape of a squared-off U, like this: ⊓. (See reconstruction drawing, p. 236.)

In the Byzantine period, the rock-cut burial benches on which bodies had initially been laid to rest in the Iron Age were carved out to form basins, or carved-in-place

* An ossuary is a stone box used to collect bones for secondary burial after the flesh had decayed. This was customary mainly in Jerusalem and its vicinity in the Second Temple period.

Text continues on p. 244

The Garden Tomb and the Misfortunes of an Inscription

Jerome Murphy-O'Connor, O.P.

On November 7, 1889, the *Northern Christian Advocate* (Syracuse, New York) published a note from an anonymous correspondent in Jerusalem: "There are strange rumors afloat about an inscription found at St. Stephen's [St. Étienne's monastery] (north of Damascus Gate). It is said that the Romanists are anxious to hush up the discovery, as it would damage the credit of the Church of the Holy Sepulchre. Its contents are to the following effect: 'I, Eusebius, have desired to be buried in this spot, which I believe to be close to the place where the body of my Lord lay.' "

Those who believed the Garden Tomb to be the burial place of Jesus were overjoyed. Here was unambiguous evidence that General Charles George Gordon had been correct, because St. Étienne's monastery lay immediately to the north of the Garden Tomb, the tomb Gordon had identified in 1883 as the burial site of Jesus. Protestants, who had never been permitted to worship in the Holy Sepulchre, scented victory. The pious fraud of the traditional site—the Church of the Holy Sepulchre—was on the verge of being exposed. Only this climate of thought explains why secondhand and highly dubious information printed in an obscure American newspaper should have been reproduced by the prestigious British-based Palestine Exploration Fund (PEF) for the benefit of English readers.[1] The PEF went further and commissioned Conrad Schick, a German architect living in Jerusalem, to look into the facts.

The cause of all this excitement was a thick stone slab measuring 51 inches (1.3 m) long and 31 inches (80 cm) wide. It came to light in the early summer of 1889. The French Dominicans were excavating the atrium of the church of St. Stephen, which had been built by the Empress Eudocia in 460 A.D. When they took down a large medieval wall, they found that it had been built across a Byzantine grave cut into the rock below the pavement of the atrium. The inscribed slab, set into the pavement, covered the steps leading down to the tomb. Although cracked by the weight of the wall, all the pieces of the slab were in place. The seven-line Greek inscription was intact. The many abbreviations made it difficult to read at first, but very quickly consensus emerged among the experts that the wording was:

Thēk(ē) diapher(ousa) Nonnou diak(onou)
Onis(imou) tēs hag(ias) tou Ch(risto)u
A(nastaseō)s k(ai) tēs mo(nēs) autēs.

"The private tomb of the deacon Nonnus Onesimus of the Holy Resurrection of Christ and of this monastery."

This text does not have a single word in common with the version reported in the *Northern Christian Advocate.* But it is easy to see what happened. In the Byzantine period the Church of the Holy Sepulchre was known as the Church of the Holy Resurrection. Those who had been looking desperately for evidence to support Gordon's theory heard the rumors of the discovery and took in only what suited them. It was enough that the inscription mentioned the Holy Sepulchre. On that they embroidered the version they wanted to find. If the deacon buried here served the Holy Resurrection, the nearby Garden Tomb *must* be the sepulcher of Jesus!

Far from identifying the church of St. Stephen with the Church of the Holy Sepulchre, the inscription does precisely the opposite. Nonnus Onesimus was a monk in the monastery attached to the church of St. Stephen; at the same time he served as deacon of the Church of the Holy Sepulchre (the Church of the Holy Resurrection). Such a combination was far from unusual. Cyril of Scythopolis, the sixth-century historian of Palestinian monasticism, mentions a "Gabriel who was both priest of the Holy Resurrection and superior (of the monastery) of St. Stephen" (*Life of St. Euthymius,* n. 39). The analogy with the Nonnus Onesimus inscription is striking.

As deacon of the Holy Sepulchre, Nonnus occupied the second highest position in the hierarchy of the Jerusalem church. This explains why he was granted the dignity of a private tomb where his remains could rest undisturbed.

In view of the highly acrimonious debate that developed between partisans of the Garden Tomb and the defenders of the traditional Holy Sepulchre,[2] mention must also be made of another inscription. It was found in 1885 in part of the tomb complex to which the Garden Tomb belongs, and reads simply, "Private tomb of the deacon Euthymius Pindiris." Since this contributed nothing to the proof that Gordon's supporters were seeking, it had attracted little attention. But the inscription remained a vague popular memory with bizarre consequences.

Confusion between the Nonnus inscription and the Euthymius inscription is already evident in the *Northern Christian Advocate* report. The place of discovery and the mention of the Holy Sepulchre belong to the Nonnus inscription. But the name Eusebius comes from the Euthymius inscription. There is enough similarity of sound between the elements of the two four-syllable names for the original Euthymius to be transmuted into the better known Eusebius.

Such confusion would have been impossible had the author of the *Northern Christian Advocate* report consulted the full publication of the Nonnus inscription by Father Germer-Durand in July 1889,[3] a full three months before the *Northern Christian Advocate* report appeared.

In a letter to the PEF, Professor Edward Hull proclaimed: "In my opinion the recent excavations in the neighborhood of 'Jeremiah's Grotto,' . . . all tend to confirm the view that this spot is without doubt the site of the Crucifixion and of the Holy Sepulchre."[4]

Hull's interpretation was of less consequence than the totally misleading use of the Nonnus inscription in a long, and apparently scientific, article by James Edward Hanauer, which the PEF published in 1892. As the clinching argument in favor of the Garden Tomb as the authentic Holy Sepulchre, Hanauer noted: "close by we have not only the ruins of the great church, dedicated in A.D. 460, to the proto-martyr Stephen, but also a medieval Christian cemetery known, whatever the reason may be, as that 'Of the Holy Resurrection (Anastasis) of Christ.' "[5]

The least of the errors in this statement by Hanauer is the presentation of the tombstone of the deacon Nonnus as if it was the sign over the gate of a cemetery! But that did not worry those who wanted to believe. A committee was formed in England to buy the Garden Tomb as the probable site of the Holy Sepulchre. The Archbishop of Canterbury, the Anglican bishops of Salisbury, Rochester, Ripon and

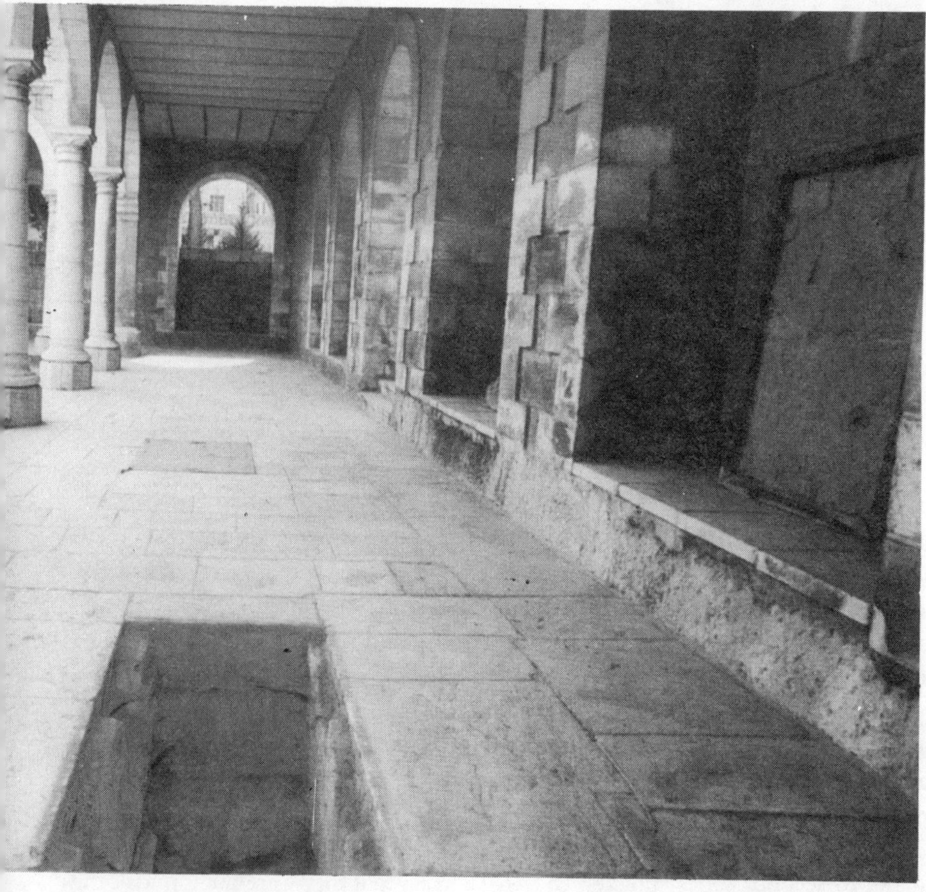
RICHARD NOWITZ

MARIE-JOSEPH LAGRANGE

St. Étienne's Church *(above) is located north of Jerusalem's Old City, just a hundred yards away from the Garden Tomb, a site that some believe to be the burial place of Jesus. In the portico surrounding St. Étienne's courtyard, steps lead down to a tomb where a Byzantine monk is buried.*

The stone slab that originally covered this tomb entrance now leans against a nearby wall, right, where its short, Greek inscription (drawing, left) can easily be read.

Cashel, and the archdeacons of London and Westminster were listed as supporters of this cause in a letter to the London *Times* (September 22, 1892) appealing for funds.[6] A wily German speculator had secured the property and was holding out for much more money than it was worth.

Religious fervor was at such a pitch that even when sanity spoke with the sonorous voice of the Thunderer it fell on deaf ears. The precise references of Claude Conder (surveyor of western Palestine for the PEF in the late 19th century) to the inscriptions that had given rise to all the trouble—"Two inscriptions giving the names of deacons of the Greek church, and, by the characters used, dating from the Byzantine period, have been found near the tomb"[7]—was ignored. Father Marie-Joseph Lagrange's detailed report in 1894 on the excavations at St. Stephen's, with a full account of the Nonnus inscription, went unread.[8] Irish archaeologist Robert Macalister's insistence that neither of the inscriptions mentioned anyone buried near his Lord was of no avail.[9]

As the arguments based on the exegesis of Gospel texts and on archaeology began to be recognized as fallacious, even to those who wanted to believe in the Garden Tomb, the argument based on the inscriptions gained in importance. It would be futile to detail all the distortions that piety demanded of facts. The culmination came in a book entitled *Palestine Depicted and Described*, published in 1911. The author, M. G. E. Franklin, claimed to have followed the excavations at the Garden Tomb from the beginning and to have participated in the discovery of the inscriptions: "Two of the slabs contained inscriptions in Greek, one referring to Nonnus and the other to Onesimus 'deacons of the Church of the Resurrection buried near my [sic] Lord.' These stones have now been placed in the land adjoining the church of St. Stephen, where they are shown to Catholic pilgrims. But they are not in their original place, since I noted their transfer."[10]

At this point farce had given way to fraud, and men of good will threw up their hands and turned to other things. The Nonnus inscription, so variously exploited in the service of a vain hope, stands today in the atrium of St. Étienne's monastery three yards from where it was discovered. Its place in the pavement has been taken by a metal plate that can be lifted with ease. In the tomb beneath rest the bones of Nonnus undisturbed by the storm that raged about his epitaph.

[1] "Notes and News," *Palestine Exploration Fund Quarterly Statement (PEFQS)*, 1890, p. 3.

[2] The ins and outs of the affair are detailed with mordant Gallic humor by Louis-Hugues Vincent, "Garden Tomb. Histoire d'un mythe," *Revue Biblique* 34 (1925), pp. 401-431.

[3] Joseph Germer-Durand, "Nouvelles Archéologiques de Jérusalem," *Cosmos*, No. 235 (July 27, 1889), p. 453.

[4] Edward Hull, letter in *PEFQS*, April 1890, p. 125.

[5] James Edward Hanauer, "Notes on the Controversy Regarding the Site of Calvary," *PEFQS*, October 1892, pp. 307-308.

[6] This letter is reprinted in *PEFQS*, January 1893, pp. 80-81, together with a selection of the letters published by the *Times* in response (pp. 81-89).

[7] Claude R. Conder, Letter to *Times* reprinted in *PEFQS*, Janaury 1893, p. 82.

[8] Marie-Joseph Lagrange, *Saint Etienne et son sanctuaire à Jérusalem* (Paris: Picard, 1894).

[9] Robert Macalister, "The Garden Tomb," *PEFQS*, July 1907, p. 232.

[10] Quoted in Vincent, "Garden Tomb," p. 422.

sarcophagi that resemble bathtubs or troughs. The carved-in-place sarcophagus opposite the entrance to the inner chamber is very short—less than 4¾ feet long on the inside. This was a result of carving out the two side burial benches to their full length, so that not enough room was left for the middle sarcophagus to extend along the full length of the wall. The traditional suggestion has been that this short resting place was intended for a child. I know of no parallel to such a short carved-out resting place.

Burial benches arranged on three walls opposite the entrance are typical of the First Temple period. Although hollowed-out sarcophagi cut into the rock, like those carved out in the Garden Tomb, are well known from the Byzantine period, in original Byzantine tombs they always appear under a vaulted ceiling, never under a flat ceiling like the ceiling in the Garden Tomb cave. Thus, on purely archaeological grounds, we can be sure that the cave was not originally hewn in the Byzantine period. Moreover, Byzantine sarcophagi are usually arranged parallel to one another, not around the three sides of the room like Iron Age burial benches. Indeed, I know of no other case where such trough-shaped sarcophagi from the Byzantine period are arranged around the room like this. It seems clear that the carving out of the rock-cut benches occurred when the cave was put to secondary use in the Byzantine period. The telltale hints of its original appearance, however, make plain that it was originally carved in the First Temple period.*

It would be nice if we knew what had been found in the Garden Tomb cave when it was cleaned and "excavated" from time to time. But our information is fragmentary at best.

I mentioned earlier that in 1924 James E. Hanauer published the results of Karl Beckholt's 1904 excavations at the Garden Tomb. Hanauer's publication includes photographs of several of the finds. In these photographs we can recognize a complete clay figurine of a four-legged animal (perhaps a horse), which is typically found in late Iron Age II sites. Such figurines have been found in other excavations both in Jerusalem and Judah. The animal figurine couldn't be accurately dated either when it was excavated by Beckholt, or when it was published by Hanauer. Now it can be dated on the basis of well-stratified and well-dated parallels. Another of Beckholt's finds was a clay model of a bed or couch, also apparently from Iron Age II.*

In the course of my own investigation of the Garden Tomb, I came across an old collection of artifacts stored in a closet at the site. These included "Greek Fire" hand grenades from the Middle Ages, pottery fragments from the Crusader period, Byzantine sherds and a sling stone shaped like a tennis ball, a type well known from Iron Age sites. Of particular importance, however, were three chipped oil lamps with thick bases, typical of the late Iron Age in Judah, and a fragment of a rim of a burnished deep bowl with a handle attached to it, belonging to the same period.

The question naturally arises as to whether these artifacts in fact came from excavations in the area of the Garden Tomb. The Iron Age finds from Beckholt's excavations in the courtyard suggest that they did.** The fact that the oil lamps were chipped and broken off, and especially the fact that a relatively small fragment of the burnished bowl rim was retained, strengthen the suggestion that this pottery was discovered at the site and was not purchased on the antiquities market. As they are, they are of little or no commerical value and would be unlikely to have been saved if they were not found at the site.

It seems likely that the closet housed a collection of items that were uncovered in excavations at the front of the cave of the Garden Tomb. It is reasonable to assume that in the Byzantine period, when many of the caves in this region were opened up for renewed use, they were cleared of bones, funerary offerings and pottery vessels in order to make room for new burials. These Garden Tomb closet artifacts were the items most probably discovered during the cleanup excavations in front of the cave conducted by the Garden Tomb Association.

If the ceramic evidence were the only basis for the dating suggested here, it would certainly be insufficient, but in conjunction with other evidence, it bears considerable weight.

On the basis of all the evidence, it seems clear that the Garden Tomb burial cave was first hewn in Iron Age II,

* Because the Garden Tomb cave was refurbished and altered for secondary use during the Byzantine period, it bears none of the other characteristics of Byzantine burial caves. Several such Byzantine caves were discovered in the courtyard of the St. Étienne Monastery near the Garden Tomb, and they all differ from the Garden Tomb cave in plan, character and architectural details.

* Hanauer also published the "Stone of Venus" I mentioned in the footnote on p. 235; Beckholt was accused of manufacturing this object himself.

** Additional support for this suggestion comes from the Late Iron Age pottery found in other excavations in the vicinity—close to the Damascus Gate in R. W. Hamilton's excavations in the 1930s, and in the German excavations under Saint Paul's Hospice adjoining the Garden Tomb, as well as in additional digs extending up to the line of the Third Wall.

the First Temple period, the eighth-seventh centuries B.C. It was not again used for burial purposes until the Byzantine period.* So it could not have been the tomb in which Jesus was buried.

* In the fifth century A.D., the Empress Eudocia (also spelled Eudoxia) built the great Church of Saint Stephen on the site of today's monastery of St. Étienne, thereby initiating a wave of development in the area. It seems that the Garden Tomb cave was emptied of its original contents at that time and prepared for use as a Christian burial site—perhaps for the clergy of St. Stephen's church. The plan of the cave was adapted to the customs of the new occupants: in place of burial benches on which to lay the deceased, burial troughs were cut out, and Christian symbols were daubed on the walls in red paint.

Still later, in the Middle Ages, the area of the Garden Tomb became a stable for the mules and donkeys of the Crusaders. To this stage, we may attribute the water cistern in the court of the Garden Tomb, as well as the soft limestone figurines of horsemen found by Beckholt in his excavations. During this period a series of vaults was built against the escarpment into which the cave is hewn. The vaults were built to create a complex of mule stables used by the Crusaders. In order to create vaults that were high enough, but would not extend above the escarpment, the Crusader builders lowered the rock surface in front of the cave entrance. As a result, today one must step up to enter the caves. Outside the entrance to the cave, a channel was cut into the rock face; this channel was most probably used in connection with the Crusader complex of vaulted structures. This late rock-cut channel was subsequently identified by 19th- and early 20th-century defenders of the authenticity of the Garden Tomb as the groove for the rolling stone covering Jesus' burial cave mentioned in the Gospels (Matthew 27:60).

[1] Conrad Schick, "Notes, Mr. Schick's Work at Jerusalem," *Palestine Exploration Fund Quarterly Statement (PEFQS)*, 1874, p. 125.

[2] Schick, "Gordon's Tomb," *PEFQS*, 1892, pp. 120-124.

[3] James Edward Hanauer, "Model of a Columbarium. An Alleged Model of a Sanctuary from the Garden Tomb Grounds," *PEFQS*, 1904, pp.143-145.

[4] Père Louis-Hugues Vincent, "Garden Tomb, Histoire d'un Mythe," *Revue Biblique* 32 (1925), pp. 401-431. Vincent argued that the tomb was Byzantine. Among those who dated it to the Second Temple period are Schick, Sir Flinders Petrie and Dame Kathleen Kenyon.

[5] W. S. McBirnie, *The Search for the Authentic Tomb of Jesus* (Montrose, California: Acclaimed Books, 1975).

[6] Amihai Mazar, "Iron Age Burial Caves North of Damascus Gate Jerusalem," *Israel Exploration Journal* 26 (1976), pp. 1-8.

[7] Kloner, "A First Temple Period Burial Cave at Ṣobah," *Hadashot Archaelogiot* 78-79 (1982), pp. 71-71 (in Hebrew).

For further reading: L. Y. Rahmani, "Ancient Jerusalem's Funerary Customs and Tombs," *Biblical Archeologist*, Summer 1981, pp. 171-177; Fall 1981, pp. 229-235; Winter 1981, pp. 43-53; Spring 1982, pp. 109-119; and A. Mazar, "Iron Age Burial Caves North of Damascus Gate Jerusalem," *Israel Exploration Journal* 26 (1976), pp. 1-8.

GARDEN TOMB ARTICLE A "REAL SHOCKER"

To the Editor:

The Garden Tomb article ("The Garden Tomb—Was Jesus Buried Here?") in your March/April issue is a real shocker. For more than 40 years, I have believed and have been teaching that this was Christ's tomb.

Franklin Lefever
Lancaster, Pennsylvania

GARDEN TOMB ARTICLE "AN OFFENSE"

To the Editor:

Most *informed* Christians are well aware that there are two tombs which are held by Catholics and Protestants (Baptists) to have received the body of Jesus when taken from the cross. My question is, why do you permit such delicate and very personal matters to be debated on the auction block of **BAR**? Aren't there any better things to write about than to dig into personal matters where they offend and damage peoples' beliefs?

Why doesn't Mr. Barkay write an expose of the Catholic tomb where they believe Jesus was buried?

I have been in each of the tombs and studied them, and to me his article is poorly researched and certainly not authentic. His article is an offense to me and every other believer, informed and uninformed, who holds the Garden Tomb in awe.

Owen E. Davis
Perrysburg, New York

THE GARDEN TOMB ASSOCIATION RESPONDS

To the Editor:

I have received several letters asking what my association feels about your article concerning the Garden Tomb.

In the field of archaeology I have no credentials to make any comment, but I do know something about the affairs of the Garden Tomb. I knew the current feature was planned, as we supplied pictures from our archives. I had also surmised that the verdict of the article would be to date the Garden Tomb as First Temple period, as this suggestion has been around for some time in Jerusalem.

We count it as a compliment that the Garden Tomb should be considered important enough to warrant "full treatment" in **BAR**.

Since the establishment of this association in 1893 we have sought to maintain the objectives defined in the Trust Deed:

> "That the Garden Tomb be kept sacred as a quiet spot, and preserved on the one hand from desecration and on the other hand from superstitious uses."

In relation to this purpose, we have sometimes suffered more from "Friends" of the Garden than from other sources!

One of your contributors has stated in another book, "It is impossible that the Garden Tomb could be the place of Christ's burial." We are content that such verbal certitude should be available for those who seek it.

If we have any disappointments over the the articles they would be:

(1) Our "skeleton in the closet" is probably the drawing by General Gordon which we have never fully understood nor accepted as relevant to our story.

(2) The "Nonnus" inscription (see "The Garden Tomb and the Misfortunes of an Inscription," Jerome Murphy-O'Connor [pp. 242-243]) was never quoted by this association as having any significance for the Garden Tomb.

(3) It is interesting to learn that Professor Barkay made a series of visits to the Garden Tomb in 1974 as no approach or request was made to our Trustees for an official investigation.

(4) The reported "sponsored excavation" in 1955 is also news to us. In the 1950s an American group called "Defenders" did help with funds to repair our cistern (we needed the water!) and their "findings" and subsequent publicity would provide material more hilarious than the Nonnus tombstone.

(5) The mention of oil lamps brings a touch of humor to the situation.They were not discovered on this site, but had belonged to an archaeological society who had been granted storage space by one of our caretakers until—after some years—we needed the room and when no one claimed the objects they remained in a corner of our premises until visitors "took" them as souvenirs.

We should want to emphasize that our ministry in this place is more concerned with the theology of Christ's Resurrection than with the archaeology of Arimathea's Tomb.

Rev. William L. White
Honorary Secretary
The Garden Tomb (Jerusalem) Association
London, England

IN DEFENSE OF THE GARDEN TOMB

To the Editor:

BAR is a fascinating magazine! And Gabriel Barkay is an able archaeologist. The article he authored with Amos Kloner on the Iron Age tombs at St. Etienne was instructive and insightful ("Jerusalem Tombs From the Days of the First Temple," March/April 1986). By contrast, his article on the Garden Tomb was unconvincing and disappointing. It did not seem to me his best work. It offered no real evidence that the Garden Tomb was cut out during the First Temple period rather than the Second Temple period, and also ignored impressive literary evidence from the New Testament in favor of the Garden Tomb being the sepulchre of Jesus.

Only about three pages of the article were devoted to the archaeology of the tomb itself. The remainder seemed overconcerned with exposing the "mystery" of General Gordon and the "psychology" of the 19th century. The "Detailed Description" on page 51 [239] lacked any reference to the outside facade of the tomb, which is so important in understanding the tomb's history. The article suggests that the Garden Tomb's close proximity to the tombs of St. Etienne (St. Stephen) is an indication that the former was cut out in the Iron Age. Illustrations and diagrams are employed to suggest that the whole area (including the Garden Tomb) was indeed one Iron Age complex. But proximity alone proves little unless supported by other similarities, and no significant similarities were exposed. In fact, the article brought to my attention a number of important dissimilarities.

The Garden Tomb boasts none of the elaborate cornices or sunken panels which were so well displayed in the article on the St. Etienne tombs. If the Garden Tomb were of the same genre as those at St. Etienne we might expect to see similar designs in the walls, but there are none. The inner chamber of the Garden Tomb has a *nefesh* (or a "soul window") which is not a feature of the St. Etienne complex; indeed, the article does not even deal with the *nefesh*.

Basic measurements of the Garden Tomb are entirely different from the St. Etienne complex. Entrances at St. Etienne were 6 feet high from the floor. By contrast the entrance to the Garden Tomb is set well above the floor, and is only 4½ feet tall. The author himself admits it was probably originally smaller (perhaps as small as 2½ feet!). It is unfortunate that the entrance to the Garden Tomb's inner chamber has been altered, so that no comparison is possible. Also, the

6-foot ceiling of the Garden Tomb's entrance chamber is much shorter than the 10-foot ceiling at St. Etienne. No dimensions were given for the height of the burial rooms at St. Etienne, but the photos indicate they are also higher than at the Garden Tomb. Certainly if the Garden Tomb were of the same period as the tombs at St. Etienne we could expect dimensional features more similar than these.

The most striking difference between the interiors of the tombs was the absence of any repository for bones in the Garden Tomb. Impressive repositories are featured in the photos from St. Etienne, and each burial room at St. Etienne had such a repository. That the Garden Tomb has none suggests it is not of the same period. Indeed, one might ask, what was to become of old bones in the Garden Tomb, since there was no repository? My guess is that they were meant to be stored in ossuaries, the small stone coffins that are a feature of the Second Temple period.

The author does make a valid point of the triple bench arrangement in the Garden Tomb's inner chamber, comparable to the triple bench plan of St. Etienne. But such an arrangement is not exclusively a First Temple period feature. Examples of triple bench chambers are also known from Second Temple period tombs, where the benches served as shelves for ossuaries. In some cases these tombs had *arcosolia* (arched niches) for the ossuaries, but in other cases, as at the Garden Tomb, they did not. The absence of *arcosolia* in the Garden Tomb may even be an indicator that the tomb was never completed, as hinted at in the New Testament.

The article points out that the Garden Tomb's inner chamber sits to the side of the entrance chamber, not behind as in many Second Temple tombs. But such an arrangement is not an ironclad requirement of Second Temple tombs. It may be that the Garden Tomb's owner knew of the close proximity of the older St. Etienne complex and did not wish to risk breaking through to it by digging behind the entrance chamber. Another possibility is that the Garden Tomb was an essentially unfinished project, as suggested above. The New Testament account of a "young man sitting on the right side" in Jesus' sepulchre would certainly coincide with the Garden Tomb's inner chamber which is also on the right.

The article also pointed out that the Garden Tomb contained no *kokhim* (perpendicular burial vaults) which are often found in Second Temple period tombs. Again, however, *kokhim* are not an inescapable feature of the period; and again, we have to consider that the Garden Tomb may never have been completed, and therefore no *kokhim* dug out. In any case, it is improbable that Jesus was laid in a *kokh*. The New Testament accounts tell of visitors peering into the sepulchre to Jesus' resting place which was visible from outside. This does not seem possible with a *kokh*.

The article's attempt to connect Iron Age lamps and other items, all found in a closet, to the interior of the Garden Tomb is a risky proposition. Mr. Barkay well knows the impropriety of judging ceramic remains out of their proper context. Who is to say where they were found? It is certainly as possible they were discovered in an area away from the tomb as that they were found inside it. As for the absence of comb chiseling, any visitor to Jerusalem can see *tons* of Second Temple period stonework devoid of comb chisel marks.

The attempt to deal with the exterior of the tomb in a footnote was disappointing. What the author calls a "Crusader channel" does not seem to go anywhere nor is it correctly cut for drainage. Much more likely is that it is a track for a huge rolling stone. The New Testament specifies a "great stone" that "rolled." It is probably not coincidental that the track is the same width as at the "Tomb of Kings" not far away. The tired and worn-out theory that the area in front of the tomb was a Crusader stable is inconceivable. The tomb was obviously used as either an early Christian shrine or a Byzantine tomb, or possibly both. When did Crusaders ever convert a Christian shrine or a Christian tomb into a stable? When did Crusaders ever lower a solid stone floor (as was laboriously done in front of the Garden Tomb track) for a structure as common as a stable? On the other hand, such labor would not be unexpected at the site of an early Christian shrine of major importance, such as the tomb of the Resurrection.

Of course, if it turns out that the Garden Tomb belongs to a period other than Jesus', it would not really matter. As the first host I ever met at the Garden Tomb expressed it: "The most remarkable thing about the tomb is that it is empty. He is arisen!" We need no shrine to know of the reality of the resurrection. To me, however, even having read Mr. Barkay's article, the Garden Tomb still remains the best candidate for the Second Temple period tomb from which the Christ rose again.

Jeffrey Chadwick
Ben Lomond LDS Seminary
Ogden, Utah

To the Editor:

In comparing the Garden Tomb with the tombs at St. Etienne, I note five points of similarity: (1) flat ceilings, (2) rectangular doorways, (3) lack of chisel marks, (4) burial troughs carved from the host rock, and (5) reuse of the tombs during Byzantine times. The fourth and fifth similarities do not directly support Mr. Barkay's dating of the Garden Tomb, however, since he argues that the burial troughs at St. Etienne were carved at the time of the tombs' construction, while the troughs at the Garden Tomb were dug out of what originally were burial shelves.

Now in the Garden Tomb I also note seven points of dissimilarity with the tombs at St. Etienne: (1) no cornices, (2) no panels, (3) differing floor levels between rooms, (4) an entrance directly from the outside, as opposed to a descending passageway carved in the rock, (5) length, breadth and height based on neither the long nor the short cubit, (6) the burial room located to the right of the entrance chamber, even though it could have been carved directly opposite the entry (in each of the St. Etienne caves, the room to the right of the entrance chamber was reserved for some function other than burial), and (7) no repository for bones.

Given these dissimilarities, it seems to me that the Garden Tomb was not formed by the same workers as those who dug the tombs at St. Etienne, in spite of proximity. The Garden Tomb carvers designed the rooms differently, used different standards of measurement, carved the floor at differing levels, omitted the extra effort of carving cornices and/or panels, and made no provision for the First Temple (and older) practice of redepositing bones in a separate burial repository.

And, if the Garden Tomb was not carved by the same workers at those at St. Etienne, can we conclude with Mr. Barkay that both were formed during the same period?

Again, my thanks for a fine publication.

Dr. John Bristow
Seattle, Washington

Does the Holy S… Mark the Burial

Dan Bahat

Since 1960, the Armenian, the Greek and the Latin religious communities that are responsible for the care of the Holy Sepulchre Church in Jerusalem have been engaged in a joint restoration project of one of the most fascinating—and complex—buildings in the world.

In connection with the restoration, they have undertaken extensive archaeological work in an effort to establish the history of the building and of the site on which it rests. Thirteen trenches were excavated primarily to check the stability of Crusader structures, but these trenches also constituted archaeological excavations. Stripping plaster from the

ɔulchre Church
ɔf Jesus?

Preceding page: *Crowded by stone buildings on all sides, the Church of the Holy Sepulchre can be identified by its prominent domes. The larger dome covers the aedicule, Jesus' tomb; the small dome stands over the intersection of the transept and the nave. Now located in the heart of the Christian Quarter of the Old City, the church seems an unlikely location for Jesus' tomb. This was true in the fourth century as well, when the site, even then within the city walls, was identified to Queen Helena as the place of Jesus' burial. The unlikely location of the site pointed out to Helena supports its authenticity, as does the fact that the site was outside the city walls during the first third of the first century, the time of Jesus' burial (see map, p. 257).*

walls revealed structures from earlier periods. A new, modern drainage system was put in place, but the work itself was also used for archaeological research. Elsewhere, soundings were made for purely archaeological purposes.

The results of all this excavation and research have now been published in a three-volume final report by Virgilio C. Corbo, professor of archaeology at the Studium Biblicum Franciscanum in Jerusalem.* Father Corbo has been intimately involved in this archaeological work for more than 20 years, and no one is better able to report on the results than he.**

Although the text itself (Volume I) is in Italian, there is a 16-page English summary by Stanislao Loffreda. Father Loffreda has also translated into English the captions to the archaeological drawings and reconstructions (Volume II) and the archaeological photographs (Volume III). So this handsome set will be accessible to the English-speaking world as well as to those who read Italian.

During the late Judean monarchy, beginning in about the seventh or eighth century B.C., the area where the Holy Sepulchre Church is now located was a large limestone quarry. The city itself lay to the southeast and expanded first westward and then northward only at a later date. The high quality, so-called meleke-type limestone has been found wherever the excavations in the church reached bedrock. Traces of the quarry have been

* *Il Santo Sepolcro di Gerusalemme, Aspetti arceologici dalle origini al periodo crociato.* Parts I-III (Jerusalem: Franciscan Printing Press, 1981-1982).

** In 1960 he was appointed archaeologist for the Latin community on the project; in 1963, for the Greek and Armenian communities as well.

Through the facade *of the Crusader church, modern pilgrims enter the Church of the Holy Sepulchre. The Crusader church was built in the 12th century on the site of the fourth-century Holy Garden, in which stood the rock of Golgotha. The Crusader church enclosed the rock within a building for the first time. As you enter the church, the rotunda surrounding Jesus' tomb (see p. 263) is on the left. Originally built around the tomb in the fourth century, the rotunda was included within the Crusader church and indeed is its focal point. Turning to the right within the Crusader church, you find a set of steps at its eastern end leading down to St. Helena's chapel where, according to tradition, she found the true cross.*

The square tower at the left of the facade is a Crusader bell tower. At the corner where the facade meets the square tower, the beginning of another decorative carved stone arch, identical to those above the two facade windows, springs to the left toward a window that no longer exists. The drawing, below, depicts in detail the decorative stone work on these arches. It is clear that the Crusaders added the bell tower after completing the facade of the church.

IL SANTO SEPOLCRO DI GERUSALEMME, VOL. II

Signs of an ancient quarry *were found everywhere beneath the Church of the Holy Sepulchre and in its vicinity. Here we see the impressions of stone blocks that were removed by the quarriers. This particular quarry is under the Chapel of St. Vartan east of St. Helena's Chapel. Pottery sherds found in the fill date the quarry to the seventh century B.C. and perhaps as much as a century earlier. The stone is a fine-quality type of limestone known as* meleke.

found not only in the church area, but also in excavations conducted nearby in the 1960s and 1970s—by Kathleen Kenyon, in the Muristan enclave of the Christian Quarter, and by Ute Lux, in the nearby Church of the Redeemer. This meleke stone was chiseled out in squarish blocks for building purposes. The artificially shaped and cut rock surface that remains reveals to the archaeologist that the area was originally a quarry. Sometimes the workers left partially cut ashlars still attached to the bedrock (Corbo photo 62). In one area (east of St. Helena's Chapel in the Holy Sepulchre Church), the quarry was over 40 feet deep. The earth and ash that filled the quarry contained Iron Age II pottery, from about the seventh century B.C.; so the quarry can be securely dated.[1]

According to Father Corbo, this quarry continued to be used until the first century B.C. At that time, the quarry was filled, and a layer of reddish-brown soil mixed with stone flakes from the ancient quarry was spread over it. The quarry became a garden or orchard, where cereals, fig trees, carob trees and olive trees grew. As evidence of the garden, Father Corbo relies on the fact that above the quarry he found the layer of arable soil.[2] At this same time, the quarry-garden also became a cemetery. At least four tombs dating from this period have been found.

The first is the tomb traditionally known as the tomb of Nicodemus and Joseph of Arimathea (No. 28 in Corbo's list). The Gospel accounts (John 19:38-41; Luke 23:50-53; Matthew 27:57-61) report that Joseph took Jesus' body down from the cross; Nicodemus brought myrrh and aloes and, together, he and Joseph wrapped Jesus' body in linen and buried him in a garden in Joseph's newly cut, rock-hewn tomb.

The tomb traditionally attributed to Nicodemus and Joseph of Arimathea is a typical *kokh* (plural, *kokhim*) of the first century. *Kokhim* are long, narrow recesses in a burial cave where either a coffin or the body of the deceased could be laid. Sometimes ossuaries (boxes of bones collected about a year after the original burial) were placed in *kokhim*.

In the course of restoration work in the Holy Sepulchre Church a hitherto unknown passage to this tomb was found beneath the rotunda.

Another type of tomb, known as an *arcosolium* (plural, *arcosolia*), was also common in this period. An *arcosolium* is a shallow, rock-hewn coffin cut lengthwise in the side of a burial cave. It has an arch-shaped top over the recess, from which its name is derived. The so-called tomb of Jesus (Nos. 1 and 2 in Corbo's plates) is composed of an antechamber and a rock-cut *arcosolium*. Unfortunately, centuries of pilgrims have completely deformed this tomb

GARO NALBANDIAN

Beneath the north wall *of the rotunda lies a tomb traditionally attributed to Nicodemus and Joseph of Arimathea. According to Gospel accounts (John 19:38-41; Luke 23:50-53; Matthew 27:57-61), Joseph took Jesus' body down from the cross and, with Nicodemus' assistance, buried him in his own newly cut tomb. Typical of first-century tombs, it has two long recesses, or* kokhim, *in which a body could be placed.*

An *arcosolium* tomb, *another typical kind of first-century tomb. A bench cut into the rock wall held the body. Over the bench, the rock was cut into an arch; hence the name* arcosolium. *This particular fourth-century example comes from the catacombs of the Via Latina in Rome; on its* arcosolium *is a depiction of the raising of Lazarus. But remains of an* arcosolium *tomb have also been found beneath the Church of the Holy Sepulchre. Early tradition identifies this tomb as that of Jesus. It is barely recognizable as a tomb, however, because over the centuries pilgrims chipped away at the rock and most of what remains has been covered by masonry.*

by pecking and chipping away bits of rock as souvenirs or for their reliquaries. Today the tomb is completely covered with later masonry, but enough is known to date it as an *arcosolium* from about the turn of the era.

A third, much larger tomb, probably of the *kokh* type was found in front of the church (in the Parvis). This tomb was greatly enlarged in Constantine's time and was used as a cistern. Very little remains of it, but Corbo's study reveals its original function as a tomb.

Finally, although not mentioned by Corbo, in the late 19th century another tomb of the *kokh* type was found in the church area under the Coptic convent.[3]

Obviously many other tombs that existed in the area were destroyed by later structures. But the evidence seems clear that at the turn of the era, this area was a large burial ground.

The tomb in front of the Church was actually cut into the rock of what is traditionally regarded as the hill of Golgotha, where Jesus was crucified. It is possible that the rocky outcrop of Golgotha was a *nefesh*, or memorial monument.* However, this hypothesis needs more study before it can be advanced with any confidence.

The next period for which we have archaeological evidence in the Holy Sepulchre Church is from the period of the Roman emperor Hadrian. In 70 A.D. the Romans crushed the First Jewish Revolt; at that time they destroyed Jerusalem and burned the Temple. Less than 70 years later, in 132 A.D., the Jews again revolted, this time under the leadership of Rabbi Akivah and Bar Kokhba. It took the Romans three years to suppress the Second Jewish Revolt. This time, however, the victorious Roman emperor Hadrian banned Jews from Jerusalem and trenched around it a *pomerium*, a furrow plowed by the founder of a new city to mark its confines. To remove every trace of its Jewish past, Hadrian rebuilt Jerusalem as a Roman city named Aelia Capitolina. (For the same reason, he also changed the name of the country from Judea to Palaestina or Palestine.)

On the site of the former seventh-century B.C. quarry and first-century B.C. orchard-garden and cemetery, where the Holy Sepulchre Church was to be built, Hadrian constructed a gigantic raised platform—that is, a nearly rectangular retaining wall filled with earth. On top of the platform, he built a smaller raised podium, and on top of the podium, he built a temple. Although the

* *Nefesh* literally means "soul." In rabbinic literature, it also refers to a monument constructed over a grave as a memorial to the deceased. In contemporaneous Greek inscriptions, the equivalent term is *stele*.

Plan of Hadrian's pagan temple. ***Built by the Roman emperor in the second century A.D., this temple stood where, two centuries later, the Church of the Holy Sepulchre would be built by Constantine. The reconstruction is by Father Corbo, who proposes that Hadrian's temple included a tripartite rectangular structure with three niches in which stood statues of Venus, Minerva and Jupiter. BAR's reviewer Dan Bahat suggests that Hadrian's temple may well have been a rotunda, similar to the Roman temple on page 261, top, rather than a rectangular structure, and that the Hadrianic rotunda was probably dedicated to Venus/ Aphrodite, rather than Jupiter, Venus and Minerva, as argued by Father Corbo.***

Of special interest is Wall 408, lower right. This is an extant portion of the Hadrianic enclosure wall. The small white indentations on the south (outer) side of that wall indicate that the wall had pilasters, or engaged columns, protruding from the wall as they did on the outer wall of Herod's Temple Mount. One of the pilasters from Wall 408 may be seen in the photograph at the right (bottom).

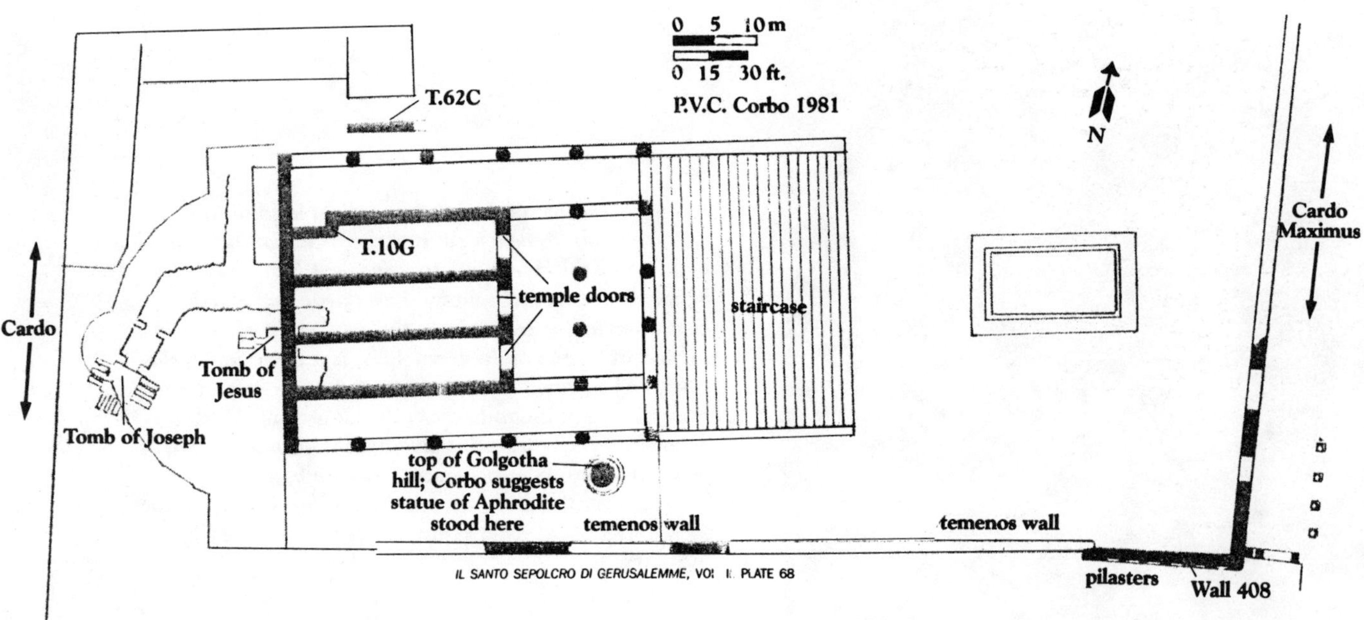

remains of the Hadrianic wall enclosing the platform are scant, its existence is clear.

Because the area had been dug as a quarry and because it had also been honeycombed with tombs and was left with depressions and protrusions of uncut rock, the building of this platform was necessary to create a level construction site.

Many of the ashlars* used by Hadrian for the retaining wall of the platform were actually old Herodian ashlars—

* An ashlar is a stone carved as a square or polygon in order to fit it into a construction.

Typical Herodian ashlars *or squared blocks of stone. The stones seen here form part of the enclosure wall of the Temple Mount platform. In the second century, the Roman emperor Hadrian used ashlars like these to build a wall enclosing a platform on the site where the Church of the Holy Sepulchre would later stand.*

GARO NALBANDIAN

Large stones *from Hadrian's enclosure (above the right edge of the staircase) were found in excavations east of the Church of the Holy Sepulchre. On several blocks the narrow margins and flat central bosses are easily seen. These ashlars come from the part of the enclosure where a pilaster began (see Wall 408 on plan, left). The pilaster is seen on top of an inwardly angled stone above steps 10-12, counting from the bottom of the staircase. This small section of Hadrian's enclosure wall, which provided a platform for a temple to a pagan goddess, demonstrates that Hadrian probably imitated the Herodian enclosure about the nearby Jewish Temple Mount.*

IL SANTO SEPOLCRO DI GERUSALEMME, VOL. III, PHOTO 120

GARO NALBANDIAN

left after the Roman destruction of Jerusalem and Herod's temple in 70 A.D. They are identical in size and facing to the Herodian ashlars in the retaining wall of the Temple Mount. Hadrian's wall therefore looked like a Herodian wall—much like the famous Western Wall of the Temple Mount which is, even today, a focus of Jewish reverence.

Although not mentioned by Corbo, the upper part of Hadrian's retaining wall even had slightly protruding pilasters or engaged pillars along the outer face of the upper part of the wall, thereby creating the appearance of regularly spaced recesses. (This can be seen in the photograph on p. 255, bottom, and on Wall 408 of Corbo's plan, p. 254.) The Hadrianic enclosure thus duplicated the Herodian Temple Mount enclosure, although unfortunately the latter did not survive to a height that included these pilasters, except in traces. This style can be seen, however, in the Herodian wall enclosing the traditional tomb of the patriarchs (the cave of Machpelah) at Hebron.*

The fact that Hadrian appears to have deliberately attempted to duplicate the Herodian enclosure at the Temple Mount has special significance. Instead of a temple to Yahweh, however, Hadrian built on his raised enclosure an elaborate temple to the goddess of love, Venus/Aphrodite.

* See Nancy Miller, "Patriarchal Burial Site Explored for First Time in 700 Years," **BAR**, May/June 1985, especially p. 31.

Built by Herod the Great, ***this monumental enclosure in Hebron encases the traditional burial site of the patriarchs Abraham, Isaac and Jacob and their wives Sarah, Rebekah and Leah. The only Herodian structure intact today, its design is identical to the enclosure Herod built about the platform of the Temple Mount in Jerusalem. Unfortunately the Jerusalem enclosure wall can no longer be seen in its original splendor. Both enclosures were built of beautifully dressed blocks of stone with narrow margins and flat central bosses. About half-way up the wall, pilasters protrude slightly from the face of the wall.***

In the second century, when the Roman emperor Hadrian built an enclosure on the Jerusalem site that would someday be the Church of the Holy Sepulchre, he built it with exactly the same design, including the pilasters that began part way up the wall. He even reused stones from Herod's Temple Mount, which the Romans had partially destroyed in 70 A.D. On the platform created by this enclosure, in imitation of the Jewish Temple Mount, Hadrian built a temple dedicated to the goddess Venus/Aphrodite.

Corbo refers to Hadrian's temple as Capitolium, that is, dedicated to Jupiter the Capitoline. For this, he relies on the fifth-century testimony of Jerome who mentions a Jerusalem temple dedicated to Jupiter. However, Eusebius in the fourth century tells us Hadrian's temple at this site was dedicated to Venus/Aphrodite. There is no reason for Corbo to choose Jupiter over Venus/Aphrodite, especially because Dio Cassio in the third century fixes the site of the temple of Jupiter on the site of the former Jewish Temple, that is, on the Temple Mount. That is the temple Jerome is referring to. A number of other ancient writers from the fifth century on refer to a temple of Venus/Aphrodite on the site where later the Church of the Holy Sepulchre was built.

To support his attribution to Jupiter, Corbo claims to have found in the rotunda of the church two fragments from a triple cella that would have accommodated statues of the Capitoline triad, Venus, Minerva and Jupiter. There is no basis, however, for suggesting that these fragmentary remains are part of a triple cella—or even that they are part of the pagan temple itself. As so often in this report, Corbo's assertion as to the date of walls is merely that—pure assertion. No evidence is given.

Parts of Hadrian's enclosure wall have survived. According to Corbo, fragments of other walls, found in cisterns and in what was the first-century B.C. garden, belonged to the substructure of Hadrian's temple (see p. 262, bottom). But for this, as before, we must rely solely on Corbo's assertion. He presents no evidence on which his conclusions can be tested. In any event, nothing of the visible parts of Hadrian's temple has been discovered. As we know from historical sources, it was razed to the ground by Constantine, so there is no hope of recovering it. Likewise, the small podium on which the temple sat, on top of the enclosure platform; the podium too has vanished without a trace.

Corbo's reconstruction of the Hadrianic temple is thus completely speculative—and unsatisfactory. In the first place, he assumes it was a three-niche structure pursuant to his mistaken theory that it was dedicated to Jupiter the Capitoline rather than Venus/Aphrodite.* But, in any event, there is no known parallel to Corbo's plan.**

Queen Helena, Constantine's mother, was shown the site on her visit to Jerusalem in 326 A.D. We do not know in what condition the site was at this time. Perhaps the pagan temple constructed by Hadrian was already in ruins—destroyed by zealous Christians.

After Queen Helena's visit, the Christian community proceeded to remove whatever was left of the Hadrianic temple, as well as the Hadrianic enclosure and the fill it contained. For the Christian community, this fill, intended by Hadrian to create a level surface for building, represented Hadrian's attempt to obliterate forever not only Jesus' tomb, but the adjacent rock of Golgotha where he had been crucified.

According to literary sources† Constantine built a rotunda *around* Jesus' tomb. In front of the rotunda was the site of the crucifixion (Golgotha or Calvary), in what is referred to in ancient literary sources as the Holy Garden. On the other side of the garden, Constantine

* Moreover, in the reconstruction itself, Wall T 62 C has no function. Wall T 10 G with two angles makes no sense at all.

** If Corbo intended as his model the Maison Carée in Nîmes, France, or the Temple of Fortuna in Rome, both of which were contemporaneous with Hadrian's temple on the site of the future Church of the Holy Sepulchre, Corbo failed to follow his models. The staircase should not occupy the whole breadth of the structure; behind the six interior columns there should be two additional columns enclosed in two *antae*, arm-like walls that extend from the main walls of the structure; and the lateral columns should not be freestanding, but only half columns attached to the side walls.

† Especially Eusebius, *Life of Constantine* (Palestine Pilgrims Texts Society, Vol. I, 1891), pp. 1-12.

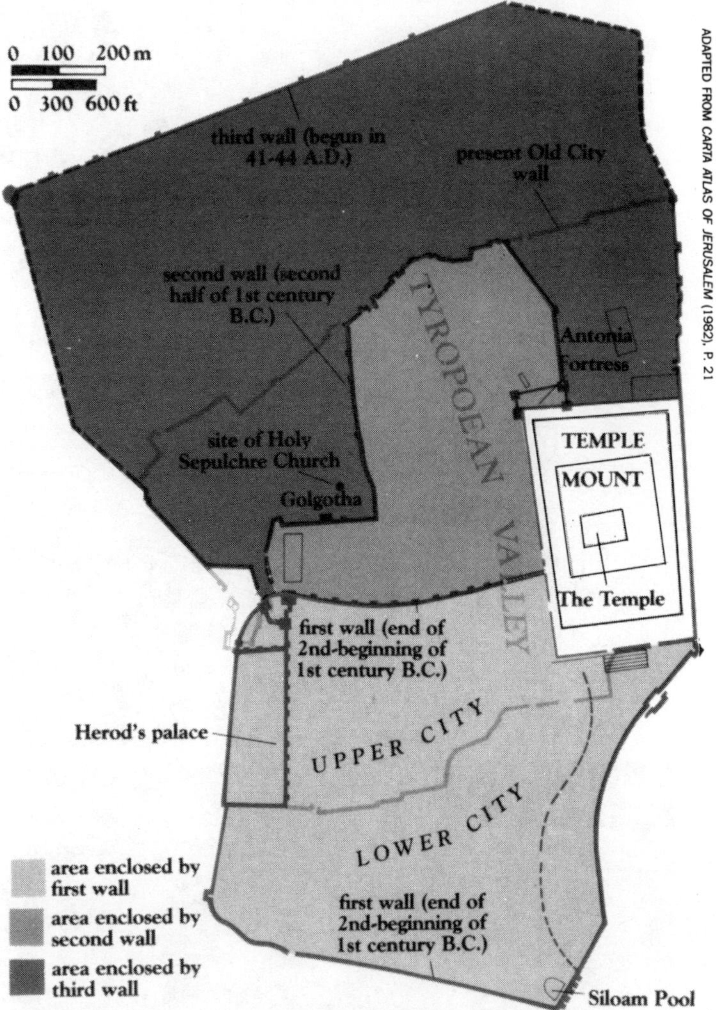

The Church of the Holy Sepulchre *in relation to nearby city walls. The so-called Third Wall was built by Herod Agrippa between 41 and 44 A.D., shortly after Jesus' crucifixion. At the time of the crucifixion, however, the site of Golgotha was outside the city wall—or "near the city," as Golgotha is described in John 19:20.*

Jerusalem on the Madaba map *(top). This mosaic depiction of sixth-century Jerusalem's streets and buildings includes the Holy Sepulchre Church. According to Dan Bahat, the details shown are those from Constantine's church, still standing when this mosaic was laid on the floor of a church in today's Jordan. The Holy Sepulchre Church is the large upside-down domed structure perpendicular to the Cardo, the colonnaded main thoroughfare running from right to left across the center of the city. The church is midway along the Cardo, interrupting the lower row of columns. Four steps abut the Cardo's central roadway. Below the full map is an enlarged detail of the church, rotated 90° to the left so that its orientation is the same as the plan (right). Referring to the detail, we may observe the following features from right to left: the steps; doorways—probably those shown in the plan between the atrium and the steps; a triangular gable with a central rhomboid window pointing into the basilica roof; five black tesserae between the roof and the dome at far left, possibly representing the Holy Garden; and the dome—probably the one covering the rotunda that surrounded the tomb of Jesus in the Constantinian church.*

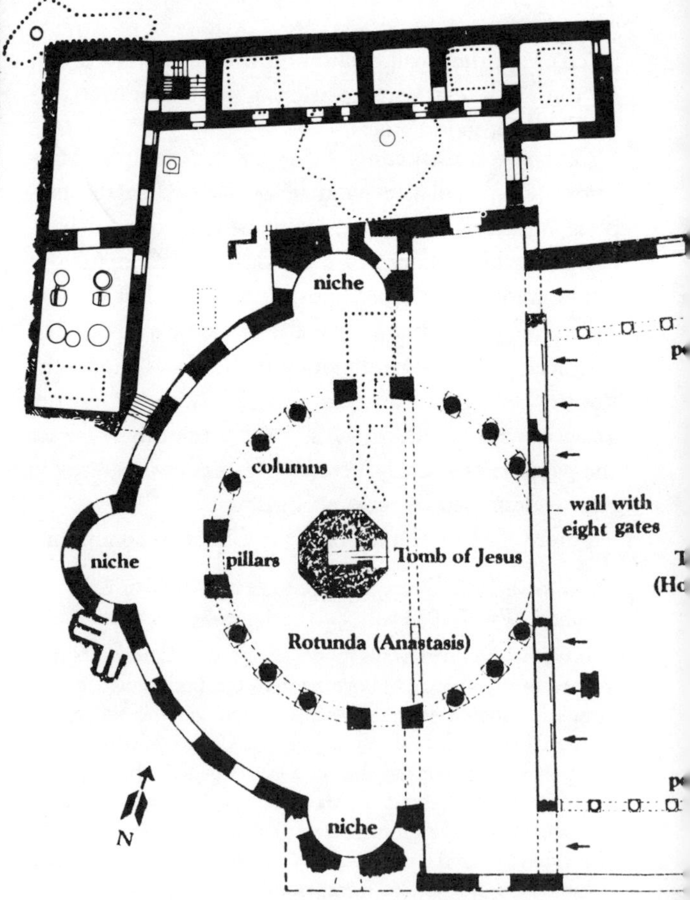

built a long church in the shape of a basilica, consisting of a nave and side aisles separated from the nave by rows of columns. Here the faithful could offer prayers. Between the rotunda and the basilica lay the hill of Golgotha.

Was the Constantinian rotunda actually built over the true site of Jesus' burial?

Although we can never be certain, it seems very likely that it was.

As we have seen, the site was a turn-of-the-era cemetery. The cemetery, including Jesus' tomb, had itself been buried for nearly 300 years. The fact that it had indeed been a cemetery, and that this memory of Jesus' tomb survived despite Hadrian's burial of it with his enclosure fill, speaks to the authenticity of the site. Moreover, the fact that the Christian community in Jerusalem was never dispersed during this period, and that its succession of bishops was never interrupted supports the accuracy of the preserved memory that Jesus had been crucified and buried here.

Perhaps the strongest argument in favor of the authenticity of the site, however, is that it must have been regarded as such an unlikely site when pointed out to Constantine's mother Queen Helena in the fourth century. Then, as now, the site of what was to be the Church of the Holy Sepulchre was in a crowded urban location that must have seemed as strange to a fourth-century pilgrim as it does to a modern one. But we now know that its location perfectly fits first-century conditions.

In the fourth century this site had long been enclosed within the city walls. The wall enclosing this part of the city (referred to by Josephus as the Third Wall) had been built by Herod Agrippa the local ruler who governed Judea between 41 and 44 A.D. (see map, p. 257). Thus, this wall was built very soon after Jesus' crucifixion—not more than 10 or 15 years afterward. And that is the crucial point.

When Jesus was buried in about 30 A.D., this area was outside the city, in a garden, Corbo tells us, certainly in a cemetery of that time. These are the facts revealed by

Plan of the Constantinian complex *from the fourth century. Black areas indicate extant remains. Dotted structures are those assumed but not found. The rotunda, with columns and pillars surrounding Jesus' tomb and three niches in the outer wall, is at far left. This rotunda probably resembled the one in Rome shown on page 261, part of a mausoleum for Constantine's daughter. The Holy Garden with a colonnaded portico on three sides is the nearly rectangular area to the right of the rotunda; the two are separated by an eight-gated wall (indicated by arrows). In the southeast corner of the Holy Garden is the rock of Golgotha or Calvary. To the right of the Holy Garden is the basilica church with a single apse toward the rotunda, and a nave with two aisles on either side. In front of the basilica is an atrium, or narthex. A set of steps leads down to the city's major north-south thoroughfare, the Cardo. At the eastern end of the basilica church, Nos. 307, 308 and 309 indicate subterranean cavities that—in part—became chapels at the time of the Crusaders. Several features of Constantine's church are represented schematically in the Madaba map (left).*

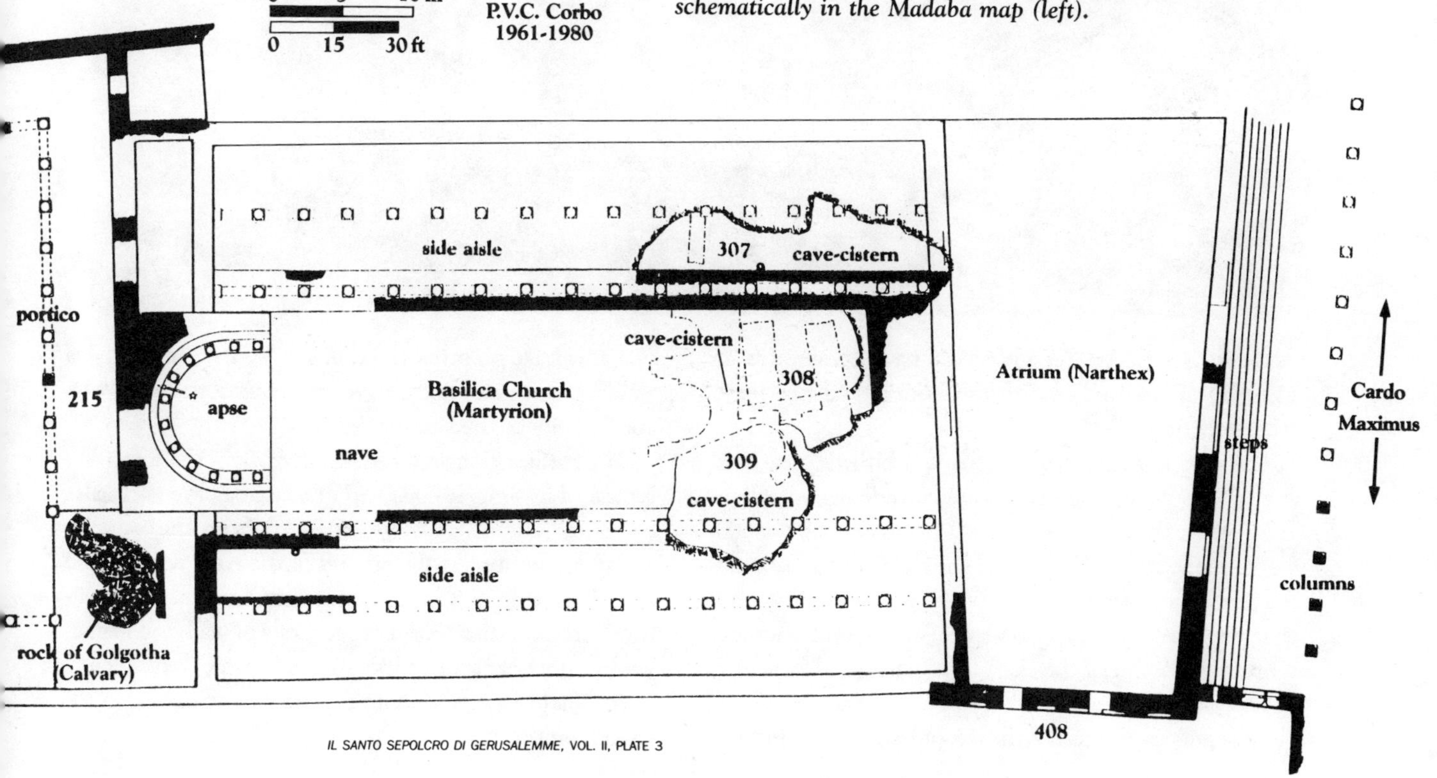

IL SANTO SEPOLCRO DI GERUSALEMME, VOL. II, PLATE 3

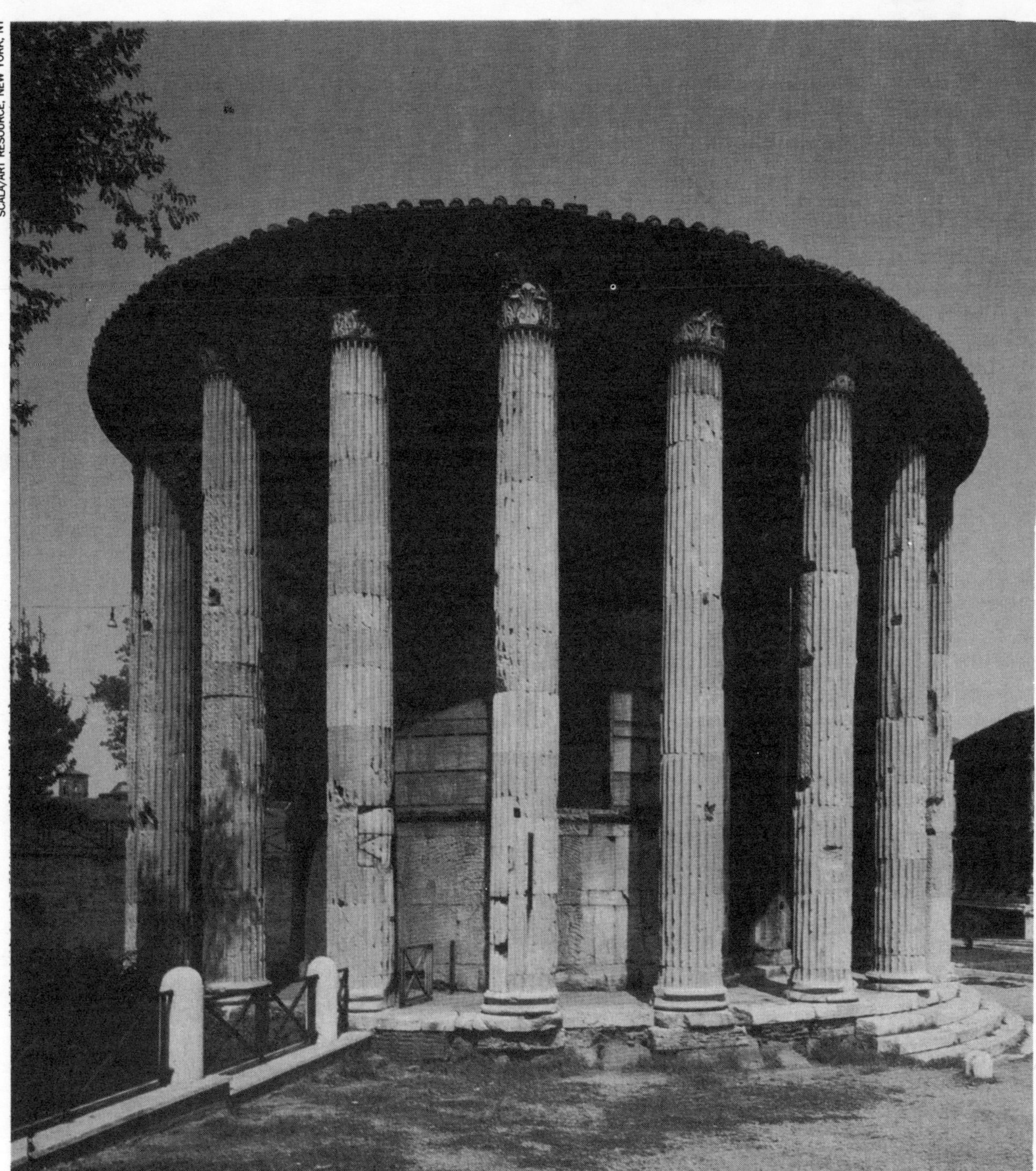
SCALA/ART RESOURCE, NEW YORK, NY

modern archaeology. Yet who could have known this in 325 A.D. if the memory of Jesus' burial had not been accurately preserved?

The Gospels tell us that Jesus was buried "near the city" (John 19:20); the site we are considering was then just outside the city, the city wall being only about 500 feet to the south and 350 feet to the east. We are also told the site was in a garden (John 19:41), which is at the very least consistent with the evidence we have of the first century condition of the site.

We may not be absolutely certain that the site of the Holy Sepulchre Church is the site of Jesus' burial, but we certainly have no other site that can lay a claim nearly as weighty, and we really have no reason to reject the authenticity of the site.

The basilica Constantine built in front of the tomb was typical of its time. It consisted of a center nave and aisles on either side of the nave separated from the nave by rows of columns. At the far end of the nave was a single apse. Unfortunately hardly a trace of Constantine's basilica church remains. From the sections of wall discovered, we can only confirm its location and former existence.

Behind (west of) Constantine's basilica was a large open garden on the other side of which, in the Rotunda, stood

A first-century B.C. round temple *(left). Already 200 years old when Hadrian built his temple in Jerusalem, this structure in the Forum Boarium in Rome is evidence that Hadrian knew round temple structures. Dedicated to Hercules Victor, this temple adds plausibility to Bahat's suggestion that Hadrian's Jerusalem temple was also round.*

A mausoleum for Constantine's daughter *(below). The rotunda of this elegant fourth-century Church of Santa Costanza in Rome may resemble the contemporaneous rotunda in Jerusalem surrounding Jesus' tomb in the Church of the Holy Sepulchre.*

More than 1,000 years after Costanza's mausoleum was built, an engraver named De Bruyn depicted the Holy Sepulchre Church rotunda (right). Here, in his work from 1681, we see that the round enclosure—probably first built by Constantine in the fourth century—persists in the Crusader reconstruction of the church.

IL SANTO SEPOLCRO DI GERUSALEMME, VOL. III, PHOTO 20

Broken columns lie *in a trench about two feet below the 12th-century Crusader pavement of the present church. Father Corbo suggests that these neatly packed sections—found below the northern side aisle of the Crusader basilica—were part of the fourth-century open-air portico built by Constantine surrounding the courtyard of the Holy Garden.*

Archaeological remains from Constantine's church *are identified by Corbo in this photograph.* A *is a section of the eastern stylobate, or column-bearing wall, of the triportico. The column base seen in the center is column 215 noted on the plan on pages 258-259.* B *designates the western edge of the apse of the basilica church.* C *and* D *are later structures;* E *is identified by Corbo as a second-century Hadrianic wall, cut by the later stylobate.*

IL SANTO SEPOLCRO DI GERUSALEMME, VOL. III, PHOTO 88

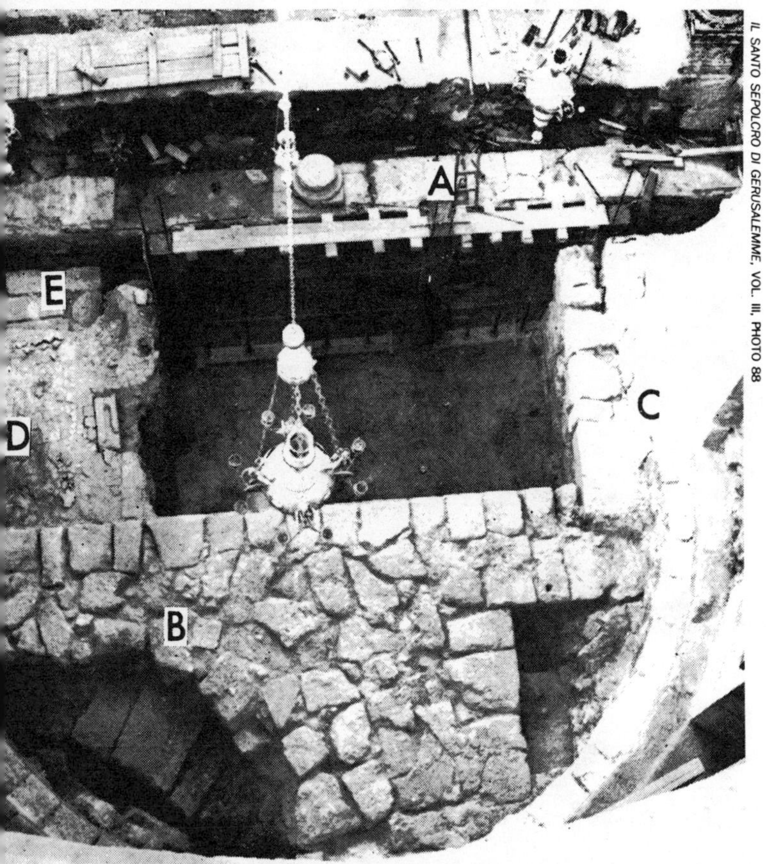

the tomb of Jesus. The apse of the basilica faced the tomb. Two principal scholars involved in the restoration disagree as to when the tomb was enclosed by a large, imposing rotunda. Corbo takes one view; Father Charles Coüasnon takes another. Coüasnon, who died in 1976, had been the architect of the Latin community in connection with the restoration work. In 1974 he published a preliminary report of the excavations, entitled *The Church of the Holy Sepulchre in Jerusalem*, (London: Oxford University Press).*

According to Coüasnon the tomb was set in an isolated square niche annexed to the Holy Garden. Coüasnon believed the tomb remained exposed to the open air until after Constantine's death, at which time the rotunda was built around it, leaving the Holy Garden between the rotunda and the back of Constantine's basilica church.

This view is rejected by Corbo who is probably correct. According to Corbo, the rotunda was part of the original Constantinian construction and design. Unfortunately, from the nature of Corbo's excavation methodology and the limited archaeological evidence in this report, it is impossible to check his dating of walls.

There is one argument Corbo fails to make, however, that might well support his position; many temples to goddesses (like Venus/Aphrodite) are round, in the form of rotundas. If it is true, as Eusebius says, that Hadrian had built a temple to Venus/Aphrodite here, it was quite probably a round temple. The Christian rotunda may well have been inspired by this pagan rotunda. (The phenomenon of a holy site from one religion being maintained as holy by subsequent religions was a common one throughout the ancient world.) If the architecture of Hadrian's pagan rotunda inspired the rotunda around Jesus' tomb, it is more likely that the later rotunda was built by Constantine himself, not by a later ruler who would not have known the pagan rotunda.

Two original columns of the rotunda built around Jesus' tomb have been preserved. Father Coüasnon suggested they were two halves of what was once a single, tall column. According to Coüasnon, this column had previously served in the portico of the Hadrianic temple; the two halves were later reused in the rotunda. In this, he is probably correct.

* See J.-P. B. Ross, "The Evolution of a Church—Jerusalem's Holy Sepulchre," **BAR**, September 1976.

The present rotunda, *often called the Anastasis ("resurrection"), is the focal point of the Church of the Holy Sepulchre. The rotunda encloses the reconstructed tomb of Jesus, shown here. The rotunda, too, has been recently reconstructed incorporating some earlier elements.*

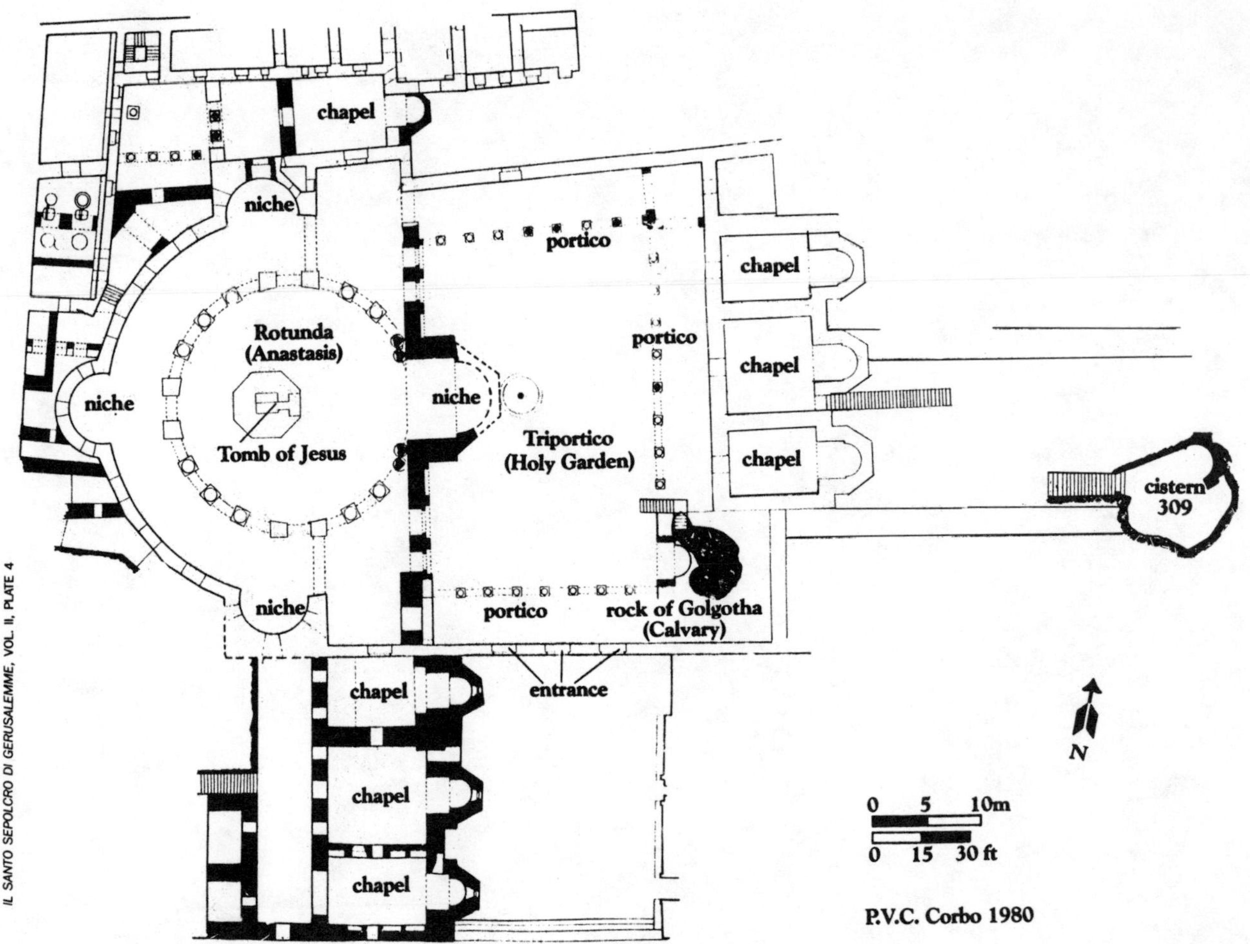

Plan of the 11th-century reconstruction *of the Church of the Holy Sepulchre, by Constantine IX Monomachus. This restoration—completed in 1048—followed the destruction of the church in 1009 by the Fatimid Caliph, El Khakim. Extant structures appear here as solid black areas. The rotunda was reconstructed and an additional niche added on the east. The Holy Garden was also retained. The Constantinian basilica, however, almost disappeared. In its place, east of the Holy Garden, were three chapels, known only from literary sources. A second group of three chapels was built south of the rotunda, and another chapel was added north of the rotunda. The entrance to the complex was from the south into the Holy Garden. The present entrance is in the same place.*

On the side of the niche that marked Jesus' tomb, a drain had been cut in the rock, apparently to allow the flow of rain water from the tomb. This might indicate that at least for some time the tomb stood in the open air. How long we cannot know.

In any event, a rotunda was soon built around the tomb where the current reconstructed tomb—the focus of the present church—now stands. This rotunda is often referred to, both now and in historical records, as the Anastasis ("resurrection").

Between the rotunda and the basilica church was the Holy Garden. According to Coüasnon, the Holy Garden was enclosed on all four sides by a portico set on a row of columns, thus creating a colonnaded, rectangular courtyard. Beyond the porticoed courtyard, on the rotunda side, was a wall with eight gates that led to the rotunda. Corbo, on the other hand, reconstructs columns on only three sides. (Thus, he calls the garden courtyard the *triportico.*) Corbo would omit the portico on the rotunda side, adjacent to the eight-gated wall. He is probably right.

Thus the complex of the Church of the Holy Sepulchre stood until the Persian invasion of 614 A.D. At that time it was damaged by fire, but not, as once supposed, totally destroyed. When the Persians conquered Jerusalem, they destroyed many of its churches, but not the Holy Sepulchre.

The situation was different, however, in 1009 A.D. On the order of the Fatimid Caliph of Cairo, El Khakim, the entire church complex—the basilica, the rotunda, the tomb inside the rotunda and the portico between the rotunda and the basilica—was badly damaged and almost completely destroyed.

The basilica was gone forever, razed to the ground. Only the 1968 discovery of the foundation of the western apse of the basilica allows its placement to be fixed with certainty (although previous reconstructions had fixed its location correctly).

The rotunda, however, was preserved to a height of about five feet. Between 1042 and 1048 the Byzantine emperor Constantine IX Monomachus attempted to restore the complex. He was most successful with the rotunda, which was restored with only slight change (see plan, p. 264). Where the Constantinian rotunda had three niches on three sides, Monomachus added a fourth. This new niche was on the east side, the direction of prayer in most churches. The new niche was the largest of the niches and was no doubt the focus of prayer in the rotunda.

In front of the rotunda, Monomachus retained the open garden. One of the old colonnades (the northern one) was rebuilt by him and has been preserved to the present time, thus enabling us to study the character of Monomachus's restoration.

Instead of a basilica, Monomachus built three groups of chapels. One group, consisting of three chapels, abutted the old baptistery; a second group, also consisting of three chapels, was built near the site of the apse of the destroyed basilica (this group is known from historical documentation only); and the third consisted of a chapel north of the rotunda.

In the course of his reconstruction, Monomachus discovered a cistern where, according to tradition, Queen Helena had discovered the True Cross. Corbo believes, probably correctly, that this tradition originated only in the 11th century. (On archaeological grounds, the cistern dates to the 11th or 12th century.) Moreover, nothing was built to commemorate Helena's supposed discovery of the True Cross here until even later, in the Crusader period. Coüasnon, on the other hand, believed the tradition that Queen Helena found the True Cross here dated from Constantinian times. According to Coüasnon, Constantine built a small crypt in the cave-cistern. Coüasnon recognized, however, that the current chapel of St. Helena dates to the Crusader period. At that time, the famous chapel of St. Helena, which is a focus of interest even now, was constructed partially in and partially adjacent to the cistern.

Overleaf: ***The Crusader Holy Sepulchre Church. The form of the church as we know it today is that given it in the 12th century by the Crusaders. The rotunda encloses the tomb of Jesus as before, but now for the first time the rock of Golgotha is enclosed within the church. In the area of the porticoed Holy Garden, the Crusaders built a basilica with a nave, a transept and a high altar at its eastern end.***

In the area of the subterranean cisterns on the eastern end of the complex, three chapels were constructed: the chapels of St. Helena, of the Finding of the True Cross and of St. Vartan. Signs of an ancient quarry may be seen in St. Vartan's chapel (see p. 252).

The Crusaders, who ruled Jerusalem from 1099 to 1187, also rebuilt the church, essentially in the form we know it today. The rotunda (or Anastasis) enclosing the tomb was maintained as the focus of the new structure. In the area of the porticoed garden in front of the rotunda, the Crusaders built a nave with a transept, forming a cross, and installed a high altar.

The traditional rock of Golgotha, where Jesus had been crucified, was enclosed—for the first time—in this church. In Hadrian's time, the rock of Golgotha had protruded above the Hadrianic enclosure-platform. According to Jerome, a statue of Venus/Aphrodite was set on top of the protruding rock. This statue was no doubt removed by Christians who venerated the rock. When Constantine built his basilica, the rock was squared in order to fit it into a chapel in the southeast corner of the Holy Garden. As noted, in the Crusader church the rock was enclosed in a chapel within the church itself. The floor level of this chapel, where the rock may still be seen, is almost at the height of the top of the rock. Because of this, a lower chapel, named for Adam, was installed to expose the lower part of the rock. This lower chapel served as a burial chapel in the 12th century for the Crusader kings of the Later Kingdom of Jerusalem. These tombs were removed after the great fire of 1808.

Father Corbo's book may well be the last word on the Church of the Holy Sepulchre for a long time to come. Despite its monumental nature, it is, alas, not beyond criticism. It is in no sense an archaeological report, despite the reference in the title of Corbo's book to the "archaeological aspects" of the site. Almost no finds are described and it is impossible to understand from Father Corbo's plates and text why a particular wall is ascribed to one period or another. This is a pity. Precise descriptions of these finds and their loci would have increased our knowledge significantly, not only with respect to the history of the church, but also with respect to the study of medieval pottery, coins and other artifacts. It is also

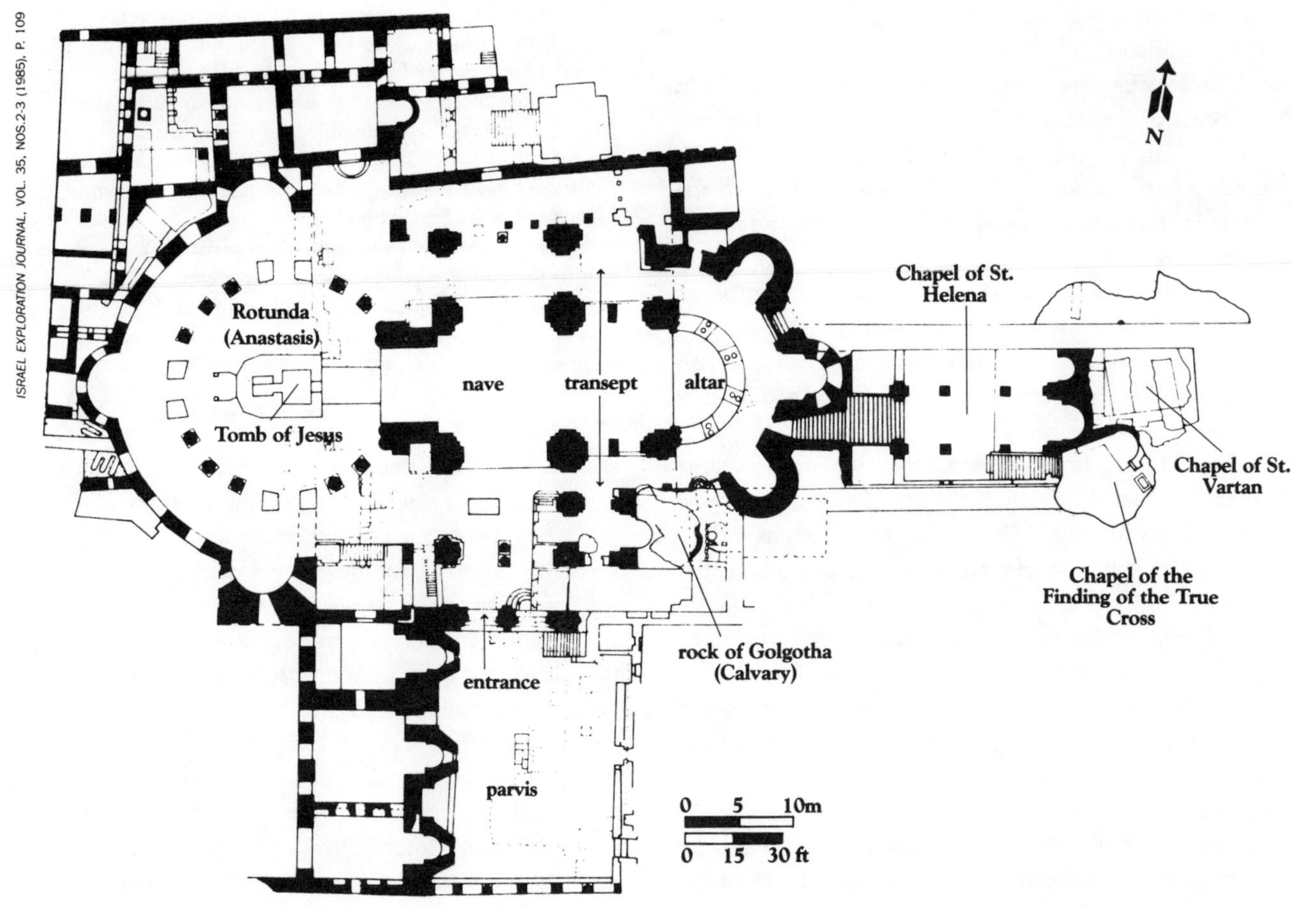

important that scholars be able to check for themselves the attribution of walls and other architectural elements. In photograph No. 207, for example, we are shown a fragment attributed by Corbo to Baldwin V's tombstone, but it is almost impossible to understand where it was found, as only a general location is mentioned.[4] Unlike many archaeological reports, Corbo gives us no loci index. Thus anyone who wishes to study thoroughly a particular locus, its contents, location and attribution to a particular period is completely stymied.

Corbo has provided no plans superimposing various periods. There is no grid where one can reconstruct the continuity of the various walls and their relation to one another. One must rely solely on the author's assumptions. He apparently justifies his attribution of walls and floors to particular periods principally on his concept of the shape of the church in a particular period.

There are other shortcomings: The meaning of the shading in some of the plates is not always given in the legend, so it is not always clear what the shading refers to. The location of the sections is not always shown on the plans, so, for example in plate 52, it is not clear where the section of the cistern in plate 53 is located.

No heights are marked on the plans. Thus, for example, when we examine the author's extremely important reconstruction of the pagan structure that preceded the rotunda, we cannot know whether a certain wall is a retaining wall, which it probably was, or a free-standing wall.

From the archaeological point of view, the book under review is definitely unsatisfactory. There is not even a discussion of the stylistic development of the building—the rotunda, for example, or the Crusader church as part of the development of the Romanesque European church. Nevertheless, no student of this great structure can afford to be without these volumes.

[1] See Magen Broshi, "Recent Excavations in the Church of the Holy Sepulchre," *Qadmoniot*, Vol. 10, No. 1, 1977, pp. 30ff (in Hebrew). More recently, see Magen Broshi and Gabriel Barkay, "Excavations in the Chapel of St. Vartan in the Holy Sepulchre," *Israel Exploration Journal* 35, Nos. 2-3 (1985), pp. 108ff.

[2] Broshi and Barkay (see note 1) do not mention this layer of arable soil; instead they found an Iron Age II floor of beaten earth above the quarry fill. Based on this floor and the large quantities of Iron Age II pottery found below, in and above this floor, they conclude this area was residential from the late eighth century to the Babylonian destruction of Jerusalem. They date the quarry mainly to the ninth-eighth centuries B.C. before the city expanded into this extramural area in the late eighth century. Corbo contends that this floor cannot be dated to Iron Age II.

[3] Conrad Schick, "Notes from Jerusalem," *Palestine Exploration Fund Quarterly Statement*, 1887, pp. 156-170.

[4] See also Corbo photographs No. 24, 25 and 204.

Evidence of Earliest Christian Pilgrimage to the Holy Land Comes to Light in Holy Sepulchre Church

By Magen Broshi

The compound of the Church of the Holy Sepulchre in Jerusalem is not only Christianity's holiest site, it is also one of the most fascinating buildings in the world. Its nucleus goes back to the 4th century A.D. — how many 4th century buildings are still in existence and in use? — and its various components represent almost every period during the last 16 centuries.*

Archaeologists have been excavating in Jerusalem for over a century, but only recently have they been allowed to dig in the Church of the Holy Sepulchre. In 1960 the three principal Communities that share the compound — the Latin Catholics, the Greek Orthodox and the Armenian Orthodox — agreed not only on a plan of extensive restoration, but also on a program of archaeological investigation and excavation. Both the restoration work and the archaeological work are still in progress.

Despite the very restricted areas available for excavation, the archaeological work has contributed substantially to our knowledge of the history of this unique edifice. Only in the past few years has sufficient archaeological evidence come to light so that we can

Magen Broshi is curator of the Shrine of the Book, the Dead Sea Scroll wing of the Israel Museum. He has conducted a number of excavations in Jerusalem and is a member of **BAR***'s Editorial Advisory Board.*

*See J.-P.B. Ross, "The Evolution of a Church —Jerusalem's Holy Sepulchre", September 1976 BAR, p. 3.

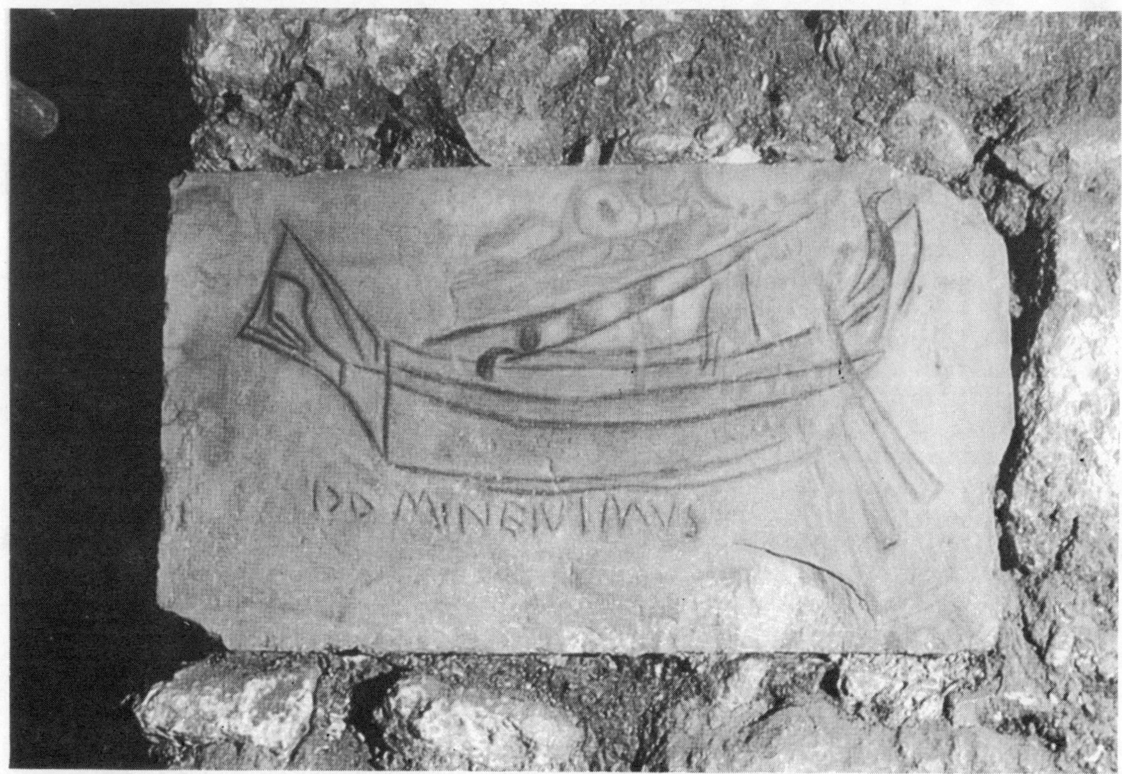

A boldly drawn graffito of a small Roman sailing vessel found on a wall beneath the Church of the Holy Sepulchre. The stern on the right tapers into a goosehead; the mast lies horizontal — either broken or lowered. Below the drawing are the Latin words, DOMINE IVIMUS, "Lord, we went" — the words which begin Psalm 122, the psalm of pilgrimage. Photo: Avinoam Glick.

locate and draw the plan of the original basilica church built by the Emperor Constantine beginning in 326 A.D. This church he constructed in front of Jesus' Tomb; the Tomb itself was venerated by pilgrims in an open courtyard. Later, Constantine built a magnificent rotunda almost 70 feet in diameter over and around the Tomb. Much of this rotunda still survives — in places up to 35 feet — in the basic structure of the present rotunda over the Tomb.

In November 1975, I was asked by the Armenian Orthodox Patriarchate to supervise clearance work at the eastern extremity of the compound (east of St. Helena's Chapel, known to Armenians as St. Krekor's [Gregory's] chapel).

Despite the confined area — only about 10 yards square — the results have been most gratifying.

The most astounding item we found was a bold drawing of a ship which we were able to date to about 330 A.D. The drawing is made on a carefully smoothed and polished stone block embedded in a wall of rougher stones (see illustration, p. 267).

Beneath the drawing is a Latin inscription "DOMINE IVIMUS": "Lord, we went."

The vessel is a small Roman sailing merchantman, typical of the kind that plied the waters of the Mediterranean Sea between different parts of the Roman Empire. Executed in firm, elegant strokes, its bow is on the left and its stern on the right. The stern tapers into a goose head, the most popular ship ornament in antiquity. The steering oars are aft. Behind the mast is a furled square mainsail.

The mast itself presents a problem: Is it lowered or is it broken? Is the ship resting in a harbor after its voyage or has it been wrecked? I incline to the belief that the artist meant to draw a broken or fallen mast — perhaps wrecked in a storm. No doubt the pilgrims made the voyage all the way from the western Mediterranean — Rome, Gaul or even Spain. We know they came from the western Mediterranean because the inscription is in Latin. Greek, not Latin, was used in the eastern part of the Roman Empire.

The furled mainsail and the lines binding it are in red (ochre-sinopia); the rest of the drawing, including the inscription, is in black (graphite). The stone block which the artist specially prepared for the drawing is about 33 inches long and 18 inches high.

The inscription "Lord, we went" may be the simple exclamation of a pilgrim that "we went to the Tomb of the Lord." More probably, however, it contains an allusion to Pslam 122, as Father Pierre Benoit, O.P. of the Ecole Biblique has suggested. Psalm 122 is the classical psalm of pilgrimage to Jerusalem. It begins: "In domum Domini ibimus" — "Let us go to the house of the Lord." By this allusion, the pilgrims have affirmed that they have gone up to the house of the Lord.

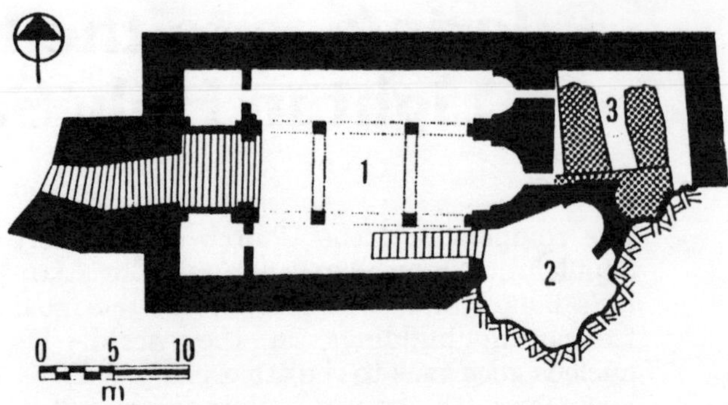

A plan of the east end of the Holy Sepulchre Church, including (1) St. Helena Chapel, (2) Grotto of the finding of the Cross, and (3) Excavated area.

The inscription is apparently the joyous exclamation of pilgrims who sailed from the western part of the Empire and finally reached the Holy City — perhaps after a perilous voyage signified by the lowered (damaged?) mast. The tableau may also be an *ex voto* — a fulfillment of a vow — commemorating the pilgrims' deliverance from the dangers and perhaps narrow excape of the arduous voyage.

The date of the drawing is determined by the type of ship, the inscription and the archaeological context. The ship is typical of the first centuries of the Christian era. The inscription implies that it was made after the conversion of the site from a pagan edifice to a Christian shrine. The archaeological evidence suggests the decade before 335 A.D. — in other words, during the first decade of Constantine's basilica which was begun in 326 A.D. The early Church Father Eusebius tells us that this area was covered with pagan shrines before Constantine built this church. It is most unlikely that a Christian would have dared to paint this inscription before 326 A.D., at a time when the area was covered with pagan shrines and Christianity was an outlawed religion. After 335 A.D. this area was filled in and inaccessible. Therefore, the ship and the inscription must have been drawn sometime during the construction of the Constantinian basilica, that is, about 330 A.D.

While some Christian pilgrimages to the Holy Land began as early as the Second Century, only after Constantine's conversion in 324 A.D. did pilgrims come in substantial numbers. The earliest extant account of a Christian pilgrim's journey to the Holy Land is by a man known to history only as the Pilgrim of Bordeaux. His Latin *Itinerarium Burdigalense* tells about a pilgrimage made in 333 A.D. To this early testimony may now be added the painting and inscription we have found in the Holy Sepulchre Church.

The pilgrim ship, although the most startling of our finds, was only a small part of what we learned in our comparatively small excavation. From a later period (12th century) we found the eastern wall of the Crusader's St. Helena Chapel.

From an earlier period (the 7th century B.C.), we learned that the area was a rock quarry. (To discover this we had to dig down almost 40 feet.) When Jerusalem expanded in the 7th century B.C., this area was inhabited for the first time. Our excavations uncovered evidence that then the area was covered with a beaten-earth floor. Seventh century pottery was found on and under the floor. Our 7th century dating was also confirmed by carbon-14 tests of the ashes in the floor.

Into that beaten-earth floor were dug the foundations of a Roman building — almost certainly the Roman Forum of Jerusalem, probably built by the Emperor Hadrian.

When Constantine built the Church of the Holy Sepulchre, he thoroughly demolished the pagan buildings, including the Roman Forum. As Eusebius tells us:

"Godless people . . . had gone to great pains to cover up this divine memorial of immortality [Jesus' tomb] so that it should be forgotten. With much labor they [the Romans] brought in soil from elsewhere and covered the whole site, and by raising the level and laying a stone pavement they concealed the divine cave under a heap of earth. And, as though this were not enough, they built above ground . . . a gloomy shrine of lifeless idols dedicated to the impure demon Aphrodite, where they poured foul libations on profane and accursed altars. . . . As soon

The worker stands on the foundation of the Roman Forum which the Emperor Hadrian erected on the site where Jesus was buried. Constantine tried, but failed, to remove every vestige of his predecessor's desecration. The walls behind the worker are from the original basilica church which Constantine built on the site. Photo: Avinoam Glick

as he [Constantine] had issued his orders, this false device was cast to the ground . . . with its images and gods. The Emperor also commanded that the stone and timber of the ruins should be removed and dumped as far away as possible, and that a large area of the foundation soil, defiled as it was by devil-worship, should be dug away to a considerable depth, and removed to some distance. At once the work was carried out, and, as layer after layer of the subsoil came into view, the venerable and most holy memorial of the Saviour's resurrection, beyond all our hopes, came into view; the holy of holies, the Cave was, like our Saviour, 'restored to life' . . . by its very existence bearing clearer testimony to the resurrection of the Saviour than any words." (Eusebius, *Life of Constantine* 3.25-3.28. J. Wilkinson's translation.)

Soundings in and around the Holy Sepulchre have confirmed that Constantine removed not only the pagan superstructures, but also the substructures. In our site, however, some of the pagan substructure was found untouched by Constantine's demolition team (see illustration).

We also uncovered the foundations of the northern stylobate of the Constantinian nave and the foundations that supported the rock ledge on which the facade of the Church was built.

Thus, in quite a small area, we were able to bring to light evidence from almost 2000 years of history — from the 8th-7th centuries B.C. to the 12th century A.D. ∎

Both Gabriel Barkay and Dan Bahat draw upon an understanding of changing styles of Jewish tomb architecture based on evidence accumulated from investigations of numerous other tombs in the area during recent years. Readers who would like more detailed descriptions, including plans and photographs, of the Iron Age and Roman-period tomb styles referred to can find them in the articles listed under For Further Reading.

While a modern reader can immediately recognize the reflections of religious bias in the remarks of Edward Robinson quoted earlier, it is not easy, even today, to be aware of one's own emotional commitment to a particular point of view. In the reprinted readers' letters attacking Gabriel Barkay's conclusions, for instance, some might consider that the writers' attacks were a bit over-zealous and reflected an already-formed attachment to the Garden Tomb. (Mr. Chadwick, for instance, continues to feel it "much more likely" that the channel in front of the tomb entrance is a track for a rolling stone, although he seems well-read enough to know that each of the several examples of tomb-entrance rolling stones that has come to light from Roman-period Palestine is set in channels that are not level—they tilt downward to a low point in front of the entrance. This includes the example at the Tomb of the Kings, which he specifically mentions!) On the other hand, if the writers are correct in only some of the omissions and logical inconsistencies with which they charge Barkay, one must ask if Barkay also has been guilty of skewing his argument by selecting only those considerations that favored a prejudged conclusion. (Why did he not discuss some of the more important dissimilarities between the Garden Tomb and his Iron Age examples—such as the absence of repository holes? And why, indeed, did he not discuss any of the features on the facade and in front of the Garden Tomb which have figured in others' arguments for its identification as an ancient shrine site? **—D.C.**)

The debate over the location of Jesus' tomb will continue. Where such an emotionally charged subject is involved, however, it is doubly important to remain alert for unacknowledged biases, both on one's own part and on the part of others. The best antidote to such lapses in objectivity, of course, is debate itself.

Those interested in truth will therefore deplore the close-minded attitude expressed in one of the other letters reprinted in **BAR**, July/August 1986:

> Most *informed* Christians are well aware that there are two tombs which are held by Catholics and Protestants (Baptists) to have received the body of Jesus when taken from the cross. My question is, why do you permit such delicate and very personal matters to be debated on the auction block of **BAR**? Aren't there any better things to write about than to dig into personal matters where they offend and damage people's beliefs?
>
> Why doesn't Mr. Barkay write an expose of the Catholic tomb where they believe Jesus was buried?
>
> I have been in each of the tombs and studied them, and to me his article is poorly researched and certainly not authentic. His article is an offense to me and every other believer, informed and uninformed, who holds the Garden Tomb in awe.

(Note that this writer was concerned about her own religious sensitivities but was quite prepared to have Roman Catholics' beliefs disturbed!)

For Further Reading

Concerning Iron Age and Roman Age Burials

Rachel Hachlili and Ann Killebrew, "The Saga of the Goliath Family—As Revealed in Their Newly Discovered 2,000-Year-Old Tomb," **BAR**, January/February 1983 (first-century A.D. tomb)

Gabriel Barkay and Amos Kloner, "Jerusalem Tombs from the Days of the First Temple," **BAR**, March/April 1986 (eighth- to seventh-centuries B.C. tombs)

Ehud Netzer, "Herod's Family Tomb in Jerusalem," **BAR**, May/June 1983

Concerning the Church of the Holy Sepulchre

J.-P. B. Ross, "The Evolution of a Church—Jerusalem's Holy Sepulchre," **BAR**, September 1976

Shulamit Eisenstadt, "Jesus' Tomb Depicted on a Byzantine Gold Ring from Jerusalem," **BAR**, March/April 1987

Concerning Crucifixion in the Roman Period

Vassilios Tzaferis, "Crucifixion—The Archaeological Evidence," **BAR**, January/February 1985

"Death by Crucifixion," Queries & Comments, **BAR**, May/June 1985

Hershel Shanks, "New Analysis of the Crucified Man," **BAR**, November/December 1985

Frederick T. Zugibe, "Two Questions About Crucifixion," **BR**, April 1989

The World of St. Paul's Missionary Journeys

Within its first generation, the Christian movement underwent a dramatic transformation from a small Jewish messianic sect to a universal missionary religion seeking converts in the gentile world to the west.

Certainly the most important person in helping to set the fledgling movement's new direction was the apostle Paul, whose missionary journeys through the Mediterranean dominate the New Testament Book of Acts (Acts 13-28). His letters to young Christian churches (along with several later letters whose authors ascribed their writings to him) became Christian scriptures in their own right and account for half the documents of the New Testament and almost one-third of its volume.

The articles in this section help to bring Paul and his missionary activity into clearer focus.

In "On the Road and on the Sea with St. Paul," Jerome Murphy-O'Connor draws upon contemporary literature, archaeological materials and a knowledge of Mediterranean topography to give an enhanced appreciation of the rigors of travel in the Mediterranean world of Paul's time and, by extension, Paul's intense determination and dedication to his ministry. Dan Cole—"Corinth & Ephesus—Why Did Paul Spend Half His Journeys in These Cities?"—integrates archaeological evidence uncovered at Corinth and Ephesus with information from the New Testament and other ancient sources to explain why Paul changed his missionary strategy when he reached Corinth and made first that city and then Ephesus bases for extended periods of time.

As a preface to reading these articles, some may wish to review the description of Paul's missionary travels through the time of his stay at Ephesus in Acts 13-19. (The map on page 274 will be helpful.)

In addition, the first two chapters of Paul's Letter to the Galatians gives some sense of the sharp differences in understanding between the initial Jewish Christian leaders—Peter (Cephas) and the others of Jesus' own disciples—and the "new wave" of leaders represented by Paul and others in the mixed Jewish-gentile congregation at Antioch. Keep in mind that the period of time of Paul's missionary journeys was approximately 48-55 A.D., only some two decades after the first Easter. It was an exciting and volatile time. As Paul made the personal decisions that shaped his itineraries, he and his associates were setting the course of the Christian movement for centuries to come.

Traveling Conditions in the First Century

On the Road and on the Sea with St. Paul

JEROME MURPHY-O'CONNOR, O.P.

In the Acts of the Apostles, we are told that Paul made three missionary journeys. In almost every introduction to the New Testament I have seen, the author discusses St. Paul's journeys in terms of places and dates; his concern is to establish the location of the cities Paul visited and to fix the exact time he visited them. But when Paul himself speaks of his travels he emphasizes, not the "where" or the "when," but the "how." For instance, in defending himself against attacks on his authority in the church of Corinth, Paul writes:

> "Three times I have been shipwrecked; a night and a day I have been adrift at sea; on frequent journeys, in danger from rivers, danger from robbers, . . . danger in the city, danger in the wilderness, danger at sea, danger from false brethren; in toil and hardship, through many a sleepless night, in hunger and thirst, often without food, in cold and exposure" (2 Corinthians 11:25-27).

By this catalogue of hardships, the Apostle underlines his dedication to his ministry. But for us, too much is left unsaid for the evocative potential of Paul's description to be fully realized. Paul's contemporaries could easily have filled in the picture from their own experiences. We who travel at great speed and in security and comfort, however, need to transport ourselves consciously to a very different world if we are to appreciate the conditions under which Paul passed a great part of his life, and that contributed to the experiences that became integral to his theology.

Since Paul himself gives us no details, we must extrapolate; what he encountered would have been similar to what others, who lived a century before or after, experienced.

With minor localized exceptions, peace reigned throughout the Roman Empire for 200 years after Augustus Caesar's (Octavian's) accession to power in 30 B.C. During this time, travel conditions remained the same. From scattered references by Greek and Roman writers, we can recreate a rather detailed picture of what it was like to travel in the first century A.D. This has been done in an excellent study entitled *Travel in the Ancient World* by Lionel Casson (London: Allen & Unwin, 1974). But Casson's material needs to be supplemented by information from a source that he inexplicably ignores; that is, from *The Golden Ass*,[1] a Latin novel written by Apuleius, who was born about 123 A.D. This novel describes the adventures of Lucius, a man turned into a donkey, who undergoes many misfortunes at the hands of a series of owners before finally recovering his own form as a man. The action takes place in the area between Corinth and Thessalonica, where Paul also went, and provides invaluable in-

© ERICH LESSING

sights into life outside the major cities, as well as conditions of travel.

Paul's first missionary journey took him from Syria to Cyprus and then to Pisidia (part of modern Turkey) (Acts 13-14). His second journey, across Asia Minor into Europe, is narrated by Luke in Acts 15-18. The journey can also be reconstructed from hints scattered throughout the Pauline Epistles. The only difference between the account in Luke and in the Epistles is the date. Luke places Paul's journey *after* the Jerusalem conference (Acts 15), which took place in 51 or 52 A.D., when the apostles worked out a compromise permitting Jewish and Gentile Christians to eat together. From Paul's own letters it is clear that this journey must have taken place *before* the Jerusalem conference, probably between 45 and 51. On his third journey, Paul revisited many of the cities where he had preached during his second journey (Acts 18:22-21:16).

In Paul's time, as today, how you traveled depended on how much money you could afford to spend. Paul was not a rich man. The impression he gives in his letters is that he had no significant personal financial resources. He seems to have had nothing beyond what he could earn and the sporadic gifts sent to him by various churches (2 Corinthians 11:8-9; Philippians 4:14). As an itinerant artisan, a tent-maker (Acts 18:3), he was far better off than an

PAUL MAY HAVE SAILED on a ship like this one during one of his journeys. Carved in relief on a mausoleum in Pompeii, Italy, this vessel is typical of merchant ships plying the Mediterranean in the first century A. D.

A female figurehead adorns the bow, left. Such figureheads sometimes represented the name of the ship. The stern, right, scoops gracefully into a gooseneck shape. Sailors clinging to long yardarms extending from the central mast work quickly to furl the sails as the ship enters port. A large oar near the stern, right, was probably one of a pair that served as rudders; they may have been operated separately or rotated together by means of a tiller bar or ropes.

From an inscription on the mausoleum, we learn that the relief was commissioned in the first half of the first century A.D. by Naevoleia Tyche for the tomb of her husband, C. Munatius Faustus, a Pompeii shipper.

unskilled worker of the laboring class, but no artisan became rich. It would have been as much as Paul could do to earn his daily bread, even if he had enjoyed a stable situation with a regular clientele. But Paul garnered much of his work from fellow travelers on the road, or he had to begin anew in a strange city where he had no reputation to attract business.

In these circumstances, Paul certainly traveled on foot. A large selection of wheeled vehicles was available to travelers, but to rent or buy one would

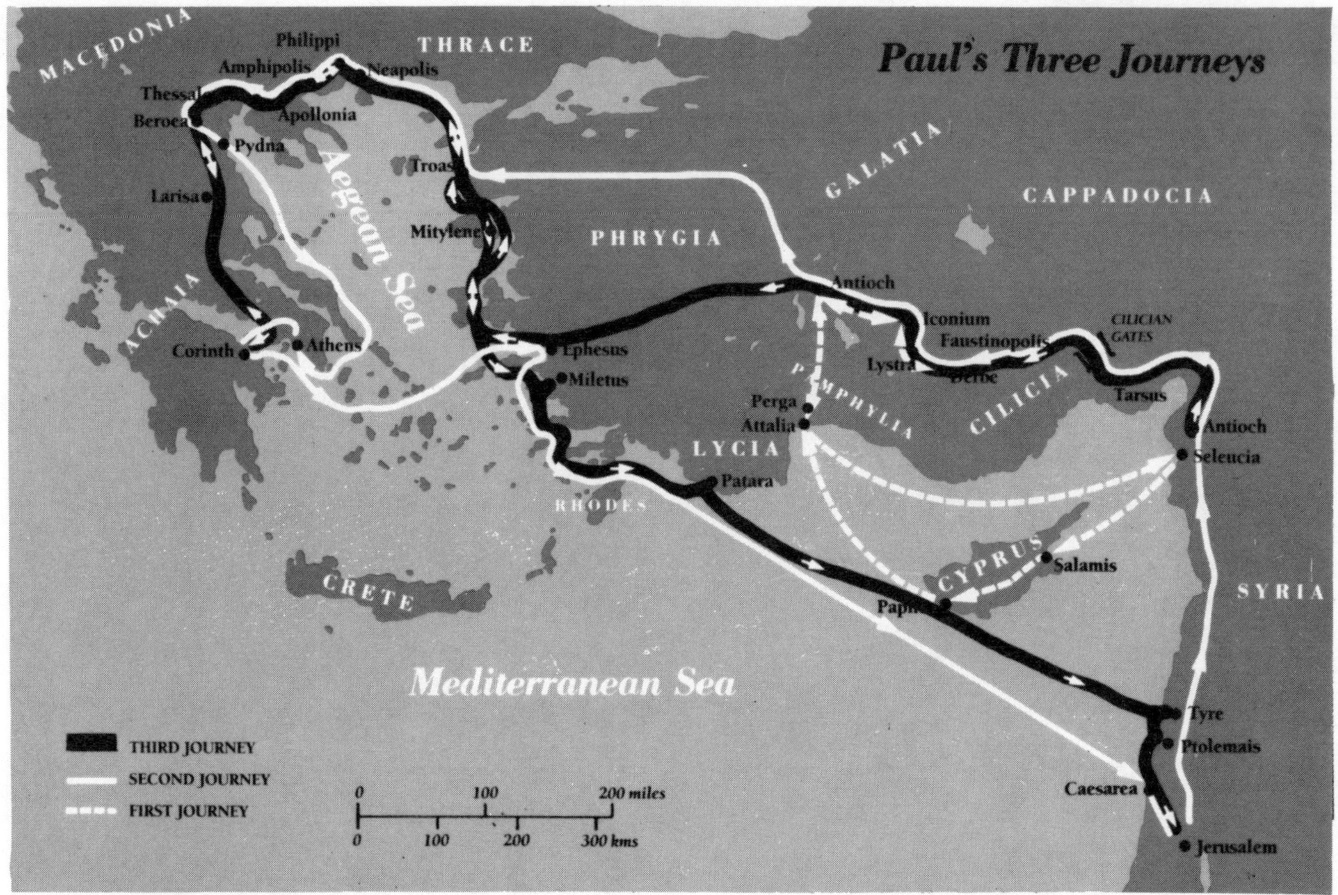

have been beyond his means. What about a horse? Except by military dispatch riders, horses were not used to travel long distances. Riding came easily only to those born on horseback, for saddles were rudimentary, and stirrups unknown. A donkey could certainly have borne some of Paul's baggage, but this would only have increased his expenses without increasing his speed. Moreover, a donkey could be requisitioned by any soldier or official who needed it. Several decades earlier, the philosopher Epictetus had advised donkey owners to surrender their beasts immediately on being requested to do so, in order to avoid being beaten up by soldiers (Discourses 4:1.79). Requisitioning by soldiers was so common that it is even illustrated by an episode in Apuleius's *Golden Ass* (9:36-10:12).

How far could Paul expect to go in a day? In some travel narratives the number of days needed to cover a known distance is recorded; the average daily distance is about 20 miles.[3] An anonymous traveler known as the Bordeaux pilgrim, who visited the Holy Land in 333 A.D., kept a famous diary that has survived. From Faustinopolis to Tarsus he followed the Roman road laid down when Pompey moved his legions into the East in 63 B.C., through the Cilician Gates. Paul took this road in reverse when he traveled from Tarsus to Galatia. According to data given by the Bordeaux pilgrim, the distances were as follows:*

City of Tarsus	to	Inn at Mascurinae—
	12 Roman miles	
Inn at Mascurinae	to	Post at Pilas—
	14 Roman miles	
Post at Pilas	to	Inn at Podanos—
	12 Roman miles	
Inn at Podanos	to	Post at Caena—
	13 Roman miles	
Post at Caena	to	City at Faustinopolis
	12 Roman miles	

From Tarsus to Faustinopolis, then, was 62 Roman miles. But in between, as the chart shows, were several inns and posts. A traveler would normally spend the night at an inn (*mansio*). A post (*mutatio*) was simply a staging-point where animals could be changed.

Thus, a normal day's journey for those traveling by carriage was from inn to inn, roughly 25 Roman miles or 22 modern miles. Those who walked, as

* Except for Tarsus, these towns are not mentioned in the Bible. But at the time the Bordeaux pilgrim lived, they existed along the route Paul took.

Acts	Epistles	Places	Distance**
15:4	Galatians 1:18	JERUSALEM TO ANTIOCH	375 miles
15:30		ANTIOCH TO TARSUS	140 miles
15:41	Galatians 1:21	TARSUS TO FAUSTINOPOLIS*	60 miles
		FAUSTINOPOLIS TO PHRYGIA AND GALATIA	435 miles
16:6		PHRYGIA AND GALATIA TO TROAS	500 miles
16:8		TROAS TO NEAPOLIS	140 miles (BY SEA)
16:11		NEAPOLIS TO PHILIPPI	15 miles
16:12	1 Thessalonians 2:2	PHILIPPI TO THESSALONICA	85 miles
17:1	Philippians 4:16	THESSALONICA TO BEROEA	45 miles
17:10		BEROEA TO PYDNA*	30 miles
		PYDNA TO ATHENS	280 miles (BY SEA)
17:15	1 Thessalonians 3:1	ATHENS TO CORINTH	50 miles
18:1		CORINTH TO EPHESUS	250 miles (BY SEA)
18:19		EPHESUS TO CAESAREA	620 miles (BY SEA)
18:22	Galatians 2:1	CAESAREA TO JERUSALEM	60 miles

Total: 3,085 miles
By land: 1,795 miles
By sea: 1,290 miles

**Towns located on Paul's route but not mentioned in the Bible.*
***The distances given in this table are rough approximations.*

Paul did, would have had to extend themselves to cover this distance. It is unlikely that Paul could have maintained such an average for long periods, particularly when the road was hilly.

If Paul says that he was "in hunger and thirst, often without food, in cold and exposure" (2 Corinthians 11:27), it is obvious that on occasion he found himself far from human habitation at nightfall. He may have failed to reach shelter because of weather conditions; an unusually hot day may have sapped his endurance; mountain passes may have been blocked by unseasonably early or late snowfalls; spring floods may have made sections of the road impassable (he claims to have been "in danger from rivers")(2 Corinthians 11:26); or fierce hailstorms may have forced him to take refuge. The average height of the Anatolian plateau (present day central Turkey) is 3,000 feet above sea-level, but great sections of it rise to double that and extreme varia-

The Second Missionary Journey of Paul

tions of temperature are the rule. The mountainous territory through which Paul passed in northern Greece would have been only marginally better.

Anyone living in the vicinity of a Roman road, and in particular near a post or an inn, was subject to requisition by Roman military, as well as civilian officials. Not only could their animals and vehicles be "borrowed," but they themselves could be pressed into service as porters or drivers. In these circumstances, the ordinary traveler did not get much sympathy. So many demands were made upon those who lived near the road that they would not be apt to offer aid gratuitously. Paul, in consequence, could not count on free hospitality. Despite the traditional generosity of the poor to their own kind, he would have had to pay for both food and lodging—which meant that he had to earn money as he traveled.

Fortunately, Paul had a trade that was much in demand among travelers. As a tent-maker he had the skill to make and repair all kinds of leather goods, not just the animal skins used to make tents. Travelers were shod in leather sandals and often wore hooded leather cloaks. They carried water and wine in leather gourds. Animals were attached to carriages and carts by leather harnesses. Sometimes, the wealthy even carried tents in case they were caught in the open at nightfall. Repairing torn pieces of leather or broken stitches no doubt provided Paul with the means to pay his way. Of course, he had no control over when the demand for his services

"Three times I have been shipwrecked; a night and a day I have been adrift at sea . . ."

would come. He could be summoned just as he was starting out from the inn in the morning. He could be involved in a breakdown on the road. He could be kept working late at night by a customer anxious to make an early start next day. Worst of all, he could be commandeered by a soldier or official to repair the soldier's or official's equipment. For this, he was unlikely to be paid and all such work meant delay—another reason why Paul sometimes found himself far from where he planned to be at nightfall.

When Paul made it to an inn, he could not look forward to a night of total repose. The average inn was no more than a courtyard surrounded by rooms. Baggage was piled in the open space, where animals were also tethered for the night. The drivers sat around noxious little fires fueled by dried dung, or slept on the ground wrapped in their cloaks.

Those who could afford better rented beds in the rooms. The snorting and stamping of the animals outside was sometimes drowned out by the snores of others who shared the room, any one of whom might be a thief. Paul's anxiety that he might lose the tools of his trade was hardly conducive to a sound night's sleep. And sound sleep was made infinitely more difficult by that perennial occupant of all inns, the bedbug.

The menace posed by the bedbug is graphically—and amusingly—described in a tale from the *Acts of John* written in the third century A.D. about a journey from Laodicea to Ephesus.[4]

> "On the first evening we arrived at a lonely inn, and while we were trying to find a bed for John we noticed a curious thing. There was one unoccupied and unmade bed, so we spread the cloaks which we were wearing over it, and begged him to lie down on it, while all the rest of us slept on the floor.
>
> "But when John lay down he was troubled by the bugs. They became more and more troublesome to him, and it was already midnight when he said to them in the hearing of us all, 'I order you, you bugs, to behave yourselves, one and all. You must leave your home for tonight and be quiet in one place, and keep your distance from the servants of God.' And while we laughed and went on talking, John went to sleep, but we talked quietly and, thanks to him, were not disturbed.
>
> "Now, as day was breaking, I got up first, and Verus and Andronicus with me, and we saw by the door of the room which we had taken an enormous mass of bugs. We were astounded at their great number. All the brethren woke up because of them, but John went on sleeping. When he woke up, we explained to him what we had seen. He sat up in bed, looked at the bugs, and said, 'Since you have behaved yourselves and listened to my correction, you may go back to your own place.' When he had said this, and had got up from the bed, the bugs came running from the door towards the bed, climbed up its legs, and disappeared into the joints" (#60-61).

"On frequent journeys, in danger from rivers, danger from robbers, danger in the city, danger in the wilderness, danger at sea, danger from false brethren . . ."

WHEN PAUL TRAVELED from Tarsus, his birthplace, on the Cilician plain to Iconium on the Anatolian plateau, he had no choice but to climb through this steep and narrow pass in the Taurus mountains. Called the "Cilician Gates," the gorge—only about 60 feet wide at its most constricted point—is cut by the Cakit River, which flows through it. As early as the eighth century B.C., travelers followed the river on a rock-cut path. Darius I of Persia and Alexander the Great both brought their armies through the narrow pass. Paul, however, walked along the Roman road laid down when Pompey moved his legions east in 63 B.C. Today, cars easily negotiate the pass on a modern roadway, right.

The rocky terrain, which may have been partially covered by snow from an unseasonal blizzard, was only a fraction of nearly 2,000 rugged miles walked by Paul on his second missionary journey. In an average day, Paul may have covered 25 miles. However, it is unlikely that he maintained that pace during his arduous climb through the 7,000-foot-high Taurus mountains.

Paul and his traveling companions must have scratched through many a weary night wishing that they had the power to rid themselves of the pest by means of a simple word!

Danger from robbers is another worry Paul mentions in his catalogue of apostolic sufferings in 2 Corinthians 11:26, and indeed robbers were almost as pervasive as bedbugs. Casson describes a commonly held, but erroneous, view of travel conditions in the Roman Empire at the time: "The through routes were policed well enough for the traveller to ride them with relatively little fear of bandits . . . Wherever he went, he was under the umbrella of a well-organized, efficient legal system."[5] This was true, however, only to the extent that the Emperor was *conceived* as a universal protector; in many instances, he did not *function* in that way. Two episodes from Apuleius's *Golden Ass* illustrate the real situation. In one, Lucius, still in the form of an ass, has been driven toward a robbers' hideout in the mountains. In a town on the way, he decides to invoke the name of the emperor, with the following result:

> "It suddenly struck me that I could use the way out open to every citizen, and free myself from

my miseries by invoking the name of the Emperor. It was already daylight, and we were going through a populous town to which a market had attracted a good crowd. In the middle of these groups, all made up of Greeks, I tried to invoke in Greek the august name of Caesar. I got as far as a distinct and powerful 'O,' but the remainder, the name of Caesar, I could not pronounce. The robbers, not liking the discordant sound of my voice, took it out of my hide" (3:29).

The point is no less clear for being made with sophistication and wit. The poor had no access to the emperor, and could not effectively claim his intervention.

Powerful and influential personalities were in a different situation. Apuleius's second story concerns a disgraced procurator who was on his way into exile on the island of Zakynthos. The procurator and his escort were spending the night at a small inn at Actium when it was attacked by robbers. The robbers were beaten off by the procurator's escort, but the procurator's wife, who had volunteered to go into exile with him, was so incensed that she returned to Rome and asked Caesar to exterminate the brigands. There was a happy ending.

"Caesar decided that the gang of the brigand Hemus should no longer exist, and it immediately disappeared; such is the power of an imperial wish. The whole gang, chased by detachments of soldiers, ended up by being cut to pieces" (7:7).

As these stories reflect, imperial authority was exercised on the personal demand of those with enough clout to reach the emperor, not by any formal institution.

It was difficult, as well, to invoke the protection of lesser officials, since provincial governors had no permanent forces to perform regular police functions. Although they moved around their territories holding judicial sessions at selected towns, and auxiliary bodyguard units could be used to intervene if necessary, the frequency of a provincial governor's visits to outlying towns depended on the whim of the official. Many were less than conscientious; even those who took their duties seriously made no effort to cover their territories systematically. [6]

Apuleius gives a picture of the small towns in northern Greece through which Paul passed that makes them sound similar to the frontier towns of the Wild West that had no sheriff. Individuals had no one but themselves to defend their rights; they often took the law into their own hands. According to *The Golden Ass*, towns were often run by influential families in their own interest. Thus, we find a poor man dispossessed with impunity "by a rich and powerful young neighbor, who misused the prestige of his ancestry, was powerful in local politics, and could easily do anything he liked in the town" (9:35). Just before being turned into an ass, Lucius is warned,

"Take care to return early from your dinner. A gang of young idiots, all from the best families, disturb public order. You will see cadavers strewn in the street. And the auxilia of the governor, far away as they are, cannot rid the city of such carnage" (2.18).

The poor were defenseless before such casual brutality. How could they appeal to the governor? And if they ever reached him, would he accept their version of events?

Neighbors could sometimes band together against outsiders. Apuleius tells the story of a group of robbers who sidle into a town and, by cautious questions in the market, discover the house of the town's moneylender. The moneylender becomes aware of what is going on, however; when the robbers come to his house that night, he is ready. As the chief robber slips his hand through the keyhole in order to pull the bolt, the owner nails it to the door, and runs to the roof to summon help (4:9-11). A similar story is narrated in 4:13-21. Such justice, of course, was highly localized. One could avoid a charge of murder simply by moving to another town (1:19). Runaway slaves were in little danger of being caught (8:15-23). On the other hand, if feelings ran high, thieves were simply executed on the spot (7:13).

Little imagination is needed to appreciate how vulnerable Paul was under such conditions. He was the stranger, the outsider. There was no one to whom he could turn for aid. He had no neighbors or friends, and could be easily victimized in innumerable ways. I think it very likely that this sense of vulnerability is what lies behind his repeated stress on his "weakness" (1 Corinthians 9:22; 2 Corinthians 11:29).

If the towns were chaotic, anarchy ruled in the countryside. Even in the relatively populous region between Athens and Corinth, the section of this road called the Sceironian Rocks was notorious for the number of its highwaymen. Highwaymen, however, were by no means the only "danger in the wilderness" (2 Corinthians 11:26) that Paul experienced.

Another danger sounds rather banal. Not all the Roman roads Paul walked were as well constructed as the famous Via Egnatia, which he took from Neapolis to Philippi and then on to Thessalonica via Amphipolis and Apollonia (Acts 17:1). The Via Egnatia was a *via silice strata*, paved with hard igneous rock and bordered with raised stones outside of which was an unpaved track for pack animals and pedestrians. Most of the other roads in the East were paved only near towns. In the countryside the road was a *via glarea strata*, an unsealed or gravel road. On these roads, the danger from flying stones thrown up by passing vehicles was a menace the walking traveler had to live with.

Wild animals were another danger. The story of the *Golden Ass* is set in an area well known to Paul, the area between Beroea and Thessalonica. As recounted by Apuleius, it was to this region that the rich man from Corinth came to collect wild beasts for his gladiatorial show (10:18). Apuleius refers explicitly to bears (4:13; 7:24), wolves (7:22; 8:15) and wild boar (8:4). Travelers in this story are armed with throwing-spears, heavy hunting-spears, bows and clubs (8:16).

Paul could have encountered some of these wild animals. When he was sent off from Beroea "as far as the sea" (Acts 17:14), presumably he went to Pydna, where the harbor may have remained functional, even though the town itself moved inland in the Roman period. As the crow flies, the distance between Beroea and Pydna is 31 miles (50 kms) over mountainous terrain, a habitat of wild animals.

Several segments of Paul's second missionary journey were by sea. He sailed from Troas to make his first European landfall at Neapolis, the port of Philippi (Acts 16:11). Certainly the return journey from Corinth via Ephesus to Caesarea was also by sea (Acts 18:18-22).

Combining land and sea travel was common in the eastern Mediterranean. At the beginning of the second century A.D., Pliny the Younger wrote to the Emperor Trajan,

> "I feel sure, Sir, that you will be interested to hear that I have rounded Cape Malea [the southern tip of Greece] and arrived at Ephesus with my complete staff after being delayed by contrary winds. My intention now is to travel on to my province [Bithynia] partly by coastal boat and partly by carriage. The intense heat prevents my traveling entirely by road, and the prevailing Etesian winds [north winds that blow from July to September] make it impossible to go all the way by sea" (Letters, 10:15, cf. also 10:17).

As an official, Pliny could requisition boats and carriages at will. Paul had to make do with what was available. When he left from Troas, it is likely that he simply took the first boat sailing to Greece, without being too particular about its specific destination. Since it was summer he could be sure of finding a boat. This would not have been true during the rest of the year, however. In winter, the Mediterranean was effectively closed to travel. Luke notes that "The voyage was already dangerous because the Fast [Yom Kippur, celebrated near the autumnal equinox] was already over" (Acts 27:9). And Pliny the Elder advises us that "Spring opens the sea to voyagers." (*Natural History*, 2:47). Storms blew regularly in winter; the violence of these winter storms is well documented. Paul's trip to Rome started so late in the season that one storm he endured lasted nearly three weeks (Acts 27:19,27). Josephus records a case where a ship sent to sea in winter on an urgent military mission hit three continuous months of storms (*Jewish War*, 2:200-203). Not unreasonably, the ancients considered sea travel highly risky between March and May and during September and October. Between November and February, however, it was extremely dangerous. We can easily understand why Paul wintered in Malta, rather than continuing his travels, after his shipwreck (Acts 28:11), and why he considered wintering in Corinth (1 Corinthians 16:6).

Storms were not the only reason the seas were usually closed in winter. Sailors plotted a course by the sun and stars, as well as by landmarks. In winter, fog or heavy cloud cover would cut off their navigational guides, easily leading to shipwreck. Therefore, ships usually did not stray far from land. Particularly in a crowded archipelago, sailors preferred to move

"In toil and hardship, through many a sleepless night . . ."

from one land sighting to another in daylight. Thus, on the run from Troas to Neapolis, Paul's ship spent the night at Samothrace (Acts 16:11), and on the trip from Troas to Miletus (Acts 20:6-16), the ship made frequent stops—at Assos, at Mitylene, at a place opposite Chios, and finally at Samos. Cicero describes a similar journey in 51 B.C.:

> "Even in July sea travel is a complicated business. I got from Athens to Delos in six days. On the 6th we left Piraeus for Cape Zoster. A contrary wind kept us there on the 7th. On the 8th we reached Kea under pleasant conditions. We had a favorable wind for Gyaros. Thence to Syros, and on to Delos, the end of the voyage, each time more quickly than we would have wished. You know the Rhodian aphracts; nothing rides the sea as badly. So I have no intention of rushing, and do not plan to move from Delos until I can see all of Cape Gyrae [the southern tip of Tinos]" (*Ad Atticum*, 5:12.1).

The prevailing wind in the sailing season was called the Etesian wind. It blew from the northern quadrant (northwest to northeast), and most consistently from the northwest. Thus, any sea journey to the southeast was likely to be a delight. When Agrippa I (10 B.C. to 44 A.D.) was returning to Palestine to take over the tetrarchy of his uncle Philip, the Emperor Caligula advised him not to take the overland route to Syria, but, as quoted by Philo,

> "to wait for the Etesian winds and take the short route through Alexandria. He told him that the ships are crack sailing craft and their skippers the most experienced there are; they drive their vessels like race horses on an unswerving course that goes straight as a die" (Philo, *In Flaccum*, 26—[trans. Casson]).

The ships referred to are the great clippers that brought Egyptian grain to Rome. These were the biggest and best ships of their day. A contemporary description gives their length as 180 feet, their beam as 50 feet, and their depth from the deck to the bottom of the hold, 44 feet.[7] From Rome to Egypt, they ran in ballast at their best point of sailing and could carry several hundred passengers. The journey from Rome to Alexandria lasted 10 to 20 days.

"*In hunger and thirst, often without food, in cold and exposure.*"

Things were very different on the return trip from Egypt to Rome. The rig of that time did not allow ships to sail close to the wind; their keels were not deep enough and they lacked jibs.[8] Thus, they could not retrace their outward route, but were forced north and east toward the southern coast of Asia Minor. They had to remain at anchor when the winds were adverse and make short dashes when conditions turned favorable.

It is obvious why Paul, of his own free will, never took a *ship* going west. When he traveled from the Middle East to Europe, he always went overland through Asia Minor, thereby avoiding the frustration of being delayed in port by adverse winds. On the return trip, however, he always took a boat. Once the island of Rhodes had been left astern, it was a straight run to the Phoenician coast (Acts 21:1-3). It certainly saved him several weeks of foot slogging.

Pliny the elder argued that "the sea-sickness caused by rolling and pitching are good for many ailments of the head, eyes, and chest" (*Natural History*, 31:33)! We will never know whether Paul agreed with this assessment.

Paul sailed west only once—to be tried by the emperor (Acts 25:12). The centurion who escorted Paul obviously knew the wind patterns. In the ports of the southern coast of Asia Minor, he looked for a ship going to Rome; in Myra in Lycia, the centurion found a grain carrier (Acts 27:5,38). Even if we were not told it was an Egyptian grain carrier, we could have deduced as much from the number of passengers, 276 in all (Acts 27:37). Luke graphically describes the difficulties caused by adverse winds (Acts 27:7-8), and the short-lived euphoria produced by a favorable breeze (Acts 27:14).

There were no passenger vessels sailing regular schedules in Paul's day. Cargo ships took passengers on a space available basis. The procedure is described by Philostratus in his *Life of Apollonius of Tyana*:

> "Turning to Danis, Apollonius said, 'Do you know of a ship that is sailing for Italy?' 'I do,' he replied, 'for we are staying at the edge of the sea, and the crier is at our doors, and a ship is being got ready to start, as I gather from the shouts of the crew and the exertions they are making over weighing the anchor!' " (8:14).

This vignette omits the haggling over the fare with a hard-eyed owner or his representative who was determined to get the maximum the market would bear. Presumably, maximum utilization of equipment was as much a concern then as it is today, but the ship's departure had to await the coincidence of a favorable wind with favorable omens. Passengers, too, had to wait; they could not afford to go too far away because the vessel might sail at any moment.

Since passengers were nothing more than an incidental benefit to the owner, the ship provided water, but neither food nor services. Passengers were expected to furnish their own provisions, other than water, for the duration of the voyage. They had to cook for themselves, which meant taking turns, after the crew had been fed, at the hearth in the galley. The fire might be doused by a stray wave, or rough conditions might mean the fire had to be extinguished before passengers had finished cooking, since loose live coals could do irreparable damage to a wooden boat in a very short time.

Passengers had to live on deck; there were no cabins on the average coastal vessel. Apart from a little shade thrown by the mainsail, no shelter was provided. The more experienced travelers brought small tents to protect themselves and their provisions. Tents would also be useful when the boat anchored for the night, often at a port where there was no inn. Frequently, the boat anchored in a small cove whose only amenity was a spring of clear water.

If Paul needed companions on the road for the slight degree of security they provided, a friend was equally necessary on board. It would be difficult for one person to carry on board the provisions necessary for an extended voyage, and it was imperative to have someone to keep an eye on them. The fact that tents were in use both ashore and on board gave Paul an opportunity to earn at least some of his passage money.

The discomfort of a sea voyage was intensified by fear. Travelers went by ship only when there was no real alternative. In the world in which Paul lived, the sea was considered dangerously alien. Farewells tended to assume that the friend taking the ship might never be seen again. Poems were written to memorialize the solemn departure. For instance, in order to wish Virgil a safe voyage to Athens, Horace composed a poem in which he evoked the invention of a boat with the words, "A heart enclosed in oak and triple-bonded bronze first committed a frail bark to the dangerous deep," and so the human race "was launched on the forbidden route of sacrilege"(*Odes,* 1:3.9 and 16). In other words, in this satirical poem, Horace is saying that the ship was first conceived by a sadistic degenerate whose mission was to destroy humanity. Without this fatal discovery Virgil would not be putting his life at risk by sailing to Athens.

Such sentiments were well warranted, for shipwrecks were common. "Three times I have been shipwrecked, a night and a day I have been adrift at sea," Paul tells us (2 Corinthians 11:25). The graphic description of a shipwreck Luke gives in Acts 27:39-44 is confirmed by other travelers. For example, listen to Dio Chrysostom (40-120 A.D):

> "It chanced that at the close of the summer season I was crossing from Chios with some fishermen in a very small boat, when such a storm arose that we had great difficulty in reaching the Hollows of Euboea in safety. The crew ran their boat up a rough beach under the cliffs, where it was wrecked. [Dio is befriended by a hunter who tells him] 'These are called the Hollows of Euboea, where a ship is doomed if it is driven ashore, and rarely are any of those aboard saved, unless like you they sail in very light craft' " (*Discourses,* 7:2-7).

Only the most urgent business justified Dio's risking 96 miles of open sea between the island of Chios and the wild, indented east coast of Euboea. He survived only because the light fishing boat could be maneuvered through the surf. A larger boat would have been pounded to pieces further out to sea so that few, if any, survivors would have made it to shore. Conditions may not have been as violent off the Malta coast where the ship carrying Paul to Rome went down, because all managed to make it ashore, either by swimming or by holding on to loose planks (Acts 27:41-44).

On at least one occasion Paul found himself "adrift on the open sea" (2 Corinthians 11:26), apparently as a result of some other kind of mishap. On the open sea, a smaller boat might be run down by a bigger one or break a plank on a heavy piece of flotsam. The survivors of an accident like this had no means of sending an SOS. Even if they were spotted by another vessel, the limited maneuverability of ancient ships made it difficult to change course to pick them up. Human life was cheap; if it was too difficult or simply too inconvenient to pick up survivors, they would be left where they were. We don't know whether Paul was rescued by a passing ship or whether a lucky current washed him ashore. In either event, he was lucky to have spent only 24 hours in the water. And he would have been less than human had he not faced his next voyage with increased trepidation.

I have tried to give something of the reality behind Paul's impassioned words in 2 Corinthians 11:25-27. When we understand this reality, we better understand Paul's dedication. I suspect our admiration for his perseverance would be even greater if we knew more about how he tried to ensure his security and earn his way.

Some of the areas through which Paul passed are spectacularly beautiful; yet this seems not to have influenced him in any way. On the other hand, his experiences as a lonely traveler almost certainly affected his theology. His pessimistic view of human nature may have been born of the ethos of his age, but it was surely reinforced by what he encountered at the inns and seaports of Greece and Asia Minor. His own poverty forced him to rub shoulders with the most downtrodden and brutalized elements in society. He no doubt felt the impact of the forces that made these elements of society what they were. He himself felt the force of a value system that the poorer elements of society could not escape. His own struggle against the insidious miasma of egocentricity would have sharpened his consciousness of sin and at the same time strengthened his dedication to the salvation of its victims. "Who is weak, and I am not weak? Who is made to fall, and I do not burn with anger?" (2 Corinthians 11:29). BR

[1] See in particular Fergus Millar, "The World of the Golden Ass," *Journal of Roman Studies* 71 (1981) pp. 63-75.

[2] J. Murphy-O'Connor, "Pauline Journeys Before the Jerusalem Conference," *Revue Biblique* 89 (1982) pp. 71-91. This table is based on the calculations presented in Robert Jewett, *A Chronology of Paul's Life* (Philadelphia: Fortress Press, 1979), pp. 59-61.

[3] Cf. R. Jewett, op. cit., p. 138, note 54.

[4] Except for minor modifications, the translation is that of G. C. Stead in E. Hennecke-W. Schneemelcher, *New Testament Apocrypha,* II (London: Lutterworth Press, 1965), pp. 243-244.

[5] Op. cit., p. 122.

[6] Cf. G. P. Burton, "Proconsuls, Assizes and Administration of Justice Under the Empire," *Journal of Roman Studies* 65 (1975) pp. 92-106.

[7] The description of Lucian in *Navigium,* 5 is cited by Casson, op. cit., pp. 158-159.

[8] On this whole question see Lionel Casson, *Ships and Seamanship in the Ancient World* (Princeton: University Press, 1971).

Corinth & Ephesus

Why Did Paul Spend Half His Journeys In These Cities?

DAN P. COLE

Paul's three missionary "journeys" form a standard feature in New Testament maps and histories. The impression that emerges from the account in Acts of the Apostles 1-21 in the New Testament is that Paul three times set out from Antioch in Syria on a succession of missionary "journeys," during which he preached and founded churches in a dozen or more cities. On his first journey, he established churches on the island of Cyprus and in Anatolia (modern Turkey); on his second journey, in Macedonia and southern Greece; and on his third journey, in Ephesus.[1]

However, a closer examination of these chapters from the Book of Acts reveals a different picture.

Although it is rarely noticed, once Paul reached Corinth on his second journey, his strategy

©SONIA HALLIDAY PHOTOGRAPHS

LIBRARY OF CELSUS at Ephesus. Thanks to restoration efforts begun in 1970 by an Austrian team, the facade of the three-storey Library of Celsus offers visitors their most impressive glimpse of the ancient city's grandeur.

According to inscriptions on its steps, the library was built in 110 A.D., after Paul's time. However, Ephesus was an established center of scholarship long before Paul arrived there, and he enjoyed the city's atmosphere of receptiveness to inquiry, debate and new ideas.

changed. For a time he stopped "journeying"; he spent approximately 18 months at Corinth (Acts 18:11) before moving on. His third "journey" was not so much a trip as an extended residence in Ephesus, where he spent at least two and one-half years (Acts 19:1-20).

Paul's three "journeys" took a total of about seven years; they began about 48 A.D. and came to an end when Paul was arrested and imprisoned about 55 A.D. The stops in Corinth and Ephesus, therefore, account for over half the time Paul was supposedly "on the road."

Before reaching Corinth Paul had established almost a dozen churches across Cyprus, Anatolia and Macedonia. On his first missionary journey he spent time at Salamis and Paphos on Cyprus, before going on to Anatolia where he visited Perge in Pamphylia; Antioch of Pisidia; and Iconium, Derbe and Listra, all in eastern Galatia (Acts 13). After a return trip to Antioch (Acts 15), he set out on his second journey, this time going all the way to Macedonia (northern modern Greece). There he established churches at Philippi, Thessalonika and Berea before heading south. He is reported to have preached in Athens, although he apparently did not establish a church there (Acts 15:36-17:34). If we allow for actual traveling time on the road,* we must conclude that Paul spent an average of only a month or two in each city!

Why did Paul spend so little time in each of these cities? In his letters, Paul expresses two dominant themes that account for the brevity of his visits in these cities. First, Paul was confident that the end of this age was coming quickly, so there was but little time left to spread the gospel before it would be too late (1 Corinthians 7:29-31; 1 Thessalonians 4:15-17).

Second, Paul had become convinced that Jesus was the "Messiah"/savior of Gentiles as well as Jews and that the gospel (literally "good news") needed to be proclaimed throughout the Gentile world (see Galatians & Romans throughout). Indeed, at one point he even conceived a definite plan to travel westward to Rome (Romans 1:13) and still farther to Spain (Romans 15:22-24), which was literally and symbolically the westernmost limit of the known world.

On his first two journeys Paul and his traveling companions—first Barnabas and then Silas—set fairly rigorous itineraries. They headed for the capital cities of districts or provinces, preached in the local synagogues, gathered those who responded—both Jews and Gentiles—into new

* See Jerome Murphy-O'Connor, "On the Road and on the Sea with St. Paul," **BR**, Summer 1985 [p. 272].

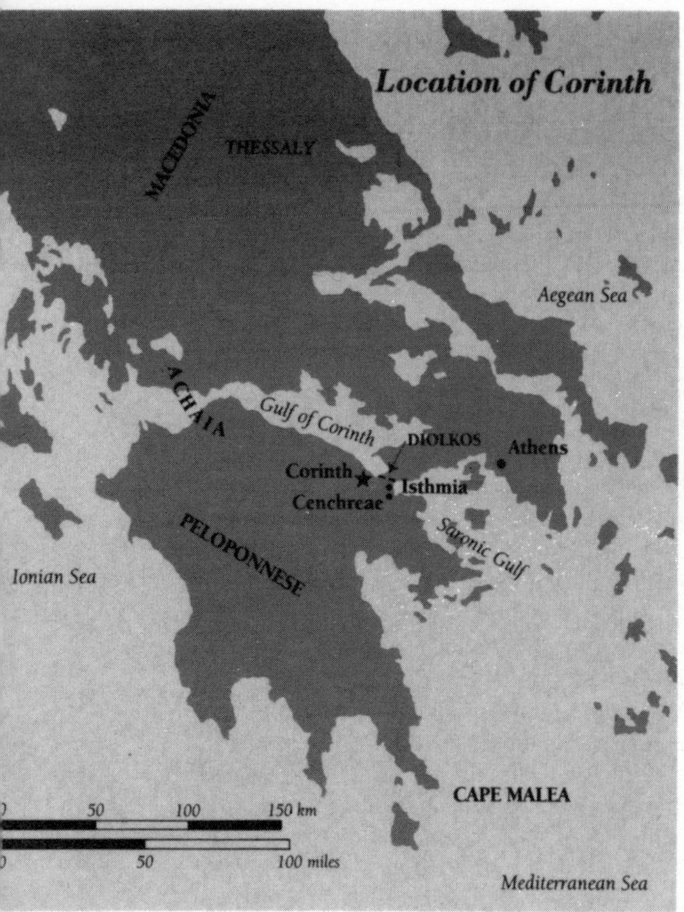

A HUB CITY through which a constant stream of travelers passed between the eastern and western halves of the Roman empire, Corinth lies on the isthmus connecting mainland Greece with the Peloponnese. The nearby port of Cenchreae offered safe anchorage to ships avoiding the rough waters around Cape Malea.

A special roadway, called the *diolkos* was built across the three-mile-wide isthmus in the early sixth century B.C.; grooves in this roadway served as tracks for wooden platforms (*holkos* in Greek) on which ships were hauled between the Gulf of Corinth and the Saronic Gulf.

church units, and then moved on. True, the opposition they engendered sometimes forced them to leave town sooner than they planned, but they would not have stayed more than a few months in any of these cities anyway. Their purpose was to remain only long enough to help a new church get established, and then leave to the new Christians in that church the task of spreading the new gospel to the smaller towns in their district.

When Paul reached Corinth, however, he broke this pattern dramatically. Despite the sense of urgency he felt about the imminence of a judgment day, he decided to "take up residence" at Corinth (and later, as we shall see at Ephesus). Why?

Is it simply that these were large, tradition-rich cities? Paul had passed through other cities impressive in size, such as Thessalonika, or rich in tradition, such as Troas. Athens had both impressive buildings and a rich classical heritage. Yet Paul did little more than pause there (Acts 17:14; 1 Thessalonians 3:1).

In fact, Corinth and Ephesus had special features that help explain Paul's decision to abandon his frenetic travel schedule and establish residency in these cities.

Corinth's strategic location was perhaps of prime importance. It was a hub city for travel between the eastern and western halves of the Roman Empire. The narrow isthmus separating the Gulf of Corinth and the Saronic Gulf had been spanned as early as the sixth century B.C. by a stone-paved roadway (the *diolkos*), making it relatively easy to pull most ships across the low, three-mile wide landstrip without even unloading them.*

The *diolkos* saved some 200 miles of extra sea travel, which a journey around the Peloponnese would have added; moreover, the sheltered waters of the Saronic and Corinthian Gulfs were far safer for sea-going ships than the treacherous winds around Cape Malea at the Peloponnese's southeastern tip. Cape Malea's reputation among sailors was as old as Homer (*Odyssey*, Book IX, lines 80ff.), who immortalized it as the point where Odysseus and his shipmates were driven off course for ten days when they were returning home from Troy.

The ship route through the more sheltered waters east and west of Corinth took on added importance because there were no convenient road systems across central or southern Greece; rugged mountain ranges there run north-south, thereby preventing easy passage.**

Corinth, therefore, was a natural funnel for traffic, receiving a steady and lively flow of travelers to and from all the Roman provinces along the northern shore of the Mediterranean.

The Romans had recognized Corinth's strategic location early. In 146 B.C. they had considered it necessary to destroy the city completely and disperse its survivors when initially those survi-

* See Victor Paul Furnish, "Corinth in Paul's Time—What Can Archaeology Tell Us?" *Biblical Archaeology Review*, May/June 1988.

** Farther north, the Roman Via Egnatia provided a shortcut across Macedonia from the Adriatic to Thessalonika and beyond for couriers and others traveling light, but for anyone with luggage or cargo the sea routes were preferable.

vors attempted to intervene in eastern Mediterranean affairs. A century later, when Rome had succeeded in extending its hegemony to the east, Caesar rebuilt Corinth as a Roman city. It was soon made the capital of the Roman province of Achaia, embracing the whole of the Peloponnese and much of central Greece.

Corinth's strategic location and the ease with which side trips could be made from this hub must have impressed Paul early in his stay. Before arriving at Corinth, Paul had been forced to leave hurriedly both Thessalonika and the next city on

THE ROAD TO CORINTH, called the Lechaeum Road, began at the port of Lechaeum on the Gulf of Corinth and terminated at the city forum two miles to the south. When Paul entered Corinth by this road, he would have seen not only the hill of Acrocorinth ahead, but, along the road, shops, a public bath, and a shrine dedicated to the god Apollo.

In the shops, shrines, and forum, a cosmopolitan mix of people—sailors, traveling salesmen, pilgrims worshipping Roman, Greek, and even Egyptian gods, and sports fans attending nearby panhellenic games—offered Paul a wealth of souls who might listen to his preaching.

his itinerary, Berea. Timothy who had stayed behind at Berea, finally caught up with Paul in Athens. Paul was so concerned about the church he had barely had time to found in Thessalonika that he sent Timothy back to Thessalonika to check on things while Paul himself went on to Corinth. Shortly after Paul arrived at Corinth, Timothy returned from Thessalonika, bringing reassuring news (1 Thessalonians 3:1-7). Paul must have been impressed with the ease with which Timothy could shuttle back and forth in a relatively short time from Berea south to Athens, from Athens back north to Thessalonika, and from there back south to Corinth. Travel conditions between Roman Achaia and Macedonia (probably using the coastal ship lanes) must have been quite efficient.

Incidentally, when Timothy arrived at Corinth and gave Paul the good news about the situation in Thessalonika, Paul was moved to write the letter known as 1 Thessalonians. This is the earliest of the Pauline letters—which means that it is also the earliest Christian document of any kind that has been preserved—before the earliest gospel. Insofar as it has survived, Christian literature begins with this letter written by Paul from Corinth to the Thessalonians. In it, Paul expresses his joy and relief at the news Timothy had brought; Paul then writes to give additional spiritual strength and guidance to the fledgling church of Thessalonika.

Once written, the letter to the Thessalonians had to be delivered, and this meant putting poor Timothy right back on ship to Thessalonika. But in this way Paul was able to keep actively in touch with the Christians there without interrupting his activities at Corinth.

Meanwhile, at Corinth Paul continued to spread the gospel to many new areas by preaching to sailors, to traveling merchants and to others who passed through the city from all over the Roman Empire. In Corinth Paul literally could spread his gospel more efficiently by staying in one place. Initially, he probably intended to move on westward from Corinth as soon as a church was firmly established there; but after he arrived at Corinth he seems to have decided that he could send the gospel on through others. He later claimed that he preached the gospel "from Jerusalem as far round as Illyricum (western Yugoslavia) (Romans 15:19), perhaps reflecting that *through his preaching at Corinth* he already had extended it this far.

In addition to being a hub for the constant stream of travelers who passed through Corinth, the city was also a destination for two types of pilgrims. The first included people suffering from all kinds of maladies who came to Corinth's *asklepieion*, a healing shrine dedicated to the deified Greek physician Asklepius. Originally worshipped at Epidaurus, Asklepius by the fourth century B.C. had several other healing shrines; the one at Corinth remained popular well into the Roman Age. Suppliants would stay in Corinth, often with family members, for a period of weeks or months, in the hope of receiving a cure. Excavations by the American School of Classical Studies have uncovered Corinth's *asklepieion*, including dining rooms, bathing facilities and the foundation of the special sleeping dormitory (*abaton*) where cures were supposed to be received through dreams. The excavations also found numerous terra cotta votive offerings to the god in the form of human body parts—arms, legs, breasts, genitals, etc.—for which cures were sought or received.

The second type of pilgrim came to Corinth to attend the Isthmian Games, which were held every two years, including the summer of 51 A.D., while Paul was there. The games were held about 10 miles from Corinth, at a shrine of Poseidon, the sea god.[2] Like the better known games at Olympia, the Isthmian Games were "panhellenic," attracting athletes and spectators from Greek settlements throughout the Mediterranean.

But the temples, theater and stadium at Isthmia also drew crowds on other occasions, between the biennial Isthmian games, when these facilities were used for lesser sports events and rituals.

The Isthmian Games and the health spa at Corinth may also have provided Paul, who was a tentmaker by trade, with a special opportunity to support himself. We know from Paul's own statements that he was anxious to be independent of support from the churches he founded, lest he be mistaken for one of the professional itinerant philosophers of his day (1 Thessalonians 4:15). We also learn from Acts that when Paul came to Corinth he sought out a Jewish couple, Aquila and Priscilla, "and because he was of the same trade he stayed with them, and they worked, for by trade they were tentmakers" (Acts 18:2-3).

Most of the people who flocked to the Corinthian *asklepieion* and the Isthmian Games stayed in tent encampments. Only aristocrats and dignitaries stayed in the limited hotel accommodations. Paul thus found a ready means of supporting himself among the very people who provided promising audiences for his preaching.

Paradoxically, Corinth offered another attractive feature for Paul—its long-standing reputation for immorality and licentiousness. The Greeks—who had a name for everything—coined the term *corinthiazesthai* to mean immorality; literally, the word means "to live a Corinthian life." To call a girl a "Corinthian lass" was to cast aspersions on her virtue.

Corinth's reputation was as notorious in Paul's day as it had been in the Classical Age five centuries before. The account by the Roman geographer Strabo that a thousand cult prostitutes (*heirodules*) once served the temple to Aphrodite on the Acrocorinth, overlooking the city, may have been exaggerated. But the steady stream of sailors, traveling salesmen and the ancient equivalent of soccer fans doubtless kept a goodly number of the cult prostitutes' secular counterparts busy in the rooms over the 33 wineshops that archaeologists have uncovered, lining the south side of the Roman forum.[3]

This is the reality that lay behind Paul's reference, in his second letter to the Corinthians, to the "impurity, immorality, and licentiousness" that characterized the behavior of some church members before their conversions (2 Corinthians 12:21). Paul knew what he was talking about when he referred to the "immoral," the "idolators," the "adulterers," the "homosexuals," the "thieves," the "greedy," the "drunkards," the "revilers" and the "robbers" (1 Corinthians 6:9-10) of Corinth. "Such," he writes to the members of the church at Corinth, "were some of you" (1 Corinthians 6:11).

Corinth also had strong associations with "pagan" religions. We have already referred to the worship of Asklepius, Poseidon and Aphrodite. The city also had a venerable connection with Apollo. A Roman-period shrine to Apollo was located prominently next to the Lechaeum Road, the main street leading from the forum to Corinth's western port. Altars and temples to other traditional Greek gods—Athena, Hera, Hermes—lined the edges of the forum. One temple was even dedicated to "all the gods."

In addition, new forms of worship had been introduced to Corinth during the century before Paul's arrival, brought by the enclaves of foreigners living at Corinth. On the road leading up to Acrocorinth, for example, was a shrine to the Egyptian gods Isis and Serapis. A shrine to Octavia, the deified sister of Emperor Augustus, was located at the west end of the forum. Some of the newer "mystery" religions also flourished in Corinth; these offered their special kinds of personal salvation and communion with savior gods.

For Paul, all this represented a special challenge—and a special opportunity. Paul had been preaching throughout his missionary journeys that Gentile converts to Christianity did not need to undertake circumcision and all the obligations of Jewish law that this ritual symbolized. Now, in Corinth of all places, if Paul could establish a church of Gentile converts who were morally upright without relying on the constraints of Torah (Jewish law), then the Christian gospel could take root anywhere—even in the most hostile soil the Gentile world could offer.

Paul's letters, later sent back to the Corinthian Christians, reflect his special zeal that their behavior be morally elevated. The church at Corinth was a "showcase" congregation for Paul; with it he hoped at last to convince the most skeptical among the Jewish Christian leaders in Jerusalem that Torah was not necessary for salvation.

Although Paul left Corinth after a year and a half, he may well have planned to return after only a brief trip back east. He seems to have left Corinth primarily to make a return visit to the church at Antioch (Acts 18:22)—it had been several years since he had started out from his sponsor-church there. He may have wanted to gain the Antioch church leaders' approval (and perhaps the approval of the Jerusalem church leaders) for the decision he had made on his own to extend his missionary activity across the Aegean from Asia to Macedonia and Greece, and he would want to share with them first-hand the successes he had achieved for the gospel on purely Gentile soil.

Paul set sail from Cenchreae, Corinth's port on the east coast of the isthmus, on a ship taking the most direct route across the Aegean Sea to Ephesus. From there he would continue by ship eastward along the coast of Asia Minor (Acts 18:18). Priscilla and Aquila, with whom he had lived in Corinth, accompanied Paul as far as Ephesus. Perhaps they originally had planned to go on with Paul to Antioch. If so, they changed their minds when they arrived at Ephesus.

Paul, who had not been to Ephesus before, was sufficiently impressed that he promised the Jews in the synagogue that he would return to them after his visit to Antioch "if God wills" (Acts 18:21).

Paul did more than keep his promise to return to Ephesus. When he did return, he stayed—for

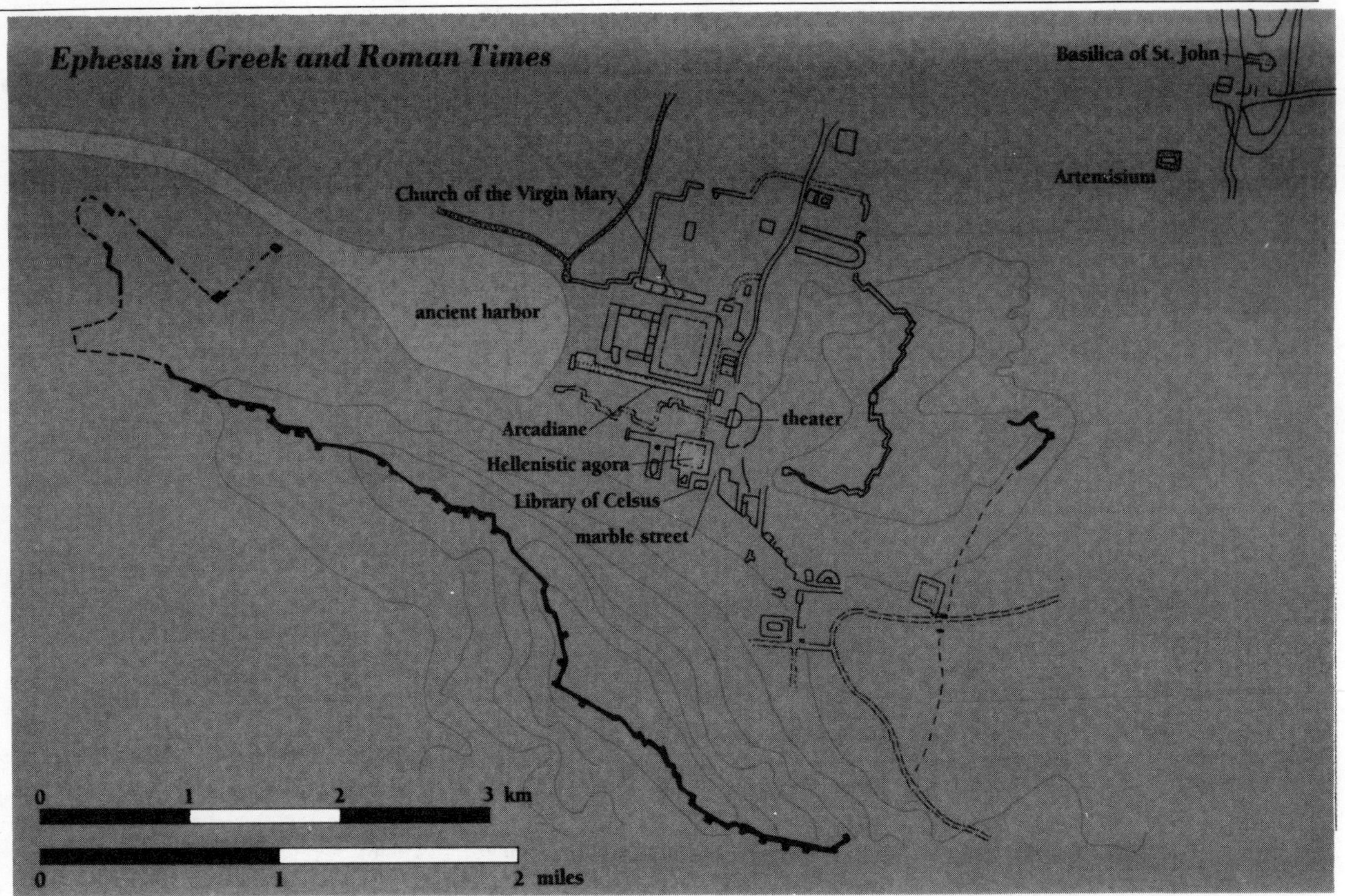

two and one-half years (Acts 19:8-10). Why so long? Not simply to establish a church there. Other Christians he trusted, such as Aquila and Priscilla, could have been counted on to do that. And it would not have taken that long anyway.

Paul found himself drawn to Ephesus because it had the same "attractions" that had detained him in Corinth—but to an even greater extent.

The modern visitor to Ephesus is immediately struck by the extent and opulence of the archaeological remains.* And only the center of the city has been exposed, although Austrian excavators have been working at the site since 1895. Ephesus was one of the three or four largest cities in the Roman world. Population estimates for Ephesus in Paul's time range up to a quarter

* The visible remains are essentially the city of the first to fourth centuries A.D., when it flourished as an important Christian center. The reason the structures have been so well preserved is, ironically, because of its rapid decline and virtual abandonment shortly thereafter. The progressive silting up of the Kayster River choked the once-bustling harbor of Ephesus beyond the point where dredging operations could maintain its contact with the sea. A growing marsh buried the precinct of Artemis and isolated the city's buildings. The dwindling populace relocated on higher ground to the north, in the area of the present-day town of Seljuk.

EPHESUS, A HARBOR CITY across the Aegean Sea from Corinth, proved even more attractive to Paul than had Corinth. He stayed in Ephesus two and a half years.

One of the largest cities in the Roman world of its day, Ephesus was built right to the edge of its magnificent natural harbor. Now silted up and planted with cotton, the ancient harbor appears as a smooth field at the foot of the mount, upper left, in the photo opposite. The broad boulevard called the Arcadiane—the main street from the harbor of Ephesus—runs diagonally across the photo, ending at the city's enormous theater (plan, above).

In this theater, 24,000 Ephesian devotees of Artemis, goddess of nature and fertility, protested against Paul's ministry. The organizer, according to the Book of Acts, was Demetrius the silversmith, whose sales to pilgrims of Artemis shrines had fallen off since Paul had begun preaching against the cult.

On the plain at the upper right in the photograph, remains of a fourth-century church are visible. Called the Church of the Virgin Mary, the building commemorates the tradition that Jesus' mother spent her final days at Ephesus.

F.H.C. BIRCH/SONIA HALLIDAY PHOTOGRAPHS

of a million people. Moreover, the city's wealth was reflected everywhere, from its marble-paved main street to recently excavated mosaic floors in aristocratic homes, that were opened to visitors only a year ago.[4]

Like Corinth, Ephesus was strategically located, and this surely accounts at least in part for its enormous size and wealth in Paul's day. As the Roman Empire stretched eastward across the Mediterranean, Ephesus's large and sheltered harbor became a major communication hub. Sea traffic from the Aegean Sea to the west, from the Bosporus and Dardanelles to the north and from Palestine to the east, stopped at Ephesus. Ephesus also served as a convenient collection point on the coast for agricultural products brought down the Maeander River Valley from the interior of Asia Minor. It's not surprising that Ephesus was designated the capital of the rich Roman province of Asia.

Ephesus also boasted one of the most popular shrines in antiquity—to the Ephesian nature/fertility/mother goddess Artemis, who was worshipped by the Romans as Diana. From all over the Mediterranean, pilgrims flocked to the great Artemisium on the shore of the Kaystros River, adjacent to Ephesus. This great temple was four times the size of the Athens Parthenon and was considered one of the "seven wonders of the world."[5]

Two life-sized marble statues of the goddess have been recovered; they undoubtedly are replicas of the huge statue that stood in the Artemisium. The many protusions on the chest of this curious-looking goddess have been variously interpreted as breasts, eggs and even dates. They are probably symbolic of fertility. Pilgrims to the shrine of Artemis in Ephesus sought the goddess's aid in becoming pregnant and her protection of mothers and children, particularly during childbirth.

The shrine to Artemis would have been one of the special challenges that attracted Paul to Ephesus. Acts records that the most hostile opposition to Paul's preaching came from adherents to this cult and from local entrepreneurs whose livelihood depended upon it. Near the end of Paul's stay at Ephesus, a local silversmith named Demetrius, who made votive shrines of the Ephesian Artemis for the pilgrim trade, organized a near-riot against Paul and his associates, filling the 24,500-seat theater of Ephesus with devotees of the goddess chanting repeatedly "Great is Artemis of Ephesus!" (Acts 19:23-41).

Local magicians and exorcists also presented a challenge for Paul. Magic practitioners and their texts had proliferated during the Roman Age, particularly out of Egypt and even from some esoteric circles within Judaism.* In 13 B.C. the Emperor Augustus unsuccessfully attempted to suppress the use of magical books. The practice of the magical arts was so closely associated with Ephesus that books of magic recipes and incantations were often referred to as "Ephesian books." According to Acts, Paul was so successful in converting Ephesians from a belief in magic that many of them threw their magic books onto a public bonfire (Acts 19:13-19).

Paul was a pugnacious warrior, and we can be sure that he was attracted rather than deterred by the presence at Ephesus of the Artemis devotees and magicians. They gave him greater opportunities to do battle for the Christian gospel. As he wrote to the Corinthians, explaining to them why he was staying so long in Ephesus, "I will stay at Ephesus until Pentacost, for a wide door for effective work has opened to me, and there are many adversaries" (1 Corinthians 16:9).

Ephesus also had a strong tradition of scholarship and intellectual inquiry. This is most dramatically suggested by the recently re-erected facade of the magnificent three-story Library of Celsus, an important scholarly archive and meeting place for intellectuals in Ephesus. Although this library was not built until 110 A.D.,

a half-century after Paul's time, the tradition of scholarly inquiry and activity in the region of Ionia surrounding Ephesus went back to pre-Classical times. The founders of both philosophy and mathematics came from Ionia in the sixth century B.C. Such giants as Thales, Anaximander and Anximenes all came from Miletus, only a few miles south of Ephesus. Herodotus, the first historian, was born a few miles farther south, at Halicarnassos (present-day Bodrum), as was Hippodamnus, who is credited with perfecting the Greek concept of city-planning. Hippocrates, the first physician, established his famous medical center on the nearby island of Kos. At Ephesus Paul could work in an atmosphere of genuine inquiry. There he could find learned scholars who were proud of a centuries-old tradition of open-minded exploration of new ideas. To Paul, this must have been a refreshing change on the one hand, from the intellectual snobbery of the Athenian Greeks (Acts 17:18,32) and on the other hand, from what Paul perceived as close-

* See the review of *The Greek Magical Papyri in Translation* in *Biblical Archaeology Review*, May/June 1987, pp. 6-8.

©SONIA HALLIDAY PHOTOGRAPHS

ARTEMIS, the Ephesian nature/fertility/mother goddess (opposite). This grotesque—but elegant—statue of the goddess, who was called Diana by the Romans, is one of several that have been uncovered in excavations. The many bulbous objects protruding from Artemis/Diana's torso may represent breasts or eggs or even clumps of dates; certainly they are emblems of the goddess's association with the mystery of fertility. This life-size statue undoubtedly is a replica of the larger cult statue that stood in the temple of Artemis in Paul's time.

The goddess's lower body is fused into a pillar shape, perhaps emulating the gigantic tree trunk from which the temple Artemis may have been carved. Signs of the zodiac encircle her neck; crowning her head is a walled edifice that may represent her sacred precinct. A menagerie of natural and mythical creatures adorns Artemis: bees, lions, bulls, stags, sphinxes and chimeras.

Scant remains from the foundation of this huge temple and one lonely column can be seen in the foreground of the photo above. A veritable forest of columns—127, each 60 feet high—stood in the temple that Paul saw. Over 360 feet long and 180 feet wide, the Artemis temple was considered one of the ancient world's "seven wonders."

mindedness of the rabbis.

Moreover, the intellectual climate of Ephesus reflected its geographical location on the threshold between East and West. Moreso than Corinth, which had been on thoroughly Greco-Roman soil, Ephesus provided a meeting place for ideas from both eastern and western cultural traditions. For Paul, who had labored hard to dissolve the barriers between east and west in the Christian fellowship and to unite Jew and Gentile, Greek and barbarian, Ephesus provided a comfortably eclectic atmosphere and a symbolic middle ground from which to preach both toward Rome and toward Jerusalem.

It has also been suggested that Paul was attracted to Ephesus because the Apostle John and Jesus' mother Mary lived there.[6] This view is based on an early tradition—though how early we can't be sure—that the apostle John eventually went to Ephesus to live. And in the Gospel of John, we are told that Jesus placed his mother Mary in the apostle John's care (John 19:26-27); on this basis she too would have ended her days at Ephesus. In the fourth century A.D., a church was built at Ephesus dedicated to the Virgin Mary to commemorate this tradition.*

Since the 19th century, modern pilgrims have been shown a shrine on a hilltop southeast of Ephesus that is supposed to mark the location of Mary's last home on earth. Excavations in 1891 revealed remains of a first-century Roman house beneath the chapel of a Byzantine monastery. The identification of the site as Mary's home, however, is based primarily on testimony from dreams of an 18th century mystic, a German nun named Katarina Emmerich.

In light of all the attractions of Ephesus, it is not difficult to understand why Paul postponed whatever plans he may have had to return to Corinth or to travel even farther west. At Ephesus Paul unpacked his traveling rucksack for the second time. The features that had led him to remain so long in Corinth were even more insistent at Ephesus. The city's strategic location, the flow of pilgrims, a famous pagan cult, infamous magicians—all provided rich opportunities and worthy challenges for Paul's preaching. And—as a bonus—at Ephesus Paul also found a stimulating community of scholars to engage in theological debate.

While at Ephesus, Paul continued his letter-writing activity. From here he wrote the letters we have in the New Testament to the Philippians, to Philemon,[7] and at least three letters to the church at Corinth.[8] Some scholars think Paul also wrote his Letter to the Galatians from Ephesus.[9] His letter to the Romans was written either shortly before he left Ephesus or just after he departed on the journey to Macedonia and Corinth.

Paul finally did leave Ephesus,[10] but he left behind him a lasting legacy. His co-workers there turned the church at Ephesus into one of the most important centers of Christian leadership during the following centuries, particularly in its production of Christian writings. Its record is impressive. The Gospel of Luke and its companion volume, the Acts of the Apostles, most probably were issued from Ephesus about 85-90 A.D. Then, between 90 A.D. and 95 A.D., someone at Ephesus gathered together Paul's own letters to individual churches and published them for general circulation.[11] The so-called Letter to the Ephesians probably was written at that time as an "introduction" to Paul's special understanding of the gospel. Some think Colossians was written from Ephesus at about the same time, if not by Paul himself earlier. The Revelation to John was issued from Ephesus about 95 A.D., and sometime in the next decade or two the Gospel of John was written at Ephesus. The four New Testament gospels were probably first published together and circulated from Ephesus.[12]

We are thus indebted to the church that Paul planted at Ephesus for the initial publication of fully half of the documents (and approximately two-thirds of the bulk) of the literature that was to comprise the New Testament scriptures.

At Ephesus Paul had indeed opened "a wide door for effective work" (1 Corinthians 16:9)! BR

* Although Acts makes no mention of Mary at Ephesus, some scholars believe Romans 16:6 is a reference to this fact. See Edgar Goodspeed, *Paul* (Nashville, TN: Abingdon, 1947), p. 233f, or his earlier *The Formation of the New Testament* (Chicago: Univ. of Chicago Press, 1926), pp. 28-29. Paul closes his letter to the Romans with various greetings, among them "Great Mary, who has worked hard among you" (Romans 16:6). The argument is that these greetings are addressed to the church at Ephesus, rather than to Rome, and that the "Mary" referred to is Jesus' mother.

[1] The details of Luke's account may not be accurate; they have been viewed suspiciously by a number of recent scholars. But most accept the general picture that emerges from Acts.

[2] An inscription at Delphi dates to the summer or fall of 51 A.D., the arrival at Corinth of Lucius Junius Gallio as proconsul. Since Paul was brought before Gallio (Acts 18:12-17) near the end of his 18-month stay in Corinth (Acts 18:11 & 18:18), he must have arrived in Corinth since sometime late in A.D. 49 or early 50 and stayed through the summer of 51.

[3] While Paul was at Corinth, a few of these wineshops aligned behind the South Stoa had been converted to administrative offices. Perhaps the city fathers were making a conscious effort to move Corinth's "red-light" district away from the city center in order to improve its image.

[4] Detailed descriptions in English of the Ephesus excavations are available in Ekrem Akurgal's *Ancient Civilizations and Ruins of Turkey* (Istanbul: Haset Kitabevi, 3rd ed. 1973), pp. 142-171 or in *Baedeker's Turkish Coast* (Norwich, England: Jarrold & Sons, Ltd., revised 1987), pp. 113-128.

[5] The other wonders were the Mausoleum of Halicarnassos, the Pyramids of Egypt, the Colossus of Rhodes, the hanging gardens of Babylon, the lighthouse of Pharos at Alexandria and Phidias's statue of Zeus in the Temple of Olympia.

[6] See, for instance, Stewart Perowne, *The Journeys of St. Paul* (New York: World, 1973), p. 72.

[7] Scholars used to assume Philemon was written from Rome because Paul is writing from prison, but there is no necessity for a Roman locale, and Edgar Goodspeed persuasively argued years ago that Ephesus is much more plausible. Paul writes the letter to entreat his friend Philemon in Laodicea to accept and forgive the runaway slave Onesimus who had come under Paul's influence while Paul was in prison. Ephesus is the nearest big city to Laodicia, a far more likely place for Paul to have encountered Onesimus than Rome. See Goodspeed, *An Introduction to the New Testament* (Chicago: Univ. of Chicago Press, 1937), pp. 109-124.

[8] In addition to 1 Corinthians, 2 Corinthians contains elements of at least three letters: (1) a fragment in 6:14-7:1, which may fit the description of a letter earlier than 1 Corinthians, which Paul mentions in 1 Corinthians 5:9-13, which may be the "painful letter" referred to in 2 Corinthians 2:3-4, 7:8; (3) the beautifully reconciliatory text in the early chapters of 2 Corinthians, which was written shortly after Paul left Ephesus on the trip that would take him back to Corinth.

[9] See, for instance, T.W. Manson, *Studies in the Gospels and Epistles* (Philadelphia: Westminster, 1962), p. 168f.

[10] Paul became convinced that it was important for him to collect contributions from the churches he had established in Macedonia and Greece for the mother church in Jerusalem and to deliver those contributions in person (1 Corinthians 16:1-4; 2 Corinthians 8:1-15; Romans 15:25-27).

In his letter to the church at Rome, Paul indicates that after delivering this collection to Jerusalem he was anxious to fulfill his earlier intention to travel westward to Rome and on to Spain (Romans 1:13; 15:23-24, 28). Arrested in Jerusalem, he did eventually reach Rome, but in chains.

[11] It may have been the publication of Acts, with the prominent place it gave to Paul's missionary activity that inspired the collection of Paul's letters. So Edgar Goodspeed first argued in *The Formation of the New Testament*, pp. 20-32.

[12] For the reasoning behind this suggestion, see Goodspeed, *Formation of the New Testament*, pp. 33-41.

Archaeological discoveries and research frequently have enriched our understanding of the Bible and of Biblical history.

Sometimes archaeology's contribution has been simply to give us a clearer picture of the Biblical world. Our new ability to envision the grandeur of Herod's Temple Mount, for instance, adds to our appreciation of the dramatic episodes in Jewish and Christian tradition that centered there, and of the impact on both Jews and Christians of the Temple's destruction.

Sometimes archaeology enables us to gain greater insight into significant forces at work in Biblical history. The documentation of Herod's mighty works in Jerusalem and elsewhere, such as at Caesarea and Herodium, provides tangible witness to his grandiose ambition and almost-unparalleled power. In this light, we can then better understand the deep divisions among the people of the Jewish state during its final century—divisions between aristocrat and peasant, between those who followed Herod in embracing Roman imperial court and culture and those whose traditional Jewish devotion led them to feel increasingly alienated in their own land—and we can better appreciate the political/religious tensions reflected in the Gospel accounts that ultimately helped to fuel the Jewish Revolt against Rome.

The Temple Scroll and others of the Dead Sea Scrolls, whatever the final assessment of their exact origins, provide vivid evidence that during the Roman period the Jewish religion was not monolithic and that the limits of its scriptures were still not set. On the fringes of the Jewish community were those who held differing views of what Torah demanded and what God's plan was for his people. The scrolls help us to understand much more graphically the deep tensions and factions within the religious community that produced John the Baptist and Jesus of Nazareth.

In some cases, archaeology allows us to retrieve the exact locales of significant events in sacred history, such as the synagogue where Jesus preached in Capernaum. In other cases, we find poignant witnesses of the faithful pilgrims from later centuries whose devotion brought them to the places made holy in the Biblical drama. The inscription discovered on the wall of the Temple Mount left by fourth century A.D. Jews who hoped for the rebuilding of the Temple, graffiti from a Capernaum house that early Christian pilgrims were convinced was Peter's house where Christ had healed the sick, the picture of the pilgrim ship deposited in the Church of the Holy Sepulchre by devout voyagers from the western Mediterranean—all this brings us closer to the pilgrims of an earlier era.

Occasionally, archaeology even enables us to supplement the information contained in the Biblical accounts, to find out something of the how and the why behind the what of Biblical events. We may use the final article as an example.

Nowhere in Paul's letters or in the Book of Acts are we told specifically what Paul's reasons were for rushing through cities such as Athens to go to Corinth, why he then abandoned his previous pattern of rapid-succession moves and established Corinth as his base or why he subsequently shifted his headquarters to Ephesus. We can only speculate on the reasons from what Paul or the author of Acts tell us.

But the archaeological remains of these two cities and a study of their setting in the geography of the first-century A.D. Roman empire make them stand out in sharp contrast to other sites. Moreover, archaeology has documented a range of activities at these cities that would have made them particularly strategic places for Paul to press forward his evangelistic plan. Whether the inspiration for this design came to Paul from within or from above, we are better able now to understand what the factors were, in human terms, that led Paul to Corinth and later to Ephesus, and to understand how these cities, in turn, may have led Paul to alter his missionary strategy.

For Further Reading

Concerning Corinth in Paul's Time

Victor Paul Furnish, "Corinth in Paul's Time—What Can Archaeology Tell Us?" **BAR**, May/June 1988

Concerning Paul

F. F. Bruce, "The Enigma of Paul," **BR**, August 1988